Cirencester College Library
Fosse Way Campus
Stroud Road
Cirencester
GL7 1XA

Cirencester College
Library

2 Week loan

7/23

15 SEP 2023 2 OCT 2023	

D1357542

XA

CIRC E

WITHDRAWN FROM

360299

THE FORMATION OF THE ENGLISH KINGDOM
IN THE TENTH CENTURY

The Formation of the English Kingdom in the Tenth Century

GEORGE MOLYNEAUX

OXFORD
UNIVERSITY PRESS

OXFORD

UNIVERSITY PRESS

Great Clarendon Street, Oxford, OX2 6DP,
United Kingdom

Oxford University Press is a department of the University of Oxford.
It furthers the University's objective of excellence in research, scholarship,
and education by publishing worldwide. Oxford is a registered trade mark of
Oxford University Press in the UK and in certain other countries

© George Molyneaux 2015

The moral rights of the author have been asserted

First Edition published in 2015

Impression: 1

All rights reserved. No part of this publication may be reproduced, stored in
a retrieval system, or transmitted, in any form or by any means, without the
prior permission in writing of Oxford University Press, or as expressly permitted
by law, by licence or under terms agreed with the appropriate reprographics
rights organization. Enquiries concerning reproduction outside the scope of the
above should be sent to the Rights Department, Oxford University Press, at the
address above

You must not circulate this work in any other form
and you must impose this same condition on any acquirer

Published in the United States of America by Oxford University Press
198 Madison Avenue, New York, NY 10016, United States of America

British Library Cataloguing in Publication Data
Data available

Library of Congress Control Number: 2014952299

ISBN 978–0–19–871791–1

Printed and bound by
CPI Group (UK) Ltd, Croydon, CR0 4YY

Links to third party websites are provided by Oxford in good faith and
for information only. Oxford disclaims any responsibility for the materials
contained in any third party website referenced in this work.

Acknowledgements

The genesis of this book can be traced to a tutorial essay on tenth- and eleventh-century English kings' dealings with the Scots and Welsh, which I wrote in November 2003, in the sixth week of my undergraduate degree. The essay evolved into a BA dissertation and then a DPhil thesis, of which this book is a heavily revised version. I have incurred many debts of gratitude during this lengthy process.

Stephen Baxter set the sixth-week essay question and sparked my interest in the Anglo-Saxon period, during a term when I had intended just to get the compulsory medieval component of my degree over and done with. Nick Karn helped me turn my initial thoughts into a dissertation, and encouraged me to apply for graduate study. George Garnett supervised my DPhil and then acted as my academic editor. I am extremely grateful for his inspiration, criticism, entertainment, patience, thoroughness, and deeply caring support. He has read numerous drafts, and tolerated my intermittent bloody-minded refusal to follow his advice.

Simon Keynes and Chris Wickham examined my DPhil, and provided valuable guidance on how I might adapt it for publication. Chris also gave me very helpful comments on the revised typescript, and I have likewise benefited from the advice of others who have read drafts of some or all of the thesis or book, notably John Hudson, Tom Lambert, Stewart Lyon, Rory Naismith, Rob Portass, Levi Roach, Alice Taylor, Gareth Williams, and OUP's anonymous readers. Among the many other people who have advised or taught me at various stages, I hope it is not invidious to record my particular gratitude to Rowena Archer, Julian Baker, Robin Fish, Diana Gotts, and John Maddicott.

Almost all of the work on both thesis and book was done during fellowships of All Souls College, Oxford. All Souls not only funded my work, but also gave me what must be near-ideal conditions in which to research and write, and I am extremely grateful to the College and its staff. In particular, Norma Aubertin-Potter and Gaye Morgan, the College librarians, have been unfailingly helpful, as have the staffs of the Bodleian and History Faculty libraries.

On other practical matters, I am grateful to the employees and contractors of OUP, especially Manikandan Chandrasekaran, Marilyn Inglis, Stephanie Ireland, Karen Parker, and Cathryn Steele, for their efficient handling of the publication process; to Henry and Louise Buglass, for drawing the maps and genealogical diagram respectively; and to the Syndics of the Fitzwilliam Museum, Cambridge, for permission to reproduce the coin images on the front cover and in Chapter 4.

On a personal level, my parents and sister have constantly encouraged me, and my father in particular was keenly interested in my work. He read an early draft of what became my article on the *Old English Bede*, published in 2009, and urged me to make it more readable; had he lived longer, I am sure he would have done the same with the typescript of the book. Lastly, I am grateful to my friends: by treating my investigations of the tenth century with a healthy mix of fascination and wry scepticism, they have helped me to maintain (I think) some semblance of sanity.

G. M.

November 2014

Contents

List of Figures

List of Maps

List of Abbreviations

ANS	*Anglo-Norman Studies*
ASC	*The Anglo-Saxon Chronicle*

MS A: *The Anglo-Saxon Chronicle: A Collaborative Edition. Volume 3: MS A*, ed. J. M. Bately (Cambridge, 1986).

MS B: *The Anglo-Saxon Chronicle: A Collaborative Edition. Volume 4: MS B*, ed. S. Taylor (Cambridge, 1983).

MS C: *The Anglo-Saxon Chronicle: A Collaborative Edition. Volume 5: MS C*, ed. K. O'B. O'Keeffe (Cambridge, 2001).

MS D: *The Anglo-Saxon Chronicle: A Collaborative Edition. Volume 6: MS D*, ed. G. P. Cubbin (Cambridge, 1996).

MS E: *The Anglo-Saxon Chronicle: A Collaborative Edition. Volume 7: MS E*, ed. S. Irvine (Cambridge, 2004).

MS F: *The Anglo-Saxon Chronicle: A Collaborative Edition. Volume 8: MS F*, ed. P. S. Baker (Cambridge, 2000).

Cited with letter symbol to indicate manuscript(s) and year, as corrected by Whitelock et al. The so-called 'Mercian Register', incorporated in manuscripts B, C, and D, is cited as 'MR'.

Translations are based on *The Anglo-Saxon Chronicle: A Revised Translation*, trans. D. Whitelock, D. C. Douglas, and S. I. Tucker (London, 1961) and *The Anglo-Saxon Chronicles*, trans. M. Swanton, revised edn (London, 2000).

ASE	*Anglo-Saxon England*
ASSAH	*Anglo-Saxon Studies in Archaeology and History*
BNJ	*British Numismatic Journal*
Cn 1018	'Cnut's Law Code of 1018', ed. A. G. Kennedy, *ASE*, 11 (1983), pp. 57–81 at 72–81.
CRF	*Capitularia regum Francorum*, ed. A. Boretius and V. Krause (2 vols, *MGH, Legum II*, Hanover, 1883–97).
CTCE	C. E. Blunt, B. H. I. H. Stewart, and C. S. S. Lyon, *Coinage in Tenth-Century England from Edward the Elder to Edgar's Reform* (Oxford, 1989).
DB	*Domesday Book*, ed. J. Morris et al. (35 vols, Chichester, 1975–86).
EETS	Early English Text Society
EHR	*English Historical Review*
EME	*Early Medieval Europe*
HE	Bede, *Ecclesiastical History of the English People*, ed. and trans. B. Colgrave and R. A. B. Mynors (Oxford, 1969).
HSJ	*Haskins Society Journal*
LE	*Liber Eliensis*, ed. E. O. Blake (London, 1962).

MGH   *Monumenta Germaniae Historica*

NC   *Numismatic Chronicle*
NCMH2   R. McKitterick (ed.), *The New Cambridge Medieval History II, c.700–c.900* (Cambridge, 1995).
NCMH3   T. Reuter (ed.), *The New Cambridge Medieval History III, c.900–c.1024* (Cambridge, 1999).
NCMH4   D. Luscombe and J. Riley-Smith (eds), *The New Cambridge Medieval History IV, c.1024–c.1198* (2 vols, Cambridge, 2004).
n.s.   new series

ODNB   H. C. G. Matthew and B. Harrison (eds), *Oxford Dictionary of National Biography* (Oxford, 2004), consulted at <http://www.oxforddnb.com/> (accessed 9 October 2014).
OEB   *The Old English Version of Bede's Ecclesiastical History of the English People*, ed. and trans. T. Miller (EETS, 95–6, 110–11, 4 vols in 2, London, 1890–8). Citations are from vol. i.

PBA   *Proceedings of the British Academy*
P&P   *Past and Present*

RC   *Regularis Concordia Anglicae Nationis*, ed. T. Symons and D. S. Spath, in K. Hallinger (ed.), *Corpus Consuetudinum Monasticarum VII.3* (Siegburg, 1984), pp. 61–147.
RS   Rolls Series

S   P. H. Sawyer, *Anglo-Saxon Charters: An Annotated List and Bibliography* (London, 1968), revised S. E. Kelly, *The Electronic Sawyer*, consulted at <http://esawyer.org.uk/about/index.html> (accessed 9 October 2014). Cited by document number only; references to editions may be obtained from *The Electronic Sawyer*, where most texts can also be viewed.
SHR   *Scottish Historical Review*
s.s.   supplementary series

TRHS   *Transactions of the Royal Historical Society*

VA   Asser, *Life of Alfred*, ed. W. H. Stevenson and revised D. Whitelock, *Asser's Life of King Alfred together with the Annals of Saint Neots Erroneously Ascribed to Asser* (Oxford, 1959), pp. 1–96.
VSÆ   Wulfstan of Winchester, *Life of St Æthelwold*, ed. and trans. M. Lapidge and M. Winterbottom, *Wulfstan of Winchester. The Life of St Æthelwold* (Oxford, 1991), pp. 1–69.
VSD   B, *Life of St Dunstan*, ed. and trans. M. Winterbottom and M. Lapidge, *The Early Lives of St Dunstan* (Oxford, 2012), pp. 1–109.
VSO   Byrhtferth of Ramsey, *Life of St Oswald*, ed. and trans. M. Lapidge, *Byrhtferth of Ramsey. The Lives of St Oswald and St Ecgwine* (Oxford, 2009), pp. 1–203.

WBEASE   M. Lapidge, J. Blair, S. Keynes, and D. Scragg (eds), *The Wiley Blackwell Encyclopedia of Anglo-Saxon England*, 2nd edn (Chichester, 2014).

Note on References and Translations

Domesday Book is cited by volume and then by folio and column. Volume i (Great Domesday) describes all shires except Essex, Norfolk, and Suffolk; these shires are described in volume ii (Little Domesday). Folio and column citations use the system of numbers and letters in *Domesday Book*, ed. J. Morris et al. (35 vols, Chichester, 1975–86).

Unless otherwise stated, English legal texts are cited from *Die Gesetze der Angelsachsen*, ed. F. Liebermann (3 vols, Halle, 1903–16), using the system of reference set out at vol. i, p. xi. Translations are, where possible, based on *The Laws of the Earliest English Kings*, ed. and trans. F. L. Attenborough (Cambridge, 1922) and *The Laws of the Kings of England from Edmund to Henry I*, ed. and trans. A. J. Robertson (Cambridge, 1925).

Other translations are, where possible, based on those in *Alfred the Great: Asser's* Life of King Alfred *and Other Contemporary Sources*, trans. S. Keynes and M. Lapidge (London, 1983); *Anglo-Saxon Charters*, ed. and trans. A. J. Robertson, 2nd edn (Cambridge, 1956); *Anglo-Saxon Wills*, ed. and trans. D. Whitelock (Cambridge, 1930); *English Historical Documents, i, c.500–1042*, trans. D. Whitelock, 2nd edn (London, 1979); and *Select English Historical Documents of the Ninth and Tenth Centuries*, ed. and trans. F. E. Harmer (Cambridge, 1914).

Introduction: The Unification of the English?

By the early eleventh century, there was an English kingdom. This is clear from the annal for 1017 in the C and E texts of the *Anglo-Saxon Chronicle*, which records its conquest by the Danish king Cnut (r. 1016–1035):

> In this year King Cnut obtained all the kingdom of the English [*eallon Angelcynnes ryce*] and divided it into four, the West Saxons for himself, the East Angles for Thorkel, the Mercians for Eadric and the Northumbrians for Erik.[1]

The annal may well have been composed very soon after, and was certainly written no later than the mid-eleventh century: it thus demonstrates that someone living in the first half of the eleventh century thought that there was such a thing as 'the kingdom of the English', *Angelcynnes rice/ryce*.[2] The D version of the *Chronicle* has the same account, except that it replaces 'eallon Angelcynnes ryce' with 'eall Englalandes rice'. D reached its current form somewhat later in the eleventh century, but the term *Englaland* was in quite common use from the reign of Cnut, whose legislation demanded that its provisions be observed 'ofer eall Englaland' ('across all England'), and described him as 'ealles Englalandes ciningc 7 Dena cining' ('king of all England and king of Danes').[3] Latin writers also recognized the existence of an English kingdom, and increasingly called it *Anglia*: to give but one example, the *Encomium Emmae Reginae*, written in 1041 or 1042, distinguishes *Anglia* from Scotland and Wales, and declares that these were three of the five *regna* ('kingdoms') of which Cnut was *imperator* ('commander' or 'emperor').[4]

---

[1] *ASC* CE 1017. The basic meaning of the noun *rice/ryce* is 'power', and by extension the territory in which power is exercised. In the context of the territory in which a king had power, 'kingdom' is the most natural translation. This is supported by Asser's use of *regnum* to translate *rice*, and Ælfric's use of the latter word to gloss *regnum*: *ASC* ABCDE 878; *VA*, lvi (p. 46); Ælfric, *Glossary*, ed. J. Zupitza, *Ælfrics Grammatik und Glossar: Text und Varianten* (Berlin, 1880), p. 299.

[2] In the C manuscript, the annals from 491 to 1048 are written by one mid-eleventh-century hand. The annal for 1017 may have formed part of a retrospective account of Æthelred II's reign, written before 1023, quite possibly in London. See S. Keynes, 'The Declining Reputation of King Æthelred the Unready', in D. H. Hill (ed.), *Ethelred the Unready: Papers from the Millenary Conference* (Oxford, 1978), pp. 229–32; *The Anglo-Saxon Chronicle: A Collaborative Edition. Volume 5: MS C*, ed. K. O'B. O'Keeffe (Cambridge, 2001), pp. xxvi–xxxii, lxiv–lxviii.

[3] *ASC* D 1017; I Cn Prol.; II Cn Prol.; P. Stafford, 'Archbishop Ealdred and the D Chronicle', in D. Crouch and K. Thompson (eds), *Normandy and its Neighbours, 900–1250: Essays for David Bates* (Turnhout, 2011), pp. 135–56. See also Cn 1018 14.6; Cn 1020 1; below, p. 201.

[4] *Encomium Emmae Reginae*, ii.19, ed. A. Campbell with supplementary introduction by S. Keynes (Cambridge, 1998), p. 34; G. Molyneaux, 'Why were some Tenth-Century English Kings Presented as Rulers of Britain?', *TRHS*, 6th series, 21 (2011), pp. 62–4. In the list of Cnut's kingdoms, *Britannia* clearly denotes Wales, since *Anglia* and *Scothia* are listed too, along with Denmark and Norway. On this sense of *Britannia*, see A. W. Wade-Evans, *Vitae Sanctorum Britanniae et Genealogiae* (Cardiff, 1944), pp. vii–viii.

This English kingdom was not a creation of Cnut: the 1017 annal presents him as having acquired an existing 'Angelcynnes ryce' or 'Englalandes rice'. Nor did his delegation of responsibility for the East Angles, Mercians, and Northumbrians cause the kingdom to fragment, since he retained overall power. The kingdom likewise remained a recognizable entity after Duke William of Normandy's victory at Hastings in 1066: by the eleventh century, the English kingdom was sufficiently well established that it could twice be conquered and taken over as a coherent unit. At the turn of the ninth and tenth centuries, by contrast, there had been no political entity which even loosely corresponded to the English kingdom of 100 years later: the West Saxon kings had power south of the Thames and in the West Midlands, but the east and north of the future English kingdom was under the domination of a variety of Scandinavian potentates. The tenth century was thus the period in which the English kingdom was formed. The aim of this book is to analyse how that happened.

Where was the eleventh-century English kingdom? To be more precise, where did contemporaries think it was? By fairly early in the twelfth century, the English kingdom could be understood as covering an area closely similar to what is now England. Listing the shires and bishoprics of *Anglia*, Henry of Huntingdon declared that its northernmost shires were Yorkshire, Northumberland ('over which the Bishop of Durham presides'), and 'that region in which there is the new bishopric of Carlisle'; bordering Wales were Gloucestershire, Herefordshire, Shropshire, and Cheshire.[5] How people in the eleventh century perceived the kingdom's extent is less clear. It is likely that few gave the matter any significant thought, and those who did need not have been unanimous. The chronicler who described Cnut dividing the newly conquered *Angelcynnes rice* into the West Saxons, the East Angles, the Mercians, and the Northumbrians seemingly understood the kingdom as encompassing everything south of the Humber (excluding Wales), plus some land further north. He may have considered the kingdom to stretch as far as the modern border on the Solway Firth and the River Tweed, or indeed beyond, but the meaning of 'Northumbrians' is ambiguous.[6] Erik, the earl to whom Cnut gave the 'Northumbrians', is said in the annal for 1016 to have taken the place of Uhtred.[7] This Uhtred had been entrusted with York by King Æthelred II (r. 978–1016), but had also been the senior representative of a dynasty that had probably been based at Bamburgh for at least a century (see Map 1).[8] One might infer from the 1016 annal that Erik succeeded Uhtred at both York and Bamburgh, but three late eleventh- or early twelfth-century texts associated with Durham name Uhtred's successor as his

---

[5] Henry of Huntingdon, *Historia Anglorum*, i.4–5, ed. and trans. D. Greenway (Oxford, 1996), pp. 16–18. This passage must postdate the foundation of an episcopal see at Carlisle in 1133.

[6] Below, pp. 24–5.　　　[7] *ASC* CDE 1016.

[8] *De obsessione Dunelmi*, ed. T. Arnold, *Symeonis Monachi Opera Omnia* (RS, 75, 2 vols, London, 1882–5), i, 216; D. Whitelock, 'The Dealings of the Kings of England with Northumbria in the Tenth and Eleventh Centuries', in P. Clemoes (ed.), *The Anglo-Saxons: Studies in Some Aspects of their History and Culture Presented to Bruce Dickins* (London, 1959), pp. 77–84; below, p. 199 n. 21. The rulers of Bamburgh are generally assumed to have been from a single dynasty, on the grounds that several of them had similar names, but my arguments would not be greatly affected if power there shifted between two or more families.

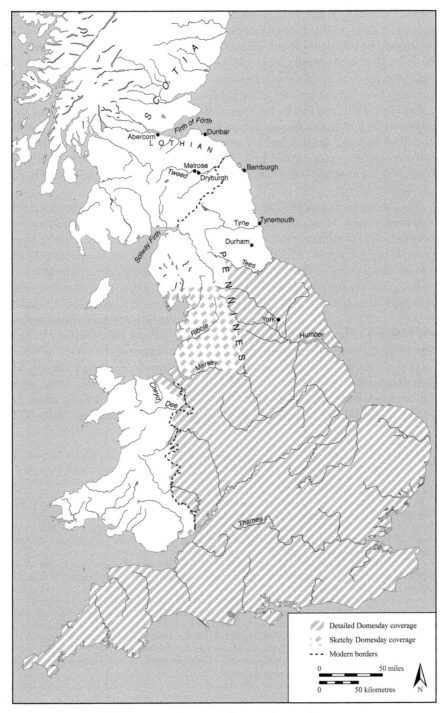

Map 1. The extent of Domesday *Anglia*.

brother Eadwulf Cudel, and say nothing of Erik.[9] Since the relevant sections of these texts focus on the rulers of Bamburgh, the apparent discrepancy is most readily resolved by postulating that Uhtred was succeeded there by Eadwulf, and at York by Erik. This would parallel what had happened about half a century before, the only previous time when a southern king is known to have given authority at York to a man from Bamburgh: two of the Durham texts state that this was followed by a division at either the Tees or the Tyne, and the man whom they name as the new appointee at York was probably not associated with Bamburgh.[10] Cnut, and the author of the 1017 annal, may have regarded Eadwulf as subordinate to Erik, but it is also eminently possible that Erik was earl only from the Humber to the Tees or Tyne, which would imply that one of the latter two rivers was the northern limit of the *Angelcynnes rice*.

The Domesday survey of 1086 sheds further light on how the kingdom's extent was perceived in the eleventh century. In the west, the limit of detailed coverage corresponds approximately to the modern Anglo-Welsh border, the greatest divergence being the survey's inclusion of a coastal strip from the Dee estuary to the Clwyd, about thirty or forty kilometres inside present-day Wales. Domesday ends well south of the Tweed and the Solway Firth, however: in the north-east, it remains reasonably detailed as far as the Tees, but then stops entirely; west of the Pennines, it becomes thinner after the Mersey, gives only terse lists of taxable lands beyond the Ribble, and says nothing about what we now call the Lake District.[11] The E text of the *Chronicle* nonetheless states that those conducting the survey were sent 'over all *Englaland*', and that 'no hide of land in *Englælande*' went unrecorded.[12] Domesday also very quickly came to be known as the *descriptio totius Anglie* ('description of the whole of *Anglia*').[13] This implies that the areas about which the survey is silent could be understood as lying outside *Englaland* or *Anglia*. One

[9] *De obsessione Dunelmi*, p. 218; *Historia Regum*, ed. Arnold, *Symeonis Monachi Opera Omnia*, ii, 197; *De primo Saxonum adventu*, ed. Arnold, *Symeonis Monachi Opera Omnia*, ii, 383; D. Rollason, 'Symeon's Contribution to Historical Writing in Northern England', in D. Rollason (ed.), *Symeon of Durham: Historian of Durham and the North* (Stamford, 1998), pp. 10–11.

[10] *Historia Regum*, p. 197; *De primo Saxonum adventu*, p. 382; below, pp. 32–3, 178–9 and n. 290. The killing of Uhtred is usually ascribed to 1016, but is placed in 1018 by A. A. M. Duncan, 'The Battle of Carham, 1018', *SHR*, 55 (1976), pp. 20–8. Duncan's date would imply that Erik gained power at York prior to Uhtred's death, but my point would be unaffected: notwithstanding Erik's appointment, Uhtred's family retained power in northern Northumbria.

[11] The extent of Domesday's coverage can be seen from the map 'England at the time of the Domesday survey 1086–87' in the map case of *Great Domesday*, ed. R. W. H. Erskine, A. Williams, and G. H. Martin (6 cases, London, 1986–92). *ASC* D 1063 suggests that at least some of the land between the Dee and the Clwyd had probably only come (back) under English domination shortly before Domesday. On Domesday's coverage of the land between the Mersey and the Ribble, and north of the latter river, see C. P. Lewis, 'An Introduction to the Lancashire Domesday', in A. Williams (ed.), *The Lancashire Domesday* (London, 1991), pp. 1–41; F. R. Thorn, 'Hundreds and Wapentakes', in Williams (ed.), *Lancashire Domesday*, pp. 42–54. See also S 1536; below, pp. 155–6.

[12] *ASC* E 1085, 1087. E is the only version of the *Chronicle* to provide more than very fragmentary coverage after 1080. On hides, see below, pp. 92–8.

[13] *Regesta Regum Anglo-Normannorum: The Acta of William I (1066–1087)*, ed. D. Bates (Oxford, 1998), no. 326; W. H. Stevenson, 'A Contemporary Description of the Domesday Survey', *EHR*, 22 (1907), p. 74; *Feudal Documents from the Abbey of Bury St. Edmunds*, ed. D. C. Douglas (London, 1932), p. 3.

might suggest that such references to Domesday were not intended to give literal descriptions of its scope, but another text from a few years later reinforces the conclusion that *Anglia* could be regarded as ending somewhere south of the Tyne, most likely at the Tees: a writ-charter issued in or soon after 1095 by William II, son of William the Conqueror, confirmed the possessions of the church of Tynemouth 'north of the Tyne, and south of the Tyne, and in *Anglia*'.[14] West of the Pennines, we have no comparable evidence to set beside Domesday, the increasing vagueness of which makes it unclear where *Anglia* was perceived to end. In particular, *Anglia* may not have encompassed the area north of the Ribble, which could perhaps have been on a broadly similar footing to the various parts of Wales that also received brief mentions in Domesday.[15]

When I refer to 'Domesday *Anglia*', I mean the area that the survey covers in detail, namely the land from the Channel to the Mersey and the Tees (excluding Wales), plus perhaps some or all of the region between the Mersey and the Lake District; I use 'northern Britain' to designate the land beyond, and 'Britain' is the name of the whole island.[16] Setting aside the ambiguity concerning the area from the Mersey to the Lakes, the key issue here is that of what the composer of the Tynemouth writ-charter and persons writing about Domesday meant when they used the words *Anglia* or *Englaland*. It is unlikely that they were referring to 'the area inhabited by the English' since, as we shall see, contemporaries regarded as English those who lived in what is now south-east Scotland. Rather, they were probably using *Englaland* or *Anglia* to denote 'the English kingdom', which would chime with these words' appearances as names of a *rice* or *regnum* ('kingdom') in the D text of the *Chronicle* and the *Encomium Emmae*: this would imply that (some) eleventh-century writers saw the English kingdom as stopping well before the Tweed and the Solway Firth.

Nonetheless, it is clear that throughout the eleventh century the kingdom was understood as extending across the bulk of what is now England. On account of this, many modern writers have characterized what happened in the tenth century as the 'unification' of the English. This label is rather misleading. To some extent, the problem with it is that the new kingdom incorporated many people who were at the time regarded not as English, but as Britons (the Cornish, for example) or Danes.[17] The more salient objection to the concept of 'unification', however, is that the eleventh-century kingdom did not encompass all those who were understood

---

[14] *Monasticon Anglicanum*, ed. W. Dugdale, J. Caley, H. Ellis, and B. Bandinel (6 vols in 8, London, 1817–30), iii, 313, datable by reference to the forfeiture of Earl Robert. Compare *ASC* E 1095.

[15] *DB*, i, 162a–162b, 179b, 183d, 186d, 253c, 254b, 255a, 269b refer to parts of Wales, although note that Archenfield is distinguished from both Wales and Herefordshire. See also H. C. Darby, *Domesday England* (Cambridge, 1977), pp. 321–33.

[16] I include London and Winchester within 'Domesday *Anglia*', although neither is described in the survey. It appears to have been intended that information about them be added, since spaces were left at appropriate points in the manuscript: V. H. Galbraith, *The Making of Domesday Book* (Oxford, 1961), pp. 195–6.

[17] D. M. Hadley, 'Viking and Native: Re-thinking Identity in the Danelaw', *EME*, 11 (2002), pp. 45–70 especially 46–53; C. Insley, 'Kings and Lords in Tenth-Century Cornwall', *History*, 98 (2013), pp. 2–22; below, pp. 44–5, 121–2. Hadley stresses that persons identified as 'Danes' need not have been biologically descended from Scandinavians.

by contemporaries to be English. West of the Pennines, where the evidence is extremely thin, one might circumvent this point by postulating that those living north of (say) the Ribble were for the most part seen as Cumbrian or Scandinavian.[18] East of the Pennines, however, the objection cannot be dodged, since there is ample evidence that the English were regarded as stretching to the Forth, which had been the northern limit of the pre-viking Northumbrian kingdom. Bede, who completed his *Ecclesiastical History* in the early 730s, and saw himself as a member of the *gens Anglorum* ('English people'), stated that the church at Abercorn, near modern Edinburgh in West Lothian, lay 'in the territory of the English [*regione Anglorum*] but in the vicinity of the sea that divides the lands of the English [*Anglorum terras*] and of the Picts'.[19] Sometime before about 900, this was rendered into the vernacular as 'in Engla londe ac hwæðre neah þæm sæ, þe Engla lond 7 Peohta tosceadaþ'.[20] This constitutes the earliest extant occurrence of the term *Englaland*; given the modern significance of the so-called 'West Lothian Question', the context is more than a little ironic.[21]

The vernacular version of the *Ecclesiastical History* appears to use *Englaland* to mean 'the land inhabited by the English', an area that was different both from the *Englaland* described in Domesday and from modern England. The word 'England' consequently risks confusion, and I generally avoid it in medieval contexts, instead using 'the English kingdom' to refer to the political entity that seems in the eleventh century to have been regarded (at least by some) as stretching from the Channel to the Tees. Setting aside this matter of terminology, two points are significant here. The first is that by the eleventh century some land south of the Forth had probably been under Scottish domination for quite a considerable time.[22] Early twelfth-century writers stated that Lothian, the land between the Forth and the

---

[18] G. Fellows-Jensen, 'Scandinavian Settlement in Cumbria and Dumfriesshire: The Place-Name Evidence', in J. R. Baldwin and I. D. Whyte (eds), *The Scandinavians in Cumbria* (Edinburgh, 1985), pp. 65–82; T. M. Charles-Edwards, *Wales and the Britons, 350–1064* (Oxford, 2013), pp. 575–8. Charles-Edwards's discussion focuses on S 1243, a mid- or late eleventh-century writ-charter in the name of one Gospatric, who may well have been from Bamburgh. The text alludes to 'the lands that were Cumbrian' in Allerdale (in the north-west of modern Cumbria). This implies that the lands in question had in some way ceased to be Cumbrian, but that this identity remained significant. The English king is not mentioned, and there is nothing to indicate that the author saw Allerdale as part of the English kingdom; Gospatric granted privileges that within the kingdom are only known to have been given by the king.

[19] *HE*, iv.26 (p. 428). On Bede's conception of the *gens Anglorum*, see especially P. Wormald, 'The Venerable Bede and the "Church of the English"', in G. Rowell (ed.), *The English Religious Tradition and the Genius of Anglicanism* (Wantage, 1992), pp. 21–2, with the caveats noted by G. Molyneaux, 'The *Old English Bede*: English Ideology or Christian Instruction?', *EHR*, 124 (2009), pp. 1296–8; G. Molyneaux, 'Did the English Really Think they were God's Elect in the Anglo-Saxon Period?', *Journal of Ecclesiastical History*, 65 (2014), pp. 721–37.

[20] *OEB*, iv.27 (p. 358).

[21] E. John, *Orbis Britanniae and Other Studies* (Leicester, 1966), p. 1 n. 1.

[22] What follows draws on M. O. Anderson, 'Lothian and the Early Scottish Kings', *SHR*, 39 (1960), pp. 98–112; G. W. S. Barrow, 'The Anglo-Scottish Border', *Northern History*, 1 (1966), pp. 21–42, reprinted in his *The Kingdom of the Scots: Government, Church and Society from the Eleventh to the Fourteenth Century*, 2nd edn (Edinburgh, 2003), pp. 119–29; B. Meehan, 'The Siege of Durham, the Battle of Carham and the Cession of Lothian', *SHR*, 55 (1976), pp. 1–19 especially 12–17; G. W. S. Barrow, 'Midlothian—or the Shire of Edinburgh?', *Book of the Old Edinburgh Club*, 35 (1985), pp. 141–8 especially 141–2; A. Woolf, *From Pictland to Alba, 789–1070* (Edinburgh, 2007), pp. 211, 234–6.

Tweed or some part thereof, had long since been given to different Scottish kings, with the donor variously named as King Edgar (r. 957/959–975), Eadwulf Cudel, or King Edward the Confessor (r. 1042–1066).[23] The gift could have been confirmed repeatedly, or revoked and reinstated, so these accounts need not be contradictory, but it is most unlikely that any of them describe the beginning of Scottish domination south of the Forth. Rather, the 'gifts' were probably recognitions of a Scottish fait accompli. As early as 685, the northern part of Northumbrian territory was under pressure: Bede's mention of Abercorn occurs in the context of its abandonment after a Pictish victory that year.[24] There are several references, mostly in the so-called *Chronicle of the Kings of Alba*, to Scottish kings active south of the Forth from the mid-ninth century onwards. Kenneth I (r. 840–858) burned Dunbar and seized Melrose. Constantine II fought against Ragnald, a Hiberno-Scandinavian potentate, on the Tyne in or around 918. Malcolm I raided as far as the Tees in 950. During the reign of Idulb (r. 954–962), 'opidum Eden', usually taken as referring to Edinburgh, was 'vacated' (by whom is unclear) and thereafter held by the Scots.[25] The result of all this was that territory south of the Forth, which Bede had regarded as within 'the lands of the English', was by the end of the tenth century under the domination of the kings of Scots.

The second important point is that, notwithstanding the southern extension of Scottish domination, the perception persisted that the land south of the Forth was in some sense English, and the term *Scotia* was until at least the early thirteenth century commonly applied only to the area further north.[26] Thus, for example, the E text of the *Chronicle* records that in 1091 Malcolm III went 'out of *Scotlande* into Lothian in *Englaland*', a statement that is all the more striking since the same text had referred a few years previously to Domesday covering all *Englaland*: in one case, *Englaland* probably meant 'the English kingdom', and in the other 'the land inhabited by the English'.[27] The distinction between kingdom and inhabitants was more explicitly articulated by Adam of Dryburgh, who wrote in 1179/1180 in what is now the Scottish Borders, and alluded to his being 'in the land of the English [*terra Anglorum*] and in the kingdom of the Scots [*regno Scotorum*]'.[28] Perceptions

---

[23] *De primo Saxonum adventu*, p. 382; *De obsessione Dunelmi*, p. 218; Orderic Vitalis, *Ecclesiastical History*, viii.22, ed. and trans. M. Chibnall (6 vols, Oxford, 1969–80), iv, 268–70.

[24] *HE*, iv.26 (p. 428).

[25] *Chronicle of the Kings of Alba*, ed. B. T. Hudson, 'The Scottish Chronicle', *SHR*, 77 (1998), pp. 148–51; *Annals of Ulster*, 918, ed. and trans. S. Mac Airt and G. Mac Niocaill, *The Annals of Ulster (to A.D. 1131). Part I: Text and Translation* (Dublin, 1983), p. 368; *Historia de Sancto Cuthberto*, xxii, xxiv, ed. T. Johnson South (Cambridge, 2002), pp. 60, 62, with comment at 105–6, 107. Kenneth I is traditionally regarded as a 'Scottish' king. This is no place to explore whether he should be described as 'Pictish'. The *Chronicle of the Kings of Alba* implies that Dunbar and Melrose were in *Saxonia*, a word that Irish writers commonly used to designate the land of the English: this mirrors the *Old English* Bede's reference to Abercorn being in *Englaland*.

[26] D. Broun, 'Defining Scotland and the Scots before the Wars of Independence', in D. Broun, R. J. Finlay, and M. Lynch (eds), *Image and Identity: The Making and Re-Making of Scotland through the Ages* (Edinburgh, 1998), pp. 4–17.

[27] *ASC* E 1085, 1087, 1091.

[28] Adam of Dryburgh, *De tripartito tabernaculo*, ii.13, in *Patrologia Latina*, ed. J. P. Migne (221 vols, Paris, 1844–64), cxcviii, column 723. For the date, see A. Wilmart, 'Magister Adam Cartvsiensis', in *Mélanges Mandonnet: Études d'histoire littéraire et doctrinale du moyen âge* (2 vols, Paris, 1930), ii, 154–5.

did eventually change, however. Thus, while the chronicle compiled at Melrose (also in the Borders) in 1173/1174 was thoroughly English in outlook, ignoring Scottish affairs and describing Bede as 'the honour and glory of our people [*gens*]', its continuations gradually shifted over the subsequent century from an English to a Scottish perspective.[29] Hence, those under Scottish rule who had once identified as English eventually came to see themselves as Scottish, just as those under English rule who had once identified as Danish eventually came to see themselves as English. This was, however, a slow process, an indication of the deep-rootedness of the belief that those who dwelt south of the Forth were English.

While Adam of Dryburgh's comment indicates that he considered Lothian part of the Scottish kingdom, others may have seen the matter differently, especially in earlier generations: this is particularly implied by a charter of 1095, in which the Scottish king Edgar referred to himself as 'possessing the whole land of Lothian [*totam terram de Lodoneio*] and the kingdom of *Scotia* [*regnum Scotiae*] by the gift of my lord William [i.e. William II], king of the English, and by paternal inheritance'.[30] Indeed, we cannot rule out the possibility that certain people held the Forth to be the northern limit of the eleventh-century English kingdom: there is no extant evidence for such a claim, but it might be thought implicit in English kings' purporting to give Lothian to their Scottish counterparts, and in William II's issuing a confirmation of the grants in Lothian that Edgar made in 1095.[31] Equally, though, some people may have asserted that the Scottish kingdom should extend south to the Tees, a possibility particularly suggested by Malcolm III's participation in the laying of the foundation stones of Durham Cathedral in 1093, an occasion at which William II is not known to have been present.[32] We should not, however, assume that the English and Scottish kingdoms were generally perceived to be separated by any linear border: certain people may have thought in such terms,

---

[29] D. Broun, 'Becoming Scottish in the Thirteenth Century: The Evidence of the Chronicle of Melrose', in B. Ballin Smith, S. Taylor, and G. Williams (eds), *West over Sea: Studies in Scandinavian Sea-Borne Expansion and Settlement before 1300. A Festschrift in Honour of Dr Barbara E. Crawford* (Leiden, 2007), pp. 19–32. For the reference to Bede, see London, British Library, MS Cotton Faustina B.ix, fo. 2ʳ, consulted in facsimile in D. Broun and J. Harrison, *The Chronicle of Melrose Abbey: A Stratigraphic Edition. I: Introduction and Facsimile* (Woodbridge, 2007).

[30] *Early Scottish Charters Prior to A.D. 1153*, ed. A. C. Lawrie (Glasgow, 1905), no. 15, the authenticity of which is defended by A. A. M. Duncan, 'Yes, the Earliest Scottish Charters', *SHR*, 78 (1999), pp. 1–38. If the charter is a later confection, and Lothian was in fact commonly regarded in the eleventh century as within the Scottish kingdom, this would only strengthen my argument that many contemporaries did not see the English kingdom as including all the English. Edgar's deference to William was at least in part a consequence of his need for support in a succession dispute: *ASC* E 1097.

[31] *Early Scottish Charters*, no. 16. That Lothian was rightfully part of the English kingdom was occasionally asserted in the thirteenth century: Gerald of Wales, *De principis instructione*, ii.1, ed. G. F. Warner, in J. S. Brewer, J. F. Dimock, and G. F. Warner (eds), *Giraldi Cambrensis Opera* (RS, 21, 8 vols, London, 1861–91), viii, 156; Matthew Paris, *Chronica Majora*, ed. H. R. Luard (RS, 57, 7 vols, London, 1872–83), v, 268. For more numerous twelfth- and thirteenth-century references to the Tweed as the border, see Barrow, 'Anglo-Scottish Border', pp. 124–6.

[32] *De iniusta vexatione Willelmi episcopi*, xx, ed. Arnold, *Symeonis Monachi Opera Omnia*, i, 195; *Historia Regum*, p. 220. G. W. S. Barrow, 'The Scots and the North of England', in E. King (ed.), *The Anarchy of King Stephen's Reign* (Oxford, 1994), pp. 231–53, reprinted in his *Kingdom*, pp. 130–47 argues that David I's southern expansion during Stephen's reign was driven by a long-standing Scottish claim to the land as far as the Tees.

but the overriding impression given by the exiguous evidence is of the ambiguous status of the land between the Tees and the Forth.[33] In the eleventh century, this area did not clearly form part of either the English or the Scottish kingdom, and was probably quite widely regarded as distinct from both: indeed, it is striking that the charter of Edgar that presents Lothian as separate from the *regnum Scotiae* is almost exactly contemporaneous with the document in which William II treated *Anglia* as stopping somewhere short of the Tyne.

Most of the extant evidence that can illuminate the extent of the eleventh-century English kingdom is from the 1080s or later, but the accumulated scraps are sufficient to make it very doubtful that many contemporaries thought of the kingdom as encompassing all the English. As such, it is inaccurate to describe what happened in the tenth century as 'the unification of the English'. Nor is it helpful to think in terms of the 'unification of the English kingdom', since the kingdom did not previously exist in some fragmented form, waiting to be assembled. The word 'unification' should therefore be eschewed, just as historians have increasingly avoided writing of a tenth-century 'reconquest', a traditional label which erroneously implied that kings were recovering something that their predecessors had once held.[34] My objection to the word 'unification' is more than terminological point-scoring, since it affects how we think about the events of the tenth century. The word is strongly associated with the so-called Italian and German 'unifications' of the nineteenth century; indeed, the *Oxford English Dictionary* records no use of the term in English before 1848, when it appears in a passage about recent and anticipated events in Italy.[35] Talk of tenth-century English 'unification' implicitly suggests that the events of that period should be compared to the much later 'unifications' of other European peoples. This is problematic, since is sometimes prompts historians to see the English as exceptional, and to feel the need to identify special causes for their peculiarly precocious 'unification'.[36] But if we dispense with the idea of 'unification', what happened in the tenth century was that a series of kings extended their domination over a relatively large territory, and intensified their hold of some of it. This was not an unusual phenomenon in early medieval Europe, and we need not seek an extraordinary explanation for it.

[33] W. M. Aird, 'Northumbria and the Making of the Kingdom of the English', in H. Tsurushima (ed.), *Nations in Medieval Britain* (Donington, 2010), pp. 45–60 emphasizes the region's ambiguous position. John of Worcester, *Chronicle*, 1093, ed. and trans. R. R. Darlington, P. McGurk, and J. Bray (2 vols so far, Oxford, 1995–), iii, 64 may allude to a linear border between the kingdoms, but need not do so, since one could translate 'in regnorum suorum confiniis' as 'in the borderlands of their kingdoms', rather than 'on the boundaries of their kingdoms': R. E. Latham et al., *Dictionary of Medieval Latin from British Sources* (Oxford, 1975–2013), s.v. 'confinium'.

[34] P. Wormald, 'Engla Lond: The Making of an Allegiance', *Journal of Historical Sociology*, 7 (1994), pp. 1–24, reprinted in his *Legal Culture in the Early Medieval West: Law as Text, Image and Experience* (London, 1999), p. 365.

[35] M. Proffitt et al., *Oxford English Dictionary Online*, s.v. 'unification', consulted at <http://www.oed.com/> (accessed 9 October 2014); L. Mariotti, *Italy, Past and Present* (2 vols, London, 1848), ii, 25.

[36] E.g. P. Wormald, 'Bede, the *Bretwaldas* and the Origins of the *Gens Anglorum*', in P. Wormald, D. Bullough, and R. Collins (eds), *Ideal and Reality in Frankish and Anglo-Saxon Society: Studies Presented to J. M. Wallace-Hadrill* (Oxford, 1983), pp. 99–129 especially 103–4.

THE ARGUMENT OF THIS BOOK

While perhaps less exceptional than often thought, the events of the tenth century remain important: Britain's political landscape was fundamentally changed by the establishment of a stable and enduring kingdom that was markedly more powerful than any other on the island. On one level, the formation of the English kingdom was a consequence of a series of campaigns and agreements during the late ninth century and the first half of the tenth: when Alfred (now often styled 'the Great') became king of the West Saxons in 871, his power stretched little north of the Thames, but over subsequent decades he and his successors extended their domination across what would later constitute Domesday *Anglia*, and indeed throughout the whole of Britain. Chapter 1 summarizes and analyses the sequence of events by which these kings increased the geographical range of their domination, but this alone is not enough to understand the English kingdom's formation. In particular, the narrative of expansion does not directly account for why, when both the area of English habitation and the power of English kings stretched significantly further than the Tees, this river was seen by at least some people in the eleventh century as the kingdom's northern frontier. There is, however, an obvious and compelling explanation for why people should have perceived the kingdom in this way: the Tees marked the limit, as James Campbell has observed, of a zone of 'uniform institutions', the most important of which were shires and their subdivisions, known as hundreds or wapentakes.[37] Since these administrative units were found throughout the area between the Channel and the Tees, but not beyond (or in Wales), there is good reason to infer that they were crucial to the definition of the eleventh-century English kingdom.

Historians have paid relatively little attention to the evidence that in the eleventh century the Tees marked (at least for some) the limit of the English kingdom; indeed, the lack of Domesday coverage further north is sometimes seen as a puzzling omission, as if the whole of modern England ought for some reason to have been included.[38] The 'uniform institutions' of shires, hundreds, and wapentakes have, by contrast, attracted considerable comment, and indeed adulation. Thanks in large part to Campbell's work, and also to that of Patrick Wormald, it is

---

[37] J. Campbell, 'The United Kingdom of England: The Anglo-Saxon Achievement', in A. Grant and K. J. Stringer (eds), *Uniting the Kingdom: The Making of British History* (London, 1995), pp. 31–47, reprinted in his *The Anglo-Saxon State* (London, 2000), pp. 47, 49.

[38] E.g. P. Chaplais, 'William of Saint-Calais and the Domesday Survey', in J. C. Holt (ed.), *Domesday Studies: Papers Read at the Novocentenary Conference of the Royal Historical Society and the Institute of British Geographers, Winchester, 1986* (Woodbridge, 1987), p. 68: 'the counties north of the Tees…unaccountably seem to have been left out'. If Chaplais is correct that the Bishop of Durham was 'the man behind the Survey', it is possible that he was entrusted with this task because the survey would not (with a few exceptions) concern his own church's lands. For recognition that the Tees may well have been regarded as the kingdom's northern boundary, see, however, W. E. Kapelle, *The Norman Conquest of the North: The Region and its Transformation, 1000–1135* (Chapel Hill, NC, 1979), pp. 12–13; W. M. Aird, *St Cuthbert and the Normans: The Church of Durham, 1071–1153* (Woodbridge, 1998), p. 227; Barrow, 'Scots and the North of England', pp. 131–2. Campbell, 'United Kingdom of England', pp. 49–50 classifies the land beyond the Tees as 'a zone…of frontier lordships', but does not address the question of whether it was considered to be outwith the English kingdom.

now well established that this administrative apparatus enabled eleventh-century kings routinely to monitor, constrain, and direct significant aspects of the behaviour of even quite ordinary people throughout the area from the Channel to the Tees.[39] It is, for example, widely recognized that shires, hundreds, and wapentakes were very probably used to assess and collect a heavy land tax across all or much of this area between 1012 and 1051;[40] to extract oaths from all (free) adult males in at least some regions from the time of Cnut (r. 1016–1035) at the latest;[41] and to organize the Domesday survey, the scope of which appears to have been unprecedented in medieval western Europe.[42] Certain claims that have been made for eleventh-century bureaucratic neatness are probably overstated; it is, for example, doubtful whether variations in the weight and fineness of coins were primarily the result of a meticulous plan.[43] Nonetheless, it is clear that by the eleventh century kings were able to affect directly and routinely the lives of a substantial proportion of the population of Domesday *Anglia*: I thus accept the broad thrust of Campbell's and Wormald's arguments, insofar as they relate to the last decades of the Anglo-Saxon period.

The caveat at the end of the previous sentence is, however, important. Despite all the significance that has been imputed to the administrative structures of what is commonly called the 'Anglo-Saxon state', there has been relatively little detailed study of when and how these became integral to royal power across what would constitute Domesday *Anglia*.[44] This is problematic, since historians frequently treat the 195 years between Alfred's succession (871) and the Norman Conquest (1066) as a block, but it is only from the second half of the tenth century onwards that we have good evidence of kings using shires, hundreds, and wapentakes for routine local regulation; those who have written surveys of royal rule in the late Anglo-Saxon period often nod to the likelihood that significant changes occurred between Alfred and 1066, without saying much about what they think changed when. This has the effect of making the late ninth and tenth centuries seem essentially similar to the eleventh, and there is sometimes

[39] See especially J. Campbell, 'Some Agents and Agencies of the Late Anglo-Saxon State', in Holt (ed.), *Domesday Studies*, pp. 201–18, reprinted in his *Anglo-Saxon State*, pp. 201–25; J. Campbell, 'The Late Anglo-Saxon State: A Maximum View', *PBA*, 87 (1994), pp. 39–65, reprinted in his *Anglo-Saxon State*, pp. 1–30; P. Wormald, 'Giving God and King their Due: Conflict and its Regulation in the Early English State', *Settimane di studio del centro italiano di studi sull'alto medioevo*, 44 (1997), pp. 549–90, reprinted in his *Legal Culture*, pp. 333–57, but on Wormald's arguments about vengeance see the literature cited below at p. 74 n. 115.

[40] Below, pp. 143, 165, 185, 197. *ASC* D 1051 makes clear that the *heregeld* was an eleventh-century innovation.

[41] II Cn 20–1; below, pp. 195–6. That only 'free' men were required to swear is not explicit, but this is implied by II Cn 20, which also provides the basis for thinking that hundreds were used to organize oath-taking. The meaning of 'free' is far from clear.

[42] For Domesday hundred juries, see the *Inquisitio Eliensis* and the *Inquisitio Comitatus Cantabrigiensis*, both in *Inquisitio Comitatus Cantabrigiensis*, ed. N. E. S. A. Hamilton (London, 1876). For Continental comparisons, see J. Campbell, 'Observations on English Government from the Tenth to the Twelfth Century', *TRHS*, 5th series, 25 (1975), pp. 39–54, reprinted in his *Essays in Anglo-Saxon History* (London, 1986), pp. 163–7; R. H. C. Davis, 'Domesday Book: Continental Parallels', in Holt (ed.), *Domesday Studies*, pp. 15–39.

[43] Below, pp. 119–20.   [44] On the term 'state', see below, pp. 232–3.

an implication or claim, notably in Wormald's work, that structures and practices visible in the eleventh century obtained from at least the reign of Alfred.[45] It is not surprising that historians have sought to project late tenth- and eleventh-century arrangements into the more distant past, since there is a strong tradition in English historiography of interpreting one period in the light of a subsequent, better-documented age.[46] It is moreover possible, if one assumes that a network of neatly organized shires and hundreds was already fundamental to how kings ruled in the late ninth and early tenth centuries, to interpret the fragmentary extant evidence in ways that are not inconsistent with this premise. The outcome, however, risks being what (in the context of Ottonian Germany) Karl Leyser called 'a shadow-history of institutions that did not really exist': a key argument of this book is that it was probably not until the mid- to late tenth century, around the time of King Edgar, that kings began to make extensive use of the administrative structures that would mark Domesday *Anglia* off from the rest of Britain.[47]

The proposition that certain developments came later than is often thought depends in large part on drawing inferences from the silence of sources, a mode of argument that cannot be entirely conclusive. The burden of proof, however, surely lies with those who believe that particular institutions *did* play major roles from an early date, and I contend that in this instance the grounds for accepting the argument from silence, while necessarily circumstantial, are cumulatively compelling. I make this case most directly in Chapter 4, which is the core of the book, but the other chapters are also important to my overall claim. As well as giving a (fairly conventional) summary of political events, Chapter 1 emphasizes that the relative calm of much of the period between the mid-950s and about 990 contrasts with the frequent campaigns of the preceding decades: thus, even if one were to suppose that an eleventh-century-style administrative apparatus already existed in Alfred's Wessex, it is far from clear that he and his successors would have been in a position to replicate it elsewhere before the second half of the tenth century. Chapters 2 and 3 then examine the power of Alfred and his successors up to the mid-tenth century, without the assumption that they used an ordered network of shires and hundreds to regulate local affairs. My aim in these chapters is less to rebut the proposition that kings ruled in such a way, and more to demonstrate two other things. First, it is possible to account for the

---

[45] Examples of accounts that combine the tenth and eleventh centuries include Campbell, 'Observations on English Government'; H. R. Loyn, *The Governance of Anglo-Saxon England, 500–1087* (London, 1984), pp. 81–171; P. Stafford, *Unification and Conquest: A Political and Social History of England in the Tenth and Eleventh Centuries* (London, 1989), pp. 134–49. Campbell acknowledges particularly clearly that changes must have taken place in his 'Late Anglo-Saxon State', pp. 16–17. The innovations that Wormald most explicitly attributed to Alfred are the extraction of oaths from all free men aged twelve or over, and the placing of all such persons in surety groups: Wormald, '*Engla Lond*', pp. 366–7. On oaths and surety groups see below, pp. 195–6.

[46] This method was pioneered by F. W. Maitland, *Domesday Book and Beyond: Three Essays in the Early History of England* (Cambridge, 1897), and has been followed by many who have been less wary of its pitfalls.

[47] K. J. Leyser, 'Ottonian Government', *EHR*, 96 (1981), p. 732.

known achievements of Alfred and his immediate successors without resorting to the hypothesis that eleventh-century conditions already obtained. Second, if one refrains from conjuring up undocumented shires and hundreds, the future Domesday *Anglia* did not yet stand as a block distinct from the rest of Britain. This paves the way for Chapter 4, in which I give detailed reasons for concluding that significant aspects of royal rule between the Channel and the Tees were transformed in the mid- to late tenth century, such that this area came for the first time to be marked by a set of broadly common characteristics. Chapter 5 in turn considers the implications and limits of these reforms, contending in particular that the combination of change and continuity in the second half of the tenth century was fundamental both to the English kingdom's definition and to its subsequent 'constitutional tradition'. The concluding chapter then returns to the historiographical issues raised in this Introduction, placing the events of the tenth century in a comparative context, and arguing that the pattern of English historical development in this period should not be seen as an exception to some kind of European norm.

Frank Stenton entitled his chapter on the period between 955 and 1016 'The Decline of the Old English Monarchy', but hardly any historians would now argue that the second half of the tenth century saw a major diminution in the power of English kings.[48] Indeed, Simon Keynes, one of the most distinguished modern authorities on the Anglo-Saxon period, has stated that the English kingdom 'did not come of age' until the 960s.[49] Keynes does not, however, go into much detail about what this coming of age entailed, and he and others who have written overviews of the kingdom's development tend to present the mid- to late tenth century as a time of incremental refinements, rather than fundamental change.[50] Alfred and his grandson Æthelstan (r. 924–939) usually receive greater attention: the latter is lauded as 'the first king of England', and the former is celebrated as the visionary who planned the kingdom that his successors would create.[51] I seek to refute the claim that the eleventh-century English kingdom represented the realization of an earlier blueprint, and my argument for the importance of the second half of the tenth century implies that the focus of the historiographical limelight should be

---

[48] F. M. Stenton, *Anglo-Saxon England*, 3rd edn (Oxford, 1971), pp. 364–93.

[49] S. Keynes, 'Re-Reading King Æthelred the Unready', in D. Bates, J. Crick, and S. Hamilton (eds), *Writing Medieval Biography, 750–1250: Essays in Honour of Professor Frank Barlow* (Woodbridge, 2006), p. 85.

[50] Stafford, *Unification and Conquest*, pp. 45–68; S. Keynes, 'England, *c.*900–1016', in *NCMH3*, pp. 456–84 especially 479–84; A. Williams, *Kingship and Government in Pre-Conquest England, c.500–1066* (Basingstoke, 1999), pp. 81–96. See also S. Keynes, 'The Cult of King Alfred the Great', *ASE*, 28 (1999), pp. 355–6; S. Keynes, 'Edgar, *rex admirabilis*', in D. Scragg (ed.), *Edgar, King of the English 959–975: New Interpretations* (Woodbridge, 2008), pp. 10–26. Insofar as major innovations are ascribed to the second half of the tenth century, attention tends to focus on the spread of Benedictine monasticism. N. Banton, 'Monastic Reform and the Unification of Tenth-Century England', *Studies in Church History*, 18 (1982), pp. 71–85 contains several stimulating observations on the period's political significance, but Banton (who died in his thirties) never developed his ideas at length.

[51] E.g. D. N. Dumville, *Wessex and England from Alfred to Edgar* (Woodbridge, 1992), pp. 141–71, 204; P. Wormald, 'Living with King Alfred', *HSJ*, 15 (2004), p. 20; S. Foot, *Æthelstan: The First King of England* (New Haven, CT, 2011).

broadened beyond the likes of Alfred and Æthelstan.[52] But this is not to say that the reign of either of these kings was insignificant: the institutional changes of the second half of the tenth century were predicated on the campaigns, alliances, and coups of Alfred and his immediate successors, and it is to the geographical extension of these kings' domination that we now turn.

[52] Below, pp. 201–13.

1

The Geographical Extension of Cerdicing Domination

ENGLISH HISTORY, c.850–1066: A BRIEF NARRATIVE

In the mid-ninth century, there were probably at least fourteen kingdoms in the island of Britain; their approximate locations are indicated on Map 2 (see page 17). Writing in 893, Asser, a Welsh clergyman in King Alfred's service, indicated the existence of at least five kingdoms in Wales, and it is likely that two more had recently been absorbed by more powerful neighbours.[1] In present-day south-west Scotland was the kingdom of Strathclyde, which increasingly came to be referred to as Cumbria, although in the mid-ninth century the power of its kings probably did not yet extend into the area that is now known by the latter name.[2] Further north-east was the Pictish kingdom, which would somehow be transformed into *Alba*, the Scottish kingdom, from about 900.[3] Unlike these nine kingdoms, the other five that are documented in the mid-ninth century all lay at least partially within what would constitute Domesday *Anglia*. One of these, Cornwall, was Brittonic, as opposed to English; it is very obscure and its last known king, Dungarth, drowned in the mid-870s.[4] The East Anglian kingdom is also poorly documented, and little can be said about it other than that it is presumed to have comprised roughly what became Norfolk and Suffolk. Somewhat more evidence survives for the other three kingdoms. That of the Northumbrians stretched from the Humber to the Forth in Bede's day, although its northern frontier was under pressure by the mid-ninth century; it also extended across the Pennines and into the far south-west of present-day Scotland. South of the Humber was the Mercian kingdom, the kings of which were probably still dominant across the Midlands but, unlike at least some

---

[1] *VA*, lxxx (pp. 66–7). On the disappearances of Ceredigion and Powys, see T. M. Charles-Edwards, *Wales and the Britons, 350–1064* (Oxford, 2013), pp. 14–17, 487, 492, 495–6, 552.

[2] P. A. Wilson, 'On the Use of the Terms "Strathclyde" and "Cumbria"', *Transactions of the Cumberland and Westmorland Antiquarian and Archaeological Society*, n.s., 66 (1966), pp. 57–92; A. Woolf, *From Pictland to Alba, 789–1070* (Edinburgh, 2007), pp. 152–7, 270–1; Charles-Edwards, *Wales*, pp. 480–2. I have been unable to take significant account of F. Edmonds, 'The Emergence and Transformation of Medieval Cumbria', *SHR*, 93 (2014), pp. 195–216, which appeared when this volume was in press.

[3] D. Broun, *Scottish Independence and the Idea of Britain from the Picts to Alexander III* (Edinburgh, 2007), pp. 71–97; Woolf, *From Pictland to Alba*, especially pp. 320–42.

[4] *Annales Cambriae, A.D. 682–954: Texts A–C in Parallel*, ed. D. N. Dumville (Cambridge, 2002), pp. 12–13. It is not known whether this drowning was accidental.

of their eighth-century predecessors, no longer enjoyed hegemony throughout Southumbria (a term of convenience for the land south of the Humber, excluding Wales). The final identifiable mid-ninth-century kingdom was that of the West Saxons. The West Saxon kings' heartlands lay in the central part of the area south of the Thames, but they had benefited from the waning of Mercian power in Kent and the south-east in the early ninth century, and had probably reduced the Cornish kings to client status well before Dungarth's death. It thus appears that by the mid-ninth century the West Saxon kings' dominance encompassed everything south of the Thames.[5]

The Cerdicings

In the central decades of the ninth century, the West Saxon kings seem to have been on at least intermittently friendly terms with their Mercian counterparts, with whom they contracted marriage alliances, fought against the Welsh, and apparently cooperated in coin production.[6] There is, however, no sign that any mid-ninth-century king wielded significant power across the bulk of what, by the eleventh century, people readily thought of as 'the English kingdom'.[7] Nor would it have been clear at the time that the West Saxon kings' successors would continue to expand as their predecessors had done in the early ninth century; indeed, their territory was partitioned in the second half of the 850s. When the West Saxon king Æthelwulf (r. 839–858) went to Rome in 855, he appears to have entrusted the western part of his kingdom to Æthelbald, his eldest surviving son, and the eastern to Æthelberht, his second son. Æthelwulf returned the next year and resumed power in the eastern portion of his former kingdom, but Æthelbald refused to relinquish the territory with which he had been charged. When Æthelwulf died in 858, he was succeeded in the east by Æthelberht, but Æthelbald retained the western lands until his death in 860, whereupon Æthelberht became king of the whole area that Æthelwulf had once ruled. The division thus turned out to be fairly brief, but this appears in large part to have been a consequence of Æthelbald's relatively swift demise: that an indefinite partition had been envisaged is suggested by an account of Æthelwulf's testamentary dispositions preserved in the will of his youngest son, Alfred. Æthelwulf had mandated that certain lands should pass between three of his sons, Æthelbald, Æthelred, and Alfred; the will does not explicitly mention a division of the kingdom, but Æthelwulf's bequests imply that Æthelberht was to retain the east, while Æthelbald, Æthelred, and Alfred were to succeed in turn in the west. On Æthelbald's death, however, Æthelred and Alfred agreed to assign

[5] S. Keynes, 'England, 700–900', in *NCMH2*, pp. 18–42 is a useful overview, although perhaps over-sceptical of the possibility of Mercian domination of Wessex in the eighth century. For the Northumbrian kingdom's extent, see D. Rollason, *Northumbria, 500–1100: Creation and Destruction of a Kingdom* (Cambridge, 2003), pp. 20–53; above, pp. 6–7. On Cornwall, see Charles-Edwards, *Wales*, pp. 431, 494.

[6] S. Keynes, 'King Alfred and the Mercians', in M. A .S. Blackburn and D. N. Dumville (eds), *Kings, Currency and Alliances: History and Coinage of Southern England in the Ninth Century* (Woodbridge, 1998), pp. 2–11.

[7] For a very fleeting exception, see *ASC* ABCDE 829, 830.

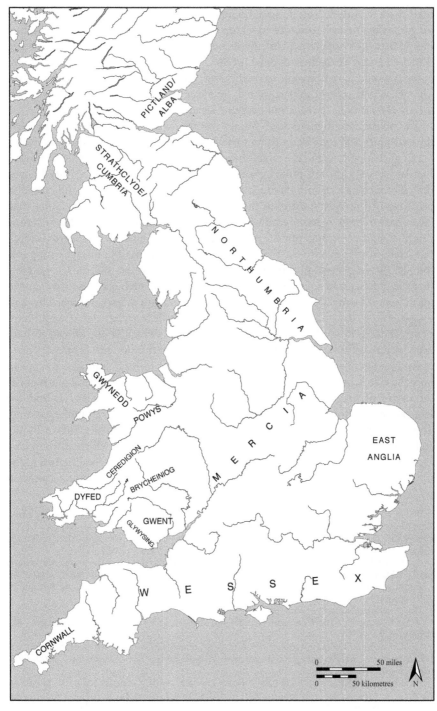

Map 2. The known kingdoms of mid-ninth century Britain.

their share to Æthelberht, perhaps because it was thought that combining the two kingdoms would aid resistance to viking raiders. Whatever the reason for modifying Æthelwulf's apparent plan, the reconstituted kingdom passed undivided to Æthelred I after Æthelberht's death in 865.[8] It is, however, unlikely that contemporaries would have been able to predict with confidence that the land south of the Thames would remain unpartitioned, let alone that Æthelred's successors would greatly extend their domination over the decades that followed.

The political configuration of Britain was fundamentally transformed between the mid-ninth and early eleventh century: this period saw the formation of an enduring English kingdom and the establishment by its kings of a Britain-wide hegemony that lasted, with various interruptions, until the early fourteenth century.[9] Given that Æthelred's successors extended their power far beyond Wessex and ceased to use 'king of the West Saxons' as their standard title, some expression other than 'West Saxon kings' is required if we are to have a consistent means of designating this royal lineage throughout the period examined in this book.[10] No term is ideal, but I refer to the dynasty as 'the Cerdicings', Cerdic being the lineage's supposed founder. Royal genealogical tracts trace descent from Cerdic (d. 534?), suggesting that the dynasty had a strong sense of its identity, and such texts use *Cerdicing* to mean 'son of Cerdic'.[11] The word was not (so far as I am aware) employed by contemporaries to designate the family as a whole, but it is nonetheless a useful term of art; indeed, it can be compared to 'Carolingian', which is not known to have been used to refer to Charles Martel's dynasty before the eleventh century.[12]

Knowledge of the narrative of high politics is not in itself sufficient to explain how the Cerdicings extended their power across Britain, but a general grasp of the succession of kings (depicted in the genealogical diagram in Fig. 1.1) and the sequence of major events is a prerequisite for an attempt at such an understanding. This requires us to consider the various texts that are traditionally known by the collective (if misleading) name 'the *Anglo-Saxon Chronicle*', on which any narrative account of the period has to rely heavily. There are five principal manuscripts of the *Chronicle*, conventionally designated by the letters A to E.[13] All share a 'common

---

[8] *VA*, xi–xviii (pp. 8–17); *ASC* ABCDE 855–858, 860, 866; S 1507; R. Abels, *Alfred the Great: War, Kingship and Culture in Anglo-Saxon England* (Harlow, 1998), pp. 68–94. *VA*, xvi (pp. 14–15) implies that Æthelwulf's will envisaged a division of the kingdom. See also *ASC* ABCDE 839; S. Keynes, 'The Control of Kent in the Ninth Century', *EME*, 2 (1993), pp. 120–31.

[9] On pan-British hegemony after the Norman Conquest and its decline in the fourteenth century, see R. R. Davies, *Domination and Conquest: The Experience of Ireland, Scotland and Wales, 1100–1300* (Cambridge, 1990); R. R. Davies, *The First English Empire: Power and Identities in the British Isles, 1093–1343* (Oxford, 2000).

[10] On royal titulature, see below, pp. 206–9.

[11] D. N. Dumville, 'The West Saxon Genealogical Regnal List: Manuscripts and Texts', *Anglia*, 104 (1986), pp. 1–32.

[12] M. Garrison, 'Divine Election for Nations—A Difficult Rhetoric for Medieval Scholars?', in L. B. Mortensen (ed.), *The Making of Christian Myths in the Periphery of Latin Christendom (c.1000–1300)* (Copenhagen, 2006), p. 306.

[13] S. Keynes, 'Manuscripts of the *Anglo-Saxon Chronicle*', in R. Gameson (ed.), *The Cambridge History of the Book in Britain. Volume I: c.400–1100* (Cambridge, 2012), pp. 537–52 is a useful survey of the vast literature on the *Chronicle*. Besides versions A to E, there are three further manuscripts, F, G, and H. F is a bilingual chronicle produced around the turn of the eleventh and twelfth centuries,

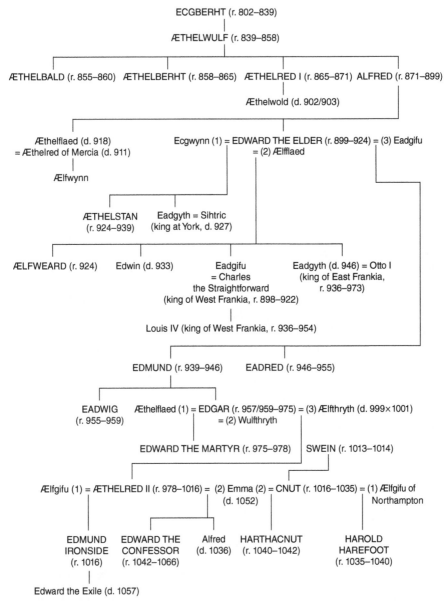

Cerdicing and Scandinavian kings are indicated in capitals, together with the dates of their reigns. For a more detailed genealogical tree, see P. Stafford, 'The King's Wife in Wessex, 800–1066', *P&P*, 91 (1981), pp. 8–9.

Fig. 1.1. The Cerdicings, 802–1066: a selective genealogical tree.

stock' of annals running from Julius Caesar's arrival in Britain to 890×892. This 'common stock' was probably put together around the latter date, drawing on oral tradition and earlier texts, and possibly the writer's personal knowledge and imagination. Whoever produced it appears to have sought to celebrate the antiquity and achievements of the Cerdicings, glossing over the dispute between Æthelbald and his father, and repeatedly stressing the dynasty's illustrious descent; this is emphasized further in the earliest extant manuscript, A, in which the 'common stock' is prefaced by a genealogical regnal list from Cerdic to Alfred.[14] The five main versions of the *Chronicle* all continue the shared set of annals, and in D and E a fair amount of additional material is also inserted within the 'common stock' itself. Each manuscript incorporates annals written by several unidentifiable authors at different times; quite often, two or more versions have the same or closely similar entries, but certain annals are unique to particular manuscripts. Parts of some of the continuations, such as the early tenth-century section of A, emulate the 'common stock' in celebrating the Cerdicings' achievements, but this is not a consistent feature of all versions: the retrospective and distinctly negative account of Æthelred II's reign found in C, D, and E is a notable counter example.[15] That the annals in the various texts are selective in what they record is highlighted at points where different versions offer contrasting perspectives on the same period: thus, for example, A's annals for the 910s focus on the deeds of Alfred's eldest son, passing over the contemporaneous actions in Mercia of the latter's sister, which are known from the so-called 'Mercian Register' that is incorporated in B, C, and D.[16] For most of the tenth century, however, all versions are terse and lacunose, and it is rare for different manuscripts to provide accounts that are both detailed and divergent. Consequently, we are, at any one time, often dependent on a single version of events, and have few or no means to ascertain what its author did not know or chose to omit. This makes it impossible to construct anything approaching a comprehensive narrative of tenth-century English history. My immediate aim, however, is simply to summarize

based in large part on a text similar to E. G is a copy of A. H is a fragment concerning the years 1113–1114. N. Brooks, ' "Anglo-Saxon Chronicle(s)" or "Old English Royal Annals"?', in J. L. Nelson, S. Reynolds, and S. M. Johns (eds), *Gender and Historiography: Studies in the Earlier Middle Ages in Honour of Pauline Stafford* (London, 2012), pp. 35–48, discusses the traditional title's shortcomings, but the label *Anglo-Saxon Chronicle* may be too firmly embedded to be discarded, and Brooks's proposed alternative privileges the texts' royal interests and associations.

[14] J. Campbell, 'Asser's *Life of Alfred*', in C. Holdsworth and T. P. Wiseman (eds), *The Inheritance of Historiography, 350–900* (Exeter, 1986), pp. 115–35, reprinted in his *The Anglo-Saxon State* (London, 2000), pp. 143–6, 150; A. Scharer, 'The Writing of History at King Alfred's Court', *EME*, 5 (1996), pp. 177–85. The 'common stock' annal concerning Julius Caesar is expanded and rewritten in the D and E texts.

[15] S. Keynes, 'The Declining Reputation of King Æthelred the Unready', in D. H. Hill (ed.), *Ethelred the Unready: Papers from the Millenary Conference* (Oxford, 1978), pp. 229–36; D. Pelteret, 'An Anonymous Historian of Edward the Elder's Reign', in S. Baxter, C. E. Karkov, J. L. Nelson, and D. Pelteret (eds), *Early Medieval Studies in Memory of Patrick Wormald* (Farnham, 2009), pp. 319–36.

[16] P. Stafford, ' "The Annals of Æthelflæd": Annals, History and Politics in Early Tenth-Century England', in J. Barrow and A. Wareham (eds), *Myth, Rulership, Church and Charters: Essays in Honour of Nicholas Brooks* (Aldershot, 2008), pp. 101–16; below, pp. 27–8. The 'Mercian Register' is cited as *ASC* MR.

the basic outlines of identifiable events, in order to provide some chronological framework for subsequent analysis of political structures.[17]

Viking Raiding and Scandinavian Settlement

Viking raiding and settlement form important parts of the background to the geographical extension of Cerdicing domination. By the mid-ninth century, several coastal areas of Britain had for some time been experiencing at least occasional viking raids, and there may already have been significant Scandinavian settlement in what is now western Scotland. The threat to the four English kingdoms increased substantially in 866, with the arrival of what appears to have been a particularly powerful viking force.[18] It killed the Northumbrian and East Anglian kings and in 871 turned on Wessex. Æthelred I, the West Saxon king, died the same year, having been defeated in battle at least three times in his final months. He was succeeded by his brother Alfred, who lost a further battle and then made peace, probably by paying tribute.[19] Thereafter, the vikings moved against Mercia, expelling its king and (according to the 'common stock') installing a certain Ceolwulf, who gave them oaths and hostages.[20] They soon returned to Wessex, however: in 878, with a substantial part of his kingdom under viking domination, Alfred took refuge at a stronghold in Somerset. From there, he mustered sufficient forces to win a significant victory at Edington in Wiltshire. As a result, the defeated viking leader Guthrum accepted baptism and his army agreed to leave Alfred's kingdom.[21]

From the mid-870s some of the vikings began to settle. The 'common stock' of the *Chronicle* refers to them sharing out land in Northumbria in 876, and says that they did the same in part of Mercia the following year, thereby depriving Ceolwulf of a chunk of what had been the Mercian kingdom. In 880, the army that had been defeated at Edington likewise divided up land in East Anglia.[22] The regions in which Scandinavian settlement took place are now often called 'the Danelaw', but the inconsistency with which this word is used risks confusion, and I therefore avoid it.[23] I also largely sidestep the long-running historiographical debates about the scale of Scandinavian settlement, and the extent to which it was the cause of certain distinctive characteristics of northern and eastern parts of the eleventh-century

---

[17] More detailed narratives are provided by F. M. Stenton, *Anglo-Saxon England*, 3rd edn (Oxford, 1971), pp. 239–76, 319–432, 560–621; P. Stafford, *Unification and Conquest: A Political and Social History of England in the Tenth and Eleventh Centuries* (London, 1989), pp. 24–128; S. Keynes, 'England, c.900–1016', in *NCMH3*, pp. 456–84.

[18] *ASC* ABCDE 866.

[19] *ASC* ABCDE 867, 870, 871; S. Keynes, 'A Tale of Two Kings: Alfred the Great and Æthelred the Unready', *TRHS*, 5th series, 36 (1986), pp. 199–200.

[20] *ASC* ABCDE 874, 877. The 'common stock' refers to Ceolwulf in disparaging terms, but see Keynes, 'King Alfred and the Mercians', pp. 12–19.

[21] *ASC* ABCDE 878.   [22] *ASC* ABCDE 876, 877, 880. See also *ASC* ABCDE 878.

[23] L. Abrams, 'Edward the Elder's Danelaw', in N. J. Higham and D. H. Hill (eds), *Edward the Elder, 899–924* (London, 2001), pp. 128–33. The expression *Dena lage* is first attested in the early eleventh century: EGu 7.2; VI Atr 37; II Cn 15, 15.1a, 15.3, 62, 65. On the significance of the distribution of Scandinavian settlement for the definition of the English kingdom, see below, pp. 213–14.

English kingdom, such as the high proportion of relatively lightly burdened peasants found in these areas at the time of Domesday. The recent tendency has been to posit a substantial (although not overwhelming) number of settlers, while being sceptical of the assumption that regional variations stem primarily from the importation of Scandinavian administrative and social structures.[24] A lack of evidence means that these controversies cannot be resolved with confidence, however, and I therefore avoid adopting definite stances on them. Instead, I seek to construct my arguments in such a way that they are not predicated on any particular view of the number of settlers, or the extent to which regional distinctiveness reflects specifically Scandinavian influence.

What is important for my argument, however, is the nature of the political structures of the eastern and northern part of what became the English kingdom. Sometime before Guthrum's death in 890, he and Alfred established a treaty that stipulated a precise linear border between their territories. This frontier is marked on Map 3; the boundary was to run along the Thames, up the Lea to its source, thence to Bedford, and up the Ouse to Watling Street.[25] This line of demarcation may well have been ephemeral, but even if it was observed for some time, it is unlikely that the territory on its north-eastern side formed a coherent unit. In the early tenth century, there were armies associated with East Anglia, Cambridge, Huntingdon, and Northampton, which sometimes cooperated, but frequently appear to have acted autonomously.[26] It is probable that the land between the Welland and the Humber rivers was similarly dominated by a number of army groups, which might collaborate from time to time, but often operated separately: when in 917 and 918 Edward the Elder and Æthelflaed (two of Alfred's offspring) obtained Derby, Leicester, Stamford, and Nottingham, resistance does not appear to have been widely coordinated.[27]

[24] Important contributions to the debates include F. W. Maitland, *Domesday Book and Beyond: Three Essays in the Early History of England* (Cambridge, 1897), pp. 339–40; F. M. Stenton, 'The Danes in England', *PBA*, 13 (1927), pp. 203–46; P. H. Sawyer, *The Age of the Vikings*, 2nd edn (London, 1971), especially pp. 148–76; O. Fenger, 'The Danelaw and Danish Law: Anglo-Scandinavian Legal Relations During the Viking Period', *Scandinavian Studies in Law*, 16 (1972), pp. 83–96; P. Wormald, 'Viking Studies: Whence and Whither?', in R. T. Farrell (ed.), *The Vikings* (Chichester, 1982), pp. 128–53; D. M. Hadley, ' "And They Proceeded to Plough and to Support Themselves": The Scandinavian Settlement of England', *ANS*, 19 (1997), pp. 69–96; D. M. Hadley, *The Northern Danelaw: Its Social Structure, c.800–1100* (London, 2000); D. M. Hadley, *The Vikings in England: Settlement, Society and Culture* (Manchester, 2006). On 'Danish' identity, and the possibility of administrative borrowing, see below, pp. 44–5, 150–1.

[25] AGu; P. Kershaw, 'The Alfred-Guthrum Treaty: Scripting Accommodation and Interaction in Viking Age England', in D. M. Hadley and J. D. Richards (eds), *Cultures in Contact: Scandinavian Settlement in England in the Ninth and Tenth Centuries* (Turnhout, 2000), pp. 43–64. Since Guthrum appears as the leader of all the people ('ðeod') in East Anglia, the agreement probably postdates the settlement of his army there in 880.

[26] *ASC* ABCD 903, ABCDE 906, ABCD 913, A 917; Hadley, *Vikings*, pp. 55–6. D. N. Dumville, *Wessex and England from Alfred to Edgar* (Woodbridge, 1992), pp. 1–23 proposes that Guthrum made the treaty as ruler of the land south-west of Watling Street. This is unlikely: the treaty clearly associates him with East Anglia and specifies no frontier between it and Essex (which, under Dumville's interpretation, was subject to Alfred).

[27] *ASC* MR 917, 918, A 918. Derby, Leicester, Stamford, Nottingham, and Lincoln later constituted some sort of bloc, known as the 'five *burhs*', but there is no evidence of this prior to the reign of Æthelred II: III Atr 1.1; *ASC* CDE 1013, 1015. King Edmund overran these five *burhs* in 942, but they need not have had any corporate existence at the time: *ASC* ABCD 942.

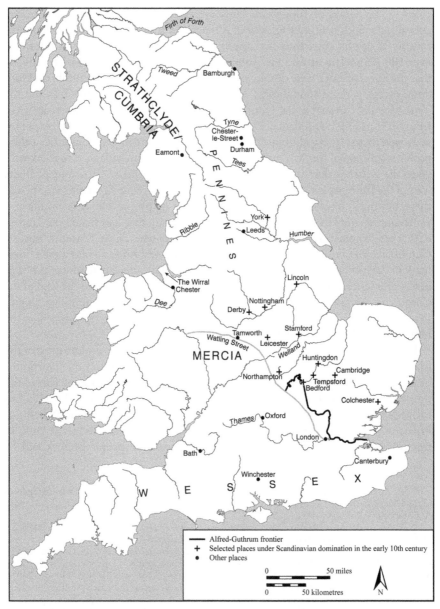

Map 3. Britain south of the Forth in the late ninth and early tenth century.

North of the Humber, we have evidence of kings with Scandinavian names ruling at York. Initially, these were probably members of the army that had settled in Northumbria in 876, but by the late 910s (if not before) they were men who, as well as having links to Scandinavia, were also active in Ireland and around the Irish Sea: such people are now often termed 'Hiberno-Scandinavians'. The power of the kings of York probably extended into Southumbria, at least intermittently: some coins in the names of York-based kings appear to have been struck at Lincoln, and the late tenth-century *Chronicle* of Æthelweard alludes to persons in late ninth-century York who apparently had significant territory in the vicinity of Stamford, over 100 kilometres or 60 miles south of the Humber.[28] It is, however, unlikely that the kings of York were dominant throughout the former Northumbrian kingdom, except perhaps sporadically. The principal power between the Tees and the Tyne was quite probably the church of St Cuthbert, located at Chester-le-Street from 883 until 995, and then at Durham. Further north, a series of English potentates were based at Bamburgh. The geographical extent of the Bamburgh rulers' power is unknown, but it is unlikely to have stretched unchallenged to the Forth, given the evidence that Scottish kings were active in Lothian.[29] The state of affairs west of the Pennines is similarly opaque. Many Scandinavian place names are attested there, but these may well mostly reflect settlement by people who came to the area via Ireland or the Hebrides, rather than with the army that had shared out land in 876. There is minimal evidence of centralized power west of the Pennines, but the Cumbrian kings brought some of what is now north-west England under their domination: describing a journey that took place in the 940s, the late tenth-century *Life* of St Cathroe refers to the saint being escorted by the Scottish king to the land of the Cumbrians ('terram Cumbrorum'), and then being taken by the Cumbrian king to Leeds, which is said to have been a frontier ('confinium') of the *Normanni* (i.e. the Hiberno-Scandinavians ruling at York) and the Cumbrians.[30]

Despite all these changes in the political configuration of the middle third of the island of Britain, people continued to write of 'Northumbria' and the 'Northumbrians'. It is, however, often likely that they were referring only to some part of the former Northumbrian kingdom. Thus, for example, the accounts of the 940s and early 950s in the various *Chronicle* manuscripts repeatedly allude to the 'Northumbrians' accepting or abandoning different kings who based themselves at York: in this context, 'Northumbrians' quite probably meant the people of York and its

---

[28] M. A. S. Blackburn, 'Currency under the Vikings. Part 2: The Two Scandinavian Kingdoms of the Danelaw, *c*.895–954', *BNJ*, 76 (2006), pp. 209–17; Æthelweard, *Chronicle*, iv.3, ed. and trans. A. Campbell (Edinburgh, 1962), p. 51.

[29] W. M. Aird, *St Cuthbert and the Normans: The Church of Durham, 1071–1153* (Woodbridge, 1998), pp. 9–59; Rollason, *Northumbria*, pp. 211–55; above, pp. 6–7.

[30] *The Life of St Cathroe*, xvi–xvii, ed. J. Colgan, *Acta Sanctorum Hiberniae* (Leuven, 1645), p. 497; D. N. Dumville, 'St Cathróe of Metz and the Hagiography of Exoticism', in J. Carey, M. Herbert, and P. Ó Riain (eds), *Studies in Irish Hagiography: Saints and Scholars* (Dublin, 2001), pp. 172–88 especially 177 n. 35; C. Downham, 'The Chronology of the Last Scandinavian Kings of York, AD 937–954', *Northern History*, 40 (2003), pp. 26–32; Charles-Edwards, *Wales*, pp. 481–2, 512, 570–1. Cathroe reached Winchester between 941 and 946, but may have begun his journey before the 940s. The word *confinium* may indicate that Leeds was on a linear frontier, or that it was within a borderland between the *Normanni* and Cumbrians: above, p. 9 n. 33. See also Rollason, *Northumbria*, pp. 249–55, although his suggestion that there may have been a Cumbrian kingdom distinct from Strathclyde is undermined by the account of Cathroe's journey, which implies that the Cumbrian kingdom that stretched to (or at least towards) Leeds also bordered the Scottish kingdom. Even if one is sceptical about the events narrated in a hagiographical text, it is notable that a tenth-century writer thought this. It is often stated that Stainmore was the Cumbrian kingdom's south-eastern limit, but see D. Broun, 'The Welsh Identity of the Kingdom of Strathclyde, *c*.900–*c*.1200', *Innes Review*, 55 (2004), pp. 173–80.

vicinity.[31] The word could, however, encompass people far from York, since the A text of the *Chronicle* for 919 refers to Manchester being 'among the Northumbrians'.[32] We encountered one ambiguous case in the Introduction to this volume, where we saw that the 'Northumbrians' over whom Cnut placed Erik may or may not have extended north of the Tees.[33] Another problematic example is the annal for 944 found in all the main versions of the *Chronicle*, which states that King Edmund (a grandson of Alfred) obtained 'all the land of the Northumbrians' ('eal Norþhymbra land'), and drove out two Hiberno-Scandinavian kings.[34] The author of the annal may have meant that Edmund re-established Cerdicing domination across the whole of what had once been the Northumbrian kingdom, but a more minimalist reading is also possible: Æthelweard indicates that it was from York that both kings were expelled, and the annalist could have been using 'eal Norþhymbra land' to refer to an area more like what became Yorkshire.[35] The confusion is only increased when we consider one of the earliest extant references to 'Yorkshire', which appears in the D text of the *Chronicle* for 1065: here, 'Eoforwicscire' is implicitly contrasted with 'Norðhymbralande', and the latter term was increasingly used to refer specifically to the area bounded by the Tees, the Tweed, and the Pennines.[36] References to 'Northumbria' and the 'Northumbrians' therefore need to be interpreted with caution.

Cerdicing Expansion

Setting aside the terminological issues just discussed, one clear effect of viking raiding and settlement was to increase the extent to which power was fragmented both north of the Humber and in eastern Southumbria. With this in mind, we can turn to the sequence of events in the decades after Alfred's defeat of Guthrum in 878, during which Cerdicing domination was extended north of the Thames, and ultimately across Britain as a whole. Alfred's victory seems to have been followed by fourteen years of relative calm, during which his forces appear to have been involved in only intermittent and fairly minor military engagements. Respite from attack afforded Alfred scope to promote learning and construct or strengthen fortifications.[37] He also acquired a degree of domination over the western part of Mercia, where Ceolwulf had by 881 been succeeded by a certain Æthelred.[38] The first definite evidence of Æthelred's submission comes from 883, when he issued a charter 'with the leave and cognisance of King Alfred'; this document gave Æthelred

---

[31] Below, p. 32. That York was the principal Northumbrian base of the Hiberno-Scandinavian kings is apparent from *ASC* DE 923, D 948; Æthelweard, *Chronicle*, iv.6 (p. 54).

[32] *ASC* A 919.   [33] Above, pp. 2–4.   [34] *ASC* ABCDE 944.

[35] Æthelweard, *Chronicle*, iv.6 (p. 54).

[36] *ASC* D 1065. See also *ASC* C 1065; *De obsessione Dunelmi*, ed. T. Arnold, *Symeonis monachi opera omnia* (RS, 75, 2 vols, London, 1882–5), i, 216, 217–18; Henry of Huntingdon, *Historia Anglorum*, i.5, ed. and trans. D. Greenway (Oxford, 1996), p. 18. S 1067, 1160 give slightly earlier references to Yorkshire.

[37] Abels, *Alfred*, pp. 169–257 is a fairly conventional survey, but on the texts commonly ascribed to Alfred see now M. Godden, 'Did King Alfred Write Anything?', *Medium Ævum*, 76 (2007), pp. 1–23.

[38] Keynes, 'King Alfred and the Mercians', pp. 12–45; Charles-Edwards, *Wales*, pp. 490–1.

no royal style, instead presenting him as an 'ealdorman', a title commonly accorded to the leading lay subordinates of a king.[39] He was ascribed the same title in the 'common stock', which reports that in 886 all the English people ('Angelcyn') who were not subject to the Danes submitted (literally 'turned'—'cirde') to Alfred, who entrusted London to Ealdorman Æthelred.[40] From around this time, Alfred was commonly styled *Angulsaxonum rex* (or some variant thereof), reflecting his power in both Anglian Mercia and Saxon Wessex.[41] Asser confirms Æthelred's submission, relates that Alfred gave the latter his daughter Æthelflaed in marriage, and records that various Welsh kings likewise accepted Cerdicing lordship; the most powerful of these kings was Anarawd of Gwynedd, who abandoned an alliance with Alfred's Northumbrian adversaries, became his godson, and promised 'that he would be obedient to the royal will in all things, just like Æthelred with the Mercians'.[42]

Following the apparent stability that had lasted for most of the period since 878, Alfred faced a renewed threat in 892, when a viking army crossed from the Continent and landed in Kent: it ranged widely for the next four years, ravaging not only along the south coast but also as far as Chester and north Wales. There are three important features of the events of 892–896, as described by the A, B, C, and D texts of the *Chronicle*. The first is that Alfred's resistance to the vikings appears to have been much more consistently successful than it had been in 871–878, probably at least in part as a result of his construction or reinforcement of fortifications in the intervening years. Strongholds could restrict enemy movement, particularly if they were sited on rivers or major land routes, and may well have been used to store supplies, thus making it harder for hostile forces to sustain themselves through plunder.[43] Second, the extension of Alfred's domination was reflected in military cooperation between the West Saxons and others who had recognized his superiority: this is most clearly seen in the defeat of a viking army by a West Saxon, Mercian, and Welsh force in 893.[44] Third, the arrival of the army from the Continent prompted the viking forces that had settled in the northern and eastern parts of what became the English kingdom to break their peace with Alfred.[45] This demonstrated that agreements were insufficient to guarantee the Cerdicing dynasty's security: an important motivation for expansion under Alfred's successors was almost certainly to subdue, expel, or destroy potentially dangerous neighbours.

---

[39] S 218. Æthelred was styled *rex* ('king') in other contexts: below, pp. 60–1.

[40] *ASC* ABCDE 886.

[41] S. Keynes, 'The West Saxon Charters of King Æthelwulf and his Sons', *EHR*, 109 (1994), pp. 1147–9. Given that Alfred was West Saxon, it is interesting that the Anglian element was placed first in the compound title. This may be a result of influence from the Continent, where there were precedents for the use of 'Anglo-Saxon' terminology to designate the Germanic inhabitants of Britain: W. Levison, *England and the Continent in the Eighth Century* (Oxford, 1946), pp. 92–3 and n. 1.

[42] *VA*, lxxv, lxxx–lxxxi (pp. 57–8, 66–7). That Anarawd became Alfred's godson is interesting, since he was presumably already Christian. His submission may only have taken place just before Asser wrote in 893, but see Charles-Edwards, *Wales*, pp. 491–4.

[43] G. Williams, 'Military and Non-Military Functions of the Anglo-Saxon *burh*, *c*.878–978', in J. Baker, S. Brookes, and A. Reynolds (eds), *Landscapes of Defence in Early Medieval Europe* (Turnhout, 2013), pp. 129–63 especially 131–2.

[44] *ASC* ABCD 893.   [45] *ASC* ABCD 893, 896.

The threat from the raiders-turned-settlers (plus, quite probably, some of those among whom they had settled) seems to have abated after 896, but was manifest again soon after Alfred's death in 899. His eldest son, Edward 'the Elder', succeeded as king, but was challenged by Æthelwold, a son of Æthelred I. Æthelwold sought support in the north and east from people whom the A, B, C, and D texts of the *Chronicle* label 'Danish', and then ravaged Mercia and part of Wessex, before being killed in battle in 902/903.[46] It is unknown what dealings (if any) Edward had in the next couple of years with the parts of Britain that were under Scandinavian domination, but he established peace with those dwelling in Northumbria and East Anglia in or around 906.[47] In 909, however, he went on the offensive, ravaging in the north. This harrying was carried out by a force comprising both West Saxons and Mercians, an indication that Edward, like Alfred, had some degree of authority in western Mercia.[48] The next year, another joint force of West Saxons and Mercians defeated a raiding army from Northumbria.[49] Between 912 and 918, Edward went most years to one or more localities in the southern East Midlands and Essex, received some sort of submission, and either took over an existing fortification or constructed a new one.[50] For the most part, there is no mention of his having encountered significant resistance: his turning up with an armed force was seemingly enough to intimidate the people of a particular area into acknowledging his superiority. So far as we know, serious violence only occurred in 917, when armies from Northampton, Leicester, Huntingdon, and East Anglia tried unsuccessfully to seize some of Edward's new fortifications. In response, Edward stormed Tempsford, Colchester, and Huntingdon, killing a substantial number of people, including an unnamed individual whom the A text of the *Chronicle* calls a king ('cyning'). The various forces south of the River Welland and in East Anglia then submitted to Edward, and there is no evidence that he or his tenth-century successors faced further armed opposition from people living in these areas.[51]

While Edward was pressing into the East Midlands, his sister Æthelflaed, described by the 'Mercian Register' as 'lady of the Mercians' after her husband Æthelred's death in 911, constructed fortifications at several locations in western Mercia. She also took Derby and Leicester, and received some kind of submission from York.[52] We have seen that Alfred and Edward obtained Mercian cooperation, but Æthelred and Æthelflaed retained a significant degree of autonomy: unlike ealdormen elsewhere, they are known to have issued charters in their own names,

---

[46] *ASC* ABCD 900, 902, 903; R. Lavelle, 'The Politics of Rebellion: The *Ætheling* Æthelwold and West Saxon Royal Succession, 899–902', in P. Skinner (ed.), *Challenging the Boundaries of Medieval History: The Legacy of Timothy Reuter* (Turnhout, 2009), pp. 51–80. The emphasis on Æthelwold's 'Danish' backers may have been intended to discredit him; it is reasonable to infer that he also had other supporters, not least the 'Byrhtsige, son of the *ætheling* Beornoth', possibly a scion of a Mercian royal dynasty, with whom he died in battle.

[47] *ASC* ABCD 906. These agreements may have had some connection to the 'peace-writings' ('friðgehwritu') relating to the east and north that are mentioned in Edward's legislation: II Ew 5.2.

[48] *ASC* ABCD 909.   [49] *ASC* ABCD 910, MR 910.

[50] *ASC* ABCD 912, 914, A 915, 916, 917, 918.   [51] *ASC* A 917.

[52] *ASC* MR 907, 910, 912, 913, 914, 915, 917, 918.

albeit sometimes with the explicit consent of the 'Anglo-Saxon' king.[53] That Æthelred and Æthelflaed's power represented a significant qualification to Edward's domination in western Mercia can be inferred from the events that followed the Mercian rulers' deaths. All of the principal versions of the *Chronicle* record that, when Æthelred died, Edward 'obtained London and Oxford and all the lands which pertained to them'.[54] This suggests that Edward's control over London and Oxford was previously more limited, and that his power in other parts of western Mercia remained restricted. After Æthelflaed's death in 918, the A text of the *Chronicle* states that Edward 'occupied [or even "seized"—*gerad*] the fortification [*burg*] at Tamworth, and all the people in the land of the Mercians which was previously subordinated [*underpeoded*] to Æthelflaed turned [or "submitted"—*cierde*] to him'.[55] The 'Mercian Register' does not mention such a submission, or the occupation of what had been a major Mercian royal centre, but records that six or eighteen months after Æthelflaed's death her daughter Ælfwynn was 'deprived of all power [*onwealdes*] among the Mercians' and taken into Wessex.[56] Edward thus exploited Æthelflaed's death, as he had previously exploited Æthelred's, to tighten his grip on western Mercia.

In his last years, Edward captured or constructed a series of fortifications in the northern Midlands and what is now north-east Wales.[57] His position in some of the areas into which he had expanded was far from secure: there are grounds to suspect that his hold on East Anglia was particularly tenuous, and a twelfth-century account (of uncertain reliability) alleges that his final act was to put down a revolt at Chester.[58] It is also likely that the area around Lincoln remained within the sphere of the Hiberno-Scandinavian kings of York until 927.[59] Nonetheless, by the time of his death in 924, Edward had acquired or built fortifications in most parts of Southumbria.[60] It appears, moreover, that towards the end of his reign he gained widespread recognition as the most powerful person in Britain. Alfred's domination in Wales may well not have continued uninterrupted into Edward's time, but the A text of the *Chronicle* records that three of the principal Welsh kings 'sought him [Edward] as lord' ('sohton him to hlaforde') after Æthelflaed's death in 918.[61]

---

[53] S. Keynes, 'Edward, King of the Anglo-Saxons', in Higham and Hill (eds), *Edward the Elder*, pp. 40–66 plays up the evidence for Mercia's subordination to Edward. P. Stafford, 'Political Women in Mercia, Eighth to Early Tenth Centuries', in M. P. Brown and C. A. Farr (eds), *Mercia: An Anglo-Saxon Kingdom in Europe* (London, 2001), pp. 44–9 is more sceptical, and plausibly posits that Edward's hold on Mercia was weaker than Alfred's had been. See also Stafford, ' "Annals of Æthelflæd" '; below, pp. 56, 137–8.

[54] *ASC* ABCD 911. See also *ASC* DE 910. Alfred had entrusted London to Æthelred twenty-five years before: *ASC* ABCDE 886.

[55] *ASC* A 918.   [56] *ASC* MR 919.   [57] *ASC* A 918, 919, 920, MR 921.

[58] Blackburn, 'Currency under the Vikings. Part 2', p. 208; L. Marten, 'The Shiring of East Anglia: An Alternative Hypothesis', *Historical Research*, 81 (2008), pp. 3–7; William of Malmesbury, *Gesta Regum Anglorum*, ii.133.1, ed. and trans. R. A. B. Mynors, R. M. Thomson, and M. Winterbottom (2 vols, Oxford, 1998–9), i, 210.

[59] Blackburn, 'Currency under the Vikings. Part 2', pp. 209–17.

[60] For a map of fortifications recorded during Edward's reign, see J. Baker and S. Brookes, *Beyond the Burghal Hidage: Anglo-Saxon Civil Defence in the Viking Age* (Leiden, 2013), p. 154.

[61] *ASC* A 918; Charles-Edwards, *Wales*, pp. 494–510.

Two years later, his superiority was similarly acknowledged by leading figures north of the Humber: the same source states that in 920 Ragnald, a Hiberno-Scandinavian potentate who had established himself at York shortly before, 'chose [Edward] as father and lord' ('geces þa to fæder 7 to hlaforde'), as did the brothers ruling at Bamburgh, and the Scottish and Cumbrian kings.[62]

Edward's intentions for the succession are not known. He had sons by three women, Ecgwynn, Ælfflaed, and Eadgifu, although his children by the last cannot have been much more than infants at his death. Ælfflaed's elder son, Ælfweard, died within a month of Edward, but appears in a West Saxon regnal list, and is said by the *Liber Vitae* of the New Minster, Winchester, to have been 'adorned with kingly badges' ('regalibus infulis redimitus'): quite what was meant by this is unclear, but Winchester appears to have backed Ælfweard as Edward's successor, at least south of the Thames, and quite possibly in Mercia too.[63] After Ælfweard's death, his elder half-brother, Æthelstan (son of Ecgwynn), became king both north and south of the Thames, although there are signs that his succession was not welcomed at Winchester, quite possibly because he had challenged Ælfweard before the latter's death. Indeed, the New Minster *Liber Vitae* ignores Æthelstan's reign, and the Bishop of Winchester is absent from his early charters, including one issued on the day of the royal coronation.[64] It is likely that Æthelstan's initial base was in Mercia, since what is probably his earliest extant charter styles him *rex Anglorum*, and is attested solely by Mercian witnesses.[65] By contrast, his next three surviving diplomas, attested by men from both sides of the Thames, call him *Angulsaxonum rex* (or a variant thereon), which implies that initially he had ruled only the Anglian portion of the 'Anglo-Saxon' realm.[66] If Æthelstan indeed sought recognition as king before Ælfweard's death, he may have claimed Mercia alone, or perhaps both Mercia and Wessex: either way, it is possible that there was a very brief *de facto* division along the Thames. While Ælfweard's demise was convenient from Æthelstan's perspective, there is no specific evidence that it was unnatural. There are, however, grounds to suspect that Æthelstan may have had a hand in the death of Ælfweard's full brother Edwin in 933: writing less than thirty years later, a monk of St-Bertin (near modern Calais) stated that Edwin had died in a shipwreck while sailing for the Continent, 'compelled by some disturbance

---

[62] *ASC* A 920; G. Molyneaux, 'Why were some Tenth-Century English Kings Presented as Rulers of Britain?', *TRHS*, 6th series, 21 (2011), pp. 88–9.

[63] *ASC* MR 924; Dumville, 'West Saxon Genealogical Regnal List', p. 29; London, British Library, MS Stowe 944, f. 9ᵛ, consulted in facsimile in S. Keynes, *The Liber Vitae of the New Minster and Hyde Abbey Winchester* (Copenhagen, 1996), with discussion at pp. 19–22. See also S. Foot, *Æthelstan: The First King of England* (New Haven, CT, 2011), pp. 37–43, 73–7.

[64] S 394; S. Keynes, *An Atlas of Attestations in Anglo-Saxon Charters, c.670–1066* (Cambridge, 2002), Table XXXVII.

[65] S 395. Note also that the 'Mercian Register' refers to Æthelstan being 'chosen by the Mercians as king': *ASC* MR 924. *ASC* AE 924 says nothing of Ælfweard and straightforwardly presents Æthelstan as Edward's successor. It is uncertain whether any weight can be placed on a twelfth-century report that Æthelstan had been brought up by Æthelred and Æthelflaed of Mercia: William of Malmesbury, *Gesta Regum*, ii.133.2 (i, 210).

[66] S 394, 396, 397.

in his kingdom', and the annals preserved in the early twelfth-century *Historia Regum* (attributed to Symeon of Durham) record that Æthelstan ordered his half-brother's drowning.[67]

After becoming king both north and south of the Thames, Æthelstan initially sought to use negotiation to neutralize the potential threat that his Scandinavian neighbours presented: in 926, he gave his sister in marriage to Sihtric, who was ruling at York in succession to Ragnald. When Sihtric died a year later, however, Æthelstan seized York and drove out one Guthfrith: Æthelstan thus pounced at a time of vulnerability, as Edward had done in Mercia.[68] Soon after, there were marked changes in the titles accorded to the king in charters: *Angulsaxonum rex*, the standard royal style since at least the 890s, was replaced by *rex Anglorum* ('king of the English'), and Æthelstan was also frequently presented as the ruler of Britain.[69] This reflects that, as well as temporarily ending Hiberno-Scandinavian rule in Northumbria, he cemented his father's position as the pre-eminent king on the island. After seizing York, he had the Scottish king, two Welsh kings, a Bamburgh potentate, and very probably the Cumbrian king meet him at Eamont (near Penrith), which prompted the author of the D text of the *Chronicle* to declare that Æthelstan 'had power over [*gewylde*] all the kings who were on this island'.[70] Æthelstan's subordination of the others who had gathered at Eamont is further indicated by their attestations of his charters, the Scottish king Constantine's attendance at his court seemingly being enforced in 934 by a campaign in which a Cerdicing fleet ravaged Caithness (the northernmost part of Britain), and land forces penetrated as far as Dunnottar (near Aberdeen).[71] The Archbishop of York witnessed Æthelstan's charters fairly frequently from 928 onwards, and there are also more occasional appearances of the Bishop of the church of St Cuthbert, in all probability the greatest landholder between the Tees and the Tyne: this underlines that Æthelstan's domination extended well beyond York itself.[72] Ten years after Æthelstan seized York and expelled Guthfrith, however, the latter's son Olaf allied with the Scottish and Cumbrian kings in an apparent attempt to re-establish Hiberno-Scandinavian rule in Northumbria. Æthelstan defeated this coalition at *Brunanburh*

---

[67] Folcwin of St-Bertin, *Gesta abbatum S. Bertini Sithiensium*, cvii, ed. O. Holder-Egger (*MGH*, Scriptores, 13, Hanover, 1881), p. 629; *Historia Regum*, ed. Arnold, *Symeonis monachi opera omnia*, ii, 93, 124. *ASC* E 933 has a bald statement that Edwin drowned at sea, but other versions of the *Chronicle* omit his death.

[68] *ASC* D 926, DE 927. Guthfrith (who is not mentioned in D) was probably in Dublin when Sihtric died, but rushed to (or at least towards) York: Charles-Edwards, *Wales*, pp. 521–2.

[69] Keynes, 'England, *c*.900–1016', pp. 468–9; Molyneaux, 'Why were some Tenth-Century English Kings Presented as Rulers of Britain?', pp. 59–60; above, p. 26; below, pp. 206–7.

[70] *ASC* D 927. Given the location, it would be very odd if the Cumbrian king were absent from Eamont, even though his presence is only mentioned by William of Malmesbury, *Gesta Regum*, ii.134.2 (i, 214): Charles-Edwards, *Wales*, p. 512.

[71] S 400, 403, 407, 412, 413, 416, 417, 418, 418a, 420, 425, 426, 427, 434, 1604, 1792; *ASC* ABCDE 934; *Historia Regum*, pp. 93, 124. The Welsh, Cumbrian, and Scottish attestations are set out at Keynes, *Atlas*, Table XXXVI. While Dunnottar was in the heartland of Constantine's kingdom, it is doubtful whether his domination extended to Caithness: Woolf, *From Pictland to Alba*, pp. 165–6. Ravaging to the very north of Britain would, however, serve to demonstrate Æthelstan's power.

[72] All episcopal attestations from Æthelstan's reign are set out at Keynes, *Atlas*, Table XXXVII. The Bishop of the church of St Cuthbert appears in S 401, 407, 412, 413, 416, 417, 418a, 425.

(perhaps on the Wirral), in what contemporaries regarded as a major battle.[73] In addition to these campaigns within Britain, Æthelstan's military activities extended to the Continent: he assisted his exiled godson Alain's campaign to wrest Brittany from Scandinavian domination in 936, and three years later sent a fleet to Flanders in an unsuccessful attempt to aid his (Æthelstan's) nephew, the Carolingian king Louis IV.[74]

So far as we know, Æthelstan neither married nor begat children. When he died in 939, he was succeeded by his half-brother Edmund (son of Edward the Elder by Eadgifu), without any known dispute. Edmund reigned until 946, when he was stabbed to death by a man whom a late tenth-century writer described as a thief.[75] Edmund's two sons were still children, and he was succeeded, again seemingly without challenge, by his full brother Eadred, who was king until his death in 955. While the successions of Edmund and Eadred were apparently smooth, their reigns were anything but calm: soon after Æthelstan died, Hiberno-Scandinavian rule was re-established at York, which then changed hands repeatedly until 954. In the first half of Edmund's reign, there was considerable military action in the northern East Midlands, and Watling Street was briefly established as a frontier: all of Æthelstan's territorial gains, and some of those of Edward the Elder, were thus for a time reversed. The sequence of events during Edmund's reign is disputed, the crux being whether or not an expedition in which he asserted control of Leicester, Lincoln, Nottingham, Stamford, and Derby preceded a campaign in which Tamworth and Leicester (and perhaps other places) were captured by one Olaf (whether Guthfrithson or Sihtricson is uncertain).[76] Either way, Edmund was soon reconciled with Olaf Sihtricson and the latter's kinsman Ragnald Guthfrithson, since in around 943 he sponsored them at their baptism and confirmation respectively: as with Guthrum's and Anarawd's acceptance of spiritual filiation to Alfred, this would symbolize Olaf's and Ragnald's friendship with Edmund, and probably some measure of deference to him.[77] This cordiality was, however, followed by a putsch, as in Mercia in 918/919 and at York in 927: in 944, Olaf and Ragnald were expelled and Edmund seized York plus, presumably, any parts of Southumbria that remained under their domination.[78]

---

[73] *ASC* ABCD 937 is the main source. For Cumbrian involvement, see *Historia Regum*, p. 93. Foot, *Æthelstan*, pp. 169–83 gives an overview of the sources and possible locations.

[74] Flodoard, *Annals*, 936, 939, ed. P. Lauer, *Les annales de Flodoard* (Paris, 1905), pp. 63, 73; *La chronique de Nantes*, xxvii, xxix, ed. R. Merlet (Paris, 1896), pp. 82–3, 87–9; Richer, *Historiae*, ii.16, ed. H. Hoffmann (*MGH*, Scriptores, 38, Hanover, 2000), pp. 108–9. Prior to becoming king, Louis had been an exile in Æthelstan's kingdom. Æthelstan supported his succession, although this did not entail military action: Flodoard, *Annals*, 936 (p. 63); Richer, *Historiae*, ii.1–ii.4 (pp. 97–100). Note also Flodoard, *Annals*, 946 (p. 101); Richer, *Historiae*, ii.49–ii.50 (pp. 134–5).

[75] Edmund's death is recorded by *ASC* ABCD 946, but only D states that he was stabbed. *VSD*, xix.1 (p. 60) is the earliest reference to the killer as a thief.

[76] The most detailed attempt to sort out the sequence of events is Downham, 'Chronology', pp. 25–43, with references to the relevant sources and other interpretations. The *Life* of St Cathroe, discussed by Downham, provides grounds to think that Erik Haraldsson may have ruled briefly at York sometime prior to Edmund's death. See also K. Halloran, 'Anlaf Guthfrithson at York: A Non-Existent Kingship?', *Northern History*, 50 (2013), pp. 180–5. For Watling Street as a border ('terminus'), see *Historia Regum*, pp. 93–4, and compare AGu 1.

[77] *ASC* ABCD 943. Olaf Guthfrithson had died by this time.

[78] *ASC* ABCDE 944; Æthelweard, *Chronicle*, iv.6 (p. 54).

It is quite likely that Edmund's seizure of York was aided by some kind of insurrection against Olaf and Ragnald: the annals preserved in the *Historia Regum* state that Olaf was expelled by 'Northumbrians', which here probably means the people of York and its environs.[79] Among these 'Northumbrians', Archbishop Wulfstan I of York may well have wielded particular influence: he and an unnamed Mercian *dux* ('leader' or 'ealdorman') are credited by Æthelweard with Olaf and Ragnald's ejection.[80] The accounts of the 940s and early 950s in the D and E versions of the *Chronicle* likewise suggest that who ruled at York was in large measure determined by Northumbrians, with Wulfstan playing a central role. The D text's annal for 941 states that the Northumbrians were false to their pledges and chose ('gecuron') Olaf (either Guthfrithson or Sihtricson) as king. D's entries for 947 and 948 state that 'Archbishop Wulfstan and all the Northumbrian wise people [*witan*]' pledged themselves to Eadred, but then accepted Erik Haraldsson as king, then deserted him in favour of Eadred. For 952, E records that the Northumbrians expelled Olaf Sihtricson, who had come to Northumbria three years before, and received Erik again instead. The same year, according to D, Eadred had Wulfstan detained, an indication that the archbishop was influential, and not someone on whom Eadred felt he could depend. Erik was driven out and killed in 954, whereupon Eadred gained power at York: both D and E attribute Erik's ejection to the Northumbrians, and Roger of Wendover states that he was betrayed by the Bamburgh potentate Oswulf.[81] Hiberno-Scandinavian rule in Northumbria was never re-established, although contemporaries cannot have known that this would be the case. The chronology of the last Hiberno-Scandinavian kings of York is uncertain, but what matters here is that York changed hands frequently, and that power there was predicated on local acceptance, which was highly mutable: Edmund and then Eadred competed with a series of Hiberno-Scandinavian kings for Northumbrian recognition, rather than necessarily attacking these kings directly. We do not know much about how the various contenders sought adherence, but in 948 Eadred induced the Northumbrians to abandon Erik by ravaging their land and making it known that he wished to inflict further damage.[82] Threatening greater destruction than one's rivals, and perhaps promising protection against their depredations, may well have been the key to power at York.

Edmund and Eadred, like Edward and Æthelstan, sought to obtain the cooperation of other non-Scandinavian rulers in Britain, most likely because the Cerdicings were anxious that such potentates should refrain from supporting any Hiberno-Scandinavian vying for power at York. Oswulf of Bamburgh is known to have attested five of Eadred's charters between 946 and 950, and Eadred entrusted York

---

[79] *Historia Regum*, p. 94; Downham, 'Chronology', pp. 37–8; above, pp. 24–5.

[80] Æthelweard, *Chronicle*, iv.6 (p. 54); S. Keynes, 'Wulfstan I', in *WBEASE*, pp. 512–13.

[81] *ASC* D 941, 947, 948, E 949, DE 952, 954; Roger of Wendover, *Flores Historiarum*, ed. H. O. Coxe (5 vols, London, 1841–4), i, 402–3. Roger wrote in the thirteenth century but had access to one or more now-lost Northumbrian texts. That his account should be taken seriously is demonstrated by his knowledge of Edgar's coin reform: below, p. 116 n. 1. On the period between 947 and 954, see Downham, 'Chronology', pp. 43–9, with references to earlier literature.

[82] *ASC* D 948.

to him after 954.[83] Welsh and (possibly) Cumbrian kings likewise witnessed a handful of times between 943×946 and 956, and there is a good chance that they (and Oswulf) were present at the Cerdicing court more often than they appear in witness lists.[84] Force, or the threat thereof, was probably important in securing cooperation. Welsh annals record that in 942 the king of Gwynedd (in north-west Wales) and his son were killed 'by the English'.[85] Edmund may have been responsible, and was certainly able to inflict destruction far from Wessex: in 945, aided by a Welsh king, he ravaged Cumbria and blinded two of its king's sons. Four versions of the *Chronicle* go on to record that Edmund then granted ('let') Cumbria to Malcolm I, the Scottish king, on condition that Malcolm be 'his co-operator [*his midwyrhta*] both on sea and on land'.[86] Up to a point, Edmund was buying Scottish cooperation, but the ravaging of Cumbria doubtless also served to warn Malcolm (and others) of the possible consequences of incurring the displeasure of the Cerdicings, who were by the mid-tenth century clearly the predominant power in Britain.

After Cerdicing Expansion

After Eadred gained power at York in 954, the narrative ceases to be one of Cerdicing expansion, and there appear to have been over thirty years without major armed conflicts. Eadred died without known offspring in 955 and was succeeded by his nephew Eadwig, the elder son of Edmund. Two years later, with Eadwig still reigning, his full brother Edgar became king north of the Thames. The division is mentioned in later narratives and is reflected in charter witness lists: persons whose principal interests lay north of the Thames ceased to attest Eadwig's diplomas during 957 and can be seen witnessing those of Edgar from 958. As with the possible split of 924, the reasons for the partition between Eadwig and Edgar are unclear. It has been interpreted as a reasonably amicable sharing of power, perhaps with Eadwig notionally remaining superior king north of the Thames.[87] But even though there is no evidence of any violent confrontation between Eadwig and Edgar, one may doubt whether relations between them were especially harmonious, since Edgar is known to have recalled Abbot Dunstan of Glastonbury from the exile into which Eadwig had had him sent.[88] Whatever the

---

[83] S 520, 544, 546, 550, 552a; *Historia Regum*, pp. 94, 197; *De primo Saxonum adventu*, ed. Arnold, *Symeonis Monachi Opera Omnia*, ii, 382.

[84] S 520, 544, 550, 552a, 566, 633, 1497; below, pp. 57–9. S 1497 preserves a witness list that may well date from 943, but could be as late as 946: *Charters of St Albans*, ed. J. Crick (Oxford, 2007), p. 159.

[85] *Annales Cambriae*, p. 16.

[86] *ASC* ABCDE 945; Roger of Wendover, *Flores Historiarum*, i, 398. *Midwyrhta* need not connote equality: Molyneaux, 'Why were some Tenth-Century English Kings Presented as Rulers of Britain?', pp. 69–70.

[87] S. Keynes, 'Eadwig (c.940–959)', *ODNB*; S. Keynes, 'Edgar, *rex admirabilis*', in D. Scragg (ed.), *Edgar, King of the English 959–975: New Interpretations* (Woodbridge, 2008), pp. 5–9; F. M. Biggs, 'Edgar's Path to the Throne', in Scragg (ed.), *Edgar*, pp. 124–39.

[88] *VSD*, xxii.1–xxiv.3 (pp. 68–76). See also G. Molyneaux, 'The *Ordinance Concerning the Dunsæte* and the Anglo-Welsh Frontier in the Late Tenth and Eleventh Centuries', *ASE*, 40 (2012), p. 267 n. 83. On the coins minted during the partition, see below, p. 138 n. 98.

cause of the division, it ended in 959, when Eadwig died and Edgar became king in Wessex, while also retaining his power north of the Thames. So far as we know, there was no significant armed conflict during Edgar's time, to which later writers looked back as a period of peace. His reign is best known for the spread of Benedictine monasticism and for two events that occurred in 973. The first was a coronation at Bath, probably intended at least in part as an assertion that Edgar was king not merely of the English, but of all Britain; the choice of location may have been influenced by Bath's visible Roman remains, which would call to mind an earlier pan-British hegemony. The second was a meeting shortly after at Chester, another Roman centre. This gathering was attended by Edgar himself, the Scottish king, and various other Insular (and possibly Breton) potentates, who are said by the D and E texts of the *Chronicle* to have promised to be cooperators ('efenwyrhtan'). Whether or not there is any sound basis for twelfth-century accounts of Edgar being ceremonially rowed along the River Dee by the other attendees, their coming to meet him demonstrates his pre-eminence among the rulers of Britain, and shows the reality underpinning the probable pretensions of the Bath coronation.[89]

When Edgar died in 975, dispute arose between the supporters of his two young sons, Edward and Æthelred, born of different women. Unlike in 924 (possibly) and 957–959 (certainly), there is no sign of a territorial partition: the elder boy, Edward 'the Martyr', was crowned as sole king, but was killed three years later in circumstances that are far from clear.[90] Little is known about his reign, save that several laypeople seized lands from religious institutions, sometimes alleging that they were reclaiming estates given under duress.[91] It is, however, unsurprising that the churchmen who wrote our extant sources dwelt on the depredations that they faced, and there is no evidence of direct armed conflict between the two half-brothers' respective backers: despite the manner of Edward's death and the losses suffered by monastic houses, we should therefore not assume that his reign was a time of rampant strife.

Following the killing of Edward, his half-brother Æthelred II became king. Æthelred's later years saw devastating Scandinavian attacks, which culminated in the

---

[89] For a survey of the reign, see Keynes, 'Edgar', pp. 9–59, with comment on the year 973 at 48–51. On the events of 973 and the word *efenwyrhta*, see also D. E. Thornton, 'Edgar and the Eight Kings, AD 973: *textus et dramatis personae*', *EME*, 10 (2001), pp. 49–79; A. Breeze, 'Edgar at Chester in 973: A Breton Link?', *Northern History*, 44 (2007), pp. 153–7; Molyneaux, 'Why were some Tenth-Century English Kings Presented as Rulers of Britain?', pp. 66–8, 69–70; below, pp. 187–8, 212–13. *ASC* ABC 973 and *ASC* DE 973 give separate accounts of the Bath coronation. The Chester meeting only appears in D and E.

[90] S. Keynes, *The Diplomas of King Æthelred 'the Unready', 978–1016: A Study in their Use as Historical Evidence* (Cambridge, 1980), pp. 163–74; B. Yorke, 'Edward, King and Martyr: A Saxon Murder Mystery', in L. Keen (ed.), *Studies in the Early History of Shaftesbury Abbey* (Dorchester, 1999), pp. 99–116.

[91] D. J. V. Fisher, 'The Anti-Monastic Reaction in the Reign of Edward the Martyr', *Cambridge Historical Journal*, 10 (1952), pp. 254–70; S. Jayakumar, 'Reform and Retribution: The "Anti-Monastic Reaction" in the Reign of Edward the Martyr', in Baxter et al. (eds), *Early Medieval Studies*, pp. 337–52.

conquest of his kingdom, but people living in the early part of his 38-year reign cannot have known how it would end; there were some viking raids in the 980s, but no indication that contemporaries saw these as a fundamental threat. Attacks became markedly more serious from the early 990s, however, and there were particularly devastating assaults in 1006–1007 and 1009–1012.[92] Repeated tribute payments brought only temporary respites, and in 1013 the Danish king Swein received a series of submissions in different parts of Æthelred's kingdom; the effect of this was, in the words of the C, D, and E texts of the *Chronicle*, that 'all the people [*þeodscype*] regarded [Swein] as full king [*fulne cyng*]'. Æthelred was expelled to Normandy, where he might have ended his days in exile, had Swein not died a few weeks later.[93] The English magnates then sent for Æthelred, saying that they would accept him back on condition that he should rule 'more justly' ('rihtlicor') than before. He returned as king in the spring of 1014, but by the end of the following year lay sick. Meanwhile, Swein's son Cnut ravaged widely and obtained the defection of the kingdom's greatest magnate, Eadric Streona.[94] When Æthelred died in April 1016, one of his sons, Edmund Ironside, was proclaimed king, but could not command Eadric's loyalty. Cnut defeated Edmund a few months later, and Æthelred's kingdom was split between them; as in 957–959 (and possibly 924), the Thames served as the boundary, with Edmund taking Wessex and Cnut the land to the north. Edmund died a few months later, however, and Cnut then became king both north and south of the Thames. He swiftly neutralized potential threats by having Eadric and other leading English magnates killed or exiled, and marrying Æthelred's widow.[95] Cnut's position can hardly have been secure while Edmund was still alive, but by 1018 he had a sufficiently firm hold on the English kingdom to extract a vast payment, put at 82,500 pounds (presumably of silver) by the C and D texts of the *Chronicle*.[96]

During the fifty years between Cnut's conquest and 1066, the English kingdom did not experience serious external attack. Welsh and Scottish kings sometimes launched frontier raids, but these did not fundamentally threaten Cnut or his successors; indeed, the Scots may not even have been seen as penetrating the English kingdom, since Durham is the furthest south that they are known to have attacked.[97] By contrast, Cnut (r. 1016–1035) and Edward the Confessor (r. 1042–1066), like several of their tenth-century predecessors, were quite capable of coercing the other kings on the island: Cnut's superiority was recognized by three northern rulers in about 1031, and English forces inflicted serious defeats on Welsh or Scottish kings in 1053,

---

[92] S. Keynes, 'Æthelred II (c.966×8–1016)', *ODNB* is a useful overview.

[93] *ASC* CDE 1013; Wulfstan of York, *Homilies*, ed. D. Bethurum, *The Homilies of Wulfstan* (Oxford, 1957), XX (B H), lines 66–71.

[94] *ASC* CDE 1014, 1015.

[95] *ASC* CDE 1016, 1017. There is no reliable evidence about the cause of Edmund's death.

[96] *ASC* CDE 1018. E's figure is 500 pounds higher. *ASC* CDE 1018 also records that the Danes and English reached an agreement at Oxford; Cn 1018 is probably a product of this settlement.

[97] For references, see K. L. Maund, *Ireland, Wales, and England in the Eleventh Century* (Woodbridge, 1991), pp. 120–41; Woolf, *From Pictland to Alba*, pp. 232–40, 254–5. On the kingdom's extent, see above, pp. 2–5.

1054, and 1063.[98] While Scottish and Welsh raiding did not represent an especially serious threat, there were times when the kingdom's stability could have been jeopardized by disputes between contenders for the throne, or between magnates and the reigning king. In 1033/1034, one of Æthelred's sons, Edward ('the Confessor'), tried to return from exile in Normandy to challenge Cnut; had a storm not prevented Edward's fleet (provided by Duke Robert of Normandy) from crossing the Channel, this could have precipitated a major conflict.[99] When Cnut died in 1035, there was a further crisis over who should succeed him: the people north of the Thames backed his elder surviving son, Harold Harefoot, while those in Wessex favoured the latter's half-brother Harthacnut (Cnut's son by Æthelred's widow), who was then in Denmark.[100] Edward and his full brother Alfred appear also to have made bids for the kingship at this time: both crossed the Channel separately, but Edward departed after a brief skirmish, and Alfred was swiftly apprehended and killed.[101] Harold was ultimately accepted as king over the whole kingdom from 1037 until his death in 1040, but the killing of Alfred demonstrates the potential for succession disputes to turn violent, and conflict between Cnut's sons' respective supporters may well only have been avoided because Harthacnut remained in Denmark.[102]

After Harold died, Harthacnut crossed the sea and was received as king. He recalled Edward, his half-brother, who was by now Æthelred's only surviving son, and may have associated him in the kingship in some way.[103] In any event, Edward became sole king on Harthacnut's death in 1042. Edward's reign saw some significant internal crises. The most serious was a dispute in 1051–1052 between the king and his most powerful subordinate, Earl Godwine (d. 1053): Godwine and his family were exiled, for reasons which are disputed, but they were reinstated after they harried the king-

---

[98] *ASC* DE 1027, D 1053, CD 1054, DE 1063; Maund, *Ireland, Wales, and England*, pp. 124–5, 138–9, 141; B. T. Hudson, 'Cnut and the Scottish Kings', *EHR*, 107 (1992), pp. 350–60; Woolf, *From Pictland to Alba*, pp. 244–8, 260–70; T. Bolton, *The Empire of Cnut the Great: Conquest and the Consolidation of Power in Northern Europe in the Early Eleventh Century* (Leiden, 2009), pp. 132–50; Molyneaux, 'Why were some Tenth-Century English Kings Presented as Rulers of Britain?', pp. 75–7.

[99] William of Jumièges, *Gesta Normannorum Ducum*, vi.9–vi.11, ed. and trans. E. M. C. van Houts (2 vols, Oxford, 1992–5), ii, 76–8; S. Keynes, 'The Æthelings in Normandy', *ANS*, 13 (1990), pp. 185–95. William states that the attempted invasion prompted Cnut to offer to divide the English kingdom with Æthelred's sons. If this proposal was indeed made, it appears that nothing came of it, perhaps because Cnut died soon after.

[100] *ASC* E 1035. The geographical distribution of Harold's and Harthacnut's respective supporters is reflected in coins being struck in the former's name north of the Thames, and in the latter's to the south: T. Talvio, 'Harold I and Harthacnut's *Jewel Cross* Type Reconsidered', in M. A. S. Blackburn (ed.), *Anglo-Saxon Monetary History: Essays in Memory of Michael Dolley* (Leicester, 1986), pp. 273–90.

[101] *ASC* CD 1036; *Encomium Emmae Reginae*, iii.2–iii.6, ed. A. Campbell with supplementary introduction by S. Keynes (Cambridge, 1998), pp. 40–6; William of Jumièges, *Gesta Normannorum Ducum*, vii.5–vii.6 (ii, 104–6); Keynes, 'Æthelings', pp. 195–6. The sources differ in assigning responsibility for Alfred's death.

[102] *ASC* CD 1037.

[103] *ASC* CDE 1040, 1041; *Encomium Emmae Reginae*, iii.13–iii.14 (p. 52); William of Jumièges, *Gesta Normannorum Ducum*, vii.6 (ii, 106); J. R. Maddicott, 'Edward the Confessor's Return to England in 1041', *EHR*, 119 (2004), pp. 650–66.

dom's southern coast.[104] Ælfgar, a member of a different family but also a powerful earl, was similarly banished in 1055 and 1058, but both times he soon returned with Welsh military support and was, like Godwine, restored.[105] The Northumbrians rebelled in 1065 against the earl whom Edward had set over them, Tostig son of Godwine, and forced the king to appoint a son of Ælfgar instead.[106] These various confrontations witnessed significant violence, but outright armed conflict between the leading magnates was avoided, and the kingdom did not fragment.[107]

Edward died on 5 January 1066, leaving no children or other close blood relatives. Harold son of Godwine, the kingdom's greatest magnate since his father's death, was crowned king the next day. A few months later, King Harold of Norway and Duke William of Normandy launched separate invasions, both challenging the succession. Harold Godwinson defeated the former at Stamford Bridge (Yorkshire) on 25 September, but was killed in battle against William at Hastings (Sussex) nineteen days later. William then proceeded around the southern part of the kingdom, receiving submissions, and was crowned king at Westminster on Christmas Day. Having imposed a heavy tax, he returned to Normandy in the spring, taking the most important surviving English magnates with him as hostages.[108] The swiftness with which William recrossed the Channel shows that he was confident of the security of his position, and the fact that he needed to put down various risings in the following years does not gainsay that he had effectively conquered the English kingdom in the ten weeks between Hastings and Christmas.[109] The speed of William's conquest is testament not only to his military strength, but also to the coherence and centralization of the eleventh-century English kingdom: it was a definite entity that one leader could seize from another.

The foregoing account leads to an end point identified with hindsight, and thus has a strong teleological savour. The Cerdicings' expansion was, however, neither inexorable nor irreversible, and contemporaries could not have known how events would unfold. Thus, for example, the long-term prospects for anyone remaining dominant throughout Britain surely looked doubtful at best in the 940s and early 950s, when York was changing hands repeatedly. There were, moreover, several times when the power built up by the Cerdicings was divided, or at least came close to being split, notably in 855–860, 924, 957–959, 1016, 1033/1034, and 1035–1037. Some of these episodes can (with varying degrees of plausibility) be interpreted as attempts at joint rule, but in the Carolingian empire what began in 817 as an agreed sharing of power became an acrimonious and lasting division: without certain fortuitous events, particularly several convenient deaths, something similar could have happened in an English context.[110] Many chance occurrences were thus necessary for

---

[104] *ASC* CDE 1051, 1052. The three versions report the events of 1051–1052 quite differently.
[105] *ASC* CDE 1055, D 1058. Again, the three versions diverge markedly in their accounts of 1055.
[106] *ASC* CDE 1065.
[107] On the reasons why conflict was averted in 1051, 1052, and 1065, see below, pp. 215–16.
[108] *ASC* CD 1065, CDE 1066.   [109] *ASC* D 1067, DE 1068, 1069, 1071, 1075.
[110] S. Patzold, 'Eine „loyale Palastrebellion" der „Reichseinheitspartei"? Zur 'Divisio imperii' von 817 und zu den Ursachen des Aufstands gegen Ludwig den Frommen im Jahre 830', *Frühmittelalterliche Studien*, 40 (2006), pp. 43–77; below, pp. 245–8.

the eleventh-century English kingdom to come into existence and then to endure, but its history should not be understood simply in terms of dynastic and military contingencies: that Domesday *Anglia* constituted a clearly identifiable political entity was also a consequence of structural changes during the tenth century. These are the central concern of this book.

HOW DID THE CERDICINGS EXTEND THEIR DOMINATION?

While the narrative of Cerdicing expansion has often been recounted, it has been somewhat less common for detailed attention to be devoted to the issues of how and why Alfred and his successors extended their domination. A lack of evidence prevents firm answers to these questions, but they are too important to be sidestepped.

Terminology

There is a preliminary matter of terminology: when analysing Cerdicing expansion, it is preferable to think in terms of an 'extension of domination' rather than a 'conquest'.[111] There are three reasons for this. First, 'conquest' is usually taken to imply quite thorough subjugation, of the kind that enabled Cnut and William to levy heavy taxes, but I argue in subsequent chapters that in the first half of the tenth century kings had little ability to regulate the conduct of the bulk of the population, including in the south of Britain. 'Domination', on the other hand, embraces everything from close control to loose hegemony. Second, 'conquest' is generally associated with warfare, but the Cerdicings often acquired some ability to mould and constrain the actions of at least the greater inhabitants of an area without using (much) force: 'extension of domination' encompasses the spread of power through both violent and non-violent means. Third, talk of the 'conquest' of the land that became the English kingdom imposes what may well be an anachronistic dichotomy between that area and other parts of Britain. Wales and northern Britain are generally (and justifiably) not thought of as being 'conquered' in the tenth century, but contemporary writers frequently conceived of the island as a single political unit, ruled by the Cerdicings, to whose 'domination' leading potentates from across the whole landmass were at least intermittently subject.[112]

The concept of 'domination' is closely related to that of 'lordship'. Indeed, Old English *hlaford* and *hlafordscipe*, from which Modern English 'lord' and 'lordship' derive, were often rendered in Latin as *dominus* and *dominium* or *dominatio*.[113] In the medieval period, kingship was commonly understood as a species of lordship: thus, for example, Edmund demanded that his subjects swear an oath that they would be faithful to him, 'just as a man ought to be to his lord [*domino suo*]', and

---

[111] Compare Davies, *Domination and Conquest*.   [112] Below, pp. 207–13.
[113] The equivalence is particularly clearly demonstrated by *ASC* F 924; Ælfric, *Catholic Homilies: The First Series*, ed. P. Clemoes (EETS, s.s., 17, Oxford, 1997), p. 374.

Æthelred II declared that he would be a 'faithful lord' ('hold hlaford') upon his return from exile in 1014.[114] The language of lordship was, moreover, used by late ninth- and tenth-century writers to describe the geographical extension of Cerdicing power: Asser relates that Welsh kings requested Alfred's *dominium*; the A version of the *Chronicle* refers to people from Bedford, Northampton, Cambridge, and Stamford seeking or choosing Edward the Elder as *hlaford*; and the same text states that Edward was subsequently sought or chosen as *hlaford* by the Hiberno-Scandinavian potentate Ragnald, the rulers of Bamburgh, and the Welsh, Cumbrian, and Scottish kings.[115] Edward's relationships with the Scottish king and the people of Bedford can hardly have been identical, but *hlafordscipe* or *dominium* was a sufficiently broad concept to encompass both, since there was plenty of scope for variation in what a person's obligations to his or her lord might be, and in how closely these duties might be defined. This is implied by an Old English formula for an oath by which, in return for being kept ('healde') appropriately, a person promised to love all that his (or potentially her) lord loved, to shun all that the lord shunned, and to do nothing that was loathsome to the lord, and to 'fulfil all that was [their] agreement' ('eall þæt læste, þæt uncer formæl wæs').[116] Detailed obligations could thus be agreed in a subsidiary pact, but the defining feature of lordship was simply a general promise that the subordinate would be loyal and refrain from acting contrary to the lord's will. Given that contemporary writers understood Cerdicing power, and its extension, in terms of *hlafordscipe* or *dominium*, it is eminently appropriate that we should use the modern equivalents of these loose and flexible words. To think of 'lordship' or 'domination' allows us to recognize the essential similarity of a range of unequal relationships, the terms of which could be nebulous or precise, and in which the inequality between the parties could be great or small.[117] The merit of thinking in terms of 'domination' rather than 'lordship' is that the latter word now tends to call to mind a bond founded upon a formally established agreement between two individuals, but the mere threat of Cerdicing coercion was often probably enough to constrain or shape the actions of others. The Cerdicings' domination could be codified in a pact, but did not need to be.

The Lack of Coordinated Resistance

Turning from terminological to substantive matters, a basic point is that it took quite a long time for Cerdicing domination to spread across what became the English kingdom, and indeed across Britain. Expansion spanned the first half of the tenth century, and there were serious counter-attacks in 917, 937, and the early 940s, the last of which resulted in a struggle for control of York that continued until 954. Campaigning was most intense in the 910s, the late 930s, and the 940s,

---

[114] III Em 1; *ASC* CDE 1014.
[115] *VA*, lxxx (pp. 66–7); *ASC* ABCD 914, A 917, 918, 920.
[116] Swer 1, which is in some respects closely similar to III Em 1.
[117] Compare R. R. Davies, 'The Medieval State: The Tyranny of a Concept?', *Journal of Historical Sociology*, 16 (2003), pp. 295–6; R. R. Davies, *Lords and Lordship in the British Isles in the Late Middle Ages*, ed. B. Smith (Oxford, 2009), especially pp. 1, 6–7, 15–18, 158–78, 197–217.

but even the years between *c.*920 and 937 were punctuated by expeditions. Edward the Elder may have put down opposition in Chester in 924, and Æthelstan drove out Guthfrith in 927, penetrated far into Scotland in 934, and supported Alain's return to Brittany in 936.[118] Expeditions will have varied considerably in scale and duration, but as a generalization the first half of the tenth century saw frequent campaigns, many of which must have been major undertakings. The three and a half decades after 954 were, however, quite different: it was probably only around 990 that renewed Scandinavian attacks became a serious problem, and Edgar's reign in particular was widely remembered as a time of peace. This contrast is of considerable significance to the arguments of this book: prolonged campaigning need not preclude simultaneous administrative innovation, and may indeed provoke it, but we should not start from the assumption that the first half of the tenth century provided a propitious context for kings to overhaul the means by which they ruled.

The extension of Cerdicing domination was a lengthy process in large part because resistance to it was usually not very widely coordinated. Unlike in 1066, power across what would become the English kingdom was highly fragmented in the late ninth and early tenth centuries, such that there was no question of a single battle or submission delivering domination over all or even most of this area. The general absence of concerted opposition made expansion protracted, but also made it possible, since the Cerdicing king only needed to be stronger than the specific party over which he was seeking to extend his domination at any particular time. Thus in the East Midlands and East Anglia Edward the Elder subdued different army groups piecemeal, and he and Æthelstan seized Tamworth and York at moments when these were vulnerable.[119] There is also little sign of collaborative attempts by potentates in Wales or northern Britain to resist Cerdicing domination, save for when the Scottish and Cumbrian kings allied with Olaf Guthfrithson in 937.[120] Given that Æthelstan managed to defeat this coalition, albeit in what may have been a close-run battle, it is likely that his military might substantially exceeded that of each individual member of the alliance.[121] Any individual attempt to resist the Cerdicings would therefore probably have stood a high chance of being crushed, which makes it unsurprising that the mere threat of force was often seemingly sufficient for them to secure cooperation.

The Extent of Expropriation

In the wake of the conquests of 1016 and (especially) 1066, large numbers of incumbent aristocratic landholders were deprived of many or all of their estates.[122] How far the extension of Cerdicing domination entailed something similar is important, but uncertain. As a preliminary, it should be noted that there was considerable

---

[118] Above, pp. 28, 30, 31.
[119] Above, pp. 27–8, 30.   [120] Above, pp. 30–1.
[121] On the basis of the Cerdicings' coercive strength, see below, pp. 79–85.
[122] A. Williams, *The English and the Norman Conquest* (Woodbridge, 1995), especially pp. 1–70; Bolton, *Empire of Cnut*, pp. 13–76.

variation in what it meant for a person to 'possess' land (or to 'have', 'hold', or 'own' it—there is no unproblematic term). Royal diplomas granting *terra* ('land') commonly declare that it was being given in perpetuity, that the recipient could bequeath or alienate it freely, and that it was to be exempt from all except specified obligations. There is debate about whether such features were peculiar to land granted by a royal charter, and about how the words *bocland* and *folcland* should be interpreted, but it is not necessary to enter these controversies to recognize the implication that some land was held only for a limited term, or with restricted freedom of disposition, or subject to the discharge of various burdens.[123] There were, moreover, geographical and chronological variations in the nature of aristocratic landholders' relationships with peasants. By the time of Domesday, what modern historians often call 'manorialism' was at least moderately well established in much of the south and west: this involved lords renting out small pieces of land to peasants in return for onerous labour services and payments. Such arrangements were, however, less common in much of the north-east of the area described by Domesday, and even in the south and west it is likely that fewer peasants had been so heavily burdened earlier in the Anglo-Saxon period. In places and periods where manorialism was less prevalent, lords did still receive payments (in cash and kind) and services from peasants, but in most cases these dues were probably occasional and fairly light, such that the majority of peasants would have had only a small proportion of their time controlled by a lord, and would only have handed over to him or her a modest share of their produce. This is a schematic summary: the contrasts just identified were not absolute, the extent of manorialism at different times is debated, and it was probably common in all periods and places for lords to have both heavily and lightly burdened subordinates.[124] Here, however, the point to bear in mind is simply that possession of what for convenience we commonly call an 'estate' might cover everything from 'ownership' of land to loose 'superiority' (Maitland's term—one might substitute 'domination' or 'lordship') over those who lived on it: indeed, when discussing possession of 'lands' or 'estates', it might be more precise, if excessively cumbersome, to talk of someone having 'a more or less circumscribed set of rights over land and its inhabitants'.[125]

The areas in which it is easiest to assess the extent to which the Cerdicings deprived incumbents of their land (or of their more or less circumscribed sets of rights over land and its inhabitants) are those furthest from Wessex. The dynasties

---

[123] Maitland, *Domesday Book*, pp. 226–58, 293–318; S. Reynolds, *Fiefs and Vassals: The Medieval Evidence Reinterpreted* (Oxford, 1994), pp. 323–42; S. Baxter and J. Blair, 'Land Tenure and Royal Patronage in the Early English Kingdom: A Model and a Case Study', *ANS*, 28 (2006), pp. 19–29; J. G. H. Hudson, *The Oxford History of the Laws of England. Volume II: 871–1216* (Oxford, 2012), pp. 94–108.

[124] This overview is based above all on R. Faith, *The English Peasantry and the Growth of Lordship* (London, 1997), pp. 1–177. See also Maitland, *Domesday Book*, pp. 107–28, 220–356; T. H. Aston, 'The Origins of the Manor in England', *TRHS*, 5th series, 8 (1958), pp. 59–83; Hadley, *Northern Danelaw*, pp. 1–215; C. Dyer, *Making a Living in the Middle Ages: The People of Britain, 850–1520* (New Haven, CT, 2002), pp. 13–42; C. Wickham, *Framing the Early Middle Ages: Europe and the Mediterranean, 400–800* (Oxford, 2005), pp. 314–26, 347–51.

[125] Compare Maitland, *Domesday Book*, pp. 226–44; Reynolds, *Fiefs and Vassals*, pp. 53–7. Wickham, *Framing*, pp. 319, 349–50 eschews the term 'estate' in non-manorial contexts.

ruling at Bamburgh and in Wales, Cumbria, and Scotland remained in place, and it is unlikely that the Cerdicings effected major changes in who held land in these areas, although donations to the church of St Cuthbert imply that some estates between the Tees and Tyne passed through their hands.[126] In those parts of Britain that had by the eleventh century become the English kingdom, on the other hand, the Cerdicings deprived several existing potentates of their positions during the tenth century: an unnamed king and various East Anglian notables were killed in 917, the Mercian ruling family was suppressed in 918/919, and Hiberno-Scandinavian kings were repeatedly driven from Northumbria between 927 and 954.[127] It is likely that the Cerdicings appropriated many or all of whatever estates such people had held: this is the simplest way to explain how by 1066 there had come to be significant royal landholdings in several shires north of the Thames.[128] In some cases, land north of the Thames that we know to have been in Cerdicing hands in the second half of the tenth century had almost certainly once been held by churches such as Ely and *Medeshamstede* (Peterborough). In Wessex, the Cerdicings are known to have extorted ecclesiastical possessions, but it is perhaps more probable that the likes of Ely and *Medeshamstede* were deprived of lands by persons unknown, either before or during the period of Scandinavian domination, and that some of those who had acquired such estates in turn lost them to the Cerdicings.[129] One can, however, only make guesses about the extent to which Cerdicing expansion entailed confiscation, from whom estates were seized, and what then happened to the lands in question. Confident conclusions are impossible, since we have neither a tenth-century Domesday Book nor any genuine diplomas from the second half of Edward the Elder's reign, and few later charters concern land north of an imaginary line between Worcester and the Wash.[130]

It is sometimes assumed that when the Cerdicings acquired estates in areas in which they had recently gained power, they granted many of these to persons from south of the Thames, such that the upper aristocracy of the early English kingdom was overwhelmingly West Saxon in origin. This hypothesis cannot be disproved, and may be correct, but it ought not to be taken for granted.[131] It is very likely that when the Cerdicings confiscated (or otherwise acquired) lands north of the Thames,

[126] *Historia de Sancto Cuthberto*, xxvi, xxix, xxxii, ed. T. Johnson South (Cambridge, 2002), pp. 64, 66, 68, but note below, p. 65 n. 82.

[127] Above, pp. 27–8, 30, 31–2.

[128] D. H. Hill, *An Atlas of Anglo-Saxon England* (Oxford, 1981), p. 101. On royal landholding, see below, pp. 51–2, 83–4.

[129] R. Fleming, 'Monastic Lands and England's Defence in the Viking Age', *EHR*, 100 (1985), pp. 247–65; Dumville, *Wessex and England*, pp. 29–54; J. Blair, *The Church in Anglo-Saxon Society* (Oxford, 2005), pp. 121–34, 323–9. Dumville contests many details of Fleming's argument, but accepts that there was a substantial transfer of land from ecclesiastical institutions to the king. Blair demonstrates that this process began before the viking attacks. S 1444 indicates that Edward the Elder had extorted land from Winchester. *VSÆ*, xxiii–xxiv (pp. 38–40) mentions Edgar's sale to Æthelwold of land at Ely and Peterborough.

[130] On the reasons for the uneven distribution of extant charters, see below, pp. 51–2.

[131] The need for caution is underlined when one notes that traditional assumptions about Carolingian domination leading to Austrasian magnates being implanted *en masse* in Neustria have been seriously qualified: K. F. Werner, 'Important Noble Families in the Kingdom of Charlemagne—A Prosopographical Study of the Relationship between King and Nobility in the Early Middle Ages',

they sometimes transferred these to West Saxon magnates. Such persons were not, however, the only recipients of estates redistributed by the Cerdicings, and may not have been the principal beneficiaries. Some lands went to new or existing ecclesiastical institutions on or (relatively) close to the territory in question. For instance, Æthelstan, Eadwig, and Edgar granted lands north of the Ribble and in what became Nottinghamshire to the church of York; Edgar gave six local estates to St Werburgh's in Chester; and the same king sold or donated various lands in the vicinities of Ely, Peterborough, and Ramsey to monastic houses in these locations.[132] Turning to the secular beneficiaries of royal largesse, there is a fair chance that Eadred gave most of whatever lands he seized in 954 not to West Saxon magnates, but to those Northumbrians who had been responsible for Erik Haraldsson's downfall: that he entrusted York to Erik's betrayer, Oswulf of Bamburgh, is suggestive in this regard.[133] Those who state that the aristocracy was largely of southern origin tend to cite as evidence Æthelstan Half-King and Ælfhere of Mercia, the two most powerful magnates of the mid-tenth century.[134] Both men are known to have held lands south of the Thames, while acting as ealdormen further north, but this does not prove that they were West Saxons who had been intruded into subjugated territory: one could alternatively hypothesize that they hailed from north of the Thames, and went on to acquire lands to the south. This would parallel the way in which, according to Asser, Alfred lavished honours and powers in Wessex on Mercian churchmen, and there would be a strong rationale for the Cerdicings to bestow lands south of the Thames upon magnates from further north: such gifts would bind the beneficiaries to Wessex and discourage them from separatism.[135] The evidence relating to the origins of Ælfhere and Æthelstan Half-King is inconclusive, and we should keep an open mind about the extent to which the tenth century saw land north of the Thames transferred to West Saxon magnates.

Even if kings gave a large proportion of whatever lands they obtained to West Saxons, however, there is good reason to suspect that very many persons who held estates north of the Thames before coming under Cerdicing domination continued

---

trans. T. Reuter, *The Medieval Nobility: Studies on the Ruling Classes of France and Germany from the Sixth to the Twelfth Century* (Amsterdam, 1979), pp. 146–73.

[132] S 407, 659, 667, 679, 776, 779, 780, 781, 782; *VSÆ*, xxiii–xxiv (pp. 38–40); *LE*, ii.7, ii.27, ii.34, ii.37, ii.39, ii.40, ii.43, ii.47 (pp. 79, 100, 109, 111–15, 116); *Chronicon Abbatiæ Rameseiensis*, xxiv, ed. W. D. Macray (RS, 83, London, 1886), pp. 47–8. In certain cases, the land in question may already have been in the beneficiary's possession, with the effect of the royal grant being to change the terms on which it was held: below, p. 65 n. 82.

[133] Eadred may indeed have had little option but to recognize Oswulf as the principal lay potentate at York.

[134] Stafford, *Unification and Conquest*, p. 157; C. Hart, *The Danelaw* (London, 1992), pp. 569–604 especially 570–2; C. Wickham, *Problems in Doing Comparative History* (Southampton, 2005), p. 25; C. Insley, 'Southumbria', in P. Stafford (ed.), *A Companion to the Early Middle Ages: Britain and Ireland, c.500–c.1100* (Chichester, 2009), p. 330. Dumville, *Wessex and England*, p. 153 cites a grant to a certain Wulfsige of land in Derbyshire as evidence of 'the creation within the Danelaw of an aristocracy of Southern orientation', but there is nothing to suggest that Wulfsige's origins or other interests lay in the south, and some basis for associating him with Mercia: P. H. Sawyer, 'The Charters of Burton Abbey and the Unification of England', *Northern History*, 10 (1975), pp. 34–8.

[135] *VA*, lxxvii (p. 62); N. Banton, 'Ealdormen and Earls in England from the Reign of King Alfred to the Reign of King Æthelred II' (D.Phil. thesis, University of Oxford, 1981), pp. 89, 96–100, 141.

to do so afterwards. We have seen that Edmund and Eadred competed with Hiberno-Scandinavian kings for recognition from the local population north of the Humber: since Northumbrian support could still have been transferred to another Hiberno-Scandinavian potentate after 954, an attempt to enforce widespread confiscations might well have been counterproductive.[136] Nor do mass land seizures seem especially probable further south. When describing how Edward the Elder extended his domination into the East Midlands, East Anglia, and Essex, the A, B, C, and D texts of the *Chronicle* refer to people 'bowing' or 'turning' to him, or 'seeking him as lord', sometimes without a fight. Similarly, the Mercians are said by the A text to have 'turned' to Edward after he occupied Tamworth.[137] Such expressions do not themselves prove that those who submitted to Edward were allowed to retain their estates, but an account of a late tenth-century Huntingdonshire land dispute implies that this had often been so. The dispute turned on whether the claimants' uncle's grandmother had submitted to Edward promptly: it was determined that she had failed to do so, and had consequently forfeited her land, but this suggests that those who made timely submissions had not suffered confiscation.[138] It is, moreover, interesting that when people in areas that had been under Scandinavian domination did cease to hold land, this was not invariably the result of forfeiture: two charters refer to estates in what became Bedfordshire and Derbyshire having been purchased 'from the pagans' at Edward's behest, and Æthelstan bought a tract north of the Ribble from an unknown vendor.[139]

Persons regarded by contemporaries as 'Danes' were among those who reached accommodations with the Cerdicings, and probably kept (much of) their land: the A version of the *Chronicle* states that Edward settled (or garrisoned) the fortification at Nottingham 'both with English and with Danish people', and refers to the submission of all those dwelling in Mercia, 'both Danish and English'.[140] Later in the century, Edgar declared that certain laws he had made should be observed 'among the English', but allowed a degree of autonomy 'among the Danes'.[141] These so-called Danes may not all have been biologically descended from Scandinavians, and their legal customs need not have been the same as those that obtained in Scandinavia, but it is notable that some inhabitants of the English kingdom could be regarded as Danish, and indeed contrasted with the English.[142] It is, moreover, striking that the witness lists of diplomas of Æthelstan and his successors include a substantial number of men with Scandinavian names and the title

---

[136] Above, p. 32.   [137] *ASC* ABCD 912, 914, A 915, 917, 918.

[138] *LE*, ii.25 (pp. 98–9); Molyneaux, 'Why were some Tenth-Century English Kings Presented as Rulers of Britain?', pp. 82–3 n. 88.

[139] S 396, 397, 407. Note also *ASC* A 916; Abrams, 'Edward the Elder's Danelaw', p. 139.

[140] *ASC* A 918.

[141] IV Eg 2.1–2.2, 12, 13.1–14. See also VI Atr 37; Cn 1018 26–7; II Cn 12–15.3, 45.3, 46, 48, 62, 65, 71.2–71.3; S 939. Edgar also referred to Britons, who could have been Welsh, Cumbrian, or Cornish.

[142] Fenger, 'Danelaw'; M. Innes, 'Danelaw Identities: Ethnicity, Regionalism, and Political Allegiance', in Hadley and Richards (eds), *Cultures in Contact*, pp. 65–88; Hadley, *Northern Danelaw*, pp. 298–309; D. M. Hadley, 'Viking and Native: Re-thinking Identity in the Danelaw', *EME*, 11 (2002), pp. 45–70 especially 46–53.

dux, a Latin equivalent of ealdorman; a person's name proves nothing about how his or her identity was perceived by contemporaries, but these attestations encourage one to suspect that there were 'Danes' of considerable wealth and status who did not suffer forfeiture.[143] Thus, while some people between the Thames and Tees suffered confiscation as the Cerdicings pushed north, there is reason to think that very many did not. To a considerable extent, Alfred and his successors seem to have left incumbent landholders in place, on condition that they recognized the Cerdicings' superiority.

WHY DID THE CERDICINGS EXTEND THEIR DOMINATION?

While the foregoing discussion emphasizes that much is uncertain about how the Cerdicings extended the geographical reach of their power, numerous other early medieval rulers did so too, and there is little reason to think that the methods used by Alfred and his successors were exceptional. It is also likely that many of the reasons why the Cerdicings sought to expand were similar to those which made contemporaneous kings want to do the same: they doubtless hoped that offensive campaigns would bring plunder, tribute, land, and prestige. There are, however, grounds to think that the Cerdicings had an additional, more specific objective. This was in all probability not, as is sometimes claimed, a particularly pressing desire to unite the English, although they may well have aspired to the even grander possibility of rulership of Britain.[144] Rather, one of their major goals was probably to obtain security from the Scandinavian potentates who had gravely threatened Wessex during the second half of the ninth century, and who had supported Æthelwold's challenge to Edward the Elder. Up to a point, the Cerdicings sought security from past or potential Scandinavian aggressors by reaching agreements with them: Alfred contracted a treaty with Guthrum and acted as his baptismal sponsor; Edward the Elder received some sort of recognition of superiority from Ragnald; Æthelstan married his sister to Sihtric; and Edmund sponsored Olaf Sihtricson and Ragnald Guthfrithson at their baptism and confirmation respectively.[145] When opportunities presented themselves, however, the Cerdicings set aside such pacts and expelled leading potentates of Scandinavian origin, thus reducing the risk that the latter might exploit moments of Cerdicing vulnerability in much the same way.[146] Nonetheless, it should not be assumed that Cerdicing kings entered agreements simply as temporary expedients, or that Alfred's specific aim was the expulsion from Britain of all Scandinavian kings: until the campaigns

---

[143] Banton, 'Ealdormen and Earls', pp. 239–42; Abrams, 'Edward the Elder's Danelaw', pp. 138–9; Keynes, *Atlas*, Tables XXXII, XXXVIII, XLII, XLV, L, LVI; L. Abrams, 'Edgar and the Men of the Danelaw', in Scragg (ed.), *Edgar*, pp. 182–7; L. Roach, *Kingship and Consent in Anglo-Saxon England, 871–978: Assemblies and the State in the Early Middle Ages* (Cambridge, 2013), pp. 38–9; below, p. 57.
[144] Below, pp. 201–13.   [145] Above, pp. 22, 29, 30, 31.
[146] Above, pp. 30, 31–2.

of the second half of Edward the Elder's reign, it may well have appeared unrealistic to hope for anything more than a *modus vivendi*.

After Edward's successes, however, he and his descendants may have begun to think in terms of ridding Britain of Scandinavian kings. Indeed, Æthelstan's ambitions probably extended beyond Britain to Brittany, from which a viking fleet had come to the Severn estuary in 914.[147] His support for Alain in 936 was most likely not just an act of a benevolent godfather, but also an attempt to stop Brittany serving as a base for future raids.[148] The Cerdicings did not, as we have seen, seek to kill or expel from Britain everyone who was regarded as a 'Dane', but they do appear to have been especially concerned about those major potentates who were of Scandinavian origin.[149] By contrast, they supplanted neither the English rulers of Bamburgh nor the existing royal lines in Scotland, Cumbria, and Wales.[150] One might suggest that Scottish kings were simply too strong or too distant to be toppled, but it is striking that Alfred and his successors do not appear to have tried to suppress the royal line of Gwent, an agriculturally fertile part of south-east Wales: the rulers of a small kingdom quite close to Wessex would probably have represented easier targets than the Hiberno-Scandinavian kings of York. The removal of Ælfwynn of Mercia shows that non-Scandinavian dynasties were not invariably allowed to retain power, but this need not undermine the hypothesis that the Cerdicings were particularly concerned to deal with what they saw as the Scandinavian threat. Tamworth is only about 100 kilometres or 60 miles north of the Thames, it was probably fairly straightforward for Edward to oust a female relative who had just succeeded her mother, and he may in any case have seen the suppression of a quasi-autonomous Mercian lineage as a means to strengthen his position vis-à-vis the Scandinavian potentates who remained in Northumbria and (probably) the northern East Midlands.

It was not necessary for the Cerdicings to displace the rulers of Bamburgh, or the Welsh, Cumbrian, or Scottish kings, in order to exclude leading Scandinavian potentates from Britain. Gaining some measure of domination over non-Scandinavian rulers was, however, integral to the achievement of this goal, since the Cerdicings needed the cooperation of those who might otherwise have aided their adversaries. That Scandinavian potentates might obtain assistance from rulers in Wales and northern Britain is demonstrated by Anarawd of Gwynedd's cooperation with Alfred's Northumbrian enemies, and by the Scottish and Cumbrian kings' backing of Olaf Guthfrithson in 937.[151] Anarawd's promise of obedience to Alfred surely encompassed a pledge not to revive his Northumbrian alliance, and comparable undertakings were probably given by Malcolm when he became Edmund's cooperator ('midwyrhta') in 945, and by the assortment of Insular rulers who promised in 973 to be cooperators ('efenwyrhtan') with Edgar.[152] The Cerdicings' apparent desire to kill or expel Scandinavian kings did not necessarily require the former to

---

[147] *ASC* ABCD 914.   [148] Above, p. 31.   [149] Above, pp. 44–5.

[150] The Cerdicings did, however, inflict serious harm on certain individuals from non-Scandinavian dynasties: e.g. Roger of Wendover, *Flores Historiarum*, i, 398.

[151] Above, pp. 26, 30–1.   [152] Above, pp. 33, 34.

have ongoing direct dealings with the bulk of the population in the areas into which they extended their domination, or for that matter in Wessex itself. The Cerdicings did, however, need at least a minimal level of cooperation from those persons in all parts of the island who were powerful enough to be valuable allies for Scandinavian potentates, or indeed for anyone else who might seek to challenge their (the Cerdicings') position. The object of the next chapter is to analyse how, during the period when the Cerdicings were extending their domination, they gained and retained the cooperation of such persons.

2

The Cerdicings and Their Greater Subordinates from the Late Ninth to the Mid-Tenth Century

ARGUMENT AND APPROACH

As we noted in the Introduction to this volume, much work on royal rule in the late Anglo-Saxon period focuses on kings' use of shires, hundreds, and wapentakes to regulate what people did at a local level, but the evidence for this comes from the mid-tenth century and after.[1] In some cases, late tenth- and eleventh-century arrangements had much earlier antecedents: thus, for example, we shall see in subsequent chapters that there were already shires south of the Thames when Alfred became king, and that certain of the hundred and wapentake districts visible in Domesday may have been recognized for centuries as territorial units for one purpose or another.[2] It is, however, unsound to infer continuity of function from continuity of territorial delimitation, and there is no good evidence that Alfred routinely regulated the lives of ordinary people through an ordered system of shires and hundreds. Moreover, even if Alfred did rule in such a way within Wessex, it is by no means obvious that shires and hundreds would have been swiftly introduced elsewhere. We have noted that throughout the first half of the tenth century the Cerdicings were frequently engaged in military action. We have also seen that a significant proportion of those who held land north of the Thames probably retained their possessions under Cerdicing domination.[3] The hypothesis that an administrative system based on shires and hundreds or wapentakes was rapidly established across what became the English kingdom consequently requires one to suppose more than just that such a system already operated in Wessex: it also entails the assumption that kings had both the desire and the capability to impose major and immediate changes on incumbent landholders over whom they had just gained power, while simultaneously pressing on with further campaigns. Such a theory is possible, but by no means probable: to accept it in spite of the lack of firm evidence would be imprudent.

In Chapter 4 I argue that it was not until the mid- to late tenth century, around the time of Edgar, that a system of shires and hundreds or wapentakes began to play a significant role in the Cerdicings' attempts to regulate the conduct of 'the

---

[1] Above, pp. 10–12.   [2] Below, pp. 146–7, 157–8.
[3] Above, pp. 42–5.

general populace'—people with whom kings rarely or never had direct dealings on an individual basis. Chapter 4 thus represents a direct challenge to the hypothesis that Alfred and his immediate successors had an eleventh-century-style administrative apparatus at their disposal. For now, however, I merely suspend the assumption that this theory is correct, and analyse the domination of kings from Alfred to Edgar without projecting back late tenth- and eleventh-century conditions. The focus of this chapter is on royal relations with leading lay and ecclesiastical figures, while Chapter 3 turns to the Cerdicings' power over more ordinary people. This pair of chapters yields two significant conclusions. The first is that one can account for the known accomplishments of Alfred and his immediate successors without positing that they had a sophisticated or standardized system of local regulation. The second conclusion is that, unless one decides to postulate the existence of an unevidenced administrative apparatus, the land between the Channel and the Tees did not yet constitute a distinct block. Within this area, the Cerdicings' domination appears to have been far from uniform, and in some ways not so very different from their power in Wales or northern Britain.

Regardless of whether an administrative apparatus of shires, hundreds, and wapentakes played any significant part in royal rule, a king's ability to retain the adherence of leading lay and ecclesiastical magnates must have been crucial: if the most powerful people of a region withdrew their allegiance, as those of York did repeatedly in the 940s and early 950s, it was hard for Cerdicing domination to survive there.[4] The need to think about the Cerdicings' relationships with the greatest English magnates of the tenth century is widely recognized, particularly by Cyril Hart and Ann Williams, who have sought to assemble all that is knowable about two of the most powerful aristocrats of the period, Æthelstan Half-King and Ælfhere of Mercia.[5] The new and very useful *Prosopography of Anglo-Saxon England* database will facilitate similar treatment of other individuals, but it is questionable whether this will in itself do much to advance understanding of how kings dealt with their greater subordinates.[6] Aside from uncertainties about whether particular charters are reliable, and about whether two occurrences of a name denote the same person, studies of this kind have fundamental limitations. One problem is that merely identifying close relationships between individuals does not prove that they pursued common goals; they may, at least at times, have been bitter rivals.[7] Even more serious is that without a tenth-century Domesday Book, our knowledge of the lands and other interests of even the greatest magnates will always be extremely incomplete. We know about estates that are mentioned in surviving wills and charters, but for most magnates we do not have a will, and the extant corpus of charters represents only a fraction of those issued. In particular, relatively

---

[4] Above, pp. 31–2.

[5] A. Williams, '*Princeps Merciorum gentis*: The Family, Career and Connections of Ælfhere, Ealdorman of Mercia, 956–83', *ASE*, 10 (1982), pp. 143–72; C. Hart, *The Danelaw* (London, 1992), pp. 569–604, the latter being a revised version of an article published in *ASE*, 2 (1973).

[6] J. L. Nelson, S. Keynes, S. Baxter et al., *Prosopography of Anglo-Saxon England*, consulted at <http://www.pase.ac.uk/index.html> (accessed 9 October 2014).

[7] For a revealing example, see S 1447, in which a man forfeits his land to the king rather than allow it to enter his brother's possession.

few records of land held on lease have been preserved, probably because such documents became redundant after the land returned to the lessor.[8] It is, moreover, quite likely that much land was never the subject of a written grant at all, but was held on a customary basis.[9] Even a will is unlikely to give us a full account of the testator's holdings: the rarity with which extant wills mention sons suggests that they concerned bequests only of those estates that could be alienated comparatively freely, and that separate arrangements governed the distribution of lands that had been in a family for a generation or more.[10] Our ignorance is such that, as we saw in the previous chapter, we are even in the dark about matters as fundamental as whether Æthelstan Half-King and Ælfhere were men of southern origin who obtained ealdordoms in East Anglia and Mercia, or whether they hailed from north of the Thames but also acquired estates in Wessex.[11] Rather than assembling fragments of information to produce further highly incomplete prosopographies of particular individuals, my aim is to sketch the general parameters within which kings from Alfred to Edgar dealt with their greater subordinates.

THE CERDICINGS' LANDS, PRESENCE, ASSEMBLIES, AND DEMANDS

Geographical Variations in the Cerdicings' Domination, Lands, and Presence

A basic starting point is that from at least the early 880s the Cerdicings had some degree of continuous domination not only over the magnates of the land south of the Thames, but also over those of western Mercia. That is not to say that all magnates in these areas were loyal all of the time: a charter of Edward the Elder indicates that an estate in Wiltshire had been forfeited by a *dux* ('leader' or 'ealdorman') named Wulfhere for breach of an oath he had sworn to Alfred.[12] Nor did all magnates always support the same Cerdicing, but from the middle of Alfred's reign until the latter part of Æthelred II's, the superiority of a member of their dynasty appears to have been recognized in western Mercia and south of the Thames. From the mid- to late 910s, the same was so with regard to the southern East Midlands and East Anglia. By contrast, the Cerdicings' position further north was precarious,

---

[8] On leases, see J. G. H. Hudson, *The Oxford History of the Laws of England. Volume II: 871–1216* (Oxford, 2012), pp. 98–102.

[9] S. Reynolds, *Fiefs and Vassals: The Medieval Evidence Reinterpreted* (Oxford, 1994), pp. 325–6, 331, 333–5. Note also Hudson, *Oxford History of the Laws of England*, p. 95.

[10] P. Wormald, 'On þa wæpnedhealfe: Kingship and Royal Property from Æthelwulf to Edward the Elder', in N. J. Higham and D. H. Hill (eds), *Edward the Elder, 899–924* (London, 2001), p. 267; J. Mumby, 'The Descent of Family Land in Later Anglo-Saxon England', *Historical Research*, 84 (2011), pp. 1–17 especially 3–4. A will would also be likely to omit lands that the testator held by virtue of some office, like that of ealdorman.

[11] Above, p. 43.

[12] S 362; below, p. 64. J. L. Nelson, '"A King Across the Sea": Alfred in Continental Perspective', *TRHS*, 5th series, 36 (1986), pp. 53–5 suggests that Wulfhere may have had familial ties to the Cerdicings.

lapsing several times between 937 and 954.[13] The Cerdicings' power in Wales may have been more continuous, but it is doubtful whether Alfred's hegemony persisted without intermission, and it is only in 918/919 that we have evidence of all the principal Welsh kings recognizing Edward the Elder's superiority; it is, moreover, entirely possible that there were major interruptions to the domination of Edward's successors.[14] Cerdicing domination of Britain was not, however, just a passing peculiarity of the decade between Æthelstan's seizure of York and the battle of *Brunanburh*, a point demonstrated by Edgar's having the Scottish king and assorted other potentates gather at Chester in 973.[15] Thus, from fairly early in the tenth century, the Cerdicings' domination intermittently extended across the whole of Britain, but their hegemony was uneven and in many regions insecure. Significantly, the areas in which they sometimes lost power included parts of the future English kingdom, and even after 954 it probably took some time before contemporaries could predict with any confidence that no more Hiberno-Scandinavian potentates would establish themselves in Northumbria. Thus, the land from the Channel to the Tees did not stand distinct from the rest of Britain as a stable political unit in the late ninth or early tenth century.

Geographical variations in the security of the Cerdicings' domination were a cause and consequence of two further contrasts. The first is the distribution of the lands that they held, whether as individuals or by virtue of their royal position.[16] Some estates between the Tees and Tyne appear to have passed through the Cerdicings' hands, but there is no reason to think that they acquired lands further north or in Wales.[17] This stands in stark contrast to the southernmost part of Britain, where the Cerdicings held numerous estates, but there were probably some regions between the Thames and Tees in which Edgar and his predecessors had little or no land. There are two reasons for this inference. First, the great bulk of these kings' surviving charters concern land near or south of the Thames. In part, this is probably a reflection of differences in the rate of document preservation, since the archives that contain the most tenth-century material are in the south. We should, however, be wary of the supposition that the low number of extant royal diplomas concerning land further north derives simply from the loss of records. In particular, it is notable that while very few extant charters relate to land in East Anglia, the region

[13] Above, pp. 30–2.

[14] *ASC* A 918; T. M. Charles-Edwards, *Wales and the Britons, 350–1064* (Oxford, 2013), pp. 494–510. For Welsh attestations of Cerdicing charters in 928–935 and 943×946–956, and the problems of interpreting their absence at other times, see below, pp. 57–9. *Annales Cambriae, A.D. 682–954: Texts A–C in Parallel*, ed. and trans. D. N. Dumville (Cambridge, 2002), p. 16 records the killing of the king of Gwynedd and his son 'by the English' in 942. This could reflect that Cerdicing domination had been challenged, or that it was being asserted with renewed vigour. It could also have had nothing to do with the Cerdicings.

[15] Above, p. 34.

[16] The evidence of a conceptual distinction between a king's personal possessions and land pertaining to the royal office is not extensive, but see G. Garnett, 'The Origins of the Crown', *PBA*, 89 (1996), pp. 184–9; Hudson, *Oxford History of the Laws of England*, pp. 108–10. S 937 indicates that certain estates were earmarked for kings' sons, and may allude to lands associated with the royal office. Note also Norðleod 1; Mirce 2–4.

[17] For lands between the Tees and Tyne, see *Historia de Sancto Cuthberto*, xxvi, xxix, xxxii, ed. T. Johnson South (Cambridge, 2002), pp. 64, 66, 68, although note below p. 65 n. 82.

accounts for a high proportion of surviving tenth-century wills. That such non-royal documents were preserved suggests that the rarity of royal diplomas is in large part a result of the area never having had many in the first place, probably because the Cerdicings had little land to grant there.[18] The second reason for concluding that the lands held by the Cerdicings were unevenly distributed is that, while Domesday records that Edward the Confessor had very substantial southern holdings, it ascribes him few or no estates in some shires, such as Cheshire, Essex, Hertfordshire, Leicestershire, and Lincolnshire.[19] Domesday cannot provide a detailed guide to periods long before its compilation, and in each of the shires just named there is evidence that at least a little land had passed through the Cerdicings' hands during the course of the tenth and eleventh centuries.[20] Nonetheless, it is hard to avoid the suspicion that there were parts of the area between the Thames and Tees in which the Cerdicings had never obtained much land, or had swiftly relinquished whatever they did acquire. This would be consistent with a hypothesis explored in the previous chapter, that Alfred and his successors permitted large numbers of incumbent landholders to keep their possessions, and also redistributed much of what they did confiscate to persons or institutions based nearby.[21] It thus appears that, at least in terms of Cerdicing landholdings, many regions between the Thames and the Tees were quite unlike the dynasty's West Saxon heartlands, and in some sense were more similar to Wales and northern Britain. This is important, since, where the Cerdicings possessed estates, they could use these to reward, strengthen, and implant their supporters; where they did not, their patronage options were narrower, and they were more dependent on the loyalty of those already *in situ*.[22]

The distribution of royal landholding also affected kings' movements, since they could most readily sustain a frequent personal presence in areas where they were able to consume the surpluses generated by their own estates. This brings us to our second contrast: there were marked disparities in the amount of time that the Cerdicings spent in different regions. It appears that they very seldom went to Wales: Alfred is not known to have set foot there, Edward the Elder's sole recorded trip was to build a fortification at the mouth of the Clwyd, and after that there is no documented visit by a reigning king until William the Conqueror.[23] Visits to northern Britain were similarly infrequent. If we discount the twelfth-century tale that Edgar had circumnavigated Britain annually, there are only five occasions on which William's predecessors are known to have ventured north of the Tees or the Ribble: Æthelstan went to Eamont in 927, and seven years later ravaged the Scottish

---

[18] L. Marten, 'The Shiring of East Anglia: An Alternative Hypothesis', *Historical Research*, 81 (2008), pp. 7–8.

[19] D. H. Hill, *An Atlas of Anglo-Saxon England* (Oxford, 1981), p. 101; J. L. Grassi, 'The Lands and Revenues of Edward the Confessor', *EHR*, 117 (2002), pp. 251–83; below, pp. 83–4.

[20] Cheshire: S 667. Essex: S 418a, 517a, 517b, 522a, 676, 717, 919, 931a, 931b, 1015, and see also S 1486. Hertfordshire: S 794a, 888, 900, 912, 916, 1031. Leicestershire: S 749. Lincolnshire: S 782.

[21] Above, pp. 40–5.   [22] Below, pp. 65–6.

[23] *ASC* MR 921, E 1081; Charles-Edwards, *Wales*, pp. 499–500. Prior to becoming king, Harold Godwinson campaigned in north Wales and considered inviting Edward the Confessor to go hunting in Gwent: *ASC* DE 1063, CD 1065.

kingdom; Edmund laid waste to the Cumbrian kingdom in 945; Eadred visited the church of St Cuthbert sometime during his reign; and Cnut went to Scotland in or around 1031.[24] There is a fair chance that there were expeditions to Wales and northern Britain that went unrecorded in extant sources, but it is reasonable to infer that such trips were rare. It is likely, however, that royal visits to large parts of the area that would be described in Domesday were not very much more frequent. Edward the Elder mounted several military expeditions in Essex and the Midlands, and struggles for power at York prompted his successors to go north on various occasions, but the places in which tenth-century Cerdicing kings are known to have issued diplomas or legislation suggest that they spent the great bulk of their time near or south of the Thames, and especially in central Wessex.[25] The normally narrow geographical range of their movements should not, however, be mistaken for sedentariness, since, within their southern heartlands, kings' presences are documented at a substantial number of locations. Nor should it be thought that kings only left the south to campaign: Æthelstan, for example, at least occasionally granted charters or issued legislation at locations in Essex and the East Midlands, and the D text of the *Chronicle* mentions that he met the Hiberno-Scandinavian king Sihtric at Tamworth, and died at Gloucester.[26] It is, moreover, highly likely that during the partition between Eadwig and Edgar, the latter was usually north of the Thames.[27] Nonetheless, it remains hard to escape the conclusion that most kings were most often in the very south of Britain, and that their presence became progressively less frequent as distance from Wessex increased.

---

[24] *ASC* D 927, ABCDE 934, 945, DE 1027; Symeon of Durham, *Libellus de Exordio atque Procursu istius, hoc est Dunhelmensis, Ecclesie*, ii.20, ed. and trans. D. Rollason (Oxford, 2000), p. 140. Æthelstan, Edmund, and Cnut are also known to have visited the church of St Cuthbert, but the first two called while proceeding north on campaigns that may have been those of 934 and 945, and Cnut's visit could likewise have been part of his expedition of *c*.1031: Symeon of Durham, *Libellus de Exordio*, iii.8 (p. 166); *Historia de Sancto Cuthberto*, xxvi–xxviii, xxxii (pp. 64–6, 68). For the claim that Edgar sailed around Britain each year, see John of Worcester, *Chronicle*, 975, ed. and trans. R. R. Darlington, P. McGurk, and J. Bray (2 vols so far, Oxford, 1995–), ii, 424–6; William of Malmesbury, *Gesta Regum Anglorum*, ii.156.2, ed. and trans. R. A. B. Mynors, R. M. Thomson, and M. Winterbottom (2 vols, Oxford, 1998–9), i, 256.

[25] L. Roach, *Kingship and Consent in Anglo-Saxon England, 871–978: Assemblies and the State in the Early Middle Ages* (Cambridge, 2013), pp. 45–76, 239–42. See also Hill, *Atlas*, pp. 84, 87–90; J. R. Maddicott, *The Origins of the English Parliament, 924–1327* (Oxford, 2010), pp. 16–17; S. Foot, *Æthelstan: The First King of England* (New Haven, CT, 2011), pp. 77–91, 259–66; S. Keynes, 'Church Councils, Royal Assemblies, and Anglo-Saxon Royal Diplomas', in G. R. Owen-Crocker and B. W. Schneider (eds), *Kingship, Legislation and Power in Anglo-Saxon England* (Woodbridge, 2013), pp. 140–57. Maddicott, *Origins*, p. 11 n. 36 uses *ASC* CDE 1006 to suggest that the diplomas may present a misleading picture of royal movements, but see below, p. 217 n. 101.

[26] S 407 (Nottingham), 412 (Colchester, Essex), 426 (Buckingham); VI As 12.1 (Whittlebury, Northamptonshire); *ASC* D 926, 940. Note, however, that S 407 appears to have been issued while Æthelstan was heading north to ravage the Scottish kingdom. For reports of Æthelstan meeting Frankish envoys at York and Welsh rulers at Hereford, see Richer, *Historiae*, ii.2, ed. H. Hoffmann (*MGH*, Scriptores, 38, Hanover, 2000), p. 98; William of Malmesbury, *Gesta Regum*, ii.134.5 (i, 214–16). William of Malmesbury, *Gesta Regum*, ii.135.1 (i, 216) may refer to Æthelstan receiving Norwegian envoys at York. Foot, *Æthelstan*, pp. 251–8 surveys the debate about William's reliability as a source for Æthelstan's reign.

[27] Edgar issued a charter at Penkridge (Staffordshire) in 958 (S 667), but his movements during the period of partition are otherwise unknown.

Historians of Ottonian Germany have sometimes presented itinerant kingship as a (poor) substitute for 'missing' local administrative institutions of the sort that existed in the eleventh-century English kingdom.[28] The limited range of Cerdicing itineration does not, however, constitute evidence that such an administrative apparatus was already in place in the first half of the tenth century. Indeed, one could argue that the pattern of Edgar's predecessors' (and successors') itineration was not so very different from that of their Ottonian contemporaries, even though the latter were kings of a much larger territory. Like the Cerdicings, the Ottonians appear to have spent the bulk of their time in fairly small regions (especially south-eastern Saxony) where they had substantial landholdings, and to have been infrequent visitors to most of the vast area in which they were recognized as kings. The rarity of the Ottonians' visits to the likes of Bavaria or even northern Saxony does not reflect that some administrative apparatus rendered their personal presence in these areas superfluous. Rather, these were regions in which they had comparatively few lands or rights to sustain extended visits, and in which such domination as they had depended on the sometimes questionable loyalty of powerful magnates.[29] Much the same was probably so of the Cerdicings' position vis-à-vis the likes of East Anglia and the northern East Midlands, in which (as far as we can tell) kings held few estates and spent little time. Indeed, the whole notion that royal itineration was a way of making up for 'missing' administrative institutions is unhelpful: it implies that the absence of such structures represents both an anomaly and a deficiency, but there is no reason why they 'ought' to have existed, either on the Continent or in Britain.

Royal Assemblies

The usually limited range of Cerdicing and Ottonian (and indeed Carolingian) itineration meant that, to a considerable extent, kings did not go to their subordinates, at least the greater of whom instead came to them.[30] In the case of the Cerdicings, the best (though not unproblematic) evidence of this is provided by charters, which document a land gift or transaction and then provide a list of witnesses; the king himself nearly always appears first, and there then follows some combination of archbishops, bishops, *duces*, and *ministri*. These last terms are very probably Latin equivalents of Old English *ealdorman* and *þegn*, the former being the powerful holder of

---

[28] E.g. J. W. Bernhardt, *Itinerant Kingship and Royal Monasteries in Early Medieval Germany, c.936–1075* (Cambridge, 1993), pp. 51–2. See also p. 48 for a comparative comment about the Cerdicings.

[29] E. Müller-Mertens, *Die Reichsstruktur im Spiegel der Herrschaftspraxis Ottos des Grossen* (Berlin, 1980), especially pp. 79–163; Bernhardt, *Itinerant Kingship*, pp. 45–70, 312–13, 318. See also K. J. Leyser, 'Ottonian Government', *EHR*, 96 (1981), pp. 721–53 especially 746–51; T. Zotz, 'Kingship and Palaces in the Ottonian Realm and the Kingdom of England', in D. Rollason, C. Leyser, and H. Williams (eds), *England and the Continent in the Tenth Century: Studies in Honour of Wilhelm Levison (1876–1947)* (Turnhout, 2010), pp. 311–30; below, p. 237.

[30] K. F. Werner, '*Missus–Marchio–Comes*. Entre l'administration centrale et l'administration locale de l'Empire carolingien', in W. Paravicini and K. F. Werner (eds), *Histoire comparée de l'administration (IVᵉ–XVIIIᵉ siècles)* (Munich, 1980), pp. 192–4; Leyser, 'Ottonian Government', pp. 748–51; T. Reuter, *Germany in the Early Middle Ages, c.800–1056* (Harlow, 1991), pp. 210–11; M. Costambeys, M. Innes, and S. MacLean, *The Carolingian World* (Cambridge, 2011), pp. 173–5, 408–9.

a prestigious royal office, and the latter someone, often a minor aristocrat, who served a superior in one way or another.[31] As well as being occasions when they could have land grants witnessed by many leading lay and ecclesiastical magnates, it is likely that kings used these assemblies in a variety of other ways. Evidence of what happened at late ninth- and tenth-century royal assemblies is scarce, but legislation is known to have been promulgated at some.[32] It also appears that judicial verdicts and appointments to major offices were determined or at least approved by those in attendance, since kings are sometimes said to have decided such things with the agreement of 'wise people' (*witan* or *sapientes*).[33] More generally, kings probably used assemblies to consult their leading subordinates about a range of issues, and to seek their consent to important decisions. It is, furthermore, a fair guess that assemblies served both to assert kings' charismatic uniqueness through ceremonial display, and to engender a sense of commonality between them and their subordinates through feasting. Neither point can be demonstrated conclusively from contemporary sources, but an interest in splendour is implied by the introduction of crowning into the royal inauguration liturgy in 925, and a late tenth-century *Life* of St Dunstan states that before Edmund's death (946) the saint had a dream in which the king fell asleep at a banquet with all his great men.[34]

[31] H. R. Loyn, 'Gesiths and Thegns in Anglo-Saxon England from the Seventh to the Tenth Century', *EHR*, 70 (1955), pp. 540–9; N. Banton, 'Ealdormen and Earls in England from the Reign of King Alfred to the Reign of King Æthelred II' (D.Phil. thesis, University of Oxford, 1981); G. Molyneaux, 'The *Ordinance concerning the Dunsæte* and the Anglo-Welsh Frontier in the Late Tenth and Eleventh Centuries', *ASE*, 40 (2012), pp. 265–7. By the early eleventh century, *þegn* had come to denote a person of noble status. Witness lists are unlikely to record all those present when a grant was made, and it is possible that they sometimes include persons who were absent, but there is no reason to think that the latter practice was common: S. Keynes, *The Diplomas of King Æthelred 'the Unready', 978–1016: A Study in their Use as Historical Evidence* (Cambridge, 1980), pp. 37, 130–4, 154–5; below, pp. 58–9.

[32] II As Epilog; VI As 10; I Em Prolog; III Em Inscr. all appear to refer to large gatherings.

[33] *VSO*, i.5 (pp. 22–4); *VSD*, xxvi.3 (p. 80); *ASC* BC 971; S 362, 414, 415, 1211, 1447. Note, however, that it is not certain that all of these decisions were made at large assemblies; it is conceivable that in some cases the 'wise people' were a small group of confidantes. A similar point applies where legislation is said to have been issued with the agreement of *witan* or *sapientes*: Af El 49.10; AGu Prol.; II Ew 1; III As 2; IV As 1; V As Prol.1; VI As 12.1; II Em Prolog; II Eg Prol.; IV Eg 1.4. Many of these may have been large gatherings, but this is not certain. See more generally Maddicott, *Origins*, pp. 25–31; Roach, *Kingship and Consent*, pp. 77–160, 212–35.

[34] *The Sacramentary of Ratoldus*, ed. N. Orchard (London, 2005), p. 52; *VSD*, xxxii (p. 94). On the introduction of crowning, see J. L. Nelson, 'The First Use of the Second Anglo-Saxon *Ordo*', in J. Barrow and A. Wareham (eds), *Myth, Rulership, Church and Charters: Essays in Honour of Nicholas Brooks* (Aldershot, 2008), pp. 117–26, and contrast J. L. Nelson, 'The Second English *Ordo*', in J. L. Nelson, *Politics and Ritual in Early Medieval Europe* (London, 1986), pp. 361–74. S 549, a charter issued at Easter 949, refers to Eadred being 'exalted with royal diadems'; this may reflect that he wore his crown at this and other assemblies, although it could be metaphorical. *VSD*, xxi.4 (p. 68) implies that Eadwig had been wearing his crown at his wedding feast. *VSÆ*, xii (pp. 22–4); *VSD*, x.3–6, xxi.2–5, xxxiii.1–2 (pp. 34–6, 66–8, 94–6); *VSO*, iv.7, v.11 (pp. 110, 178); Wulfstan of Winchester, *Narratio Metrica de S. Swithvno*, lines 61–114, ed. and trans. M. Lapidge, *The Cult of St Swithun* (Oxford, 2003), pp. 376–80 give further references to kings and magnates feasting together. The role of rituals and symbolic behaviour in relationships between kings and magnates is considered by M. Hare, 'Kings, Crowns and Festivals: The Origins of Gloucester as a Royal Ceremonial Centre', *Transactions of the Bristol and Gloucestershire Archaeological Society*, 115 (1997), pp. 44–8; J. Barrow, 'Demonstrative Behaviour and Political Communication in Later Anglo-Saxon England', *ASE*, 36 (2007), pp. 127–50; Maddicott, *Origins*, pp. 18–25; L. Roach, 'Public Rites and Public Wrongs: Ritual Aspects of Diplomas in Tenth- and Eleventh-Century England', *EME*, 19 (2011), pp. 182–203; Roach, *Kingship and Consent*, pp. 161–211. Parts of these works are necessarily speculative.

Here, however, the details of what happened at assemblies are less important than the basic point that turning up at such a gathering amounted to recognition of the superiority of the person at whose behest it had been organized. Who attended, and how consistently they did so, are therefore matters of considerable importance.[35] The evidence from Alfred's reign is, however, minimal, since few genuine charters survive, and their witness lists are relatively short. Alfred is known to have held at least one assembly attended by persons based in both Wessex and Mercia: in 889 he and Æthelred of Mercia jointly granted land in London to the Bishop of Worcester, in the presence of the recipient, Æthelflaed, and the Bishops of Lichfield, Dorchester-on-Thames, Winchester, and Sherborne.[36] It may, however, have been more common for separate meetings to be held north and south of the Thames, since charters in Alfred's sole name include no witnesses known to have been based in Mercia, while certain grants of Æthelred are said to have been witnessed by Alfred and the 'wise people' of Mercia.[37] There is more evidence from Edward the Elder's early years of bishops from the south-east, western Mercia, and the West Saxon heartlands all attending the same assemblies, but this may well not have been frequently mirrored among the laity. Æthelred and Æthelflaed, the most readily identifiable Mercian laypeople, only appear in those charters of Edward that they issued jointly with him, and these concern estates either north of the Thames or in northern Somerset, where a few decades previously the Mercian king Burgred (r. 852–874) had held an assembly and granted land.[38] Even if some of the laymen who witnessed Edward's other grants were from north of the Thames, the general absence from his charters of Æthelred and Æthelflaed suggests that the land subject to them was far from fully integrated with Wessex.[39]

It is unclear how long this partial division between southern and Mercian assemblies persisted, since no royal diplomas survive from the second half of Edward the Elder's reign and only a handful are extant from Æthelstan's early years.[40] From fairly soon after Æthelstan's seizure of York, however, it is clear that leading ecclesiastical

---

[35] Maddicott, *Origins*, pp. 4–11; Roach, *Kingship and Consent*, pp. 27–44 provide overviews of assembly attendance.

[36] S 346. See also S 1628.

[37] S 218, 223. See also S 217, 1441, 1442. Æthelred and Æthelflaed sometimes made grants without reference to Alfred or Edward the Elder: S 219, 220, 221, 222, 224, 225.

[38] S 361, 367, 367a, 371. Compare S 210, 1701. For bishops' attestations, see S. Keynes, *An Atlas of Attestations in Anglo-Saxon Charters, c.670–1066* (Cambridge, 2002), Table XXXIII.

[39] Setting aside the charters that Edward issued jointly with Æthelred and Æthelflaed, S 362 is the most likely of his diplomas to include at least one Mercian lay witness: the Æðelferd *dux* who attests it may be the man of the same name who appears in several of Æthelred and Æthelflaed's grants (and who may have been Æthelstan Half-King's father). S 362 states that the *dux* Wulfhere had been deprived of his lands by the judgement of the wise people of the *Gewisse* (i.e. West Saxons) and Mercians, although it is not clear whether it was under Alfred or Edward that this sentence had been imposed. Nor is it certain whether the West Saxon and Mercian wise people had given judgement in a single meeting; they could conceivably have done so separately.

[40] D. N. Dumville, *Wessex and England from Alfred to Edgar* (Woodbridge, 1992), pp. 151–3; Wormald, 'On þa wæpnedhealfe', especially p. 275. The all-Mercian witness list of what appears to be Æthelstan's earliest extant diploma (S 395) need not indicate that the holding of separate assemblies had continued throughout Edward's reign, since the charter may well reflect the particular conditions of a succession dispute: above, p. 29.

and lay magnates from across the lands that would be described in Domesday, and beyond, were attending the same royal assemblies. The Archbishop of York is first known to have attested (at Exeter) in 928, and successive holders of this see thereafter appeared fairly frequently, joining the Archbishop of Canterbury and the bishops whose episcopal seats lay on or south of the Thames, or in western Mercia.[41] From the early 930s onwards we have attestations in the same documents by *duces* who can be associated with Wessex, western Mercia, and East Anglia, and this title is also accorded to several witnesses with Scandinavian names, most or all of whom were probably men of considerable power, based in the East Midlands, East Anglia, or north of the Humber.[42] Potentates from Wales and northern Britain likewise travelled to meet Æthelstan on the latter's ground: five Welsh kings appear in several charters dating from between 928 and 935, two men who were probably successive rulers of Bamburgh attested frequently from 930 to 935, and the Cumbrian and Scottish kings witnessed more occasionally in the same period.[43] It is also from around this time that we have the first appearances in Cerdicing charters of the Bishop of the church of St Cuthbert, then at Chester-le-Street, who was probably the most powerful figure between the Tees and the Tyne.[44] Although Scottish kings did not subsequently witness Cerdicing charters, there were further Welsh attestations between 943×946 and 956, and possible Cumbrian attestations in 946 and 949.[45] Bishops of the church of St Cuthbert and Bamburgh potentates witnessed several times in the 940s and 950s too, and, unlike the Welsh kings, they also occasionally appeared later in the tenth century, and in the eleventh.[46]

---

[41] S 399, 400; Keynes, *Atlas*, Tables XXXVII, XLI, XLIV, XLVIII, LIV. There does not appear to have been a bishopric in East Anglia in the first half of the tenth century, and at that time the diocese of Dorchester-on-Thames covered the whole of the East Midlands: below, p. 110.

[42] Banton, 'Ealdormen and Earls', pp. 92–105; Keynes, *Atlas*, Tables XXXII, XXXVIII, XLII, XLV, L, LVI. On the Scandinavian-named *duces*, see the literature cited above at p. 45 n. 143.

[43] Keynes, *Atlas*, Tables XXXVI, XXXVIII; Charles-Edwards, *Wales*, pp. 514–18. Welsh kings: S 400, 407, 413, 416, 417, 418a, 420, 425, 427, 434, 1792. Ealdred and Oswulf of Bamburgh: S 403, 407, 412, 413, 416, 418, 418a, 425, 434, 1604. Owain, Cumbrian king: S 413, 434, 1792. Constantine, Scottish king: S 426, 1792. The reliability of these charters, and those cited in subsequent footnotes, varies, with a few being clear fabrications. They nonetheless collectively establish that the men in question were at least sometimes present at royal assemblies, and were at least sometimes accorded particular titles: even late concoctions are likely to have taken names and titles from authentic witness lists. My arguments for the most part do not depend on whether any particular witness was present, or styled in any particular way, on any particular occasion. For an earlier example, note that Asser stated that Anarawd of Gwynedd came to Alfred's presence: *VA*, lxxx (pp. 66–7).

[44] S 401, 407, 412, 413, 416, 417, 418a, 425; Keynes, *Atlas*, Table XXXVII.

[45] S 520, 544, 550, 552a, 566, 633, 1497; Keynes, *Atlas*, Table XXXVI. Charles-Edwards, *Wales*, pp. 516–17 suggests that the Cadmon who appears in S 520 and S 544 may have been a Cumbrian king. S 779, a diploma of disputed reliability that purports to be from 970, is attested by Malcolm *dux*, possibly another Cumbrian or Scottish potentate.

[46] Chester-le-Street/Durham attestations, with names of bishops and date ranges of attestations: S 544, 549, 550, 552a, 569, 675, 679, 681 (Ealdred, 949–959); S 781 (Ælfsige, 970); S 922 (Aldhun, 1009); S 1011 (Æthelric, 1045); S 1036 (Æthelwine, 1062). See also *Rituale Ecclesiae Dunelmensis: The Durham Collectar*, ed. U. Lindelöf (Durham, 1927), p. 185; *De primo Saxonum adventu*, ed. T. Arnold, *Symeonis Monachi Opera Omnia* (RS, 75, 2 vols, London, 1882–5), ii, 382. Bamburgh attestations: S 520, 544, 546, 550, 552a (Oswulf, 946–950); S 766, 771, 779, 806 (Eadwulf, 968–970); S 881 (Waltheof, 994); S 921, 922, 926, 931, 931b, 933, 934 (Uhtred, 1009–1015). The compilation of these lists was greatly facilitated by Keynes, *Atlas*, Tables XLIV, XLV, LIV, LVI, LXb, LXII, LXVI, LXXII.

The frequency with which these witnesses are recorded varies widely. To assess how far this reflects similarly wide variations in the frequency with which they actually attended the Cerdicings' assemblies, we need to consider the drafting of charters. Despite the importance that has been attached to the possible existence of what is now often called a royal 'writing office', we can largely sidestep the debate about whether tenth-century diplomas were commonly produced by permanent members of kings' households, rather than by persons whom kings commissioned on an ad hoc basis, or by the beneficiaries of the grants in question.[47] This debate does not fundamentally affect interpretation of charters' content: whether in the service of the king or that of someone who had just benefited from his patronage, the drafter of a diploma would have had every reason to couch a grant in terms of which the reigning king would be expected to approve. Nor does the controversy contribute significantly to evaluation of the nature of royal power, since the putative so-called 'writing office' was no vast secretariat: the very basis for thinking that it existed is that in some periods (notably 928–935) a small number of people seem to have drafted a high proportion of known royal documents. It would hardly be remarkable if, as seems likely, kings had within their entourages a handful of people (or perhaps just one person) capable of producing diplomas. The problem of who drafted royal charters is therefore not one with which it is necessary to engage here.

Whether or not those who drafted charters were permanent members of the royal household, it is significant that the main clusters of attestations by men from Wales and north of the Tees appear in two highly distinctive corpora of documents, known respectively as the 'Æthelstan A' and 'alliterative' charters. Each of these two groups is marked by a different set of unusual features of formulation and vocabulary, the details of which need not concern us at this point.[48] What does matter here, however, is that the 'Æthelstan A' charters are the sole source of the Welsh, Cumbrian, Scottish, Bamburgh, and Chester-le-Street attestations from Æthelstan's reign, and that the 'alliterative' charters account for all but one of the

---

[47] For major contributions to the debate, see R. Drögereit, 'Gab es eine angelsächsische Königskanzlei?', *Archiv für Urkundenforschung*, 13 (1935), pp. 335–436; P. Chaplais, 'The Origin and Authenticity of the Royal Anglo-Saxon Diploma', *Journal of the Society of Archivists*, 3.2 (1965), pp. 48–61; P. Chaplais, 'The Anglo-Saxon Chancery: From the Diploma to the Writ', *Journal of the Society of Archivists*, 3.4 (1966), pp. 160–76; Keynes, *Diplomas*, pp. 14–153; P. Chaplais, 'The Royal Anglo-Saxon "Chancery" of the Tenth Century Revisited', in H. Mayr-Harting and R. I. Moore (eds), *Studies in Medieval History Presented to R. H. C. Davis* (London, 1985), pp. 41–51; *Charters of Abingdon Abbey*, ed. S. E. Kelly (2 vols, Oxford, 2000–1), vol. i, pp. lxxi–cxxxi; S. Keynes, 'Edgar, *rex admirabilis*', in D. Scragg (ed.), *Edgar, King of the English 959–975: New Interpretations* (Woodbridge, 2008), pp. 12–23; Keynes, 'Church Councils, Royal Assemblies, and Anglo-Saxon Royal Diplomas'. F. M. Stenton, *Anglo-Saxon England*, 3rd edn (Oxford, 1971), pp. 353–4 treated the alleged establishment of the 'writing office' in Æthelstan's reign as the start of 'the history of the English civil service'.

[48] Drögereit, 'Gab es eine angelsächsische Königskanzlei?', pp. 345–8, 361–9; Keynes, *Diplomas*, p. 82 and n. 165; S. Keynes, 'King Athelstan's Books', in M. Lapidge and H. Gneuss (eds), *Learning and Literature in Anglo-Saxon England: Studies Presented to Peter Clemoes on the Occasion of his Sixty-Fifth Birthday* (Cambridge, 1985), pp. 156–9; Hart, *Danelaw*, pp. 431–45; Keynes, 'Church Councils, Royal Assemblies, and Anglo-Saxon Royal Diplomas', pp. 53–5, 93–5; D. A. Woodman, '"Æthelstan A" and the Rhetoric of Rule', *ASE*, 42 (2013), pp. 217–48.

Welsh, Bamburgh, Chester-le-Street, and (possible) Cumbrian attestations of 943×946–956.[49] This is significant because it may be that potentates from Wales and northern Britain were present at assemblies more often than the extant texts indicate, but that those who drafted other charters for some reason chose not to include them in witness lists. Since the 'Æthelstan A' charters are confined to the years 928–935 and all but one of the known 'alliterative' charters are from 940–957, the (near) absence at other times of attestations by Scottish, Welsh, and Cumbrian rulers should not in itself be taken as proof of diminutions in Cerdicing domination.[50] Nonetheless, since Welsh, Bamburgh, Chester-le-Street, and (possibly) Cumbrian attestations are recorded between 943×946 and 956, it is probably reasonable to infer that Scottish kings did not commonly attend Cerdicing assemblies during these years. This would not be surprising, given that for substantial parts of this period York was under Hiberno-Scandinavian domination.

While witness lists may understate the frequency with which potentates from Wales and northern Britain were present at assemblies, it is still very likely that most great magnates from the area between the Channel and the Tees showed up more often. There were, however, disparities in attendance rates within the latter area. The appearances of the Scandinavian-named *duces* are somewhat less frequent than those of persons with the same title from Wessex or western Mercia, including in the period when Æthelstan's domination of York and the East Midlands is not known to have been challenged. Since most attestations by Scandinavian-named *duces* occur in the 'Æthelstan A' and 'alliterative' charters, this can in part be attributed to drafting practices, but even within the 'Æthelstan A' series there are cases of at least moderately lengthy witness lists with few or no Scandinavian-named *duces*.[51] It is, moreover, notable that while Archbishop Wulfstan I of York witnessed consistently from 931 to 935, his next appearance was not until 942, and there are gaps in his attestations between then and his death in 956: it is very likely that the lacunae are linked to intermittent Hiberno-Scandinavian domination at York.[52] Even a leading magnate from the heart of Wessex could on occasion seemingly be absent from royal assemblies: Bishops of Winchester usually attested with great reliability, but Bishop Frithestan does not appear in Æthelstan's earliest charters, most likely because Winchester had probably backed Ælfweard's claim to kingship.[53] The attestations of many *ministri* are intermittent too, although this may not usually reflect shifts in their relationships with the king, since the majority of lesser magnates may only have attended assemblies if they

---

[49] The exception is S 546, which pertains to a third distinctive group, the 'Dunstan B' charters.

[50] Keynes, *Atlas*, Tables XXVII, XXVIII; Keynes, 'Edgar', pp. 26–7, 50–1. S 931 is a charter of 'alliterative' style dated 1013, presumably modelled on an earlier 'alliterative' charter; it has a moderately lengthy witness list, but those named all appear to have been English. For a possible Scottish or Cumbrian attestation in 970, see above, p. 57 n. 45.

[51] S 379, 400, 422, 423, 1604. Less weight can be placed on absences from short witness lists, since they are more likely to reflect selectivity on the part of the drafter or later copiers.

[52] Keynes, *Atlas*, Tables XXXVII, XLI, XLIV, XLVIII; S. Keynes, 'Wulfstan I', in *WBEASE*, pp. 512–13.

[53] Keynes, *Atlas*, Table XXXVII; above, p. 29. Frithestan is absent from S 394, 396, 397. He is also absent from S 395, but this is unremarkable, since all the bishops who attested had Mercian dioceses.

were already in the vicinity, and there is also a good chance that the drafters of charters recorded merely a selection of the *ministri* present.[54] Setting the *ministri* aside, what matters here is that in the second quarter of the tenth century potentates from across Britain at least intermittently showed up at the Cerdicings' assemblies, and that the Tees did not mark a simple dichotomy between consistent and sporadic attendees.

One could distinguish between the Welsh, Cumbrian, and Scottish witnesses on the one hand, and those from the rest of Britain on the other, on the grounds that the former group consisted of kings and the latter did not. This distinction is not, however, entirely clear-cut. Those who drafted diplomas almost always accorded only qualified kingliness to Welsh, Cumbrian, and Scottish witnesses: while the reigning Cerdicing was usually *rex* or *basileus* (both 'king'), no witness from Wales or northern Britain received either of these titles, save for in one 'alliterative' charter where the Welsh king Hywel Dda appears as *rex*.[55] Rather, the Welsh, Cumbrian, and Scottish witnesses were styled *subregulus* ('under-ruler') in the 'Æthelstan A' charters, and, with the sole exception just noted, the Welsh and (possibly) Cumbrian rulers who attested 'alliterative' charters did so either without any title, or as *regulus* ('ruler').[56] The switch from *subregulus* to *regulus* could denote a substantive rise in the status of certain witnesses, although it may alternatively just reflect a difference in the semantic preferences of the respective drafters of 'Æthelstan A' and 'alliterative' charters. Whatever the reason for the change, *regulus* was still clearly inferior to the titles sported by the Cerdicings: as a diminutive form of *rex*, it could be translated 'little king' or 'petty king'.

The drafters of charters very rarely accorded even such qualified regal status to leading English magnates, who usually attested as *dux*, but we should be wary of assuming any very sharp distinction between the power of so-called *duces* and so-called *subreguli* or *reguli*. That there was no great gulf between them is implied by a charter of Offa from 778, which refers to a certain Ealdred as both *subregulus* and *dux* of the people of the Hwicce.[57] Similarly, the Old English version of Bede's *Ecclesiastical History* rendered 'subreguli' as 'aldormen'.[58] Much the same is suggested by Asser's statement that Anarawd, the king of Gwynedd, submitted to Alfred on the same terms as the Mercian ealdorman Æthelred.[59] Furthermore, while Æthelred was often styled *ealdorman* or *dux*, he once attested a charter as 'subregulus et patricius Merciorum' ('under-ruler and leader of the Mercians'); appears as the final name in a list headed 'de regibus Merciorum' ('concerning the kings of the Mercians'); and was twice styled *rex* by the late tenth-century chronicler

---

[54] Keynes, *Atlas*, Tables XXI, XXXV, XXXIX, XLIII, XLVI, LI, LVII; Maddicott, *Origins*, pp. 8–10.

[55] S 550. *Basileus* may have had particularly 'imperial' connotations, but see G. Molyneaux, 'Why were some Tenth-Century English Kings Presented as Rulers of Britain?', *TRHS*, 6th series, 21 (2011), p. 63.

[56] S 427, a charter of dubious authenticity in the style of 'Æthelstan A', calls Hywel *vndercyning*, a vernacular rendering of *subregulus*.

[57] S 113; Stenton, *Anglo-Saxon England*, pp. 45–6, 305. The Hwicce were located in the southern West Midlands, and were subordinated by the Mercians during the seventh and eighth centuries. Note also S 89 and S 1429, in which *subregulus* and *comes* are used of the same individuals.

[58] *HE*, iv.12 (p. 368); *OEB*, iv.15 (p. 298).   [59] *VA*, lxxx (pp. 66–7).

Æthelweard.[60] As the first Mercian ruler to be clearly subject to more than fleeting Cerdicing domination, Æthelred's position may well have been unusual, but the leading English magnate of the second quarter of the tenth century was also at least occasionally represented in quasi-regal terms, apparently being known as Æthelstan *semi-rex* ('half-king').[61] Similar considerations apply to Bamburgh potentates, who were styled *dux* or *hæhgerefa* (literally 'high-reeve') in charters, but appear in Irish annals of the first half of the tenth century as 'kings of the north Saxons'.[62] All of this suggests that kingliness was to some extent in the eye of the beholder, and that there was no great gulf between the power of stronger *duces* and that of at least some *subreguli* or *reguli*. It cannot plausibly be maintained that all persons accorded one of these three titles were equals in strength or status, but they were all subordinates of the Cerdicing kings, and in the second quarter of the tenth century they all attended the same assemblies in southern Britain, albeit with varying frequency: they thus all had something very important in common.

The Cerdicings' Other Demands

The obligations that the Cerdicings imposed on their subordinates were not limited to attendance at assemblies, but there is relatively little detailed evidence about the precise nature and extent of their other demands. At a bare minimum, the Cerdicings surely insisted that no aid be given to their adversaries, but even from the potentates of Wales and northern Britain they appear to have sought more than mere neutrality. It is likely that at least three Welsh *subreguli* participated in Æthelstan's Scottish expedition of 934, since their charter attestations suggest that they accompanied him as he headed north.[63] A Welsh king also aided Edmund's ravaging of Cumbria in 945.[64] Edmund subsequently gave Cumbria to the Scottish king in return for cooperation 'both on sea and on land', which sounds like a formula for

---

[60] S 346; *Hemingi Chartularium Ecclesiæ Wigorniensis*, ed. T. Hearne (2 vols, Oxford, 1723), i, 242; Æthelweard, *Chronicle*, iv.3, ed. and trans. A. Campbell (Edinburgh, 1962), pp. 49, 50. For Æthelred as *ealdorman* or *dux*, see S 217, 218, 222, 223, 349, 361, 396, 397, 1280, 1282, 1441, 1507; *ASC* ABCDE 886, ABCD 893, 911; Æthelweard, *Chronicle*, iv.3 (p. 46). Æthelflaed is styled *regina* ('queen') by *Annales Cambriae*, pp. 14–15; *Annals of Ulster*, 918, ed. and trans. S. Mac Airt and G. Mac Niocaill, *The Annals of Ulster (to A.D. 1131). Part I: Text and Translation* (Dublin, 1983), p. 368.

[61] *VSO*, iii.14 (pp. 82–4).

[62] *Annals of Ulster*, 913 (p. 360); *The Annals of Clonmacnoise*, ed. D. Murphy (Dublin, 1896), pp. 145, 149. The word *hæhgerefa* is fairly rare, but also appears in a gloss added during the second half of the tenth century to Mark xiii.9 in the Lindisfarne Gospels: the glossator, a member of the church of St Cuthbert and thus near neighbour of Bamburgh, gave both 'undercyningum' and 'hehgeroefum' as renderings of 'praesides'. His bracketing of high-reeves with subordinate kings may reflect that he regarded these ranks as equivalent, although it does not prove this. See London, British Library, MS Cotton Nero D.iv, f. 121ᵛ, consulted in facsimile in T. D. Kendrick et al., *Evangeliorum quattuor Codex Lindisfarnensis* (2 vols, Olten and Lausanne, 1956–60), i; N. R. Ker, *Catalogue of Manuscripts Containing Anglo-Saxon* (Oxford, 1957), no. 165. For other occurrences of the term 'high-reeve', see *ASC* DE 778, 779, A 1001, CDE 1002; III Em 5; Norðleod 4.

[63] S 407, 425. There may well also have been a Welsh component to the force with which Æthelstan drove out Guthfrith in 927: Charles-Edwards, *Wales*, pp. 511–12.

[64] Roger of Wendover, *Flores Historiarum*, ed. H. O. Coxe (5 vols, London, 1841–4), i, 398.

a promise of military assistance.[65] The potentates who gathered at Chester in 973 likewise pledged to work together 'on sea and on land'.[66] Welsh and Scottish rulers are, in addition, known to have handed over movable wealth to the Cerdicings: John of Worcester records that the Scottish king gave Æthelstan 'worthy gifts' after the 934 campaign, and *Armes Prydein*, a Welsh poem that most likely dates from the second quarter of the tenth century, complains about the tribute being collected for an unnamed English king.[67]

Turning to the evidence relating to magnates within the area that would constitute Domesday *Anglia*, there is reason to think that military assistance was again central to the demands that the Cerdicings laid upon their greater subordinates. The paramount importance of military aid is indicated by the routine reservation of army service (*exercitus* or *expeditio*), along with labour on bridges and fortifications, in royal charters that state that land should otherwise be exempt from all burdens.[68] Implicit in such grants, however, is that ordinarily more was owed than just army, bridge, and fortification service. The nature of the additional burdens is a matter of surmise, and it is highly likely that different landholders aided kings in different ways, providing a variety of types of movable wealth and services. This is suggested by a tenth- or eleventh-century passage about the duties of a thegn, which in this context probably means someone of noble status, although not necessarily of really exceptional wealth or power. The text states that, as well as army, fortification, and bridge service, a thegn might be obliged by the king to discharge other responsibilities, such as equipping a ship, guarding the coast, acting as a bodyguard, doing some further form of military guard duty ('fyrdweard'), performing service pertaining to royal deer fences, rendering alms and church dues, 'and many other diverse things'.[69] While stressing the variety of tasks that a thegn might perform, this passage also underlines the importance of military service: in addition to the three obligations commonly reserved in charters, a substantial proportion of the other duties listed are in some sense martial. Despite the shortage of evidence, it can hardly be doubted

---

[65] *ASC* ABCD 945. Roger of Wendover, *Flores Historiarum*, i, 398 states that Malcolm agreed to defend the northern parts of *Anglia*; this may well derive from an early source, although it could just be an inference from whatever version of the *Chronicle* Roger was using.

[66] *ASC* DE 973.

[67] John of Worcester, *Chronicle*, 934 (ii, 388–90); *Armes Prydein: The Prophecy of Britain from the Book of Taliesin*, ed. I. Williams and trans. R. Bromwich (Dublin, 1982), especially lines 17–22, 69–86; Charles-Edwards, *Wales*, pp. 519–35. John also states that the Scottish king gave his son as a hostage. While it is unknown what source (if any) John had for this or the reference to 'worthy gifts', there are grounds to accept his account, since verifiable sources are usually rendered quite faithfully in sections of his *Chronicle* prior to about 970: R. R. Darlington and P. McGurk, 'The "Chronicon ex Chronicis" of "Florence" of Worcester and its Use of Sources for English History before 1066', *ANS*, 5 (1982), pp. 185–96.

[68] W. H. Stevenson, 'Trinoda Necessitas', *EHR*, 29 (1914), pp. 689–703; N. Brooks, 'The Development of Military Obligations in Eighth- and Ninth-Century England', in P. Clemoes and K. Hughes (eds), *England Before the Conquest: Studies in Primary Sources Presented to Dorothy Whitelock* (Cambridge, 1971), pp. 69–84; below, p. 81.

[69] Rect 1; P. Wormald, *The Making of English Law: King Alfred to the Twelfth Century. Volume I: Legislation and its Limits* (Oxford, 1999), pp. 387–9. On the term 'thegn', see the literature cited above at p. 55 n. 31.

that the Cerdicings obtained a somewhat wider range of renders and services, in greater measure and more frequently, from people based in or near Wessex than from those living further away. The key demand of a measure of military assistance was, however, common to all the Cerdicings' subordinates: indeed, it is striking that the pledges obtained by Edmund and Edgar from some of the greatest potentates in Britain echoed Edward the Elder's Exeter legislation, which records that he had asked those present at its issue to affirm that they would cooperate with him, and 'love what he loved and shun what he shunned, both on sea and on land'.[70]

THE CERDICINGS' MEANS OF SECURING OBEDIENCE

Oaths

The question we now need to consider is how the Cerdicings induced other powerful people to recognize their superiority, attend their assemblies, and contribute to the advancement of their objectives. One significant way in which the Cerdicings sought to secure adherence was through oaths, the breach of which could be expected to incur divine punishment.[71] Several of Alfred's agreements with his Scandinavian adversaries were accompanied by such solemn promises, and the various versions of the *Chronicle* repeatedly mention oaths when recounting how his successors extended their domination. Thus the army ('here') in East Anglia swore in 917 that 'they willed all that [Edward the Elder] willed'; in the same year the army of Cambridge sealed its acceptance of Edward's lordship with oaths ('aþum'); in 927 the rulers who gathered at Eamont established peace 'with pledge [*wedde*] and with oaths [*aþum*]'; in 946 the Scots gave Eadred oaths ('aþas') 'that they willed all that he willed'; and the next year Archbishop Wulfstan and the Northumbrians gave both pledge and oaths ('ge wed 7 eac aþas').[72] As well as extracting oaths when they extended their domination into new areas, it appears that from time to time the Cerdicings had at least the greater of their existing subordinates make formal professions of loyalty. This is clearest in an ordinance of

---

[70] II Ew 1.1; above, pp. 61–2. *ASC* A 917 refers to the army ('here') in East Anglia swearing that 'they willed all that [Edward the Elder] willed, and would keep peace with all with whom the king wished to keep peace, both on sea and on land'.

[71] What follows draws on P. Wormald, 'Oaths', in *WBEASE*, pp. 345–6; D. Pratt, *The Political Thought of King Alfred the Great* (Cambridge, 2007), pp. 232–8; T. B. Lambert, 'Protection, Feud and Royal Power: Violence and its Regulation in English Law, *c*.850–*c*.1250' (PhD thesis, Durham University, 2009), pp. 214–19; M. Ammon, '"Ge mid wedde ge mid aðe": The Functions of Oath and Pledge in Anglo-Saxon Legal Culture', *Historical Research*, 86 (2013), pp. 515–35. I have also consulted a draft for the second volume of *The Making of English Law*, in which Wormald set out in detail his case for tracing a general loyalty oath back to Alfred. Wormald's draft was made available online while this volume was in press: see now P. Wormald, 'Papers Preparatory to *The Making of English Law: King Alfred to the Twelfth Century. Volume II: From God's Law to Common Law*', ed. S. Baxter and J. G. H. Hudson (London, 2014), pp. 112–29, consulted at <http://www.earlyenglishlaws.ac.uk/reference/wormald/> (accessed 9 October 2014).

[72] AGu Prol.; *ASC* ABCDE 876, 877, 878, ABCD 893, A 917, D 927, ABCD 946, D 947. On the problems of getting non-Christian vikings to adhere to oaths, see R. Abels, 'King Alfred's Peace-Making Strategies with the Vikings', *HSJ*, 3 (1991), pp. 27–9.

Edmund, preserved only in a later Latin version, which gives the text of the oath that 'all' ('omnes') were to swear in God's name, promising to be faithful to the king as one ought to be to one's lord, to love what he loved, to shun what he shunned, and to refrain from concealing any breach of the oath by another.[73] Undertakings of a broadly similar nature had, however, quite likely been extracted for some time by Edmund's reign. Æthelstan complained that 'the oaths [*aþas*] and the pledges [*wedd*] and the sureties [*borgas*]' given at an assembly held at Grately (Hampshire) had been disregarded, and pledges are also known to have been given at Thunderfield (Surrey) later in the same king's reign.[74] Edward the Elder's Exeter legislation, as well as alluding to a promise of cooperation on sea and on land, referred to an oath ('að') and pledge ('wæd') that the 'whole people' ('eal ðeod') had given.[75] Moreover, while Alfred's much-discussed demand that people abide by their 'oath and pledge' may have been a general injunction to keep one's word, rather than an allusion to a specific promise, he evidently received professions from certain of his subjects, since the *dux* Wulfhere suffered forfeiture for breaching an oath to him.[76] Indeed, it is possible that Alfred's predecessors had sought comparable undertakings: there is no specific evidence that they did so, but Carolingian kings are known to have demanded loyalty oaths from their subordinates since at least the late eighth century, and the promise prescribed by Edmund is similar to that which Charlemagne had stipulated.[77]

It is uncertain how many people from different parts of Britain swore oaths to the Cerdicings. When recording that Welsh and northern rulers sought or chose Edward the Elder as lord in 918 and 920, the A text of the *Chronicle* states that they did so with 'all the Welsh people', 'all the Scottish people', 'all who live among the Northumbrians', and 'all the Strathclyde Welsh'.[78] It is, however, implausible that more than a very small proportion of those living in Wales or northern Britain personally took oaths to recognize Edward's lordship: rather, it sounds as if the chronicler considered the promises given by rulers, probably along with members of their entourages, to be binding on their respective peoples. Within at least some of what had by the eleventh century become the English kingdom, Cnut demanded that all free males aged twelve or over swear to abjure theft, but it is very doubtful whether a comparably large segment of the population had personally given loyalty oaths in the first half of the tenth

---

[73] III Em 1. Compare Swer 1, a formula for an oath to a lord. On kingship as a form of lordship, see above, pp. 38–9.

[74] V As Prol.3; VI As 10.   [75] II Ew 1.1, 5.

[76] Af 1; S 362; Ammon, ' "Ge mid wedde ge mid aðe" ', especially pp. 518–20, with references to earlier literature.

[77] *CRF*, no. 34 (c. 19); III Em 1; C. E. Odegaard, 'Carolingian Oaths of Fidelity', *Speculum*, 16 (1941), pp. 284–96; F. L. Ganshof, 'Charlemagne's Use of the Oath', in F. L. Ganshof, *The Carolingians and the Frankish Monarchy*, trans. J. Sondheimer (London, 1971), pp. 111–24; M. Becher, *Eid und Herrschaft. Untersuchungen zum Herrscherethos Karls des Großen* (Sigmaringen, 1993). The similarity of the oaths could, but need not, reflect that it was in Charlemagne's day that the Cerdicings began to emulate this Frankish practice; they could alternatively have been inspired considerably later by a text of Charlemagne's legislation, or by the oaths demanded by his successors.

[78] *ASC* A 918, 920.

century.[79] It is clear that those present at Grately and Thunderfield had sworn oaths to Æthelstan, and on the latter occasion it was decreed that reeves should extract pledges of obedience in their own districts.[80] Æthelstan thus made some attempt to extend oath-taking beyond those present at his assemblies, but there is no need to infer from Edward's and Edmund's references to the 'whole people' and 'all' that promises had been given by the entire (free adult male) population. As with the account of the Welsh and northern rulers' choosing Edward as lord, such language may well reflect that promises made by those at royal assemblies could be seen as binding on the general populace.[81] It is highly probable that the proportion of the population from which the Cerdicings received oaths decreased as distance from Wessex increased, and also that there was considerable variation in the precise nature of the undertakings given by people in different parts of Britain. All across the island, however, oaths were important to the Cerdicings' attempts to secure adherence.

Patronage: Land, Office, and Movable Wealth

Observing that the Cerdicings received oaths does not go far in explaining the basis of their domination: rather, it raises the questions of how they induced people to swear oaths, and how they dealt with those for whom the prospect of divine retribution was an insufficient deterrent to disloyalty. One dimension of their attempts to secure adherence was through the dispensing of patronage, which historians have mostly examined in terms of grants of land, office, or movable wealth. These were all undoubtedly significant in the Cerdicings' manipulation of their subordinates, although the relative importance of these forms of patronage varied in different regions. Taking land first, diplomas record numerous grants in perpetuity to lay and ecclesiastical beneficiaries, although we know almost nothing about the many loans of land that kings probably made. The diplomas of early tenth-century kings concern estates scattered across Southumbria, and Æthelstan and Edgar are known to have made some grants north of the Humber, and indeed the Tees.[82]

---

[79] II Cn 20–1, which refers to a 'freoman' over twelve winters old, although the meaning of 'free' is uncertain. Old English *mann* (like Latin *homo*) meant 'person', rather than necessarily 'male person', but there are grounds to infer that the obligation was (at least largely) confined to males, since this was the case with frankpledge (which built on basic loyalty oaths) in later centuries, when the evidence is fuller. Frankpledge was largely absent north of the Humber and in the shires bordering Wales, and the same may have been so of earlier loyalty oaths. See W. A. Morris, *The Frankpledge System* (London, 1910), pp. 43–59, 81; below, pp. 195–6. Oaths were to have been central to the second volume of Wormald's *Making of English Law*, but his published comments are scattered and fragmentary. His belief that an oath taken by all free adult males went back to Alfred's day is, however, clear at Wormald, '*Engla Lond*', p. 366.

[80] V As Prol.3; VI As 10. Hungary offers a parallel for an oath being taken by magnates at an assembly, then administered more widely: below, p. 242.

[81] II Ew 5; III Em 1; Pratt, *Political Thought*, p. 236; Maddicott, *Origins*, p. 54.

[82] For grants north of the Humber by Æthelstan and Edgar, see S 407, 681, 712, 716; *Historia de Sancto Cuthberto*, xxvi (p. 64). S 451 and S 456 are late fabrications. Note that some royal diplomas may well not have conveyed estates from the possession of the king to that of another, but instead have changed the status of land that the beneficiary already held, exempting it from obligations or making it more freely alienable. Such grants could, however, still represent a form of royal patronage. See Hudson, *Oxford History of the Laws of England*, p. 96; R. Naismith, 'Payments for Land and Privilege in Anglo-Saxon England', *ASE*, 41 (2012), pp. 281, 284–5. S 1458 seems to describe something along such lines. Note also S 298, 715, 727, in which kings granted land to themselves, probably to change its status.

There is, on the other hand, no evidence that the Cerdicings influenced the distribution of land in Wales or north of the Tyne. This did not, however, mean that the area between the Channel and the Tyne, or even just Southumbria, stood apart from the rest of the island as a block in which royal landed patronage was evenly spread: the bulk of the estates that the Cerdicings are known to have granted lay near or south of the Thames.[83]

Turning to appointments to bishoprics, abbacies, and secular offices, royal patronage was important because the Cerdicings could use such preferments to reward or encourage loyalty, and because major churches and (probably) secular offices had substantial lands associated with them.[84] The royal role in appointments can be demonstrated most clearly in the cases of senior ecclesiastical positions. Prior to the Gregorian reform movement, it was generally accepted as unproblematic that kings should appoint prelates: the earliest *Lives* of Æthelwold, Dunstan, and Oswald, written around the turn of the tenth and eleventh centuries, refer without awkwardness to kings choosing bishops and abbots, and the number of priests closely associated with Alfred who entered the episcopate suggests that royal influence over appointments to bishoprics was no tenth-century novelty.[85] This is not to say that kings had an entirely free hand: the pool of plausible candidates for high ecclesiastical office may well have been limited in practice, accounts of kings deciding whom to appoint sometimes allude to the advice or consent of counsellors, and non-royal aristocratic patrons of many religious houses may have had at least as much influence as the Cerdicings on the selection of their heads.[86] Nonetheless, the saints' *Lives* imply that in many cases the Cerdicings had a substantial degree of discretion to determine who should occupy bishoprics and certain abbacies.

The evidence relating to major secular positions, notably that of ealdorman, is somewhat thinner. It is a fair guess that appointments were again made by the king, with a greater or lesser amount of consultation, although this cannot clearly be demonstrated before the eleventh century.[87] There appears, however, to have been a significant element of heredity in succession to some ealdordoms: most notably, both Æthelstan Half-King and Ælfhere became ealdormen in regions where their fathers had probably held such office, and these men were in turn

---

[83] Above, pp. 51–2.

[84] S. Baxter and J. Blair, 'Land Tenure and Royal Patronage in the Early English Kingdom: A Model and a Case Study', *ANS*, 28 (2006), pp. 19–46 especially 23–6; S. Baxter, *The Earls of Mercia: Lordship and Power in Late Anglo-Saxon England* (Oxford, 2007), pp. 141–5, 147–9; M. F. Giandrea, *Episcopal Culture in Late Anglo-Saxon England* (Woodbridge, 2007), pp. 124–55; A. Williams, *The World Before Domesday: The English Aristocracy, 900–1066* (London, 2008), pp. 21–3. For a Hungarian parallel, see below, p. 242.

[85] *VSÆ*, xi, xvi (pp. 18–20, 28–30); *VSO*, i.5, iii.5, iv.5 (pp. 22–4, 58, 102–4); *VSD*, xiv.5–6, xix.2–4, xxv, xxvi.3 (pp. 48–50, 60–2, 76–8, 80). On evidence from the various versions of the *Chronicle*, see below, pp. 177–8. For the ninth-century evidence, see Pratt, *Political Thought*, pp. 56–8, and more generally T. Vogtherr, 'Zwischen Benediktinerabtei und bischöflicher Cathedra. Zu Auswahl und Amtsantritt englischer Bischöfe im 9.–11. Jahrhundert', in F.-R. Erkens (ed.), *Die früh- und hochmittelalterliche Bischofserhebung im europäischen Vergleich* (Cologne, 1998), pp. 287–320.

[86] *VSO*, i.5 (pp. 22–4); *VSD*, xxvi.3 (p. 80); *ASC* BC 971 refer to advice or consent.

[87] For evidence of kings appointing earls in the eleventh century, see Baxter, *Earls*, pp. 68–70.

followed by a son and brother-in-law respectively.[88] This need not indicate any recognized right to bequeath or inherit office, since it could simply reflect that close relatives of previous incumbents generally had lands and personal connections that would assist them in fulfilling the role of ealdorman, and were therefore strong candidates for appointment. Either way, though, the tendency towards heredity implies that in practice kings had restricted options when appointing to secular offices. This does not, however, negate the importance of royal patronage in appointments. For one thing, it is far from clear that hereditary succession was automatic, and a determined king would probably have been able to deny it.[89] Furthermore, even if a king had little choice but to appoint one of the previous incumbent's kinsmen, he may have had some scope to select amongst them; it is, for example, suggestive that Ælfhere appears to have become an ealdorman before the man who may well have been his elder brother, and also to have achieved greater prominence than him.[90] The appointment of ealdormen was thus another way in which the Cerdicings could exercise patronage.

As with land, there were considerable geographical variations in the scope that the Cerdicings had to select who should hold offices. There is no sign of their making appointments to any position in Wales or north of the Tees during the tenth century, save for a late and uncertain account of Edgar investing a Welsh bishop.[91] Again, however, we should be wary of positing a dichotomy at the Tees. It is likely that the Cerdicings had greatest discretion to choose office holders in or close to their Wessex heartlands, and it is notable in this regard that the clearest cases of early to mid-tenth-century heredity in successions to ealdordoms, namely those of Æthelstan Half-King and Ælfhere, are from north of the Thames. It is, moreover, doubtful whether the Cerdicings had a significant role in determining who should be Archbishop of York before the 950s. The only evidence to the contrary is a charter that refers to Æthelstan granting land to Wulfstan at the time when he established ('constitui') the latter as archbishop, but the diploma appears to date from 934, three years after Wulfstan had assumed office.[92] In any case, even if

---

[88] Banton, 'Ealdormen and Earls', pp. 96–100, 109–10, 129–32, 138–40, 144; Williams, '*Princeps Merciorum gentis*', especially pp. 145–7, 170–1; Hart, *Danelaw*, pp. 569–604 especially 569–70, 584–6. Hereditary succession to ealdordoms remained common in the eleventh century. Episcopal office does not appear to have been hereditary, although bishops were not necessarily celibate: *ASC* A 1001; *De obsessione Dunelmi*, ed. Arnold, *Symeonis Monachi Opera Omnia*, i, 215–17.

[89] The clearest examples of established families losing their prominence are, however, from the late tenth and early eleventh centuries: Williams, '*Princeps Merciorum gentis*', pp. 170–2; R. Fleming, *Kings and Lords in Conquest England* (Cambridge, 1991), pp. 39–51; Hart, *Danelaw*, p. 597.

[90] Williams, '*Princeps Merciorum gentis*', p. 155.

[91] W. Davies, 'The Consecration of Bishops of Llandaff in the Tenth and Eleventh Centuries', *Bulletin of the Board of Celtic Studies*, 26 (1976), pp. 53–73 especially 67–8. Eadred entrusted York to Oswulf of Bamburgh, but it was not until the eleventh century that we can see southern kings determining who held power at Bamburgh itself, or indeed who occupied the bishopric of Durham: *Historia Regum*, ed. Arnold, *Symeonis monachi opera omnia*, ii, 94, 197; *De primo Saxonum adventu*, p. 382; below, pp. 199–200 n. 21.

[92] S 407; *Charters of Northern Houses*, ed. D. A. Woodman (Oxford, 2012), pp. 89–92. The charter gives an incarnational date of 930, but the indiction, epact, concurrence, and witnesses point to 934. On the appointment of Oscytel in the 950s, see below, pp. 177–8.

Æthelstan did more than merely ratify Wulfstan's appointment, he did not thereby acquire a reliable subordinate.[93]

When we turn to the disbursement of movable wealth, the geographical range of the Cerdicings' patronage is wider: Asser alluded to the Welsh kings gaining riches by submitting to Alfred, referring specifically to the latter showering gifts on Anarawd; the *Historia de Sancto Cuthberto* lists various precious objects that Æthelstan and Edmund bestowed on the church at Chester-le-Street; and Symeon of Durham states that Eadred likewise brought 'royal gifts' to this establishment.[94] One need not question the sincerity of these kings' devotion to St Cuthbert to recognize that such generosity would have encouraged the church's members to support Cerdicing interests in northern Britain with the practical power derived from extensive landholdings, as well as with their prayers. The Cerdicings also made gifts of movable wealth to institutions and individuals within what would constitute Domesday *Anglia*: thus, for example, Asser noted that Alfred made annual payments to those who served him, and to monastic houses in 'Saxonia' (i.e. Wessex) and Mercia, while the wills of both Alfred and Eadred prescribed that substantial quantities of precious metal be given to certain leading church-men and lay magnates.[95] The geographical distribution of royal handouts is uncertain, but there are grounds to suspect that recipients in southern Britain, and Wessex in particular, received a hefty share of such largesse. Asser mentions that in some years Alfred made gifts to churches in Wales, Cornwall, and Northumbria (plus Gaul, Brittany, and Ireland), but clearly presents these as being of lower priority than the annual donations to houses in Wessex and Mercia.[96] Similarly, when Eadred left funds for the alleviation of famine or heathen attack, he allocated at least 1,000 pounds (presumably of silver) for the land south of the Thames, as against a mere 400 pounds for the Mercians, and seemingly nothing for Essex, East Anglia, or Northumbria.[97] The Cerdicings' patronage was thus neither limited to the part of Britain between the Channel and the Tees, nor uniformly distributed within that area.

Patronage: Assistance in Disputes

While the significance of grants of land, office, and movable wealth is widely recognized, other kinds of patronage may well have been at least as important. In particular, kings' ability to exploit rivalries or enmities between weaker parties was potentially of great significance to their domination, both in what became the English kingdom, and in other parts of Britain. We may begin with four tenth-century narratives concerning lands south of the Thames or in the southern East

---

[93] Above, pp. 32, 59.

[94] *VA*, lxxx–lxxxi (p. 67); *Historia de Sancto Cuthberto*, xxvi–xxviii (pp. 64–6); Symeon of Durham, *Libellus de Exordio*, ii.20 (p. 140). Note also *VA*, lxxvi (pp. 59–60).

[95] *VA*, c, cii (pp. 86, 88–9); S 1507, 1515.   [96] *VA*, cii (p. 89).

[97] S 1515. The references in Eadred's will to 'the archbishop' in the singular suggest that it was composed at a time when York was under Hiberno-Scandinavian domination, which would explain the lack of provision for Northumbria, although not Essex or East Anglia.

Midlands. These accounts are all highly partial, being written from the perspective of a party closely connected to the dispute in question, but they reveal prevailing assumptions about how disputes could be conducted, and particularly the role that kings could play. The first is a letter addressed to Edward the Elder in the context of a dispute between the Bishop of Winchester and a certain Æthelm, concerning an estate at Fonthill (Wiltshire).[98] The sender of the letter had given Fonthill to the bishop, and wrote to Edward to explain how he (the sender) had come to be in legitimate possession of it. The letter thus represents an attempt to secure Edward's support in opposition to Æthelm's claim, and the sender evidently anticipated that royal backing would be of paramount importance, since he concluded with a statement that he would have to be satisfied with whatever the king decided. The earlier events related in the letter likewise show the king as pivotal to the outcome of disputes. During Alfred's reign, Æthelm had challenged the claim of Fonthill's then holder, a certain Helmstan, a godson of the sender of the letter. Helmstan, whose word was possibly considered unreliable because he had previously committed theft, was only allowed to establish his claim to the land after the sender of the letter petitioned the king, who instructed various men, including the sender, to reconcile the disputants. After these men favoured Helmstan's version of events, Æthelm, too, petitioned Alfred, but he was unsuccessful. Helmstan then formally established his claim, swearing an oath with the support of the sender of the letter, to whom he gave Fonthill in return for this assistance. The sender then leased Fonthill back to Helmstan on condition that the latter keep out of trouble, but in due course he committed another theft. The sender induced Edward, who had succeeded Alfred as king, to exempt Helmstan from forfeiture, but revoked the lease of Fonthill, giving the estate to the Bishop of Winchester instead. Since Edward would have received Helmstan's forfeited possessions, it is perhaps unremarkable that the remission of this punishment required the solicitation of his favour. In addition, however, the letter presents kings as fundamental to the outcome of disputes in which they seemingly had no direct material interests: opposing parties saw obtaining royal favour as a means to victory.

The second document is a will dating from sometime in the second half of the tenth century, but which refers to events that had probably taken place in the 950s. The testatrix was a wealthy widow named Æthelgifu, who mandated the distribution of twelve estates in the East Midlands, a holding in London, and various movable possessions.[99] Æthelgifu addressed her will to the king and his wife (both unnamed), a feature comparable to the Fonthill letter, which was directed to

[98] S 1445. My discussion draws on S. Keynes, 'The Fonthill Letter', in M. Korhammer (ed.), *Words, Texts and Manuscripts: Studies in Anglo-Saxon Culture Presented to Helmut Gneuss on the Occasion of his Sixty-Fifth Birthday* (Cambridge, 1992), pp. 53–97; Wormald, *Making*, pp. 144–8; N. Brooks, 'The Fonthill Letter, Ealdorman Ordlaf and Anglo-Saxon Law in Practice', in S. Baxter, C. E. Karkov, J. L. Nelson and D. Pelteret (eds), *Early Medieval Studies in Memory of Patrick Wormald* (Farnham, 2009), pp. 301–17. It is probable, but not certain, that the letter was written by Ealdorman Ordlaf. It cannot be securely dated within Edward's reign.

[99] S 1497; D. Whitelock, 'Examination of the Will', in D. Whitelock, N. R. Ker, and F. Rennell (eds), *The Will of Æthelgifu: A Tenth-Century Anglo-Saxon Manuscript* (Oxford, 1968), pp. 18–37; *Charters of St Albans*, ed. J. Crick (Oxford, 2007), pp. 91–100, 152–4.

Edward the Elder. The address was not a formality: after declaring her wishes, Æthelgifu begged the king that no one be allowed to overturn her testament, and outlined why she was particularly worried about this possibility: her late husband's kin had refused to recognize what she claimed were his bequests to her. In spite of Æthelgifu's producing 2,000 oaths, quite possibly in about 956, her husband's nephew, Eadelm, had seized her land at Standon (Hertfordshire).[100] Continuing her narrative, Æthelgifu stated: 'Then I appealed to the king, and gave him 20 pounds; then [Eadelm] gave me back my land against his will'. It is not clear whether Æthelgifu's payment was to the king in return for his intervention, or to Eadelm to soften the blow of losing Standon. Even if Æthelgifu had not bought royal support against Eadelm, it is revealing that she pleaded that no one be allowed to change her testament 'with riches [*feo*]', thereby anticipating the possibility that the king might be swayed by the bribes of others. It is also notable that, as well as leaving the king 30 mancuses of gold and two stallions, as she was apparently required to do, she also threw in her deerhounds, and gave 30 mancuses of gold to his wife: these additional bequests were very probably intended to encourage the king to resist any challenges to the will.[101] Regardless of what Æthelgifu may have given the king during her dispute with Eadelm, that episode will have demonstrated the value of royal support: it is not surprising that she sought similar royal assistance for after her death, and that she was willing to pay for it.

The third narrative concerns land at Cooling and Osterland (Kent) between 896 and *c*.959, and was probably written down soon after the latter date.[102] The document is in the name of Eadgifu, whose father, Sigelm, died in battle in 902/903, fighting for Edward the Elder against Æthelwold.[103] Seven years previously, Sigelm had given Cooling to a certain Goda as security for a loan. According to Eadgifu, Sigelm had repaid the loan and bequeathed Cooling to her before going to battle, but Goda kept the estate, claiming that he had not been repaid. A man called Byrhtsige Dyring protested until certain wise people ('witan') directed Eadgifu to clear her father by an oath.[104] Despite swearing this oath, Eadgifu did not obtain possession of Cooling until six years after her father's death, when her friends induced Edward the Elder to declare that Goda would forfeit all his lands unless he restored the estate to her. Thus, as in the Fonthill letter and Æthelgifu's will, royal intervention was (at least for a time) decisive, but it had to be sought. For reasons that are obscure, Edward later declared all of Goda's lands forfeit, and gave them and the relevant charters to Eadgifu. She, however, returned most of the estates to Goda, ostensibly for fear of God, although she kept the charters and

---

[100] On the gathering at which these oaths were sworn, see below, pp. 170–1.

[101] Whitelock, 'Examination', p. 21 lists further examples of testators making payments to kings and their wives. On the term 'mancus', see M. A. S. Blackburn, 'Gold in England during the "Age of Silver" (Eighth–Eleventh Centuries)', in J. Graham-Campbell and G. Williams (eds), *Silver Economy in the Viking Age* (Walnut Creek, CA, 2007), pp. 57–9.

[102] S 1211.

[103] Sigelm's death is also recorded in *ASC* ABCD 903. On Æthelwold's challenge to Edward the Elder, see above, p. 27.

[104] 'Witan' may, but need not, refer to those present at a royal assembly.

also a holding at Osterland. At some point during or after these events, Edward married Eadgifu: this may well explain why he assigned Goda's lands to her, but it is quite possible that Goda's forfeiture preceded the marriage, which was probably contracted in Edward's later years.[105] After Edward had been succeeded by Æthelstan, his son by another woman, Goda persuaded the new king to ask Eadgifu to return the charters, which she did, retaining only those concerning Osterland. Why Æthelstan assisted Goda in this way is uncertain, but it is plausible that the former's relationship with his stepmother was strained, since she had her own sons to promote. In any case, though, the key point here is that we have another instance of a disputant's object being achieved through a petition to a king. Eadgifu held Cooling and Osterland undisturbed during the reigns of her sons, Edmund and Eadred, with whom she appears to have had close and cooperative relationships.[106] In such circumstances, her tenure could not be challenged, but after Eadred's death and Eadwig's succession she was 'deprived of all her possessions': two of Goda's sons seized Cooling and Osterland, telling Eadwig that they had a better claim to them. Following Edgar's accession, he and his counsellors ('wytan') restored the estates to Eadgifu, who then granted them to Christ Church, Canterbury.[107] That at least some of Eadgifu's possessions were seized during Eadwig's reign and returned by Edgar is confirmed in the earliest *Life* of Dunstan, which states that Edgar restored her and others whom Eadwig had 'ordered to be plundered by an unjust judgement'.[108] Eadgifu's narrative suggests that Goda's sons seized the estates on their own initiative, and then told Eadwig of their claim to them, rather than implementing a royal command, but it is clear that her loss and recovery of the land was closely linked to her relationships with Eadwig and Edgar. Following her marriage to Edward, Eadgifu is likely to have been so inextricably identified with particular members of the Cerdicing dynasty that either she had little need to petition the reigning king, or any lobbying she might have attempted would have had little hope of success. The whole case nevertheless demonstrates that kings could be central to disputes between magnates, and the early part of the narrative reveals that someone who had not yet married into the royal dynasty needed six years of friends' lobbying to gain the royal intervention that would prove crucial.

---

[105] Eadgifu's account does not refer to her marriage to Edward. Her eldest known child, Edmund, was born in 920 or 921, which implies that she and Edward married towards the end of the latter's reign (924): *ASC* ABCD 940. This would be consistent with Edward's already having had children by two other women.

[106] On Eadgifu's relationships with Edmund and Eadred, and especially her attestations of their charters, see P. Stafford, 'The King's Wife in Wessex, 800–1066', *P&P*, 91 (1981), pp. 25–6; P. Stafford, *Queen Emma and Queen Edith: Queenship and Women's Power in Eleventh-Century England* (Oxford, 1997), pp. 199–204; Keynes, *Atlas*, Table XXXIa. Given the rarity with which West Saxon royal women appeared in witness lists prior to Edmund's reign, nothing should be read into Eadgifu's absence from Æthelstan's charters. Eadgifu persuaded Eadred first to prevent Æthelwold from leaving the kingdom and then to give him Abingdon: *VSÆ*, x–xi (p. 18). She was also named as a major beneficiary in Eadred's will, which Eadwig probably did not implement: S 1515; S. Keynes, 'The "Dunstan B" Charters', *ASE*, 23 (1994), pp. 188–90.

[107] Here, unlike before, it is clear that 'wytan' refers to royal counsellors.

[108] *VSD*, xxiv.3 (p. 76).

The fourth case concerns the estate of Sunbury (Middlesex).[109] The end point of the narrative can be dated to 968 and the text was probably written soon after. The train of events began with the theft of a woman, probably a female slave. This happened before the end of Eadred's reign (955), but the king was not involved at the outset. It was established that, sometime after the theft, the woman had been in the possession of one Æthelstan of Sunbury, who failed to prove that he had acquired her legally. Æthelstan surrendered the woman and paid compensation to the original owner, but an ealdorman named Byrhtferth demanded that Æthelstan also pay his *wer* (the value of his life) to the king as a penalty. Æthelstan could not afford to do so and forfeited Sunbury. Later, in the words of the narrative, 'fortune changed' ('wendun gewyrda'): Eadred died and Eadwig became king. Æthelstan seemingly saw this as an opportunity to challenge the confiscation and returned to Sunbury without paying his *wer*. Eadwig was not willing to accept this, however, and gave Sunbury to a certain Beornric, who threw Æthelstan out and took possession of it. We thus see a king licensing one of his subordinates to use force against another. After Edgar became king north of the Thames, Æthelstan again tried to recover Sunbury: he went to Edgar and requested judgement, but the wise people of Mercia ('Myrcna witan') declared that he could only recover the estate if he paid his *wer*. Since Æthelstan still could not do so, Edgar gave the land to a different Æthelstan, who was an ealdorman; it is not known what had happened to Beornric. Ealdorman Æthelstan subsequently sold Sunbury to a certain Ecgferth, who committed the estate to Archbishop Dunstan on condition that the latter act as guardian to his widow and child. After Ecgferth drowned in uncertain circumstances, Dunstan reminded the king of the earlier arrangement, but Edgar replied that his counsellors ('mine witan') had pronounced Ecgferth's possessions forfeit. Dunstan offered to pay Ecgferth's *wer*, but Edgar declared that this could only obtain a consecrated grave for the dead man, since the whole 'spæce' (which means something like 'case' or 'judgement') had been left to Ealdorman Ælfheah.[110] The narrative concludes with a statement that, six years later, this Ælfheah sold Sunbury to Dunstan, along with an estate in Surrey that had also been held by Ecgferth. As in the account of Eadgifu's dispute with Goda and his family, this case indicates that the succession of a new king signalled the opportunity to attempt to reverse previous decisions: Æthelstan did not succeed, but he considered it worth trying with both Eadwig and Edgar. The final part of the narrative is also interesting, since we see Dunstan petitioning Edgar unsuccessfully: the archbishop enjoyed a close relationship with this king, who had recalled him from exile, elevated him to the episcopate, and ultimately appointed him to Canterbury, but even Dunstan could not take Edgar's favour for granted.[111]

These accounts show that the Cerdicings' patronage extended far beyond doling out land, offices, and movable wealth. In the first place, the Fonthill and Sunbury

---

[109] S 1447; P. Stafford, 'King and Kin, Lord and Community: England in the Tenth and Eleventh Centuries', in P. Stafford, *Gender, Family and the Legitimation of Power: England from the Ninth to the Early Twelfth Century* (Aldershot, 2006), VIII, pp. 5–11.

[110] A charter dated 962 records Edgar granting land at Sunbury to Ælfheah: S 702.

[111] *VSD*, xxiv.2, xxv, xxvi.3 (pp. 74–80).

cases suggest how kings' use of forfeiture to punish wrongdoing could create opportunities for patronage: Helmstan obtained mercy from the king and Æthelstan seemingly thought he had a chance. There are references elsewhere to payments being made for the remission of punishments: Edgar rescinded a man's forfeiture upon payment of 100 mancuses of gold, and, in a separate case, restored several confiscated estates in return for 120 mancuses of gold.[112] Depriving someone of his or her lands would have entailed exertion and caused resentment, so it is quite explicable that kings only implemented sentences of forfeiture selectively, leaving the recipients of mercy beholden to them. Perhaps more importantly, the narratives that we have considered demonstrate that the favour of the reigning king was of great value for magnates who were in dispute with one another: royal interventions could cause incumbents to relinquish what they held, or challengers to drop their claims. Æthelgifu's will suggests that disputants might give movable wealth to procure royal backing, but it is quite possible that loyalty and (if necessary) military support, while harder to document, were even more important forms of reciprocation. Aiding one magnate against another could have been a particularly efficient form of royal patronage. In part, this was because, unlike with grants of land, movable wealth or (in many cases) office, a king could often have lent support to a disputant without diminishing the material resources that he (the king) directly controlled. It is, however, also significant that support for a disputant was fairly readily reversible: the last two narratives indicate that a change of king was an opportunity for reopening old quarrels, and the sender of the Fonthill letter implies that Æthelm had similarly resurrected a case that had been settled (for the time being) during Alfred's reign. That kings might reverse their predecessors' actions meant that a disputant who initially failed to obtain royal support had not necessarily lost decisively: such a person could bide his or her time and seek to gain the favour of the next king, as Goda and his sons appear to have done. Conversely, a winner remained vulnerable to challenge, and therefore needed to continue to cultivate relationships with the reigning king and the latter's successors.

Assistance in a dispute was in some ways a more powerful form of patronage than a simple grant of land, office, or movable wealth, since it would probably have been less difficult to withdraw. It was quite possible for kings to revoke grants of these latter kinds: thus, for example, Edward the Elder gave to a third party an estate that the *dux* Wulfhere had forfeited, Eadred imprisoned the Archbishop of York, and Edgar dismissed the Archbishop of Canterbury to make way for Dunstan, who had himself previously been ejected from Glastonbury by Eadwig.[113] But it might require a major effort on a king's part to deprive someone of what he or she had previously been granted, not least because possession of the land, office, or movable wealth would have augmented that person's power. The difficulty of

---

[112] *LE*, ii.19 (p. 95); S 687. These payments sound much like post-Conquest amercements.

[113] S 362; *ASC* D 952; *VSD*, xxii–xxiii.1, xxvi.3 (pp. 68–72, 80). Note also S. Keynes, 'Eadwig (*c*.940–959)', *ODNB*; below, p. 75. Wulfhere may have retained (or he or his descendants may have recovered) some land, but he was evidently at least temporarily deprived of at least one estate: B. Yorke, 'Edward as Ætheling', in Higham and Hill (eds), *Edward the Elder*, pp. 35–7, although Yorke here presents possibility as 'fact'.

dislodging an incumbent landholder is illustrated by a somewhat later example, from the reign of Æthelred II: Wulfbald, a Kentish magnate, repeatedly disobeyed the king and was sentenced to forfeit all that he had, but nonetheless managed to keep hold of his possessions until he died.[114] A person who only held an estate because of prior royal backing in a dispute was probably at least a little more vulnerable to expropriation, however, since the king could transfer his support to the other disputant, and license the latter to eject the incumbent. Thus, for example, Eadwig could inflict harm on Eadgifu without needing to deploy his own coercive strength, either ordering or permitting her enemies to seize her possessions. A person who had received royal assistance in a dispute, and his or her heirs, therefore needed to work especially hard to retain royal favour.

The extant narratives show kings' interventions being sought in land disputes, but it is likely that their favour was just as valuable in enmities where a party feared that there was a threat to his or her life or person. Until well into the twelfth century, kings do not seem to have regarded most forms of assault or homicide as meriting royal punishment in and of themselves. Instead, kings appear, to a considerable extent, to have left victims of violence, or their kin and associates, to use the threat of vengeance to obtain compensation from the perpetrators. Alfred and his pre-Conquest successors made some attempts to promote the payment of compensation and limit violent reprisals, but did not fundamentally challenge the basic principles of feuding.[115] From very early in the Anglo-Saxon period, however, royal legislation indicates that kings demanded substantial fines for breaches of protection that they had granted, and Edmund took this further, declaring that violators of his protection should forfeit all their possessions, and be at his mercy for their lives.[116] If a king declared a certain person or space to be under royal protection, an act of violence committed against that person or in that space made the perpetrator liable not only to the victim's attempts to obtain vengeance or compensation, but also to severe punishments ordained by the king. Potential aggressors might therefore be more likely to think twice about causing injury if doing so would violate royal protection, and a person who feared attack consequently had every reason to seek to procure a grant of protection from the king.

Even if we focus on disputes over land, for which the Southumbrian evidence is richest, there was no shortage of disagreements that kings could exploit. Recent research has emphasized the flexibility and variety of inheritance practices in the

---

[114] S 877. The lands ascribed to Wulfbald would have been sufficient to make him a locally powerful figure, but nothing more. For a case from Edward the Confessor's reign of a man disobeying a royal order to relinquish land, see *LE*, ii.96 (pp. 165–6).

[115] T. B. Lambert, 'Theft, Homicide and Crime in Late Anglo-Saxon Law', *P&P*, 214 (2012), pp. 3–43. See also P. R. Hyams, *Rancor and Reconciliation in Medieval England* (Ithaca, NY, 2003), especially pp. 71–110; Lambert, 'Protection, Feud and Royal Power', pp. 18–55, 149–99; Hudson, *Oxford History of the Laws of England*, pp. 171–5. Contrast Wormald, 'Giving God and King their Due', pp. 336–42.

[116] Lambert, 'Theft, Homicide and Crime', pp. 26–32; Lambert, 'Protection, Feud and Royal Power', pp. 4–9, 56–110. For punishments for breaches of royal protection, see, for example, Abt 8; Wi 2; Af 3, 5; II Em 6; VI Atr 34; VIII Atr 3, 5.1; I Cn 2.5, 3.2; II Cn 12, 15, 42; *Leges Edwardi Confessoris*, 12–12.7, 26–27.2, ed. and trans. B. R. O'Brien, *God's Peace and King's Peace: The Laws of Edward the Confessor* (Philadelphia, PA, 1999), pp. 168–70, 184–6.

Anglo-Saxon period: there was consequently much scope for disappointed expectations and contention over the proper distribution of a deceased person's possessions.[117] In particular, a widow (like Æthelgifu) was vulnerable to claims from the kin of her deceased husband, children she had by him, and any step-children. It is therefore significant that widowhood was probably common in early medieval societies, as a result of male involvement in violence, the likelihood that women often married young, and the practice of men having a succession of wives of child-bearing age.[118] The leasing of land was another likely cause of disputes: the lessee might dispute the lessor's demands for reversion, especially if the loan was for a long term, such as the three-life leases that were common in the late Anglo-Saxon period.[119] The actions of kings themselves could engender or entrench disagreements, especially if they took land from one person and gave it to another. We have already noted that Eadwig deprived Eadgifu of land, and that the earliest *Life* of Dunstan indicates that she was not alone in being treated in this way.[120] Eadwig's charters give further grounds to think that he deprived many people of estates, since a substantial number of the holdings that he granted are known to have been given to other beneficiaries in the preceding decades.[121] Certain persons who had been prominent during Eadwig's reign appear in turn to have had lands expropriated by Edgar, and the latter restored at least some estates to those who had formerly held them.[122] The reasons for Eadwig's (and to some extent Edgar's) land seizures are unclear, but what matters here is that they would have fomented disputes between the dispossessed and those to whom confiscated estates were transferred. There were thus multitudinous quarrels between magnates, and plentiful opportunities for kings to grant or withhold their favour.

The accounts of disputes discussed above contain no clear references to shire, hundred, and wapentake meetings, which (as we shall see) became important from the mid- to late tenth century.[123] This does not mean that the fashion in which disagreements were pursued was chaotic: given the similarities between the cases we have examined, it is likely that all parties well knew how the outcome might be determined, and that the result was likely to be favourable if royal support could be obtained. Dispute settlement based on the solicitation (or indeed purchase) of

[117] Mumby, 'Descent of Family Land'.

[118] J. Crick, 'Men, Women and Widows: Widowhood in Pre-Conquest England', in S. Cavallo and L. Warner (eds), *Widowhood in Medieval and Early Modern Europe* (Harlow, 1999), pp. 24–36 especially 24–9. On the frequency of widowhood, see K. J. Leyser, *Rule and Conflict in an Early Medieval Society: Ottonian Saxony* (Oxford, 1979), pp. 51–8, with discussion of serial monogamy by Stafford, 'King's Wife', pp. 13–14; C. J. Morris, *Marriage and Murder in Eleventh-Century Northumbria: A Study of 'De obsessione Dunelmi'* (York, 1992), pp. 16–18. For disputes involving widows, in addition to Æthelgifu's will, see S 877, 1200 (probably), 1457, 1458, 1462 (probably). Note also Keynes, 'Fonthill Letter', p. 72.

[119] E.g. S 884, 1404, with S. Baxter, 'Archbishop Wulfstan and the Administration of God's Property', in M. Townend (ed.), *Wulfstan, Archbishop of York* (Turnhout, 2004), pp. 161–205 especially 165–76; Hudson, *Oxford History of the Laws of England*, pp. 99–102.

[120] S 1211; *VSD*, xxiv.3 (p. 76); above, p. 71.   [121] Keynes, 'Eadwig'.

[122] S. Jayakumar, 'Eadwig and Edgar: Politics, Propaganda, Faction', in Scragg (ed.), *Edgar*, pp. 91–5.

[123] The gathering at which Æthelgifu and 2,000 supporters swore oaths is a possible exception, but see below, pp. 170–1.

royal backing does not correspond to modern notions of justice, but it could have done much to maintain and cement a king's position. With plenty to keep aristocrats quarrelling, and royal support being an effective route to victory, a king would have had considerable scope to manipulate rivalries among his greater subordinates and compel them to compete for his favour.[124] Divisions among aristocrats could, on the other hand, expose a king to danger, since those who did not enjoy his favour might well support any plausible challenger for the throne; thus, for example, discord within the elite hampered Æthelred II's ability to resist external attack.[125] What should not be overlooked, however, is that disagreements between magnates were for kings as much a source of strength as of vulnerability, since disputants had reason to cultivate royal favour. If a king could thereby have at least the bulk of aristocrats eager to do his will, he would have been in a strong position, whether or not he had any administrative apparatus with which to regulate the conduct of more ordinary people.

The disputes that we have considered thus far concerned land no further north than what would become Hertfordshire, but when we turn our attention to areas more distant from Wessex we likewise see the Cerdicings encouraging acceptance of their domination through the exploitation of divisions between competing parties. Thus, for example, after ravaging Cumbria and blinding two sons of its king in 945, Edmund granted it to the Scottish king Malcolm I in return for a promise of cooperation.[126] Given that the Cerdicings had never had more than a loose hegemony over Cumbria, Edmund was not relinquishing much, but the damage he had inflicted would have assisted attempts by Malcolm to extend his domination south-west. Cooperation could, moreover, be secured through promises of assistance in the event of an attack by a third party: Asser reports that the southern Welsh kings were primarily attracted to Alfred's lordship by the prospect of protection from their northern neighbours and Æthelred of Mercia.[127] Similarly, there is a fair chance that the Scottish king and the rulers of Bamburgh chose Edward the Elder as lord in 920 in return for a commitment that he would come to their aid should there be a resumption of their recent hostilities with the Hiberno-Scandinavian

---

[124] My thinking on the structural significance of aristocratic discord is influenced by N. Elias, *The Civilizing Process*, trans. E. Jephcott (2 vols, Oxford, 1978–82), ii, 161–201; N. Elias, *The Court Society*, trans. E. Jephcott (Oxford, 1983), especially pp. 78–213, 276–83. Note also Leyser, *Rule and Conflict*, especially pp. 28–31, 102, although my argument is somewhat different from Leyser's. A significant part of Leyser's argument is that members of the Ottonian dynasty struggled (with the aid of their respective aristocratic backers) for the throne, but did not seek to divide the Reich. By contrast, territorial partition appears at least sometimes to have been an option in English succession disputes, which would therefore not necessarily have had centripetal effects (see above, pp. 37–8). My argument concentrates not on discord between Cerdicings, but on discord between magnates, and the Cerdicings' exploitation of this.

[125] On the circumstances leading up to Cnut's conquest, see P. Stafford, 'The Reign of Æthelred II, a Study in the Limitations on Royal Policy and Action', in D. H. Hill (ed.), *Ethelred the Unready: Papers from the Millenary Conference* (Oxford, 1978), pp. 15–46; M. K. Lawson, *Cnut: England's Viking King* (Stroud, 2004), pp. 25–52.

[126] *ASC* ABCD 945; Roger of Wendover, *Flores Historiarum*, i, 398.

[127] *VA*, lxxx (p. 66). That it was the hope of protection which prompted these kings to recognize Alfred's superiority is not gainsaid by his apparent failure to prevent Anarawd from ravaging south-west Wales (with the support of unidentified Englishmen) in or around 893: *Annales Cambriae*, p. 14.

potentate Ragnald.[128] These enmities were not (so far as we know) articulated in terms of legal principles, they involved higher stakes than the likes of Fonthill or Sunbury, and the range of people with whom the Cerdicings dealt personally decreased with distance from Wessex: Helmstan and Æthelstan of Sunbury do not appear to have been from the very uppermost ranks of the English elite, but the disputes in which the Cerdicings are known to have become involved in Wales and northern Britain concerned only the greatest potentates of these areas. Nonetheless, the basic technique of exploiting divisions between antagonistic parties was broadly similar: discord in Wales and northern Britain presented the Cerdicings with opportunities to dispense patronage, much as it did within the part of the island that would be described in Domesday.

Coercion

The reigning Cerdicing was not the only person who could give support to disputants: according to another vernacular text, similar to those analysed above, successive ninth-century Bishops of Worcester complained that the family of one Eastmund was wrongfully occupying an episcopal estate, but it was only when Æthelred became lord of the Mercians that Bishop Wærferth managed to obtain satisfaction.[129] The support of the likes of Æthelred would, however, have been less valuable than that of the Cerdicings, since the latter had greater coercive capabilities with which to compel adherence to their commands. The Cerdicings' military strength, and the role that force played in their hegemony, is most clearly demonstrated by Æthelstan's ravaging to the very north of Britain in 934. Immediately after, Constantine II paid tribute, surrendered his son as a hostage, and made the only two known appearances by a Scottish king in the witness lists of Cerdicing charters.[130] It is not known what prompted Æthelstan's expedition, or that of Edmund against the Cumbrian kingdom eleven years later.[131] These campaigns may very well have been to exact revenge for specific acts or omissions, but even if they were unprovoked displays of violence, they would most likely have served to terrify the victims, and indeed other potentates, into seeking to cultivate the

---

[128] *ASC* A 920. For Ragnald's hostilities with the rulers of Bamburgh and the Scottish king, see *Chronicle of the Kings of Alba*, ed. B. T. Hudson, 'The Scottish Chronicle', *SHR*, 77 (1998), p. 150; *Annals of Ulster*, 918 (p. 368); *Historia de Sancto Cuthberto*, xxii, xxiv (pp. 60, 62), with discussion at pp. 105–6, 107. Much the same consideration may well have motivated the Cumbrian king, since Strathclyde had suffered viking attacks in the preceding decades, and may have been plundered by Ragnald: C. Downham, *Viking Kings of Britain and Ireland: The Dynasty of Ívarr to A.D. 1014* (Edinburgh, 2007), pp. 162–4, with a possible reference to a raid by Ragnald at *Fragmentary Annals of Ireland*, ed. and trans. J. N. Radner (Dublin, 1978), p. 182. Ragnald himself probably wanted an assurance that Edward would not seek to dislodge him from York. M. R. Davidson, 'The (Non)submission of the Northern Kings in 920', in Higham and Hill (eds), *Edward the Elder*, pp. 200–11 gives a useful discussion of the context, although his attempt to play down the disparities in power between the parties is dubious.

[129] S 1446. It is not explicit that Æthelred's support had been decisive, although this is the obvious implication. There are tentative grounds to date the resolution of the dispute to *c*.903, but it could have been somewhat earlier or later. Note also S 1441.

[130] *ASC* ABCDE 934; S 426, 1792; John of Worcester, *Chronicle*, 934 (ii, 388–90).

[131] *ASC* ABCDE 945; Roger of Wendover, *Flores Historiarum*, i, 398.

Cerdicings' goodwill. While it seems to have been rare for the Cerdicings to go to Wales or northern Britain, the mere threat of a campaign was probably sufficient to induce fear, and a punitive expedition would not necessarily have required the king's personal leadership: in the eleventh century, earls seemingly acting on Edward the Confessor's behalf inflicted serious defeats on Scottish and Welsh kings.[132]

Force was also fundamental to the Cerdicings' domination within what would constitute the *Anglia* of Domesday. The case of Wulfbald, who kept his possessions despite ignoring Æthelred II's commands, suggests that a magnate might gamble that the king would not go to the effort of enforcing his will.[133] This was, however, a risky approach, since the Cerdicings intermittently unleashed crude but terrifying displays of coercive power. Thus Eadred ordered what the D text of the *Chronicle* describes as a 'great slaughter' ('mycel wæll') in Thetford (Norfolk) in 952, to avenge the killing of an abbot, and in 969 Edgar had all Thanet (Kent) ravaged, probably to punish the detention and robbery of some merchants from York.[134] Interestingly, these accounts may imply that Eadred and Edgar did not personally participate on either occasion, but ordered or permitted others to inflict devastation; there was quite probably no shortage of people who were keen to engage in royally authorized predation and violence. It is, moreover, notable that when recording the punishment of Thanet, the D and E texts of the *Chronicle* employed the verb *oferhergian* ('to ravage'), the same word as had been used to narrate what Æthelstan and Edmund did to the Scottish and Cumbrian kingdoms.[135] It was doubtless easier for the Cerdicings to arrange a ravaging of Thanet than of Cumbria or Scotland, but coercive tactics that they employed against the recalcitrant in the southernmost part of Britain probably did not differ much from those by which they enforced their domination right across the island.

Oferhergian could connote very serious devastation, like that which had in the previous century been inflicted by plundering raiders from across the North Sea: the same verb is used in the notices of viking ravaging in the 'common stock' of the *Chronicle*, and the prose preface to the *Old English Pastoral Care* alludes to the viking period as the time when 'all was *forheregod* [ravaged] and burned'.[136] *Oferhergian* also occurs in the D text of the *Chronicle*'s account of Eadred's punishment of the Northumbrians for their acceptance of Erik Haraldsson as king in 948: that Ripon Minster was burned down during this expedition gives some impression of

---

[132] *ASC* CD 1054, DE 1063; Molyneaux, 'Why were some Tenth-Century English Kings Presented as Rulers of Britain?', pp. 76–7. See also *ASC* D 1053.

[133] S 877.

[134] *ASC* D 952, DE 969; Roger of Wendover, *Flores Historiarum*, i, 414–15. Roger is the sole source for Edgar's motivation in ravaging Thanet. He assigned the episode to 974, but his chronology is unreliable and he was probably referring to the ravaging mentioned in the D and E texts of the *Chronicle* under 969: M. Dolley, 'Roger of Wendover's Date for Eadgar's Coinage Reform', *BNJ*, 49 (1979), pp. 3–7.

[135] *ASC* ABCDE 934, 945, DE 969; above, pp. 30, 33. See also *ASC* ABCD 903, D 948.

[136] *ASC* ABCDE 835, 865; *King Alfred's West-Saxon Version of Gregory's Pastoral Care*, ed. and trans. H. Sweet (EETS, 45, 50, London, 1871–2), pp. 4–5. Note also *ASC* CDE 1001, where a Scandinavian rout of the people of Devon and Somerset is described as a 'mycel wæll', the same words used with regard to Thetford in 952.

the kind of destruction that ravaging entailed.[137] Ravaging will have seriously harmed both the magnates and the general population of an area. Ordinary people almost certainly had possessions destroyed, seized, or damaged, and may well have suffered death or physical injury. If crops were devastated, moreover, starvation would probably follow.[138] Even if magnates escaped bodily harm and managed to preserve sufficient wealth to obtain what little food was available in a time of famine, they would have suffered major material loss through the diminution in the productive capacity of their lands and subordinates. The threat of a ravaging expedition is thus likely to have been a powerful deterrent to disobedience, even for the greatest of the Cerdicings' subordinates. The Cerdicings' domination was thus founded on military might, both in what would constitute the eleventh-century English kingdom, and in the rest of Britain.[139]

THE BASIS OF THE CERDICINGS' COERCIVE STRENGTH

The foregoing argument raises a problem: how did kings from Alfred to Edgar procure the warriors, sailors, and military equipment with which they enforced their domination? There is little evidence with which to answer this question, but the issue is too important to be dodged, even if one can only offer a sketch of the parameters of possibility. A preliminary point is that the Cerdicings were not unusual in being able to raise powerful military contingents, and there may have been little qualitative difference between their forces and those of other potentates in northern Europe: that Æthelstan obtained ships and warriors to ravage as far as Caithness is not necessarily remarkable, given that various Scandinavians had in the previous century obtained ships and warriors to ravage many parts of the British Isles. Moving to the substantive question, however, one thing that seems securely knowable about how the Cerdicings raised military forces is that at all times during the Anglo-Saxon period at least some of those who gave kings armed support did so in return for (or in the hope of) reward. Thus Bede (writing in 734) worried that warriors would go overseas unless they received lands, Asser stated that Alfred distributed a sixth of his annual income to his fighters, there is significant circumstantial evidence that Edgar hired Scandinavian sailors, and successive kings paid a fleet from 1012 to 1050.[140] We have, moreover, already noted the likelihood that military cooperation was the most important demand that the Cerdicings made of all of their subordinates, and it is likely that those who provided it were rewarded in a range

---

[137] *ASC* D 948. See also *ASC* D 1069.

[138] For famine as a potential consequence of ravaging, see W. E. Kapelle, *The Norman Conquest of the North: The Region and its Transformation, 1000–1135* (Chapel Hill, NC, 1979), pp. 118–19.

[139] Compare J. Campbell, 'Was it Infancy in England? Some Questions of Comparison', in M. Jones and M. Vale (eds), *England and her Neighbours, 1066–1453: Essays in Honour of Pierre Chaplais* (London, 1989), pp. 1–17, reprinted in his *Anglo-Saxon State* (London, 2000), p. 185.

[140] Bede, *Letter to Ecgberht*, xi, ed. and trans. C. Grocock and I. N. Wood, *Abbots of Wearmouth and Jarrow* (Oxford, 2013), pp. 142–6; *VA*, c (p. 86); S. Jayakumar, 'Some Reflections on the "Foreign Policies" of Edgar "the Peaceable"', *HSJ*, 10 (2001), pp. 17–37; *ASC* CDE 1012, CDE 1040, C 1049, CE 1050, D 1051.

of ways, aside from grants of land and movable wealth: possibilities include assistance in disputes, remission of punishments, appointments to office, and invitations to feasts.[141] In many cases, it is probable that those who received (or hoped for) royal patronage did not just serve in person, but also (or instead) placed members of their own military retinues at the reigning king's disposal; thus, for example, some of those who fought on Æthelred II's behalf at Maldon in 991 are described in the poetic account of the battle as the household force ('heorðwerod') of Ealdorman Byrhtnoth.[142] In some instances, such as the fleet hired by Æthelred and his successors, it may well have been explicitly stipulated what personnel and equipment would be supplied to the king and what he would give in return. Such spelling out need not have been the norm, however, and may indeed have been regarded as dishonourable. In many cases, people quite possibly served the king in the hope that they would at some point be rewarded in some way, rather than in the knowledge that they would at a particular time be rewarded in a particular way; equally, kings may well have bestowed largesse without detailing the favours that they might later seek to call in.[143]

Few, if any, historians would dispute that kings obtained warriors, ships, weapons, and other equipment at least in part through such reciprocal personal relationships.[144] What is contested is whether there was in addition a general obligation to contribute to royal armed forces. That there was not is argued by Richard Abels, who adopts the minimalist position that throughout the Anglo-Saxon period only those who had benefited from their king's largesse, or commended themselves to his lordship, were obliged to contribute.[145] Abels's case challenges that of Warren Hollister, who contended that there was a general obligation, and that it had two manifestations. First, Hollister argued that in times of dire emergency a king could require anyone in any part of his kingdom to serve in what he (Hollister) called the 'great *fyrd*', *fyrd* being an Old English word for a military force. The second form of general obligation in Hollister's scheme, labelled the 'select *fyrd*', did not entail a universal muster: instead, any district could be required to supply a stipulated quantity of people and equipment, responsibility for which lay with the landholders of the area in question.[146] Hollister's argument for the principle of a general

---

[141] Above, pp. 61–3.

[142] *The Battle of Maldon*, line 24, ed. D. G. Scragg (Manchester, 1981), p. 57; R. Abels, *Lordship and Military Obligation in Anglo-Saxon England* (London, 1988), pp. 146–8; S. Baxter, 'The Earls of Mercia and their Commended Men in the Mid Eleventh Century', *ANS*, 23 (2001), pp. 23–46 especially 29–31. The date of the poem is unknown; it may have been composed soon after the battle, but this is far from certain.

[143] Compare R. Abels, 'Household Men, Mercenaries and Vikings in Anglo-Saxon England', in J. France (ed.), *Mercenaries and Paid Men: The Mercenary Identity in the Middle Ages* (Leiden, 2008), pp. 143–65.

[144] Despite their many differences, this much is common ground for C. W. Hollister, *Anglo-Saxon Military Institutions on the Eve of the Norman Conquest* (Oxford, 1962), pp. 9–24 and Abels, *Lordship and Military Obligation*, although Hollister's discussion here focuses on those who probably served in return for defined wages.

[145] Abels, *Lordship and Military Obligation*.

[146] Hollister, *Anglo-Saxon Military Institutions*, pp. 7–8, 25–115. Hollister concentrated on the eleventh century, but regarded both forms of the general obligation as long-standing. His arguments develop those of F. W. Maitland, *Domesday Book and Beyond: Three Essays in the Early History of England* (Cambridge, 1897), pp. 156–64, 235–6, 294–5.

obligation has considerable force. From the late eighth century in Mercia and Kent, and the mid-ninth century in Wessex, royal charters granting land in perpetuity routinely stated that it should be exempt from all burdens, except army service (*exercitus* or *expeditio*) and labour on bridges and fortifications. Some charters include a statement to the effect that these three obligations were common to the whole people, which suggests that kings were claiming a right to the service of everyone, or at least all 'free' adult males, in their kingdoms: some rather contrived reasoning is necessary if one wants to believe that these duties only pertained to estates held by virtue of a royal grant.[147] Furthermore, two texts from the eleventh century seem to refer to kings exploiting general obligations, levied on the basis of 'hides': we shall in due course examine hides in more detail, but for now it is enough to say that they were units in which land was reckoned.[148] The first reference is in the annal for 1008 in the C, D, and E texts of the *Chronicle*, which records that Æthelred ordered that ships be built 'throughout all the English' ('ofer eall Angelcyn'), with a ship being due from 310 hides, and a helmet and corselet from eight hides: on the face of things, it sounds as if these obligations applied generally throughout Æthelred's kingdom.[149] The second is in Domesday's account of the customs of Berkshire in Edward the Confessor's day, which states that from five hides one *miles* ('soldier') would go to the royal army, and that the five hides would give this *miles* 20 shillings for two months' service.[150] Again, there is no particular reason to think that such quotas were confined to land held as a result of a royal grant. It would not be surprising if kings asserted a right to military service from the population as a whole, while also receiving service from those who had benefited from (or who hoped for) royal largesse: kings could then have directed their patronage at those able to supply highly skilled and well-equipped warriors, and attempted to exploit the general obligation if they needed to raise large numbers of troops.[151]

---

[147] Stevenson, 'Trinoda Necessitas', especially pp. 689–90 n. 3; Brooks, 'Development of Military Obligations'. Contrast Abels, *Lordship and Military Obligation*, pp. 43–57.

[148] Below, pp. 92–8.

[149] *ASC* CDE 1008. There were parts of the kingdom, notably Kent and the north-east, where units of reckoning other than the hide were commonly used (see below, pp. 93–4). In such areas, Æthelred's demands were probably apportioned by alternative units, but even if his order only pertained to regions where reckoning in hides was practised, the basic point would stand: this does not sound like a levy restricted to land held by royal grant.

[150] *DB*, i, 56c. The word *miles* could denote a soldier of widely varying status, skill, and experience; it is uncertain what sort of soldier is envisaged here. Maitland, *Domesday Book*, pp. 156–7 collects references in Domesday to military service.

[151] That such methods of raising forces could be combined is demonstrated by the fuller evidence available from the twelfth- and thirteenth-century Scottish kingdom: G. W. S. Barrow, *The Anglo-Norman Era in Scottish History* (Oxford, 1980), pp. 161–8; A. Taylor, 'Common Burdens in the *Regnum Scottorum*: The Evidence of the Charter Diplomatic', in D. Broun (ed.), *The Reality behind Charter Diplomatic in Anglo-Norman Britain* (Glasgow, 2011), pp. 166–234, consulted at <http://paradox.poms.ac.uk/ebook/index.html> (accessed 9 October 2014). Barrow pointed out the relevance of his work to debates about pre-Norman English military organization, but predicted that historians of the Anglo-Saxon period would make no use of his insight. For the likelihood that in the post-1066 English kingdom knight service obligations coexisted with a general duty of military service, the latter surviving from before the Conquest, see C. W. Hollister, '1066: The "Feudal Revolution"', *American Historical Review*, 73 (1968), pp. 708–23, although the Scottish evidence is clearer.

It thus seems probable that eleventh-century English kings at least occasionally required that all land in their kingdom supply military personnel and equipment. A key argument of this book is that one should not assume that eleventh-century arrangements were applicable in earlier periods, but in this case the charter formulae provide good grounds for thinking that by the mid-ninth century at the very latest the principle that a king might demand military resources from any land in his kingdom applied across much (and perhaps all) of the future Domesday *Anglia*.[152] Nonetheless, it is possible that forces raised by this obligation made little or no contribution to the armies with which the Cerdicings extended and maintained their domination in the late ninth and tenth centuries.[153] The prospect of sharing in the spoils of success may have meant that plenty of capable warriors were keen to participate in offensive campaigns or plundering expeditions, for which kings may in consequence not have had much need to insist on the fulfilment of obligations of any sort. In particular, the Cerdicings may have seen little reason to exploit a general obligation, if this would have yielded persons who were less experienced and worse equipped than the warriors they could assemble through more personal ties. This is not to say that the putative 'select *fyrd*' would necessarily have been an ill-equipped rabble: the fairly substantial payment that the Berkshire *milites* received for two months' service perhaps suggests that such persons tended to have some military skills and gear.[154] But except in specific (mostly defensive) circumstances, it is quite conceivable that the logistical challenges of raising and supplying even a 'select' form of general levy may have outweighed the potential strategic benefits of such a force. One could therefore maintain that the principle of general liability for military service was recognized throughout the late Anglo-Saxon period, but also hypothesize that most royal armies were probably composed predominantly of those who had received the king's patronage (or hoped to do so), plus their retinues: in practical terms one would then arrive at a position not vastly different from that of Abels.

Even on such a minimalist view, however, the military capabilities of Alfred and his successors would have been considerable. The key to this is the Cerdicings' wealth. It is impossible to compile a comprehensive inventory of any Cerdicing's assets, but they were clearly rich in both land and movables. We have already noted that wills appear not to list all of a testator's estates, and it is unclear whether the same was so for wealth in the form of precious metal, but very considerable quantities of gold and silver are mentioned in the testaments of Alfred and Eadred,

---

[152] No charters of the Northumbrian or East Anglian kings survive, so it is impossible to say whether they reserved military service when granting land, but they may have done so. It is also quite possible that the notion of a universal obligation existed before the appearance of reservation clauses in charters.

[153] What follows owes much to the stimulation of T. Reuter, 'Plunder and Tribute in the Carolingian Empire', *TRHS*, 5th series, 35 (1985), pp. 75–94; T. Reuter, 'The End of Carolingian Military Expansion', in P. Godman and R. Collins (eds), *Charlemagne's Heir: New Perspectives on the Reign of Louis the Pious (814–840)* (Oxford, 1990), pp. 391–405.

[154] Compare Abels, *Lordship and Military Obligation*, pp. 132–45. 20 shillings would probably have been enough to buy a few oxen or perhaps twenty sheep: D. L. Farmer, 'Prices and Wages', in H. E. Hallam (ed.), *The Agrarian History of England and Wales. Volume II: 1042–1350* (Cambridge, 1988), pp. 716–17.

the only two Cerdicing kings for whom such documents survive.[155] The legacies in Alfred's will include 1,800 pounds (presumably of silver) and 800 mancuses (presumably of gold); he also left 100 mancuses to each of his ealdormen, suggesting that his total bequests of gold substantially exceeded 1,500 mancuses.[156] Eadred left 2,090 pounds (presumably of silver) and 2,240 mancuses of gold, plus 120 mancuses for each bishop or ealdorman; 80 mancuses for each seneschal, chamberlain, or butler; 50 mancuses and 5 pounds of silver for each mass-priest in charge of the king's relics; 5 pounds of silver for every other priest; and 30 mancuses for each steward, other member of the royal household, or priest appointed since his accession.[157] Neither the precise totals nor the relative values of gold and silver are crucial here; the basic point is simply that a late ninth- or mid-tenth-century Cerdicing king could bequeath well over 1,500 mancuses of gold and 1,500 pounds of silver. By contrast, the amounts listed in the will of Ealdorman Æthelmaer (d. 982) total 800 mancuses of gold and 56 pounds of silver, and the sums mentioned in other surviving wills of ealdormen are lower.[158] The figures just quoted omit chattels for which Æthelmaer's will does not specify a value, and his wealth may well have been exceeded by that of certain ealdormen for whom no testament is extant, notably Æthelstan Half-King and Ælfhere. Nonetheless, the very wide gap between the sums mentioned in the wills of Æthelmaer and Eadred suggests that a king's movable wealth would have been considerably greater than that of an ealdorman of a similar period.[159]

An analogous point can be made with respect to land. Contrary to what has sometimes been claimed, Domesday shows that in 1066 Edward the Confessor had more valuable landholdings than anyone else in his kingdom; he had estates in most shires, albeit with a strong concentration south of the Thames.[160] Over the preceding two centuries, the Cerdicings had both acquired and alienated considerable quantities of land, and it is impossible to make any comprehensive assessment of the scale or distribution of the holdings of any of Edward's predecessors. It is,

---

[155] S 1507, 1515; above, p. 50. Alfred stated that, while he thought he had sufficient resources to pay the stipulated bequests, he was not certain. He also said that anything left over should be shared between those to whom he had left legacies. This may imply that the bequests listed in his will were an estimate of his total wealth in precious metal.

[156] S 1507. *ASC* ABCD 896, 897, 900 give reason to suspect that in Alfred's day each shire south of the Thames (and Essex) had an ealdorman. On the term 'mancus', see Blackburn, 'Gold', pp. 57–9.

[157] S 1515. Eadred's charters were typically attested by seven or more bishops, and anything from two to eleven ealdormen: Keynes, *Atlas*, Tables XLIV, XLV. The size of Eadred's household is unclear, but see Williams, *World Before Domesday*, pp. 25–6.

[158] S 1498, which also mentions that Æthelmaer had previously bought an estate from the king for 120 mancuses of gold. See also S 1483, 1485, 1504, 1508.

[159] Blackburn, 'Gold', p. 56 uses John of Worcester, *Chronicle*, 1040 (ii, 530) to suggest that Earl Godwine possessed more gold than Eadred had bequeathed, but John's account may be based on a poem the literal accuracy of which is highly questionable: H. Summerson, 'Tudor Antiquaries and the *Vita Ædwardi regis*', *ASE*, 38 (2009), pp. 157–63, 170–2; S. Keynes and R. Love, 'Earl Godwine's Ship', *ASE*, 38 (2009), pp. 185–223. It is nonetheless quite possible that Godwine and certain other eleventh-century earls were richer than at least some tenth-century kings. The key point, though, is that royal wealth had probably increased even more dramatically than aristocratic wealth, such that the king was at all times the richest person in the kingdom: below, pp. 183–5, 224 n. 138.

[160] Hill, *Atlas*, p. 101; Baxter, *Earls*, pp. 128–38; above, p. 52. Contrast Fleming, *Kings and Lords*, pp. 58–71.

however, very interesting that a substantial proportion of the places listed in King Alfred's will were in some way linked to Edward the Confessor over a century and a half later. This continuity is all the more striking when one considers that Alfred bequeathed several estates to persons other than Edward the Elder, although he stipulated that the beneficiaries should only pass the lands they received to their own children or the royal kin.[161] That there was a significant element of continuity in the lands held by the Cerdicings is, moreover, implied by the general distribution of the estates ascribed to Edward the Confessor in Domesday: their strong southern focus suggests that the core of his holdings had been in his ancestors' hands prior to the extension of their domination in the late ninth and tenth centuries. If that inference is correct, Alfred and his successors would almost certainly have held substantially more land than anyone else south of the Thames, as Edward did in 1066.[162] It is, moreover, a fair guess that from at least the late ninth century onwards the reigning Cerdicing always had more resources at his disposal than anyone else in Britain. Earlier in the ninth century, this may not have been so, but viking attacks and settlement had resulted in a shrunken Mercian kingdom, and the fragmentation of power in East Anglia, the East Midlands, and Northumbria, such that it is unlikely that any individual in these areas matched the Cerdicings' wealth.[163] Nor is it probable that any of the Welsh, Cumbrian, or Scottish kings could have done so, given the limited agricultural potential of large parts of Wales and northern Britain. We can therefore conclude, albeit tentatively, that Alfred and each of his successors probably had greater resources than any of their contemporaries in Britain.

This is significant, since estates and treasure could be used to reward warriors: if the foregoing inferences are correct, the Cerdicings would from at least the late ninth century onwards have been in a position to maintain the biggest and best military retinue on the island. Thus, even on Abels's minimalist interpretation, which holds that kings did not draft members of the general populace into their armies, the Cerdicings' coercive capabilities would have surpassed those of any other person in Britain. This is not to say that Abels's stance is necessarily correct. Alfred was undoubtedly able (as we shall see in the next chapter) to obtain large numbers of people to labour on fortifications, and the members of such construction gangs could plausibly have been forced to fight, rather than undertake building work.[164] There is no specific evidence that the Cerdicings used mass levies to recruit people into their armies in the late ninth to mid-tenth centuries, and there may usually have been little point in dragooning hordes of peasants with little fighting experience, but it would be incautious to discount the possibility that Alfred and his successors at least occasionally did so. If they did, this would only have increased their already considerable coercive strength. The key point, however, is that, whether or not the Cerdicings used such levies, their wealth probably

---

[161] S 1507; Wormald, '*On þa wæpnedhealfe*', especially pp. 270–6.

[162] Most of the Cerdicings' estates probably yielded less wealth in the ninth century than the eleventh, but this would also apply to the holdings of non-royal magnates: above, pp. 41, 83 n. 159; below, pp. 183–5, 224 n. 138.

[163] Above, pp. 21–5.   [164] Below, pp. 86–104.

enabled them to wield more powerful military forces than anyone else in Britain. Given that other potentates rarely combined against them, this meant that they could establish and maintain at least a loose and intermittent hegemony over all the other leading figures on the island. One can thus account for late ninth- and early tenth-century kings' domination over their greatest subordinates without conjuring up an apparatus of uniform administrative institutions, of the sort that would later set one part of Britain off from the rest. The issue that we now need to consider is whether this argument also holds with regard to the power that kings—from Alfred to Edgar—had over the great mass of the population below the level of the aristocratic elite.

3

The Cerdicings and the General Populace from the Late Ninth to the Mid-Tenth Century

THE IMPOSITION OF BURDENS

In the previous chapter, we saw that there is no need to posit the existence of an eleventh-century-style administrative apparatus to account for the power that kings from Alfred to Edgar had over their greater subordinates, and that variations in royal domination over such people did not serve to mark the future Domesday *Anglia* off from other parts of Britain. In this chapter, I advance similar arguments with regard to the power that Alfred and his immediate successors had over more ordinary people, of the sort who rarely or never went to royal assemblies outside their own locality, and with whom the Cerdicings rarely or never dealt on an individual basis. As before, my aim (for now) is not to refute the contention that late ninth- and early tenth-century kings used a network of hundreds and wapentakes to regulate what happened at a local level; rather, my objective in this chapter is simply to show that there is no compelling reason to posit that later administrative arrangements were already in place, and that there are other plausible hypotheses that could account for the Cerdicings' known achievements. These alternative theories involve a fair amount of inference and speculation, and I do not claim that they amount to proof of how kings ruled. A similar or greater degree of speculation is, however, involved if one wishes to project the administrative structures of the late tenth and eleventh centuries back into earlier periods: the point is simply that there is more than one way to interpret the fragmentary extant evidence.

Fortifications and the Burghal Hidage

The Cerdicings were, by the time of Æthelstan (r. 924–939), able to have pretty much any part of Britain ravaged, and they were therefore in a position to inflict suffering on anyone on the island. It was, however, in all likelihood only occasionally that such treatment was meted out on any particular locality, and my concern here is with the more ongoing effects that the Cerdicings had on the lives of ordinary people. Little is known about what agricultural and other surpluses kings extracted from their subordinates, but fortifications (*burhs*) provide clear evidence that Alfred and his immediate successors were beneficiaries of the service of a substantial segment of the population, at least across much of southern Britain. Given how many fortifications they had built, and the magnitude of the defences that have been identified in some locations, kings were evidently able to obtain labour from large numbers of people.[1]

There are two issues to consider here. The first is that the burdens that Cerdicing domination imposed on ordinary people were neither confined to the area between the Channel and the Tees, nor evenly distributed within this area. We saw in the previous chapter that, from the time of Æthelstan if not before, powerful people from across Britain supplied the Cerdicings with at least occasional tributes and military aid.[2] Since such potentates will have needed to exploit those beneath them to do so, the Cerdicings were the indirect beneficiaries of some of the labour of ordinary people throughout the island, not just in the area that became the English kingdom. Within Domesday *Anglia*, the distribution of fortifications implies that the Cerdicings were the beneficiaries of far more labour service in some regions than others: known Cerdicing strongholds are more closely spaced in the south and west than in the northern East Midlands or East Anglia, and York is the only one north of the Humber.[3] To some extent, variations in the burdens associated with the Cerdicings' domination were probably a direct consequence of the southern focus of royal estates, since there is a fair chance that kings could most readily extract services from the inhabitants of lands that they themselves held.[4] More broadly, however, we saw in the previous chapter that as distance from Wessex increased, and royal estates became fewer, the Cerdicings' grip on great magnates loosened: the south would in consequence have been the region in which such people could most readily have been induced to place their own subordinates' labour at the Cerdicings' disposal.[5]

The second issue to examine is that of how the Cerdicings organized the extraction of labour (and potentially other goods and services) from ordinary people, and in particular whether the undertaking of major construction projects implies the existence of a uniform eleventh-century-style administrative apparatus. The obvious place to start is the text known as the Burghal Hidage, the manuscripts of which belong to two groups. Common to both is a list of about thirty locations, each of which is assigned a number of hides, ranging from 100 for Lyng (Somerset) to 2,400 for each of Winchester and Wallingford. All the places listed lie south of or on the Thames, except Buckingham. It is usually thought that the list as it stands dates from soon after Edward the Elder's construction there of two fortifications in 914, but Buckingham could be an addition to an earlier version; conversely, it is conceivable that the text originated somewhat later. In the branch of the manuscript tradition represented by the sole pre-Conquest manuscript, which dates from the

---

[1] D. H. Hill, 'Gazetteer of Burghal Hidage Sites', in D. H. Hill and A. R. Rumble (eds), *The Defence of Wessex: The Burghal Hidage and Anglo-Saxon Fortifications* (Manchester, 1996), pp. 189–231; J. Baker and S. Brookes, *Beyond the Burghal Hidage: Anglo-Saxon Civil Defence in the Viking Age* (Leiden, 2013).

[2] Above, pp. 61–3.

[3] G. Williams, 'Military and Non-Military Functions of the Anglo-Saxon *burh*, *c*.878–978', in J. Baker, S. Brookes, and A. Reynolds (eds), *Landscapes of Defence in Early Medieval Europe* (Turnhout, 2013), pp. 151–7.

[4] On the distribution of the Cerdicings' lands, see above, pp. 51–2.

[5] Above, pp. 48–85 especially 50–1.

early eleventh century, the list is followed by a formula for calculating the number of hides needed for the establishment ('wealstillinge') and 'wære' of a given length of wall. We shall return shortly to the meaning of 'wære', but for now it is enough to note that the formula assumes that four people were required for each *gyrd* (about 16 feet or 5 metres) of wall, and that each hide would supply one person.[6]

Archaeologists have calculated the length of wall that the formula would imply for each hidage listed, and then attempted to compare the results to the places' actual defences. At Winchester, the length inferred from the formula matches up very closely with the remains, and reasonable fits can be demonstrated without difficulty at a few other sites. Much excitement has been expressed at what is often thought to have been a general rule. In most cases, however, the rule only holds if one employs all manner of contrivances. Thus, it is suggested that sometimes not all known defences were in use at the time (e.g. Exeter), and in many other places defences for which there is no evidence are conjured up. Where a site was partly adjacent to a river or the sea, the conjectured length of the defences sometimes includes the water's edge (e.g. Wallingford) and elsewhere excludes it (e.g. Wareham). It has been postulated that one definition of the length of a *gyrd* was used in some cases, a different one in others. Such variations are eminently plausible, but the notion of a general correspondence rests on circular arguments: commentators want the figures to match up, so manipulate them until they do.[7] There is, however, no good reason for thinking that the formula ought to yield neat results, especially given that it only appears in one branch of the manuscript tradition, and may have originated separately from the list of places. The formula could, for example, have been derived by a person who knew the length of the defences at Winchester and the number of hides pertaining thereto, but was largely ignorant about many of the other locations in the list.

Although historians and archaeologists are often excited by the possibility that a standard ratio may have been used to calculate how many hides should pertain to

---

[6] N. Brooks, 'The Unidentified Forts of the Burghal Hidage', *Medieval Archaeology*, 8 (1964), pp. 86–8; A. R. Rumble, 'An Edition and Translation of the Burghal Hidage, together with Recension C of the Tribal Hidage', in Hill and Rumble (eds), *Defence*, pp. 24–35; A. R. Rumble, 'The Known Manuscripts of the Burghal Hidage', in Hill and Rumble (eds), *Defence*, pp. 36–59; J. McN. Dodgson, 'OE *Weal-stilling*', in Hill and Rumble (eds), *Defence*, pp. 176–7. The manuscripts that do not contain the formula append a total of the hides listed, a statement that 30,000 hides pertained to the West Saxons, and hidages for Worcester and Warwick. With the possible exception of the alleged total (which does not accord with the figures listed in the extant manuscripts), these are probably late additions: N. Brooks, 'The West Saxon Hidage and the "Appendix"', in Hill and Rumble (eds), *Defence*, pp. 87–92. A *gyrd* was either just over or just under 16 feet (about 5 metres): D. A. Hinton, 'The Fortifications and their Shires', in Hill and Rumble (eds), *Defence*, pp. 153–4.

[7] J. Campbell, 'Observations on English Government from the Tenth to the Twelfth Century', *TRHS*, 5th series, 25 (1975), pp. 39–54, reprinted in his *Essays in Anglo-Saxon History* (London, 1986), p. 155; Hinton, 'Fortifications and their Shires', pp. 153–4; Hill, 'Gazetteer'. D. H. Hill, *An Atlas of Anglo-Saxon England* (Oxford, 1981), p. 85 provides a graph illustrating the supposed general rule. Contrast the more cautious comments in N. Brooks, 'The Administrative Background to the Burghal Hidage', in Hill and Rumble (eds), *Defence*, pp. 128–50 especially 128–32; D. H. Hill, 'The Shiring of Mercia—Again', in N. J. Higham and D. H. Hill (eds), *Edward the Elder, 899–924* (London, 2001), p. 158, although the latter article propounds another theory involving the manipulation of figures to fit known targets. Note also Baker and Brookes, *Beyond the Burghal Hidage*, pp. 120–1.

each fortification, the issue is peripheral here: even if a formula was used to compute the number of people desirable for particular sets of defences, this would reveal nothing about how service was extracted. Somewhat more important in the present context is Nicholas Brooks's widely accepted contention that the fortifications listed in the Burghal Hidage were garrisoned by something like one fifth of all able-bodied adult males in Wessex.[8] This conclusion is unsound. Setting aside Brooks's speculations about the overall population, which we may for the sake of argument accept, his case started with the observations that the Burghal Hidage list assigns roughly 27,000 hides, and that the formula is premised on each hide providing one person. Brooks assumed that these people performed garrison service, and suggested that they did so continuously. It is clear that fortifications were guarded, since the annal for 893 in the A, B, C, and D texts of the *Chronicle* refers to Alfred having divided his army in two 'except for those who had to hold the fortifications [*burga*]', but Brooks's assumption that there was a link between these garrisons and the Burghal Hidage is questionable.[9] The key here is the word 'wære', mentioned in the Burghal Hidage formula. The basic meaning of this noun is 'defence', and that of the related verb *werian* is 'to defend', but these words were also used to refer more generally to the discharge of obligations.[10] Thus, for example, a Northamptonshire tax collection record from soon after the Norman Conquest contrasts land from which not a penny had been received with that which had been 'gewered' (i.e. acquitted of its dues).[11] This implies that the 'wære' mentioned in the Burghal Hidage need not have related to garrison duty, and might instead have concerned some other form of obligation, such as repair work. Domesday strengthens this suspicion, referring to a requirement that each hide in Cheshire supply one person for the rebuilding ('reædificandum') of the wall and bridge at Chester.[12] It is consequently doubtful whether the mass levies envisaged by the Burghal Hidage had anything to do with those 'who had to hold the fortifications'. Those performing this latter task could instead have been the same kind of people as probably formed the core of the king's mobile forces, namely individuals who had personal ties to him, and their dependents. This would chime with a reference in the A, B, C, and D texts of the *Chronicle* to 'the king's thegns [*cinges þegnas*] who were then at home at the fortresses [*æt ham æt þæm geweorcum*]' pursuing a raiding army in 893.[13]

[8] N. Brooks, 'England in the Ninth Century: The Crucible of Defeat', *TRHS*, 5th series, 29 (1979), pp. 17–20. That the text concerns garrisoning is taken for granted by Baker and Brookes, *Beyond the Burghal Hidage*, p. 32; Williams, 'Military and Non-Military Functions', p. 133. Note, however, the scepticism of J. Campbell, 'Stenton's *Anglo-Saxon England*, with Special Reference to the Earlier Period', in D. Matthew, A. Curry, and E. Green (eds), *Stenton's* Anglo-Saxon England *Fifty Years On* (Reading, 1994), p. 51.

[9] *ASC* ABCD 893.

[10] A. R. Rumble, 'OE *Waru*', in Hill and Rumble (eds), *Defence*, pp. 178–81; R. Faith, *The English Peasantry and the Growth of Lordship* (London, 1997), pp. 90–1. Latin *defensio* and *defendere* were also used in connection with the discharge of obligations that did not specifically relate to 'defence'.

[11] *Anglo-Saxon Charters*, ed. and trans. A. J. Robertson, 2nd edn (Cambridge, 1956), pp. 230–6.

[12] *DB*, i, 262d.

[13] *ASC* ABCD 893. See also *ASC* A 917 for references to forces being assembled from fortifications. On military organization see above, pp. 79–85.

Whether or not 'wealstillinge' and 'wære' encompassed garrison duty is not crucial, however: more important is the question of how long it took to discharge these obligations each year. Even if every hide was to produce one person for garrison duty, it is unlikely that any individual so supplied served for more than a limited period per year, since the hypothesis that all but the smallest strongholds were permanently guarded by several hundred (and, in many cases, over a thousand) people would sit uneasily with archaeological evidence that most of the places fortified around the turn of the ninth and tenth centuries were not very densely populated until at least the second half of the tenth.[14] Nor would construction and repair be likely to have required year-round service. The Burghal Hidage formula envisages one person for roughly 4 feet (1.2 metres) of wall: even if in practice the ratio were doubled, repairs would quite probably have taken no more than a week or two each year.[15] The establishment of a new set of defences would have taken longer, although it was not always necessary to start from scratch: at some sites, including Winchester, Roman walls were reused.[16] Even in a case where there is no evidence of existing defences, however, construction could have been completed within a month: the A, B, C, and D texts of the *Chronicle* refer to Edward the Elder staying in Buckingham for four weeks while fortifications were built on both sides of the river.[17] The plausibility of this is demonstrated by an experiment which indicated that, using only extremely primitive tools, a ditch could be dug and the spoil used to make a bank at a steady rate of about 5 cubic feet (0.14 cubic metres) per person-hour:

[14]   G. G. Astill, 'Towns and Town Hierarchies in Saxon England', *Oxford Journal of Archaeology*, 10 (1991), pp. 103–9; R. Holt, 'The Urban Transformation in England, 900–1100', *ANS*, 32 (2010), pp. 57–78. See also N. Christie, O. Creighton, M. Edgeworth, and M. Fradley, ' "Have you Found Anything Interesting?" Exploring Late-Saxon and Medieval Urbanism at Wallingford: Sources, Results, and Questions', *Oxoniensia*, 75 (2010), pp. 45–6.

[15]   Above, pp. 87–8 and n. 6. That the maintenance of fortifications was an annual task, not a continuous one, is apparent from the command that every fortification be repaired by fourteen nights after Rogation Days in II As 13. This provision appears in a part of Æthelstan's Grately legislation that may well reproduce an ordinance from the mid-910s, which is also a likely date for the received version of the Burghal Hidage list: above, p. 87; below, pp. 137–40. See also M. A. S. Blackburn, 'Mints, Burhs, and the Grately Code, cap. 14.2', in Hill and Rumble (eds), *Defence*, pp. 169–72.

[16]   While Winchester's defences may have needed relatively little work, a new street grid was established there, probably before the early tenth century: M. Biddle and D. H. Hill, 'Late Saxon Planned Towns', *Antiquaries Journal*, 51 (1971), pp. 70–8, although one of Biddle and Hill's supporting arguments erroneously assumes that regular demonetization was practised in the first half of the tenth century. It has been estimated that the new street plan entailed the surfacing of 8.63 kilometres of road with perhaps 8,000 tonnes of flint cobbles. This was a considerable undertaking, but it is important not to be dazzled by large numbers. The width of Winchester's streets varied, but 9 metres would probably serve as a generous average. This would imply a total surface area of 77,670 square metres. The Burghal Hidage states that 2,400 hides pertained to Winchester. If 2,400 labourers each laid just over 1 square metre per day, they could have surfaced all the streets within a month. For estimated measurements, see M. Biddle and D. Keene, 'Winchester in the Eleventh and Twelfth Centuries', in M. Biddle (ed.), *Winchester in the Early Middle Ages: An Edition and Discussion of the Winton Domesday* (Oxford, 1976), p. 282; M. Biddle and D. Keene, 'General Survey and Conclusions', in Biddle (ed.), *Winchester*, p. 450. Note, too, that the laying of the cobbles need not have been completed in one stint of work, even if Biddle and Hill are correct that the street grid was the result of a single plan: Baker and Brookes, *Beyond the Burghal Hidage*, pp. 66–70 and n. 35.

[17]   *ASC* ABCD 914. No remains of these fortifications have yet been identified: Hill, 'Gazetteer', pp. 194–5.

given one person for every 4 feet (1.2 metres) of length, as anticipated by the formula, this would suggest that seven hours' work per day would have enabled the construction within four weeks of a bank as wide and high as those identified at many Burghal Hidage sites.[18] Brooks may have been correct that a fifth of able-bodied adult males in Wessex personally performed some sort of fortification work but, whether or not this entailed garrison duty, each person would probably have been required for only a limited period per year. If a fifth of able-bodied adult males did four weeks' annual fortification work, this would have represented about 1.5 per cent of the time of the total able-bodied adult male population.[19] The extent of the burden that the Cerdicings imposed on the general populace, while still significant, would then have been very considerably lower than Brooks suggested.

Our wonderment at the Cerdicings' fortifications should also be tempered by recognition that there are many examples from other parts of early medieval Europe of construction projects that must have required substantial labour forces. The dyke generally ascribed to Offa is but one of several massive prehistoric and medieval linear earthworks that survive in Britain and on the Continent.[20] Defences that may well antedate the late ninth century have been found at Hereford, Tamworth, and Winchcombe, and it is possible that similar works were undertaken at other places in the Midlands during the period of Mercian hegemony.[21] Contemporary annals refer to the West Frankish king Charles the Bald (r. 840–877) summoning men and carts from across his kingdom to construct defences in the 860s.[22] Many fortifications were built or reinforced in tenth-century East Frankia.[23] A canal 500 metres (1,640 feet) long and 11 metres (36 feet) wide was dug across the

---

[18] P. A. Jewell (ed.), *The Experimental Earthwork on Overton Down, Wiltshire, 1960* (London, 1963), pp. 50–8. The experiment can only give the roughest of impressions of how long work may have taken: the rate of progress would have been affected by numerous factors, including the workers' physical capabilities, the tools available, the soil type, and the weather. For typical measurements at Burghal Hidage sites, see Baker and Brookes, *Beyond the Burghal Hidage*, p. 75. My time calculation is based on a width of 8 metres (26.2 feet) and a height of 2.5 metres (8.2 feet); for every 1.2 metres (4 feet) of length, these dimensions would entail the movement of 24.3 cubic metres (859 cubic feet) of earth, or 172 person-hours of work. My calculation assumes an average height of 2.5 metres (8.2 feet) across the entire width; if a bank sloped away from a 2.5 metre (8.2 foot) peak, less earth (and therefore labour time) would have been required.

[19] While historians tend to assume that labourers were male, a passage in the *Life* of St Brigit about the construction of a road (discussed below, pp. 103–4) suggests that one should not reject out of hand the possibility that some were female, although it is unclear whether the hagiographer imagined Brigit herself to have participated in the physical labour. Old English *mann* did not refer exclusively to males.

[20] P. Squatriti, 'Digging Ditches in Early Medieval Europe', *P&P*, 176 (2002), pp. 11–65.

[21] S. Bassett, 'The Middle and Late Anglo-Saxon Defences of Western Mercian Towns', *ASSAH*, 15 (2008), pp. 180–239. Baker and Brookes, *Beyond the Burghal Hidage*, pp. 49–52, 74–5; Williams, 'Military and Non-Military Functions', p. 147 are somewhat more cautious.

[22] S. Coupland, 'The Fortified Bridges of Charles the Bald', *Journal of Medieval History*, 17 (1991), pp. 1–12.

[23] E. J. Schoenfeld, 'Anglo-Saxon *Burhs* and Continental *Burgen*: Early Medieval Fortifications in Constitutional Perspective', *HSJ*, 6 (1994), pp. 49–66; M. Innes, *State and Society in the Early Middle Ages: The Middle Rhine Valley, 400–1000* (Cambridge, 2000), pp. 162–4; P. Ettel, 'Frankish and Slavic Fortifications in Germany from the Seventh to the Eleventh Centuries', in Baker, Brookes, and Reynolds (eds), *Landscapes of Defence*, pp. 261–84.

Danish island of Samsø in or around 726, a date established by tree-ring analysis of the timber with which its banks were reinforced.[24] Five large circular ramparts dating from the late tenth century have been found in Denmark and what is now southern Sweden.[25] Bridges, some of considerable size, were erected throughout Europe in the early medieval period, including in Scandinavia and the Slavic lands.[26] The Cerdicings were thus not unusual in being able to carry out major construction projects, and it is notable that many substantial works were undertaken in regions and periods in which most historians have not been inclined to postulate the existence of administrative systems akin to those of the eleventh-century English kingdom.

Hides and the Assessment of Obligations

Arguments like those just presented only take us so far, however: lowering our estimates for the number of person-hours required to build and maintain fortifications, and acknowledging that other early medieval potentates also accomplished major construction projects, does not explain how the Cerdicings managed to obtain the labour of thousands of people, even if only for fairly short periods each year. Nor is it enough to observe that since well before Alfred's reign it had probably been an established principle that a king might demand bridge and fortification work, as well as army service, from any land in his kingdom: this simply begs the question of how the principle was given practical effect.[27] To pursue this problem, we first of all need to analyse the 'hide', which, as we have seen, appears in the Burghal Hidage and elsewhere as a unit of reckoning on which obligations were levied. In particular, we need to consider whether the levying of obligations on hides compels us to postulate that Alfred, and indeed earlier kings, had elaborate administrative apparatuses with which to survey their kingdoms, assess how many hides each landholder possessed, and check whether the burdens incumbent on each hide had been discharged.

Eight preliminary points are necessary. First, when we talk of the 'hide', we are conflating at least three Old English words, *hid*, *hiwisc*, and *hiwscipe*, but this is justifiable since the terms were used synonymously as units of reckoning.[28] Second, it appears that the root from which all these words derive meant something like 'family', and *hiwisc* and *hiwscipe* are attested as translations of Latin *familia* in contexts that have nothing to do with reckoning. It has been argued that the hide was in origin probably linked to a 'nuclear family' or

---

[24] A. Nørgård Jørgensen, 'The Kanhave Canal on Samsø—New Investigations', *Château Gaillard*, 18 (1998), pp. 153–8.

[25] E. Roesdahl, 'The Danish Geometrical Viking Fortresses and their Context', *ANS*, 9 (1987), pp. 208–26; M. K. Lawson, *Cnut: England's Viking King* (Stroud, 2004), pp. 21–2.

[26] N. Brooks, 'European Medieval Bridges: A Window onto Changing Concepts of State Power', *HSJ*, 7 (1995), pp. 11–29.

[27] Above, p. 81.

[28] F. W. Maitland, *Domesday Book and Beyond: Three Essays in the Early History of England* (Cambridge, 1897), pp. 358–9. *Hiwscipe* is rarely attested as a unit of reckoning, but see S 1492.

'household', but the specific nature of the 'family' is not critical here.[29] Third, the hide was used in Wessex as a unit of reckoning by around the turn of the seventh and eighth centuries at the latest, and could by then serve as a measure of land: the legislation ascribed to Ine (r. 688–726) stipulated wergelds (compensation tariffs) on the basis of how many 'hida' or '*hida* of land' a victim had, mentioned circumstances in which oaths of different numbers of 'hida' were required, and listed agricultural renders due from ten 'hidum'.[30] Fourth, it is probable that the hide was likewise used as a unit of reckoning, including for land, across most of the rest of the future English kingdom from early in the Anglo-Saxon period. The so-called 'Tribal Hidage', which perhaps dates from the seventh or eighth century, lists numbers of 'hyda' pertaining to population groups across Southumbria, and Bede reckoned land (*terra*) in terms of *familiae* ('families'), stating that this was 'the custom of reckoning of the English [*Anglorum*]'.[31] Bede was probably employing Latin *familia* to render *hid*, *hiwisc*, or *hiwscipe*, and these words were used when his work was translated into the vernacular sometime before about 900.[32] Fifth, the use of hides to reckon obligations implies that a hide was not simply whatever land any 'family' (however defined) happened to have, but that the measuring unit reflected the typical or minimum holding of a family of a certain type and status. Sixth, a hide of land was not a standardized measure of surface area, and is more likely to have been an expression of productive capability, such that reckoning a piece of land in hides would require consideration of both size and fruitfulness. This accords with Bede's commenting that Anglesey was both larger and more fertile than Man, before stating that they respectively constituted 960 and 'over 300' *familiae*.[33] Seventh, while counting in hides was widespread, the *hid*, *hiwisc*, or *hiwscipe* was probably never the name of the principal unit for reckoning land in every part

[29] T. M. Charles-Edwards, 'Kinship, Status and the Origins of the Hide', *P&P*, 56 (1972), pp. 5–8; E. G. Stanley, 'The *Familia* in Anglo-Saxon Society: "Household", rather than "Family, Home Life" as now Understood', *Anglia*, 126 (2008), pp. 37–64. For *hiwisc* and *hiwscipe* in contexts unrelated to reckoning, see, for example, the use of 'faeder hiuisc' and 'hioscipes fæder' to gloss *pater familias* ('father of a family' or 'master of a household'): London, British Library, MS Cotton Nero D.iv, ff. 173ʳ, 175ᵛ, 177ᵛ, 194ʳ, consulted in facsimile in T. D. Kendrick et al., *Evangeliorum quattuor Codex Lindisfarnensis* (2 vols, Olten and Lausanne, 1956–60), i; *HE*, v.12 (p. 488); *OEB*, v.13 (p. 422).

[30] Ine 14, 19, 24.2, 32, 44.1, 46, 52, 53, 54, 54.2, 64, 65, 66, 70.1. P. Wormald, *The Making of English Law: King Alfred to the Twelfth Century. Volume I: Legislation and its Limits* (Oxford, 1999), pp. 103–6 points out that the text that has come down to us may have evolved over a considerable period, but the initial core can be dated to 688×694. On the reckoning of oaths in hides, see H. M. Chadwick, *Studies on Anglo-Saxon Institutions* (Cambridge, 1905), pp. 134–53.

[31] W. Davies and H. Vierck, 'The Contexts of the Tribal Hidage: Social Aggregates and Settlement Patterns', *Frühmittelalterliche Studien*, 8 (1974), pp. 223–93; D. N. Dumville, 'The Tribal Hidage: An Introduction to its Texts and their History', in S. Bassett (ed.), *The Origins of Anglo-Saxon Kingdoms* (London, 1989), pp. 225–30; *HE*, i.25, ii.9, iii.4, iii.24, iii.25, iv.3, iv.13, iv.16, iv.19, iv.23, v.19 (pp. 72, 162, 222, 292, 294, 298, 336, 372, 374, 382, 396, 406, 520).

[32] *OEB*, i.14, iii.18, iv.3, iv.17, iv.18, iv.21, iv.24, v.17 (pp. 56, 236, 238–40, 262, 300–2, 304, 306, 324, 332, 456).

[33] *HE*, ii.9 (p. 162). Maitland, *Domesday Book*, pp. 357–520 provides the fullest discussion, proposing 120 acres as a typical area for a hide, while recognizing wide variation. While Bede assigns roughly three times as many hides to Anglesey as to Man, the former island is only about 25 per cent larger.

of what had by the eleventh century become the English kingdom. In Kent, the basic unit appears from early in the Anglo-Saxon period to have been the 'sulung' (cognate with Old English *sulh*, meaning 'plough'), and Scandinavian settlement in the north and east seems to have resulted in the 'ploughland' (*plogesland*, Latinized in Domesday as *carrucata*) taking the hide's place, although this may have been a case of renaming rather than substantive change.[34] Eighth, while references to the quantification of landholdings are unusually (although not uniquely) pervasive in English sources, other medieval societies also had units of reckoning on which military obligations might be levied.[35] One fairly well-evidenced parallel is that early ninth-century Frankish capitularies demanded army service from persons who possessed given numbers of *mansi*, the root meaning of which is 'dwellings'.[36] Another is that what appears to have been a seventh- or early eighth-century text ascribed different numbers of *tige*, that is 'houses', to various kindreds and locations in Argyll and the Inner Hebrides, with two ships due from every twenty *tige*.[37] Reckoning in hides, sulungs, ploughlands, *mansi*, and *tige* may spring from a common prehistoric root, with possession of a plough, a residence, and a certain quantity of land all being markers of status, but one could alternatively postulate that similar circumstances had prompted different societies to develop at least loosely analogous reckoning practices, with or without knowledge of each other.[38] Either way, however, the English were not extraordinary in having units of reckoning on which obligations could be levied.

Even if a hide of land were traditionally associated with an area that could be cultivated by a single plough team, what represented a landholding of appropriate size and fertility for a family of a certain type and status was probably somewhat impressionistic, and the potential uncertainty about what constituted a hide is underlined by an account of a late tenth-century dispute over whether an estate

---

[34] Maitland, *Domesday Book*, pp. 395–6; P. Vinogradoff, 'Sulung and Hide', *EHR*, 19 (1904), pp. 282–6; W. H. Stevenson, 'Yorkshire Surveys and Other Eleventh-Century Documents in the York Gospels', *EHR*, 27 (1912), pp. 15–24; Charles-Edwards, 'Kinship, Status and the Origins of the Hide', pp. 14–15.

[35] C. Wickham, *Framing the Early Middle Ages: Europe and the Mediterranean, 400–800* (Oxford, 2005), p. 319. Quantification of landholdings also appears to have been very common in at least the south-eastern part of Wales, since the charters preserved in the *Liber Landavensis* routinely reckon land in units known as *unciae* and *modii*: W. Davies, '*Unciae*: Land Measurement in the *Liber Landavensis*', *Agricultural History Review*, 21 (1973), pp. 111–21. It is uncertain to what extent *unciae* and *modii* were linked to the assessment of obligations.

[36] *CRF*, nos. 44 (c. 6), 48 (c. 2), 50 (c. 1); J.-P. Devroey, *Puissants et misérables. Système social et monde paysan dans l'Europe des Francs (VIᵉ–IXᵉ siècles)* (Brussels, 2006), pp. 421–41. See also *Annales de Saint-Bertin*, 860, 864, 866, 869, 877, ed. F. Grat, J. Vielliard, and S. Clémencet (Paris, 1964), pp. 82–3, 105, 125–6, 153, 213. Frankish charters sometimes refer to the conveyance of one or more *mansi*, but such quantification is less ubiquitous than in English diplomas.

[37] J. Bannerman, *Studies in the History of Dalriada* (Edinburgh, 1974), pp. 27–156; J. E. Fraser, *From Caledonia to Pictland: Scotland to 795* (Edinburgh, 2009), pp. 349–55.

[38] For arguments in favour of a common origin, see Charles-Edwards, 'Kinship, Status and the Origins of the Hide'; J. Campbell, 'Archipelagic Thoughts: Comparing Early Medieval Polities in Britain and Ireland', in S. Baxter, C. E. Karkov, J. L. Nelson, and D. Pelteret (eds), *Early Medieval Studies in Memory of Patrick Wormald* (Farnham, 2009), pp. 47–63 especially 52–8.

amounted to as many hides as its vendor claimed.[39] Given this ambiguity, it is necessary to consider how the hidages used for assessment purposes were determined. It is often assumed that they were imposed from above, and in many instances this probably was indeed the case. Thus, it appears that, by the end of the Anglo-Saxon period, kings (or their agents) sometimes assigned hidage assessments on the basis of hundredal districts, since there were many hundreds, especially in the Midlands, to which Domesday attributed a round number of hides, often 100.[40] Moreover, one can also hardly doubt that from very early in the Anglo-Saxon period it was often kings who made the subjective judgement that a given piece of land constituted a particular number of hides, and should render obligations accordingly. Thus, when kings granted land by charter, they stated that they were giving the recipient a certain number of *familiae, tributarii, mansiones, mansae, manentes,* or *casati,* these all probably being Latin renderings of 'hide'.[41] This does not, however, indicate that early kings had sophisticated mechanisms to survey their kingdoms. For one thing, it is eminently possible that kings often co-opted hidage assessments allocated by other powerful individuals or churches, who likewise claimed rights to renders and services.[42] Moreover, even if it was kings who determined assessments, it is unlikely that each individual hide represented a specific, discrete piece of land: if a king reckoned a given estate at (say) 20 hides, he would probably not have needed to demarcate its constituent hides. Perhaps most importantly, however, reckoning in hides dates back to a time when kingdoms were fairly small. For many kings of the early Anglo-Saxon period, it would not have been a very major undertaking to travel around their territories and allot hidages in person, and assessments so determined could have been preserved when stronger kingdoms absorbed their weaker neighbours.

We need not, moreover, assume that hidages were usually (let alone always) imposed from above. Historians have tended to overlook the possibility that landholders, particularly those who had never received royal charters, may to a large extent have assessed their own liability for royal (and other) dues, and would not necessarily have sought to minimize their burdens by adopting conservative estimations of

---

[39] *LE,* ii.11a (pp. 89–90). The link of hide and plough team is proposed by Charles-Edwards, 'Kinship, Status and the Origins of the Hide', pp. 14–15, although this requires the explaining away of a reference to a sulung (compare *sulh,* i.e. 'plough') being equivalent to two *manentes* (S 169). As Charles-Edwards acknowledges, this would suggest that the putative link of hide and plough team varied in practice.

[40] Maitland, *Domesday Book,* pp. 451–60; J. H. Round, *Feudal England: Historical Studies on the XIth and XIIth Centuries* (London, 1909), pp. 44–98; below, pp. 142–3. There were also a great many hundreds, especially in the south, which did not have 100 hides. See also *Anglo-Saxon Charters,* pp. 230–6; below, pp. 162–3.

[41] Maitland, *Domesday Book,* pp. 359–60. On the equivalence of such Latin terms, see (in addition to the evidence cited by Maitland) S 259, 543; Stephen of Ripon, *The Life of Bishop Wilfrid,* viii, ed. and trans. B. Colgrave (Cambridge, 1927), p. 16; *HE,* v.19 (p. 520).

[42] Bede complained that those living in remote places paid episcopal dues but rarely saw a bishop, although it is only a guess that such impositions were assessed in hides: Bede, *Letter to Ecgberht,* vii, ed. and trans. C. Grocock and I. N. Wood, *Abbots of Wearmouth and Jarrow* (Oxford, 2013), pp. 134–6. P. S. Barnwell, '*Hlafæta, ceorl, hid* and *scir*: Celtic, Roman or Germanic?', *ASSAH,* 9 (1996), pp. 53–61 explores the possibility of continuity in assessments from the Roman period, or indeed before.

their holdings. In this regard, the key point is that, for the purposes of legal status, it would have been desirable for a person to be regarded as possessing more hides, rather than fewer, since this would potentially increase the value of his or her wergeld and oath.[43] Given that what constituted a hide of land was probably somewhat ambiguous, it may well have been that one way in which a person could have laid claim to the legal status associated with a certain number of hides would have been to make a public show of acquitting the obligations incumbent on that number of hides, even if his or her estate had never been allocated a hidage by any king or royal agent. That status could be intimately connected with the discharge of royal burdens assessed on hides is clearly expressed in an early eleventh-century text associated with Archbishop Wulfstan II of York. It states that a Welsh holder of a hide of land who brought forth the king's tribute ('cyninges gafol forðbringan') should have a wergeld of 120 shillings, and that compensation of 2,000 *thrymsas* should be paid for the slaying of a non-noble ('ceorlisc man') who had prospered sufficiently to obtain 'five hides of land to the king's *utware*'.[44] Two further references suggest that this link between status and burdens already obtained much earlier in the Anglo-Saxon period. The treaty of Alfred and Guthrum prescribed a wergeld of 200 shillings for a non-noble occupying tributary land ('ceorle ðe on gafollande sit'), and the legislation ascribed to Ine set the wergeld of a Welsh tribute-payer ('gafolgelda') at 120 shillings.[45] Interestingly, the latter text gives the same figure for the wergeld of a Welsh holder of one hide of land: this reinforces the inference that rendering certain dues was a way to demonstrate worthiness of the status associated with possession of a hide.[46]

It would be fanciful to suppose that landholders commonly rushed to hand over to kings all that they could afford in the hope of enhancing their legal status. Most obviously, people are likely to have wanted both wealth and status, and to have varied in how they prioritized these. In addition, there may well have been limits on the extent to which paying royal dues could buy status: a holder of land generally reckoned at (say) three-quarters of a hide might have convinced others that he or she had a whole hide by discharging the corresponding burden, but it is less likely that even an extremely extravagant payment to the king would have persuaded this hypothetical person's neighbours that the land in question amounted to five hides. Furthermore, the extant legal texts imply that for English people there were only two main levels of wergeld, 200 and 1200 shillings, and that possession

---

[43] Ine 19, 24.2, 32; Geþyncðo 2–3; Norðleod 7–12; Að 1. A high wergeld would provide some deterrent against assault, and a powerful oath would assist a person in gaining and retaining clients: S. Baxter, 'Lordship and Justice in Late Anglo-Saxon England: The Judicial Functions of Soke and Commendation Revisited', in Baxter et al. (eds), *Early Medieval Studies*, pp. 401, 417. The nature of the relationship between oath value and possession of a certain number of hides of land is unclear, but a link can be inferred, since wergelds were linked to landholding, and Ine 19 and Að 1 indicate that there was a connection between a person's wergeld and the strength of his or her oath. See Chadwick, *Studies*, pp. 134–53.

[44] Norðleod 7, 9, discussed by Wormald, *Making*, pp. 391–4. See also Geþyncðo 3. On *thrymsas*, see Chadwick, *Studies*, pp. 20–3. The precise meaning of *utware* is unclear, but the etymological link with *waru* (on which see above, p. 89) leaves little room for doubt that it relates to the discharge of obligations.

[45] Ine 23.3; AGu 2. See also Ine 6.3.   [46] Ine 32.

of five hides of land was sufficient to qualify for the latter.[47] If taken literally, this would suggest that holding five hides rather than four would have been very advantageous, but that having six rather than five, or four rather than three, would have had no effect on a person's wergeld.[48] This does not, however, negate my overall point: even if the only burdens that landholders discharged voluntarily were those that assisted them in claiming wergelds of either 200 or 1200 shillings, this would have resulted in a great many people rendering dues and services on the basis of hides, and kings could probably have dealt on an individual basis with those who held well in excess of five hides. The link between burdens and status thus makes it quite unnecessary to posit that kings in the early Anglo-Saxon period had eleventh-century-style administrative systems with which to survey their kingdoms, allocate assessments, or enforce the discharge of obligations levied on hides. It is, moreover, notable that similar arguments can be applied to *tige*, which were not solely used to assess obligations: in early Irish law, grades of non-noble status were associated with possession of a *tech* (the singular of *tige*) of a particular size, plus sufficient resources to make payments to a lord, and grades of noble status corresponded to the number of *tech*-possessing clients from whom a person received renders.[49]

The hypothesis that during the early Anglo-Saxon period landholders were often willing to adopt reasonable (or even inflated) hidage assessments is rendered particularly plausible when one notes that the corresponding burdens may initially not have been especially heavy. Here a key piece of evidence is the statement in the legislation ascribed to Ine of the agricultural produce due from ten hides, which is

---

[47] Chadwick, *Studies*, pp. 76–114; Charles-Edwards, 'Kinship, Status and the Origins of the Hide', pp. 10–11. The importance of 200- and 1200-shilling wergelds is assumed in the legislation ascribed to Ine (Ine 19, 34.1, 70), which nonetheless discusses the wergelds of the Welsh more explicitly, assigning them what seems to be a parallel, lower tariff (Ine 23.3, 24.2, 32): that more attention was devoted to the Welsh probably reflects that they constituted an exception to well-known norms, which did not need to be spelt out. The link between possession of five hides and a 1200-shilling wergeld is first clear in early eleventh-century texts (Geþyncðo 2; Mirce 1.1; Að 1), and the criteria for a 200-shilling wergeld are not certain in any period, but the legislation ascribed to Ine accords the highest known tier of Welsh wergeld to holders of five hides, which gives grounds to suspect that for English people such a holding was already sufficient (if not necessarily necessary) for a 1200-shilling wergeld early in the Anglo-Saxon period. Likewise, the same text's attribution of a 120-shilling wergeld to Welsh holders of one hide may reflect that for English people such a holding was sufficient (if not necessarily necessary) for a 200-shilling wergeld. We have already noted that AGu 2 implies a close link between this wergeld and the discharge of dues, presumably at some minimum level. Whether the level in question was associated with one hide is not critical to my argument. The point is simply that a person would have had an incentive to discharge whatever dues would support a claim to a 200-shilling wergeld. Until the time of Alfred, 600-shilling wergelds are also mentioned frequently, although Welsh holders of five hides are the only persons to whom they are explicitly assigned (Ine 24.2; compare Ine 70; Af 10, 18.2, 30, 39.2, 40). If the 600-shilling wergeld reflects a third major tier of social status, with possession of a certain number of hides being a sufficient or necessary condition for each, this would only help my argument.

[48] My argument would be strengthened if the tiered system implied by the legal texts was schematic, and in practice wergelds increased gradually depending on (among other things) how many hides a person had.

[49] Bannerman, *Studies*, pp. 133–40; T. M. Charles-Edwards, '*Críth Gablach* and the Law of Status', *Peritia*, 5 (1986), pp. 53–73. See also Charles-Edwards, 'Kinship, Status and the Origins of the Hide', p. 18. It is unclear whether (and, if so, how) sulungs, ploughlands, and *mansi* related to legal status.

usually assumed to relate to a levy that the king might impose to provision himself and his entourage for one day and one night. The list includes specified quantities of honey, loaves, ale, animals, cheese, and various other items, but does not appear unduly onerous, when taken in conjunction with rough estimates of the potential annual agricultural output of definite geographical areas for which hidage reckonings are known.[50] Kings probably punished persons whom they identified as avoiding obligations, but there may well not have been all that much need for detailed auditing or heavy-handed enforcement: landholders were quite possibly content to deliver a relatively modest share of their agricultural surplus to a nearby royal residence, and to make a point of doing so in the witness of their neighbours, since neglect of this might have enabled others to question whether they actually had as many hides as they claimed.[51] Over time, the repetition of such payments would probably have resulted in it being generally accepted (at least among local people) that particular estates should be reckoned at specific numbers of hides, even if these hidages had at first been adopted through self-assessment, rather than imposed by a king.

The Organization of Labour Gangs

While kings may have had relatively little difficulty in obtaining sufficient resources to sustain themselves and their entourages in the early Anglo-Saxon period, attempts to extract more onerous burdens appear to have led to problems in securing compliance. This was evident in Alfred's reign, when, according to Asser, royal demands for the construction of fortifications sometimes went unheeded.[52] The mere fact that reckoning in hides was long-established is therefore not sufficient to explain how, in practice, Alfred and his successors obtained enough labourers to have fortifications built and maintained. Asser implies that the key to the actual implementation of Alfred's commands was aristocratic cooperation. He states that Alfred sought, and ultimately managed, to have defences constructed by instructing ('docendo'), cajoling ('adulando'), urging ('hortando'), commanding ('imperando'), and chastising ('castigando') bishops, ealdormen ('comites'), nobles ('nobilissimos'), thegns ('ministros'), and reeves ('praepositos').[53] This laundry list suggests that construction work was not organized through a uniform administrative system,

---

[50] Ine 70.1; Wickham, *Framing*, pp. 318–19, 321. See also C. Dyer, *Lords and Peasants in a Changing Society: The Estates of the Bishopric of Worcester, 680–1540* (Cambridge, 1980), pp. 28–30. R. Lavelle, '*Ine* 70.1 and Royal Provision in Anglo-Saxon Wessex', in G. R. Owen-Crocker and B. W. Schneider (eds), *Kingship, Legislation and Power in Anglo-Saxon England* (Woodbridge, 2013), pp. 268–70 interprets the burden as somewhat heavier, although still manageable. F. M. Stenton, *Anglo-Saxon England*, 3rd edn (Oxford, 1971), p. 288 took the list as describing what a lord (not necessarily a king) might extract from ten hides of his own land. If so, this would suggest that the dues that the king received from estates held by others were probably lower.

[51] Evidence of enforcement is minimal, but penalties for neglect of military service are specified at Ine 51. In the eleventh century, it appears that a person could establish a claim to an estate by discharging the burdens due from it, if the incumbent failed to do so: M. K. Lawson, 'The Collection of Danegeld and Heregeld in the Reigns of Æthelred II and Cnut', *EHR*, 99 (1984), pp. 723–5. There is no evidence that this practice obtained earlier, but it may have done so.

[52] *VA*, xci (pp. 78–9).   [53] *VA*, xci (p. 78).

but through a series of contacts between the king and a variety of persons who could have compelled substantial numbers of subordinate peasants to work on royal construction projects. There is, moreover, a fair likelihood that magnates and reeves not only supplied labourers from estates that they held or managed, but also organized and enforced contributions from neighbouring landholders. One indication of such a possibility is that there are references in ninth-century 'common stock' annals to ealdormen fighting with the people of Berkshire, Devon, Dorset, Hampshire, Kent, Somerset, Surrey, or Wiltshire: this shows that shires already existed south of the Thames in the ninth century, and suggests that each had an ealdorman who could assemble a fighting force from it.[54] Such contingents may have been raised through general levies on each hide (or group of hides) in a shire, or gathered from those with whom an ealdorman had some personal tie, but either way the implication seems to be that an ealdorman might lead a force from a shire, rather than just from his own estates and household. In light of this, one might guess that ealdormen, operating at the level of the shire, could have played a significant role in assembling people to labour on fortifications. It should, however, be noted that the Burghal Hidage is not arranged by shires, and it is therefore no more than a plausible possibility that these units were significant in the organization of labour gangs.[55]

Further possibilities about the kinds of districts in which magnates may have arranged and directed labour forces are raised by a text concerning Rochester Bridge. The text details which estates were responsible for maintaining the bridge's constituent sections, and the core of the document probably dates from the first half of the eleventh century. Certain parts of the bridge are said to have pertained to the king or to the Archbishop of Canterbury, but in each case only the first one or two estates assigned to the section are likely to have belonged to the king or archbishop, and Brooks was probably correct to infer that major landholders (or their local representatives) coordinated service from several estates, only some of which need have been in their own hands.[56] The area covered by the estates listed

[54] *ASC* ABCDE 802, 840, 845, 851, 853, 860. See also *ASC* ABCDE 757, 865, 878, ABCD 896, 897, 900, 903, E 1097; S 1211; *VA*, i, lii (pp. 1, 40). Several of these shires previously constituted kingdoms. The 802 and 878 annals refer to 'Wilsætan' (compare *Sumorsæte*, *Dornsæte*) rather than 'Wiltunscire' (which appears in Asser and the 897 annal), but this does not seriously affect my general point. B. Eagles, ' "Small Shires" and *regiones* in Hampshire and the Formation of the Shires of Eastern Wessex', *ASSAH* (forthcoming) suggests that the 'shires' named in the 'common stock' may have been much smaller than those of Domesday, with the Domesday shires of eastern Wessex only being formed in the late ninth century. There are two reasons to doubt this intriguing hypothesis. First, the 'common stock' refers to no *scir* not named in Domesday, which would be odd if the likes of *Hamtunscir* or *Bearrucscir* were just two of many 'small shires'. Second, the 'common stock' associates these shires with ealdormen: the same is so of Kent and Surrey, which suggests that these units were all analogous.

[55] For attempts to link the Burghal Hidage's figures with Domesday shires, see Maitland, *Domesday Book*, pp. 502–6; Brooks, 'Administrative Background', pp. 133–41.

[56] S 1481d; N. Brooks, 'Rochester Bridge, AD 43–1381', in N. Yates and J. M. Gibson (eds), *Traffic and Politics: The Construction and Management of Rochester Bridge, AD 43–1993* (Woodbridge, 1993), pp. 16–20, 26–34. The text as we have it suggests that the sections of the bridge assigned to the Bishop of Rochester were to be maintained almost entirely by estates of his church, but there are grounds to suspect that this is a consequence of alterations during the twelfth century.

in the Rochester document corresponds closely to that of the lathe of Aylesford, lathes being subdivisions of Kent that are first clearly documented in Domesday, where each lathe appears with two or more component hundreds. The text thus provides evidence of labour services being apportioned among the inhabitants of a district considerably smaller than a shire, but larger than a hundred. The origin of the Kent lathes is uncertain, but they are widely thought to have existed in some form from early in the Anglo-Saxon period, or possibly even before.[57]

Whether or not that was so, there is plenty of evidence that people in the early to mid-Anglo-Saxon period could think in terms of territorial units that were very probably smaller than the shires of Domesday, and are often referred to as *provinciae* or *regiones* in Latin texts. Thus, for example, Bede mentioned the '*provincia* of the Meonware' (probably in the Meon Valley, Hampshire), the '*provincia* which is called Oundle' (in Northamptonshire), the '*regio* which is called Leeds' (in West Yorkshire), 'the *regio* which is called Ely' (in Cambridgeshire), and 'the *provincia* of the Gyrwe' or 'the *regio* of the Gyrwe' (in which Peterborough lay).[58] These last references are of particular interest, since the Tribal Hidage includes both the South Gyrwe and the North Gyrwe, ascribing each 600 hides, which raises the possibility that other comparably assessed groups whom it lists were also associated with *provinciae* or *regiones*.[59] Notwithstanding various speculative studies, the bounds of these *provinciae* and *regiones* are largely unknowable, but that matters little here.[60] Nor is it certain what made them recognizable units, although the *Old English Bede* gives grounds to suspect that in many cases the identities of *provinciae* and *regiones* were closely linked to those of their inhabitants, who might be conceived of as a people: it renders *provincia* as *mægð* (the root meaning of which is 'kindred') and *regio* as *ðeodlond* ('people-land').[61]

---

[57] S. Brookes, 'The Lathes of Kent: A Review of the Evidence', in S. Brookes, S. Harrington, and A. Reynolds (eds), *Studies in Early Anglo-Saxon Art and Archaeology: Papers in Honour of Martin G. Welch* (Oxford, 2011), pp. 156–70, with references to earlier literature. See also Chadwick, *Studies*, pp. 249–62. The Domesday survey of Sussex indicates the existence there of units called rapes, which were of broadly comparable size to the Kent lathes. The Sussex rapes may have been of pre-Conquest origin, but there is no firm evidence: F. R. Thorn, 'Hundreds and Wapentakes', in A. Williams and R. W. H. Erskine (eds), *The Sussex Domesday* (London, 1990), pp. 29–33.

[58] *HE*, ii.14, iii.20, iv.6, iv.13, iv.19, v.19 (pp. 188, 276, 354, 372, 392, 516). For further examples and discussion, see P. F. Jones, *A Concordance to the Historia Ecclesiastica of Bede* (Cambridge, MA, 1929), pp. 429–31, 448; Stenton, *Anglo-Saxon England*, pp. 293–301; J. Campbell, *Bede's Reges and Principes* (Jarrow, 1979), reprinted in his *Essays*, pp. 86–7; B. Yorke, *Wessex in the Early Middle Ages* (London, 1995), pp. 39–43. Note that *regio* appears in contexts where it may well refer to a lathe: J. E. A. Jolliffe, *Pre-Feudal England: The Jutes* (Oxford, 1933), p. 46; N. Brooks, 'The Creation and Early Structure of the Kingdom of Kent', in Bassett (ed.), *Origins*, p. 72.

[59] Dumville, 'Tribal Hidage', p. 227. *HE*, iv.19 (p. 390) refers specifically to the South Gyrwe.

[60] E.g. N. Brooks, 'Alfredian Government: The West Saxon Inheritance', in T. Reuter (ed.), *Alfred the Great: Papers from the Eleventh-Centenary Conferences* (Aldershot, 2003), pp. 163–73.

[61] *Provincia* translated *mægð*: *HE*, iii.20, iv.13, v.19 (pp. 276, 372, 528); *OEB*, iii.14, iv.17, v.17 (pp. 220, 302, 464). *Regio* translated *ðeodlond*: *HE*, preface, iii.21, iv.19, v.12 (pp. 2, 280, 392, 488); *OEB*, preface.2, iii.15, iv.21, v.13 (pp. 2, 222, 318, 422). *Regio* is sometimes translated simply as *lond*: *HE*, ii.14, iii.24, iv.6, iv.19 (pp. 188, 292, 354, 394, 396); *OEB*, ii.11, iii.18, iv.7, iv.21 (pp. 140, 238, 280, 320, 324). These references are not comprehensive, and Bede also used *regio* and *provincia* with regard to much larger areas. There is no need to suppose that the inhabitants of a *provincia* or *regio* descended from a common ancestor: the important point is simply that they could be imagined as a people or kindred.

When considering the nature of these *provinciae* and *regiones*, and their possible relationships to the organization of labour forces, one can do little more than speculate. Nonetheless, it is hard to see how the *provinciae* and *regiones* to which Bede alluded could have been established as a coherent or comprehensive administrative system across what would become the English kingdom. At most, they could represent divisions systematically imposed by the rulers of individual early Anglo-Saxon kingdoms, perhaps to demarcate zones whose inhabitants were to render royal dues in particular locations.[62] It is, however, at least as likely that in many cases *provinciae* and *regiones* developed from a variety of other origins, reflecting (for example) zones of settlement during the migration period, territories in which a single potentate was or had been dominant, parishes pertaining to major churches, or some combination of these.[63] There was nothing peculiarly English about the existence in the early medieval period of districts considerably smaller than a typical Domesday shire, and in some sense associated with a 'people': this is the literal translation of the names of a local territorial unit in Brittany, *plebs*, and of an Irish petty-kingdom, *túath*, both *plebes* and *túatha* usually being closer in size to Domesday hundreds and wapentakes than to shires.[64] Within Britain, moreover, it is unlikely that identifiable territories of this kind of scale were confined to what would become the English kingdom. When evidence becomes available in and after the late eleventh century, one finds references from other parts of the island (notably eastern Scotland) to comparably sized districts, in each of which many of the inhabitants owed renders and services to a particular lord. It is likely that arrangements along these lines were for the most part not recent innovations: rather, as has long been recognized, such 'extensive lordships' had probably existed in many lowland areas of Britain in the early medieval period, but by the time of Domesday they had often been split up into smaller units of more intensive exploitation in most of the English kingdom, except the north-east.[65] It is a fair

[62] J. Campbell, 'Bede's Words for Places', in P. H. Sawyer (ed.), *Places, Names and Graves: Early Medieval Settlement* (Leeds, 1979), pp. 34–54, reprinted in his *Essays*, pp. 108–16 seems to reflect thinking along such lines: 'what sounds like a tribe may have been only an administrative district' (p. 113). See also Campbell, *Bede's Reges and Principes*, pp. 95–6.

[63] S. Bassett, 'In Search of the Origins of Anglo-Saxon Kingdoms', in Bassett (ed.), *Origins*, pp. 3–27 especially 17–23; D. M. Hadley, *The Northern Danelaw: Its Social Structure, c.800–1100* (London, 2000), pp. 94–164; Brooks, 'Alfredian Government', pp. 163–73.

[64] W. Davies, *Small Worlds: The Village Community in Early Medieval Brittany* (London, 1988), pp. 63–7; T. M. Charles-Edwards, 'The Pastoral Role of the Church in the Early Irish Laws', in J. Blair and R. Sharpe (eds), *Pastoral Care before the Parish* (Leicester, 1992), pp. 64–5; T. M. Charles-Edwards, *Early Christian Ireland* (Cambridge, 2000), pp. 12–13, 97–8, 102–6, 248. Breton *plebes*, Irish *túatha*, and English hundreds and wapentakes all varied considerably in size. *Túath* was usually rendered in Latin as *plebs*. For Welsh *tud*, cognate with *túath*, see T. M. Charles-Edwards, 'Some Celtic Kinship Terms', *Bulletin of the Board of Celtic Studies*, 24 (1971), pp. 115–19, but note W. Davies, *Patterns of Power in Early Wales* (Oxford, 1990), p. 19.

[65] E. W. Robertson, *Historical Essays in Connexion with the Land, the Church &c* (Edinburgh, 1872), pp. 112–30; W. Rees, 'Survivals of Ancient Celtic Custom in Medieval England', in H. Lewis (ed.), *Angles and Britons* (Cardiff, 1963), pp. 148–68; G. R. J. Jones, 'Multiple Estates and Early Settlement', in P. H. Sawyer (ed.), *Medieval Settlement: Continuity and Change* (London, 1976), pp. 15–40; Faith, *English Peasantry*, pp. 1–14; Hadley, *Northern Danelaw*, pp. 84–164; G. W. S. Barrow, 'Pre-Feudal Scotland: Shires and Thanes', in G. W. S. Barrow, *The Kingdom of the Scots: Government, Church and Society from the Eleventh to the Fourteenth Century*, 2nd edn (Edinburgh, 2003), pp. 7–56. While arguing

guess (although nothing more) that many English *provinciae* and *regiones* developed as 'extensive lordships', the inhabitants of which rendered goods and services to a powerful person or religious institution. An individual dominant over an 'extensive lordship' may have been regarded (at least by some people) as a king, and would in any case have had a position somewhat analogous to the king (*rí*) of a *túath*. It is likely that such a person could, if cajoled or threatened, have diverted his or her subordinates into performing labour or other services for the reigning Cerdicing, much as the kings of individual *túatha* did for superior kings.[66]

Many *provinciae* and *regiones* that had once constituted 'extensive lordships' may well already have been divided before the end of the ninth century, however, and others possibly acquired their identity without ever having been subordinate to a single potentate. There is a fair chance that many were districts whose inhabitants gathered periodically to socialize, trade, witness transactions, resolve disputes, manage shared resources (e.g. pasture), and so on. That local assemblies were at least occasionally held in some places is apparent from Alfred's legislation and Asser's *Life* of the same king, which both allude to meetings in the presence of a royal reeve or ealdorman.[67] There is, however, no need to assume that such gatherings were usually (let alone always) convened by royal agents. Indeed, there are numerous examples from societies past and present of neighbours congregating to deal with matters of mutual concern, without necessarily being instructed to do so by anyone from outside their locality.[68] Thus, for example, the king of a *túath* could summon its inhabitants to an assembly (*óenach*), and documents from the early medieval Rhine valley describe meetings that seem to have been orchestrated by a variety of local potentates.[69] Aristocratic initiative is not, moreover, a prerequisite for people to gather: the Redon cartulary suggests that the peasant inhabitants of ninth-century Breton *plebes* sometimes met without any powerful figure instructing them to do so, and the Norwegian *Gulathing* law code (extant only in thirteenth-century and later manuscripts, but incorporating earlier material) states that anyone should have the right to summon a *þing* (assembly).[70]

It is impossible to prove that the holding of local meetings was a widespread practice in the early Anglo-Saxon period. The hypothesis that in at least some parts of what became the English kingdom there were districts with long-standing

that the phenomenon of 'extensive lordship' was old by the time of Domesday, Hadley stresses that the bounds of individual 'extensive lordships' probably changed over time, but this does not fundamentally affect my argument.

[66] Charles-Edwards, *Early Christian Ireland*, pp. 525–30.

[67] Af 22, 34, 38–38.2; *VA*, cvi (p. 92). See also S 1186a.

[68] A. Richards and A. Kuper (eds), *Councils in Action* (Cambridge, 1971); S. Reynolds, *Kingdoms and Communities in Western Europe, 900–1300*, 2nd edn (Oxford, 1997), especially pp. 67–78, 101–54.

[69] Charles-Edwards, *Early Christian Ireland*, p. 560; B. Jaski, *Early Irish Kingship and Succession* (Dublin, 2000), pp. 49–56; Innes, *State and Society*, especially pp. 94–140.

[70] Davies, *Small Worlds*, especially pp. 63–7, 134–60, 201–13; *Gulathing Law*, cxxxi, ed. B. Eithun, M. Rindal, and T. Ulset, *Den eldre Gulatingslova* (Oslo, 1994), p. 102; S. Bagge, *From Viking Stronghold to Christian Kingdom: State Formation in Norway, c.900–1350* (Copenhagen, 2010), pp. 179–84.

assembly customs would, however, explain why accounts of the late tenth century and after mention gatherings attended by persons from several neighbouring hundreds. No extant pre-Conquest legislative text ordains that there should be assemblies of groups of hundreds, but this practice would be readily explicable if those hundreds that sometimes met jointly had been formed through the division of territories the inhabitants of which had congregated for generations. One example of a group of hundreds that appears repeatedly is the 'eight hundreds of Oundle', and we should at least countenance the possibility that this district was related to the '*provincia* of Oundle' mentioned by Bede.[71] If it was indeed common for the inhabitants of certain localities to assemble, kings (or powerful persons acting on their behalf) could have exploited such existing assembly customs to publicize their demands and coordinate levies of people to perform labour, or indeed to discharge other burdens. Given the lack of direct evidence for the nature of the units that Bede called *provinciae* and *regiones*, much of the foregoing is necessarily speculative. The key point, though, is that such modestly sized districts were found across and, it should be stressed, beyond the future English kingdom. They can hardly have been created as a uniform administrative network, and it appears that an assortment of loosely comparable units developed in different areas, quite possibly from a variety of origins.

We cannot know by what means Edgar's predecessors obtained the labour of large numbers of people to construct and maintain fortifications, but the fact that they evidently did so in no way compels us to posit that they had a slick, sophisticated, or standardized administrative system at their disposal. Rather, Asser's comments lead one to suspect that Alfred dealt directly with a relatively small number of powerful people, who in turn probably cajoled and threatened others into carrying out the work. Such arrangements may well have entailed uneven distributions of responsibilities, and have been somewhat haphazard in organization, but this need not preclude their having been effective in getting tasks done.[72] In this regard, it is instructive to consider a passage from a seventh-century *Life* of Brigit, an Irish saint, which relates that a certain king ordered that 'peoples' (*populi* and *plebes*, probably translating *túatha*) from all his *regiones* and *provinciae* should come together and build a solid road across a sodden bog, through which a river flowed. The workforce that assembled is said to have divided the task among kindreds (*cognationes*) and families (*familiae*), and an especially onerous section fell by chance to a certain people (*natio*). This group then browbeat Brigit's people (who were weaker and less numerous) into swapping, but the river miraculously changed

[71] H. Cam, 'Early Groups of Hundreds', in J. G. Edwards, V. H. Galbraith, and E. F. Jacob (eds), *Historical Essays in Honour of James Tait* (Manchester, 1933), pp. 13–26; C. Hart, *The Danelaw* (London, 1992), pp. 141–76; J. G. H. Hudson, *The Oxford History of the Laws of England. Volume II: 871–1216* (Oxford, 2012), p. 55. For late evidence of lathe meetings, see Jolliffe, *Pre-Feudal England*, pp. 60–3, 68; Brooks, 'Creation and Early Structure', pp. 69–70. The eight hundreds of Oundle are indicated on Map 4, for which see below, p. 142.

[72] Compare A. Taylor, 'Common Burdens in the *Regnum Scottorum*: The Evidence of the Charter Diplomatic', in D. Broun (ed.), *The Reality behind Charter Diplomatic in Anglo-Norman Britain* (Glasgow, 2011), pp. 204–33, consulted at <http://paradox.poms.ac.uk/ebook/index.html> (accessed 9 October 2014).

course during the night: the section that had been forced on Brigit's people became less difficult, and the most arduous work was shifted back to those who had bullied them.[73] In view of the evidence that in much of what became the English kingdom burdens were levied on 'families' (i.e. hides), and the possibility that labour forces there were extracted from *regiones* and *provinciae* that were in some way associated with 'peoples', the writer's assumptions are very revealing: it was evidently thinkable to him that a king might obtain a labour force from the 'peoples' of *regiones* and *provinciae*, that he might leave those assembled to arrange the division of labour themselves, that they might do so on the basis of kindreds and families, and that they might then get on with the task. There is in consequence no need for us to suppose that the Cerdicings required an eleventh-century-style administrative apparatus to undertake major construction projects: if a king, or those acting for him, could induce a number of magnates, *regiones*, and *provinciae* to supply labourers, it mattered little who those labourers were, or how equitably the task was split between them.

THE DETECTION AND PUNISHMENT OF THEFT

The Importance of Theft and the Problems of the Sources

That the Cerdicings imposed burdens on the general populace, especially south of the Thames, does not prove that in any part of Britain, kings—from Alfred to Edgar—routinely regulated how individual persons below the highest echelons of society acted in relation to each other. The legislation of Alfred, and especially his successors, does, however, show that these kings desired that even very ordinary people should behave in particular ways. For the Cerdicings, the mere fact that they were declaring law and exhorting people to righteous conduct may have been more important than the detailed content of their decrees, but their legislation nonetheless reveals something of their priorities.[74] In particular, it implies that they were especially concerned to try to curb theft, and it is therefore on this that we need to focus.[75] When seeking to account for the Cerdicings' achievements, one might, however, try to sidestep the issue, since the prevalence or otherwise of theft is unlikely to have had much bearing on kings' ability to extend and then maintain their power across Britain. Moreover, while in some cases we have definite archaeological evidence that the Cerdicings managed to have fortifications constructed, there is very little basis on which to assess how common theft was, and one could postulate that royal legislation was widely ignored. Such a hypothesis would

---

[73] Cogitosus, *Life of St Brigit*, vii, ed. I. Bollandus and G. Henschenius, *Acta Sanctorum Februarii* (3 vols, Antwerp, 1658), i, 140. On the date, see Charles-Edwards, *Early Christian Ireland*, p. 438.

[74] P. Wormald, '*Lex Scripta* and *Verbum Regis*: Legislation and Germanic Kingship from Euric to Cnut', in P. H. Sawyer and I. N. Wood (eds), *Early Medieval Kingship* (Leeds, 1977), pp. 105–38, reprinted in his *Legal Culture in the Early Medieval West: Law as Text, Image and Experience* (London, 1999), pp. 1–44; Wormald, *Making*, especially pp. 29–143, 416–65.

[75] T. B. Lambert, 'Theft, Homicide and Crime in Late Anglo-Saxon Law', *P&P*, 214 (2012), pp. 3–43.

perhaps be convenient, but it cannot safely be assumed correct; indeed, a text from London implies that during Æthelstan's reign many people were sufficiently unconcerned about thieves that they let their livestock wander, and Edmund expressed thanks for 'the peace that we now have from thefts'.[76] We therefore need to take seriously the possibility that, at least in certain places, royal demands for actions against thieves met with some measure of success.

Whether or not the Cerdicings managed to reduce theft, it is instructive to examine what their legislation implies about the ways in which they sought to advance this aim. Normative legal sources pose many interpretive challenges, in addition to the obvious uncertainty about whether they were obeyed. One largely insurmountable problem is that the extant texts probably do not fully reflect the legislation that kings issued, especially since some of their decrees may never have been written down. A further difficulty is that we often have no way of knowing to what geographical area a legal text was intended to relate. Given the importance attached (as we shall see in a moment) to fortified locations in royal legislation, it is reasonable to infer that the Cerdicings did not envisage the practical provisions of their ordinances taking effect in Wales or northern Britain, but we should also bear in mind that the anticipated applicability of at least some of their decrees may have been considerably more restricted.[77] Yet another pitfall is that legislation may represent an attempt to introduce change, a statement of existing practice, an evocation of idealized custom, or a mixture of all these things. This last obstacle can, however, to some extent be circumvented by focusing less on the detail of specific decrees, and more on how the assumptions implicit in royal ordinances changed over time. The legislation of late tenth- and eleventh-century kings assumes, as we shall see in the next chapter, that hundreds or wapentakes should be at the heart of royal attempts to regulate the conduct of ordinary people, and some of Edgar's decrees presuppose that these administrative structures existed across the land from the Channel to the Tees.[78] By contrast, the legislation of Edgar's predecessors says nothing of wapentakes, and yields just one reference (from Edmund's reign) to a hundred: even if hundreds and wapentakes already existed in some form, their absence from royal legislation suggests that prior to the mid-tenth century they were not especially important to the Cerdicings' attempts to obtain adherence to their commands.[79] My immediate aim, however, is not to argue that hundreds and wapentakes were insignificant before the mid-tenth century, but to consider the evidence for how Edgar's predecessors *did* seek to regulate the conduct of ordinary people at a local level.

---

[76] VI As 8.7; II Em 5, but note that Æthelstan complained that his decrees were disregarded: IV As 3–3.2; V As Prol.–Prol.3.

[77] The uncertainty about geographical applicability is highlighted by two complementary ordinances of Æthelred II, issued at Woodstock (I Atr) and Wantage (III Atr) respectively. The Wantage text seems to have been for an area of Scandinavian settlement, and, had it been lost, historians might well have been oblivious to the likelihood that the Woodstock decrees were not meant to apply throughout Æthelred's kingdom. See C. Neff, 'Scandinavian Elements in the Wantage Code of Æthelred II', *Journal of Legal History*, 10 (1989), pp. 285–316; Wormald, *Making*, pp. 324–7.

[78] Below, pp. 122–3.   [79] III Em 2; below, pp. 144–55.

Ports, Burhs, and Reeves

A notable feature of the legislation of Edward the Elder and Æthelstan is that they assumed that it would be desirable to confine certain activities to a limited set of locations, referred to as *ports* or *burhs*.[80] These kings ordered that trade, or at least trade in goods worth more than the fairly modest threshold of 20 pence, should only take place in a *port*, where transactions were to be witnessed by either a '*port-reeve*' (*portgerefa*) or some other trustworthy person, the intention probably being to impede the sale of stolen goods, and to facilitate the collection of tolls.[81] In a similar vein, Æthelstan's Grately ordinance incorporates a ban on the minting of coins outside a *port*, which may well derive from a decree of Edward; this prohibition is followed by quotas of moneyers for various named locations, and a statement that there could (or possibly should) be one moneyer in other *burhs*.[82] This suggests that, in the context of early tenth-century royal legislation, *burh* and *port* denoted much the same sort of place, and the desire to limit minting and (high-value) transactions to *ports* or *burhs* implies that early tenth-century kings sought to use reeves based in such locations to secure adherence to their commands.[83] This inference is corroborated by Æthelstan's tithe ordinance, which is addressed to 'the reeve in every *burh*'; these reeves were ordered to render tithes from the king's own possessions, and (in cooperation with bishops) to instruct other people to do like-wise.[84] That Æthelstan regarded *burhs* as central to the enforcement of his legisla-tion is further underlined by two passages in his Grately decrees, concerning the punishment of persons who committed theft or failed to attend meetings: in each case, the possessions of wrongdoers were to be seized by 'all the senior people [*yld-estan men*] pertaining to the *burh*'.[85]

The question of what Edward and Æthelstan meant when they referred to *ports* and *burhs* is therefore of some importance. These words could designate places with substantial populations, which might reasonably be called 'towns', but both (and especially *burh*) could simply denote a site that was in some way fortified.[86] It is therefore problematic to settle on a translation, but the Grately ordinance's asso-ciation of minting with *ports* or *burhs* suggests that the locations in which coins

---

[80] The nominative plurals are *portas* and *byrig*, but '*ports*' and '*burhs*' are used here for simplicity.

[81] I Ew 1–1.1; II As 12, 13.1. On Æthelstan's relaxation of these restrictions, see below, p. 108. 20 pence might have bought a cow, or two or three pigs, but probably not an ox: D. L. Farmer, 'Prices and Wages', in H. E. Hallam (ed.), *The Agrarian History of England and Wales. Volume II: 1042–1350* (Cambridge, 1988), pp. 716–17. That tolls were collected on trade in fortifications is clear from S 223, 346.

[82] II As 14–14.2; below, pp. 136–40.

[83] The potential equivalence of *burh* and *port* is also implied by their twice being offered as alter-native glosses to *civitas* in the Lindisfarne Gospels: London, British Library, MS Cotton Nero D.iv, ff. 20ᵛ, 21ʳ, consulted in facsimile in Kendrick et al., *Evangeliorum quattuor Codex Lindisfarnensis*, i.

[84] I As Prol.–1.   [85] II As 20–20.1, 20.3–20.4. Compare Blas 3; S 1497; *ASC* ABCD 914.

[86] On the term *burh*, see Maitland, *Domesday Book*, pp. 183–6; A. H. Smith, *English Place-Name Elements* (2 vols, Cambridge, 1956), i, 58–62; D. H. Hill and A. R. Rumble, 'Introduction', in D. H. Hill and A. R. Rumble (eds), *Defence*, p. 3; S. Draper, 'The Significance of Old English *Burh* in Anglo-Saxon England', *ASSAH*, 15 (2008), pp. 240–53; Baker and Brookes, *Beyond the Burghal Hidage*, pp. 37–41, 95–9. *Port* is less discussed, but see Smith, *English Place-Name Elements*, ii, 70–1. The contexts in which *port* appears in legislation suggest its primary connotation was of a trading place.

were struck during the reigns of Edward and Æthelstan are likely to provide a rough guide (albeit only a rough guide) to the kinds of places that these kings meant when they used these words in their legislation. Æthelstan's reign was the first time that it became common for coins to state their place of issue, and moneyers are known to have minted in his name at York and at over thirty locations south of the Mersey and the Humber.[87] Since there is no evidence that the Cerdicings controlled fortifications in Wales or north of York, one might contend that for substantial periods from 927 onwards their domination in the land between the Channel and the Tees was qualitatively different from in other parts of the island. This argument cannot, however, bear great weight, not least because the Cerdicings' hold on York and the northern East Midlands was far from continuous.[88] Moreover, while both coins and written sources imply that during the first half of the tenth century there were many *ports* or *burhs* south of the Thames (although not in Cornwall), and a fair number in the southern and western Midlands, rather fewer are identifiable in the northern East Midlands and East Anglia, and York is the sole example beyond the Humber: there were thus substantial contrasts within the land that would be described by Domesday.[89]

Even in areas where there were many *ports* or *burhs*, however, it is doubtful whether most of these had much significance for the bulk of the population, except as places where they might be forced to labour from time to time. It has been argued that Alfred sought to promote commercial activity in at least some of the places that he fortified, the principal basis for this contention being that the rectilinear layout of Winchester's streets dates to the late ninth or very early tenth century, and that similar grids identifiable in a few other places may have been established around the same time.[90] But even if we leave aside the significant possibility that Winchester was atypical, a regular layout need not indicate that a place is a major centre of population or trade, whatever the aspirations of its planners may have been. Indeed, archaeologists have in recent decades emphasized for a whole series of fortified places the lack of evidence of dense habitation or substantial artisanal activity before the second half of the tenth century (or later); the main exceptions, principally York and Lincoln, lay in regions of Scandinavian settlement, and were major trading centres well before they came under Cerdicing domination.[91] The region in which *ports* or *burhs* probably exerted greatest commercial

[87] C. E. Blunt, 'The Coinage of Athelstan, King of England, 924–939: A Survey', *BNJ*, 42 (1974), pp. 35–160 especially 40–5, 61–104, with maps of named minting locations at 42–3. See also Hill, *Atlas*, pp. 127–8. Coins struck in parts of the East Midlands very rarely state their place of issue before the last years of Edgar's reign; there is therefore some uncertainty about the locations in which moneyers worked there.

[88] Above, pp. 31–2, 50–1.

[89] Williams, 'Military and Non-Military Functions', pp. 151–7. For a map, see Baker and Brookes, *Beyond the Burghal Hidage*, p. 154.

[90] Biddle and Hill, 'Late Saxon Planned Towns'; M. Biddle, 'Towns', in D. M. Wilson (ed.), *The Archaeology of Anglo-Saxon England* (London, 1976), pp. 124–37. See also D. H. Hill, 'Athelstan's Urban Reforms', *ASSAH*, 11 (2000), pp. 173–86.

[91] For overviews and references to detailed studies, see Astill, 'Towns and Town Hierarchies', pp. 103–14; D. A. Hinton, 'The Large Towns, 600–1300', in D. M. Palliser (ed.), *The Cambridge Urban History of Britain. Volume I: 600–1540* (Cambridge, 2000), pp. 225–35; Holt, 'Urban Transformation';

magnetism was thus the area in which they were fewest, which raises the suspicion that most people rarely (if ever) set foot in one, unless they were compelled to construct or repair it. As such, orders that all (high-value) transactions be conducted in *ports* or *burh*s probably proved unenforceable, and this is likely to be the reason why Æthelstan rescinded these restrictions.[92] That he lifted a ban on Sunday trading at the same time suggests that the limitations were removed because they had proved unworkable, not because they had lost their rationale, and it does not appear that any very systematic new witnessing arrangements were established instead: Æthelstan's successor, Edmund, ordered that no one should acquire cattle without the witness of a high-reeve, priest, *hordarius* ('treasurer'?), or *port*-reeve, essentially a list of persons of standing.[93]

Given that Æthelstan presumably did not want only the inhabitants of *burh*s to pay tithes, but entrusted enforcement of his tithe ordinance to 'the reeve in every *burh*', he may well have intended that such reeves should each oversee some sort of hinterland.[94] Even so, it is unlikely to have been practical for reeves based in *ports* or *burh*s to regulate with much consistency the behaviour of persons who did not live in the immediate vicinity, especially if the reeve was to be readily available in the *port* or *burh* to witness transactions. There are, however, several references in royal legislation to reeves who are not explicitly associated with *ports* or *burh*s. Thus Æthelstan ordered that every reeve ('ælc gerefa') should extract a pledge of obedience from his own district ('his agenre scire'), Alfred and Edward the Elder referred to assemblies being held in the presence of reeves, and the latter king specifically ordered that every reeve ('ælc gerefa') should hold a meeting ('gemot') every four weeks, and see that justice was done.[95] One could speculate that these stipulations primarily concerned reeves of *ports* or *burh*s, and assemblies held in these places. Such an interpretation would help my argument that *ports* and *burh*s were central to early tenth-century kings' efforts to secure compliance with their commands, and might be supported by Æthelstan's reference to non-attendance at meetings being punished by 'all the senior people pertaining to the *burh*'.[96] This reading is, however, somewhat forced, and the use of *burh*s to organize enforcement posses need not indicate that such places were the only locations in which kings wished reeves to convene meetings.[97] Rather, there is a fair chance that many injunctions in royal legislation were directed not just to the king's own reeves, whether in *burh*s or elsewhere, but also to the reeves of other landholders.[98] It is,

Baker and Brookes, *Beyond the Burghal Hidage*, pp. 66–72, 89–90. See also Christie et al., ' "Have you Found Anything Interesting?" ', pp. 45–6.

[92] IV As 2; VI As 10.

[93] III Em 5. See II As 10 for a similar list of approved witnesses, who may have been those authorized to witness the low-value transactions that II As 12 implicitly permitted to take place outwith a *port*.

[94] I As Prol. On the hinterlands of *burh*s and the development of shires, see below, pp. 157–64, 171.

[95] Af 22, 34; I Ew Prol., 2; II Ew 8; VI As 10. See also V As 1.5; *VA*, cvi (p. 92). Note that *scir* need not mean 'shire': below, pp. 170, 181.

[96] II As 20–20.1. See also Maitland, *Domesday Book*, p. 185; Chadwick, *Studies*, pp. 219–20.

[97] The 'senior people pertaining to the *burh*' need not all have resided in the *burh*: below, p. 171.

[98] That persons other than the king might have reeves is apparent from Ine 63.

moreover, quite likely that local assemblies were held in many locations besides *port*s and *burh*s, whether or not kings mandated this: as we have noted, it is eminently possible for the inhabitants of a locality to gather without any royal or other external prompting, to address matters of mutual concern.[99] Nonetheless, the attempts of early tenth-century kings to limit trade outside *port*s and *burh*s suggest that they had minimal confidence in many of those through whom they might otherwise have sought to achieve the local implementation of their commands elsewhere. In this regard, it is notable that, even after Æthelstan permitted trade outside *port*s, the only reeves to figure in Edmund's list of approved witnesses were high- and *port*-reeves: it is unclear quite what a high-reeve was, but the implication is that Edmund was reluctant to rely on ordinary reeves based outside *port*s.[100] It is therefore very doubtful whether the Cerdicings were able to use reeves to regulate closely the behaviour of more than a small proportion of the population between the Channel and the Tees.

Bishops and Ealdormen

In addition to *port*s, *burh*s, and reeves, the legislation of Alfred and his successors repeatedly mentions bishops, and reveals a clear expectation that they should contribute to the implementation of royal decrees. Alfred, Æthelstan, and Edmund envisaged that bishops should prescribe punishments for pledge-breakers and homicides, and Æthelstan enjoined both bishops and reeves to order the payment of tithes.[101] Æthelstan also instructed bishops to extract fines from any reeves who neglected his commands, and this may explain why he was seemingly more willing to rely on reeves in *port*s or *burh*s than those based elsewhere: the former need not have exceeded their rural counterparts in trustworthiness, but may well have been easier for bishops to monitor.[102] Further evidence of bishops' contribution to the implementation of royal commands is provided by their being named among those responsible for two texts from Kent and London, which outline arrangements to give local effect to Æthelstan's legislation.[103] These assorted references are collectively significant, since bishops would have had more than just

---

[99] Above, pp. 102–3.

[100] III Em 5. On high-reeves, see above, p. 61 and n. 62. Legal texts from both the tenth and eleventh centuries frequently prescribe penalties for reeves who disobeyed orders, took bribes, or were complicit in theft, which implies that many were far from reliable: II Ew 2, 8; I As 4; As Alm 2; II As 3.2, 25–25.1; III As 7.3; IV As 7; V As 1.2–1.3; VI As 8.4, 11; III Em 7.2; IV Eg 13.1; IV Atr 7.3; VII Atr 6.3; II Cn 8.2, 69.2. See also Wulfstan of York, *Institutes of Polity*, ed. K. Jost, *Die «Institutes of Polity, Civil and Ecclesiastical». Ein Werk Erzbischof Wulfstans von York* (Bern, 1959), pp. 81–2.

[101] Af 1.2; I As 1; II As 26–26.1; II Em 4. See also VI As 12.2. Bishops remained important in the attempts of Edgar and later kings to enforce their will: below, pp. 172–3.

[102] As Alm 2; II As 25–25.1. The seats of some bishoprics were in places that may not have been regarded as *burh*s or *port*s (e.g. Crediton, Dorchester-on-Thames, and Sherborne), but bishops would still probably have been more able to oversee those reeves who were based in a limited number of *port*s or *burh*s than others scattered throughout their dioceses. Note, however, that the apparent limitation of minting to *port*s or *burh*s quite probably did not result in its being under a high level of royal control before the very end of Edgar's reign: below, pp. 130–40.

[103] III As Prolog; VI As Prolog; below, pp. 113–15.

moral authority with which to enforce their will, and potentially that of the king: the extensive lands of many episcopal sees would have enabled them to support substantial armed retinues.[104] Indeed, Bishop Theodred of London bequeathed an unnamed mid-tenth-century king his four best horses, his two best swords, four shields, and four spears.[105] It is likely that bishops used (as well as possessed) such war gear: since there are references to them leading armies or dying in battle both during the ninth century and in (and after) the reign of Æthelred II, it is probable that they also acted as military commanders in the intervening period.[106] The coercive power of early tenth-century bishops need not, however, only have been deployed on the battlefield: they would also have been able to force reeves and other individuals to comply with the Cerdicings' demands.

As with *ports* and *burhs*, geographical variation is important when considering the role of bishops in the implementation of royal commands. We have already seen that by the mid-tenth century the Cerdicings had closer ties to bishops between the Channel and the Tees than further north or in Wales: this is reflected both in royal influence over episcopal appointments, and in bishops' attendance at assemblies.[107] There was, however, no stark dichotomy between the area that would be covered by Domesday and the rest of the island. In the first place, Archbishop Wulfstan I of York was anything but a pliant tool of the Cerdicings.[108] There were, moreover, wide variations in the size of dioceses. From sometime during Edward the Elder's reign onwards, those south of the Thames were all fairly small, being no bigger than a couple of shires. The dioceses of Hereford and Worcester were comparable to this in scale, but that of Lichfield stretched across the whole of north-west Mercia. Those of York and Dorchester-on-Thames were even bigger, the latter covering much or all of the East Midlands. In East Anglia, the bishopric of Elmham disappeared during the viking attacks, and there is no evidence that it was re-established before the 950s; in the first half of the tenth century, the whole of East Anglia may at least notionally have been within the see of London.[109] The diocesan structure of the land between the Channel and the Tees was thus highly uneven, and the bishops of the larger sees are unlikely to have been able to enforce royal orders consistently at a local level across the areas for which they were responsible.

[104] On bishoprics' landed endowments, see M. F. Giandrea, *Episcopal Culture in Late Anglo-Saxon England* (Woodbridge, 2007), pp. 124–55, with comments on bishops' military activities at 35–6, 67–8.
[105] S 1526. See also S 1492.
[106] *ASC* ABCDE 825, 836, 845, 871, CDE 992, 1016, D 1051, CD 1056.
[107] Above, pp. 57, 66, 67–8.   [108] Above, pp. 32, 59, 67–8.
[109] For maps, see Hill, *Atlas*, p. 148. On the division of the West Saxon sees during Edward the Elder's reign, see N. Brooks, *The Early History of the Church of Canterbury: Christ Church from 597 to 1066* (Leicester, 1984), pp. 210–13; A. R. Rumble, 'Edward the Elder and the Churches of Winchester and Wessex', in Higham and Hill (eds), *Edward the Elder*, pp. 238–44. From at least 953 until at least 1011, there was at times a Bishop of Lindsey, which implies at least intermittent diminutions in the size of the diocese of Dorchester-on-Thames: P. H. Sawyer, *Anglo-Saxon Lincolnshire* (Lincoln, 1998), pp. 150–2, 238. On East Anglia, see L. Marten, 'The Shiring of East Anglia: An Alternative Hypothesis', *Historical Research*, 81 (2008), pp. 5–6.

The evidence for ealdormen is thinner than for bishops, but some rather similar considerations apply. Like bishops, ealdormen appear to have led armies, and probably had sufficient wealth to support large numbers of warriors themselves. Indeed, Lantfred of Winchester, who wrote in the early 970s, alluded to one of Edgar's ealdormen travelling with a sizeable retinue 'as is the custom among the Anglo-Saxons [*Anglosaxonum*]'.[110] Ealdormen at least sometimes acted on kings' behalf at a local level: we glimpsed one doing so in the Sunbury case, in which Ealdorman Byrhtferth first demanded that a man deemed guilty of theft pay Eadred the value of his (the thief's) life, and then declared at least one of his estates forfeit when he failed to do so.[111] There are a handful of references to ealdormen in Alfred's legislation, which allocated them compensation payments for various infractions, and envisaged that they might preside at meetings, assist victims of wrongdoing in besieging their adversaries, and authorize people to go from one district ('boldgetale') to another. Any lord who received someone who had moved without the appropriate permission was liable to pay 60 shillings to the king in the district ('scire') that the person had left, and the same amount in the district into which he (or presumably she) had come.[112] If all 120 shillings actually went to the king, this division would seem rather odd: it suggests that in each of the two districts a proportion of the payment went to some other party, probably the ealdorman, presumably reflecting that he was responsible for extracting the fine, and would be more likely to do so if permitted to take a cut.[113] In the extant legislation of the decades after Alfred's death, however,

---

[110] As with bishops, the evidence comes from the ninth century and then the late tenth and later, but it is likely that ealdormen acted as military leaders in the interim: *ASC* ABCDE 802, 840, 845, 851, 853, 860, 871, ACDE 991, CDE 992, 1003, 1015, 1016, DE 1051, E 1052, CD 1054, 1055, DE 1063, CDE 1066; Lantfred of Winchester, *Translatio et Miracvla S. Swithvni*, xxxi, ed. and trans. M. Lapidge, *The Cult of St Swithun* (Oxford, 2003), pp. 318–20. For discussion, see N. Banton, 'Ealdormen and Earls in England from the Reign of King Alfred to the Reign of King Æthelred II' (D.Phil. thesis, University of Oxford, 1981), pp. 17–24; S. Baxter, 'The Earls of Mercia and their Commended Men in the Mid Eleventh Century', *ANS*, 23 (2001), pp. 23–46 especially 29–31; S. Baxter, *The Earls of Mercia: Lordship and Power in Late Anglo-Saxon England* (Oxford, 2007), pp. 79–89.

[111] S 1447; above, p. 72. That the payment was due to the king is apparent from a comment made by a brother of the alleged wrongdoer.

[112] Af 3, 15, 37–37.1, 38–38.1, 40, 42.3. Compensation payments for ealdormen were often equal to those due to bishops, which suggests that they were in some sense secular and spiritual equivalents, and in this regard note also Norðleod 3. For ealdormen presiding at meetings, see too *VA*, cvi (p. 92). The nature, frequency, and regularity of the meetings at which ealdormen presided are uncertain, as is the meaning in this context of *scir*, which could refer to districts of many sizes and kinds: below, pp. 170, 181.

[113] It may be that ealdormen already received a third of many royal revenues, as many earls did by the time of Domesday: Banton, 'Ealdormen and Earls', pp. 30–3; Baxter, *Earls*, pp. 89–97, both of whom are inclined to see this practice as emulation of Frankish precedent. They may well be correct, but it is worth noting that early Irish (and later Welsh) legal texts refer to a person who assisted another in enforcing a right receiving a third of the proceeds: this raises the possibility that the third-share's origins may not have been specifically Frankish. The parallel is not exact, however, since the Irish (and Welsh) texts envisage the enforcer being a powerful lord (or king) who aided a subordinate, rather than a subordinate to whom the collection of dues was delegated. See D. A. Binchy, *Celtic and Anglo-Saxon Kingship* (Oxford, 1970), pp. 18–19, 22; D. Jenkins and M. E. Owen, 'Glossary', in D. Jenkins and M. E. Owen (eds), *The Welsh Law of Women* (Cardiff, 1980), p. 219; F. Kelly, *A Guide to Early Irish Law* (Dublin, 1988), p. 126; T. M. Charles-Edwards, 'Celtic Kings: "Priestly Vegetables"?',

ealdormen hardly appear. Æthelstan stated that they could grant fugitive thieves three days' respite, and enjoined them to pay tithes and obey royal commands, but otherwise they go unmentioned until Edgar ordered that shire meetings be held in the presence of an ealdorman and a bishop.[114] The paucity of evidence means that little can be said about the functions of ealdormen in the period from Alfred to Edgar, and their responsibilities may indeed not have been closely defined. Whatever it was that kings wanted ealdormen to do, however, the latter were not always reliable; thus, for example, a *dux* named Wulfhere suffered forfeiture for breaching an oath to Alfred, as we saw in the previous chapter.[115] Moreover, while there is some reason to think that in the south ninth-century ealdormen may well have had only one shire each, tenth-century ealdordoms appear to have stretched across the equivalent of several shires: as with the bishops of large dioceses, this probably meant that many an ealdorman would have been unable to maintain a sufficiently frequent personal presence throughout his area of responsibility to monitor compliance with the king's commands closely.[116]

Local Policing Arrangements

While we can infer that reeves, bishops, and ealdormen were able to advance (or obstruct) royal interests, at least in particular localities, the foregoing arguments suggest that these figures are unlikely to have enabled late ninth- and early tenth-century kings to regulate systematically the actions of ordinary people, especially away from *ports* or *burhs*. It is nonetheless entirely possible that the Cerdicings obtained a fair degree of compliance with their demands that tough action be taken against thieves, since such calls would probably have been popular with the great majority of those who had enough possessions to be at risk of theft. In this regard, it should be recalled that, as elsewhere in early medieval Europe, the inhabitants of many localities in lowland Britain are quite likely to have held periodic gatherings, and cooperated on a variety of matters, without necessarily being told to do so by anyone from outside the area in question.[117] Local groups of this sort may well have made arrangements for the pursuit of thieves since long before the tenth century, or at least have required only minimal encouragement from kings to add policing to such activities as they already undertook collectively. After all, people can (and in some places still do) form 'neighbourhood watch' groups to apprehend and punish persons whom they identify as thieves, without necessarily

in Baxter et al. (eds), *Early Medieval Studies*, p. 69. For Norwegian and Hungarian parallels, which could represent borrowings from English and Frankish practices respectively, see Snorri Sturluson, *Heimskringla*, ed. F. Jónsson (4 vols, Copenhagen, 1893–1901), i, 104; below, pp. 242, 243.

[114] I As Prol.; IV As 6.2; VI As 11; III Eg 5.1–5.2. On shire meetings, see below, pp. 165–72.

[115] S 362; above, p. 50. See also *VA*, xii (pp. 9–10); *ASC* CDE 992, 1002, 1003, 1015, 1016.

[116] Banton, 'Ealdormen and Earls', especially pp. 62, 93–5, 198–9, 368–9. For the apparent link between ealdormen and southern shires in the ninth century, see *ASC* ABCDE 802, 840, 845, 851, 853, 860, ABCD 896, 897, 900; above, p. 99 and n. 54.

[117] Above, pp. 102–3.

needing any external prompt to do so.[118] Except in unevenly distributed *port*s or *burh*s, Edward the Elder and Æthelstan may well have had little by way of a systematic administrative framework with which to organize how thieves were identified, detained, and punished, but this need not imply that these kings' calls for a crackdown on theft were futile: royal injunctions could have prompted a variety of local groups to establish, reinforce, or modify their own arrangements to catch wrongdoers.

That no royal impetus was necessarily required for such initiatives is indicated by a decree issued by the West Frankish king Carloman II in 884, which banned locally organized policing groups, presumably for fear that they might be turned to purposes prejudicial to the existing social hierarchy.[119] There is, by contrast, no sign that the Cerdicings sought to prohibit thief-catching associations, and Æthelstan appears to have encouraged them, at least in cases where such groups were directed by magnates: two texts from his reign suggest that he called on the more important inhabitants of individual localities to take responsibility for working out much of the detail about how his commands might be implemented.[120] One of these texts runs in the name of the bishops and thegns of Kent, and is explicitly addressed to the king. It expresses enthusiasm for what Æthelstan had decreed at Grately, Faversham, and 'in western parts' (i.e. at Exeter), and states that everyone should act as surety for his (or, conceivably, her) own subordinates, or delegate this responsibility to a reliable reeve. It concludes with a request that Æthelstan prescribe alterations to it, if he judged that it contained too much or too little.[121] The other text declares itself to be a set of ordinances established 'in our peace guilds' by the bishops and reeves pertaining to London, as a supplement ('ecan') to what had been decreed at Grately, Exeter, and Thunderfield. While the text is not addressed to Æthelstan, the authors appear to have envisaged that its content would be communicated to him, since there is a statement that any additions that he recommended would be gladly accepted. The regulations describe an insurance scheme to compensate any guild member whose possessions were stolen, coupled with a requirement to cooperate in the pursuit of thieves; members were to be placed into groups of 100 persons, subdivided into tens, for the organization of their financial and pursuit obligations. The text also refers, in what appears to be an addendum, to Æthelstan having declared that pledges should be exacted by reeves in their districts of responsibility.[122]

---

[118] A. Reynolds, *Anglo-Saxon Deviant Burial Customs* (Oxford, 2009) demonstrates that there are many cases where the remains of what appear to be executed corpses date to early in the Anglo-Saxon period. Reynolds tends to assume that execution burials reflect royal activity, but capital sentences need not always have been imposed by kings or their agents.

[119] *CRF*, no. 287 (c. 14). See also *Annales de Saint-Bertin*, 859 (p. 80).

[120] These texts are discussed in greater detail by L. Roach, 'Law Codes and Legal Norms in Later Anglo-Saxon England', *Historical Research*, 86 (2013), pp. 465–86. See also D. Pratt, 'Written Law and the Communication of Authority in Tenth-Century England', in D. Rollason, C. Leyser, and H. Williams (eds), *England and the Continent in the Tenth Century: Studies in Honour of Wilhelm Levison (1876–1947)* (Turnhout, 2010), pp. 331–50.

[121] III As.

[122] VI As. The reference to bishops in the plural can be explained in various ways: it could reflect that the Bishop of London had one or more auxiliary bishops, that more than one bishop who held

The Kent and London texts both set out arrangements to implement the calls for action against thieves that Æthelstan had made at Grately and elsewhere, and they envisaged that the king might review their content. These general similarities suggest that the two sets of regulations were probably not spontaneous local initiatives, but responses to a royal instruction or invitation to draw up procedures along such lines. The texts do, however, reveal that Æthelstan left local notables considerable latitude to decide how best to go about countering theft: the Kent document gives no hint of anything resembling the groups of ten and 100 prescribed in London, and it is clear that the king had not dictated the content of either text, since both anticipate that he might propose revisions. These two sets of regulations thus suggest that Æthelstan ordered that there be a crackdown on theft, and stipulated certain ways in which this could or should be done, but that such efforts as were made to implement the objective in practice relied less on any standardized system than on a patchwork of locally devised arrangements. This is all the more striking when one notes that Kent and London were probably among the places where Æthelstan would have had most scope to dictate what should happen at a local level. Surviving coins suggest that Kent had at least four *burh*s or *port*s, and Canterbury and Rochester made it unique in being a shire with more than one bishopric.[123] London was likewise the seat of an episcopal see, and the 'common stock' and *Chronicle* continuations suggest that it was already a place of unusual importance to the Cerdicings, even though it was probably rather less commercially significant than it would become by the end of the tenth century.[124] There is no way to ascertain how (if at all) the inhabitants of other areas responded to royal calls for action against thieves, but, given that Kent and London were locations in which Æthelstan was relatively powerful, it is likely that local notables elsewhere had at least as much discretion as the magnates of these places to decide how (and indeed whether) to give effect to his demands.[125] We can only guess at the extent to which measures prescribed by leading figures in Kent, London, and perhaps other places resulted in a diminution in theft, but it should not be assumed that locally devised procedures were ineffective. Indeed, arrangements agreed by the very people who would have to implement them may often have achieved more than any standardized system that a king could have tried to impose. Nonetheless,

---

land in London (see S 346 for a grant there in favour of the Bishop of Worcester) was involved, or that the arrangements described were intended to apply in some areas outwith the diocese of London. The use of the plural in the Kent text is unsurprising, since Kent included both Canterbury and Rochester.

[123] Blunt, 'Coinage of Athelstan', pp. 42–3, 64–5, 69, 76, 77–8; Hill, *Atlas*, p. 148.

[124] *ASC* ABCDE 886, DE 910, ABCD 911; T. Dyson, 'King Alfred and the Restoration of London', *London Journal*, 15 (1990), pp. 99–110; R. Naismith, 'London and its Mint, *c.*880–1066: A Preliminary Survey', *BNJ*, 83 (2013), pp. 44–74.

[125] Roach, 'Law Codes', especially pp. 472–4 argues that IV As constitutes a third text concerned with applying Æthelstan's demands in some particular (unidentified) locality. This may well be correct, although the document could alternatively be a third-person version of an ordinance that the king himself had issued. Pratt, 'Written Law', pp. 345–8 treats the *Ordinance concerning the Dunsæte* as another response to Æthelstan's legislation, but see G. Molyneaux, 'The *Ordinance concerning the Dunsæte* and the Anglo-Welsh Frontier in the Late Tenth and Eleventh Centuries', *ASE*, 40 (2012), pp. 249–72.

the key issue here is not the extent to which early tenth-century kings managed to curb theft, but that their efforts, whether successful or otherwise, appear to have been based on the encouragement of a series of local arrangements, rather than on a uniform administrative apparatus.

It is impossible to establish for certain that eleventh-century-style administrative arrangements did not exist prior to the second half of the tenth, but then there is very often no way to prove a negative. What the foregoing does show, however, is that kings could have been very powerful without having any particularly sophisticated administrative apparatus: it is possible to account for the known accomplishments of Edgar's predecessors without resorting to the unevidenced hypothesis that they used an ordered system of shires and hundreds or wapentakes to regulate ordinary people's lives. Rather, it appears that the Cerdicings' exploitation of peasant labour, and their campaign against theft, were both predicated on the cooperation of a range of people who were in one way or another locally powerful. This underlines the arguments of the previous chapter: the Cerdicings' position rested on their ability to constrain and mould the actions of their greater subordinates. These two chapters also highlight the likely geographical variability of the Cerdicings' domination in the late ninth and early tenth centuries: as distance from Wessex increased, there appears to have been a decrease in their grip on great potentates, a narrowing of the range of persons with whom they dealt personally, and a decline in their capacity to monitor and direct the conduct of members of the general populace. There may well have been quite marked contrasts east and west of (roughly) the dyke commonly ascribed to Offa, where a major linguistic frontier was probably mirrored by a significant difference in Cerdicing domination: unlike in Wales, there appear to have been a fair number of *port*s or *burh*s in western Mercia, and magnates from the latter area attested the Cerdicings' charters with much greater consistency than Welsh *subreguli*. Elsewhere, however, it is doubtful whether contrasts in the Cerdicings' power created a sharp dichotomy to mark any very substantial part of Britain off from the rest, since there were wide variations in the intensity of Cerdicing domination within, as well as beyond, what would become Domesday *Anglia*. Indeed, one could argue that in the decades immediately after 927 (if not 920) there were some significant common features to the Cerdicings' power all across the island. Throughout Britain, they used a mixture of patronage and coercion to secure at least a modicum of intermittent cooperation from their greater subordinates, while probably doing fairly little (even in the south) to regulate closely the lives of the general populace. By the end of the tenth century, however, the Cerdicings were using an administrative system of hundreds and wapentakes to shape significant aspects of how quite ordinary people interacted with each other in one part of Britain, the part that would be described in Domesday. There thus came to be a significant element of uniformity to their domination within this portion of the island, such that their power there was markedly different from elsewhere. The aim of the next chapter is to consider more closely when and why this shift took place.

4

Administrative Change in the Mid- to Late Tenth Century

COINS

Thus far, I have sought to show that one can account for the Cerdicings' known accomplishments between the late ninth and mid-tenth centuries without positing a neat or uniform administrative system, and that during this period there was probably not a very sharp dichotomy between their domination within what would constitute Domesday *Anglia* on the one hand, and the rest of Britain on the other. In this chapter, the focus shifts to the second half of the tenth century: I argue that it was around then that the Cerdicings implemented a series of administrative changes, the overall effect of which was to intensify their domination between the Channel and the Tees, and to mark that area off from Wales and northern Britain. My claims about the timing of these changes are in large part founded on silence. It is only from the second half of the tenth century onwards that we have clear evidence that hundreds, wapentakes, shire meetings, and sheriffs were important, and I contend that the absence or near-absence of comparable references in earlier sources reflects that previously these things were non-existent, or at least of relatively little significance to how kings ruled. While I argue that there are strong circumstantial grounds for inferring that, across the land from the Channel to the Tees, late tenth- and eleventh-century kings exercised power in ways that were in some respects quite different from those of their predecessors, arguments from silence cannot be entirely conclusive—practices and institutions may have existed earlier without being recorded, and that which was written down may not have been preserved. One particularly clear illustration of the limitations of the textual sources at our disposal is that the surviving coins reveal that a major numismatic reform was implemented towards the end of Edgar's reign, but the earliest extant reference to this is in a thirteenth-century chronicle.[1] At least as importantly, however, Edgar's coin reform underpins the argument of this chapter: since coins are plentiful both before and after the reform, it is clear that Edgar had

---

[1] Roger of Wendover, *Flores Historiarum*, ed. H. O. Coxe (5 vols, London, 1841–4), i, 416. Roger's knowledge of the reform indicates that he had a reliable, now-lost source, but his statement that the change was a response to coin-clipping is not borne out by the coins themselves. It may have been a guess based on the circumstances of his own day. Roger placed the reform in 975, but this dating is not reliable: M. Dolley, 'Roger of Wendover's Date for Eadgar's Coinage Reform', *BNJ*, 49 (1979), pp. 1–11.

both the desire and the capacity to impose numismatic uniformity in place of ear-lier diversity. This is a change that can be proved, rather than merely inferred from silence, and it underlines that major administrative reforms need not necessarily have been described in surviving written sources from the period. In light of this, we should be open to the possibility that fundamental changes were made to hun-dreds, shire meetings, and the like, notwithstanding the lack of explicit references in extant texts.

Post-Reform Coins

The establishment of uniformity in production was fundamental to Edgar's coin reform: sometime in his later years, all moneyers working between the Channel and the Tees—which is the same as saying all moneyers in Britain—began to strike coins of the design depicted on this volume's cover. Earlier in Edgar's reign, by contrast, coins of quite widely varying appearance had been struck contemporaneously in different locations, and this had also been so during the preceding decades.[2] There is no very sound basis for the now-widespread belief that the reform took place in 973, but the quantity of pre-reform coins bearing Edgar's name allows one to infer that the change was effected late in his reign.[3] Thus, even if one declines to pin the introduction of the new type to a specific year, it constitutes a clear and quite closely datable case of diversity being replaced with uniformity from the Channel to the Tees. Uniformity was especially marked in the reform issue itself: the dies used to strike the new type were almost all so similar that it seems likely that the vast major-ity were cut in one workshop.[4] Under Edgar's successors, small regional variations suggest that dies were often made in several locations, although these differences are generally detectable only by close examination, and the striking of a single type at any one time remained the norm until Stephen's reign (r. 1135–1154).[5] Following Edgar's reform, the design being struck changed every few years, but almost always

[2] R. H. M. Dolley and D. M. Metcalf, 'The Reform of the English Coinage under Eadgar', in R. H. M. Dolley (ed.), *Anglo-Saxon Coins: Studies Presented to F. M. Stenton on the Occasion of his 80th Birthday* (London, 1961), pp. 136–68; K. Jonsson, *The New Era: The Reformation of the Late Anglo-Saxon Coinage* (Stockholm, 1987).

[3] Dolley, 'Roger of Wendover's Date'; J. D. Brand, *Periodic Change of Type in the Anglo-Saxon and Norman Periods* (Rochester, 1984), pp. 9–17; Jonsson, *New Era*, pp. 83–4; I. Stewart, 'Coinage and Recoinage after Edgar's Reform', in K. Jonsson (ed.), *Studies in Late Anglo-Saxon Coinage in Memory of Bror Emil Hildebrand* (Stockholm, 1990), pp. 461–2.

[4] Jonsson, *New Era*, pp. 86–94.

[5] For the sequence of types, see D. M. Metcalf, *An Atlas of Anglo-Saxon and Norman Coin Finds, c.973–1086* (London, 1998), pp. 103–90, 307–9. Æthelred II's Second Hand, Intermediate Small Cross, Agnus Dei, and (possibly) Benediction Hand types, and a variant on Edward the Confessor's Pyramids type, were exceptional in not being minted throughout the kingdom. During the disputed succession to Cnut, some coins were struck in the name of Harold Harefoot and others in that of Harthacnut. On die variations, see Jonsson, *New Era*, pp. 86–95; M. A. S. Blackburn and S. Lyon, 'Regional Die-Production in Cnut's *Quatrefoil* Issue', in M. A. S. Blackburn (ed.), *Anglo-Saxon Mon-etary History: Essays in Memory of Michael Dolley* (Leicester, 1986), pp. 223–72; S. Lyon, 'Die-Cutting Styles in the *Last Small Cross* Issue of *c.*1009–1017 and Some Problematic East Anglian Dies and Die-Links', *BNJ*, 68 (1998), pp. 21–41; M. Allen, *Mints and Money in Medieval England* (Cambridge, 2012), pp. 115–16. For Stephen's reign, see M. A. S. Blackburn, 'Coinage and Currency', in E. King (ed.), *The Anarchy of King Stephen's Reign* (Oxford, 1994), pp. 145–205.

incorporated a stylized royal portrait, together with the reigning king's name and the title *Rex Anglorum* (frequently abbreviated).[6] Coins also invariably bore the name of the moneyer (i.e. the person who was responsible for the coin's manufacture), and the location in which he worked. As well as uniformity of output at any time, there also seems to have been something approaching uniformity within the currency circulating between the Channel and the Tees. The rarity of finds of coins struck outwith this area suggests that these were usually melted down and reminted, and most post-reform coin hoards consist of a single type, or at least a small number of chronologically close types, which implies that a large proportion of the coins in circulation was converted each time a new variety was issued.[7]

This is all well known to historians. Indeed, the evidence that kings could enforce the minting of a single design, and additionally induce the frequent conversion of a large proportion of the circulating currency into a new type, is often taken as a barometer of administrative sophistication, and used to justify maximalist interpretations of the sometimes exiguous sources for other aspects of royal activity.[8] Two significant aspects of the organization of the post-reform coinage are, however, less clear than sometimes assumed. The first problem concerns the withdrawal from circulation of earlier coins when a new type was issued. In 1961, Michael Dolley and Michael Metcalf argued that Edgar and his successors demanded that all coins be reminted each time a new design was issued, and Dolley in particular came to believe that these recoinages were initially conducted at regular six-yearly intervals.[9] Few if any numismatists would now adhere to Dolley's sexennial theory, however, and there is no particular reason to infer that Edgar planned that his reform be repeated frequently.[10] More importantly, the presence of coins of Æthelred and Cnut in certain hoards deposited in or after the reign of Edward the Confessor indicates that, at least from the time of Æthelred, many coins were not reminted when a new type was introduced.[11] In light of this, Ian Stewart has hypothesized that there may have been no general prohibition on the

---

[6] Metcalf, *Atlas*, pp. 307–9. Æthelred's short-lived Agnus Dei type was exceptional in not bearing a royal portrait.

[7] Metcalf, *Atlas*, pp. 85–9; B. Cook, 'Foreign Coins in Medieval England', in L. Travaini (ed.), *Moneta locale, moneta straniera. Italia ed Europa XI–XV secolo* (Milan, 1999), pp. 236–8, 269–70; Allen, *Mints*, pp. 35–40, 346–9, 515–19. The presence of several types is more common in hoards concealed after the 1040s.

[8] J. Campbell, 'Observations on English Government from the Tenth to the Twelfth Century', *TRHS*, 5th series, 25 (1975), pp. 39–54, reprinted in his *Essays in Anglo-Saxon History* (London, 1986), pp. 155–6; J. Campbell, 'The Significance of the Anglo-Norman State in the Administrative History of Western Europe', in W. Paravicini and K. F. Werner (eds), *Histoire comparée de l'administration (IVᵉ–XVIIIᵉ siècles)* (Munich, 1980), pp. 117–34, reprinted in his *Essays*, pp. 186–8; S. Keynes, *The Diplomas of King Æthelred 'the Unready', 978–1016: A Study in their Use as Historical Evidence* (Cambridge, 1980), p. 196; H. R. Loyn, 'Progress in Anglo-Saxon Monetary History', in Blackburn (ed.), *Anglo-Saxon Monetary History*, p. 10; A. Williams, *Kingship and Government in Pre-Conquest England, c.500–1066* (Basingstoke, 1999), p. 96.

[9] Dolley and Metcalf, 'Reform', pp. 152–8; S. Lyon, 'Dr Michael Dolley, MRIA, FSA', *BNJ*, 52 (1982), pp. 268–9.

[10] The most devastating assault on the sexennial theory (and on Dolley's character) is Brand, *Periodic Change*. See also Stewart, 'Coinage and Recoinage', pp. 462–3, 471–80.

[11] Allen, *Mints*, pp. 516–19.

use of old coins, and that the preponderance in many hoards of a single type per-haps arose because kings themselves accepted payment only in the current issue.[12] This would have forced a significant degree of reminting, but the replacement of previous types would have been less complete and less rapid than Dolley and Met-calf envisaged. In response, Metcalf argues that hoards with long age structures are unlikely to represent the currency in circulation at the time of concealment: had they done so, natural wastage would probably have caused older types to be poorly represented relative to recent ones, but this is not always the case. Metcalf therefore interprets these caches as savings hoards, accumulated over decades, and infers that the currency in circulation was largely homogeneous, with obsolete types being retained only for their intrinsic metal value.[13] The hypothesis that relative homo-geneity within the circulating currency primarily arose from a need to pay royal dues in the latest issue would require one to postulate that kings had a very domin-ant role within the cash economy; this is not out of the question, but nor can it be safely assumed, especially prior to the introduction of the *heregeld* (army-tax) in 1012.[14] Although there can be no certainty, it is likely that Edgar and his succes-sors did not merely insist that they be paid in coins of the current type, but also sought (with partial success) to ban the use of old coins in other transactions: the plausibility of this interpretation is strengthened when one notes that this is what earlier Frankish kings had demanded.[15]

The second major area of uncertainty concerns the intrinsic values of post-reform coins. There were substantial variations in the median weights of the types issued consecutively after Edgar's reform.[16] At least in part, this was probably because kings sometimes ordered a change in weight at the same time as a change in design: the suspicion that they did so is strengthened by the late tenth- or early eleventh-century Old English *Legend of the Seven Sleepers*, whose anonymous writer assumed that the introduction of new coin dies might be accompanied by a weight adjustment.[17] There were, however, also manifold weight variations within individual types: the median weights of coins struck in different places varied for any given type, multiple weight standards were used in certain locations, and, in many (but by no means all) periods and places, weights were progressively reduced over the course of an issue.[18] In addition, there was at times a modicum of diversity

---

[12] Stewart, 'Coinage and Recoinage', especially pp. 463–8, developing a suggestion of P. Grierson, 'Numismatics and the Historian', *NC*, 2 (1962), pp. viii–xiv.

[13] Metcalf, *Atlas*, pp. 94–9. See also Allen, *Mints*, pp. 38–9.

[14] On the *heregeld*, see below, p. 197.

[15] *CRF*, nos. 90 (c. 9), 150 (c. 20), 273 (cc. 10–11, 15–16).

[16] H. B. A. Petersson, *Anglo-Saxon Currency: King Edgar's Reform to the Norman Conquest* (Lund, 1969); S. Lyon, 'Variations in Currency in Late Anglo-Saxon England', in R. A. G. Carson (ed.), *Mints, Dies and Currency: Essays Dedicated to the Memory of Albert Baldwin* (London, 1971), pp. 101–20; H. B. A. Petersson, 'Coins and Weights: Late Anglo-Saxon Pennies and Mints, c.973–1066', in Jonsson (ed.), *Studies*, pp. 207–433.

[17] *The Anonymous Old English Legend of the Seven Sleepers*, ed. H. Magennis (Durham, 1994), p. 47; D. Whitelock, 'The Numismatic Interest of an Old English Version of the Legend of the Seven Sleepers', in Dolley (ed.), *Anglo-Saxon Coins*, pp. 188–94; C. Cubitt, ' "As the Lawbook Teaches": Reeves, Lawbooks and Urban Life in the Anonymous Old English Legend of the Seven Sleepers', *EHR*, 124 (2009), pp. 1025–7.

[18] Jonsson, *New Era*, pp. 95–100; Petersson, 'Coins and Weights'; Metcalf, *Atlas*, pp. 56–69.

in the alloys used: most post-reform coins contained over 90 per cent silver, but there was some sporadic debasement in the first half of the eleventh century, with a significant minority of coins dipping below this fineness threshold.[19] Given that it appears that within the English kingdom coins were usually traded on the basis of their face value, manipulation of weights and metal content would have been a source of profit for those who controlled minting.[20] Some adjustments may have been made for kings' advantage, but it is doubtful whether royal instructions were the principal cause of the variations in intrinsic values: that unauthorized debasement took place is suggested by legislative strictures against those who struck impure coins, or paid bribes to have good coins converted into ones defective in weight or fineness.[21] Moreover, even if many of the variations were prescribed or explicitly permitted by kings, the existence of widely varying standards would probably have impeded the detection of persons who manipulated intrinsic values for their own advantage. The idea that variations in coins' intrinsic values were predominantly attributable to some meticulous royal scheme ought therefore to be treated with considerable caution.

In view of these uncertainties, historians should temper their wonderment at the coinage of Edgar and his successors, and be more careful about building arguments on the premise that minting was under very close royal control. Nonetheless, there remains a marked contrast with the situation in tenth- and eleventh-century West Frankia, where coins were often struck anonymously or in the names of deceased kings, and occasionally in the names of non-royal persons: that the coins produced in the names of Edgar and his successors were subject to a significant level of central regulation is amply demonstrated by the near uniformity of design within each issue, and the at least partial withdrawal from circulation of previous types.[22] It is, moreover, noteworthy that Edgar's reform took place in the context of what appears to have been a very substantial increase in the volume of the English currency, possibly caused in large part by an influx of silver from mines discovered in Germany in the 960s.[23] That the number of coins in circulation was growing

---

[19] D. M. Metcalf and J. P. Northover, 'Interpreting the Alloy of the Later Anglo-Saxon Coinage', *BNJ*, 56 (1986), pp. 35–63; R. J. Eaglen and R. Grayburn, 'Gouged Reverse Dies in the Quatrefoil Issue of Cnut', *BNJ*, 70 (2000), pp. 22–6; D. M. Metcalf and J. P. Northover, 'Sporadic Debasement in the English Coinage, *c*.1009–1052', *NC*, 162 (2002), pp. 217–36.

[20] Metcalf, *Atlas*, pp. 56–69.

[21] III Atr 8–8.2; IV Atr 5–9.3; Cn 1018 20–20.2; II Cn 8–8.2. Persons who induced moneyers to debase coins would presumably have received more coins than they handed in, thus gaining if others accepted their coins at face value. On the dates of different parts of IV Atr, see M. K. Lawson, *Cnut: England's Viking King* (Stroud, 2004), pp. 186–7; D. Keene, 'Text, Visualisation and Politics: London, 1150–1250', *TRHS*, 6th series, 18 (2008), pp. 93–4.

[22] On West Frankish coins, see J. Lafaurie, 'Numismatique. Des Carolingiens aux Capétiens', *Cahiers de civilisation médiévale*, 13 (1970), pp. 132–7; F. Dumas, 'Le début de l'époque féodale en France d'après les monnaies', *Cercle d'études numismatiques*, 10 (1973), pp. 65–77; P. Grierson and M. A. S. Blackburn, *Medieval European Coinage with a Catalogue of the Coins in the Fitzwilliam Museum, Cambridge. I: The Early Middle Ages (5th–10th Centuries)* (Cambridge, 1986), pp. 243–9; P. Spufford, *Money and its Use in Medieval Europe* (Cambridge, 1988), pp. 55–60.

[23] R. Naismith, 'The English Monetary Economy, *c*.973–1100: The Contribution of Single-Finds', *Economic History Review*, 66 (2013), pp. 201–12, 219–20. See also Allen, *Mints*, pp. 252–3; P. H. Sawyer, *The Wealth of Anglo-Saxon England* (Oxford, 2013), pp. 98–105; R. Naismith, 'The Social Significance of Monetization in the Early Middle Ages', *P&P*, 223 (2014), pp. 18–19. Sawyer

rapidly makes it all the more striking that the Cerdicings were able to impose and maintain a significant measure of numismatic uniformity.

There is no direct written evidence for how Edgar and his successors implemented recoinages, and in making guesses about the means by which they did so we should distinguish relative uniformity of production from relative uniformity in circulating currency. The first required the cooperation of moneyers, of whom around 120 are known at the time of Edgar's reform.[24] Securing their compliance may well have been far from straightforward, especially with regard to standards of fineness and weight, but would have been facilitated by the fact that moneyers only worked in a few dozen locations, most (if not all) of which would probably have been regarded as *port*s or *burh*s. We saw in the previous chapter that early tenth-century kings probably had somewhat more reliable means to regulate what went on in such places than elsewhere, and this suggests a hypothesis about how Edgar could have established relative uniformity in production: he may well have managed to use a fairly well-established network of reeves based in *port*s and *burh*s to compel moneyers to adhere to prescribed standards, at least in coin design.[25]

Achieving a semblance of uniformity in the circulating currency probably represented a greater challenge: if, as seems likely, Edgar and his successors sought to ban the use of obsolete coins in all transactions, this would have required the compliance of many thousands of coin-users, including people who lived far from *port*s or *burh*s, and in regions well outside the Cerdicings' heartlands.[26] The key to understanding how late tenth- and eleventh-century kings forced the withdrawal of old coins may be provided by the legislation that Edgar issued at an unidentified location called *Wihtbordesstan*, probably sometime between 966 and his death in 975.[27] The ordinance declares that

hypothesizes that English traders acquired German silver in exchange for wool and other goods, but there is little contemporary evidence to indicate what commodities the English exported, the record of London tolls that Sawyer cites may date from the twelfth century (Keene, 'Text, Visualisation and Politics', pp. 93–4), and massive imports of German silver are conjectural. New silver supplies could, for example, also have been obtained by melting down plate: *VSÆ*, xxix (p. 44). Note too that, while the volume of coins in circulation appears to have been markedly greater in the years between Edgar's reform and *c*.1100 than between *c*.880 and the reform, it was lower than in the early Anglo-Saxon period.

[24] K. Jonsson and G. van der Meer, 'Mints and Moneyers, *c*.973–1066', in Jonsson (ed.), *Studies*, pp. 54–119. For instructions relating to a ninth-century West Frankish recoinage, see *CRF*, no. 273 (especially cc. 10–19); below, pp. 133–4.

[25] Above, pp. 106–9.

[26] On the extent of coin use, see Metcalf, *Atlas*, especially pp. 100–1; R. Naismith, *Money and Power in Anglo-Saxon England: The Southern English Kingdoms, 757–865* (Cambridge, 2012), pp. 252–92; Naismith, 'English Monetary Economy'.

[27] The date is based on the reference to Earl Oslac as one of those responsible for the implementation of the decrees, since the D and E texts of the *Chronicle* give 966 as the year in which he 'obtained the ealdordom': IV Eg 15; *ASC* DE 966. There are some grounds for positing a date in the 970s: N. Banton, 'Monastic Reform and the Unification of Tenth-Century England', *Studies in Church History*, 18 (1982), p. 79; P. Wormald, *The Making of English Law: King Alfred to the Twelfth Century. Volume I: Legislation and its Limits* (Oxford, 1999), pp. 441–2; S. Keynes, 'Edgar, *rex admirabilis*', in D. Scragg (ed.), *Edgar, King of the English 959–975: New Interpretations* (Woodbridge, 2008), pp. 11–12 and n. 41. See also D. Whitelock, 'The Dealings of the Kings of England with Northumbria in the Tenth and Eleventh Centuries', in P. Clemoes (ed.), *The Anglo-Saxons: Studies in Some Aspects of their History and Culture Presented to Bruce Dickins* (London, 1959), pp. 77–8; below, pp. 178–9. Oslac

'Danes' should generally be permitted to determine their own laws, but also represents the first known case of a Cerdicing issuing legislation that explicitly covered areas of Scandinavian settlement, since it demands that one particular measure apply to all people, 'English and Danes and Britons'. In order to impede the sale of stolen goods, at least twelve sworn witnesses were to be appointed in each *burh*, hundred, or wapentake (*wæpengetac*), and all transactions were to be conducted in the presence of two or three such persons.[28] At the time of Domesday and after, the phenomena denoted by the words 'hundred' and 'wapentake' were clearly equivalent, and both terms were occasionally used in relation to the same district.[29] Rather than indicating a major substantive contrast between hundreds and wapentakes, the semantic distinction reflected that areas in which there had been considerable Scandinavian settlement had somewhat different vocabulary to regions in which there had been little or none. It appears, moreover, that the two terms were already interchangeable when the *Wihtbordesstan* ordinance was issued: when demanding that all transactions be conducted in the presence of nominated witnesses, the text in one place uses the formulation 'either in a *burh* or in a wapentake', and in another 'either in a *burh* or in a hundred'.[30]

This decree was to be observed in every part of Edgar's *anweald*, which means 'power' or 'authority', or (by extension) the area in which power or authority is enjoyed.[31] Edgar's use of the word is, however, somewhat ambiguous: he declared that this provision should apply 'in common to all of us who dwell in these islands', but his orders can hardly have taken effect throughout Britain, since even after the end of the Anglo-Saxon period there were neither hundreds nor wapentakes in Wales and north of the Ribble and the Tees.[32] It can, however, be inferred that Edgar envisaged that the measures should be implemented between the Humber and the Tees: he demanded that their observance be promoted by Earl Oslac 'and all the army [*here*] dwelling in his ealdordom', and we know from two early

appears as *dux* in a charter of 963 (S 716), but the 966 annal implies that it was only then that he became the principal lay potentate at York.

[28] IV Eg 2.1–13.1. That IV Eg 5 applied to wapentakes as well as hundreds is implicit in IV Eg 6. On 'Danes', see above, pp. 44–5.

[29] F. M. Stenton, *Anglo-Saxon England*, 3rd edn (Oxford, 1971), p. 505. For the equivalence of the terms, see also *Leges Edwardi Confessoris*, 30.1, 31.1, ed. and trans. B. R. O'Brien, *God's Peace and King's Peace: The Laws of Edward the Confessor* (Philadelphia, PA, 1999), pp. 188–90. On the term 'wapentake', see below, pp. 150–1.

[30] IV Eg 6, 10.

[31] IV Eg 2.2; A. Cameron, A. C. Amos, and A. diP. Healey et al., *Dictionary of Old English* (Toronto, 1986–), s.v. 'anweald', consulted at <http://tapor.library.utoronto.ca/doe/> (accessed 9 October 2014).

[32] IV Eg 14.2. One possible exception is Sadberge wapentake, immediately north of the Tees, which is first mentioned in 1185 but may have been regarded as a wapentake at an earlier date: O. S. Anderson, *The English Hundred-Names* (3 vols, Lund, 1934–9), i, 1. Domesday describes two hundreds (Ati's Cross and Exestan) in the far north-east of modern-day Wales, but at the time these seem to have been within Cheshire. The Cheshire folios also briefly mention Arwystli (in central Wales), and call it a hundred, but the scribe was probably just using a familiar term in place of Welsh *cantref*. See *DB*, i, 268d–269b; F. Thorn, 'Hundreds and Wapentakes', in A. Williams and R. W. H. Erskine (eds), *The Cheshire Domesday* (London, 1991), pp. 34–5.

twelfth-century Durham texts that Oslac wielded power at York, while a Bamburgh potentate had charge of the land beyond either the Tees or the Tyne.[33] Edgar also commanded that written copies of the decrees be distributed by Ealdormen Ælfhere and Æthelwine, who can be associated with Mercia and East Anglia respectively, and the emphasis on the universality of its witnessing provisions allows us to infer that these were to apply throughout the land from the Channel to the Tees.[34] It thus appears that phenomena known as hundreds or wapentakes existed across this area by the end of Edgar's reign, and that they could be used for the monitoring of transactions. This provides a potential way to explain how Edgar could have secured the withdrawal from circulation of obsolete coins: as part of his numismatic reform, he may have ordered that the nominated witnesses in each *burh*, hundred, and wapentake check that those engaging in trade used only coins of the current type.[35]

Pre-Reform Coins

While the means by which late tenth- and eleventh-century kings enforced relative uniformity are uncertain, it is clear that the coinage of Edgar and his successors was markedly different from what had gone before. This is not to say that the reformed coinage was innovatory in all respects. There seems to have been a significant degree of continuity in personnel, since many of the moneyers named on Edgar's early coins likewise appear after the reform.[36] Coins may well have been produced in more locations than before, but the reform entailed no major change in the distribution of places with one or more moneyers: the striking of coins at York and certain Southumbrian locations, but nowhere else in Britain, goes back to very early in the Anglo-Saxon period, and the number of places with moneyers had increased progressively during the late ninth and early tenth centuries.[37] Another

---

[33] IV Eg 15; *Historia Regum*, ed. T. Arnold, *Symeonis Monachi Opera Omnia* (RS, 75, 2 vols, London, 1882–5), ii, 197; *De primo Saxonum adventu*, ed. Arnold, *Symeonis Monachi Opera Omnia*, ii, 382.

[34] IV Eg 15.1; A. Williams, '*Princeps Merciorum gentis*: The Family, Career and Connections of Ælfhere, Ealdorman of Mercia, 956–83', *ASE*, 10 (1982), pp. 143–72; C. Hart, *The Danelaw* (London, 1992), pp. 591–8. The text does not stipulate any arrangements for its distribution south of the Thames, and Edgar may have issued a complementary ordinance for that region: Wormald, *Making*, pp. 125–8, 369–70.

[35] That the *Wihtbordesstan* decrees say nothing about monitoring coins need not undermine this hypothesis, since the legislation may antedate the numismatic reform.

[36] Jonsson, *New Era*, pp. 119–80. More generally, R. Naismith, 'Prelude to Reform: Tenth-Century English Coinage in Perspective', in R. Naismith, M. Allen, and E. Screen (eds), *Early Medieval Monetary History: Studies in Memory of Mark Blackburn* (Farnham, 2014), pp. 39–83 emphasizes points of similarity before and after the reform, while acknowledging the changes it introduced.

[37] For post-reform minting locations, see Jonsson, *New Era*, pp. 119–80. On the trend since the late ninth century, which was not restricted to areas under Cerdicing domination, see Jonsson, *New Era*, pp. 23–6, 71–6; M. A. S. Blackburn, 'Expansion and Control: Aspects of Anglo-Scandinavian Minting South of the Humber', in J. Graham-Campbell, R. Hall, J. Jesch, and D. N. Parsons (eds), *Vikings and the Danelaw: Select Papers from the Proceedings of the Thirteenth Viking Congress* (Oxford, 2001), pp. 125–42 especially 125, 132–3, 137, 139; M. A. S. Blackburn, 'Alfred's Coinage Reforms in Context', in T. Reuter (ed.), *Alfred the Great: Papers from the Eleventh-Centenary Conferences* (Aldershot, 2003), pp. 207–8; Naismith, 'Social Significance', p. 16. On minting locations prior to the

way in which the reform continued long-standing practice was the naming on coins of a king and a moneyer. This had been the norm both at York and in Southumbria since the mid-eighth century, although during periods of Scandinavian domination certain coins from the East Midlands, East Anglia, and Northumbria had omitted one or both of these details, and until the early tenth century some minting had been in the names of senior churchmen.[38] Notwithstanding the significant continuities from the pre-reform period, however, the new coinage was quite different from that which it replaced: a marked contrast is evident with regard to diversity both in moneyers' output, and in circulating currency.

Taking diversity of output first, the fundamental work on pre-reform coins, Blunt, Stewart, and Lyon's *Coinage in Tenth-Century England* (1989), uses three categories to classify the vast majority of the coins minted in the names of Cerdicings from Edward the Elder's accession to Edgar's reform. Coins of all three types give the king's name in a circle on one side. On coins of 'circumscription' and 'horizontal' types, this circle encloses a cross (or occasionally another ornament); these types are distinguished from each other by the first stating the moneyer's name in another circle on the reverse, and the second giving it in a horizontal inscription. In the third main category, the 'portrait' type, the king's name encloses not a cross but a stylized image of a royal bust; the moneyer's name appears on the reverse, during Edward the Elder's reign in horizontal format, but thereafter almost always in a circle.[39] Differences within each of these types are important for numismatic taxonomy, but here we will focus just on the three broad categories, since many coin-users may not have noticed that they had a mixture of (say) 'horizontal trefoil' and 'horizontal rosette' coins. By contrast, as is apparent from Figs. 4.1, 4.2, and 4.3, coins of 'circumscription', 'horizontal', and 'portrait' types can be distinguished at a glance.

Prior to Edgar's reform, it was fairly unusual for coins to state the location in which they had been struck. There are quite a few exceptions from Edgar's

---

late ninth century, all of which were close to the Channel or the North Sea, see D. M. Metcalf, *Thrymsas and Sceattas in the Ashmolean Museum, Oxford* (3 vols, London, 1993–4), iii, 297–300; Naismith, *Money*, pp. 7–9, 128–32. Modern writers often refer to 'the London mint', 'the mint of Canterbury', and so on, but I avoid this practice, since it is doubtful whether all moneyers in a particular settlement worked on the same premises: M. Biddle and D. Keene, 'Winchester in the Eleventh and Twelfth Centuries', in M. Biddle (ed.), *Winchester in the Early Middle Ages: An Edition and Discussion of the Winton Domesday* (Oxford, 1976), pp. 397–400, 422; Brand, *Periodic Change*, pp. 45–50.

[38] Blackburn, 'Expansion and Control'; M. A. S. Blackburn, 'Currency under the Vikings. Part 1: Guthrum and the Earliest Danelaw Coinages', *BNJ*, 75 (2005), pp. 18–43; M. A. S. Blackburn, 'Currency under the Vikings. Part 2: The Two Scandinavian Kingdoms of the Danelaw, *c*.895–954', *BNJ*, 76 (2006), pp. 204–26; Naismith, *Money*, pp. 87–155; R. Naismith, 'Kings, Crisis and Coinage Reforms in the Mid-Eighth Century', *EME*, 20 (2012), pp. 291–332. Moneyers working under Scandinavian domination sometimes substituted the name of a saint or non-royal person for that of a king. They also sometimes imitated Alfred's coins, thereby naming a king, albeit not one to whom they were subordinate. The last churchman known to have had coins struck in his own name was Archbishop Plegmund of Canterbury (d. 923).

[39] *CTCE*, pp. 10–19. Logically, there should be four categories: since coins with cross obverses are placed into two categories depending on whether they have a horizontal or circumscription reverse, one ought to divide coins with portrait obverses in the same way. But it would perhaps be pedantic to insist on this, since at any particular time the great majority of portrait types used the same reverse.

Fig. 4.1. Pre-reform circumscription type coin in Edgar's name. Moneyer Heremod; minted at Wallingford. © The Fitzwilliam Museum, Cambridge.

Fig. 4.2. Pre-reform horizontal type coin in Edgar's name. Moneyer Beneðiht; place of minting unknown. © The Fitzwilliam Museum, Cambridge.

Fig. 4.3. Pre-reform portrait type coin in Edgar's name. Moneyer Ælfnoth; minted at London. © The Fitzwilliam Museum, Cambridge.

pre-reform years, but before his overhaul of the coinage the only reign during which the practice was widespread (although still not universal) was that of Æthelstan. The evidence from Æthelstan's reign did, however, enable Christopher Blunt to demonstrate that at that time contrasting designs were struck contemporaneously in different regions.[40] It has since been shown that this was also the case both before and after: geographical variations in the styles minted in the time of Edward the Elder can be inferred through analysis of those moneyers' names and coin designs that are known for both him and his successor, and one can do the same for the decades after Æthelstan by looking forward from the styles and moneyers of his reign, and backwards from the names of post-reform moneyers.[41] We do not need to enter into the detail of how stylistic regions shifted and overlapped to grasp the basic points that during the decades prior to the reform divergent styles were minted contemporaneously in different places, with the style minted changing more often in some areas than in others. In western Mercia, for example, Edgar's reform appears to have been the first time since very early in the tenth century that coins bearing a royal portrait had been minted, but such types were widespread in other regions in Æthelstan's later years. After Æthelstan, circumscription or horizontal styles were more common, although portrait coins were struck intermittently in some places, and in East Anglia their minting appears to have continued uninterrupted from Edward the Elder's later years until Edgar's reform.[42] Turning to what was written on coins, the location of minting was commonly stated for much of Æthelstan's reign, and intermittently thereafter, but before Edgar's reform this practice was very rare in the East Midlands.[43] Similarly, the royal title was frequently just *rex* ('king'), but *rex totius Britanniae* ('king of the whole of Britain'), *rex Anglorum* ('king of the English'), and *rex Saxonum* ('king of the Saxons') also appear, often in various abbreviations.[44] There were times when a single type was minted across substantial parts of the land from the Channel to the Tees, but at no point prior to Edgar's reform was a homogeneous design struck throughout this area.

When the geographical range of the Cerdicings' domination had been narrower, however, there had been much less diversity in the designs struck at any particular time. Under Alfred's predecessor Æthelred, almost all coins produced south of the

[40] C. E. Blunt, 'The Coinage of Athelstan, King of England, 924–939: A Survey', *BNJ*, 42 (1974), pp. 35–160.

[41] Jonsson, *New Era*, pp. 31–6, 44–62; I. Stewart, 'English Coinage from Athelstan to Edgar', *NC*, 148 (1988), pp. 192–214; *CTCE*, pp. 20–96, 108–210; H. Pagan, 'Mints and Moneyers in the West Midlands and at Derby in the Reign of Eadmund (939–46)', *NC*, 155 (1995), pp. 139–61; S. Lyon, 'The Coinage of Edward the Elder', in N. J. Higham and D. H. Hill (eds), *Edward the Elder, 899–924* (London, 2001), pp. 67–78; H. Pagan, 'The Pre-Reform Coinage of Edgar', in Scragg (ed.), *Edgar*, pp. 192–207.

[42] Stewart, 'English Coinage', pp. 210–13 tabulates the sequence of types in different regions.

[43] *CTCE*, pp. 255–63. For an exception, see M. A. S. Blackburn and K. Leahy, 'A Lincoln Mint-Signed Coin from the Reign of Edgar', *NC*, 156 (1996), pp. 239–41. Lincoln had also been named on some coins struck while it was under Scandinavian domination: Blackburn, 'Currency under the Vikings. Part 2', pp. 210–12.

[44] Blunt, 'Coinage of Athelstan', pp. 47–8, 68; *CTCE*, pp. 26, 134–5, 172–81; C. S. S. Lyon, '206', in M. Allen and S. Moorhead (eds), 'Coin Register 2010', *BNJ*, 80 (2010), p. 226.

Thames appear to have been of a type now known as 'Lunettes', and the same design was struck in Mercia in the name of King Burgred (r. 852–874).[45] This continued into Alfred's reign but, to judge from the hoard evidence, coordinated recoinages were conducted in the mid-870s in Wessex and western Mercia, the latter by then ruled by Ceolwulf II. The lightweight and debased Lunettes type was withdrawn from circulation in both kingdoms, and replaced with heavier and purer coins that bore a design conventionally called 'Cross-and-Lozenge'.[46] There seems to have been a further recoinage a few years later, perhaps around 880, by which time Ceolwulf had disappeared: the Cross-and-Lozenge coinage was withdrawn, a still heavier issue of horizontal type was introduced, and Alfred was thenceforth the only layperson named on coins produced south of the Thames or in western Mercia.[47] Small quantities of other styles (e.g. the London Monogram) were also struck in Alfred's name, but coins of horizontal type appear to have been strongly dominant for the rest of his reign, and this remained the most common design under Edward the Elder.[48] There was, however, greater stylistic diversity under Edward than there had been at any time during his father's reign: a few portrait types were minted in Edward's name both north and south of the Thames, west Mercian moneyers switched to a variety of exceptional styles during the 910s, and, when coins began to be struck in Edward's name in East Anglia, they bore a portrait (and were light in weight). Towards the end of Edward's reign, West Mercian moneyers reverted to striking coins of horizontal type, which had never ceased to be dominant in the south, and a similar design was introduced in the southern East Midlands, but this did not lead to uniformity of output: the new East Anglian type was produced on a substantial scale, and was quite unlike the majority of the coins minted in Edward's name.[49] Over the decades that followed, stylistic heterogeneity if anything increased, but south of the Thames, and in and near London, it remained usual for output to be strongly dominated by a single type at any particular time: uniformity of design was thus in large measure maintained within the core area of the Cerdicings' power, but it was only inconsistently that the designs used there were emulated in other regions.[50]

Somewhat analogous points can be made about trends in coins' intrinsic values. The median weight of Alfred's later coins, and of the non-East Anglian issues in

---

[45] A. W. Lyons and W. A. Mackay, 'The Coinage of Æthelred I (865–871)', *BNJ*, 77 (2007), pp. 71–118.

[46] Blackburn, 'Alfred's Coinage Reforms', pp. 205–6, 212–14; A. W. Lyons and W. A. Mackay, 'The Lunettes Coinage of Alfred the Great', *BNJ*, 78 (2008), pp. 38–110.

[47] M. A. S. Blackburn, 'The London Mint in the Reign of Alfred', in M. A. S. Blackburn and D. N. Dumville (eds), *Kings, Currency and Alliances: History and Coinage of Southern England in the Ninth Century* (Woodbridge, 1998), pp. 105–23 especially 107, 109–10, 120–3; Blackburn, 'Alfred's Coinage Reforms', pp. 206, 214. Alfred was already named on some coins probably struck at London (i.e. north of the Thames) during the Lunettes and Cross-and-Lozenge issues.

[48] Blackburn, 'London Mint', p. 107; *CTCE*, pp. 20–96, 264–6; Lyon, 'Coinage of Edward the Elder'.

[49] *CTCE*, pp. 20–96, 264–6; Lyon, 'Coinage of Edward the Elder'. The exceptional Mercian coins bear a range of images, including of buildings, birds, and plants.

[50] Stewart, 'English Coinage', pp. 195–7, 210. Output within the south became somewhat less homogeneous during Eadwig's reign, and the early part of Edgar's.

Edward the Elder's name, lay between 1.55 grams and 1.59 grams, with over 80 per cent falling within a relatively narrow 0.25 gram range.[51] During the decades that followed, however, weights became progressively more variable, and on average lighter: by Edgar's reign, the median had declined to between 1.25 grams and 1.29 grams, and the range needed to encompass 80 per cent had widened to about 0.45 grams.[52] At the same time, silver content became significantly less consistent, and on average lower: a standard in excess of 85 per cent was maintained in the late ninth and early tenth centuries, but by the time of Eadred some coins had a much lower proportion of silver, and Edgar's pre-reform coins ranged from under 50 to over 90 per cent fine.[53] Too few metal analyses have been undertaken to permit conclusions about how fineness differed from place to place, but it is apparent that variations in weight were to some extent regional. Thus, the median weight of the East Anglian issue in Edward the Elder's name was about 0.2 grams below that of his other coins, and in Æthelstan's reign the standards used in the East Midlands and at York were lighter than elsewhere.[54] That these were areas that only came under the Cerdicings' domination during the tenth century underlines the point that the geographical extension of their power was associated with increasing variety in the coins struck in their names. Weights remained variable after Edgar's reform, but the median for the reform type was 1.58 grams, a level not seen since the early tenth century, and it became the norm for silver content to exceed 90 per cent: variations in intrinsic value were thus not eliminated, but the reform greatly increased uniformity of output through the establishment of a single design and a much more consistent standard of fineness.[55]

A similarly marked shift from heterogeneity to (relative) homogeneity is evident when we consider the designs within the circulating currency. Admittedly, even before the reform, it appears that after about 880 (at the latest) the only coins to

---

[51] *CTCE*, pp. 236–8. The range needed to encompass 80 per cent is calculated from the outer limits of the 0.05 gram intervals within which the *CTCE* tables indicate the lowest and highest deciles to fall.

[52] *CTCE*, pp. 236–45.

[53] J. S. Forbes and D. B. Dalladay, 'Composition of English Silver Coins (870–1300)', *BNJ*, 30 (1960–1), pp. 82–7; E. J. Harris, 'The Stuff of Coins', *Seaby's Coin and Medal Bulletin*, 521 (October 1961), pp. 389–90; E. J. Harris, 'Debasement of the Coinage', *Seaby's Coin and Medal Bulletin*, 524 (January 1962), pp. 5–7; H. McKerrell and R. B. K. Stevenson, 'Some Analyses of Anglo-Saxon and Associated Oriental Silver Coinage', in E. T. Hall and D. M. Metcalf (eds), *Methods of Chemical and Metallurgical Investigation of Ancient Coinage* (London, 1972), pp. 195–209; D. M. Metcalf and J. P. Northover, 'Debasement of Coinage in Southern England in the Age of King Alfred', *NC*, 145 (1985), pp. 164–5; Metcalf and Northover, 'Interpreting the Alloy', pp. 52–3; *CTCE*, p. 245; D. M. Metcalf, 'The Rome (Forum) Hoard of 1883', *BNJ*, 62 (1992), pp. 64–5. The bulk of the data available for the period after Edmund concern coins of northern origin, and may therefore be unrepresentative, but the trend would still be significant, even if debasement were predominantly associated with northern moneyers.

[54] Blunt, 'Coinage of Athelstan', pp. 58–9; *CTCE*, pp. 237–9, 241; Metcalf, 'Rome (Forum) Hoard', pp. 77, 89–90; Blackburn, 'Currency under the Vikings. Part 2', pp. 206–8, 217. From Æthelstan's reign onwards, East Anglian coins were usually no longer of below average weight. Coins struck in the East Midlands and at York ceased to be so distinctive in weight as standards elsewhere declined and became more variable.

[55] Petersson, 'Coins and Weights', p. 347; above pp. 117–18, 119–20. Coins from the reform issue itself appear to have been struck to a standard in excess of 95 per cent silver.

circulate widely in areas of Cerdicing domination were those bearing the name of either a Cerdicing king or an archbishop of Canterbury, and the last archbishop to be so named died in 923.[56] It is particularly notable that two hoards from Norfolk and Suffolk contain only coins of Edward the Elder, which raises the possibility that he enforced the removal from circulation of other coins soon after extending his domination into East Anglia.[57] The extension of Cerdicing power was not, however, always followed by the immediate reminting of non-Cerdicing types: a hoard concealed after 920 in the vicinity of Leicester mixes Edward's coins with Anglo-Scandinavian and Islamic issues, despite the area having very probably been under his domination since 918; and a hoard deposited in the hinterland of York quite soon after Æthelstan's seizure of power there combines Cerdicing, Anglo-Scandinavian, Carolingian, and Islamic coins, along with metal in uncoined forms.[58] Areas newly brought under Cerdicing domination can hardly be taken as typical, but even in regions where the overwhelming majority of coins in circulation bore a Cerdicing's name, the currency was far from uniform. Diversity in the circulating currency is apparent both within and between regions. Within regions, diversity arose in part because coins sometimes moved from their region of origin to one in which a different style was being produced, and in part because, after the reform of *c.*880, there does not appear to have been any systematic attempt to remove older types from circulation when new designs began to be struck.[59] Indeed, large hoards are rarely restricted to coins bearing the name of a single Cerdicing, let alone coins of a single issue.[60] Nonetheless, hoards and single finds suggest that within a region the circulating currency was often slanted towards relatively recent issues of the area in question; this is hardly surprising, given that older types would gradually drop out of circulation through loss or export, and that a substantial proportion of trade was probably local.[61] Thus a mixture of types circulated within any given

---

[56] C. E. Blunt, 'A Penny of the English King Athelstan Overstruck on a Cologne Denier', in T. Fischer and P. Ilisch (eds), *Lagom. Festschrift für Peter Berghaus zum 60. Geburtstag am 20. November 1979* (Münster, 1981), pp. 119–21; Jonsson, *New Era*, pp. 29–30; Cook, 'Foreign Coins', pp. 233–6, 268–9. For the movement of coins between Southumbrian kingdoms in the ninth century and before, see D. M. Metcalf, 'The Monetary Economy of Ninth-Century England South of the Humber: A Topographical Analysis', in Blackburn and Dumville (eds), *Kings, Currency and Alliances*, pp. 167–97; Naismith, *Money*, pp. 203–9.

[57] Blackburn, 'Currency under the Vikings. Part 2', pp. 207–8. Note, however, that the coins struck in Edward's name in East Anglia were light in weight.

[58] Blackburn, 'Currency under the Vikings. Part 2', p. 209; B. Ager and G. Williams, 'The Vale of York Viking Hoard: Preliminary Catalogue', in T. Abramson (ed.), *Studies in Early Medieval Coinage, Volume 2: New Perspectives* (Woodbridge, 2011), pp. 135–45; G. Williams, 'Coinage and Monetary Circulation in the Northern Danelaw in the 920s in the Light of the Vale of York Hoard', in Abramson (ed.), *Studies*, pp. 146–55.

[59] Evidence that some coins moved long distances is discussed by Naismith, 'Prelude to Reform', pp. 58–66.

[60] For details of hoards, see M. A. S. Blackburn, H. Pagan et al., *Checklist of Coin Hoards from the British Isles, c.450–1180*, consulted at <http://www-cm.fitzmuseum.cam.ac.uk/dept/coins/projects/hoards/index.list.html> (accessed 9 October 2014).

[61] D. M. Metcalf, 'The Monetary History of England in the Tenth Century Viewed in the Perspective of the Eleventh Century', in Blackburn (ed.), *Anglo-Saxon Monetary History*, pp. 145–50; Naismith, 'Prelude to Reform', pp. 58–66. Note also Jonsson, *New Era*, pp. 36–68, 77–8; K. Jonsson, 'The Pre-Reform Coinage of Edgar—The Legacy of the Anglo-Saxon Kingdoms', in

region, and the balance of that mixture varied from region to region. This represents a clear contrast to the post-reform period, when at any time the bulk of coins in circulation between the Channel and the Tees appear to have been of one design.[62]

The Control of Minting and Coin Use Before Edgar's Reform

Considered in the light of the decades that preceded it, the reform was not the culmination of a sustained progression towards numismatic uniformity: rather, it represented a break from what had gone before. The most straightforward way to interpret this is to hypothesize that, at least to the north of the Thames, the extent to which the Cerdicings regulated minting and coin use loosened as the geographical scope of their domination increased, and that Edgar then reversed the trend. Such an interpretation would run along the following lines. From *c.*880 onwards, coins of fairly uniform design and intrinsic value, and bearing Alfred's name, were minted both south of the Thames and in western Mercia, and he appears to have been able to enforce the removal from circulation of earlier types.[63] This suggests that Alfred regulated coin production and use in western Mercia and the south. We need not, however, suppose that he required a network of hundreds to do so, since his recoinages were much more geographically restricted than Edgar's, and levels of coin use were considerably lower than in the late tenth and eleventh centuries.[64] Given that Alfred probably held very substantial lands south of the Thames, and had a reasonably firm grip on the leading magnates both there and in western Mercia, he may have been able to use a congeries of personal ties to arrange that those managing estates should force peasants who used coins to exchange them for the current type.[65]

There are grounds to suspect that in the southernmost part of Britain Alfred's successors maintained a substantial level of control over minting, since near and south of the Thames output continued at most times in subsequent decades to be dominated by one design. They did not, however, continue to enforce uniformity in the circulating currency: until Edgar's reform, changes of type were not associated with the widespread systematic withdrawal from circulation of previous issues. Nor did the Cerdicings impose uniformity in coin production across their expanding territory.[66] They may from time to time have concentrated on a particular area and induced its moneyers to conform to southern practices. Thus, for example, horizontal types began to be struck in the East Midlands in the wake of Edward's campaigns there, and the reversion to similar designs in western Mercia in the

B. Cook and G. Williams (eds), *Coinage and History in the North Sea World, c.500–1250: Essays in Honour of Marion Archibald* (Leiden, 2006), pp. 325–46, although Jonsson's theory about local recoinages goes significantly beyond the evidence.

[62] In some regions, locally struck coins made up a large proportion of the circulating currency after Edgar's reform, but this does not affect the point that in all areas the coins in circulation were of the same design: Naismith, 'English Monetary Economy', pp. 215–16.

[63] Above, p. 127.   [64] Naismith, 'English Monetary Economy', pp. 201–12, 219–20.

[65] Above, pp. 50–2, 84, 87.   [66] Above, pp. 126–8.

same king's last years could reflect a tightening of his domination after Æthelflaed's death.[67] But this did not mean that emulation of southern styles would continue reliably when royal priorities shifted elsewhere: western Mercia's divergence from southern practices during the 910s may reflect that Edward's domination there had loosened while he was campaigning in the southern East Midlands and East Anglia. Nor was the extension of Cerdicing domination into a region always followed by its moneyers being brought into conformity with the south: the first coins minted in Edward's name in East Anglia, and in Æthelstan's at York, were distinctive in design and light in weight.[68] Particularly when one considers the proliferation of coin types alongside the growing variability in intrinsic values, it looks as if the Cerdicings' regulation of minting in most places north of the Thames became increasingly tenuous as the geographical scope of their domination widened.[69]

If in many areas the Cerdicings had little role in determining the specifications to which coins were struck, the question arises of who did decide. That moneyers within a region tended to strike the same style at any one time may reflect that they worked under the direction of some regional potentate, such as an ealdorman or bishop, but this is very far from certain. Instead, one could account for the regional pattern with the simple hypothesis that there were fewer die-cutters than moneyers, and that the latter usually obtained their dies from the nearest manufacturer: if so, moneyers themselves may well have had considerable latitude to decide numismatic standards, being constrained mainly by the choice of conveniently available dies, and (perhaps more importantly) by what their clients were willing to accept.[70] Whoever was responsible for the heterogeneity, however, the reform was quite possibly not the first attempt by a Cerdicing to promote greater uniformity in coin production across what would constitute Domesday *Anglia*: it may have been a royal command that led during Æthelstan's reign to coins from many (but not all) areas naming their place of production, and an unrealized project to establish a single design could likewise explain the widespread striking in Edgar's pre-reform years of circumscription coins that again stated their location of origin.[71] But such schemes, if schemes they were, proved neither durable nor universal: it was only towards the close of Edgar's reign that anything approaching uniformity

---

[67] Lyon, 'Coinage of Edward the Elder', p. 73.

[68] *CTCE*, pp. 52–3; Lyon, 'Coinage of Edward the Elder', pp. 74, 77; Blackburn, 'Currency under the Vikings. Part 2', p. 217. The coins that are probably the first issued in Æthelstan's name at York depict a building.

[69] *CTCE*, p. 245 interprets the increasing weight diversity and variable debasement as implying 'a laxity, not to say a breakdown, in the control of the coinage'.

[70] Naismith, 'Kings, Crisis and Coinage Reforms'; Naismith, 'Prelude to Reform', pp. 77–8. Contrast Jonsson, *New Era*, pp. 65–8, 185–8.

[71] *CTCE*, pp. 172–85, 255–63; Blackburn and Leahy, 'Lincoln Mint-Signed Coin'; S. Lyon and S. Holmes, 'The Circumscription Cross Penny of Edgar from Middleton on the Wolds', *Numismatic Circular*, 110 (2002), p. 192; M. Lessen, 'A Presumed "Hampshire" Hoard of Eadgar CC Coins', *Numismatic Circular*, 111 (2003), pp. 61–2; Pagan, 'Pre-Reform Coinage', p. 196; C. S. S. Lyon, 'The Earliest Signed Penny of Cricklade: A Local Find of Edgar's "Circumscription Cross" Issue', in Abramson (ed.), *Studies*, pp. 181–2. Naming the location of issue, as well as the moneyer, would have increased accountability: given the limited stock of Old English personal names, it would often have been impossible to identify from the moneyer's name alone who had produced a coin.

of moneyers' output, and indeed uniformity of circulating currency, was established between the Channel and the Tees.

Most modern commentators have been very reluctant to conclude that pre-reform diversity reflects that in many regions the Cerdicings had minimal ability to regulate the specifications to which coins were struck, and by implication that they probably had little control over what happened to the profits of minting.[72] One standard survey of medieval numismatics simply glides over the heterogeneity of the pre-reform coinage: its author states that 'with the West Saxon reconquest [*sic*] a uniform coinage was imposed on the whole of England, with only slight regional deviations', and goes on to assert that under Æthelstan minting was subject to 'very strict royal control'.[73] Other writers have been more ready to acknowledge that there was variety, but take refuge in the supposition that it arose from some orderly process, by which kings delegated responsibility for coin design and production: thus, for example, we read of 'deep-rooted diversity, albeit under overall royal control', and are assured that numismatic variations were 'indications of practical administrative procedures rather than of political diversity or particularism'.[74] The assumption that kings already had significant capacity to regulate minting prior to Edgar's reform was questioned in the 1980s by Kenneth Jonsson, but unfortunately he yoked his arguments concerning the production of coins to a dubious theory about ealdormen restricting their movement between regions.[75] This hypothesis was immediately challenged by Michael Metcalf, and Jonsson's claims have been accorded little credence since.[76] But while Metcalf mauled the theory that ealdormen regulated circulation, his grounds for rejecting the hypothesis that, before the reform, persons other than kings had a substantial degree of control over coin production are weak: he offers no explanation for the 'mystery' of why heterogeneous designs were struck simultaneously, and resorts to the confident but ill-justified assertion that minting was 'by long and unquestioned tradition a royal prerogative', an expression that is not (so far as I am aware) contemporary.[77]

---

[72] On minting profits, for which there is no direct evidence before the eleventh century, see below, p. 185.

[73] Spufford, *Money*, p. 92. See also D. N. Dumville, *Wessex and England from Alfred to Edgar* (Woodbridge, 1992), pp. 149, 170; J. R. Maddicott, *The Origins of the English Parliament, 924–1327* (Oxford, 2010), p. 20. On the word 'reconquest', see above, p. 9.

[74] H. R. Loyn, 'Numismatics and the Medieval Historian: A Comment on Recent Numismatic Contributions to the History of England, *c*.899–1154', *BNJ*, 60 (1990), p. 31; Keynes, 'Edgar', p. 24. See also R. Fleming, *Britain after Rome: The Fall and Rise, 400 to 1070* (London, 2010), pp. 274–5.

[75] Jonsson, *New Era*, especially pp. 65–8, 185–8.

[76] D. M. Metcalf, 'Were Ealdormen Exercising Independent Control over the Coinage in Mid Tenth Century England?', *BNJ*, 57 (1987), pp. 24–33. Jonsson, 'Pre-Reform Coinage' does not deal with Metcalf's salient objections.

[77] Metcalf, 'Were Ealdormen Exercising Independent Control over the Coinage in Mid Tenth Century England?', pp. 27, 32. The basis for Metcalf's premise that Æthelstan controlled minting (pp. 31–2) is not explicit; it perhaps rests on the Grately legislation (discussed below, pp. 136–40), or on a vague notion that he was a 'strong' king. Metcalf's conclusion that kings regulated coin production closely in the early Anglo-Saxon period is disputed: Metcalf, *Thrymsas and Sceattas*, i, 10–25; Grierson and Blackburn, *Medieval European Coinage*, pp. 158–9; A. Gannon, *The Iconography of Early Anglo-Saxon Coinage, Sixth to Eighth Centuries* (Oxford, 2003), pp. 16–17, 188–93; Naismith, *Money*, pp. 90–6.

English writers' unsubstantiated reluctance to conclude that diversity in the design, weight, and fineness of pre-reform coins is likely to reflect limited royal control over minting is all the more notable when one glances across the Channel, and considers the prevailing interpretation of the coins struck in the name of the West Frankish king Charles the Bald (r. 840–877) before his recoinage of 864. The coins of Charles's grandfather Charlemagne (r. 768–814) had at any time been of largely uniform appearance, and moderately consistent intrinsic value, especially in the second half of his reign. This was to a significant extent sustained under Charlemagne's son, Louis the Pious (r. 814–840). Charlemagne and Louis also implemented recoinages in 793/794, 813, 816–818/819, and 822/823–825, thereby enforcing relative uniformity within the circulating currency.[78] There was much greater diversity after Charles became king. Several hoards include coins in the names of both Louis and Charles, suggesting that there were no recoinages in the latter's reign until 864. In Aquitaine, coins were for a time minted in the name of Charles's rebellious nephew, Pippin II. Elsewhere, although Charles's name was used consistently, contrasting designs were produced contemporaneously, lightweight coins were struck in some places, and there was widespread variable debasement.[79] Modern writers have taken all this numismatic heterogeneity as evidence that in the first twenty-four years of his reign Charles failed to assert more than minimal control over coin production.[80] That they have drawn this conclusion is unsurprising, since it is an obvious way to interpret the material, and accords with the traditional 'grand narrative' of the withering of West Frankish royal power after the zenith of Charlemagne's reign.[81] In 864, however, Charles reformed the West Frankish coinage: he ordered in his Edict of Pîtres that all coins in circulation be replaced with a new type of uniform design, good metal, and full weight, and that every coin

---

[78]   D. M. Metcalf and J. P. Northover, 'Coinage Alloys from the Time of Offa and Charlemagne to *c*.864', *NC*, 149 (1989), pp. 106, 108–9; S. Coupland, 'Money and Coinage under Louis the Pious', *Francia*, 17 (1990), pp. 23–54; S. Coupland, 'Charlemagne's Coinage: Ideology and Economy', in J. Story (ed.), *Charlemagne: Empire and Society* (Manchester, 2005), pp. 211–29; G. Sarah, M. Bompaire, M. McCormick, A. Rovelli, and C. Guerrot, 'Analyses élémentaires de monnaies de Charlemagne et Louis le Pieux du Cabinet des Médailles. L'Italie carolingienne et Venise', *Revue numismatique*, 164 (2008), pp. 355–406; G. Sarah, 'Analyses élémentaires de monnaies de Charlemagne et de Louis le Pieux du Cabinet des Médailles. Le cas de Melle', in A. Clairand and D. Hollard (eds), *Numismatique et archéologie en Poitou-Charentes* (Paris, 2009), pp. 63–83; S. Coupland, 'Carolingian Single Finds and the Economy of the Early Ninth Century', *NC*, 170 (2010), pp. 287–319 especially 297–300. A lapse in Louis's regulation of minting when he was deprived of power in 833–834 is the most likely context for an issue in his son Lothar's name: S. Coupland, 'The Coinage of Lothar I (840–855)', *NC*, 161 (2001), pp. 160–4.

[79]   Metcalf and Northover, 'Coinage Alloys', pp. 114–20; S. Coupland, 'The Coinages of Pippin I and II of Aquitaine', *Revue numismatique*, 6ᵉ série, 31 (1989), pp. 194–222; S. Coupland, 'The Early Coinage of Charles the Bald, 840–864', *NC*, 151 (1991), pp. 121–58.

[80]   Coupland, 'Early Coinage', pp. 152–5; M. A. S. Blackburn, 'Money and Coinage', in *NCMH2*, p. 553; I. H. Garipzanov, 'Metamorphoses of the Early Medieval Ruler in the Carolingian World', *EME*, 14 (2006), p. 449.

[81]   Coupland's conclusions about the coinage of Louis the Pious qualify the narrative of decline, but still stand within a well-established historiographical camp, since challenges to the traditional characterization of Louis as a hapless weakling have been gathering momentum since the 1950s: Coupland, 'Money and Coinage', especially pp. 23–4, 48. Compare F. L. Ganshof, 'Louis the Pious Reconsidered', *History*, 42 (1957), pp. 171–80.

henceforth state its location of issue.[82] Except in Aquitaine, the reform appears to have been implemented with considerable success.[83] The introduction of a uniform design, the raising of weight and fineness, and the naming of coins' places of origin (presumably to aid accountability) are obvious parallels with Edgar's reform. We should, however, consider not only the similarities of the coins introduced by the two reforms, but also the similarities of what they replaced. On the Continent, pre-reform variations in design, weight, and fineness are interpreted straightforwardly as reflections of limited central control; north of the Channel, comparable variations prior to Edgar's reform are either ignored or shoehorned into a theory of overall royal regulation. The coins struck in Charles's name before 864 cannot prove that the Cerdicings' control of minting was (in many regions) limited in the decades before Edgar's reform. But the comparison does highlight elements of circularity in the prevailing interpretations of coins from both sides of the Channel. Traditional historiographical paradigms about when royal administration either developed or decayed predispose numismatists to believe that minting either was or was not under close royal regulation, and historians then use conclusions predicated on such premises to support their conventional narratives. We should therefore be very wary of the assumption that coin production prior to Edgar's reform was consistently subject to a high level of Cerdicing control across the land that would be described in Domesday.

The basis for challenging this widely held premise is simple: after the early tenth century, the coins issued in the Cerdicings' names became increasingly varied in design, weight, and fineness, which could well reflect that no single party had much control over minting throughout the land between the Channel and the Tees. Against this, two main lines of argument can be deployed. The first is to play down the diversity, and to see it as being outweighed by certain common features: coins consistently named both the king and the moneyer, only a handful of designs were used, and weights and finenesses appear to have been fairly stable until well into the second quarter of the century.[84] Even setting aside that near-uniformity in intrinsic value did not last, however, these features do not amount to a compelling case for positing a high degree of royal regulation of minting. That many moneyers struck coins of similar weight and fineness does not prove that they did so at the behest of a single authority, since they could have adopted common standards, whether by agreement or by emulation, in order to facilitate exchange. Such a

---

[82] *CRF*, no. 273 (especially cc. 10–19).

[83] S. Coupland, 'L'article XI de l'Edit de Pîtres du 25 juin 864', *Bulletin de la société française de numismatique*, 40 (1985), pp. 713–14; D. M. Metcalf and J. P. Northover, 'Carolingian and Viking Coins from the Cuerdale Hoard: An Interpretation and Comparison of their Metal Contents', *NC*, 148 (1988), pp. 98–106; P. Grierson, 'The *Gratia Dei Rex* Coinage of Charles the Bald', in M. T. Gibson and J. L. Nelson (eds), *Charles the Bald: Court and Kingdom*, 2nd edn (Aldershot, 1990), pp. 52–64; Coupland, 'Early Coinage', p. 155. There is one respect in which the numismatic provisions in the Edict appear not to have been implemented: it states that coins should only be struck 'in our palace' and nine stipulated locations (c. 12), but coins of the reformed type bear the names of over 100 places.

[84] Metcalf, 'Were Ealdormen Exercising Independent Control over the Coinage in Mid Tenth Century England?', pp. 27, 29, 32 argues along such lines.

possibility is demonstrated by times during the early and mid-Anglo-Saxon periods when coins were struck to comparable standards in different English kingdoms and on the Continent, even though no party would have been in a position to regulate all the moneyers concerned.[85] It is, moreover, important to bear in mind that people are often reluctant to accept currency of unfamiliar appearance, as anyone who has attempted to pay with a Scottish or Northern Irish banknote in an English shop probably knows. In consequence, even if a moneyer worked without royal licence or oversight, he would have had reason to select from the repertoire of designs presently or recently in use, and to continue long-standing practice by naming himself and a king: introducing substantial idiosyncrasies would probably have served little purpose, and would have risked making clients suspicious. Thus in tenth- and eleventh-century West Frankia, where kings had largely ceased to be able to regulate production standards and the allocation of minting profits, coins were nonetheless commonly struck in the name of the reigning king or one of his predecessors, and earlier royal issues were widely imitated.[86] Similarly, the *Liber Eliensis*, William of Newburgh, and Roger of Howden relate that during Stephen's reign barons usurped control of minting, but very few are known to have had their names put on coins: instead, the names of 'William' or 'Henry' (Stephen's predecessors) were quite widely used, and many magnates probably appropriated coining revenues without removing Stephen's name.[87] The coins from the decades prior to Edgar's reform thus do not themselves demonstrate any consistent ability on the part of Alfred's successors to control numismatic production standards (or indeed the distribution of minting profits) throughout their expanding area of domination. Nor is there good evidence that they regulated the circulating currency, except perhaps briefly in East Anglia, where Edward the Elder may have enforced the replacement of the existing coin stock.[88] There were no general recoinages between the middle of Alfred's reign and Edgar's last years, and the apparent reminting of foreign coins could have been necessitated by popular suspicion of unfamiliar money, rather than a royal command. Even if there was a ban on the import of foreign coins, enforcement of this would only have required the Cerdicings to have had reliable agents at a relatively small number of commonly used entry points to their territory: this does not imply any significant capacity to monitor coin use across the land subject to their domination.

[85] Grierson and Blackburn, *Medieval European Coinage*, pp. 107–10, 150, 157, 168; Naismith, *Money*, pp. 156–80.

[86] Lafaurie, 'Numismatique', p. 135; Grierson and Blackburn, *Medieval European Coinage*, pp. 246–9; Spufford, *Money*, pp. 55–7. Numismatists studying the period before Edgar's reform tend to assume that any given coin was minted during (or at least very soon after) the reign of the king named on it, but we should not reject out of hand the possibility that certain moneyers struck in the names of deceased kings. If this were the case, it might invalidate my statements about when particular types were minted in particular places, but my overall arguments would be reinforced.

[87] *LE*, iii.73 (p. 322); William of Newburgh, *Historia rerum Anglicarum*, ed. R. Howlett, *Chronicles of the Reigns of Stephen, Henry II and Richard I* (RS, 82, 4 vols, London, 1884–9), i, 69–70; Roger of Howden, *Chronica*, ed. W. Stubbs (RS, 51, 4 vols, London, 1868–71), i, 211; Blackburn, 'Coinage and Currency'.

[88] For the possibility of an East Anglian recoinage, albeit to introduce a lightweight issue, see above, pp. 128, 129.

The second way in which one could try to justify the contention that the Cerdicings had a significant degree of control over coin production or use prior to Edgar's reform would be to invoke two passages of royal legislation. One is a statement in the legislation that Æthelstan issued at Grately (Hampshire), namely that there should be *an mynet* over all the king's *anweald* ('þæt an mynet sy ofer eall ðæs cynges onweald'), *an mynet* meaning 'one money' or 'one coinage', and *anweald* something like 'area of power or authority'.[89] The other relevant passage appears in an ordinance of Edgar that probably antedates the reform: the king declared that *an mynet* should go over all his *anweald* ('ga an mynet ofer ealne þæs cynges anweald'), echoing the Grately decrees, and added that measures should accord with those in use at Winchester.[90] These excerpts are often quoted as if their meanings were unambiguous, but it is unclear both how contemporaries understood the *anweald* of different kings, and how *an mynet* may have been defined. On the latter problem, one possibility is that, before the reform, kings were indifferent to the appearance of coins, and Æthelstan and Edgar were merely expressing the desire that all coins minted or used should bear the name of a past or present Cerdicing king, and conform to a standard weight and alloy.[91] If so, Æthelstan's wishes were to a considerable extent realized, at least during his own reign, when intrinsic values remained fairly homogeneous. His putative aspirations for uniformity would, however, have been pretty modest: it should be recalled that elements of homogeneity could have developed or persisted even without royal enforcement, and under this interpretation Æthelstan did not object to stylistic diversity that would have been immediately visible to all coin users. On the other hand, however, these calls for *an mynet* could reflect that Æthelstan and Edgar did not regard contemporary moneyers' products as sufficiently uniform, and wished to effect change: far from describing existing reality, a legislative demand can be a response to a perceived problem. The Cerdicings may thus have desired that the coins struck in their names be of a single design, without being able to enforce this until Edgar's last years. On this reading, one might postulate a connection between Edgar's call

---

[89] II As 14. This reference may lie behind Metcalf's premise that minting was under royal control during Æthelstan's reign: Metcalf, 'Were Ealdormen Exercising Independent Control over the Coinage in Mid Tenth Century England?', pp. 31–2. For *anweald/onweald*, see above, p. 122. It is not known when during Æthelstan's reign the Grately meeting was held, but it is likely to have been considerably before his death, since it preceded most of his other known legislation: Wormald, *Making*, pp. 439–40.

[90] III Eg 8–8.1. In manuscripts associated with Archbishop Wulfstan II of York (d. 1023), London is named alongside Winchester: D. Whitelock, *English Historical Documents, i, c.500–1042*, 2nd edn (London, 1979), p. 433 n. 6. The date of this legislation is uncertain, but it appears that the texts known as II Edgar and III Edgar emanate from a single meeting, held at Andover (Hampshire) sometime prior to the gathering at *Wihtbordesstan* (see IV Eg 1.4, which seems to refer to II Edgar), the date of which is also uncertain (see above, p. 121 and n. 27). If one postulated that the *Wihtbordesstan* meeting was at the very end of Edgar's reign, and that the Andover assembly was only slightly earlier, one could then associate the latter's reference to 'an mynet' with the reform itself, but this chronology would be extremely compressed. For similar later references, see VI Atr 32.1–32.2; Cn 1018 20.2–21; II Cn 8–9.

[91] For interpretation along such lines, see Metcalf, 'Were Ealdormen Exercising Independent Control over the Coinage in Mid Tenth Century England?', p. 29; Naismith, 'Prelude to Reform', pp. 56–68.

for *an mynet* and the minting in several regions of a circumscription type during the part of his reign which antedated the reform.[92] Similarly, one might associate the Grately reference to *an mynet* with the fairly widespread production of horizontal, circumscription, and then portrait types in successive phases of Æthelstan's reign, and with the partial and temporary adoption of the practice of naming the location of issue.[93] These possibilities are speculative, but the key point is that royal legislation does not prove that kings had much control over minting or coin use. One can only argue that the coins struck (or circulating) during Æthelstan's reign or Edgar's pre-reform years constituted *an mynet* if one posits that these kings conceived of numismatic uniformity in somewhat limited terms.

We might leave the matter at that, but consideration of the textual context of the Grately reference to *an mynet* renders its import even more ambiguous. The relevant words appear within a part of the text which is marked out from the rest by the explicit numbering of its clauses, and which therefore looks as if it may have had some separate existence before being incorporated into the Grately legislation.[94] This suspicion is reinforced when one notes that the numbered section contradicts a statement found just before it, that no one should trade in goods worth over 20 pence except in a *port*: by contrast, the clause introduced 'second' declares that all trade, not merely transactions over 20 pence, should take place in a *port*.[95] This more stringent rule also appears in the legislation of Edward the Elder, which gives a basis for suggesting that the numbered clauses may have originated in his reign.[96] Such a possibility affects interpretation of the demand for *an mynet* in the king's *anweald*, since the geographical scope of Edward's domination was smaller than Æthelstan's, and the coins minted in the former's name less diverse. It is eminently possible that contemporaries differed markedly in how they conceived of Edward's *anweald*, but it is hard to see how anyone could have understood it to stretch very far into the East Midlands, or to East Anglia, until the mid- to late 910s.[97] Edward's domination in western Mercia was, moreover, to

---

[92] Above, p. 131.

[93] For the sequence of types in different regions, see Stewart, 'English Coinage', pp. 210–13. Wormald, *Making*, pp. 439–40 posits a link between the Grately legislation and the naming on coins of their place of issue.

[94] II As 13–18; *Die Gesetze der Angelsachsen*, ed. F. Liebermann (3 vols, Halle, 1903–16), iii, 100; M. A. S. Blackburn, 'Mints, Burhs, and the Grately Code, cap. 14.2', in D. H. Hill and A. R. Rumble (eds), *The Defence of Wessex: The Burghal Hidage and Anglo-Saxon Fortifications* (Manchester, 1996), pp. 167–72. Blackburn canvassed the possibility that the numbered clauses, while possibly originating before the Grately meeting, were only inserted into the text after it. There are, however, two indications that they were added at Grately, or at least soon after. First, although there are significant variations between the manuscripts of the Grately legislation, the numbered section is absent only from Cambridge, Corpus Christi College, MS 383, which had broken off earlier in the text (Wormald, *Making*, pp. 291–5, 440 n. 77). Second, the Kentish response to the Grately legislation seems to refer to a provision within the numbered section (II As 15; III As 8).

[95] II As 12, 13.1. On *port*s, see above, pp. 106–9.   [96] I Ew 1.

[97] At the beginning of 917, Northampton, Leicester, Huntingdon, and East Anglia were bases of armies hostile to Edward, but his *anweald* may have been perceived to extend into at least parts of the southern East Midlands and Essex by this time; between 912 and 916 he constructed fortifications in Hertford, Witham, Buckingham, Bedford, and Maldon, and some of the principal inhabitants of Northampton (or its vicinity) also accepted him as lord in 914: *ASC* ABCD 912, 914, A 915, 916, 917. We should, however, keep an open mind about whether Edward's *anweald* was considered to

some extent qualified until his sister Æthelflaed's death in 918, and the fact that coins struck there consistently bore his name does not in itself prove that everyone (or indeed anyone) regarded that region as within his *anweald*.[98] In the present context, it is particularly interesting that the 'Mercian Register' states that Æthelflaed died in 'the eighth year in which she held *anweald* among the Mercians', and then relates that the next year her daughter Ælfwynn was 'deprived of all *anweald* among the Mercians'.[99] The attribution to Æthelflaed and Ælfwynn of *anweald* in Mercia need not preclude Edward's having been perceived (especially by West Saxons) to enjoy *anweald* there too, but it should alert us to the possibility that until 918/919 at least certain people may have regarded (much of) western Mercia as outwith his *anweald*. There is, moreover, some reason to suspect that this view may not have been confined to Mercians: all the main manuscripts of the *Chronicle* record that on the death in 911 of Æthelflaed's husband Æthelred, Edward obtained London and Oxford, which implies that his (Edward's) power elsewhere in Mercia remained limited.[100] It is therefore conceivable that, if the numbered section of the Grately text originated before the late 910s, its author may have seen the 'king's *anweald*' as extending little north of the Thames. Such an understanding of the royal *anweald* would, however, be much less likely at any later date.

That the writer of the numbered clauses may indeed have thought of the 'king's *anweald*' as being confined to the southernmost part of Britain is suggested by what follows the demand for *an mynet*. After ordering that no one mint except in a *port*, the text assigns quotas of moneyers to eleven or twelve locations, and declares that other unnamed *burh*s could (or perhaps should) have one moneyer.[101] All of the named places are south of or on the Thames, and the list of locations with more than one moneyer seems at first glance manifestly incomplete, with Chester being an especially notable omission: it had well over a dozen moneyers working concurrently during Æthelstan's reign, and several of them

extend to these various places, not least because of the doubts (to which we turn next) about whether his dominance over Æthelflaed was sufficient to place Mercia within his *anweald*. Note, moreover, that the A text of the *Chronicle* alludes to persons in Essex (and East Anglia) being under Danish *anweald* as late as autumn 917: *ASC* A 917, and compare *ASC* ABCD 912.

[98] On Edward's position vis-à-vis western Mercia, see above, pp. 27–8, 56. Moneyers' naming of Edward could be no more than an acknowledgement of his very nominal authority: note that coins were minted in the name of Louis the Pious in Italy, even when it was under the *de facto* control of Lothar, his son and (from *c*.829 until 839) adversary. See J. Jarnut, 'Ludwig der Fromme, Lothar I. und das Regnum Italiae', in P. Godman and R. Collins (eds), *Charlemagne's Heir: New Perspectives on the Reign of Louis the Pious (814–840)* (Oxford, 1990), pp. 349–62; Coupland, 'Money and Coinage', pp. 43–4, 45–8; Coupland, 'Coinage of Lothar', pp. 160–4. The case of Louis and Lothar also warns against the inference that the division between Eadwig and Edgar was harmonious, just because coins appear to have continued to be struck in the former's name north of the Thames. See *CTCE*, pp. 278–80.

[99] *ASC* MR 918, 919.

[100] *ASC* ABCDE 911. On the other hand, *ASC* ABCD 914 alludes to forces from Hereford and Gloucester compelling raiders to promise to leave Edward's *anweald*, which may imply that the author of this annal saw the king's *anweald* as including at least the south-western part of Mercia.

[101] II As 14–14.2. The uncertainty about the number of places arises because Dorchester only appears in a Latin rendering of the list from around the turn of the eleventh and twelfth centuries.

appear also to have struck coins in Edward the Elder's name.[102] The list's scope would, however, cease to be surprising if it were compiled prior to the late 910s by someone who saw the northern limit of Edward's *anweald* as being not very far beyond the Thames. Given that coins rarely named their place of origin before Æthelstan's reign, much guesswork is involved in estimating how many moneyers worked in particular locations during Edward's time, but a few tentative observations are possible. First, the list in its current form is probably not significantly earlier than the 910s, since it is unlikely that coins were struck in some of the named locations until well into Edward's reign.[103] Second, most of the quotas in the list would be broadly plausible figures for the approximate numbers of moneyers working at the named places in the mid-910s, with the most marked exception perhaps being Rochester (where the figure given would also fit ill with the evidence from Æthelstan's reign).[104] Third, there are no particular grounds to conclude that during the 910s two or more moneyers were active concurrently at any location south of (or on) the Thames unmentioned in the list, except perhaps Oxford.[105] Given how little is known about the numbers of moneyers working in different places during Edward's reign, one cannot claim that the stated quotas strengthen the theory that the numbered clauses were written in the mid-910s, but nor do they tell against it.

If the numbered clauses were written in the mid-910s by someone who regarded Edward's *anweald* as stretching little north of the Thames, the statement that there should be *an mynet* over all the king's *anweald* could readily be reconciled with the coins of that period: while west Mercian moneyers struck pictorial designs during the 910s, production in the south was (as we have seen) strongly dominated by coins of horizontal type, and weights and finenesses there appear to

---

[102] Blunt, 'Coinage of Athelstan', pp. 97–9; Naismith, 'Prelude to Reform', pp. 70–4. Where the same two (or more) moneyers' names occur on coin types issued in consecutive periods, one can infer that for at least some time those moneyers probably worked concurrently. Note also that the names of five moneyers who struck at Shrewsbury in Æthelstan's reign had appeared on coins bearing Edward's name: Blunt, 'Coinage of Athelstan', pp. 99–100; Naismith, 'Prelude to Reform', p. 72.

[103] *CTCE*, pp. 25–34, 43–51, 54–5; Blackburn, 'Mints, Burhs, and the Grately Code', pp. 162–5, 172. The level of coin production appears to have been very low during the early years of Edward's reign.

[104] Naismith, 'Prelude to Reform', p. 71. There is often some discrepancy between the quota and the number of moneyers that can be associated with a place, but where more moneyers are known, one can (to some extent) posit that they did not all work concurrently; where fewer, that there were moneyers of whom no coins have yet been found. One can also hypothesize that the quotas were not observed in practice. The list attributes three moneyers to Rochester, but only one is known to have worked there during Æthelstan's reign, and there are no particular grounds to associate any with it in Edward's day. Naismith, 'Prelude to Reform', pp. 74–5 suggests that the quotas for Rochester and Canterbury best fit the early ninth century: the list may have grown by accretion after that, without its figures being consistently updated.

[105] Naismith, 'Prelude to Reform', p. 72. *CTCE*, pp. 21, 26, 29, 46 suggests that there may have been two moneyers at Oxford from early in Edward's reign, but only one of the moneyers associated with Oxford during Æthelstan's reign appears on coins from Edward's. Blackburn, 'Mints, Burhs, and the Grately Code', p. 170 expresses some puzzlement at the list's omission of Bath, Langport, and Wallingford, since each may have had two moneyers during Æthelstan's reign, but there is no evidence that any of them had more than one under Edward.

have been fairly uniform throughout Edward's reign.[106] The significance of this hypothesis about the origin of the numbered clauses is that it means that we cannot even be sure that Æthelstan aspired to have *an mynet* (whatever that might mean) throughout his *anweald* (however defined), since a king did not need to subscribe to every particular of a predecessor's legislation to incorporate it into his own. The best known evidence of this is Alfred's appending to his legislation that attributed to Ine, which was in some respects inconsistent with his own, but the Gratley text itself illustrates the point equally well: the numbered section contains a demand that all trade be conducted in a *port*, but is preceded by a provision that implicitly permitted low-value transactions to take place in other locations.[107] As such, the numbered clauses embedded within the Gratley legislation should not be relied on as evidence for the organization or regulation of minting during Æthelstan's reign: the already slender basis for believing that he had consistent overarching control of the production of the coins that bore his name is thus undermined still further.

Ultimately, however, it is not critical to my argument whether minting was subject to close royal regulation in any given region during the decades prior to Edgar's reform. That the coins struck in the name of the reigning Cerdicing were diverse in appearance from the mid-910s, and from fairly soon after also increasingly diverse in weight and fineness, could have been a consequence of kings' being unable to impose uniformity, or of having limited interest in doing so. Either way, what matters here is that Edgar was the first king who had both the desire and the capability to enforce anything approaching homogeneity in moneyers' output, and indeed relative homogeneity in the circulating currency, all across the land from the Channel to the Tees. This does not mean that his predecessors should be deemed in some way deficient: most of them (unlike Edgar) were frequently engaged on major military campaigns, pre-existing minting practices within the territory that they brought under their domination varied considerably, and they may not have seen the imposition of numismatic uniformity as a priority. But while the pre-reform coinage should not be used to denigrate those in whose names it was issued, its diversity does need to be recognized: many modern writers invoke Edgar's recoinage as a prime demonstration of the administrative prowess of the so-called 'Anglo-Saxon state', but by ignoring or talking down the heterogeneity of what went before, they understate the reform's transformational significance. With

---

[106] Above, pp. 127–8. My hypothesis would not necessarily be undermined if the writer of the numbered clauses perceived Edward's *anweald* to extend into the southern East Midlands or Essex. When coins began to be struck in Edward's name in these areas, they were of horizontal types, as in the south. Since coins from the East Midlands so rarely state their place of production, it is particularly hard to assess how many moneyers worked in which locations at different times: the most that can be said is that there is no particular reason to think that two or more moneyers concurrently struck coins in Edward's name at any place in the East Midlands or Essex in the mid-910s. A single moneyer (or two with the same name) is known for Hertford and Maldon in Æthelstan's reign, and the coins struck in these locations were often in stylistic affinity with those from London and south of the Thames: Blunt, 'Coinage of Athelstan', pp. 76–7, 78; *CTCE*, p. 112.

[107] Wormald, *Making*, pp. 267, 278; II As 12, 13.1. The bishops and thegns of Kent appear, however, to have taken at least one of the numbered clauses as an expression of Æthelstan's will: II As 15; III As 8.

coins, we know that towards the end of Edgar's reign there was a dramatic switch from diversity to relative uniformity between the Channel and the Tees. Why this reform was implemented is a matter to which we shall return towards the end of this chapter.[108] First, however, we need to consider whether other similarly fundamental changes, for which the evidence is more exiguous, may have been effected around the same time.

HUNDREDS AND WAPENTAKES

Early References to Hundreds and Wapentakes

We have already seen that the *Wihtbordesstan* decrees indicate that by the end of Edgar's reign phenomena known as 'hundreds' or 'wapentakes' were to be found across at least the vast majority of what would constitute Domesday *Anglia*, including between the Humber and the Tees. In addition, the text shows that the words 'hundred' and 'wapentake' had equivalent meaning; that they denoted fora in which witnesses might be appointed and trade conducted; that hundreds (and by implication wapentakes) were entities to which confiscated goods could be allocated; and that each had a senior figure (the 'hundrodes ealdor', or 'leader of the hundred') who was to be notified if people failed to make it known that they had purchased goods.[109] Much about hundreds and wapentakes is, however, first clear in Domesday Book, which was founded on the sworn testimony of representatives from each hundred and wapentake, and usually lists landholders' estates under the hundred or wapentake in which they lay.[110] The survey thus uses these two terms to refer to districts, the approximate boundaries of which can be mapped; by way of example, Map 4 (on page 142) illustrates the Domesday hundreds of Northamptonshire.[111] From Domesday we learn that hundreds and wapentakes varied considerably in size and shape, but that they were usually fairly modest in scale: it would in many cases be possible to walk across a hundred or wapentake in a few hours.[112] Domesday also affords indications that such units were used for assessing and extracting burdens: in some cases, the hidage of every manor in a hundred had changed by a uniform percentage between 1066 and 1086, which suggests that an assessment

---

[108] Below, pp. 182–94 especially 185, 189, 191, 192.

[109] IV Eg 3.1, 5–6, 8.1, 10; above, pp. 121–3. We have no way of ascertaining whether in the northwest hundreds existed all the way to the Ribble during Edgar's reign, or indeed at any time before 1066.

[110] The names of the individuals who testified for certain hundreds are recorded in the *Inquisitio Eliensis* and *Inquisitio Comitatus Cantabrigiensis*, both in *Inquisitio Comitatus Cantabrigiensis*, ed. N. E. S. A. Hamilton (London, 1876).

[111] The challenges associated with mapping hundreds and wapentakes are discussed by F. R. Thorn, 'Hundreds and Wapentakes', in A. Williams and G. H. Martin (eds), *The Bedfordshire Domesday* (London, 1991), pp. 54–64, and in corresponding articles in each volume of the same series. Detailed maps are contained in the map case of *Great Domesday*, ed. R. W. H. Erskine, A. Williams, and G. H. Martin (6 cases, London, 1986–92).

[112] Anderson, *English Hundred-Names*, vol. i, pp. xl–xlv; H. R. Loyn, 'The Hundred in England in the Tenth and Eleventh Centuries', in H. Hearder and H. R. Loyn (eds), *British Government and Administration: Studies Presented to S. B. Chrimes* (Cardiff, 1974), pp. 1–2; S. Brookes and A. Reynolds, 'The Origins of Political Order and the Anglo-Saxon State', *Archaeology International*, 13/14 (2009–11), p. 85.

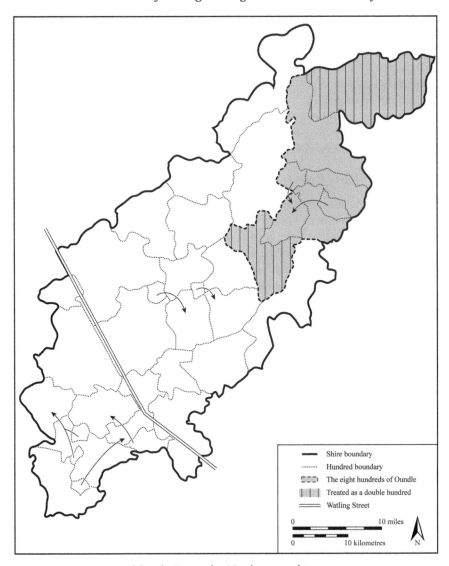

Map 4. Domesday Northamptonshire.

could be imposed on a hundred (or, by analogy, a wapentake), and then apportioned among the estates within it.[113] It is also notable that there are many instances, especially in the Midlands, where Domesday attributes 100 hides to a hundred: such round numbers are very far from being a general rule, and are rare south of the Thames, but they imply that in some cases assessments had been

[113] J. H. Round, *Feudal England: Historical Studies on the XIth and XIIth Centuries* (London, 1909), pp. 49–54.

allocated systematically.[114] Confirmation that hundreds were used for the collection of royal dues during William the Conqueror's reign is provided by a text that details the tax due and paid from each of the hundreds of Northamptonshire, and records closely contemporaneous with Domesday give similar information for hundreds in Wiltshire, Dorset, Devon, Cornwall, and Somerset.[115]

In view of the significance that is accorded to hundreds and wapentakes in modern assessments of the late Anglo-Saxon period, we need to examine the chronology of their development closely. Prior to the Norman Conquest, there are only a few pieces of evidence about individual hundreds and wapentakes. Edward the Confessor granted judicial rights in eight and a half Suffolk hundreds to the abbey of Bury St Edmunds.[116] An Old English text from Peterborough records the tithes that certain hundreds owed at an unknown date.[117] Another document from the same abbey alludes to a whole wapentake acting as surety for a purchase, and refers to transactions being witnessed by groups of hundreds between *c*.971 and 992.[118] The *Libellus Æthelwoldi*, a twelfth-century Latin text compiled from late tenth-century vernacular records, mentions several instances from the general vicinity of Ely of transactions being concluded, or disputes settled, in the presence of one or more hundreds; almost all occurred during or after the reign of Edgar, although in one case what is described as a gathering of 'two hundreds' probably took place a few years before he became king.[119] Aside from meagre references of this sort, however, very little is known for certain about any specific hundred or wapentake before the Norman Conquest, and we should be cautious about projecting the evidence of Domesday into the distant past.

---

[114] F. W. Maitland, *Domesday Book and Beyond: Three Essays in the Early History of England* (Cambridge, 1897), pp. 451–60; Stenton, *Anglo-Saxon England*, pp. 298–9; Loyn, 'Hundred', p. 2. Domesday wapentakes commonly contain a multiple of twelve carucates, but interpretation of this is complicated by the division of many wapentakes into units known as hundreds, often assessed at twelve carucates apiece. These units should not be confused with the hundreds found elsewhere. It is possible that each wapentake was allocated a multiple of twelve carucates, and that this liability was then apportioned among hundreds, which may or may not have been newly created for the purpose. Alternatively, one could hypothesize that assessments were in the first instance allotted to a wapentake's constituent hundreds, not to the wapentake as a whole. For discussion, see Round, *Feudal England*, pp. 69–82; Stenton, *Anglo-Saxon England*, pp. 647–8; D. Roffe, 'The Lincolnshire Hundred', *Landscape History*, 3 (1981), pp. 27–36; O'Brien, *God's Peace and King's Peace*, pp. 88–93; D. M. Hadley, *The Northern Danelaw: Its Social Structure, c.800–1100* (London, 2000), pp. 101–4.

[115] *Anglo-Saxon Charters*, ed. and trans. A. J. Robertson, 2nd edn (Cambridge, 1956), pp. 230–6; *Exon Domesday*, ed. H. Ellis, *Libri censualis vocati Domesday-Book additamenta ex codic. antiquiss.* (London, 1816), pp. 1–11, 12–26, 59–75, 489–90. The Northamptonshire Geld Roll states that the hidage assessments it records had also pertained in Edward the Confessor's day. See also S 1131 for a scrap of evidence from just before the Conquest.

[116] S 1069, 1070, 1078, 1084; R. Sharpe, 'The Use of Writs in the Eleventh Century', *ASE*, 32 (2003), pp. 262–6.

[117] S 1448.   [118] S 1448a.

[119] *LE*, ii.11, ii.11a, ii.12, ii.15, ii.16, ii.17, ii.18, ii.24, ii.25, ii.31, ii.34, ii.35, ii.38, ii.48 (pp. 85, 86, 89, 90, 91, 92, 93, 94, 97, 99, 104, 109, 110, 111, 116); A. Kennedy, 'Law and Litigation in the *Libellus Æthelwoldi Episcopi*', *ASE*, 24 (1995), pp. 137–41, 144, 146, 148. For the meeting of two hundreds, which was held some fifteen years before the uncertain date during Edgar's reign when Æthelwold acquired Ely, see *LE*, ii.18, ii.24 (pp. 93–4, 97); below, p. 155. Gifts, sales, or leases of hundreds or fractions thereof are mentioned at *LE*, ii.4, ii.5, ii.41, ii.75 (pp. 75, 77, 114, 144). *LE*, ii.32 (p.106) refers to a man recovering stolen items with the aid of *centuriones*, who may have been persons in some way associated with a hundred.

In consequence, our knowledge of hundreds and wapentakes in the late Anglo-Saxon period largely rests on the *Wihtbordesstan* decrees and other legislative texts. The only one of these that mentions hundreds or wapentakes and definitely ante-dates the time of Edgar is the legislation that Edmund issued at Colyton (Devon), in which he declared that a person who failed to assist in the pursuit of a thief should pay 120 shillings to the king, and 30 to the hundred ('hundreto').[120] It is not known when during his reign (939–946) Edmund made this order, or to what geographical area it pertained, but it indicates that in at least part of his territory there existed an entity known as a hundred, which could receive payments, and which was probably in some way concerned with the apprehension of wrongdoers. A much more detailed description of the workings of a hundred is provided by an anonymous text, which calls itself 'the ordinance on how one should hold the hundred [*hundred*]'.[121] Since this 'Hundred Ordinance' states that thieves should be treated in accordance with Edmund's decree, it cannot be earlier than that king's reign, and is perhaps unlikely to be from very many decades later.[122] A date of origin in Edgar's reign would, however, be well within the bounds of possibility, and it is worth noting that the *Wihtbordesstan* legislation likewise refers back to Edmund's day.[123]

Turning to the content of the Ordinance, it begins by stating that 'they', which appears to mean the inhabitants of the hundred, or perhaps certain of the inhabitants of the hundred, should assemble every four weeks and do justice ('riht') to each other; later, it says that 'in the hundred just as in another meeting [*oðer gemote*]' each case should have a day appointed for its just resolution.[124] The bulk of the text is, however, concerned not with meetings but with arrangements for the pursuit of thieves, seemingly under the leadership of a 'hundredman' and 'tithing men', who were also to act as witnesses when anyone acquired goods.[125] It is apparent that hundreds could be geographical districts, since there is a reference to a trail being traced from one hundred into another, but a 'hundred' was also an entity that could receive wealth: the hundred was to take half of the confiscated possessions of thieves, and was to be paid 30 pence by anyone who neglected pursuit obligations.[126] The nature of the wealth-receiving hundred is ambiguous, especially when one notes that in Merovingian legislation the term *centena* ('hundred') means 'that which is under the command of a *centenarius*', and is used to denote both a geographical area and the posse that a *centenarius* led in pursuit of thieves: the wealth-receiving hundred may at least notionally have encompassed all or much

---

[120] III Em 2. The text survives only in a Latin translation from around the turn of the eleventh and twelfth centuries.

[121] Hu Inscr. Hu 8–9 may well have originated separately. Wormald, *Making*, pp. 378–9 discusses the text.

[122] Hu 2, which may refer to III Em 2, 4.

[123] IV Eg 2a. The *Wihtbordesstan* reference concerns royal and thegnly rights, and reveals nothing about hundreds or wapentakes in Edmund's reign.

[124] Hu 1, 7–7.1.   [125] Hu 2–6.1.

[126] Hu 2.1, 3, 5. A second failure to join a posse was punishable by a payment of 60 pence (split equally between the hundred and a *hlaford*, i.e. a 'lord'), a third by a payment of half a pound (the recipient is not specified), and a fourth by full forfeiture and outlawry. These punishments are much lower than those specified by III Em 2 (120 shillings to the king and 30 to the hundred), which may imply that the Hundred Ordinance is not closely contemporaneous with Edmund's Colyton legislation.

of the population of the geographical hundred, but it may alternatively have been restricted to those directly involved in chasing malefactors.[127] Nor is it clear whether the Hundred Ordinance is a piece of royal legislation, but at least some of its provisions probably embody royal commands, since a hundredman who failed to assist after a track had been traced to the edge of his hundred was to pay the king 30 shillings.[128] Despite these uncertainties, the text strongly suggests that by around the time of Edgar (and possibly a little before) there were, at least in certain areas, districts known as 'hundreds' in which regular assemblies were held, and policing groups organized.

These conclusions from the Hundred Ordinance go beyond what we had established from the *Wihtbordesstan* legislation: while the latter indicates that 'hundreds' or 'wapentakes' existed across all or most of the future Domesday *Anglia*, it does not prove that they were districts, or indeed tell us very much about how they functioned. Legislation that Edgar had issued at Andover (Hampshire) on some earlier occasion also mentions hundreds in quite elliptical terms: like the Hundred Ordinance and the *Wihtbordesstan* decrees, it alludes to the hundred as a recipient of forfeited goods, but also states that the hundred meeting ('hundredgemot') should be attended 'as was previously ordained'.[129] If the Hundred Ordinance is a piece of royal legislation, the Andover decrees could here be invoking its demand that hundred meetings be held every four weeks, but it is also possible that both of these texts drew separately on instructions about the frequency of hundred meetings, issued by Edgar or one of his predecessors, of which there is no extant record.[130] Four-weekly meetings and thief-catching posses may well have been common features of the hundreds and wapentakes that existed across the land from the Channel to the Tees by the end of Edgar's reign, although the uncertainties about the nature and applicability of the Hundred Ordinance mean that this cannot be demonstrated. Nor is it easy to interpret all of the references to hundreds and wapentakes in the legislation of Æthelred II and Cnut, but that is not critical here. What matters much more is that there are many such references. Æthelred alluded to oath-helpers being drawn from within one or more hundreds, envisaged that protection ('grið') might be established in a wapentake, ordered that meetings be held in every wapentake to identify and punish wrongdoers, and prescribed payments to be made to wapentakes as security.[131] Cnut mentioned hundreds as bodies that might receive fines or confiscated possessions, reiterated the obligation to attend hundred meetings, stated that cases should only be taken to the king if justice could not be obtained in a hundred, declared that forcible recovery of property was permitted only after justice had thrice been demanded in a hundred,

---

[127] A. C. Murray, 'From Roman to Frankish Gaul: "Centenarii" and "Centenae" in the Administration of the Merovingian Kingdom', *Traditio*, 44 (1988), pp. 59–100 especially 80–4, 88–9, 100. See also below, pp. 243–4.

[128] Hu 5.1.   [129] III Eg 5, 7.1.

[130] Under the latter scenario, it would be possible for the Hundred Ordinance to postdate the Andover legislation. *Leges Henrici Primi*, vii.4, ed. and trans. L. J. Downer (Oxford, 1972), p. 100 states that hundred and wapentake meetings should be held twelve times per year.

[131] I Atr 1.2–1.3; III Atr 1.2, 3.1–3.3. Note also Northu 57.2.

mandated that every free male over 12 years old be in a hundred and under surety, and referred to oath-helpers being chosen from within one or more hundreds.[132] We could easily become mired in trying to elucidate what each of these provisions meant, and in speculating about whether specific commands were widely observed in practice, but that would risk obscuring a much more significant point: royal legislation of the late tenth and eleventh centuries assumes that hundreds and wapentakes existed; that they had meetings associated with them; and that they should play an integral part in attempts to detect, punish, and prevent behaviour that kings deemed undesirable. By contrast, the legislation of Alfred, Edward the Elder, Æthelstan, and Edmund makes no mention of wapentakes, and only that of Edmund yields even a single reference to a hundred. It is well known that 'absence of evidence is not evidence of absence', but here we are dealing not with absent sources, but with silent sources: the extant decrees of Alfred, Edward the Elder, and Æthelstan constitute a sizeable corpus of evidence, in which neither hundreds nor wapentakes appear. This silence strongly suggests that phenomena known as hundreds and wapentakes played no significant role in late ninth- and early tenth-century kings' attempts to implement their legislation.

Possible Antecedents of Hundreds and Wapentakes

While the silence of legislation from before the mid-tenth century suggests that hundreds and wapentakes were not previously important to kings' attempts to implement their decrees, it is quite likely that hundreds or wapentakes (or both) existed in some form before these words began to appear in extant sources. In considering this issue, it is important to distinguish territory, function, and terminology: even if continuity from the early tenth century (or before) can be inferred in one of these, continuity in the others does not necessarily follow. We may begin with territory. Despite the paucity of evidence, some historians have argued that certain of the districts represented by Domesday hundreds and wapentakes had probably constituted recognizable blocks since early in the Anglo-Saxon period. It has, for example, been suggested that the boundaries of Domesday hundreds and wapentakes may in some cases have been based on those of the shadowy *regiones* and *provinciae* that we considered in the previous chapter, or of early minster parishes, or of areas that were at some point under the domination of a single potentate.[133] While we know extremely little about the size and shape of *regiones*, *provinciae*, and other early units, such theories have much to commend them. For one thing, the hypothesis that hundred and wapentake boundaries were influenced by those of a heterogeneous collection of earlier districts would explain why Domesday hundreds and wapentakes vary considerably in size and shape. Moreover,

---

[132] Cn 1018 26.3; II Cn 15.2, 17–17.1, 19, 20–20a, 22–22.1, 25.1, 27, 30–30.2, 31a.

[133] For suggestions along such lines, see S. Bassett, 'The Administrative Landscape of the Diocese of Worcester in the Tenth Century', in N. Brooks and C. Cubitt (eds), *St Oswald of Worcester: Life and Influence* (London, 1996), pp. 157–73; N. Brooks 'Alfredian Government: The West Saxon Inheritance', in Reuter (ed.), *Alfred*, pp. 162–73; J. Blair, *The Church in Anglo-Saxon Society* (Oxford, 2005), pp. 299–304, 308–10; T. M. Charles-Edwards, *Wales and the Britons, 350–1064* (Oxford, 2013), p. 23.

the frequency with which Domesday attributes round numbers of hides to Midland hundreds may have resulted from the Cerdicings systematically imposing regular assessments on either existing or newly demarcated districts, at some point after they extended their domination north of the Thames; if so, this may suggest that the more irregular assessments south of the Thames had earlier origins, and by implication that the territories to which they pertain probably antedated the tenth century.[134] Furthermore, sources from after the Norman Conquest associate the lordship of certain hundreds with particular manors, especially in the south-west, which may well reflect that the hundredal districts in question had originated as territories that delivered renders to a single collection point, whether for the king or for some other recipient.[135] It may also be significant that three cemeteries containing late seventh- or eighth-century executed corpses are on or very near the boundaries of Domesday hundreds, as are certain other early burials that appear in some way abnormal. Early burials could have been used as landmarks when later boundaries were set out, but it is perhaps more likely that the boundaries were recognized before the burials, and deemed suitably liminal for the interment of outcasts.[136] None of this is conclusive, but it would hardly be surprising if, whenever it was that the districts represented by Domesday hundreds and wapentakes were demarcated, use was often made of whatever boundaries were already recognized for one purpose or another. This would not, however, necessarily mean that the hundreds and wapentakes of Domesday all preserve units of very great antiquity: as we noted in the previous chapter, references to several hundreds meeting together prompt one to suspect that the hundreds in question had been formed through the partition, rather than the continuation, of earlier blocks.[137] The territories of certain Domesday hundreds and wapentakes may therefore be very old indeed, but there is no secure basis for concluding that this was always or usually the case. Indeed, while the *Wihtbordesstan* legislation indicates the existence across the land between the Channel and the Tees of phenomena known as hundreds and wapentakes, and the Hundred Ordinance allows us to infer that these were districts, there is no way to ascertain how far the boundaries of the hundreds and wapentakes of Edgar's day corresponded to those of Domesday.[138]

---

[134] Stenton, *Anglo-Saxon England*, pp. 298–9; Loyn, 'Hundred', p. 2.

[135] H. Cam, '*Manerium cum Hundredo*: The Hundred and the Hundredal Manor', *EHR*, 47 (1932), pp. 353–76, especially 370–6; P. H. Sawyer, 'The Royal *Tun* in Pre-Conquest England', in P. Wormald, D. Bullough, and R. Collins (eds), *Ideal and Reality in Frankish and Anglo-Saxon Society: Studies Presented to J. M. Wallace-Hadrill* (Oxford, 1983), pp. 280–3.

[136] A. Reynolds, *Anglo-Saxon Deviant Burial Customs* (Oxford, 2009), pp. 109–11, 131–4, 150–1, 153–5, 209–12, 217–19. These execution cemeteries are at Chesterton Lane (Cambridgeshire), Sutton Hoo (Suffolk), and Walkington Wold (Yorkshire). Given the small corpus of evidence, little weight can be placed on this hypothesis, especially when one notes that in the case of Sutton Hoo the boundary was a natural one, the River Deben. Reynolds's concept of 'deviance' is also problematically broad. For further comment on executions, see above, p. 113 n. 118.

[137] H. Cam, 'Early Groups of Hundreds', in J. G. Edwards, V. H. Galbraith, and E. F. Jacob (eds), *Historical Essays in Honour of James Tait* (Manchester, 1933), pp. 13–26; above, pp. 102–3.

[138] When considering the antiquity or otherwise of Domesday hundreds, it is tempting to use the theories of W. J. Corbett, 'The Tribal Hidage', *TRHS*, n.s., 14 (1900), pp. 208–11, 223–30, which are discussed by H. M. Chadwick, *Studies on Anglo-Saxon Institutions* (Cambridge, 1905), pp. 209–10; H. R. Loyn, *The Governance of Anglo-Saxon England, 500–1087* (London, 1984), pp. 137–8. Corbett

Even if a hundred or wapentake district had constituted a recognizable territory long before the tenth century, it need not have served all, or indeed any, of the purposes of a late tenth- or eleventh-century hundred or wapentake. We therefore need to consider precedents for the functions associated with hundreds and wapentakes. An obvious first point is that there was in all likelihood nothing new about the imposition of burdens on districts, including in some cases districts corresponding to later hundreds and wapentakes: indeed, we have already noted that the irregular hidages of many southern Domesday hundreds may well reflect that the territories in question had been used for the extraction of obligations since before the tenth century.[139] Similarly, the idea that trade should be conducted in particular places in the presence of particular people was no novelty, although in this respect hundreds and wapentakes came to fulfil a function which Edward the Elder and (initially) Æthelstan had sought to restrict to *ports*.[140] There were also precedents for the holding of local assemblies: texts from the early tenth century and before assume that such meetings would be held, and, as we saw in the previous chapter, analogy with other parts of Europe suggests that the inhabitants of many localities may well have long gathered from time to time, potentially with no external prompting.[141] We cannot establish with confidence where local assemblies were held during or before the early tenth century, but it is eminently possible that the meeting places of certain hundreds and wapentakes had a considerable history as gathering points.[142] If this were indeed the case, then the legislation on hundreds and wapentakes issued by Edmund, Edgar, and

---

sought to count Domesday hundreds, and showed that his figures for various groups of shires could be combined to give round totals of 120 or 140 hundreds. If Corbett's reckoning of hundreds is correct, and if the resultant totals are more than coincidence, this could imply that at least some Domesday hundreds had been formed quite recently; had much time passed, the apparent symmetry would probably have been disrupted by the amalgamation and division of hundreds, as happened in several shires between Domesday and the early fourteenth century (the next time at which lists of hundreds can be compiled). Little weight can be placed on this argument, however, as there are uncertainties about the number of hundreds in some shires, and there must be a suspicion that Corbett's choice of which shires to group together was driven by a desire to produce totals that yielded a pleasing symmetry. For another attempt to count the hundreds in each Domesday shire, and details of how they related to fourteenth-century hundreds, see Thorn, 'Hundreds and Wapentakes', in Williams and Martin (eds), *Bedfordshire Domesday*, and equivalent contributions to other Alecto Domesday volumes. Thorn's figures sometimes, but not always, corroborate Corbett's.

[139] Above, p. 147. Regular hidages of Midland hundreds need not indicate that such territories were first used to assess obligations in the late Anglo-Saxon period: even if the round hidages were established by the Cerdicings, at least certain of the territories on which these quotas were imposed may have had some prior history as assessment districts. For speculation along such lines, see Corbett, 'Tribal Hidage', especially pp. 198–201, 208–11, but contrast Chadwick, *Studies*, pp. 241–4.

[140] I Ew 1–1.1; II As 12, 13.1. On the loosening of these restrictions, see above, p. 108.

[141] Hl 8; Ine 8; Af 22, 34, 38–38.2; I Ew 2; II Ew 8; II As 2, 12, 20, 20.3; V As 1.1; *VA*, cvi (p. 92); S 1186a; above, pp. 102–3.

[142] Anderson, *English Hundred-Names*, especially iii, 213–15 infers that the holding of gatherings at certain hundredal meeting points went back to the pre-Christian period because the names of the locations in question (e.g. *Wodneslaw* and *Thunreslaw*) were most likely coined then. Anderson's conclusion may well be correct, but his reasoning is dubious: an early place name need not indicate early use as a meeting site. Contrast A. Pantos, 'Assembly-Places in the Anglo-Saxon Period: Aspects of Form and Location' (3 vols, D.Phil. thesis, University of Oxford, 2001), i, 95–104. Pantos tentatively argues for the early formation of certain other place names at i, 38–46.

their successors may in many regions not have required people to start doing entirely new things, but to continue or adjust their existing practices, and perhaps perform them within a modified territorial framework. Kings' cooption, and probably reshaping, of long-standing structures of communal organization would still have constituted a very significant development, however, not least because it would have established a framework through which varied local practices could be made more standardized.[143]

Two specific precedents for features of hundredal organization require fuller comment. The first is Edward the Elder's order that reeves should hold meetings every four weeks, with each person being worthy of *folcriht* ('common justice'), and each case being dealt with on an *andaga* ('appointed day').[144] Since this foreshadows the Hundred Ordinance's prescriptions that four-weekly meetings be held, and that each case be settled in accordance with *folcriht* on an *andaga*, some historians have concluded that Edward had mandated the holding of hundred assemblies in all but name.[145] That a king should order the frequent and regular holding of what were probably fairly local meetings is significant, but caution is in order: Edward may in some instances have envisaged four-weekly meetings being organized on the basis of districts that were similar to (or even coterminous with) those of later hundreds, but there is little reason to think that this was generally the case.[146] His order could, for example, have been directed not to reeves responsible for hundreds, or equivalent districts known by other names, but to the reeves of *ports* and royal lands, and potentially also those of non-royal estates. If so, some of the practices associated with late tenth- and eleventh-century hundred and wapentake assemblies would not have been new, but the places in which they had previously applied would have been different, and possibly fewer in number. This would be consistent with the Hundred Ordinance, which implies that at least certain aspects of hundred meetings were based on arrangements relating to some other, probably better-established, form of assembly: its declaration that every case should be determined according to *folcriht* on an *andaga* is preceded by a phrase indicating that this should be so 'in the hundred just as in another meeting [*swa on oðer gemote*]'.[147] It is therefore likely that elements of hundredal administration drew on practices that went back to at least the reign of Edward the Elder, but his demand for four-weekly meetings does not indicate that the hundred system of Edgar's day was already functioning in the early tenth century.

An analogous point can be made about the resemblances between the provisions of the Hundred Ordinance and the thief-catching arrangements that the bishops and reeves of London established (or codified) during Æthelstan's reign. Most of

---

[143] Below, pp. 195–9.   [144] II Ew 8.

[145] Hu 1, 7–7.1; H. Cam, *Local Government in Francia and England: A Comparison of the Local Administration and Jurisdiction of the Carolingian Empire with that of the West Saxon Kingdom* (London, 1912), pp. 49, 59; Stenton, *Anglo-Saxon England*, p. 299; Loyn, 'Hundred', pp. 3–4. Contrast Chadwick, *Studies*, pp. 233–5, 240, 244–62.

[146] That the meetings were fairly local is implied by their being convened by reeves, rather than any more exalted figures.

[147] Hu 7.

the similarities between the texts are fairly general, and it is unsurprising that two sets of regulations concerning the pursuit of thieves should both address such matters as the organization of posses, the following of trails from one district ('scyre' in the London text) into another, and the distribution of confiscated goods.[148] In addition to such broad resemblances, however, the texts share a detail that is perhaps less likely to be coincidence: both prescribe a penalty of 30 pence for neglect of pursuit duties.[149] There may, moreover, have been some connection between the 'hundred' of the Hundred Ordinance, and the London practice of organizing policing and other responsibilities on the basis of groups of 100 people: the Hundred Ordinance says nothing about 100-person groups, and the London regulations use 'hundred' only in a numerical sense, but we should be open to the possibility of a link, not least because the 'hundred' and the 100-person contingent each had a senior figure known as a *hyndenman* or *hundredesman* ('hundredman').[150] It may also be significant that the 100-strong units of the London text were formed from ten ten-person groups, each of which had a senior member ('se yldesta'): this figure may have been in some way analogous to the 'tithingman' of the Hundred Ordinance, although it is uncertain whether the latter led ten subordinates.[151] A further point of interest is that the London regulations state that the leaders of the 100- and ten-person groups should meet each month, a frequency that resembles the four-weekly assemblies prescribed by the Hundred Ordinance.[152] Even if the policing arrangements to which the two texts relate were similar, however, it is likely that during Æthelstan's reign the London provisions obtained in only a fairly limited geographical area: while the inhabitants of certain other localities may well have organized posses, his extant legislation neither demands the establishment of policing associations, nor assumes their existence. In this regard, it is particularly notable that Æthelstan made no reference to any organized pursuit group when he ordered that fugitive thieves be chased and killed by all 'who want what the king wants'.[153] Nor did he refer to such a body when he declared that any person to whose land missing livestock had been tracked should seek to show that the trail could be traced beyond the bounds of the estate.[154] Thus, while precedents can be found for some of the activities of hundreds and wapentakes, we should be wary of taking this as evidence that mid- and late tenth-century kings merely perpetuated, and perhaps renamed, existing administrative structures: rather, their legislation on hundreds and wapentakes may well have served to appropriate and apply more widely practices that had previously been specific to particular places.

Moving to matters of terminology, the difficulties posed by the word 'wapentake' are perhaps less intractable than those associated with 'hundred'. 'Wapentake'

---

[148] VI As 1.1, 3–4, 8.3–8.4; Hu 2–2.1, 5; Chadwick, *Studies*, p. 247 n. 1. On the London text, see above, pp. 113–14. On the term *scir*, see below, pp. 170, 181.

[149] VI As 8.5; Hu 3.   [150] VI As 3, 8.1; Hu 2, 4, 5.

[151] VI As 3, 8.1; Hu 2, 4. After the Norman Conquest, tithingmen are documented as heads of districts, as well as of groups of ten (or more) people: W. A. Morris, *The Frankpledge System* (London, 1910), pp. 11–14, 86–90, 103–11.

[152] VI As 8.1; Hu 1.   [153] IV As 6.3.   [154] V As 2.

is first attested in Edgar's *Wihtbordesstan* legislation, but appears to be of Old Norse derivation, formed from elements meaning 'weapon' and 'the act of taking'.[155] Later Scandinavian sources use the word *vápnatak* to refer both to the end of an assembly, when those present resumed arms that they had laid aside during the meeting, and to a custom whereby people indicated consent by clashing or brandishing weapons.[156] It is, however, uncertain whether 'wapentake' ever had either of these meanings in Britain, and we cannot even be sure that the word was already used by Scandinavians when they settled in the future English kingdom.[157] Whatever rationale underlay the formation of the term, though, its etymology suggests that it either came from Scandinavia, or was coined in Britain by speakers of Old Norse. Either way, one can infer that the Cerdicings adopted, rather than created, the word, which in turn implies that phenomena in some way similar to late tenth-century wapentakes were already present prior to the northern extension of their domination. Given the lack of early evidence, we cannot now establish how the phenomena denoted by the term 'wapentake' originated: they could have existed in Britain before Scandinavian settlement but then have been renamed, or have developed in Britain at some point after the settlement, or have been introduced by settlers in imitation of a practice from across the North Sea. Nor can we determine whether the similarity between late tenth-century and at least some earlier wapentakes was territorial, functional, or both. We can, however, conclude that the means by which late tenth- and eleventh-century Cerdicing kings sought to regulate local affairs in the north-east of what would constitute Domesday *Anglia* were in some way based on the cooption or reorganization of earlier arrangements: for present purposes, this is more important than the irresolvable question of whether those earlier arrangements had antecedents in Scandinavia.

How and when the term 'hundred' came to be used in non-numerical contexts is very uncertain. One possibility is that the widening of its range of meanings was prompted by Londoners' use of 100-person groups to organize policing during Æthelstan's reign.[158] Alternatively, territories (sometimes) reckoned at 100 hides apiece may have come to be known by the numerical value of their (typical or idealized) hidage: such a semantic development might have been associated with the putative imposition by the Cerdicings of regular assessments in the Midlands, but could have been much older, and it is worth noting that the Tribal Hidage assessments are all multiples of 100 hides.[159] A further theory is that hundreds may have been based, both in substance and in name, on a Frankish model; the word *centena* ('hundred') appears in Merovingian legal texts as a

---

[155] IV Eg 6; C. T. Onions, G. W. S. Friedrichsen, and R. W. Burchfield, *The Oxford Dictionary of English Etymology* (Oxford, 1966), s.v. 'wapentake'.

[156] R. Cleasby, G. Vigfusson, and W. A. Craigie, *An Icelandic–English Dictionary*, 2nd edn (Oxford, 1957), s.v. 'vápna-tak'.

[157] A somewhat different explanation of the word was given by one twelfth-century writer: *Leges Edwardi Confessoris*, 30.2–30.4 (p. 188).

[158] VI As.

[159] D. N. Dumville, 'The Tribal Hidage: An Introduction to its Texts and their History', in S. Bassett (ed.), *The Origins of Anglo-Saxon Kingdoms* (London, 1989), pp. 225–30; above, pp. 95, 142–3.

term for both a district and a policing group, and also crops up in subsequent centuries, although it is increasingly unclear what it denoted.[160] There was thus a long period during which *centenae* could in principle have been transplanted north of the Channel, but the evidence is too sketchy to permit the kind of detailed comparison that could substantiate (or refute) the hypothesis that they provided the inspiration for English hundreds. Another potential hypothesis is that there was a prehistoric origin to the lexical (and perhaps conceptual) pairing of the number 100 and some sort of territory. This could explain why Alemannia, Frisia, and Sweden yield evidence of districts called *hundare*, *huntari*, or *hunderi*, although one could alternatively posit that in each case Frankish *centenae* were the direct or indirect inspiration.[161] Insufficient evidence survives to permit secure conclusions about these various lines of speculation: there is no compelling reason to infer that 'hundred' had any non-numerical meaning in Old English before the tenth century, but we have too few earlier texts to be confident of the contrary.[162]

Despite this quagmire of uncertainties, we can be fairly sure that between Æthelstan's reign and the latter part of Edgar's there was a significant shift in the means by which the Cerdicings sought to monitor, constrain, and direct the behaviour of ordinary people across the land from the Channel to the Tees. By the time of his *Wihtbordesstan* legislation, Edgar could take for granted the existence throughout this area of units called hundreds or wapentakes, for which he sought to establish standardized procedures. Given the ubiquity of the terms 'hundred' and 'wapentake' in the legislation of Edgar and his successors, it is hard to account for the absence of at least the former word (except as a number) from the fairly copious legislation of Alfred, Edward the Elder, and Æthelstan, unless one posits a major

---

[160] That hundreds were modelled on *centenae* is argued by H. Dannenbauer, 'Hundertschaft, Centena und Huntari', *Historisches Jahrbuch*, 62–9 (1942–9), pp. 163–5, 184–5, 218; Campbell, 'Observations on English Government', pp. 159, 161–2. Contrast Cam, *Local Government*, pp. 60–2, who hypothesized that the word 'hundred' was borrowed from Scandinavia; this is unlikely, since a different term (i.e. 'wapentake') was used in the regions of greatest Scandinavian influence. For the Merovingian evidence, see Murray, 'From Roman to Frankish Gaul'. The parallels between these sixth-century texts and the Hundred Ordinance are not sufficiently close to permit the inference that whoever wrote the latter knew the former. For later references to *centenae*, see *CRF*, nos. 139 (c. 10), 193 (c. 7); Ch.-E. Perrin, 'Sur le sens du mot «centena» dans les chartes lorraines du moyen âge', *Archivum Latinitatis Medii Aevi*, 5 (1930), pp. 167–98; L. Génicot, 'La *centena* et le *centenarius* dans les sources «belges» antérieures à 1200', in E. Magnou-Nortier (ed.), *Aux sources de la gestion publique. Tome I. Enquête lexicographique sur fundus, villa, domus, mansus* (Lille, 1993), pp. 85–102. According to a diploma of 1070, the 'Theutonici' used 'hunnenduom' to refer to what were in Latin called 'centunis': *Heinrici IV. Diplomata*, ed. D. von Gladiss and A. Gawlik (*MGH, Diplomata regum et imperatorum Germaniae*, 6, 3 vols, Weimar, 1952–3 and Hanover, 1978), no. 236 (i, 299).

[161] T. Andersson, 'Die schwedischen Bezirksbezeichnungen *hund* und *hundare*. Ein Beitrag zur Diskussion einer germanischen Wortfamilie', *Frühmittelalterliche Studien*, 13 (1979), pp. 88–124 posits a common root for the Swedish, Alemannic, and Frisian 'hundreds'. At 122–3, Andersson rejects the suggestion that the English term 'hundred' derived from this root, but his conclusion is predicated on the assumption that the word did not denote a district in Old English before the tenth century. See also P. MacCotter, *Medieval Ireland: Territorial, Political and Economic Divisions* (Dublin, 2008), pp. 109–24.

[162] There is, however, some basis to suspect that 'hundred' was not a ninth-century translation of *regio* or *provincia*, since the *Old English Bede* only uses the word in a numerical sense.

substantive change during the intervening years.[163] This argument holds whether or not 'hundred' had been used as a term for a district in earlier periods. If territories (of whatever size, shape, and nature) called hundreds existed in at least some places before the mid-tenth century, the lack of references to them in legislation suggests that they were of minimal importance to the Cerdicings, except perhaps as units for the reckoning of obligations, about which extant legal texts say almost nothing.[164] If, on the other hand, 'hundred' first acquired a non-numerical meaning around the time of Edmund, it is unlikely that the phenomena it thenceforth denoted had previously existed and functioned in much the same way: had they done so, it is hard to see what would have prompted a new name to be coined for them. Whatever prior existence (some) hundreds and wapentakes may have had, it appears that it was from the mid-tenth century onwards that they became really significant to the Cerdicings' rule.

This inference is strengthened when one recognizes that many of the functions which legal texts ascribe to hundreds and wapentakes had, under Edward the Elder and Æthelstan, been associated with *port*s or *burh*s, terms which appear to have been used fairly synonymously in royal legislation.[165] Thus, whereas Edward and (for a time) Æthelstan had demanded that *port*s be the venue for trade, or at least trade over 20 pence, Edgar presented *burh*s, hundreds, and wapentakes as equally acceptable fora for the witnessing of transactions.[166] Similarly, it is only from London that we have earlier evidence of pursuit groups comparable to those described by the Hundred Ordinance, and possibly assumed in Edmund's Colyton legislation. Perhaps most striking of all, however, are the differences between two similar passages from the decrees that Æthelstan and Edgar issued at Grately and Andover respectively:

If anyone fails to attend a meeting three times, that person shall pay the king's *oferhyrnesse* [elsewhere put at 120 shillings]. And the meeting shall be announced seven days before it is held. If anyone will not do right and pay the *oferhyrnesse*, then *all the senior people who pertain to the burh shall ride* and take all that that person has, and place him [or potentially her] under surety.

If anyone is unwilling to ride with his companions, that person shall pay the king's *oferhyrnesse*.

And it shall be proclaimed in the meeting, that people should observe everything that the king wishes to be respected, and refrain from theft on pain of death and [the loss of] all they possess.

And if anyone who has a bad reputation and is untrustworthy to the people fails to attend those meetings, [people] shall be chosen from the meeting who shall ride to that person, and he [or potentially she] may still find a surety if he can.

---

[163] The lack of references to wapentakes is less significant, since it was only from towards the end of Edward's reign that Cerdicing domination extended into areas in which wapentakes were later found.

[164] For an exceptional reference in legislation to the assessment of obligations, see Ine 70.1.

[165] Above, pp. 106–9.   [166] IV Eg 6, 10.

Again, if anyone is unwilling to desist, *all the senior people who pertain to the burh shall ride and take all that that person has, and the king shall receive half,* and those who rode half, and they shall place him [or potentially her] under surety.[167]

And if that person cannot do so, *they shall seize him [or potentially her] however they can, whether alive or dead, and take all that he has*, and pay to the accuser the singlefold value of the [stolen] goods, and *the lord shall receive half of the rest, and the hundred half.*

And if anyone, kinsman or stranger, refuses to ride, that person shall pay the king 120 shillings [i.e. the king's *oferhyrnesse*].[168]

Thus, while Æthelstan had envisaged that *burh*s should be the basis for organizing the enforcement of his commands, Edgar made no such assumption, and allocated to the hundred the share of confiscated goods that had previously been assigned to 'the senior people who pertain to the *burh*'. The point is not merely that the extant legislation of Edward and Æthelstan says nothing of hundreds, although that is in itself highly suggestive. Rather, what is really telling is that, in contexts where later legal texts would refer to hundreds and wapentakes, sometimes alongside *burh*s, early tenth-century kings had mentioned *burh*s or *port*s alone. This implies that, even in their southern heartlands, Edward and Æthelstan had had no consistent means by which to replicate more widely the administrative functions associated with a limited set of fortified locations.

The likelihood that, when developing their system of hundreds and wapentakes, the mid- to late tenth-century Cerdicings drew on such local arrangements as they found does not undermine the contention that the innovations these kings introduced were of considerable significance: a similar consideration applies to Edgar's numismatic reform, which was in large part implemented by existing moneyers, but nonetheless represented a major change.[169] Indeed, the proposition that the Cerdicings transformed within a relatively short period the means by which they sought to secure local compliance with their commands is rendered more plausible if one acknowledges that their reforms probably built on some precedents, such as existing practices of communal organization. The key point, however, is that, some time between the issues of Æthelstan's Grately ordinance and Edgar's *Wihtbordesstan* decrees, the Cerdicings appear to have supplemented their unevenly distributed *port*s and *burh*s by starting to make extensive use of a set of local administrative structures all across the land from the Channel to the Tees. When during the intervening decades this development took place cannot now be established, and it

[167] II As 20–20.4. For the level of the king's *oferhyrnesse*, see I Ew 2.1; II Ew 2. On *oferhyrnesse*, the basic meaning of which is 'disobedience', see A. Taylor, '*Lex Scripta* and the Problem of Enforcement: Anglo-Saxon, Welsh, and Scottish Law Compared', in F. Pirie and J. Scheele (eds), *Legalism: Community and Justice* (Oxford, 2014), pp. 47–75 especially 54–60.

[168] III Eg 7–7.2. In some manuscripts, it is stated that the posse was to ride after someone missed three meetings, but there is some basis to suspect that originally no figure was specified: Whitelock, *English Historical Documents*, p. 433 n. 3. The person who was to split the confiscated goods with the hundred appears in different manuscripts as *hlaford* (lord) or *landhlaford* ('land-lord'). The division of confiscated goods between the hundred and a *hlaford* also appears in Hu 2.1, and the whole passage is echoed in II Cn 25–25.2. On lords' receipt of judicial profits, see below, pp. 168–9, 175–7.

[169] Above, pp. 123–4.

is quite possible that the change was effected in phases. The Colyton decrees imply that bodies known as hundreds had some royally sanctioned role in policing before Edmund's death, but we do not know to what region or regions this legislation related. The same problem attaches to the Hundred Ordinance and, in addition, the dating parameters of that text are wide. Nor is it possible to infer much from the *Libellus Æthelwoldi*'s reference to the inhabitants of two hundreds meeting at Ely during the years before Edgar's accession, as there is no indication that gatherings of these people had been mandated by any king.[170] At least in certain regions, it may well have been a little before Edgar's reign that hundreds and wapentakes began to constitute a coherent network of royal administrative districts, but it is only with that king's *Wihtbordesstan* legislation that we have any good basis for thinking that this was the case across the land from the Channel to the Tees. To judge from Domesday, hundreds and wapentakes were very far from uniform: in addition to their obvious twofold terminology, they came in multifarious shapes and sizes, had a wide range of assessments, and may well have varied in many other ways that we cannot now determine. Nonetheless, they all had enough in common that they could be designated by one or other of these equivalent words: thus, during or shortly before the reign of Edgar, at least the vast majority of what would constitute Domesday *Anglia* came to have structures of Cerdicing administration that made the area in which they were found different from the rest of Britain.

SHIRES

The Domesday Shires

At the time of Domesday, almost all the land between the Channel, the Ribble, and the Tees was not only divided into hundreds or wapentakes, but also into shires (see Map 5, on page 156). One possible exception is the two wapentakes of Rutland (between Leicestershire, Lincolnshire, and Northamptonshire), which may not have been part of any shire: they are described at the end of the account of Nottinghamshire, and pertained for tax purposes to the *vicecomitatus* ('sheriffdom') of Nottingham, but Domesday provides discrete lists of those who held land 'in Snotinghamscire' and 'in Roteland'.[171] The six hundreds between the Ribble and the Mersey, surveyed at the end of the account of Cheshire, are another possible exception, since Domesday does not present them as a shire, yet implies that they were outwith Cheshire. Near the beginning of the Cheshire folios, it is stated that,

---

[170] *LE*, ii.18, ii.24 (pp. 93–4, 97). Strictly speaking, we cannot even be sure that the 'two hundreds' were known as 'hundreds', or recognized as two distinct units, at the time when the meeting took place, since the relevant passages (and quite possibly the records on which they are based) are written from the perspective of someone looking back from after Æthelwold's acquisition of Ely.

[171] *DB*, i, 280d, 293c–294a; F. Thorn, 'Hundreds and Wapentakes', in A. Williams and R. W. H. Erskine (eds), *The Nottinghamshire Domesday* (London, 1990), pp. 40–2. The wives of several kings are known to have held substantial lands in Rutland, and its anomalous status may have been in some way linked to this. See T. C. Cain, 'An Introduction to the Rutland Domesday', in A. Williams and R. W. H. Erskine (eds), *The Northamptonshire and Rutland Domesday* (London, 1987), pp. 18–34.

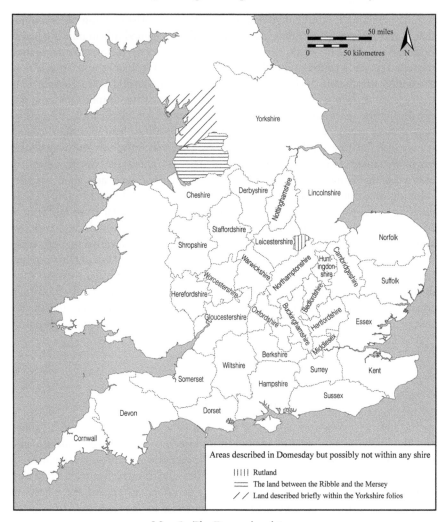

Map 5. The Domesday shires.

aside from episcopal estates, Earl Hugh and his men had 'all the rest of the land of the shire [*comitatus*]', while 'the land between the Ribble and the Mersey' was held by the king. In its description of one of the hundreds north of the Mersey (Derby hundred) Domesday does, however, mention a fine for failure to attend a shire meeting ('siremot'), which suggests that at least part of this area was in some way incorporated into the shire system.[172] A further potential mismatch is the land north of the Ribble and west of the Pennines, which appears briefly within the

---

[172] *DB*, i, 262d, 269c–270b; C. P. Lewis, 'An Introduction to the Lancashire Domesday', in A. Williams and G. H. Martin (eds), *The Lancashire Domesday* (London, 1991), pp. 1–41 especially 1, 12. The shire meeting may have been that of Cheshire, or a separate assembly for land north of the Mersey.

account of Yorkshire, but was not divided into hundreds or wapentakes. The account is, however, extremely terse, and the 'summary' that concludes the Yorkshire folios omits this region, which leads one to suspect that it may not have been regarded as part of any shire.[173] In spite of these uncertainties, though, a basic point is clear: in general, the presence or absence of shires reinforced the distinction between the parts of Britain in which hundreds or wapentakes did or did not exist.

The thirty-three Domesday shires varied considerably. Yorkshire was over twice the size of Lincolnshire or Devon, the next biggest shires, each of which was in turn over seven times as large as Middlesex or Huntingdonshire, the two smallest.[174] Domesday sometimes records customs that were apparently peculiar to a particular shire.[175] In the Midlands, each shire was clearly focused on a fortified place from which it was named, hence *Bedford*shire, *Northampton*shire, *Stafford*shire, *Worcester*shire, and so on, but this was fairly rare in East Anglia and the south.[176] Despite such differences, however, shires evidently had enough in common to constitute a recognizable species of district that could be used as the basis for the survey. They are also known to have served a variety of other important functions during the eleventh century, notably the organization of meetings, taxation, and military forces.[177] The problem that we need to consider now is that of when shires began to play a significant role in the Cerdicings' rule over a substantial part of what would constitute Domesday *Anglia*, and I again contend that the mid- to late tenth century was crucial. This is not, however, a necessary corollary of my arguments about hundreds and wapentakes, and must be justified separately: indeed, we shall see that in a couple of regions shires may well have been established well after Edgar's *Wihtbordesstan* decrees, by which time hundreds or wapentakes appear already to have existed in the areas in question.[178]

The Establishment of Shires

When considered simply as identifiable blocks of land, some shires were much older than others. Those of the south-east, namely Essex, Kent, Middlesex, Surrey, and Sussex, take their names from kingdoms or other districts mentioned in the early Anglo-Saxon period, and are therefore likely to correspond fairly closely to territorial units that were already very old by the tenth century.[179] The same is probably

---

[173] *DB*, i, 301d–302a, 379a–382b; D. Roffe, 'The Yorkshire Summary: A Domesday Satellite', *Northern History*, 27 (1991), pp. 242–60 especially 245, 257 and n. 63; F. Thorn, 'Hundreds and Wapentakes', in Williams and Martin (eds), *Lancashire Domesday*, pp. 47–54; D. M. Palliser, 'An Introduction to the Yorkshire Domesday', in A. Williams and G. H. Martin (eds), *The Yorkshire Domesday* (London, 1992), pp. 4–5, 14; F. Thorn, 'Hundreds and Wapentakes', in Williams and Martin (eds), *Yorkshire Domesday*, pp. 55–60; above, pp. 4–5.

[174] H. C. Darby, *Domesday England* (Cambridge, 1977), p. 359. Yorkshire is easily double the size of Devon or Lincolnshire even if land west of the Pennines is excluded.

[175] R. W. Finn, *An Introduction to Domesday Book* (London, 1963), pp. 266–71.

[176] The link between fortification name and shire name may not be immediately obvious for Shropshire, but Shrewsbury appears in Domesday as 'Sciropesberie': *DB*, i, 252a.

[177] Below, pp. 165–72.   [178] Below, pp. 159, 160.

[179] Chadwick, *Studies*, pp. 269–80.

so of Cornwall, which had been a Brittonic kingdom.[180] The origins of the other shires south of the Thames, that is Berkshire, Devon, Dorset, Hampshire, Somerset, and Wiltshire, are more obscure, but they are all mentioned in the 'common stock' of the *Chronicle* or its late ninth-century continuations; these names may well already have denoted territories with extents at least roughly similar to those of the Domesday shires.[181] Aside from Essex and Middlesex, however, there is no particular basis for thinking that any Domesday shire north of the Thames corresponded to a unit of such antiquity, and the first extant references to any of them relate to the last three decades of the tenth century. The earliest of which I am aware is a report by Lantfred of Winchester, who probably wrote between 972 and 974, that a woman from 'Bedefordscire' was cured of blindness at some point after 971, the year in which the relics of St Swithun had been moved into Winchester's Old Minster.[182] Further evidence comes from the *Libellus Æthelwoldi*, which relates that on various occasions between 975 and 984 there were meetings involving the whole '*provincia* or *vicecomitatus*' at Northampton, the entirety of 'comitatus Huntendune', and all the better assembly speakers ('concionatores') of 'comitatu Grantebrygge'.[183] Since *provincia, comitatus*, and *vicecomitatus* were common Latin terms for 'shire', it is likely that the underlying vernacular texts referred to Northamptonshire, Huntingdonshire, and Cambridgeshire. Similarly, the Ramsey *Liber Benefactorum*, which was compiled and translated from earlier materials in the second half of the twelfth century, alludes to a gathering of the greater and wiser people ('majores et prudentiores') of 'comitatu Cantebriggiæ' sometime between 975 and 991.[184] It also relates that in 991 the consecration of Ramsey's new church was attended by the great men of the East Angles and the powerful people ('potentes') of 'Cantebruge scira', 'Hertford scira', 'Bedeford scira', 'Huntendune scira', 'Hamptone scira', and Kesteven ('Kestesna').[185] Most other Midland shires are first named in the account of the years from 1006 to 1016 in the C, D, and E texts of the *Chronicle*, the only earlier instance being a reference

---

[180] O. J. Padel, 'Cornwall', in *WBEASE*, p. 124.

[181] *ASC* ABCDE 757, 802, 825, 840, 845, 851, 860, 878, ABCD 896, 897; Chadwick, *Studies*, pp. 282–90; B. Yorke, *Wessex in the Early Middle Ages* (London, 1995), pp. 84–92; above, p. 99 n. 54.

[182] Lantfred, *Translatio et Miracula S. Swithvni*, viii, ed. and trans. M. Lapidge, *The Cult of St Swithun* (Oxford, 2003), p. 290 with discussion of the date of composition at 235–7. Lantfred also refers to Hampshire ('prouincia . . . quae eorum lingua Hamne dicitur'—vii, p. 290), Essex ('Eastsexan'—xix, p. 300), Somerset ('prouincia quadam que Sumersætan nuncupatur'—xxxvii, p. 330), and possibly Huntingdonshire ('prouincia Anglorum que uocatur Hunum'—xviii, p. 300).

[183] *LE*, ii.11, ii.25, ii.34 (pp. 85, 98–9, 109). There are various other possible allusions to shire meetings in the text, such as *LE*, ii.8, ii.10 (pp. 81, 83). See also *LE*, ii.49a (p. 116), for a reference to an estate being 'in vicecomitatu de Bedeforde'. The memories of old people after Edgar's death of when Edward the Elder had gained control of 'Huntendunensem provinciam' and 'comitatum de Grantebruge' (*LE*, ii.25 (pp. 98–9)) do not demonstrate that Huntingdonshire and Cambridgeshire existed in Edward's time: the witnesses may well have used terms from their own day to describe geographical areas that had not previously been understood as shires.

[184] *Chronicon Abbatiæ Rameseiensis*, xxv, ed. W. D. Macray (RS, 83, London, 1886), p. 50; A. Gransden, 'Traditionalism and Continuity during the Last Century of Anglo-Saxon Monasticism', *Journal of Ecclesiastical History*, 40 (1989), pp. 194–8.

[185] *Chronicon Abbatiæ Rameseiensis*, lviii (p. 93). Hart, *Danelaw*, pp. 178–81 offers some speculations on Kesteven.

in the C version to the ravaging of 'Legeceasterscir' (Cheshire) by a northern naval force in 980.[186] Since a single scribe wrote the C text's annals for 491 to 1048, it is conceivable that the area around Chester was not understood as a 'shire' until well after 980, but such scepticism is probably misplaced, given that Bedfordshire existed by 974 and that other shires in the southern East Midlands are attested soon after.[187] If Cheshire was indeed a recognizable unit in 980, it is likely that more southerly parts of the West Midlands had been divided into shires by that time too. Shire divisions may also have been imposed on the northern East Midlands by 980, but it is best to keep an open mind on this point, since there is no evidence until 1016, when Lincolnshire and Nottinghamshire are mentioned in the C, D, and E texts of the *Chronicle*.[188]

In spite of the lack of evidence about the northern East Midlands, we can reasonably infer that by 980 shires existed across a substantial proportion of the area in which they were to be found at the time of Domesday. Two caveats are necessary, however. First, the boundaries of these shires may sometimes have been quite different from those of 1086. There is usually no firm evidence either way, but in one case we can be fairly sure that a major change was effected by Eadric Streona, who was ealdorman of Mercia from 1007 to 1017: an early eleventh-century Worcester cartulary (i.e. document collection) indicates the existence of 'Winchcombeshire', which had disappeared by the time of Domesday, and another cartulary from the end of the century attributes to Eadric the amalgamation of the *vicecomitatus* of Winchcombe with that of Gloucester.[189] That shire boundaries could be altered,

---

[186] *ASC* C 980. The first mentions of the other Midland shires in one or more versions of the *Chronicle* are: Shropshire in 1006 (CDE); Buckinghamshire, Cambridgeshire, and Oxfordshire in 1010 (CDE); Bedfordshire, Hertfordshire, and Huntingdonshire in 1011 (CDE); Northamptonshire in 1011 (CD); Gloucestershire, Lincolnshire, Nottinghamshire, Staffordshire, and Warwickshire in 1016 (CDE); Worcestershire in 1038 (E); Derbyshire in 1048 (D); and Herefordshire in 1051 (E). Leicestershire is first named in Domesday. The account of the period between *c.*983 and 1016 in the C, D, and E manuscripts was composed before 1023: S. Keynes, 'The Declining Reputation of King Æthelred the Unready', in D. H. Hill (ed.), *Ethelred the Unready: Papers from the Millenary Conference* (Oxford, 1978), pp. 229–32.

[187] On the scribe's hand, see *The Anglo-Saxon Chronicle: A Collaborative Edition. Volume 5: MS C*, ed. K. O'B. O'Keeffe (Cambridge, 2001), pp. xxvii–xxxii. C. S. Taylor, 'The Origin of the Mercian Shires', *Transactions of the Bristol and Gloucestershire Archaeological Society*, 21 (1898), pp. 32–57 argued that the Midland shires were formed in association with Æthelred II's ship levy of 1008. Taylor discounted the earlier reference to Cheshire, and did not consider Lantfred, the *Libellus Æthelwoldi*, and the *Liber Benefactorum*. He later sought to buttress his case by arguing that Gloucestershire's northern border postdates 981, but the shire could have been formed at an earlier date and then had its boundaries modified: C. S. Taylor, 'The Northern Boundary of Gloucestershire', *Transactions of the Bristol and Gloucestershire Archaeological Society*, 32 (1909), pp. 109–19.

[188] *ASC* CDE 1016. The *Liber Benefactorum*'s juxtaposition of Kesteven with a list of shires (*Chronicon Abbatiæ Rameseiensis*, lviii (p. 93)) does not constitute decisive negative evidence, since at the time of Domesday Kesteven was a significant and recognizable district within Lincolnshire (*DB*, i, 376d–377d). It is even possible that Kesteven was regarded as a shire in the late tenth and early eleventh centuries. See Hart, *Danelaw*, pp. 177–94.

[189] *Hemingi chartularium ecclesiæ Wigorniensis*, ed. T. Hearne (2 vols, Oxford, 1723), i, 50, 280. The first cartulary organizes documents geographically, under the headings 'INTO VVEOGERNA CESTRE [Worcester]', 'INTO VVINCELCVMBE [Winchcombe] SCIRE', 'INTO OXENA FORDA [Oxford] SCIRE', 'INTO GLEAWECESTRE [Gloucester] SCIRE', and 'INTO WÆRINCG WICAN [Warwick]', although it should be noted that the three *-scire* suffixes appear to have been added a little after the rubrics were initially written: F. Tinti, *Sustaining Belief: The Church of Worcester*

even to the extent of one shire absorbing another, does not, however, particularly matter here: for my argument, the dimensions of individual shires are much less important than the basic point that by the end of the tenth century shires probably existed across at least the bulk of the Midlands, as well as in the south. The second caveat is more significant: even if the uncertainties about the northern East Midlands are set aside, it is doubtful whether any shire divisions were imposed in East Anglia or north of the Humber until well into the eleventh century. There is no extant mention of Norfolk or Suffolk from before the early 1040s, and one must wait until the 1060s for references to Yorkshire.[190] In both cases, the argument from silence is strengthened by the way in which annals concerning Æthelred II's reign in the C, D, and E versions of the *Chronicle* mention numerous shires in the Midlands and the south, while referring to 'East Anglia' and 'the Northumbrians'.[191] Indeed, these expressions are sometimes directly juxtaposed with long lists of shires, which implies that in the early eleventh century 'Norfolk', 'Suffolk', and 'Yorkshire' were not recognized as such: when describing where Swein's army had ravaged, the 1011 annal in the C, D, and E texts records East Anglia alongside fifteen named shires, and in 1016 Cnut is said to have gone from Buckinghamshire to Bedfordshire to Huntingdonshire to Northamptonshire, then along the fen to Stamford, into Lincolnshire, Nottinghamshire, 'and so into the Northumbrians towards York'.[192] East Anglia may have functioned as one large shire before being split into Norfolk and Suffolk, and some part of the land north of the Humber could have been regarded as a shire without being called 'Yorkshire', but there is a significant chance that shire organization was only introduced into these areas during or after the reign of Cnut. Nonetheless, the point remains that we can be reasonably sure that at least the bulk of Southumbria had been divided into shires twenty or more years before the end of the tenth century.

The problem that we now confront is that of whether some or all of the Midland shires had been established considerably before the 970s. Frank Stenton considered that the shires of the West Midlands were 'the work of a king who had no respect for the ancient divisions of Mercia', and hypothesized that they were demarcated

---

from c.870 to c.1100 (Farnham, 2010), pp. 85–150 especially 90 and n. 28, 102–5. See also J. Whybra, *A Lost English County: Winchcombeshire in the Tenth and Eleventh Centuries* (Woodbridge, 1990).

[190] S 1067, 1160, 1531; *ASC* CD 1065. The territories of Norfolk and Suffolk may have resembled those of the two dioceses into which the East Anglian kingdom had been divided between the late seventh century and the viking attacks, but this would not indicate that either Norfolk or Suffolk had functioned as a shire before the eleventh century. See J. Campbell, 'The East Anglian Sees before the Conquest', in I. Atherton, E. Fernie, C. Harper-Bill, and H. Smith (eds), *Norwich Cathedral: Church, City and Diocese, 1096–1996* (London, 1996), pp. 3–21, reprinted in his *The Anglo-Saxon State* (London, 2000), pp. 107–16.

[191] *ASC* C 978, 980, 981, 982, CDE 988, 992, 993, 994, 997, 998, 999, 1001, A 1001, CDE 1003, 1004, 1006, 1009, 1010, 1011, 1013, 1015, 1016. See also L. Marten, 'The Shiring of East Anglia: An Alternative Hypothesis', *Historical Research*, 81 (2008), pp. 1–27 especially 13–17.

[192] *ASC* CDE 1011, 1016. It is intriguing, although perhaps coincidental, that in both cases E omits Northamptonshire. The phrasing of the 1016 annal can be construed as implying that Stamford was not then within Lincolnshire, and perhaps not in Northamptonshire either. At the time of Domesday, the town of Stamford was split between these two shires, but it is possible that it had been the focus of a shire of its own in the early eleventh century. See Hart, *Danelaw*, pp. 177–94.

by Edward the Elder in the wake of his putsch of 918/919.[193] Stenton based this conclusion on the observation that these shires split the conjectured territories of the likes of the Hwicce and the Magonsæte, which had been kingdoms or provinces in the time of Mercian hegemony. The differences from older blocks are indeed notable, and it is particularly striking that the Domesday boundary between Staffordshire and Warwickshire ran straight through Tamworth, which had been a major seat of former Mercian rulers.[194] Stenton's theory is, however, far from compelling. In the first place, it is arguable that shire boundaries may have followed earlier frontiers more than they departed from them.[195] In any case, sporadic tenth- and eleventh-century references to long-defunct kingdoms do not demonstrate that local people still held these in high affection, or that they would have constituted a suitable framework for Cerdicing administration.[196] Nor need the bisecting of Tamworth have been motivated by a desire to symbolize the termination of Mercian autonomy by disregarding a place which had been significant to its former rulers. Such a theory sits awkwardly with Gloucester being made the focal point of a shire, since the burial there of both Æthelred and Æthelflaed suggests that it was at least as important as Tamworth to them.[197] Moreover, Tamworth was not unique in straddling a shire border: Stamford and Thetford did so too, and there is no particular reason to suppose that this was intended to weaken or belittle them.[198] Indeed, if the boundaries were laid out some decades after 918/919, Tamworth might well have had little claim to be the focus of a shire: without the patronage of a Mercian court, it seems to have descended into obscurity and, to judge from the meagre archaeological record, poverty.[199] These objections do not disprove Stenton's hypothesis, but they substantially undermine its rationale.

---

[193] Stenton, *Anglo-Saxon England*, p. 337. See also M. Gelling, *The West Midlands in the Early Middle Ages* (Leicester, 1992), pp. 139–42, 152, 156; D. H. Hill, 'The Shiring of Mercia—Again', in Higham and Hill (eds), *Edward the Elder*, pp. 144–5; D. Pratt, 'Written Law and the Communication of Authority in Tenth-Century England', in D. Rollason, C. Leyser, and H. Williams (eds), *England and the Continent in the Tenth Century: Studies in Honour of Wilhelm Levison (1876–1947)* (Turnhout, 2010), pp. 344–5. On the events of 918/919, see above, pp. 28, 137–8.

[194] For a map illustrating the bisection of Tamworth, see Gelling, *West Midlands*, p. 152.

[195] Bassett, 'Administrative Landscape', pp. 151–7.

[196] S 677, 712a, 723, 891, 1290, 1297, 1316, 1318, 1324; *ASC* CDE 1016; John of Worcester, *Chronicle*, 1041, ed. and trans. R. R. Darlington, P. McGurk, and J. Bray (2 vols so far, Oxford, 1995–), ii, 532.

[197] *ASC* MR 918; Æthelweard, *Chronicle*, iv.4, ed. and trans. A. Campbell (Edinburgh, 1962), pp. 53–4; A. Thacker, 'Chester and Gloucester: Early Ecclesiastical Organization in Two Mercian Burhs', *Northern History*, 18 (1982), pp. 207–11; C. Heighway, 'Gloucester and the New Minster of St Oswald', in Higham and Hill (eds), *Edward the Elder*, pp. 102–11. That Æthelflaed died in Tamworth makes her burial in Gloucester all the more notable. The possible shift in the relative importance of Gloucester and Tamworth would be readily explicable if, as has recently been suggested, the latter was under Scandinavian domination for some or all of the period 877–913: S. Bassett, 'Anglo-Saxon Fortifications in Western Mercia', *Midland History*, 36 (2011), pp. 16–17.

[198] *DB*, i, 336d; ii, 118b. It has been suggested that the bisection of Thetford represents an attempt by Cnut to undermine it, but this hypothesis seems to be inspired by the assumption that Edward the Elder divided Tamworth with a similar motive: Marten, 'Shiring', pp. 17–19 and n. 86.

[199] J. Gould, 'Third Report of the Excavations at Tamworth, Staffs., 1968—The Western Entrance to the Saxon Borough', *South Staffordshire Archaeological and Historical Society Transactions*, 10 (1969), pp. 38–41; Gelling, *West Midlands*, pp. 151–3.

Turning to the East Midlands, Stenton asserted that the shires there were based on different zones of Scandinavian settlement, since in the early tenth century we hear of armies associated with Cambridge, Huntingdon, Leicester, and Northampton.[200] Caution is in order, as there is no specific evidence for the territories of these armies, and the lands over which they were dominant may well not have neatly interlocked. Nonetheless, it is possible that these armies had power over areas comparable in size and shape to Cambridgeshire, Huntingdonshire, Leicestershire, and Northamptonshire. In a similar vein, one can speculate that at least some shires in the East and West Midlands perpetuated districts that Edward the Elder, Æthelflaed, or indeed earlier rulers had made responsible for maintaining fortifications.[201] But even if territories of similar size and shape to late tenth-century shires had constituted recognizable blocks decades before the 970s, which is itself no more than a possibility, it may not be helpful for us to think of these earlier units as 'shires'. Just because somewhere like Cambridge had an identifiable hinterland, it would not necessarily follow that contemporaries regarded the area in question as a shire, in the sense of being a member of a particular species of district that also included the likes of Devon, Kent, and Wiltshire.

An alternative argument for the early demarcation of the Midland shires is advanced by Cyril Hart, who contends that the text known as the County Hidage originated before Edmund's recovery of the territory north of Watling Street in the early 940s.[202] The County Hidage assigns hidages to Wiltshire and twelve Midland shires, namely Bedfordshire, Cambridgeshire, Huntingdonshire, Northamptonshire, Gloucestershire, Worcestershire, Herefordshire, Warwickshire, Oxfordshire, Shropshire, Cheshire, and Staffordshire; in most cases, the figures listed are fairly close to the number of hides that can be counted in the shire in Domesday.[203] Hart's argument focuses on Northamptonshire, one of four shires where there is a substantial discrepancy. Three of the four extant versions of the County Hidage assign Northamptonshire 3,200 hides (the fourth has 4,200), but a text known as the Northamptonshire Geld Roll shows that it had 2,663½ in 1066, and Hart estimates that this had fallen to about 1,244 by the time of Domesday itself.[204] Hart observes that the Geld Roll divides Northamptonshire

---

[200] *ASC* ABCD 913, A 917; Stenton, *Anglo-Saxon England*, p. 338.

[201] Bassett, 'Administrative Landscape', pp. 147–57; S. Keynes, 'Edward, King of the Anglo-Saxons', in Higham and Hill (eds), *Edward the Elder*, p. 59; Hill, 'Shiring of Mercia'.

[202] C. Hart, *The Hidation of Northamptonshire* (Leicester, 1970), especially pp. 12–21, 39–46. For the events of the 940s, see above, pp. 31–2.

[203] The text survives in three thirteenth-century manuscripts, plus a seventeenth-century edition of a now-lost manuscript of unknown date: Hart, *Danelaw*, p. 298 n. 23. The hidage figures vary between manuscripts, sometimes considerably; they are tabulated, along with totals calculated from Domesday, by Maitland, *Domesday Book*, p. 456.

[204] *Anglo-Saxon Charters*, pp. 230–6. The Geld Roll dates from William the Conqueror's reign, but states that the hidages were the same in the time of Edward the Confessor. The text is not preserved in a roll, but the name has become conventional. The other shires for which the Domesday hidage is markedly lower than that in the County Hidage are Cambridgeshire, Cheshire, and Shropshire. Hart argues that Cambridgeshire was reassessed at the same time as Northamptonshire, but offers no explanation for the changes in Cheshire and Shropshire: C. Hart, *The Hidation of Cambridgeshire* (Leicester, 1974), especially pp. 30–2. Hart buttresses his case by claiming that the reduction in Cambridgeshire's hidage must antedate the foundation of Ramsey and the refoundation of Ely, since estates they

into thirty-two hundreds, that it ascribes those hundreds lying wholly or partially south of Watling Street 100 hides apiece, and that its assessments of many of the hundreds to the north are considerably lower.[205] Given that the County Hidage assigns Northamptonshire 3,200 hides, Hart very reasonably infers that it was composed at a time when each of the shire's hundreds had 100 hides, as those in the south still did in 1066; it follows that there had been an unevenly distributed cut in Northamptonshire's assessment sometime between the date of the County Hidage and the Norman Conquest. The flaw in Hart's argument is his assumption that this selective reduction reflects an attempt by Edmund to secure support following his recovery of the land beyond Watling Street: this proposition is unsound, since there is no need to pin the reassessment to an event mentioned in a narrative source. Even if one wished to do so, Edmund's reign would not be the only option, since the C, D, and E texts of the *Chronicle* record that in 1013 Swein received the submission of those living north of Watling Street, and only ravaged to the south; one could, for example, postulate that Cnut rewarded those who had submitted promptly by reducing their assessments.[206] There is, therefore, no need to suppose that the County Hidage or the shires it names (except Wiltshire) antedated the 940s. Indeed, there are grounds to suspect that the text may be considerably later, since it attributes Gloucestershire a hidage that corresponds reasonably closely to that which can be estimated from Domesday. This implies that the County Hidage reflects a situation no earlier than 1007, the earliest date for the amalgamation of Gloucestershire and Winchcombeshire.[207]

The foregoing merely demonstrates that it is not necessary to accept the arguments of Stenton and Hart about when the Midland shires were formed. There are, however, two points that provide a more positive basis for suspecting that in both the East and West Midlands shires may well be only a little older than the earliest clear evidence of their existence. The first is the way in which they relate to episcopal sees. We noted in Chapter 3 that, while southern bishoprics were of fairly modest extent from the early tenth century onwards, much of the Midlands was covered by two vast dioceses, the seats of which were at Dorchester-on-Thames and Lichfield.[208] This contrast arose because at some point during the reign of Edward the Elder (probably 908×918) the dioceses of Sherborne and Winchester were split into five, the resultant bishoprics corresponding closely to shires: Sherborne appears henceforth to have covered just Dorset; Winchester,

---

obtained soon after appear in Domesday with the same hidage as at the time of acquisition. Hart lists various transactions (p. 30 n. 2), but it is the exception, rather than the rule, that an estate of the same name occurs in Domesday with the same hidage.

[205] The figure of 32 is reached by reckoning 'double hundreds' as two hundreds, and 'hundreds-and-a-half' at one and a half hundreds. Hart's claim that hidage reductions correlate with the incidence of Scandinavian place names is dubious. For a map of the Domesday hundreds of Northamptonshire, see above, p. 142.

[206] *ASC* CDE 1013.

[207] Maitland, *Domesday Book*, pp. 455–60; S. Keynes, 'County Hidage', in *WBEASE*, pp. 128–9; above, p. 159.

[208] Above, p. 110.

Hampshire and Surrey; Wells, Somerset; Ramsbury, Wiltshire and Berkshire; and Crediton, Devon and Cornwall.[209] The apparent linkage of diocese and shire (or shires) was reinforced during Æthelstan's reign, when a separate see for Cornwall was established (or reestablished) at St Germans.[210] In view of this, it is striking that the tenth century saw no fundamental reorganization of the large Midland sees, and that Gloucestershire, Shropshire, and Warwickshire straddled dioceses.[211] At the very least, this should caution against the assumption that Edward and Æthelstan rushed to remould Mercia in Wessex's image. We can, however, go further: since the southern bishoprics appear to have been refashioned to correspond with shires during these kings' reigns, the divergences between boundaries further north suggest that it was not Edward or Æthelstan who established the Midland shires.

The second indication that the Midland shires may well have been formed no earlier than the mid-tenth century comes from a passage in the will of King Eadred, written sometime between 951 and 955, in which he distributed precious metal that was to be used if it became necessary to alleviate famine or buy off heathen attackers.[212] Since the other extant sources from the first three quarters of the tenth century rarely name any of the shires that we know to have existed in the south, little weight can be placed on their silence about those of the Midlands, but Eadred's will refers to every Domesday shire south of the Thames except Cornwall. He left 400 pounds (presumably of silver) for Kent, Surrey, Sussex, and Berkshire, 200 pounds for Hampshire, the same for Somerset and Devon, and 100 pounds for each of Wiltshire and Dorset. In addition, Bishop Ælfsige of Winchester was to have custody of 200 pounds for whichever 'scire' needed it. Given that Eadred arranged his southern bequests by shire, it is very interesting that he then allocated 400 pounds for the Mercians ('Myrcum'), making no prescriptions about how this gift should be apportioned among them. The lack of reference to the Midland shires could just reflect that Eadred was being less generous to the Mercians, and that splitting up the 400 pounds would have given each shire relatively little. Equally, however, the silence about the Mercian shires could reflect that they did not exist in the early 950s, or at least that they did not yet constitute units that were significant to the Cerdicings. If Eadred's will is taken in conjunction with the pattern of diocesan boundaries, we have just enough evidence to draw the tentative conclusion that in the Midlands shire divisions were probably only established in the third quarter of the tenth century.

[209] D. H. Hill, *An Atlas of Anglo-Saxon England* (Oxford, 1981), p. 148; N. Brooks, *The Early History of the Church at Canterbury: Christ Church from 597 to 1066* (London, 1984), pp. 210–13; A. R. Rumble, 'Edward the Elder and the Churches of Winchester and Wessex', in Higham and Hill (eds), *Edward the Elder*, pp. 238–44. Selsey remained the episcopal see of Sussex. Kent continued to have seats at both Canterbury and Rochester.

[210] C. Insley, 'Athelstan, Charters and the English in Cornwall', in M. T. Flanagan and J. A. Green (eds), *Charters and Charter Scholarship in Britain and Ireland* (Basingstoke, 2005), pp. 20–3.

[211] Bassett, 'Administrative Landscape', pp. 151–5 plays down the differences between shire and diocesan boundaries in the West Midlands, but the pattern is still strikingly different from that in Wessex.

[212] S 1515.

The Functions of Shires

At least as important as the question of when particular territories began to be classed as 'shires' is that of what purposes these shires served at different dates. In the south, shires existed in the ninth century, but the only function that they are known to have performed is the organization of armed forces: the 'common stock' of the *Chronicle* records several occasions when a contingent from Berkshire, Devon, Dorset, Hampshire, Kent, Somerset, Surrey, or Wiltshire fought, and usually notes that it did so under the leadership of a named ealdorman.[213] Shires likewise acted as units of military organization in the eleventh century, and it is notable that annals concerning Æthelred II's reign refer not only to forces from various southern shires, but also to Cambridgeshire standing firm against a Scandinavian army in 1010.[214] There is hardly any definite evidence from before the Norman Conquest that kings used shires to organize such other services and renders as they extracted from their subordinates, but this is clearly indicated by a text in which Edward the Confessor granted the beneficiary exemption from *scot* and *gafol*, both of which denote some form of payment, 'in hundred and in shire [*scire*]'.[215] It is, moreover, highly likely that the *heregeld* levied from 1012 to 1051 had been collected on a shire-by-shire basis: this is known to have been the case very shortly after the Conquest, and is perhaps suggested by Harthacnut's having all Worcestershire ravaged to punish the killing of two tax-gatherers.[216] We should, moreover, be open to the possibility that shires had played some role in the Cerdicings' extraction of labour services and other dues since at least the ninth century. Given that we have so few sources concerning the imposition of burdens, an argument from silence would be weak, and it is eminently plausible that a method by which military forces were organized may also have been employed in connection with the assessment and discharge of other duties.[217]

By the eleventh century, however, the Cerdicings used shires not only to obtain things from their subordinates, but also to regulate the dealings that the latter had with one another. Key to this was the routine holding of shire meetings, which served (among other things) as royally ordained fora for dispute settlement. Evidence for these assemblies comes in three main forms. The first is royal legislation: Edgar declared in his Andover decrees that the *scirgemot* ('shire meeting') and *burhgemot* ('*burh* meeting') should be held twice and thrice per year respectively, in the presence of the ealdorman and bishop.[218] Cnut repeated these provisions, adding

---

[213] *ASC* ABCDE 802, 840, 845, 851, 853, 860, 878. Note also *ASC* ABCD 903; S 1211; above, p. 99 n. 54.

[214] *ASC* A 1001, CDE 1001, 1003, 1010. See also II Cn 79; *ASC* CD 1052.

[215] S 1131, which can be dated to 1049×1066. For the same formulation in documents of at best doubtful authenticity, see S 1120, 1130, 1137.

[216] *ASC* CD 1041; John of Worcester, *Chronicle*, 1041 (ii, 532). The Northamptonshire Geld Roll and the records preserved in *Exon Domesday* provide the clearest evidence for the use of shires to organize tax collection soon after the Norman Conquest: *Anglo-Saxon Charters*, pp. 230–6; *Exon Domesday*, pp. 1–11, 12–26, 59–75, 489–90.

[217] Above, p. 99.

[218] III Eg 5.1–5.2. The *burhgemot* is very obscure: all that can really be said about it is that it was presumably a meeting associated with a fortified location, and that it was different from a *scirgemot*.

that more frequent meetings could be convened if necessary, and also stipulating that no one should forcibly recover disputed property without seeking justice three times in a hundred and once in a *scirgemot*.[219] The second type of evidence is that of short formulaic vernacular documents, now often known as 'writ-charters', which served as evidence of a grant of some kind, and survive from around the turn of the tenth and eleventh centuries onwards. Writ-charters in the name of the reigning king are very frequently addressed to a bishop, an ealdorman or earl, and the thegns of a shire, which implies that shire meetings were indeed held in the form that Edgar and Cnut prescribed.[220] References to specific shire meetings, which frequently occur in accounts of land disputes, constitute the third, and in some ways most significant, body of material. The relevant texts tend to be written from the perspective of one of the contending parties, but the partiality of the sources causes little difficulty here, since we are concerned with the fora in which matters were considered, not with the substance of the disagreements. Prior to the Norman Conquest, such accounts of shire meetings survive for Berkshire, Cambridgeshire, Dorset, Gloucestershire (possibly), Herefordshire, Huntingdonshire, Kent, Lincolnshire, Northamptonshire, and Worcestershire.[221]

No unequivocal account of a shire meeting relates to a period before the mid-960s at the earliest, but the half-century from then until Æthelred II's death yields references for six different shires.[222] We have already noted that the *Libellus Æthelwoldi* mentions Cambridgeshire, Huntingdonshire, and Northamptonshire assemblies held during the nine years after Edgar's death, and that the Ramsey *Liber Benefactorum* alludes to a Cambridgeshire meeting that took place sometime between 975 and 991.[223] An arch-sceptic could object that the compilers of these

---

See J. G. H. Hudson, *The Oxford History of the Laws of England. Volume II: 871–1216* (Oxford, 2012), p. 56.

[219] II Cn 18–19.2. Note also II Atr App 8.1, 8.3; Forf 1–2, which may be fragments of a lost royal ordinance from the late tenth century: Wormald, *Making*, pp. 369–70.

[220] *Anglo-Saxon Writs*, ed. F. E. Harmer (Manchester, 1952, reprinted Stamford, 1989), especially pp. 45–54; Sharpe, 'Use of Writs'. Old English *gewrit* denoted a piece of writing, rather than just this class of document. The term 'writ-charter' is not contemporary, but usefully enables one to distinguish documents that represent a grant or confirmation from other forms of writing. Under Sharpe's definition, the address to one or more shires is an essential feature of a 'writ-charter', but it seems unhelpful to exclude documents of much the same formulation that notified other recipients (e.g. the inhabitants of *burhs*) of grants: e.g. S 996, 1096, 1103, 1119, 1149, 1150, 1153.

[221] *LE*, ii.11, ii.25, ii.34 (pp. 85, 98–9, 109); *Chronicon Abbatiæ Rameseiensis*, xxv, xc (pp. 50, 154); S 1422, 1454, 1456, 1458, 1460, 1462; *The Life and Miracles of Saint Kenelm*, xviii, xix, ed. and trans. R. C. Love, *Three Eleventh-Century Anglo-Latin Saints' Lives* (Oxford, 1996), pp. 72–4. S 1394, 1399, 1402, 1403, 1406, 1409, 1469, 1473, 1474, 1476 provide further evidence of shire meetings in Devon, Gloucestershire, Hampshire, Herefordshire, Kent, and Worcestershire, although not (explicitly) of their use for dispute resolution. For additional possible references, see P. Wormald, 'A Handlist of Anglo-Saxon Lawsuits', *ASE*, 17 (1988), pp. 247–81, reprinted in his *Legal Culture in the Early Medieval West: Law as Text, Image and Experience* (London, 1999), p. 285; P. Wormald, 'Giving God and King their Due: Conflict and its Regulation in the Early English State', *Settimane di studio del centro italiano di studi sull'alto medioevo*, 44 (1997), pp. 549–90, reprinted in his *Legal Culture*, p. 347 n. 48.

[222] For possible earlier examples, see below, pp. 169, 170–1.

[223] *LE*, ii.11, ii.25, ii.34 (pp. 85, 98–9, 109); *Chronicon Abbatiæ Rameseiensis*, xxv (p. 50); above, p. 158.

twelfth-century Latin 'cartulary-chronicles' may have recast the documents that they used and translated, but there is no specific reason to think that the accounts of shire meetings were later inventions. There are, moreover, four further references to shire assemblies held before 1016: these are found in discrete vernacular texts, two of which are written in hands approximately contemporary with the events they describe. The earliest of the four relates that, sometime between 964 and 988, Archbishop Dunstan of Canterbury secured a contested bequest at a meeting attended by various named dignitaries and 'all the people of East Kent and West Kent'.[224] In the second case, datable to 990×992, it is reported that Æthelred II ordered a *scirgemot* in Berkshire to assess a certain Wynflæd's claim that she had a right to two estates that someone else had seized.[225] The third account concerns a meeting held sometime between 995 and 1005, after Æthelred sent a written message and seal to Archbishop Ælfric of Canterbury and the 'thegns of East Kent and West Kent', instructing them to consider the Bishop of Rochester's contention that a certain Leofwine was in wrongful possession of the episcopal estate of Snodland.[226] The last of the four documents records that 'all the senior thegns in Dorset', along with assorted named magnates, witnessed a settlement agreed by the church of Sherborne and Edmund *ætheling* (one of Æthelred II's sons, and future king) at some point between 1007 and 1014, under which Edmund would pay 20 pounds (presumably of silver) to lease the estate of Holcombe for the rest of his life. This text is a little coy about the preceding chain of events, but a separate letter from the Bishop of Sherborne indicates that he was parting with Holcombe involuntarily, and it is clear that the lifetime loan was a compromise to resolve a dispute. According to the lease agreement, Sherborne had 'not dared' to refuse the *ætheling*'s initial request that he receive Holcombe in perpetuity, but the king had refused to ratify such a deal, ordering instead that some arrangement be reached whereby the church would not lose the land forever.[227] There is thus good evidence that in and after the final quarter of the tenth century shire assemblies were held both north and south of the Thames, and that they were used to arrange dispute settlement, as the Cerdicings commanded.

---

[224] S 1458, which survives in a near-contemporary manuscript. The distinction between East Kent and West Kent goes back to the early Anglo-Saxon period (when Kent was often ruled by two joint-kings), and was reflected in its being the only shire with two episcopal sees (Canterbury and Rochester): B. Yorke, 'Joint Kingship in Kent, *c*.560 to 785', *Archaeologia Cantiana*, 99 (1983), pp. 1–19.

[225] S 1454, which survives in a near-contemporary manuscript. For discussion, see A. Kennedy, 'Disputes about *bocland*: The Forum for their Adjudication', *ASE*, 14 (1985), pp. 187–8; Wormald, 'Giving God and King their Due', pp. 343–52; Wormald, *Making*, pp. 151–3.

[226] S 1456. The text survives in an early twelfth-century Rochester collection, but there is no reason to doubt that what we have is an accurate copy of a document written around the time of the events described. The case is discussed by P. Wormald, 'Charters, Law and the Settlement of Disputes in Anglo-Saxon England', in W. Davies and P. Fouracre (eds), *The Settlement of Disputes in Early Medieval Europe* (Cambridge, 1986), pp. 149–68, reprinted in his *Legal Culture*, pp. 289–311 especially 303–5.

[227] S 1383, 1422. The letter was copied into a pontifical book in a near-contemporary hand, and the lease agreement survives in a mid-twelfth-century cartulary. There is no reason to doubt that the extant texts are accurate copies of documents written in the early eleventh century. It is not explicitly stated that Edmund had demanded a permanent grant, but this can be inferred from Æthelred's response. For the date, see *Charters of Sherborne*, ed. M. A. O'Donovan (Oxford, 1988), pp. 49–51. Note also S 1474.

We now need to consider whether any inferences can be drawn from the lack of comparable evidence for shire meetings in texts concerning the period before Edgar. Of the three sets of sources just discussed, writ-charters reveal least in this regard, since the earliest possibly genuine examples date from the reign of Æthelred II.[228] If we had examples from the preceding decades that were silent about shires, this would have implied (but not proved) that shire meetings began or became more important in the late tenth century, but the straightforward absence of writ-charters permits no such inference, since shire assemblies could have been held without being sent documents of this (or any other) nature. It is, moreover, possible that writ-charters, and indeed other missives, had been addressed to shire meetings in earlier periods, but that all such texts have been lost; there would have been especially little reason to preserve a document such as that which Æthelred is said to have sent in the Snodland case, since this merely conveyed an order, and did not (in contrast to a writ-charter) constitute proof of a grant.[229] The evidence of writ-charters is, however, not entirely insignificant in the present context. While it is impossible to prove that documents of this type were first written around the turn of the tenth and eleventh centuries, we can at least be confident that they were thenceforth issued with much greater frequency than before. It would otherwise be very hard to explain why we have several dozen examples in the names of kings from Æthelred to Harold II, but absolutely none from earlier reigns. The proliferation of writ-charters is important when we consider that, unlike other vernacular missives, they served as evidence of a grant, frequently of the right to various judicial profits.[230] Maitland saw such grants as

---

[228] S 945, 946. S 456, which runs in Æthelstan's name, is clearly a post-Conquest confection.

[229] S 1456. In the Berkshire case (S 1454), Æthelred is said to have sent his seal ('insegel') to the *scirgemot*; this seal may well have been attached to a document, but it is possible that the seal-matrix itself (or an impression thereof) had been given to the bearer of an oral message as a means of authentication. There may also have been no need to preserve in perpetuity writ-charters that conveyed fiscal or judicial privileges, since there is reason to suspect that in the eleventh century fresh grants were required when either the king or the beneficiary died: Sharpe, 'Use of Writs', especially pp. 283–4. A passing reference in the *Old English Soliloquies* (which has no equivalent in the Latin) implies that written messages, authenticated with seals, were commonly sent before the late tenth century, but the remark in question does not indicate that such documents were directed to shires, or that they were used to make grants: *King Alfred's Version of St. Augustine's Soliloquies*, ed. T. A. Carnicelli (Cambridge, MA, 1969), p. 62. The traditional attribution of this text to Alfred is uncertain, but it is unlikely to be much later than the mid-tenth century, since it appears to have been written by the same person as the *Old English Boethius*, which is extant in a mid-tenth-century manuscript, and of which a now-lost fragment in a slightly earlier hand apparently existed in the late nineteenth century: *The Old English Boethius: An Edition of the Old English Versions of Boethius's De Consolatione Philosophiae*, ed. M. Godden and S. Irvine (2 vols, Oxford, 2009), i, 18–24, 34–41, 135–51. More generally, see *Anglo-Saxon Writs*, ed. Harmer, pp. 1–34.

[230] On the nature of the rights granted, see Maitland, *Domesday Book*, pp. 80–107, 258–92; J. Goebel, *Felony and Misdemeanor: A Study in the History of English Criminal Procedure* (New York, NY, 1937), pp. 339–78; N. D. Hurnard, 'The Anglo-Norman Franchises', *EHR*, 64 (1949), pp. 289–327, 433–60; *Anglo-Saxon Writs*, ed. Harmer, pp. 73–85; P. Wormald, 'Lordship and Justice in the Early English Kingdom: Oswaldslow Revisited', in W. Davies and P. Fouracre (eds), *Property and Power in the Early Middle Ages* (Cambridge, 1995), pp. 114–36, reprinted in his *Legal Culture*, pp. 313–32; S. Baxter, 'Lordship and Justice in Late Anglo-Saxon England: The Judicial Functions of Soke and Commendation Revisited', in S. Baxter, C. E. Karkov, J. L. Nelson, and D. Pelteret (eds), *Early Medieval Studies in Memory of Patrick Wormald* (Farnham, 2009), pp. 383–419; T. B. Lambert,

'reckless liberality', but this interpretation can be stood on its head.[231] For one thing, permitting magnates to take fines would have been a pragmatic way for kings to incentivize cooperation in the detection and conviction of wrongdoers. Moreover, as we shall shortly see, some judicial profits went to non-royal recipients long before writ-charters entered (routine) use.[232] In consequence, rather than indicating that kings were losing control of judicial profits, the multiplication of writ-charters from Æthelred's time onwards could reflect that it had become necessary (or at least much more desirable) for those who received fines to obtain specific warrants of their entitlement to do so.[233] If this was indeed the case, it would suggest that kings had become more assertive of their own right to take fines, and more capable of enforcing such penalties in practice. Hence, while the appearance of writ-charters cannot prove that there had been a major increase in the Cerdicings' use of shire assemblies for local judicial regulation, it is eminently congruent with such a hypothesis.

Turning to prescriptive legal texts, the basic point is that shire meetings are explicitly mandated in the decrees of Edgar and Cnut, but not in the fairly voluminous surviving ordinances of previous kings. Mentions of shire assemblies are, however, hardly abundant in late tenth- and eleventh-century legislation, which makes the argument from silence less immediately compelling than for hundreds and wapentakes, for which a complete absence of references prior to Edmund's reign contrasts with a profusion from Edgar's time onwards.[234] It should, moreover, be borne in mind that since at least the ninth century the southern shires appear to have been used for military musters.[235] In view of this, it would be rash to deny that certain of the inhabitants of a shire may on occasion have gathered for other reasons. In particular, there is reason to think that at least one assembly of the magnates of Kent was held during Æthelstan's reign, since the bishops and thegns of that shire ('Centescyre thaini') sent him a message outlining how they proposed to implement his commands.[236] A further possibility is that Alfred's legislation and Asser's *Life* of the same king were alluding to gatherings much like shire assemblies when they mentioned meetings held in the presence of ealdormen, especially given that ninth-century annals in the 'common stock' and its continuations frequently

---

'Protection, Feud and Royal Power: Violence and its Regulation in English Law, *c*.850–*c*.1250' (PhD thesis, Durham University, 2009), pp. 79–102, 111–47; T. B. Lambert, 'Royal Protections and Private Justice: A Reassessment of Cnut's "Reserved Pleas"', in S. Jurasinski, L. Oliver, and A. Rabin (eds), *English Law before Magna Carta: Felix Liebermann and* Die Gesetze der Angelsachsen (Leiden, 2010), pp. 157–75; Hudson, *Oxford History of the Laws of England*, pp. 56–63.

[231] Maitland, *Domesday Book*, p. 282.   [232] Below, p. 176.

[233] Goebel, *Felony and Misdemeanor*, pp. 361–78 especially 373; H. Cam, 'The Evolution of the Mediaeval English Franchise', *Speculum*, 32 (1957), pp. 427–33; Lambert, 'Protection', pp. 133–6; Hudson, *Oxford History of the Laws of England*, p. 60.

[234] III Eg 5.1–5.2; II Cn 18–19.2. For the references to hundreds and wapentakes, see above, pp. 144–6.

[235] Above, pp. 99, 165.

[236] III As Prolog. This text is known only in a Latin translation from around the turn of the eleventh and twelfth centuries, but 'Centescyre' may well be taken from the underlying vernacular version. On this text, see above, pp. 113–14.

associate ealdormen with specific shires.[237] Shire meetings may even have gone back to the time of Ine, whose legislation envisages that a person might seek justice before someone known as a *scirman*.[238] It is, however, far from certain that this was a person associated with a 'shire' such as Hampshire or Wiltshire, since the word *scir* was a general term for an office or geographical area, and could be used in connection with districts or spheres of authority of many sizes and kinds, including dioceses, parishes, and areas of lordship.[239] There are thus some possible indications in legal texts that gatherings similar to shire assemblies may have been held before Edgar's reign, but nothing to demonstrate that such meetings were routine. Edgar, by contrast, ordered that the *burhgemot* and *scirgemot* be held thrice and twice annually: shire meetings were thenceforth to be regular, and distinct from assemblies organized on the basis of *burh*s.[240] It is, moreover, very interesting that Edgar had just stipulated that hundred meetings should be attended 'as it was previously ordained': that he did not say the same with regard to shire assemblies rather implies that his prescription that the latter be held twice per year represented an innovation of the Andover decrees.[241]

The case for thinking that the holding of shire assemblies began during the second half of the tenth century, or at least that they became significantly more routine around that time, is strengthened when we consider references to actual meetings. Had our only accounts of late tenth-century shire assemblies been those in the *Libellus Æthelwoldi* and the *Liber Benefactorum*, an argument from previous silence would have been unsound, since there are no extant cartulary-chronicles that provide similar coverage of earlier periods. A little more weight can be placed on the four discrete Old English dispute narratives, however, since five documents of broadly similar nature, plus one will, describe disagreements from between the very end of the ninth century and Edgar's early years.[242] We considered all but one of these texts in Chapter 2, noting that they reveal how disputing magnates could obtain their objectives by gaining the support of the reigning Cerdicing, or in one case Æthelred of Mercia.[243] Here, however, the key point is that none of these six texts contains a clear reference to a shire meeting. In two cases, this is unremarkable, since they concern lands near Gloucester around the turn of the ninth and tenth centuries, prior to even Stenton's early date for the demarcation of the Mercian shires.[244] The other four texts are more interesting, as they relate to periods and places in which shires are either known or widely believed to have existed. Of

---

[237] Af 38–38.1; *VA*, cvi (p. 92); *ASC* ABCDE 802, 840, 845, 851, 853, 860, ABCD 896, 897, 900; above, p. 99 n. 54. Note also Ine 36–36.1; Af 37–37.1.

[238] Ine 8, discussed below, p. 81.

[239] Taylor, 'Origin', pp. 32–4; T. N. Toller, *An Anglo-Saxon Dictionary Based on the Manuscript Collections of the Late Joseph Bosworth* (Oxford, 1898), with *Supplement* (Oxford, 1921), s.v. 'scir'; L. M. Larson, *The King's Household in England Before the Norman Conquest* (Madison, WI, 1904), p. 105; A. H. Smith, *English Place-Name Elements* (2 vols, Cambridge, 1956), ii, 109–11; R. Faith, *The English Peasantry and the Growth of Lordship* (London, 1997), pp. 9–11.

[240] III Eg 5.1.   [241] III Eg 5.

[242] S 1211, 1441, 1445, 1446, 1447, 1497. For early ninth-century examples, see S 1432, 1437.

[243] Above, pp. 68–77. The case not previously discussed is S 1441, which is similar to S 1446, although Æthelred's significance is implied more strongly in the latter.

[244] S 1441, 1446.

these four, the only one that even comes close to mentioning anything sounding like a shire meeting is Æthelgifu's will, which refers to a gathering at Hitchin, tentatively dated to *c*.956, where she had produced the oaths of 2,000 supporters, including 'all the senior [*yldestan*] men [pertaining] to Bedford [*to Bedanforda*] and to Hertford [*to Heortforda*] and their wives'.[245] In view of the numbers involved, it is very likely that some of these people came from the hinterlands of Bedford and Hertford, rather than just these two specific locations, but it is striking that neither 'Bedfordshire' nor 'Hertfordshire' is mentioned.[246] In consequence, Æthelgifu's will if anything strengthens the case for suspecting that in the mid-950s the southern East Midlands had not yet been divided into clearly demarcated districts, seen by contemporaries as equivalent to the shires south of the Thames.

Both before and after the time of Edgar, extant free-standing Old English dispute narratives are far from formulaic, and they frequently allude to third parties in whose presence disagreements were discussed or resolved. It is therefore unlikely to be the result merely of some change in drafting fashion that such texts mention shire assemblies in the context of the late tenth and eleventh centuries, but not the preceding decades.[247] Still less can the contrast be explained by a difference in the kinds of issues with which the surviving documents are concerned: all describe land disputes involving substantial lay or ecclesiastical magnates. Nor indeed should the appearance of shire assemblies be attributed to any very dramatic increase in the quantity of discrete vernacular dispute narratives that have come down to us: there are only eight such texts from between the middle of Edgar's reign and Æthelred's death, and shire meetings are explicitly mentioned in four.[248] Nonetheless, the evidence of Old English dispute narratives would not by itself be

---

[245] S 1497. On the possible date of the Hitchin meeting, see *Charters of St Albans*, ed. J. Crick (Oxford, 2007), pp. 92–4. Hitchin is roughly equidistant between Bedford and Hertford. The reference to the 'yldestan men' associated with two places where there are known to have been fortifications (*ASC* ABCD 912, A 915) calls to mind Æthelstan's order that persons who failed to attend meetings should be punished by 'all the *yldestan men* who pertain to the *burh*': I As 20–20.4. A late twelfth- or thirteenth-century reviser of the twelfth-century Abingdon cartulary-chronicle added a miracle story about a gathering of many people from Berkshire and Oxfordshire ('tam Berrocensis pagi quam Oxenefordensis'), which allegedly took place during the reign of Edmund, but such a narrative cannot constitute evidence for the operation of shire assemblies in the tenth century: *Historia Ecclesie Abbendonensis*, ed. and trans. J. G. H. Hudson (2 vols, Oxford, 2002–7), i, 284–6, with discussion of the revised version at vol. i, pp. xxxvii–lv.

[246] Accounts of late tenth-century Huntingdonshire and Kent shire meetings refer to 1,000 or more persons taking oaths: *LE*, ii.25 (p. 99); S 1458.

[247] On the potentially deceptive effect of changes in drafting practice, see S. Keynes, 'Crime and Punishment in the Reign of King Æthelred the Unready', in I. Wood and N. Lund (eds), *People and Places in Northern Europe, 500–1600: Essays in Honour of Peter Hayes Sawyer* (Woodbridge, 1991), pp. 76–81. My argument is not dependent on the texts that Keynes discusses.

[248] In addition to the four accounts that mention shire meetings, the documents most comparable to the dispute narratives from the preceding decades are S 939, S 1242 (compare the Fonthill letter), S 1457, and the Old English section of S 877. Since Old English dispute narratives are somewhat heterogeneous in form, there is scope for debate about what to include in this corpus, which is a subset of the cases listed by Wormald, 'Handlist', pp. 267–9. My total of eight excludes S 1377 (which is brief, mentions no meeting of any sort, and concerns alleged witchcraft rather than an aristocratic land dispute), S 1448a (which contains no sustained narrative), S 1453 (again no sustained narrative), and various Latin diplomas that include passing references to disputes or statements about why land had been forfeited.

enough to sustain the hypothesis that shire assemblies had been rare or non-existent prior to Edgar's reign, since we have too few such texts to be confident that
those that survive are representative. The argument does, however, gain greater
force when one considers that documents of this sort start to refer to shire meetings
very soon after the word *scirgemot* first appears in surviving royal legislation.[249]
That two quite different kinds of source break their silence at much the same time
makes it hard to resist the inference that the routine holding of shire assemblies
only became standard practice with Edgar's Andover decrees, which may indeed
also have been contemporaneous with the demarcation of the Midland shires.
These changes probably did not in themselves produce even a semblance of uniformity throughout the whole area from the Channel to the Tees, since there is a
fair likelihood that it was only in the eleventh century that shire organization was
introduced north of the Humber and in East Anglia, and perhaps also in the
northern East Midlands. But in a large part of Domesday *Anglia* it is probable that
the mid-tenth century saw not only the systematic organization of hundreds or
wapentakes, but also the establishment of a second layer of standard administrative
divisions and associated assemblies, through which the Cerdicings could likewise
seek to monitor and shape the conduct of their subordinates.

ROYAL AGENTS

Continuities

While the mid- to late tenth century appears to have seen major changes in the
institutional framework of local administration, there were considerable continuities in the kinds of people through whom the Cerdicings sought to enforce
their will. The legislation of Edgar, Æthelred II, and Cnut, like that of their
predecessors, refers repeatedly to reeves, envisaging that they should play a key
role in implementing royal instructions. Thus, for example, all three of these
kings ordered that reeves punish persons who failed to pay tithes, Æthelred and
Cnut demanded that they place under surety those who were subject to suspicion, and the latter king enjoined them to pronounce just judgements.[250] Similarly,

---

[249] Wormald sometimes drew attention to the fact that the earliest unequivocal accounts of shire
assemblies come soon after the first occurrence of the word *scirgemot* in legislation, but his papers for
the second volume of *The Making of English Law* indicate that he wanted to trace shire meetings back
to at least the early tenth century, and he had tentatively suggested in print that the Fonthill letter
(S 1445) may allude to such a gathering in Edward the Elder's reign: Wormald, 'Handlist', pp. 284–5;
Wormald, 'Giving God and King their Due', p. 347 and n. 48; Wormald, *Making*, p. 152; P. Wormald, 'Courts', in *WBEASE*, p. 129; P. Wormald, 'Papers Preparatory to *The Making of English Law:
King Alfred to the Twelfth Century. Volume II: From God's Law to Common Law*', ed. S. Baxter and
J. G. H. Hudson (London, 2014), pp. 192–8, consulted at <http://www.earlyenglishlaws.ac.uk/reference/
wormald/> (accessed 9 October 2014). There is no particular reason to think that the Fonthill letter
refers to any meeting organized on the basis of a shire; on the events it narrates, see above, p. 69.

[250] II Eg 3.1; IV Eg 1.5, 13.1; I Atr 1.14, 4; III Atr 1.1, 3.1–3.2, 7, 13; IV Atr 3, 7.3, 8; VII Atr
2.5, 6.3; VIIa Atr Poen. 2.3; VIII Atr 8, 32; Cn 1020 11; Cn 1027 12, 16; I Cn 8.2; II Cn 8.2, 33,
69.1–69.2. Compare above, pp. 106–9.

bishops continued to figure prominently in royal ordinances: among other things, they were expected to attend *burh* and shire meetings, prescribe penalties for wrongdoers, and exact fines from persons who judged unjustly.[251] Ealdormen remained important too: they led military contingents, probably collected various royal revenues, were entrusted with the distribution of the *Wihtbordesstan* decrees, and (like bishops) were to be present at shire and *burh* meetings.[252] From the time of Cnut onwards, the word *ealdorman* was increasingly replaced by *eorl*, but it is doubtful whether this terminological shift was associated with substantial changes in the kinds of things that ealdormen or earls were expected to do: both before and after Cnut's conquest, they appear to have been powerful secular magnates responsible for upholding royal interests across a sizeable area, often equivalent to several shires.[253] If the earlier arguments of this chapter are correct, there were significant changes during the tenth century in some of the key administrative structures within which reeves, bishops, and ealdormen operated, but the holders of all three of these offices continued to be fundamental to the implementation of royal commands. More generally, kings will also have continued to need the cooperation of persons of wealth and power, who did not necessarily have any specific office, but were capable of advancing or obstructing royal objectives. Within this context of broad continuity in the kinds of people responsible for giving effect to the Cerdicings' commands, the second half of the tenth century did, however, see four notable developments, and it is to these that we now turn.

The Proliferation of Benedictine Monasteries

The first development, to which particular historiographical attention has been devoted, is the proliferation of Benedictine monasteries during Edgar's reign. While stressing, surely correctly, that Edgar's reasons for promoting such establishments were primarily religious, Eric John claimed that his actions had the effect of reducing royal dependence on the cooperation of lay magnates, especially ealdormen, and transferred some of their responsibilities to abbots or monk-bishops.[254]

---

[251] III Eg 3, 5.1–5.2; IV Atr 8; VIII Atr 27; Cn 1020 8–9, 11; Cn 1027 16; I Cn 5.3; II Cn 18–18.1, 43, 53–54.1, 56–56.1. Compare above, pp. 109–10. Ælfric argued that clergy should not sit in judgement on thieves and robbers, but Archbishop Wulfstan wrote that bishops should collaborate with secular judges ('worulddeman') in giving judgements: Ælfric, *Pastoral Letters*, ed. B. Fehr, *Die Hirtenbriefe Ælfrics in altenglischer und lateinischer Fassung* (Hamburg, 1914), 3.80–90, II.201, 2a.xv (pp. 66–7, 140–1, 226–7); Episc 4, 9.

[252] III Eg 5.1–5.2; IV Eg 15–15.1; II Atr 6; III Atr 1.1; IV Atr 8; Cn 1020 8; II Cn 18–18.1; S. Baxter, *The Earls of Mercia: Lordship and Power in Late Anglo-Saxon England* (Oxford, 2007), pp. 61–124. Compare above, pp. 111–12.

[253] Williams, *Kingship and Government*, pp. 131–2; Baxter, *Earls*, especially pp. 72–4. Contrast R. Fleming, *Kings and Lords in Conquest England* (Cambridge, 1991), especially pp. 21–2. The word *eorl* is attested before Cnut's reign, notably in IV Eg 15.

[254] E. John, *Orbis Britanniae and Other Studies* (Leicester, 1966), pp. 154–80 especially 174–80. The number of bishoprics held by monks rose markedly under Edgar, but declined in the eleventh century: T. Vogtherr, 'Zwischen Benediktinerabtei und bischöflicher Cathedra. Zu Auswahl und Amtsantritt englischer Bischöfe im 9.–11. Jahrhundert', in F.-R. Erkens (ed.), *Die früh- und hochmittelalterliche Bischofserhebung im europäischen Vergleich* (Cologne, 1998), pp. 289–304.

John's case is undermined by his use of unreliable documents that mention a right to exclude royal agents from territories allegedly placed under ecclesiastical jurisdiction, but a more dilute version of his argument has some merit.[255] Setting aside later claims to immunity from interventions by royal officers, writ-charters clearly show that by the mid-eleventh century at the latest many monasteries had the right to certain judicial profits, most commonly those known as 'sake and soke'.[256] There is dispute about quite what offences this phrase covered, and about whether it implied a right to convene a judicial tribunal.[257] These problems are not crucial here, however, since even if 'sake and soke' only amounted to an entitlement to some of the fines imposed by an ordinary hundred meeting, holders of the privilege would have had a financial incentive to promote the implementation of royal demands for the apprehension of malefactors. Given the lack of earlier writ-charters, it cannot be proved that monastic houses commonly received such profits before the eleventh century, although they may well have done: we know that estates were given to Abbot Ealdwulf of Peterborough (*c.*972–992) to redeem sentences of outlawry that he had imposed, and it should be noted that institutions may have taken fines without specific royal authorization.[258]

Even if monasteries rarely benefited from judicial penalties, however, there would still be grounds to suspect that they and their abbots were often willing to further the interests of the Cerdicings, with whom they frequently had strong ties. The *Regularis Concordia*, composed during Edgar's reign very probably by Bishop Æthelwold of Winchester, prescribed that psalms for the king and queen be said several times a day in all monasteries, and stated that royal consent should be obtained for abbatial elections.[259] That kings could, at least in some cases, determine who became abbot is indicated by a charter in which Æthelred II confessed to accepting payment from an ealdorman in return for giving the latter's brother the abbacy of Abingdon.[260] Whether or not royal interventions in elections were common, it is clear that kings were in close contact with abbots, since large numbers appear in charter witness lists from the late 960s onwards.[261] Monastic houses probably hoped that kings would dispense largesse to them, and they sometimes also needed royal protection, not least against the depredations of laypeople who alleged that they or their relatives had been coerced or tricked into parting with their lands: that Edgar had shielded monasteries against such challenges is suggested by the large number of claims raised in the aftermath of his

---

[255] On the documents used by John, see Wormald, 'Lordship and Justice', especially pp. 323–6.

[256] E.g. S 986, 1069, 1071, 1072, 1077, 1080, 1082, 1083, 1088, 1090, 1091, 1096, 1099.

[257] For debate, see the literature cited above at p. 168 n. 230.

[258] S 1448a; above, pp. 168–9; below, p. 176.

[259] *RC*, viii, ix, x, xvii, xix, xxi, xxiv, xxv, xxxi, xxxiii, xxxiv, xxxvii (pp. 74–6, 81–2, 83, 84, 86, 90, 91–2, 93); M. Lapidge, 'Æthelwold as Scholar and Teacher', in B. Yorke (ed.), *Bishop Æthelwold: His Career and Influence* (Woodbridge, 1988), pp. 98–100.

[260] S 876. The case also illustrates that churches were not necessarily a counterweight to the secular aristocracy, given the close ties between certain senior churchmen and lay magnates. See also above, p. 66; below, pp. 227–8.

[261] Banton, 'Monastic Reform', pp. 73–5; S. Keynes, *An Atlas of Attestations in Anglo-Saxon Charters, c.670–1066* (Cambridge, 2002), Tables LV, LVIII, LXI, LXVII, LXXIII, and compare Tables XX, XXXIV, XXXVII, XLI, XLIV, XLVIII.

death.[262] In consequence, whatever judicial privileges monasteries may or may not have enjoyed, they would have had reason to cultivate the Cerdicings' favour.

This is significant, since many monastic houses were extremely rich: Domesday shows that several possessed lands worth as much as those of all but the greatest lay magnates, and the evidence from Abingdon, Ely, and Ramsey suggests that each acquired a large proportion of its endowment in the second half of the tenth century.[263] Since wealth could be used to encourage, and ultimately compel, obedience, many monasteries thus had the means as well as a motive to promote adherence to the Cerdicings' commands. The distribution of Benedictine houses was, however, uneven, with the great majority being in the south, the south-west Midlands, or the Fens.[264] In addition, it should be noted that certain monasteries may have been more anxious to please their aristocratic benefactors than Edgar and his successors.[265] Nonetheless, it is important that in the second half of the tenth century substantial quantities of land were transferred from laypeople to institutions that sometimes had particularly close ties to the Cerdicings: this very probably boosted kings' ability to secure compliance with their will in certain specific localities.

The Regulation of Judicial Profits

The second development is perhaps of wider significance: the granting to monasteries of judicial privileges took place in the context of a marked increase in the frequency with which kings explicitly permitted other institutions and individuals to enjoy similar rights.[266] Whatever 'sake and soke' entailed, the earliest documented recipients of this privilege are not known to have made monastic professions: the expression first appears in two diplomas of the 950s, which grant 'sake and soke' in parts of (what would become) Nottinghamshire and Yorkshire to a bishop and a *matrona* (a married or widowed woman).[267] Similarly, the earliest

---

[262] S. Jayakumar, 'Reform and Retribution: The "Anti-Monastic Reaction" in the Reign of Edward the Martyr', in Baxter et al. (eds), *Early Medieval Studies*, pp. 337–52.

[263] For convenient tables, see D. Knowles, *The Monastic Order in England*, 2nd edn (Cambridge, 1963), p. 702; Hill, *Atlas*, p. 154; P. A. Clarke, *The English Nobility under Edward the Confessor* (Oxford, 1994), p. 14. On Abingdon, Ely, and Ramsey, see E. Miller, *The Abbey and Bishopric of Ely: The Social History of an Ecclesiastical Estate from the Tenth Century to the Early Fourteenth Century* (Cambridge, 1951), pp. 16–25; J. A. Raftis, *The Estates of Ramsey Abbey: A Study in Economic Growth and Organization* (Toronto, 1957), pp. 1–21; *Historia Ecclesie Abbendonensis*, vol. i, pp. cxxxvii–cliii. Given the losses that many monasteries suffered after Edgar's death, some may have been wealthier in 975 than at the time of Domesday.

[264] For maps, see Hill, *Atlas*, pp. 151, 153.

[265] Baxter, *Earls*, pp. 152–203 discusses one family's monastic patronage. S. Wood, *The Proprietary Church in the Medieval West* (Oxford, 2006), pp. 408–12 stresses that even houses founded by aristocrats often had significant royal connections.

[266] This subsection draws on Maitland, *Domesday Book*, pp. 258–92; Goebel, *Felony and Misdemeanor*, pp. 339–78; Wormald, 'Lordship and Justice', pp. 328–9; Baxter, 'Lordship and Justice'; Lambert, 'Protection', pp. 27–30, 125–36. Some of the more unusual privileges appear to have been largely restricted to a handful of particularly favoured monasteries: Lambert, 'Royal Protections', especially p. 172.

[267] S 659, 681.

surviving possibly genuine writ-charter to convey 'sake and soke', a document in the name of Æthelred II, concerns not a monastery, but the priests of St Paul's (London).[268] Furthermore, there are many references in legal texts from the mid-tenth century onwards to circumstances in which fines or confiscated goods should go to a lord, variously termed a *hlaford*, *landhlaford*, or *landrica*.[269] Such references may reflect that kings were allowing lords to take fines that they had previously collected (or aspired to collect) themselves: this is suggested by Edgar's prescription that forfeited possessions should be divided between a *hlaford* and a hundred, when Æthelstan had referred in a very similar passage to the goods being split between the king and an enforcement posse.[270] That Edgar or one of his immediate predecessors appears to have forsaken a source of income which Æthelstan had claimed should not be taken as an indication of weakness or profligacy. Given their moral responsibility to uphold order, it may well have seemed less important to kings that they themselves should profit, than that those with local power should be incentivized to bring wrongdoers to justice.[271]

The substantial number of references to lords receiving judicial profits in late tenth- and eleventh-century legislation need not, moreover, imply the wholesale renunciation by kings of rights that they had hitherto exercised for their own financial benefit, since there are several indications that certain judicial profits had long gone to non-royal recipients. Æthelstan's Grately ordinance mentioned a penalty being paid 'either to the king or to the person to whom it rightfully pertains'.[272] Some early charters imply that their beneficiaries were to take judicial penalties.[273] The legislation ascribed to Ine suggests that lords usually received fines from their dependants, declaring that they would not do so if they had previously failed to enforce discipline.[274] The late seventh-century decrees of the Kentish king Wihtred mention payments to a lord (*dryhten*) for Sabbath violation or wrongful sexual relationships.[275] Thus, the ordinances of Edgar and his successors may have served less to afford lords new rights, than to confirm or adjust existing practices whereby magnates took fines. Indeed, as was perhaps the case with many writ-charters, the effect may often have been to assert that what had formerly been a customary entitlement was now a privilege granted, and potentially limited, by the king.[276] In this respect, it is notable that late tenth- and eleventh-century legislation does not simply reveal in passing that magnates received judicial profits,

---

[268] S 945. For further examples of non-monastic holders of 'sake and soke', see S 1101, 1102, 1111, 1112, 1115, 1116, 1163, 1241; *DB*, i, 1c, 280c, 298c, 336d, 337a.

[269] Hu 2.1, 3; II Eg 3.1; III Eg 7.1; IV Eg 8.1; I Atr 1.5, 1.7; III Atr 3.3, 4.1, 4.2; VIII Atr 8; I Cn 8.2; II Cn 25.1, 30.3b, 30.8, 36, 37, 42, 48.1. Note also IV Eg 11; I Atr 3.1; III Atr 3.2, 5, 7; II Cn 24.1, 30.6, 63, 66, 71.3, 73.1; Northu 49. It is doubtful whether there were rigid distinctions in meaning between *hlaford*, *landhlaford*, and *landrica*: Baxter, 'Lordship and Justice', pp. 405–6.

[270] II As 20.4; III Eg 7.1; above, pp. 153–4. See also II Cn 25.1.

[271] On royal duties, see below, pp. 187–8, 224–9.

[272] II As 1.5. Note also II As 21; VI As 1.1, although the latter reference is in the specific context of London. Comparison with IV Eg 11 and I Atr 3.1 suggests that the *londhlaford* in II As 10 may only have been a temporary custodian of confiscated goods.

[273] For references and discussion, see Maitland, *Domesday Book*, pp. 274–7, 290–2; Goebel, *Felony and Misdemeanor*, pp. 344–58; Lambert, 'Protection', pp. 133–4.

[274] Ine 50. See also Ine 39.   [275] Wi 5, 9, 10.   [276] Above, pp. 168–9.

but frequently states that a lord should have a specific fraction of a specific fine or forfeiture.[277] It thus appears that during the second half of the tenth century the Cerdicings defined more closely their subordinates' rights to take penalties from wrongdoers: whether or not kings also raised the financial incentives for cooperation in implementing their legislation, this is suggestive of a significant tightening in royal regulation of local judicial administration.

Cerdicing Agents in York

The third important shift is the establishment of closer relationships between the Cerdicings and those who held power at York. In the 940s and 950s, Archbishop Wulfstan's attestations of Cerdicing charters had been somewhat intermittent, most probably because of his cooperation with Hiberno-Scandinavian potentates.[278] By contrast, Wulfstan's successors appear in witness lists with reasonable consistency, and almost all can be shown to have had substantial Southumbrian ties.[279] In many cases they had been promoted from a southern bishopric that they then held concurrently with York, a practice that probably began with Wulfstan's immediate successor, Oscytel (d. 971), who seems to have remained Bishop of Dorchester-on-Thames after becoming archbishop sometime in the 950s.[280] That Oscytel and three out of the next four archbishops had previously held episcopal office in Southumbria strongly suggests that they were not York insiders, but instead owed their elevation to the Cerdicings, and it is likely that one reason why these prelates were allowed to keep their southern sees was to deter them from promoting separatism.[281] In two of these cases, we have confirmation of Cerdicing involvement in the appointment: Oscytel's death notice in the B text of the *Chronicle* states that he had been consecrated to the archbishopric with King Eadred's consent, and Byrhtferth of Ramsey attributed to Edgar the choice of Oswald as Bishop of Worcester (961–992) and Archbishop of York (971–992).[282] There are grounds to suspect that the B text's reference to 'Eadred' is an error for Eadwig or Edgar, but either way it is interesting that whoever composed the annal chose to mention Cerdicing participation in Oscytel's elevation.[283] Several dozen notices of

---

[277] Hu 2.1, 3; II Eg 3.1; III Eg 7.1; IV Eg 8.1; III Atr 3.3; VIII Atr 8; I Cn 8.2; II Cn 25.1, 36.

[278] Keynes, *Atlas*, Tables XLI, XLIV, XLVIII; above, pp. 32, 57, 59.

[279] Whitelock, 'Dealings', pp. 72–6; Keynes, *Atlas*, Tables LIV, LVIII, LXa, LXb, LXVI, LXXII. The exception is Edwald, briefly archbishop in 971: Whitelock, 'Dealings', p. 75 n. 6.

[280] That Oscytel continued to hold Dorchester is argued by Whitelock, 'Dealings', pp. 73–5. Even if he relinquished it, however, my basic point would not be fundamentally affected, since from 971 York was definitely held in plurality with a southern see.

[281] Edwald is again the exception. Archbishops Oswald (971–992) and Ealdwulf (995–1002) initially held just the bishopric of Worcester, which they retained after their elevations to York. Archbishop Wulfstan II (1002–1023) had been Bishop of London, then received Worcester and York simultaneously. There appears to have been a short vacancy at York between Oswald and Ealdwulf.

[282] *ASC* B 971; *VSO*, iv.5 (p. 102). The B manuscript is in a hand of the second half of the tenth century, and appears to have been written 977×c.1000: *The Anglo-Saxon Chronicle: A Collaborative Edition. Volume 4: MS B*, ed. S. Taylor (Cambridge, 1983), pp. xxiii–xxiv. Note also *ASC* C 971.

[283] Since Eadred and Wulfstan died in 955 and 956 respectively, a plain reading of the B annal implies that Oscytel became archbishop while Wulfstan was still alive, but this sits awkwardly with witness lists: Wulfstan appears as archbishop at the end of Eadred's reign and the beginning of

the deaths or successions of bishops appear in the various versions of the *Chronicle*, but very few such references say anything about kings approving episcopal appointments, and there is no parallel within the B text itself.[284] The reason why royal involvement was rarely mentioned is probably because it could usually be taken for granted, but there is a ready explanation for this exceptional feature of Oscytel's obit: he may very well have been the first Archbishop of York in whose selection a Cerdicing had played a major role.[285]

Oscytel's elevation was mirrored in the secular sphere by the installation at York of Oslac as ealdorman. We have already seen that Oslac was charged by Edgar with the implementation of the *Wihtbordesstan* decrees, and that later Durham sources record that he was based at York while the land beyond the Tees or Tyne was subject to a Bamburgh potentate.[286] The D and E texts of the *Chronicle* record that Oslac 'obtained the ealdordom' in 966, which is interesting, since, as with royal approval of episcopal consecrations, the dates at which people became ealdormen or earls are rarely noted in any version of the *Chronicle*: this is the earliest such record, and they only became common during the 1050s.[287] The resultant suspicion that Oslac's appointment may have been of unusual significance is strengthened when one considers his appearances in charters. He attested a handful of times during the 960s, and then witnessed almost all extant royal documents from the last five years of Edgar's reign.[288] Subsequent ealdormen and earls with power at York likewise attested Edgar's successors' charters with at least moderate frequency.[289] This contrasts markedly with Oswulf of Bamburgh, to whom York had been entrusted following the killing in 954 of Erik Haraldsson: Oswulf had

Eadwig's, while Oscytel continued to attest as bishop. With one possible exception from 956 (S 659), Oscytel's genuine attestations as archbishop begin in 959 (S 681). The suspicion that the B text's 'Eadred' is an error increases when one notes that the equivalent entry in the C text gives 'Eadweard'. There was no King Edward in the relevant period, and both texts quite possibly derive from a manuscript in which the second part of either Eadwig or E(a)dgar's name was unclear. See J. Barrow, 'Oscytel (*d.* 971)', *ODNB* and contrast *Charters of Northern Houses*, ed. D. A. Woodman (Oxford, 2012), pp. 102–3.

[284] There are several references to royal involvement in episcopal appointments in the decade after Edward the Confessor's accession: *ASC* CE 1044, C 1045, 1047, 1049, CD 1050, E 1051. The only examples in earlier annals are *ASC* E 667, 685, DE 780, AF 959, E 963, CDE 1013, although there is reason to think that all these entries were added during the eleventh or twelfth centuries. The burst of references in the early part of Edward's reign may be a consequence of the controversy known to have been associated with certain of his appointees.

[285] S 407 may imply that Æthelstan had had a hand in selecting Wulfstan, although he possibly did no more than ratify the appointment of a York insider: see above, pp. 67–8.

[286] IV Eg 15; *Historia Regum*, p. 197; *De primo Saxonum adventu*, p. 382; above, pp. 122–3.

[287] *ASC* DE 966; above, p. 121 n. 27. For other references, see *ASC* CDE 983, 1007, 1016, E 1051, CDE 1052, 1053, DE 1055, 1057, CDE 1065. The cluster in the 1050s may result from the rivalries between the families of Godwine and Leofric, in which gaining and retaining earldoms was important.

[288] N. Banton, 'Ealdormen and Earls in England from the Reign of King Alfred to the Reign of King Æthelred II' (D.Phil. thesis, University of Oxford, 1981), pp. 154, 241–2, 247; Banton, 'Monastic Reform', p. 78; Keynes, *Atlas*, Table LVI.

[289] See the attestations of Thored (witnesses 979–*c.*989), Ælfhelm (993–1005), Uhtred (1009–1015), Erik (1018–1023), Siward (1033–1053×1055), Tostig (1059–1065), and Morcar (1065) in Keynes, *Atlas*, Tables LXII, LXIX, LXXIV, with Whitelock, 'Dealings', pp. 79–84; Banton, 'Ealdormen and Earls', pp. 249–60.

intermittently witnessed charters of Æthelstan and Eadred, but does not attest after 950.[290] He may have continued to visit Eadred and his successors from time to time, but there is no reason to think that his ties to the Cerdicings were close, and he did not owe his power at Bamburgh to them.[291] Indeed, given that Oswulf is said to have had a hand in Erik's death, it is possible that Eadred had little choice but to recognize him as the principal lay potentate in York.[292] Since Oslac's consistent appearances in witness lists cannot be attributed to any marked change in drafting practices, the contrast with Oswulf at very least indicates that those who composed royal charters regarded the two men differently, and probably reflects that Oslac attended Cerdicing assemblies much more frequently than his predecessor. Either way, however, the disparity between the attestations of Oswulf and Oslac can be explained by the hypothesis that the latter had much closer ties to the Cerdicings, and that his power was far more reliant on their backing. There are some slight grounds for thinking that Oslac may have been of Southumbrian origin, and his dependence on the support of the reigning Cerdicing is implied by his being driven across the sea by persons unknown immediately after Edgar's death.[293] Thus it appears that the third quarter of the tenth century saw the installation at York of an ealdorman and archbishop who owed their positions to the Cerdicings' patronage, and were in frequent personal contact with them. Thenceforth, royal assemblies were consistently attended by magnates from across the whole of what would constitute Domesday *Anglia*, and there was probably a significant increase in kings' ability to have their commands implemented throughout the land between the Humber and the Tees.

Sheriffs

The fourth significant change in royal agents that can be placed in the second half of the tenth century is the development of the office of shire-reeve or sheriff (*scirgerefa*). In the eleventh century, when evidence concerning sheriffs first becomes extensive, they are known to have collected royal dues, given judgements, and organized military forces: their functions thus overlapped with those of earls, and to some extent bishops.[294] Sheriffs, bishops, and earls could in consequence

---

[290] *Historia Regum*, p. 197; *De primo Saxonum adventu*, p. 382; Keynes, *Atlas*, Tables XXXVIII, XLV. The date of Oswulf's death is unknown; the *Historia Regum* explicitly places Oslac's appointment within Oswulf's lifetime, but the *De primo Saxonum adventu* simply says that Oswulf was succeeded by Oslac at York and by Eadwulf Evilchild between the Tees and 'Myreford'. Various men with Scandinavian names, some of whom may have been from north of the Humber, appear as *duces* in charters of Edgar and his predecessors, but none attested consistently: above, pp. 44–5, 57, 59.

[291] On the problems with using lack of attestations to infer absence from assemblies, see above, pp. 58–9. Note, however, that alliterative charters, which Oswulf had previously witnessed, continued to be issued after his disappearance (S 556, 566, 569, 633), which makes it harder to dismiss the end of his attestations as a mere change in drafting fashion.

[292] Roger of Wendover, *Flores Historiarum*, i, 402–3.

[293] On Oslac's possible Southumbrian origin, see Whitelock, 'Dealings', pp. 78–9, but contrast Banton, 'Ealdormen and Earls', pp. 239–43. For his expulsion, see *ASC* ABCDE 975.

[294] W. A. Morris, *The Medieval English Sheriff to 1300* (Manchester, 1927), pp. 23–39; Baxter, *Earls*, pp. 121–3.

have kept each other's power in check, although we should not assume that they were constantly at loggerheads, as their roles were also complementary.[295] In particular, sheriffs will often have been more able than either bishops or ealdormen to attend to the local detail of royal administration, since they did not have obligations associated with high ecclesiastical office, and were usually responsible for just a single shire.[296]

No genuine surviving text terms a specific person *scirgerefa* before Cnut's reign, from which we have evidence of sheriffs of Herefordshire, Kent, Staffordshire, and Worcestershire.[297] The word was, however, in use earlier, and was already familiar enough to be employed metaphorically: Archbishop Wulfstan II of York's *Institutes of Polity*, the earliest version of which antedates 1016, refers to 'Christ's *scirgerefa*', probably meaning a bishop, sitting in judgement on a priest.[298] Furthermore, the two accounts of late tenth- or very early eleventh-century Kent shire meetings discussed above furnish evidence of persons whom we can reasonably regard as sheriffs: Wulfsige 'the *scirigman*', active sometime between 964 and 988; and Leofric 'sciresman', active sometime between 995 and 1005.[299] That *scirman* could be used as an alternative to *scirgerefa* is clear from two documents relating to Kent and datable to 1016×1020: the Æthelwine 'scirman' addressed in a writ-charter is almost certainly the same person as the Æthelwine 'sciregerefan' who witnessed a marriage agreement, together with two of the other addressees.[300] We shall see that *scirman* did not always mean 'sheriff', but Wulfsige and Leofric can confidently be classed thus, since both are presented as important participants in shire meetings. In Wulfsige's case, moreover, it is clear that he was acting as a royal representative, since he accepted Archbishop Dunstan's oath 'to the king's hand'. In Kent, although not necessarily elsewhere, it thus seems safe to trace the position of sheriff back to at least the 980s, and possibly the 960s.

There is, as we have seen, plenty of earlier evidence of royal reeves, who are known, like later sheriffs, to have performed judicial and financial tasks.[301] The office of sheriff can therefore be regarded as a development of existing practices, but there are no good grounds to infer that any of the reeves mentioned in legislation of the early tenth century or before had responsibility for a shire, as opposed to a *port*, *burh*, or estate.[302] One scrap of evidence that has been taken to imply the

---

[295] That earls and sheriffs could complement each other is stressed by Baxter, *Earls*, pp. 247–50.

[296] For occasional instances of sheriffs with more than one shire, see Morris, *Medieval English Sheriff*, p. 24. On the sizes of dioceses and ealdordoms, see above, pp. 110, 112, 163–4. Sheriffs are also likely to have been more able than early tenth-century *port*- or *burh*-reeves to enforce royal commands throughout a shire, since they would not have needed to be available in the *port* or *burh* to witness transactions: see above, pp. 106–9.

[297] S 985, 991, 1461, 1462; *Hemingi chartularium*, i, 277. The authenticity of S 991 is uncertain, but comparison with S 1423 and S 1460 suggests that the Leofric it names was sheriff of Worcestershire.

[298] Wulfstan of York, *Institutes of Polity*, ed. K. Jost, *Die «Institutes of Polity, Civil and Ecclesiastical». Ein Werk Erzbischof Wulfstans von York* (Bern, 1959), pp. 144–5, with discussion of the date at 33–4; P. Wormald, 'Archbishop Wulfstan: Eleventh-Century State-Builder', in M. Townend (ed.), *Wulfstan, Archbishop of York* (Turnhout, 2004), pp. 16–19. The text does not, however, have a section devoted to sheriffs.

[299] S 1456, 1458; above, p. 167. For another possible 'scireman' from around the turn of the tenth and eleventh centuries, see S 1495, although the text is not authentic in its current form.

[300] S 985, 1461.   [301] Above, pp. 106–9.

[302] Morris, *Medieval English Sheriff*, pp. 1–23. On a reference to a supposed mid-tenth-century sheriff in a late eleventh-century miracle collection, see Marten, 'Shiring', pp. 11–13.

contrary is that the London peace regulations of Æthelstan's reign allude to the *scir* for which a *gerefa* ('reeve') was responsible.[303] It should, however, be recalled that *scir* could denote territories or offices of many types, and did not refer exclusively to a 'shire' such as Kent or Warwickshire; indeed, it is notable that the London text appears to use *scir* interchangeably with *manung*, which seems to be another generic term for a sphere of authority.[304] Similar considerations apply to the reference in Ine's legislation to a person seeking justice before a *scirman*, since the *scir* with which such a figure was associated need not have been a shire.[305] Indeed, an account of the duties of an estate reeve uses *scirman* synonymously with *gerefa* to refer to a person responsible for directing workers, making repairs, providing tools, and so on.[306]

If the references from the London text and Ine's legislation are set aside, there is no sound basis for thinking that sheriffs existed before at least the reign of Edgar. The argument that the office was only established around that time is founded on silence, but it can be buttressed by considering a change in the pattern of attestations by ealdormen. Until 970, Edgar's charters were often witnessed by half a dozen or more such figures, but during the last five years of his reign all reliable attestations by ealdormen come from just four men, each of whom was primarily associated with an area north of the Thames.[307] The number of ealdormen witnessing increased after Edgar's death, but three or four attestations became the norm again for substantial parts of the period between 985 and 1016.[308] These reductions suggest that Edgar had marginalized or dismissed certain southern ealdormen, or decided not to replace them when they died, and that Æthelred later emulated him. In light of this, it is interesting that both annals and documentary sources from the years around the millennium yield a profusion of references to reeves and high-reeves: this may well reflect that such figures were being charged with tasks previously undertaken by ealdormen.[309] All this suggests that the late tenth century is a very plausible period for the introduction of sheriffs, especially

[303] VI As 8.4, 10. Dumville, *Wessex and England*, p. 148 states that 'we first meet the sheriff here'.

[304] VI As 8.2, 8.4, and compare V As 1.5. On the term *scir*, see above, p. 170. Note also that York was composed of seven 'scyrae' in 1066: *DB*, i, 298a.

[305] Ine 8; above, p. 170.

[306] Ger 5, 12, with Wormald, *Making*, pp. 387–9. The Old English version of Gregory's *Pastoral Care* uses *scirman* to translate *praepositus*, a general term for a person with authority, which was often used to denote a reeve: Gregory, *Pastoral Care*, ii.6, ii.10, ed. F. Rommel, *Règle pastorale* (2 vols, Paris, 1992), i, 204, 240; *King Alfred's West-Saxon Version of Gregory's Pastoral Care*, ed. and trans. H. Sweet (EETS, 45, 50, London, 1871–2), pp. 108–9, 152–3.

[307] Banton, 'Ealdormen and Earls', pp. 153–9; Banton, 'Monastic Reform', p. 78; Keynes, *Atlas*, Table LVI. The attestations of S 784 by Ælfheah and S 800 by Æthelweard are dubious: E. E. Barker, 'The Anglo-Saxon Chronicle Used by Æthelweard', *Bulletin of the Institute for Historical Research*, 40 (1967), p. 85; Banton, 'Ealdormen and Earls', p. 153 and n. 2.

[308] Keynes, *Atlas*, Tables LVIII, LXII.

[309] *ASC* A 1001, CDE 1002, 1003, 1011; S 883, 893, 894, 910, 915, 918, 925, 926, 1215, 1454, 1456, 1457, 1654. Comparison of *ASC* CDE 1002 and S 926 implies that *prefectus* could denote a high-reeve. For comment, see P. Stafford, 'The Reign of Æthelred II, a Study in the Limitations on Royal Policy and Action', in Hill (ed.), *Ethelred*, pp. 29, 31; Keynes, *Diplomas*, p. 198 n. 165; Banton, 'Ealdormen and Earls', pp. 153–9, 176–82. Some of those described as reeves or high-reeves may in effect have been sheriffs: J. Blair, *Anglo-Saxon Oxfordshire* (Stroud, 1994), pp. 103–4. This cannot, however, be taken as a general rule: *ASC* A 1001 implies that Hampshire had at least two royal high-reeves.

in the south, where they are first documented: their appointment could either have obviated the need to fill vacant ealdordoms, or checked the power of ealdormen who remained in office.

If these hypotheses about royal agents are correct, Edgar sought to increase his control of York through the installation of Oslac as ealdorman, but at the same time aimed to reduce his reliance upon ealdormen in the south, either replacing or complementing them with less exalted figures. On one level, this would imply that the Cerdicings' rule became more, rather than less, heterogeneous in the third quarter of the tenth century, with different types of people representing the king in different regions. Much the same argument could be made on the basis that Benedictine monasteries were unevenly distributed, although the significance of this is lessened when one notes that other powerful institutions and persons played comparable roles in the local implementation of royal commands. These geographical variations are important, but there is a broader consideration: all of the changes that we have just examined would have served to increase the extent to which Edgar and his successors could regulate the behaviour of those living between the Channel and the Tees, while altering nothing about the Cerdicings' relationships with the inhabitants of Wales or northern Britain.

THE REASONS FOR CHANGE

It thus appears that several fundamental administrative changes were effected in the mid- to late tenth century: we know that relative uniformity was established in coin production and circulation, and we can infer that kings started to make extensive use of hundreds and wapentakes; that several new shires were demarcated; that shire meetings became more routine; that powerful institutions and individuals were more systematically incentivized to enforce royal legislation at a local level; that men with strong ties to the Cerdicings were installed at York as ealdorman and archbishop; and that the first sheriffs were appointed. The numismatic changes are especially significant to this interpretation of the period. In part, this is because they are the best evidenced: since we know for sure that there was one major standardizing reform at this time, we should be receptive to the possibility that there were others. Equally, however, they are important because they are so poorly documented: given that a profound overhaul of coin production and circulation could be implemented without being mentioned in any surviving contemporary or near-contemporary text, we should not expect to find more than the most exiguous evidence for such other changes as may have taken place in the same period. The sequence of arguments from silence presented above should be seen in this light: they do not purport to constitute categorical proof, but there are grounds to accept each one individually, and together they permit us to conclude with reasonable confidence that the mid- to late tenth century in general, and Edgar's reign in particular, saw substantial changes in the character of Cerdicing rule between the

Channel and the Tees. This conclusion prompts a question: why were these putative reforms implemented?

Possible Preconditions

There is no direct evidence for why the reforms that I posit were implemented, which is hardly surprising, given that in most cases the changes themselves can only be inferred. Some tentative hypotheses are, however, possible. One obvious proposition is that the end of frequent campaigning may have been a precondition for widespread, comprehensive, and enduring change in administrative practices. It is conceivable that early tenth-century kings could have implemented reforms while also mounting military expeditions, or at least have done so during gaps in campaigning. Indeed, Edgar may well have built on, or been inspired by, more limited changes effected by his predecessors, such as the four-weekly meetings mandated by Edward the Elder, and the widespread (but short-lived) naming of minting locations under Æthelstan. Nonetheless, the level of attention and resources that kings could have devoted to administrative reorganization would almost certainly have been higher in periods when they were not contending with armed opposition, and the prolonged period of relative calm after 954 may well have been a prerequisite for far-reaching and lasting reforms. This is especially likely to have been so with regard to land north of the Humber and in the northern East Midlands: even if the Cerdicings had been able to impose new administrative structures in these areas during the 920s and 930s, it is questionable whether these would have persisted through the struggles of the 940s and early 950s.[310] In addition, one could suggest that the decades following a long series of expansionary campaigns may have been a time when institutional innovation was not only possible, but also desirable, given that territorial enlargement would have decreased kings' ability to maintain a frequent personal presence throughout the area under their domination. There are, however, plenty of examples from early medieval Europe of long-running offensive campaigns not being followed by major administrative change. Thus, while the end of expansion was perhaps a necessary condition for the reforms that the Cerdicings implemented, it is not in itself sufficient to account for them.

Somewhat similar arguments apply to the significance of the increase in the Cerdicings' wealth that probably took place before and during the second half of the tenth century. We saw in Chapter 2 that there is reason to think that from at least the late ninth century onwards the reigning Cerdicing had more land and movable wealth than any other person in Britain.[311] This position is likely to have been reinforced in subsequent decades, in part through confiscations from those

---

[310] On the events of the 940s and early 950s, see above, pp. 31–2.
[311] Above, pp. 83–4.

who resisted Cerdicing expansion.[312] As well as acquiring new lands and treasure, it is probable that Alfred's successors obtained more wealth from their existing estates, since the tenth century appears to have fallen within a long period of rising agricultural extraction in many lowland parts of southern Britain. That this was so is implied by the increasing number and size of towns, in which a substantial proportion of the population undertook non-subsistence activities: artisans must have been able to buy others' food surpluses and to sell their own wares. The causes of growing agricultural productivity need not concern us here, although the most important was probably the increasingly intensive exploitation of land and its inhabitants, especially as large estates were divided into smaller units.[313] Whatever the reasons for increased output, the point that matters here is that the Cerdicings, as (in all likelihood) the largest landholders in Britain, were probably the greatest beneficiaries.[314] It is therefore probable that the disparity in wealth between the reigning Cerdicing and any of his subordinates increased over the course of the tenth century. This would in turn have enhanced the Cerdicings' ability to reward those who were cooperative, and to punish those who were not.

This is significant, since the changes that appear to have been implemented in the mid- to late tenth century were probably not universally popular. Moneyers may have been far from enthusiastic about the imposition of a single design, especially if the centralization of die-cutting was exploited to force them to pay higher prices. Coin-users quite possibly resented changes of type, since converting coins into a new issue probably entailed transaction costs. Those who had long participated in customary local assemblies may well have been reluctant to replace time-honoured practices with Cerdicing prescriptions, and persons who had not hitherto attended such meetings may have been even less enthusiastic. The despoliation of many monasteries after Edgar's death implies widespread resentment of the ways in which they had been endowed, and Oslac's expulsion likewise suggests that his installation at York was unwelcome to some. There may, moreover, have been significant aristocratic resentment of the appointment of sheriffs, if such men served as a check on ealdormen, or indeed replaced them outright. The Cerdicings' ability to overcome such opposition as they faced was in the last resort founded on

---

[312] On land confiscations, see above, pp. 42, 44. Direct evidence for the confiscation of movable wealth is minimal, but *ASC* A 917 refers to the seizure of 'everything that was inside' Tempsford and Colchester. See also Sawyer, *Wealth*, pp. 94–5.

[313] Other factors probably included greater use of water mills and heavy ploughs, the clearance or drainage of new land, and the beginning of the so-called 'medieval warm period'. On increasing agricultural extraction and its possible causes, see Maitland, *Domesday Book*, especially pp. 318–40; H. H. Lamb, *Climate, History and the Modern World*, 2nd edn (London, 1995), pp. 171–82; Faith, *English Peasantry*, especially pp. 153–77; C. Dyer, *Making a Living in the Middle Ages: The People of Britain, 850–1520* (New Haven, CT, 2002), pp. 11–70; A. Burghart and A. Wareham, 'Was there an Agricultural Revolution in Anglo-Saxon England?', in J. Barrow and A. Wareham (eds), *Myth, Rulership, Church and Charters: Essays in Honour of Nicholas Brooks* (Aldershot, 2008), pp. 89–99; C. Wickham, *The Inheritance of Rome: A History of Europe from 400 to 1000* (London, 2009), pp. 467–71; Fleming, *Britain after Rome*, pp. 241–317.

[314] While the growing productivity of the lands that the Cerdicings themselves held would probably have been the main cause of the increase in their wealth, they would also have derived more income from tolls on trade, as all manner of landholders sold agricultural surpluses and bought artisanal goods.

their coercive strength, which ultimately derived from their wealth.[315] That the Cerdicings were greatly enriched during the tenth century may therefore have been a prerequisite for the administrative changes that they appear to have imposed in the latter part of that period. We should, however, be wary of the assumption that medieval kings were forever yearning to rule in more standardized ways: that the Cerdicings were capable of effecting administrative reform is not enough to explain why they chose to do so.

Resource Extraction and Military Recruitment

When considering the Cerdicings' possible motives, it should be borne in mind that they may have had a range of objectives: there is no need to fixate on a single hypothesis about why they introduced reforms. One obvious potential explanation is that they may have wanted to develop mechanisms to extract more from their subordinates. At first glance, the numismatic reforms appear especially susceptible to such an interpretation: kings could profit from selling approved dies, and were therefore the indirect recipients of a proportion of whatever fees moneyers charged their clients. It is, however, far from certain that Edgar envisaged that his reform should be repeated at frequent intervals; he may simply have intended to replace the existing coin stock with a currency of uniform design and less varied intrinsic value. Moreover, even when frequent type changes had become established practice, it appears that kings received relatively little income from minting. On the basis of the limited information provided by Domesday, it has been estimated that Edward the Confessor's average annual revenue from this source was probably around 125 to 150 pounds, while his lands generated over 6,000 pounds.[316] In the longer term, shires, hundreds, and wapentakes made a contribution to royal income that far outstripped that of minting. These units probably served as the administrative framework for the assessment and collection of the onerous annual land tax that was instituted in 1012, and they may have been used in much the same way to raise the sums paid to Scandinavian attackers on various occasions from 991 onwards.[317] Earlier than that, the assemblies associated with shires, hundreds, and wapentakes would have yielded fines and forfeitures, but many judicial

---

[315] Above, pp. 79–85.

[316] D. M. Metcalf, 'The Taxation of Moneyers under Edward the Confessor and in 1086', in J. C. Holt (ed.), *Domesday Studies: Papers Read at the Novocentenary Conference of the Royal Historical Society and the Institute of British Geographers, Winchester, 1986* (Woodbridge, 1987), pp. 279–93 especially 286–90; J. L. Grassi, 'The Lands and Revenues of Edward the Confessor', *EHR*, 117 (2002), pp. 251–83; Baxter, *Earls*, pp. 128–38. Metcalf's estimation of Edward's average annual minting revenue takes account of the likelihood that he received much more from moneyers in years when there was a change of type. The average was probably lower in the late tenth century, when type changes were less frequent.

[317] M. K. Lawson, 'The Collection of Danegeld and Heregeld in the Reigns of Æthelred II and Cnut', *EHR*, 99 (1984), pp. 721–38; above, pp. 141–3, 165; below, p. 197. A reference to a large tribute payment does not, however, necessarily indicate that a tax had been imposed on the general populace, let alone that such a tax had been levied on the basis of shires, hundreds, and wapentakes: payments could have been funded through less systematic forms of extortion, and (as S 1515 suggests) from the king's own wealth. See also J. L. Nelson, *Charles the Bald* (Harlow, 1992), p. 186.

profits probably went to magnates, and there is no specific evidence that these administrative structures were immediately employed to extort wealth from the general populace.[318] It is, however, eminently possible that they were so used, and kings were almost certainly alert to opportunities to increase their income; it appears, for example, that in the second half of the tenth century they demanded progressively larger payments of precious metal and war gear (heriots) from the assets of dead magnates.[319]

As well as a potential means to raise revenue, the Cerdicings quite possibly saw administrative reforms as a way to improve military recruitment. In particular, the establishment of shires in the Midlands could have been intended to replicate north of the Thames a unit of military organization that had long existed in the south, and hundreds may well also have been used to muster forces.[320] That the thirty-five years after 954 appear to have been without major armed conflict does not undermine this interpretation: comparison with Alfred's actions after his victory in 878 suggests that kings might well have used a period of calm to prepare for a possible resumption of hostilities.[321] Indeed, there is some circumstantial evidence that Edgar made new arrangements for the provision of ships by bishops. It is well established that the charter that purports to record him granting Worcester three hundreds as a 'ship-soke', along with assorted anachronistic jurisdictional privileges, was confected in the twelfth century.[322] There may, however, be some genuine basis for the claim that Edgar gave Worcester land and certain rights in these three hundreds, which were collectively reckoned at 300 hides in Domesday, in return for naval service. This possibility is strengthened by a letter in which Bishop Æthelric of Sherborne complained that various estates were not rendering the 'scypgesceote' ('ship payment') that his predecessors had received, and that he consequently lacked at least 33 of the 300 hides that other bishops had.[323] The document cannot be earlier than Æthelric's elevation to the episcopate in 1001×1002, but the reference to his predecessors implies that the allocation to bishops of 300 hides in return for ship service went back a decade or more.[324] This does not prove that any military reorganization took place in Edgar's time, but we should be open to the possibility that a desire to facilitate the raising of armed

---

[318] On magnates' receipt of judicial profits, see above, pp. 175–7.

[319] N. Brooks, 'Arms, Status and Warfare in Late-Saxon England', in Hill (ed.), *Ethelred*, pp. 87–90.

[320] On the military functions of shires, see above, pp. 99 and n. 54, 165. The scanty evidence relating to hundreds is discussed by R. Abels, *Lordship and Military Obligation in Anglo-Saxon England* (Berkeley, CA, 1988), p. 182, although the oft-cited reference in Æthelweard's *Chronicle* to the 'centurias' of Wiltshire going into battle (Æthelweard, *Chronicle*, iii.3 (p. 28)) may simply reflect a taste for classicizing vocabulary.

[321] Above, pp. 25, 26.   [322] S 731; Wormald, 'Lordship and Justice', pp. 323–4.

[323] S 1383; N. Hooper, 'Some Observations on the Navy in Late Anglo-Saxon England', in C. Harper-Bill, C. J. Holdsworth, and J. L. Nelson (eds), *Studies in Medieval History Presented to R. Allen Brown* (Woodbridge, 1989), pp. 208–13; P. Taylor, 'The Endowment and Military Obligations of the See of London: A Reassessment of Three Sources', *ANS*, 14 (1992), pp. 293–303. See also Tinti, *Sustaining Belief*, pp. 157–64. Domesday's description of Worcester's triple-hundred is at *DB*, i, 172c.

[324] Æthelric's two immediate predecessors were Wulfsige and Æthelsige, who died in 1001×1002 and 990×993 respectively.

forces may have provided some of the impetus for the administrative changes that can be ascribed to the second half of the tenth century.

Moral Motivations

The system of shires and hundreds was in all likelihood greatly entrenched by its use to extract wealth and service in the face of early eleventh-century Scandinavian attacks. This need not, however, imply that those responsible for the administrative changes of the preceding decades had foreseen all the uses to which their innovations would be put, or that they had been thinking solely in terms of revenue collection and military recruitment. Indeed, a substantial part of the impetus (or at least the stated justification) for mid- to late tenth-century administrative reforms may well have been moral, and it is notable that the *Wihtbordesstan* legislation presents itself as an attempt to propitiate God and thereby gain relief from a pestilence. Edgar identified tithe payment as the most important remedy for the situation, but the whole ordinance is said to be 'for all our souls'.[325] There was nothing new about the idea that Christian kings had onerous moral responsibilities, including the correction of their people; such thinking is, for example, implicit in Asser's *Life* of Alfred.[326] But the belief that kings owed their office to God, and were morally obliged to discipline those under their rule, appears to have become more pervasive and insistent in and after the mid-tenth century. Writing sometime between 941 and 946, Archbishop Oda of Canterbury explicitly warned Edmund that at Judgement Day he would need to render an account both for himself and for those subject to him.[327] From the 950s onwards, the frequency with which titles accorded to kings in royal charters included 'gratia Dei' ('by the grace of God') or similar words increased markedly.[328] Manuscript paintings from Edgar's reign and after assimilate the king to an abbot, and indeed to Christ, thereby asserting that he must be a model for, and corrector of, his people.[329] A Christological view of kingship also very probably played some part in Edgar's second (or, less likely, delayed) consecration in 973, even if this was in large measure intended as a celebration of his power throughout Britain: two quite different accounts of the occasion survive in separate branches of the *Chronicle*, but the fact that both

---

[325] IV Eg, especially Prolog–1.8, 15.

[326] M. Kempshall, 'No Bishop, No King: The Ministerial Ideology of Kingship and Asser's *Res Gestae Aelfredi*', in R. Gameson and H. Leyser (eds), *Belief and Culture in the Early Middle Ages: Studies Presented to Henry Mayr-Harting* (Oxford, 2001), pp. 106–27. See more generally D. Pratt, *The Political Thought of King Alfred the Great* (Cambridge, 2007), especially pp. 134–66.

[327] *Councils and Synods with Other Documents Relating to the English Church, I, A.D. 871–1204*, ed. D. Whitelock, M. Brett, and C. N. L. Brooke (2 vols, Oxford, 1981), no. 20 (i, 70).

[328] C. Insley, 'Charters, Ritual and Late Tenth-Century English Kingship', in J. L. Nelson, S. Reynolds, and S. M. Johns (eds), *Gender and Historiography: Studies in the Earlier Middle Ages in Honour of Pauline Stafford* (London, 2012), pp. 84–5.

[329] R. Deshman, '*Christus rex et magi reges*: Kingship and Christology in Ottonian and Anglo-Saxon Art', *Frühmittelalterliche Studien*, 10 (1976), pp. 367–405; R. Deshman, '*Benedictus monarcha et monachus*: Early Medieval Ruler Theology and the Anglo-Saxon Reform', *Frühmittelalterliche Studien*, 22 (1988), pp. 204–40; R. Deshman, *The Benedictional of Æthelwold* (Princeton, NJ, 1995), pp. 192–214.

stress that Edgar was then just short of thirty years old indicates that his age was perceived to be important, probably because it called to mind Luke's statement that Jesus was about thirty when he was baptized and began his ministry.[330]

The most striking demonstration of the heightening concern with royal obligations is, however, a small but significant change that was made around the time of Edgar to the liturgy for consecrating a king. At the conclusion of the earliest known English consecration rite, which dates back to at least the first half of the ninth century, the newly enthroned king issued three commands, namely that the Church of God and all Christian people observe true peace, that robberies and injustices be forbidden, and that there be justice and mercy in all judgements.[331] This remained the case in the new liturgy that very probably had its first use at Æthelstan's inauguration, which Janet Nelson labels 'Version A' of the 'Second English *ordo*'.[332] The change with which we are concerned here came with what Nelson calls 'Version B', which must have been in use by the succession of Æthelred at the very latest, but is unlikely to have been employed before Edgar's reign. The revised liturgy recast the three commands as three promises, and moved them from the end to the beginning of the ceremony.[333] Thus, what the king had previously ordered after his enthronement, he now promised before it: from sometime in (roughly) the third quarter of the tenth century onwards, consecration came to require a prior undertaking to forbid wrongdoing and to promote peace and justice.[334]

---

[330] *ASC* ABCDE 973; J. L. Nelson, 'Inauguration Rituals', in P. H. Sawyer and I. N. Wood (eds), *Early Medieval Kingship* (Leeds, 1977), pp. 63–70; Deshman, '*Benedictus monarcha et monachus*', pp. 234–6; Deshman, *Benedictional*, pp. 212–13.

[331] *The Leofric Missal*, ed. N. Orchard (2 vols, London, 2002), ii, 432; J. L. Nelson, 'The Earliest Surviving Royal *Ordo*: Some Liturgical and Historical Aspects', in B. Tierney and P. Linehan (eds), *Authority and Power: Studies in Medieval Law and Government Presented to Walter Ullmann* (Cambridge, 1980), pp. 29–48.

[332] *The Sacramentary of Ratoldus*, ed. N. Orchard (London, 2005), p. 54; J. L. Nelson, 'The Second English *Ordo*', in J. L. Nelson, *Politics and Ritual in Early Medieval Europe* (London, 1986), pp. 361–74; J. L. Nelson, 'The First Use of the Second Anglo-Saxon *Ordo*', in Barrow and Wareham (eds), *Myth, Rulership, Church and Charters*, pp. 117–26.

[333] *The Benedictional of Archbishop Robert*, ed. H. A. Wilson (London, 1903), p. 140, with Nelson, 'Second English *Ordo*', pp. 369–74, who suggests that Æthelwold was responsible for the change. Since an anonymous homily states that the three promises were administered to an unnamed king by Dunstan (d. 988), they must have been introduced by the time of Æthelred's consecration: M. Clayton, 'The Old English *Promissio regis*', *ASE*, 37 (2008), pp. 148–9. 'Version A' appears to have referred initially to rule over two peoples (i.e. the Saxons and either the Angles or Mercians), which was subsequently expanded to encompass the Saxons, Mercians, and Northumbrians, and then changed to refer to the whole of Albion. There are grounds to suspect that the 'three peoples' variant was introduced for Eadred, since it is most closely paralleled in the royal styles used in his diplomas, including one issued on (or soon after) the day of his consecration (S 520, 549, 569, 572). This would imply that the 'Albion' variant was not used until Eadwig's consecration at the earliest, which would be consistent with the charter evidence, since references to Albion were common in and after the second half of Eadred's reign (e.g. S 555, 556, 557, 560, 561, 562, 563, 564, 568, 593, 598, 609). It would then follow that 'Version B' is unlikely to have been used until at least Edgar's putative first consecration at the beginning of his reign. See C. E. Hohler, 'Some Service Books of the Later Saxon Church', in D. Parsons (ed.), *Tenth-Century Studies: Essays in Commemoration of the Millennium of the Council of Winchester and Regularis Concordia* (London, 1975), pp. 67–9; Nelson, 'Second English *Ordo*'.

[334] 'Version A' included a pre-consecration promise, but this specifically concerned churches and their privileges: *Sacramentary of Ratoldus*, pp. 47–8.

In light of this, the elaboration of mechanisms for local policing and dispute settlement can be interpreted as an attempt by Edgar and other members of his dynasty to obtain prosperity and salvation by discharging their moral obligations to extirpate wrongdoing and ensure justice. Indeed, insofar as mid- to late tenth-century kings saw hundredal administration as a means of wealth extraction, they may have been at least as concerned with ecclesiastical as royal income; there is no proof of this, but royal legislation demands the payment of church dues, and a significant number of parishes were coterminous with hundreds.[335] Further-more, although the lack of contemporary written accounts precludes certainty about the motivations for Edgar's coin reform, it may well have had a strong moral dimension, since false weights and measures were by the time of Æthelred being bracketed with perjury, adultery, and other 'devilish deeds'.[336] All this may be rele-vant to understanding not only the Cerdicings' probable motivations, but also their ability to realize their objectives: that people could have been cajoled into accepting possibly unpopular decrees through warnings of divine punishment is suggested by Edgar's *Wihtbordesstan* legislation, which urged his subjects to pay tithes, on pain of confiscation of their possessions by the king's reeve, temporal death through God's wrath, and then eternal torment in Hell.[337]

If there was a strong moral dimension to the administrative reforms apparently undertaken in the second half of the tenth century, it may well have been Bishop Æthelwold of Winchester who did most to persuade the Cerdicings, and Edgar in particular, that they needed to intensify their efforts to discipline their people. Æthelwold's ties to the ruling dynasty were tight. In his youth, he spent time in the household of Æthelstan, who ordered that he be tonsured as a cleric.[338] Later, after Æthelwold had become a monk at Glastonbury, Eadred made him Abbot of Abingdon, and subsequently visited him there.[339] Less is known about Æthel-wold's relationship with Eadwig, but there is abundant evidence of his closeness to Edgar, who is known to have been to Abingdon as a boy, and whom the abbot very probably tutored.[340] This is likely to have established a strong bond between them, and would explain why Æthelwold witnessed almost all of Edgar's extant charters issued after Eadwig's death, initially being the only abbot to make more than very occasional appearances.[341] The close ties between the two men are further demon-

---

[335] Blair, *Church*, pp. 299–303, 308–10, 433–51.

[336] V Atr 24–5; VI Atr 28.2–28.3. See also III Eg 8–8.1; V Atr 26.1; VI Atr 31–32.2; Cn 1018 20–1; II Cn 8–9.

[337] IV Eg 1.4–1.5a. Compare II Eg 3.1. Tithe-payment was more clearly a matter of moral concern than hundredal administration, but the *Wihtbordesstan* legislation is nonetheless suggestive of the way in which the prospect of divine punishment could have been invoked to promote compliance with the Cerdicings' commands.

[338] *VSÆ*, vii (p. 10).   [339] *VSÆ*, xi–xii (pp. 18–24).

[340] On Æthelwold and Eadwig, see B. Yorke, 'Æthelwold and the Politics of the Tenth Century', in Yorke (ed.), *Æthelwold*, pp. 79–80. Æthelwold did not desert Eadwig during the latter's territorial split with Edgar; this is unsurprising, given Abingdon's location south of the Thames. For the evidence that Æthelwold tutored Edgar, see below, p. 192 and n. 358.

[341] Keynes, *Atlas*, Tables LIV, LV. For the possibility that Æthelwold played a significant role in charter production during Edgar's reign, see *Charters of Abingdon Abbey*, ed. S. E. Kelly (2 vols, Oxford, 2000–1), vol. i, pp. cxv–cxxxi, but contrast Keynes, 'Edgar', pp. 15–18.

strated by Edgar's patronizing Æthelwold's abbey of Abingdon, appointing him Bishop of Winchester, aiding him in the establishment there and elsewhere of Benedictine monasticism, and giving him an estate in return for producing a vernacular version of the Rule of St Benedict.[342] Æthelwold also appears to have had close links to Edgar's consecrated queen, Ælfthryth, naming her as the protectoress of nunneries in the *Regularis Concordia*, and supporting her sons' claims to the royal succession.[343] This may have resulted in his losing some influence during the brief reign of Edward the Martyr, Edgar's child by another woman, although he continued to witness charters.[344] Even if Æthelwold was somewhat marginalized under Edward, however, he was almost certainly extremely prominent after the succession of Ælfthryth's surviving son, Æthelred, who was probably no older than about twelve when he became king.[345] Æthelred's charters were consistently attested by both Ælfthryth and Æthelwold until the latter's death in 984.[346] Ælfthryth is then not known to have witnessed until 993, when she reappeared in a charter in which Æthelred attributed unspecified tribulations to wrongs that he had perpetrated because of youthful folly and poor counsel. Significantly, Æthelred stated that these afflictions had been manifest since the death of Æthelwold, 'whose industry and pastoral care counselled not only for my benefit but also for that of all of this land'.[347] From this, it can be inferred that Æthelwold had played a major role in moulding or dictating Æthelred's actions, and it is interesting that Ælfthryth should resurface in a charter that invoked the bishop's memory: this suggests that Æthelwold's power had been such that only his death enabled Æthelred to escape maternal tutelage.

Thus, for a quarter of a century, Æthelwold was one of the Cerdicings' most significant associates. It is well known that he used his influence to promote adherence to a strict form of religious observance, outstripping Dunstan and Oswald in his zeal to replace clerks with monks.[348] It is also securely established that one of Æthelwold's sources of inspiration was the religious reforms that Louis the Pious, acting on Benedict of Aniane's advice, had prescribed in the late 810s: when writing the *Regularis Concordia*, Æthelwold chose a title that echoes Benedict's *Concordia Regularum*, and drew (among other sources) on texts associated with Louis's monastic programme.[349] Like Edgar, Charlemagne's heir has often been seen as a king whose principal achievements lay in the promotion of Benedictine monasticism, but in recent decades it has been stressed that Louis had broader reforming

---

[342] *Councils and Synods*, no. 33 (i, 147–52); *VSÆ*, xiii, xvi–xviii, xx–xxv, xxvii (pp. 24, 28–32, 36–44); *LE*, ii.37 (p. 111). On the Old English Rule, see M. Gretsch, *The Intellectual Foundations of the English Benedictine Reform* (Cambridge, 1999), pp. 226–60.

[343] *RC*, iii (p. 70); Yorke, 'Æthelwold', pp. 81–4.   [344] Keynes, *Atlas*, Table LVIII.

[345] For this and what follows, see Keynes, *Diplomas*, pp. 164, 174–5, 176–7, 181–2; Yorke, 'Æthelwold', pp. 85–6.

[346] Keynes, *Atlas*, Tables LIX, LXa.   [347] S 876, on which see below, pp. 227–8.

[348] Brooks, *Early History*, pp. 251–60; J. Barrow, 'The Community of Worcester, 961–c.1100', in Brooks and Cubitt (eds), *St Oswald*, pp. 84–99; C. Cubitt, 'Review Article: The Tenth-Century Benedictine Reform in England', *EME*, 6 (1997), pp. 93–4; N. Robertson, 'Dunstan and Monastic Reform: Tenth-Century Fact or Twelfth-Century Fiction?', *ANS*, 28 (2006), pp. 153–67.

[349] Deshman, '*Benedictus monarcha et monachus*', pp. 228–30; *VSÆ*, pp. li–lx; Deshman, *Benedictional*, pp. 209–14.

objectives. His legislation, notably that of 818–819, is much concerned with the regularization of judicial procedures, and with the practicalities of how his commands should be implemented.[350] It should, moreover, be noted that Louis's reign saw two recoinages, and it may be no coincidence that both were conducted at times of especial moral significance: the first was contemporaneous with the legislation of the late 810s, and the second followed closely the public penance that Louis performed in 822 to atone for his part in his nephew's death.[351] That Louis promoted Benedictine observance as part of a wider effort at societal reform makes it all the more plausible that Edgar's backing of monasticism was coupled with an overhaul of the means of royal rule.

Æthelwold may not have been aware that administrative and numismatic reforms were undertaken in the 810s, but there is every reason to think that his conception of royal office had much in common with that which had shaped Louis's actions, namely the belief that a king's position was akin to that of an abbot, charged with correcting those under his authority.[352] For one thing, it may well have been Æthelwold who was responsible for 'Version B' of the 'Second English *ordo*', which required the king to promise before his consecration that he would root out wrongdoing.[353] More securely, Æthelwold can be identified as the author of the *Regularis Concordia*, which calls Edgar 'shepherd of shepherds' ('pastorum pastor'), an expression that metaphorically cast the king as abbot of abbots.[354] Æthelwold was, moreover, very probably the composer of the New Minster Winchester refoundation charter, in which Edgar is styled 'vicar of Christ' ('Christi uicarius'), like the monastery's abbot, and presented as responsible for rooting out wrongdoing in his kingdom.[355] It is likely that Æthelwold developed such ideas about kingship in response to multiple stimuli, but one specific source may well have been Abbot Smaragdus of St-Mihiel's *Via regia* ('Royal Way'), an admonitory tract that had probably been intended for Louis, and of which there are a couple of apparent verbal echoes in the *Regularis Concordia*.[356] In this text, Smaragdus

---

[350] Ganshof, 'Louis the Pious Reconsidered', pp. 176–80; F. L. Ganshof, 'Les réformes judiciaires de Louis le Pieux', *Comptes-rendus des séances de l'Académie des Inscriptions et Belles-Lettres*, 109 (1965), pp. 418–27; K. F. Werner, '*Hludovicus Augustus*. Gouverner l'empire chrétien—idées et réalités', in Godman and Collins (eds), *Charlemagne's Heir*, pp. 3–123 especially 69–92. Louis's concern with the specific mechanisms by which his decrees should be put into practice continued a trend evident in Charlemagne's later years: see below, p. 236 n. 18.

[351] Coupland, 'Carolingian Single Finds', pp. 297–300. On Louis's penance of 822, see M. de Jong, *The Penitential State: Authority and Atonement in the Age of Louis the Pious, 814–840* (Cambridge, 2009), especially pp. 35–7, 122–31.

[352] T. F. X. Noble, 'The Monastic Ideal as a Model for Empire: The Case of Louis the Pious', *Revue bénédictine*, 86 (1976), pp. 235–50; Deshman, '*Benedictus monarcha et monachus*', pp. 221–5.

[353] Nelson, 'Second English *Ordo*', pp. 369–71; above, p. 188.

[354] *RC*, iii (p. 70); Lapidge, 'Æthelwold', pp. 98–100; Deshman, '*Benedictus monarcha et monachus*', pp. 207–8.

[355] S 745; Lapidge, 'Æthelwold', pp. 95–8; Deshman, '*Benedictus monarcha et monachus*', pp. 221–5. Note, however, that in the Carolingian period the king was more often presented as vicar of God than Christ: E. H. Kantorowicz, *The King's Two Bodies: A Study in Mediaeval Political Theology* (Princeton, NJ, 1957), pp. 77, 89–90.

[356] Smaragdus, *Via regia*, in *Patrologia Latina*, ed. J. P. Migne (221 vols, Paris, 1844–64), cii, columns 933–70; J. Bovendeert, 'Royal or Monastic Identity? Smaragdus' *Via regia* and *Diadema monachorum* Reconsidered', in R. Corradini, R. Meens, C. Pössel, and P. Shaw (eds), *Texts and*

referred to the king being 'in place of Christ' ('vice Christi'), and urged him to discipline himself and those under his rule; among other things, Smaragdus called for the prohibition of false weights and measures, which underlines the possible moral dimension to coin reforms.[357] The administrative changes wrought around the time of Edgar's reign can readily be interpreted as an attempt to give practical effect to exhortations like those of Smaragdus's *Via regia*: it is therefore highly significant that Æthelwold was very probably referring to himself when he declared in the *Regularis Concordia* that a certain abbot had instructed the youthful Edgar in the '*via regia* of catholic faith'.[358]

The administrative innovations that I attribute to Edgar's time were more fundamental than those demanded by Louis. A possible reason for this is that Æthelwold may have added to the general stock of Carolingian ideas about kingship a belief that homogeneity was desirable in and of itself, since he not only called for the observance of a single monastic Rule in the *Regularis Concordia*, but also appears to have cultivated standardized Old English spelling and vocabulary, with set translations of particular Latin words.[359] Even if Æthelwold was not obsessed with uniformity for its own sake, however, the far-reaching nature of the administrative changes may still be linked to his influence, since he is known to have been exceptionally uncompromising in his zeal to overhaul that which he deemed defective. In particular, his immediate establishment of a monastic cathedral chapter at

---

Identities in the Early Middle Ages (Vienna, 2006), pp. 239–51. The foreword to the *Regularis Concordia* twice refers to 'uiam regiam', once in the context of 'mandatorum Domini', the latter being an apparent echo of Smaragdus's second chapter: *RC*, i, v (pp. 69, 72); Deshman, '*Benedictus monarcha et monachus*', pp. 230–3; Deshman, *Benedictional*, pp. 198–9, 201, 210–13. These similarities of wording are not sufficiently numerous to prove that Æthelwold knew the *Via regia*, but the likelihood that he did so is strengthened when one notes that he certainly had access to another of Smaragdus's works, a commentary on the Benedictine Rule: M. Gretsch, 'Æthelwold's Translation of the *Regula Sancti Benedicti* and its Latin Exemplar', *ASE*, 3 (1974), pp. 144–6. Even if Æthelwold had not read Smaragdus's *Via regia*, he could have encountered broadly similar ideas in several other texts, notably *On the Twelve Abuses of the World*, an early medieval Irish tract. Æthelwold's identifiable writings do not quote the *Twelve Abuses*, but he is known to have possessed a copy, and his pupil Ælfric made extensive use of the text: S 1448; below, pp. 224–6.

[357] Smaragdus, *Via regia*, xviii, xxix (columns 958, 966–7).

[358] *RC*, i (p. 69); John, *Orbis Britanniae*, pp. 159–60. John identified the abbot as Æthelwold primarily on the strength of Byrhtferth's statement that Æthelwold had instructed Edgar (*VSO*, iii.11 (pp. 76–8)), and also noted that what appears to be the preface to the Old English Benedictine Rule refers to Edgar being at Abingdon as a boy, and promising its abbot (i.e. Æthelwold) that he would be generous to the monastery (*Councils and Synods*, no. 33 (i, 147–8)). John's case is materially strengthened by Dorothy Whitelock's demonstration that the latter text was almost certainly composed by Æthelwold, since this shows him referring to himself in the third person when writing about Edgar's education: D. Whitelock, 'The Authorship of the Account of King Edgar's Establishment of Monasteries', in J. L. Rosier (ed.), *Philological Essays: Studies in Old and Middle English Language and Literature in Honour of Herbert Dean Meritt* (The Hague, 1970), pp. 125–36.

[359] *RC*, especially iv (pp. 70–1); H. Gneuss, 'The Origins of Standard Old English and Æthelwold's School at Winchester', *ASE*, 1 (1972), pp. 63–83; W. Hofstetter, 'Winchester and the Standardization of Old English Vocabulary', *ASE*, 17 (1988), pp. 139–61; M. Gretsch, 'Winchester Vocabulary and Standard Old English: The Vernacular in Late Anglo-Saxon England', *Bulletin of the John Rylands University Library of Manchester*, 83 (2001), pp. 41–87. For a possible link between late tenth-century Benedictine reform and another kind of standardization, see J. Blair, 'Grid-Planning in Anglo-Saxon Settlements: The Short Perch and the Four-Perch Module', *ASSAH*, 18 (2013), pp. 18–61 especially 54.

Winchester surpassed not only Dunstan and Oswald, but also Benedict of Aniane, on whose example he demonstrably drew.[360] In light of this, it would be in no way surprising if Æthelwold spurred Edgar to effect administrative changes that outstripped those of Louis, but which were driven by much the same logic. Ultimately, one cannot prove why either Louis or Edgar implemented administrative reforms, but the parallels between their circumstances suggest that similar factors were relevant in each case: both men began to reign fairly soon after lengthy spells of expansionary campaigning had given way to relative stability, both lived during prolonged periods of growing productivity and trade, and both ruled at times when there was acute concern with kings' duty to discipline their peoples.[361] To take the comparison one step further, one might note that each had a son who, in the face of Scandinavian attack, employed the tools of local administration to extract vast sums from his subordinates.[362] It is uncertain how far either Louis or Edgar had anticipated that their reforms might be used in such ways, although it would be perverse to suppose that either was unmindful of the possibilities for financial gain. Equally, however, we should not assume that raising revenue was the sole (or even necessarily dominant) rationale for administrative innovations: moral concerns may well have been a genuine motivation, rather than just a cover for rapacity.

Ultimately, the objectives of those who demanded or implemented reform cannot now be established with confidence, but the key point of this chapter is that the period after the expansionary campaigns of the first half of the tenth century very probably witnessed substantial changes in how the Cerdicings ruled between the Channel and the Tees. The year 955 did not, *pace* Stenton, mark the beginning of six decades of Cerdicing 'decline'.[363] Nor, in all likelihood, was the mid- to late tenth century a time when kings simply refined some largely pre-existing administrative apparatus. Rather, this period, far more than the reigns of either Alfred or Æthelstan, was probably the most pivotal phase in the development of the institutional structures that were fundamental to royal rule in the eleventh-century English kingdom. If my argument be accepted, some might be tempted to take it a stage further, and to laud Edgar in the way that Alfred has often been fetishized. This temptation should be resisted, for three reasons. First, even if one assumes that institutional standardization is something to celebrate, it is uncertain how far Edgar as an individual was the main instigator of whatever changes took place during his reign, and his personal character is (like that of every other tenth-century English king) largely unknowable. Second, while Edgar's reign was probably the most significant period of administrative reform, some important developments

---

[360] P. Wormald, 'Æthelwold and his Continental Counterparts: Contact, Comparison, Contrast', in Yorke (ed.), *Æthelwold*, pp. 15–19, 30–42; above, p. 190.

[361] Noble, 'Monastic Ideal'; T. Reuter, 'The End of Carolingian Military Expansion', in Godman and Collins (eds), *Charlemagne's Heir*, pp. 391–405; A. Verhulst, *The Carolingian Economy* (Cambridge, 2002); de Jong, *Penitential State*.

[362] E. Joranson, *The Danegeld in France* (Rock Island, IL, 1923), pp. 26–117, 189–204; above, p. 165; below, p. 197.

[363] Stenton, *Anglo-Saxon England*, pp. 364–93; above, p. 13.

took place before and after: in particular, the use of hundreds for policing appears in at least some places to have gone back to Edmund's time, there is no particular reason to think that sheriffs existed outside the south-east until well after Edgar's death, and it was only from Cnut onwards that writ-charters become abundant. Third, despite the major administrative innovations of the mid- to late tenth century, important aspects of the Cerdicings' domination remained largely unchanged, and it is to the implications of this mix of innovation and continuity that we now turn.

5

The Implications of Administrative Change

THE INTENSIFICATION OF CERDICING DOMINATION
BETWEEN THE CHANNEL AND THE TEES

The previous chapter argued that the Cerdicings implemented a series of administrative reforms in the mid- to late tenth century. The aim of this chapter is to analyse the implications of these innovations and to draw attention to their limits. In particular, it seeks to show that the geographical and substantive limits of reform had significant consequences, doing much to define the English kingdom and stimulate attempts to circumscribe royal arbitrariness. We begin, however, with the most direct implication of the developments identified in the last chapter: during the mid- to late tenth century, there was probably a significant intensification in the Cerdicings' domination between the Channel and the Tees. Since there is so little evidence relating to individual localities, either before or after the mid-tenth century, we cannot assess the precise nature or extent of change in specific places. It is, however, highly likely that the reforms increased the Cerdicings' scope to mould the conduct of ordinary people throughout this area. Earlier, when there were fewer standardized administrative structures, it would probably have been hard for kings to formulate stipulations that were both detailed and suitable for general application, and this suspicion is strengthened when one notes that Æthelstan appears to have wanted local notables to devise arrangements to give effect to his commands. By the end of Edgar's reign, however, there was in all parts of the future Domesday *Anglia* a common framework within which precise instructions could (at least in principle) be implemented.

Edgar's *Wihtbordesstan* legislation, with its stipulations about the way in which trade was to be monitored, illustrates how hundreds and wapentakes could provide a framework for procedural standardization, and his successors likewise used these units to organize the implementation of their commands.[1] Thus, for example, Æthelred prescribed processes involving hundreds or wapentakes to establish the guilt or otherwise of those accused of wrongdoing, and Cnut ordered that every freeman ('freoman') over twelve winters old be 'brought within a hundred and a tithing', and 'within a hundred and under surety'.[2] This last reference has attracted particular attention, since it may describe something much like the 'frankpledge' law enforcement system, which by the twelfth century operated in a large part of

---

[1] IV Eg 3–12.1.
[2] I Atr 1–1.14; III Atr 3.1–3.3; II Cn 20–20a. Compare II Cn 22–22.1, 30–30.9.

the English kingdom, although neither north of the Humber nor in most of Cheshire, Shropshire, and Herefordshire.[3] It relied on hundred and wapentake meetings to place most lay males over the age of twelve into groups called tithings, which served as units for policing and collective surety: the members of a tithing were liable to punishment if they failed to apprehend and produce for trial any of their number who had been accused of an offence.[4] Entry into a frankpledge tithing was accompanied by an oath to abjure theft, and it is noteworthy that the relevant passage of Cnut's legislation is followed by an order that every man over twelve winters old swear to be neither a thief nor a thief's accomplice: we therefore have a good basis for suspecting that the essentials of frankpledge were already in place under Cnut.[5] There is, however, no proof, and Cnut's separate mentions of 'hundred and tithing' and 'hundred and surety' may reflect that tithing and surety were distinct in his time: one could hypothesize that, while all free men were to be in a policing tithing and to have a surety, it need not have been the other members of a man's tithing who stood surety for him.[6] The question of whether twelfth-century arrangements already obtained is not, however, crucial here; what matters much more is that the legislation of Edgar, Æthelred, and Cnut presupposes that hundreds and wapentakes existed, and that these units constituted an administrative framework for which detailed procedures could be prescribed. How far the decrees of these kings took effect is largely unknowable, but we should be very wary of any suspicion that their legislation was a dead letter: the implementation of coin reforms demonstrates that

---

[3] What follows draws on W. A. Morris, *The Frankpledge System* (London, 1910); P. Wormald, 'Frederic William Maitland', *Law and History Review*, 16 (1998), pp. 1–25, reprinted in his *Legal Culture in the Early Medieval West: Law as Text, Image and Experience* (London, 1999), pp. 54–7; P. Wormald, 'Frankpledge', in *WBEASE*, pp. 197–8; J. G. H. Hudson, *The Oxford History of the Laws of England. Volume II: 871–1216* (Oxford, 2012), pp. 74–5, 169–71, 391–5.

[4] Tithings could comprise either ten or more men, or all the men of a particular area: Morris, *Frankpledge*, pp. 86–90.

[5] II Cn 21; Morris, *Frankpledge*, pp. 70–1, 130. Such arrangements may have antedated Cnut, but there is no specific evidence. Oaths were demanded by earlier kings, although Cnut's reign is the first point at which it is clear that these were to be sworn by all adult males (above, pp. 63–5). The obligation on tithings to apprehend fugitives is probably related to the policing responsibilities with which tithingmen are associated in the Hundred Ordinance, which is likely to date to the mid- to late tenth century (Hu 2; above, pp. 144–5 and n. 130). The demand that every man have a surety was prefigured in the legislation of both Edgar and Æthelred, but there is no particular reason to think that either of these kings envisaged sureties being organized on the basis of tithings (III Eg 6–6.2; IV Eg 3; I Atr 1). William of Malmesbury, *Gesta Regum Anglorum*, ii.122.1, ed. and trans. R. A. B. Mynors, R. M. Thomson, and M. Winterbottom (2 vols, Oxford, 1998–9), i, 188 credits Alfred with the establishment of frankpledge. It is noteworthy that William thought the system antedated the Conquest, but no reliance should be placed on his claim that it went back to Alfred. Contrast P. Wormald, '*Engla Lond*: The Making of an Allegiance', *Journal of Historical Sociology*, 7 (1994), pp. 1–24, reprinted in his *Legal Culture*, pp. 366–7; Wormald, 'Frederic William Maitland', pp. 54–7; Wormald, 'Frankpledge'. D. Pratt, 'Written Law and the Communication of Authority in Tenth-Century England', in D. Rollason, C. Leyser, and H. Williams (eds), *England and the Continent in the Tenth Century: Studies in Honour of Wilhelm Levison (1876–1947)* (Turnhout, 2010), pp. 337–49 suggests that frankpledge was set up during Æthelstan's reign. Pratt places particular emphasis on the text of the London peace regulations (discussed above, pp. 113–14), but there is no evidence that the ten-person policing groups it describes acted as mutual sureties. Indeed, the text presupposes that sureties for a convicted thief would be provided by the person's lord or kindred: VI As 1.4, 12.2.

[6] Morris, *Frankpledge*, pp. 1–41 argues along such lines.

Edgar and his successors were quite capable of securing widespread compliance with their commands.

The intensification of Cerdicing domination is further manifested in Æthelred's institution of the *heregeld* (army tax). The requirement that a king's subordinates discharge obligations imposed by him was not itself new, but the account of Edward the Confessor's (temporary) abolition of the *heregeld* in the D text of the *Chronicle* makes clear that this tax represented an especially oppressive burden, and that it had first been levied in 1012.[7] There is no proof that its collection was organized through shires, hundreds, and wapentakes from the outset, but there is every reason to think that this was so, as would be the case after the Norman Conquest.[8] There are, moreover, grounds to conclude that from at least the time of Cnut the tax was probably levied across all or much of what would constitute Domesday *Anglia*: a document from St Peter's, Gloucester, indicates that the abbot resorted to leasing out land in order to raise funds when Cnut made a 'great exaction of *heregeld* through the whole of *Anglia* [*per totam Angliam*]', and a late eleventh-century Worcester cartulary details estates that had been lost when the same king imposed an 'unbearable tax [*vectigal*] on the whole kingdom of the English [*toti Anglorum regno*]'.[9] It thus appears that, within a few decades, the administrative innovations of the mid- to late tenth century were being used to impose novel and onerous burdens on the inhabitants of at least the bulk of the land between the Channel and the Tees.

The establishment of a particular set of relatively standardized structures did not eliminate diversity within the future Domesday *Anglia*; obvious examples include variations in the sizes of shires, and the twofold terminology of hundreds and wapentakes.[10] There were also many continuities from earlier periods. Kings did not cease to require magnates' cooperation if their commands were to take effect at a local level.[11] *Burh*s remained prominent in royal legislation, being supplemented rather than replaced by the development of hundred, wapentake, and

---

[7] *ASC* D 1051. See also *ASC* CDE 1012, C 1049, CE 1050; M. K. Lawson, 'The Collection of Danegeld and Heregeld in the Reigns of Æthelred II and Cnut', *EHR*, 99 (1984), pp. 721–38; J. Gillingham, '"The Most Precious Jewel in the English Crown": Levels of Danegeld and Heregeld in the Early Eleventh Century', *EHR*, 104 (1989), pp. 373–84; M. K. Lawson, '"Those Stories Look True": Levels of Taxation in the Reigns of Æthelred II and Cnut', *EHR*, 104 (1989), pp. 385–406; J. Gillingham, 'Chronicles and Coins as Evidence for Levels of Tribute and Taxation in Late Tenth- and Early Eleventh-Century England', *EHR*, 105 (1990), pp. 939–50; M. K. Lawson, 'Danegeld and Heregeld Once More', *EHR*, 105 (1990), pp. 951–61. On burdens in earlier periods, see above, pp. 86–104. A tax much like the *heregeld* was levied after the Norman Conquest, and it may (but need not) have been reintroduced sometime between 1051 and 1066: F. Barlow, *Edward the Confessor*, 2nd edn (New Haven, CT, 1997), p. 106 n. 5; D. Pratt, 'Demesne Exemption from Royal Taxation in Anglo-Saxon and Anglo-Norman England', *EHR*, 128 (2013), pp. 7–8.

[8] Above, pp. 141–3, 165, 185.

[9] S 1424; *Hemingi chartularium ecclesiæ Wigorniensis*, ed. T. Hearne (2 vols, Oxford, 1723), i, 277–8; Lawson, 'Collection of Danegeld', pp. 724–5 and n. 8. Losses occurred because land could be assigned to anyone who paid the tax due from it, if the holder did not do so.

[10] Above, pp. 122, 157. Note, too, the limited distribution of twelfth-century frankpledge: above, pp. 195–6.

[11] Powerful individuals and institutions were given (or permitted to retain) financial incentives to identify and convict wrongdoers: above, pp. 174–7.

shire administration.[12] Assemblies did not suddenly start to operate according to abstract conceptions of legal fairness; much, for example, still depended on whether a litigant had sufficient connections to gather large numbers of oath-helpers.[13] Nor did royally mandated local meetings acquire a monopoly on dispute settlement: the legislation of Æthelred and Cnut states that the kin of a churchman accused of homicide must pay compensation or bear the enmity ('fæhðe') with him, an implicit acknowledgement that victims of at least some forms of wrongdoing might still use the threat of vengeance to obtain redress.[14] Cases that did not involve physical violence could likewise be resolved by the parties and their associates: while the *Libellus Æthelwoldi* several times mentions meetings of hundreds, it also describes a land dispute being settled by compromise, without apparent recourse to any royally mandated assembly.[15] Perhaps most importantly, the newly prominent administrative structures of shires, hundreds, and wapentakes were not always entirely novel, with much probably being founded on the appropriation and modification of long-standing local assembly customs.[16] We should therefore not assume that the innovations of the mid- to late tenth century introduced order where there had previously been chaos. Rather, their main effect was probably to increase the extent to which it was the king, as opposed to a range of local notables, who determined what constituted order, and how it should be upheld.

This conclusion may prompt some to question the importance of the reforms discussed in the previous chapter: for most people, it may have mattered little to what extent it was the king, rather than one or more local magnates, who decided how (and how far) their conduct should be regulated. This does not, however, mean that the changes were insignificant. In the first place, the impact on the general populace was probably far from trivial: kings seem to have imposed some demands that were quite unlike anything seen in the preceding decades, the apparent restriction of the use of obsolete coins being a clear and early example. Moreover, kings soon began to use the apparatus of shire, hundred, and wapentake administration to extract unprecedentedly heavy financial burdens. In any case, however, even if the lives of ordinary people were not fundamentally transformed, the reforms would have been important to the Cerdicings. Given the perceived moral responsibility of rulers to discipline their subjects, it probably mattered a great deal to kings that they

---

[12] III Eg 5.1; IV Eg 2a, 3–6, 10; II Atr 2.1, 5.2–6; III Atr 1.1–1.2, 6.1, 7; II Cn 18, 22.1, 24, 34.

[13] P. Wormald, 'Charters, Law and the Settlement of Disputes in Anglo-Saxon England', in W. Davies and P. Fouracre (eds), *The Settlement of Disputes in Early Medieval Europe* (Cambridge, 1986), pp. 149–68, reprinted in his *Legal Culture*, pp. 308–9; S. Baxter, 'Lordship and Justice in Late Anglo-Saxon England: The Judicial Functions of Soke and Commendation Revisited', in S. Baxter, C. E. Karkov, J. L. Nelson, and D. Pelteret (eds), *Early Medieval Studies in Memory of Patrick Wormald* (Farnham, 2009), p. 417.

[14] VIII Atr 23–5; I Cn 5.2b–5.2d. See also *Diplomatarium Anglicum Ævi Saxonici*, ed. B. Thorpe (London, 1865), pp. 610–13; P. R. Hyams, *Rancor and Reconciliation in Medieval England* (Ithaca, NY, 2003); T. B. Lambert, 'Theft, Homicide and Crime in Late Anglo-Saxon Law', *P&P*, 214 (2012), pp. 3–43.

[15] *LE*, ii.33 (pp. 107–8); above, p. 143. A. Kennedy, 'Law and Litigation in the *Libellus Æthelwoldi Episcopi*', *ASE*, 24 (1995), pp. 131–83 stresses the variety and flexibility of the means of dispute settlement described by the *Libellus*. That disputants sometimes reached settlements outside the official framework of judicial institutions should come as no surprise: this remains common today.

[16] Above, pp. 148–50, 154.

should be the ones who directed how order was maintained.[17] While the extant evidence is too thin to permit any very full assessment of the details of how administrative change affected ordinary people, it is highly probable that kings became significantly more able to shape and constrain what happened at a local level: it thus appears that the mid- to late tenth century saw a major intensification in the Cerdicings' domination between the Channel and the Tees.

THE DEFINITION OF THE ENGLISH KINGDOM

The Geographical Limits of Reform

While substantial, the Cerdicings' reforms were geographically limited. Edgar's numismatic innovations only applied within what would constitute Domesday *Anglia*: in the rest of the island, minting remained absent, and hoards sometimes still combined English, Hiberno-Scandinavian, and Continental issues, along with uncoined bullion.[18] Similarly, while hundreds or wapentakes seem by the end of Edgar's reign to have been used for administrative purposes throughout the area from the Channel to the Tees, these units were (with very few exceptions) never introduced further north or in Wales.[19] Likewise, although most (but not all) of the Domesday shires probably existed by the end of the tenth century, it was not until significantly after the Norman Conquest that the system was extended north of the Tees and west of the Pennines.[20] Furthermore, while the Cerdicings appear to have been able to install both ealdormen and archbishops at York from Edgar's reign onwards, it was not until well into the eleventh century that there is good evidence of southern kings intervening in episcopal elections at Durham or determining who had power at Bamburgh.[21] This contrast was reflected in witness lists:

[17] Above, pp. 187–93; below, pp. 224–9.

[18] M. A. S. Blackburn, H. Pagan et al., *Checklist of Coin Hoards from the British Isles, c.450–1180*, consulted at <http://www.cm.fitzmuseum.cam.ac.uk/dept/coins/projects/hoards/index.list.html> (accessed 9 October 2014); M. A. S. Blackburn, 'Currency under the Vikings. Part 3: Ireland, Wales, Isle of Man and Scotland in the Ninth and Tenth Centuries', *BNJ*, 77 (2007), pp. 119–49.

[19] J. C. Holt, *The Northerners: A Study in the Reign of King John* (Oxford, 1961), pp. 197–8; above, pp. 122–3 and n. 32.

[20] R. Sharpe, *Norman Rule in Cumbria, 1092–1136* (Kendal, 2006); above, pp. 157–60.

[21] On the appointments of Oscytel and Oslac in the 950s and 966, see above, pp. 177–9. Cnut is the first king known to have played any role in the appointment of a Bishop of Durham: Symeon of Durham, *Libellus de Exordio atque Procursu istius, hoc est Dunhelmensis, Ecclesie*, iii.6, ed. and trans. D. Rollason (Oxford, 2000), p. 160; *Charters of Northern Houses*, ed. D. A. Woodman (Oxford, 2012), pp. 310–16. Harthacnut's betrayal of Eadwulf of Bamburgh may reflect that he had backed Siward's extension of his power beyond the Tees, but the earliest clear-cut case of a southern king choosing who had power at Bamburgh is Edward the Confessor's (far from successful) installation of Tostig as earl from the Humber to the Tweed: *ASC* CD 1041, CDE 1065; *Historia Regum*, ed. T. Arnold, *Symeonis Monachi Opera Omnia* (RS, 75, 2 vols, London, 1882–5), ii, 198; *De primo Saxonum adventu*, ed. Arnold, *Symeonis Monachi Opera Omnia*, ii, 383. *De obsessione Dunelmi*, ed. Arnold, *Symeonis Monachi Opera Omnia*, i, 216 has Æthelred II replacing Waltheof of Bamburgh with the latter's son Uhtred, and at the same time granting Uhtred authority at York. The entrusting of York to a man from Bamburgh echoes what Eadred had done (above, pp. 32–3), and probably followed the killing in 1006 of Ealdorman Ælfhelm (*ASC* CDE 1006), but little reliance can be placed on *De obsessione*'s implication that Æthelred removed Waltheof from his position in Bamburgh. The text gives an impossible date

from Edgar's later years onwards, leading magnates from throughout the land between the Channel and the Tees were routinely present at Cerdicing assemblies, but Welsh, Cumbrian, and Scottish rulers do not seem to have attested late tenth- and eleventh-century charters, and appearances by Bishops of Chester-le-Street (Durham after 995) and Bamburgh potentates were sporadic.[22] It is doubtful whether the second half of the tenth century saw major change in the Cerdicings' dealings with Wales or northern Britain. English kings continued to have only a loose and intermittent dominance over the great potentates of these areas, and cannot have had more than an extremely occasional impact on the general popu-lace.[23] Indeed, it is notable that, following the gathering at Chester in 973, there is no specific evidence of a Welsh, Cumbrian, or Scottish ruler acknowledging the superiority of a southern king until about 1031.[24] If anything, the Cerdicings' episodic island-wide hegemony entered one of its more tenuous phases soon after they intensified their grip on the land between the Channel and the Tees.

We saw in Chapters 2 and 3 that in the early tenth century there was relatively little to mark out the land from the Channel to the Tees as a block, coherent in itself and distinct from the rest of Britain. This did not preclude the existence of a concept of an English kingdom, or at least of an English kingship; indeed, the title *rex Anglorum* ('king of the English') was in common use from early in the reign of Æthelstan.[25] The tendency of some modern historians to celebrate Æthelstan as 'the first king of England' is, however, problematic, since there is little sign that in his day the title *rex Anglorum* was closely or consistently tied to an area similar to that which we consider England.[26] Indeed, when Æthelstan's rule was associated with any definite geographical expanse, the territory in question was usually the whole island of Britain. By the eleventh century, however, as we noted in the Intro-duction to this volume, the English kingdom was being conceptualized in terms quite readily recognizable to us, although at least some writers appear to have regarded the Tees as its northern limit. *Anglia* and *Englaland* are both known to have been used as names for the kingdom, and it was probably with this sense that these words were employed to designate the land described in Domesday.[27] This was a territory that did not encompass all the English, but whose greater magnates

(969), and Symeon of Durham describes Uhtred as *comes Northanhymbrorum* in the context of 995, which suggests that he was already the leading figure at Bamburgh a decade before receiving York: Symeon of Durham, *Libellus de Exordio*, iii.2 (p. 148).

[22] Above, pp. 57 and n. 46, 177–9.

[23] G. Molyneaux, 'Why were some Tenth-Century English Kings Presented as Rulers of Britain?', *TRHS*, 6th series, 21 (2011), pp. 75–7. T. M. Charles-Edwards, *Wales and the Britons, 350–1064* (Oxford, 2013), pp. 536–52 argues that Cerdicing domination in Wales weakened substantially after the mid-tenth century. The contrast between the century's two halves is less marked when one consid-ers Britain as a whole, however, since Cerdicing hegemony in the north of the island had never been more than intermittent. There may well also have been interruptions to Cerdicing power in substantial parts of Wales during the first half of the tenth century: Charles-Edwards, *Wales*, pp. 494–510, 526.

[24] *ASC* DE 1027, although note *ASC* CDE 1000.   [25] Above, p. 30; below, pp. 207–9.

[26] D. N. Dumville, *Wessex and England from Alfred to Edgar* (Woodbridge, 1992), pp. 141–71, 204; S. Foot, *Æthelstan: The First King of England* (New Haven, CT, 2011); below, pp. 208–9. My argument owes much to the stimulation of E. John, *Orbis Britanniae and Other Studies* (Leicester, 1966), pp. 1–63 especially 48.

[27] Above, pp. 1, 2, 4–5.

routinely attended royal assemblies, and in which there was numismatic uniformity and some measure of administrative standardization. It thus seems that, at least for some, the eleventh-century English kingdom was defined by features that appear to date from the mid- to late tenth century.

This is not to say that a clear and unequivocal conception of 'the English kingdom' necessarily followed hard on the heels of the developments that can be ascribed (approximately) to Edgar's reign. The perception that the presence of hundreds or wapentakes set one part of Britain off from the rest may, for example, only really have become entrenched when these units were used to levy taxation each year from 1012 to 1051. More generally, although resistance was often far from cohesive, the experience of fighting against a common enemy under Æthelred II may have contributed to the consolidation of a sense of collective feeling.[28] In addition, Cnut's conquest probably did much to crystallize the idea of the English kingdom as a definite geographical unit, and it is from his reign onwards that we find frequent appearances of the explicitly territorial term *Englaland*. It is particularly striking that all versions of the *Chronicle* use this word as the standard term for that which Cnut and his successors ruled, whereas earlier annals had usually presented Æthelred as king of the *Angelcynn* ('English people').[29] This shift from an ethnic to an overtly geographical term may reflect that most of those over whom Cnut was king (outside Scandinavia) were English, while he and many of his close associates were Danish. He referred to his subjects with couplets such as 'Danes or English', and statements that he ruled *Englaland* expressed the idea that he was king of all the inhabitants of a territory, whatever their ethnicity.[30] It may therefore only have been in the eleventh century that a conception of the English kingdom broadly similar to ours became firmly embedded in the minds of many of its inhabitants, but this idea developed within parameters that were most probably established in the mid- to late tenth century.

The Realization of an Alfredian Vision?

Few (if any) historians would dispute that the experience of being ruled by a single king through a common set of administrative structures played a significant role in fixing the idea of an English kingdom in the heads of those who dwelt within it. Likewise, it can hardly be doubted that the identity and cohesion of the kingdom

[28] On evidence of collective feeling in the account of Æthelred's reign in the C, D, and E texts of the *Chronicle*, see P. Stafford, 'The Anglo-Saxon Chronicles, Identity and the Making of England', *HSJ*, 19 (2007), pp. 32–5. For the mutable loyalties of the kingdom's greatest magnate, see S. Keynes, 'Eadric Streona (*d.* 1017)', *ODNB*. *ASC* CDE 1010 says that no shire would help the next.

[29] J. A. Stodnick, 'The Interests of Compounding: *Angelcynn* to *Engla land* in the Anglo-Saxon *Chronicle*', in H. Magennis and J. Wilcox (eds), *The Power of Words: Anglo-Saxon Studies Presented to Donald G. Scragg on his Seventieth Birthday* (Morgantown, WV, 2006), pp. 337–67; G. T. Beech, 'The Naming of England', *History Today*, 57(10) (October, 2007), pp. 30–5; Stafford, 'Anglo-Saxon Chronicles', especially pp. 32–5, 47. *Angelcynn* sometimes appears to denote a territory, but *Englaland* is much less ambiguous.

[30] Cn 1018 Prol.; Cn 1020 9; II Cn 83; Cn 1027 6. See also *ASC* CDE 1018, E 1026; S 1394, 1406, 1409.

owed much to the attendance at royal assemblies of persons from across the area between the Channel and the Tees. It is, however, now quite widely believed that the idea of an English kingdom corresponding at least loosely to modern England was not just a consequence, but also a cause, of the events of the tenth century; Patrick Wormald in particular argued that much of the impetus for the Cerdicings' actions stemmed from an Alfredian vision of 'a kingdom of all the English'.[31] What Wormald skirted round, however, is that this was not what Alfred's successors actually achieved: the kingdom of the eleventh and subsequent centuries did not include all the English, and therefore can hardly have been defined (at least at any level of detail) by a prophetic vision of English unity.[32] This does not, however, necessarily mean that we should characterize what happened in the tenth century as a failed unification project. Rather, the whole notion that the Cerdicings set out to create a kingdom with bounds corresponding to those of English habitation is ripe for reconsideration.

There is plentiful evidence that from early in the Anglo-Saxon period there was a fairly widespread belief that the Northumbrians, East Angles, Mercians, West Saxons, and so on were all in some sense a single people, known as the *Angli* or (less commonly) the *Saxones*; when used in such a collective context, both of these terms can be translated as 'the English'.[33] This sense of common identity is, for example, clear in the 'ecclesiastical history of the English people [*gentis Anglorum*]' that Bede completed in 731, and probably arose through use of one language, shared recognition of Gregory the Great as apostle, and belief in an ancestral migration from the Continent.[34] The existence of a collective identity need not, however, prompt an impulse to political consolidation, and the proposition that

---

[31] P. Wormald, 'Living with King Alfred', *HSJ*, 15 (2004), p. 20. See also P. Wormald, 'Bede, the *Bretwaldas* and the Origins of the *Gens Anglorum*', in P. Wormald, D. Bullough, and R. Collins (eds), *Ideal and Reality in Frankish and Anglo-Saxon Society: Studies Presented to J. M. Wallace-Hadrill* (Oxford, 1983), pp. 99–129; P. Wormald, 'The Venerable Bede and the "Church of the English"', in G. Rowell (ed.), *The English Religious Tradition and the Genius of Anglicanism* (Wantage, 1992), pp. 13–32; Wormald, '*Engla Lond*', pp. 371–81.

[32] Wormald wrote little about Lothian, but suggested that there was Bedan sanction for its being left out of the English kingdom, since the *Ecclesiastical History* 'revealed' that Abercorn 'had been abandoned by the "Angli" as a matter of policy' (Wormald, '*Engla Lond*', p. 378). This is an odd way to describe flight from the Picts, and in any case the belief persisted that Lothian's inhabitants were English: above, pp. 7–8. One could cling to the idea that the English were unified in the tenth century by pointing out that those living in what is now south-east Scotland were in some measure subject to Cerdicing domination, but so too was pretty much everyone else in Britain: the area in which the English lived did not constitute a discrete political unit.

[33] Wormald, 'Bede, the *Bretwaldas* and the Origins of the *Gens Anglorum*', especially pp. 120–9; M. Richter, 'Bede's *Angli*: Angles or English?', *Peritia*, 3 (1984), pp. 99–114; Wormald, 'Venerable Bede', especially pp. 18–22; S. Foot, 'The Making of *Angelcynn*: English Identity before the Norman Conquest', *TRHS*, 6th series, 6 (1996), pp. 25–49 especially 38–45; N. Brooks, 'English Identity from Bede to the Millennium', *HSJ*, 14 (2003), pp. 33–51.

[34] *HE*, preface (p. 2); N. Howe, *Migration and Mythmaking in Anglo-Saxon England* (New Haven, CT, 1989; reprinted with new introduction, Notre Dame, IN, 2001), pp. 8–71, 108–42; A. Thacker, 'Memorializing Gregory the Great: The Origin and Transmission of a Papal Cult in the Seventh and Early Eighth Centuries', *EME*, 7 (1998), pp. 59–84 especially 75–82; T. M. Charles-Edwards, 'The Making of Nations in Britain and Ireland in the Early Middle Ages', in R. Evans (ed.), *Lordship and Learning: Studies in Memory of Trevor Aston* (Woodbridge, 2004), pp. 12–24, although Howe's book should be used with caution.

Alfred and his successors wanted to unite the English cannot be accepted without specific justification. Attempts to supply such justification have proceeded along two main lines. The first is a contention that an aspiration to achieve unification was a corollary of an allegedly pervasive belief that the English were a people whom God had chosen to have a special covenant, much like the Israelites of the Old Testament. Having convinced himself (and many others) that such a notion was prevalent during the Anglo-Saxon period, Wormald concluded that the Cerdicings believed that political unification was imperative if the English were to avoid travails like those that had followed the division of the twelve tribes of Israel.[35] Even if Wormald were correct that the English thought they had a special covenant, his inference that unification was considered necessary for divine favour would require a large leap of logic. It would, moreover, face the problem that the Cerdicings made no concerted attempt to incorporate Lothian into their kingdom. The effort required to do so would have been considerable, but the Cerdicings' acceptance of Scottish rule south of the Forth would be most peculiar if they believed that English disunity risked incurring God's displeasure. In any case, however, I have argued elsewhere that the notion that the English considered themselves to be the special successors of the Old Testament Israelites is without foundation.[36] The first of the two main bases for the claim that the Cerdicings set out to unite the English thus crumbles.

The second argument for thinking that the Cerdicings aimed to establish a kingdom more or less coterminous with the area inhabited by the English starts from the observation that certain texts associated with Alfred use the word *Angelcynn* ('English people').[37] That this was a direct vernacular equivalent of *gens Anglorum* is clear from the Old English version of the *Ecclesiastical History*, and it is well established that Bede's apparent lexical preference was a major cause of the eventual predominance (at least within areas of English habitation) of 'Anglian' over 'Saxon' terminology for the collective designation of the English.[38] The fact that people wrote of *Angli*, *gens Anglorum*, or *Angelcynn* is not inherently remarkable, since they could simply have been referring to a population group that was, like the Irish, identifiable by its language and certain other shared features. Nonetheless, it has been claimed that the word *Angelcynn* was charged with some particular political significance, and that its use during Alfred's reign reflects a desire on his part 'to promote a nascent conception of one people', with a view to bringing this people under his dynasty's domination.[39] This contention is problematic. In the first place, if *Angelcynn* were a word with some powerful ideological resonance, the alleged trumpeting of this concept would not necessarily have facilitated the

---

[35] Wormald, 'Venerable Bede', pp. 23–7; Wormald, '*Engla Lond*', pp. 375–81.

[36] G. Molyneaux, 'The *Old English Bede*: English Ideology or Christian Instruction?', *EHR*, 124 (2009), pp. 1289–323; G. Molyneaux, 'Did the English Really Think they were God's Elect in the Anglo-Saxon Period?', *Journal of Ecclesiastical History*, 65 (2014), pp. 721–37.

[37] Foot, 'Making of *Angelcynn*'; A. Scharer, *Herrschaft und Repräsentation. Studien zur Hofkultur König Alfreds des Großen* (Vienna, 2000), especially pp. 123–6.

[38] Wormald, 'Bede, the *Bretwaldas* and the Origins of the *Gens Anglorum*', especially pp. 120–9; Richter, 'Bede's *Angli*'; Wormald, 'Venerable Bede', especially pp. 18–22; Foot, 'Making of *Angelcynn*', pp. 35, 38–45; Brooks, 'English Identity'.

[39] Foot, 'Making of *Angelcynn*', p. 30.

formation of a kingdom encompassing all the English. Such a kingdom would have needed to embrace many who regarded themselves as 'Danes', to whom rhetoric of this sort might well not have appealed.[40] The more fundamental objection, however, is that over a fifth of all attested mentions of *Angelcynn*, and a clear majority of those which antedate the turn of the ninth and tenth centuries, are accounted for by the vernacular version of Bede's *Ecclesiastical History*, whose author appears to have been strikingly uninterested in cultivating any sort of English ideology, even passing up an opportunity to call the English 'God's people whom he foreknew'.[41] This seriously undermines the assumption that references to *Angelcynn* elsewhere indicate a project to promote English unification, and suggests that we should look more closely at the other contexts in which this word appears.

The extant references to *Angelcynn* fall into two main chronological groups, one roughly contemporaneous with Alfred's reign, and the other from the late tenth and early eleventh centuries.[42] When considering whether Alfred and his immediate successors aimed to unite the English, it is on the earlier cluster that we need to focus. Three preliminary points are necessary. First, the word was not unknown before Alfred's reign, being attested in a mid-ninth-century charter of the Mercian king Burgred, which contrasts 'angelcynnes monna' ('English persons') and foreigners ('ælðeodigra').[43] Second, there was precedent for a West Saxon king using 'Anglian' terminology, since the legislation ascribed to Ine contrasts 'Englisc' (English) and 'Wilisc' (British).[44] Third, Alfred's reign is one of the two richest periods for surviving Old English prose, the other being the decades around the turn of the tenth and eleventh centuries. That these two phases account for most *Angelcynn* references may therefore simply be a function of general peaks in textual production and preservation. As such, while the apparent burst of appearances of *Angelcynn* in Alfred's reign probably reflects his promotion of vernacular writing, it need not indicate that he deliberately fostered the term, which may have long been in common use, without being written in the few earlier extant texts that contain Old English.

In addition to the *Old English Bede* and the Mercian charter, there are thirty occurrences of *Angelcynn* in texts from before about 900. None provides good grounds to think that Alfred harboured a specific aspiration to rule all the English. The *Old English Martyrology* accounts for nine, every one of which is strikingly banal: the text uses *Angelcynn* seven times when invoking Bede's *Ecclesiastical*

---

[40] On 'Danes', see above, pp. 44–5.

[41] Molyneaux, '*Old English Bede*', especially pp. 1316–18. Note also D. Pratt, *The Political Thought of King Alfred the Great* (Cambridge, 2007), pp. 106–7.

[42] This statement is based on searches of A. diP. Healey, J. P. Wilkin, and X. Xiang, *Dictionary of Old English Web Corpus* (Toronto, 2009), consulted at <http://tapor.library.utoronto.ca/doecorpus/> (accessed 9 October 2014). It is necessary to check under each of the variant spellings of *Angelcynn* recorded at A. Cameron, A. C. Amos, and A. diP. Healey, *Dictionary of Old English* (Toronto, 1986–), s.v. 'angel-cynn', consulted at <http://tapor.library.utoronto.ca/doe/> (accessed 9 October 2014).

[43] S 207. The charter survives in eleventh-century manuscripts, but there is no reason to doubt its authenticity. Given the Mercian context, it is conceivable that 'angelcynnes monna' denoted not the English in general, but specifically the inhabitants of Burgred's kingdom, who were Anglian; this is unlikely, however, since 'Mierce' (Mercians) would have conveyed such a meaning much more clearly.

[44] Ine 24–24.2, 46.1, 54.2, 74.

History, notes that the founding abbot of Wearmouth was an 'Angelcynnes man' ('English person'), and states that one of his successors was lamented by both 'Angelcynnes monna' ('English persons') and inhabitants of the region where he died (Burgundy).[45] A will from Alfred's reign assigned land to a beneficiary for as long as Christianity remained 'on Angelcynnes ealonde' ('in the island of the English'), a formulation which again has no apparent connection to the cultivation of English political unity, and in any case associates *Angelcynn* with Britain, not with a territory even remotely similar to the later English kingdom.[46] The other twenty references are in four texts that appear to be closely linked to Alfred, and these have attracted the greatest comment. One occurs in the treaty of Alfred and Guthrum, which presents itself as an agreement between these two leaders, 'ealles Angelcynnes witan' ('all the wise people of the English'), and all the people in East Anglia.[47] *Angelcynn* is used here to refer to those subject to Alfred, including the Anglian inhabitants of western Mercia, but need not imply any aim or claim to rule all the English. The same is so of the two references in the introduction to Alfred's legislation, which mentions that synods had been held 'geond Angelcyn' ('throughout the English'), and that Æthelberht of Kent had been the first to be baptized 'on Angelcynne' ('among the English').[48] It is most unlikely that the writer was hoping to foster English political unity by using the word *Angelcynn*, since the same text styles Alfred 'Westseaxna cyning' ('king of the West Saxons').[49] There are then seven occurrences in the prose preface to the Old English version of the *Pastoral Care*, which states that there had once been wise people and happy times 'geond Angelcynn' ('throughout the English'), that learning had since decayed, and that Alfred proposed to remedy this by translating books for study by the youth 'on Angel kynne' ('among the English'): the problem identified is thus a lack of wisdom, not of political unity, and the text evokes as a golden age a period in which there were multiple English kingdoms.[50] The remaining ten instances are in the 'common stock' of the *Chronicle*, or its early continuations. The most famous is in the annal for 886, which records the submission to Alfred of all the *Angelcynn* not subject to the Danes, and this is echoed in his obit in the A, B, and C versions.[51] As in the treaty with Guthrum, the choice of the word *Angelcynn* may well reflect that Alfred's domination extended beyond Wessex, but there is no reason to infer an aspiration to unite the English. Still less is such a desire implied by any of the other eight occurrences, where the word is simply used as a convenient term for the

---

[45] *The Old English Martyrology*, xvii, xxxvii, xcii, cxli, cxcvi, cci, cciv, ccxiv, ccxxxvii, ed. and trans. C. Rauer (Cambridge, 2013), pp. 46, 60, 108, 150, 190, 196, 198, 206, 226. The earliest extant manuscript of the *Martyrology* is dated on palaeographical grounds to the late ninth century, but the text may have been composed earlier.

[46] S 1508. On Britain as an English island, see below, pp. 210–11.   [47] AGu Prol.

[48] Af El 49.7, 49.9. Bede stated that Æthelberht was the first of the kings of the *gens Anglorum* to enter heaven: *HE*, ii.5 (p. 148).

[49] Af El 49.10.

[50] *King Alfred's West-Saxon Version of Gregory's Pastoral Care*, ed. and trans. H. Sweet (EETS, 45, 50, London, 1871–2), pp. 2–9. Compare *HE*, iv.2 (p. 334). The references to *Angelcynn* do not prove a unificatory aspiration, but may reflect that the texts Alfred intended to supply would have been usable wherever English was spoken.

[51] *ASC* ABCDE 886, ABC 900.

non-Scandinavian Germanic inhabitants of Britain.[52] Indeed, when one considers the length of the 'common stock', what is striking is the infrequency with which *Angelcynn* appears, especially by comparison to the ubiquitous references to *Franci* in the *Royal Frankish Annals*.[53] The author of the 'common stock' was (as we noted in Chapter 1) much concerned with glorifying Alfred's dynasty, but seems to have been little interested in promoting an image of an English nation, let alone enunciating the idea that such a people should have a single king.[54] In sum, the use of the word *Angelcynn* during Alfred's reign does not justify the inference that he aspired to establish a kingdom coterminous with the area inhabited by the English.

The proposition that the Cerdicings set out with the aim of forming a kingdom with such dimensions is further undermined when one examines the titles that they were accorded. We have already noted that Alfred is styled 'Westseaxna cyning' in his legislation, and this reference does not stand alone: he issued his will as 'Westseaxena cingc', with the witness of 'ealra Westseaxena witena' ('all the wise people of the West Saxons'), and in diplomas appears initially with the traditional title *Occidentalium Saxonum rex* ('king of the West Saxons').[55] In the latter part of his reign, Alfred's standard charter style switched to *Angulsaxonum rex* ('king of the Anglo-Saxons'), and Asser also accorded him this title, while describing earlier kings as *Occidentalium Saxonum rex*: this shift reflects that Alfred's domination over Æthelred had brought him power in Anglian Mercia, in addition to Saxon Wessex.[56] Some variant on *Angulsaxonum rex* remained the norm until soon after

---

[52] *ASC* ABCE 597, ABCDE 789, 817, 839, 866, 874, 885, ABCD 896. The 597 annal mentions a West Saxon king fighting against the 'Angelcyn', Britons, Picts, and Scots. The 789 annal refers to the first ships of Danish men coming to 'Angelcynnes lond'. Those for 817, 874, and 885 concern the English school or quarter in Rome. That for 839 alludes to Ecgberht having been driven from 'Angelcynnes lande' to Frankia. In 866 the 'great army' came 'on Angelcynnes lond'. Under 896 it is stated that the viking army had not afflicted the 'Angelcyn' very greatly.

[53] R. McKitterick, 'Constructing the Past in the Early Middle Ages: The Case of the Royal Frankish Annals', *TRHS*, 6th series, 7 (1997), pp. 127–8.

[54] Above, p. 20. J. M. Wallace-Hadrill, 'The Franks and the English in the Ninth Century: Some Common Historical Interests', *History*, 35 (1950), p. 213 concluded that the 'common stock' reflects 'the need not of a people but of a dynasty'. Contrast Foot, 'Making of *Angelcynn*', pp. 35–6. The 'common stock' includes some coverage of English dynasties other than the Cerdicings, but this need not imply a vision of a kingdom encompassing all their territories. Rather, the intention may well have been to emphasize the Cerdicings' success and durability in comparison with their neighbours. This interpretation is strengthened when one notes that the 'common stock' was not solely concerned with English dynasties, recounting the Carolingians' travails in the 880s: see especially *ASC* ABCDE 887.

[55] S 1507; S. Keynes, 'The West Saxon Charters of King Æthelwulf and his Sons', *EHR*, 109 (1994), pp. 1147–8. This paragraph is indebted to Susan Kelly's unpublished catalogue of royal styles, a copy of which she kindly sent me, and also to H. Kleinschmidt, 'Die Titulaturen englischer Könige im 10. und 11. Jahrhundert', in H. Wolfram and A. Scharer (eds), *Intitulatio III. Lateinische Herrschertitel und Herrschertitulaturen vom 7. bis zum 13. Jahrhundert* (Vienna, 1988), pp. 75–129.

[56] Keynes, 'West Saxon Charters', p. 1148; S. Keynes, 'King Alfred and the Mercians', in M. A. S. Blackburn and D. N. Dumville (eds), *Kings, Currency and Alliances: History and Coinage of Southern England in the Ninth Century* (Woodbridge, 1998), pp. 1–45 especially 25–6, 36–9, 40, 43–4 and n. 199; S. Keynes, 'Edward, King of the Anglo-Saxons', in N. J. Higham and D. H. Hill (eds), *Edward the Elder, 899–924* (London, 2001), pp. 40–66. On the order of the Anglian and Saxon elements in the title, see above, p. 26 n. 41.

the seizure of York and the Eamont meeting in 927.[57] Thenceforth, however, Æthelstan was frequently styled *rex Anglorum* ('king of the English'), or presented as the ruler of Britain, these ideas commonly being combined in such titles as *rex Anglorum per omnipatrantis dexteram totius Brytanie regni solio sublimatus* ('king of the English elevated by the right hand of the Almighty to the throne of the kingdom of all Britain').[58] Edmund and Eadred were sometimes characterized as rulers of the whole island, but such claims were less common in their reigns, during which York was intermittently in Hiberno-Scandinavian hands. Instead, these kings were frequently described as ruling a collection of peoples, with such titles as *rex Anglorum ceterarumque gentium in circuitu persistentium gubernator et rector* ('king of the English and governor and ruler of other peoples dwelling round about'), or *rex Ængulsæxna ond Norðhymbra imperator paganorum gubernator Brittonumque propugnator* ('king of the Anglo-Saxons and *imperator* of the Northumbrians, governor of the pagans and defender of the Britons').[59] Under Eadwig and especially Edgar, however, the motif of rulership of all Britain became ubiquitous again, and as before it often appears in conjunction with *rex Anglorum*; frequently, one finds the latter title in a charter's witness list, and a claim to the entire island in the dispositive section.[60] These concepts continued to be paired in subsequent reigns, but over time the notion of rulership of all Britain became less prominent in royal documents, especially after the Norman Conquest.[61] Such ideas still appeared in literary and historical texts, and were boosted in the twelfth century by Geoffrey of Monmouth's pseudo-history of the rulers of the ancient Britons, but claims to the whole island had by then become very rare in the titulature of contemporary kings.[62]

---

[57] S 394, 396, 397.

[58] For charters of Æthelstan containing *rex Anglorum* (or *basileus Anglorum*) and a claim to all Britain, see S 407, 411, 412, 413, 416, 418, 418a, 419, 422, 423, 425, 426, 429, 430, 431, 437, 438, 441, 442, 446, 447, 448, 449, 458. Sometimes one element appears near the beginning of the charter, and another in the witness list.

[59] For claims to Britain, see S 505, 509, 511, 546, 555, 556, 557, 560, 561, 562, 563, 564, 568, 570. For references to titles invoking a collection of peoples, see Kleinschmidt, 'Titulaturen', pp. 93–103, 106, 110–11. On the word *imperator*, see Molyneaux, 'Why were some Tenth-Century English Kings Presented as Rulers of Britain?', pp. 62–4.

[60] Numerous instances could be cited, e.g. S 591, 596, 598, 609, 613, 615, 617, 618, 641, 646, 683, 693, 697, 698, 700, 706, 709, 711, 714, 716.

[61] For a selection of references to Æthelred II, Cnut, Harthacnut, and Edward the Confessor as rulers of Britain, see S 835, 840, 848, 853, 859, 865, 869, 886, 888, 895, 955, 963, 977, 994, 998, 1001, 1003, 1006, 1008, 1012. For exceptional post-Conquest examples, see *Regesta Regum Anglo-Normannorum: The Acta of William I (1066–1087)*, ed. D. Bates (Oxford, 1998), no. 286; F. H. Dickinson, 'Charter of William the Second, Granting Bath to Bishop John de Villula', *Proceedings of the Somersetshire Archaeological and Natural History Society*, 22 (1876), pp. 114–19. Note also *English Episcopal Acta XI: Exeter, 1046–1184*, ed. F. Barlow (Oxford, 1996), no. 17.

[62] R. R. Davies, *The First English Empire: Power and Identities in the British Isles, 1093–1343* (Oxford, 2000). In the high medieval period (and after) *Britannia* was sometimes used to designate only part of the island: A. MacColl, 'The Meaning of "Britain" in Medieval and Early Modern England', *Journal of British Studies*, 45 (2006), pp. 248–69. So far as I am aware, this usage is not attested in the Anglo-Saxon period, and tenth-century royal titles sometimes explicitly refer to Britain as an island: e.g. S 591, 598, 615, 724, 736.

It is uncertain to what extent, if at all, rulers stipulated how they were to be styled in charters, but it is unlikely that any person drafting a royal diploma would have accorded the king a title to which the latter was known to object, and the foregoing survey permits two observations.[63] The first is that changes in titulature seem to have followed, rather than anticipated, shifts in kings' power. Specifically, *rex Anglorum* only appeared after Æthelstan had taken York, with the exception of one instance at the start of his reign, where it seems to refer to rule over the Anglian component of the Anglo-Saxon kingdom, not the English in general.[64] There is, moreover, no reason to think that the 'Anglo-Saxon' styles used before the capture of York implied a claim to anything more than the land south of the Thames plus (some of) Mercia; indeed, the Northumbrians were distinguished from the Anglo-Saxons when Eadred was called *rex Ængulsæxna ond Norðhymbra imperator*. The second point is that *rex Anglorum* had no monopoly in the decades after 927, being used alongside titles referring to rule over an assemblage of peoples, or all Britain. This is underlined when one broadens one's focus beyond charters. The liturgy employed at Æthelstan's coronation in 925 seems to have presented him as the ruler of two peoples, and this was subsequently expanded to three, named as the Saxons, the Mercians, and the Northumbrians.[65] On coins, the royal style was often plain *rex*, but variants on *rex totius Britanniae* ('king of the whole of Britain'), *rex Saxonum*, and *rex Anglorum* also appear, and the last of these only became standard after Edgar's reform.[66] Edgar's obit in the D and E texts of the *Chronicle* calls him 'ruler of the Angles, friend of the West Saxons and protector of the Mercians', the A, B, and C texts meanwhile styled him 'king of the English' ('Engla cyning'), he appears in the chronicle ascribed to Æthelweard as 'monarchus Brittannum' ('monarch of the people of Britain'), and Byrhtferth of Ramsey referred to him as 'totius Albionis imperator' ('*imperator* of all Britain').[67] It would not be difficult to heap up further examples: royal titulature was highly diverse in and after the second quarter of the tenth century.

The 'West Saxon' and 'Anglo-Saxon' styles used before the seizure of York give no hint that the Cerdicings aimed to create a kingdom corresponding to the area of English habitation, and those employed subsequently are arguably even more telling. Had the Cerdicings been animated by a desire to unite the English, one might have expected the achievement of this end to be clearly and consistently trumpeted. The potential was there: given that Æthelstan was presented as 'king of all Britain' (*rex totius Britanniae*), he could have been 'king of *all* the English'. A few writers did indeed characterize the Cerdicings' position in such terms: Æthelstan once appears as 'tocius gentis Anglorum rex' ('king of the whole people of the English'); similar titles crop up in some late tenth- and eleventh-century diplomas; a poem from 927 or just after celebrates Æthelstan's ruling '*Saxonia* made whole'

---

[63] On the debate about who drafted royal charters, see above, p. 58.
[64] S 395; above, p. 29.   [65] Above, p. 188 n. 333.   [66] Above, pp. 117–18, 126.
[67] *ASC* ABCDE 975; Æthelweard, *Chronicle*, iv.9, ed. and trans. A. Campbell (Edinburgh, 1962), p. 56; *VSO*, iv.17 (p. 136). It is interesting that the obit in the D and E texts distinguishes the Mercians and the Angles; the latter may perhaps have been intended to denote the East Angles.

('perfecta Saxonia'); Wulfstan of Winchester wrote in the 990s that Edgar had had power over 'all the peoples of the English' ('omnibus Anglorum... gentibus'); and a late tenth- or eleventh-century relic list described Æthelstan as having 'ruled all of *Englaland [ealles Englalandes]* alone which before him many kings held among themselves'.[68] Such statements are, however, strikingly rare, and the last in particular was made with the benefit of hindsight. Moreover, the occasional appearances of such styles as *totius gentis Anglorum rex* merely underline that the much more common *rex Anglorum* passed up a clear opportunity to stress that Cerdicing domination extended over all the English. That such connotations were not inherent in *rex Anglorum* can be inferred from Æthelstan's being accorded this title in a context where it appears to refer to his being king only to the north of the Thames.[69] Furthermore, even when claims to rule all the English were made, they were often accompanied by references to pan-insular domination: thus, for example, the charter that styles Æthelstan 'tocius gentis Anglorum rex' also calls him 'totius Bryttanniæ orbis curagulus' ('guardian of all the world of Britain'), and the poetic reference to '*Saxonia* made whole' is followed by an allusion to him arming for battle 'throughout all Britain' ('per totum Bryttanium').[70] Such juxtapositions, not to mention the general diversity of royal titulature, imply that there was considerable uncertainty about how best to characterize the Cerdicings' newly extended domination. Had there been a deep wish for a kingdom coterminous with English settlement, which could plausibly have been declared fulfilled in 927, such doubts would hardly have been likely.

The Idea of a Kingdom of Britain and its Eclipse

The principal reasons why Alfred and his successors sought to extend their domination were probably quite prosaic: aside from the general aim of increasing their wealth and power, the Cerdicings' main objective was probably to take pre-emptive action against potential aggressors by driving out major Scandinavian potentates and depriving them of possible allies.[71] This is not to exclude the possibility that the Cerdicings harboured some wider aspirations, but there is little reason to think that such ambitions as they had were focused on the creation of a kingdom with bounds based on those of existing English habitation. Indeed, there are some grounds to think that the Cerdicings may well have been at least as interested in the possibility of establishing a kingdom encompassing all Britain. From very soon after the seizure of York and the Eamont meeting, Æthelstan was explicitly and repeatedly presented as the ruler of the whole island, and similar titles were even

---

[68] S 430, 739, 748, 798, 827, 851, 863, 880, 881, 884, 885, 953, 958, 961, 962, 963, 971, 976, 998, 1003, 1006, 1019, 1022 (some of which are not authentic); M. Lapidge, 'Some Latin Poems as Evidence for the Reign of Athelstan', *ASE*, 9 (1981), pp. 83–93, 98; Wulfstan of Winchester, *Narratio Metrica de S. Swithvno*, preface, lines 163–4, ed. and trans. M. Lapidge, *The Cult of St Swithun* (Oxford, 2003), p. 408 (with discussion of the date at 336); P. W. Conner, *Anglo-Saxon Exeter: A Tenth-Century Cultural History* (Woodbridge, 1993), p. 176.

[69] S 395; above, pp. 29, 208.   [70] S 430; Lapidge, 'Some Latin Poems', p. 98.

[71] Above, pp. 45–7.

more ubiquitous during Edgar's reign. That such claims were articulated despite the tenuousness of Cerdicing power in some parts of Britain suggests that the idea of domination over the entire landmass held particular allure. This was probably because there were precedents for the idea of a single individual being hegemonic throughout the island: Bede (and his translator) had portrayed the power of the seventh-century Northumbrian kings Edwin and Oswald in such a way, and in the eighth century Æthelbald and Offa of Mercia had been styled 'king of Britain' and 'king and glory of Britain'.[72] The nature and extent of these kings' power is less important here than that Britain was perceived as a territory over which one person might be dominant; given that the island is a clearly delimited geographical unit, this is not particularly surprising, especially when one considers that similar ideas were articulated about Ireland.[73] It is, in addition, noteworthy that claims to pre-eminence throughout Britain had been made in the ecclesiastical sphere. Bede referred to Augustine (d. 604) as 'Archbishop of Britain', the decrees of the Council of Hatfield (679) gave Theodore the title 'Archbishop of the island of Britain and of the city of Canterbury', the legislation of the Kentish king Wihtred (695) styled Berhtwald 'high Bishop of Britain', and Alcuin addressed Archbishop Æthelheard of Canterbury (792–805) as 'the light of all Britain'.[74] Linked to such royal and archiepiscopal titles may well have been a belief in some circles that the English had a right to the entire landmass: we have already noted that a late ninth-century will refers to 'the island of the English', similar thinking is suggested by allusions to 'our island' in the writings of Bede and Alcuin, and Æthelweard was probably building on such ideas when he declared that 'Britain [*Brittannia*] is now called

---

[72] *HE*, ii.5, ii.9, iii.6 (pp. 148–50, 162, 230); *OEB*, ii.5, ii.8, iii.4 (pp. 108–10, 120, 164); S 89, 155; Alcuin, *Epistolae*, ed. E. Dümmler (*MGH, Epistolae Karolini Aevi*, ii, Berlin, 1895), no. 64 (p. 107). See also Adomnán, *Life of Columba*, i.1, ed. and trans. A. O. Anderson and M. O. Anderson (Oxford, 1991), p. 16.

[73] F. J. Byrne, *Irish Kings and High-Kings* (London, 1973), pp. 254–74; M. Herbert, '*Rí Éirenn, Rí Alban*, Kingship and Identity in the Ninth and Tenth Centuries', in S. Taylor (ed.), *Kings, Clerics and Chronicles in Scotland, 500–1297: Essays in Honour of Marjorie Ogilvie Anderson on the Occasion of her Ninetieth Birthday* (Dublin, 2000), pp. 62–72 especially 64–6. The island of Britain is known to have been recognized as a geographical entity since Antiquity, although for administrative purposes the Romans also used *Britannia* to designate a province or diocese that did not encompass the whole landmass: Strabo, *Geography*, iv.5, ed. and trans. H. L. Jones (8 vols, Cambridge, MA, 1917–32), ii, 252–8; Pliny, *Natural History*, iv.16, ed. and trans. H. Rackham, W. H. S. Jones, and D. E. Eichholz (10 vols, Cambridge, MA, 1938–63), ii, 196–8; P. Salway, *Roman Britain* (Oxford, 1981), Map VII (after p. xxi).

[74] *HE*, ii.3, iv.17 (pp. 142, 384); Wi Prolog; Alcuin, *Epistolae*, no. 17 (p. 47). See also *OEB*, ii.3, iv.19 (pp. 104, 310); Stephen of Ripon, *Life of St Wilfrid*, ed. and trans. B. Colgrave, *The Life of Bishop Wilfrid by Eddius Stephanus* (Cambridge, 1927), liii, lx (pp. 110, 128); *Councils and Ecclesiastical Documents Relating to Great Britain and Ireland*, ed. A. W. Haddan and W. Stubbs (3 vols, Oxford, 1869–78), iii, 229–31; *Liber Pontificalis*, lxxxvi, ed. L. Duchesne (2 vols, Paris, 1886–92), i, 376; P. Chaplais, 'The Letter from Bishop Wealdhere of London to Archbishop Brihtwold of Canterbury: The Earliest Original "Letter Close" Extant in the West', in M. B. Parkes and A. G. Watson (eds), *Medieval Scribes, Manuscripts and Libraries: Essays Presented to N. R. Ker* (London, 1978), p. 22; S 155; Alcuin, *Epistolae*, nos. 129, 231 (pp. 191, 376). That such titles became less common after the early eighth century may reflect that York was raised to archiepiscopal status in 735. Compare the claims of both Armagh and Kildare to primacy over all Ireland: T. M. Charles-Edwards, *Early Christian Ireland* (Cambridge, 2000), pp. 416–40.

Anglia, taking the name of the victors'.[75] Definite evidence of interest in the idea of rulership of Britain is scarce in the decades preceding the Eamont meeting: all we really have is Asser's reference to Alfred as 'ruler of all the Christians of the island of Britain', and an assertion in the 'common stock' (compiled during Alfred's reign) that Ecgberht of Wessex (d. 839) and seven earlier kings had been 'bryten-walda', which is most likely to mean 'Britain ruler'.[76] Nonetheless, it is likely that Æthelstan and his predecessors had been at least vaguely conscious of Britain as a territorial unit over which they might aspire to establish dominance: precedents for such claims were readily available, and the swift adoption of pan-insular titles after 927 suggests that ideas of this nature had already been contemplated.

Æthelstan's and Edgar's claims to rule Britain are now often seen as wishful thinking, but this is to apply an anachronistic standard: tenth-century kings had a loose but real hegemony throughout the island, and their titles only appear inflated if one assumes that kingship ought to involve domination of an intensity like that seen within the English kingdom of the eleventh and later centuries.[77] From the perspective of those living in the years following the Eamont meeting, by contrast, it was probably possible to conceive of Britain as a single kingdom without too much difficulty. The intensity of Æthelstan's power decreased with distance from central Wessex, but even in far-flung parts of the island it never quite disappeared, and (especially in the north) Cerdicing domination did not impose a stark dividing line between one portion of Britain and the rest.[78] As Cerdicing rule between the Channel and the Tees became somewhat more uniform, however, and at the same time qualitatively different from their power in other parts of the island, it probably grew harder to sustain the notion that Britain was a unitary realm. This would explain the gradual shift in the styles accorded to Edgar's successors: assertions that they ruled Britain did not disappear from royal documents forthwith, but such

---

[75] S 1508; *HE*, v.24 (p. 570); Alcuin, *Epistolae*, nos. 17, 19, 189 (pp. 47, 55, 316); Æthelweard, *Chronicle*, i.4 (p. 9). See also *OEB*, v.22 (p. 484); Brooks, 'English Identity', pp. 41–3, 45–6; above, p. 205. Davies, *First English Empire*, pp. 49, 202 may overstate Æthelweard's originality. Island-wide power did not need to be coupled with an assertion that all Britain had become English: thus, for example, Edgar was presented as 'illustrious king of the English and of the other peoples dwelling within the bounds of the island of Britain' by *RC*, i (p. 69). The Welsh also aspired to domination over the whole of Britain, or at least the whole of the Roman diocese of *Britannia*: H. Pryce, 'British or Welsh? National Identity in Twelfth-Century Wales', *EHR*, 116 (2001), pp. 775–801.

[76] *VA*, i (p. 1); *ASC* BCDE 829. Compare *ASC* A 829. That 'brytenwalda', not 'bretwalda', was the original reading is argued by D. N. Dumville, 'The Terminology of Overkingship in Early Anglo-Saxon England', in J. Hines (ed.), *The Anglo-Saxons from the Migration Period to the Eighth Century: An Ethnographic Perspective* (Woodbridge, 1997), pp. 352–3. On its meaning, see T. M. Charles-Edwards, '"The Continuation of Bede", *s.a.* 750: High-Kings, Kings of Tara and "Bretwaldas"', in A. P. Smyth (ed.), *Seanchas: Studies in Early and Medieval Irish Archaeology, History and Literature in Honour of Francis J. Byrne* (Dublin, 2000), pp. 144–5. Charles-Edwards's case is strengthened by S 427, which renders 'rex et rector totius huius britannie insule' as 'brytænwalda eallæs ðyses iglandæs'. There is no reason to think that 'brytenwalda' was a recognized office.

[77] For a fairly typical judgement, see S. Keynes, 'The Cult of King Alfred the Great', *ASE*, 28 (1999), p. 270: 'the kingship of Britain became a political commonplace (if not exactly a reality) in the tenth century'.

[78] There may have been a relatively pronounced split between Cerdicing domination in Wales and western Mercia, but even this would have been less clear than after hundred and shire administration had become entrenched: above, p. 115.

claims became less ubiquitous and insistent, and by the time of William the Conqueror the normal kingly title was *rex Anglorum* or variants thereon.[79] This shift may have been influenced by a loosening of Cerdicing domination in Wales and northern Britain in the decades after Edgar's death, but the move towards more modest royal styles did not mark some malaise in English kingship: rather, it primarily reflected that royal power had intensified significantly, but only in one part of the island.[80]

Those responsible for mid- to late tenth-century administrative reform are unlikely to have intended that their actions should lead to the eclipse of the idea of a kingdom of Britain. Indeed, it was during Edgar's reign, just when the greatest institutional changes were probably being implemented, that Cerdicing claims to the whole island reached their zenith. Thus, for example, the *Wihtbordesstan* ordinance, which appears to have been a key reforming text, declared that its provisions should apply to 'all of us who dwell in these islands'.[81] This ambition sat uneasily with the content of the decrees themselves, however, since their implementation was predicated on a framework of hundreds or wapentakes that did not exist beyond the Tees. A similar tension can be seen in the events of 973: the liturgy probably used at Edgar's Bath consecration prayed that he be honoured 'above all kings of Britain', but Byrhtferth described those present as 'all the nobility of the English', and there is no evidence that Welsh, Cumbrian, or Scottish potentates were in attendance; rather, such men acknowledged Edgar's authority by turning up at a subsequent meeting in Chester.[82] The holding of two gatherings in 973 suggests that there was by then a clear, if perhaps implicit, distinction between those of the Cerdicings' subordinates who lived within (roughly) what would constitute Domesday *Anglia*, and those who did not. Such a division had probably been less marked in the second quarter of the tenth century: while the Eamont and Chester meetings may well have been analogous in their attendees, Æthelstan's charters show that leading figures from across the island were all at least occasionally present at the same assemblies. There is, moreover, reason to think that Eadred's consecration in 946, unlike Edgar's in 973, was attended by at least two Welsh kings, and possibly a Cumbrian potentate, as well as Oswulf of Bamburgh and the leading magnates of the land between the Channel and the Tees.[83] Such gatherings would have been clear embodiments of the image of a single kingdom stretching

[79] *Regesta Regum Anglo-Normannorum*, pp. 85–96. Documents issued in William's name sometimes combine *rex Anglorum* with titles reflecting his Continental possessions (e.g. *dux Normannorum*), but references to Britain are extremely rare. The number of diplomas issued declined during the eleventh century, and writ-charters simultaneously proliferated. The shift in documentary form does not, however, seriously affect my argument: writ-charters could have articulated claims to Britain, but did not do so.

[80] Contrast John, *Orbis Britanniae*, pp. 60–3.   [81] IV Eg 14.2.

[82] *The Claudius Pontificals*, ed. D. H. Turner (Chichester, 1971), p. 93; *VSO*, iv.7 (p. 110); above, p. 34, with J. L. Nelson, 'Inauguration Rituals', in P. H. Sawyer and I. N. Wood (eds), *Early Medieval Kingship* (Leeds, 1977), p. 70. If the Welsh, Cumbrian, and Scottish potentates were present at Bath, it would seem odd for Edgar to have met them in another location immediately afterwards.

[83] S 520. It is not explicit that the persons named in the witness list attended the inauguration, but the charter states that the grant was made at Kingston-upon-Thames, and that Eadred had been consecrated there shortly before. On the possible Cumbrian witness, see above, p. 57 n. 45.

over all or much of Britain; by contrast, the two separate assemblies of 973 can, in retrospect, be seen as a sign that the idea of pan-insular kingship was being undermined, even as it was exalted.

The key point to come out of all this is that the idea of an English kingdom covering an area loosely similar to that which we consider England was not a cause but a consequence of the changes wrought during the tenth century. The cohesion of the eleventh-century English kingdom was doubtless assisted by the fact that most of its inhabitants could see themselves as members of a single people, of which the Cerdicings were also part, but it is most unlikely that Alfred and his successors set out with the objective of establishing a realm of all the English. Nor did they seize on such a notion when it would have been plausible to describe their power in this way, seemingly being at least as keen on the idea of a kingdom of Britain. Indeed, rather than being defined by a sense of Englishness, the eleventh-century English kingdom was primarily demarcated by the spatial limits of the administrative innovations that appear to have taken effect around the time of Edgar. These limits in turn owed much to the geographical range of Scandinavian potentates' domination, especially in the north-east. York was a major seat of a series of Hiberno-Scandinavian kings, whom the Cerdicings sought (and ultimately managed) to eject, but there appears to have been rather less Scandinavian settlement beyond the Tees, and neither Æthelstan nor his successors seem (until the mid-eleventh century) to have felt the need to try to dislodge the English rulers of Bamburgh.[84] Thus, while the Cerdicings appear by the time of Edgar to have been able to install ealdormen and archbishops at York, their domination further north (and in Wales) was based on looser relationships with established figures. Such incumbent potentates appear to have been (at most) sporadic attendees at assemblies convened by the Cerdicings, and it is likely that the latter had little scope to compel their clients to implement administrative reforms such as the establishment of hundredal organization. To judge from the rhetoric of the *Wihtbordesstan* ordinance and the numerous references to Britain in tenth-century royal charters, the Cerdicings did not intend that their practice of leaving non-Scandinavian potentates in place should result in the formation of a kingdom the size and shape of Domesday *Anglia*. Their strategy nonetheless had the ironic consequence that the eleventh-century English kingdom's dimensions were moulded at least as much by where Scandinavians had acquired power in Britain, as by where the English themselves lived. Scandinavian influence on the kingdom's definition was,

---

[84] D. Rollason, *Northumbria, 500–1100: Creation and Destruction of a Kingdom* (Cambridge, 2003), pp. 213, 244; D. M. Hadley, *The Vikings in England: Settlement, Society and Culture* (Manchester, 2006), pp. 37–44. There is also little evidence of any concerted Cerdicing attempt to eject Hiberno-Scandinavians from the land west of the Pennines, and hundredal organization stretched no further than the Ribble at the time of Domesday, but the Hiberno-Scandinavians based in this region do not appear to have been great potentates of the kind who represented a major threat to the Cerdicings. One might try to explain the eleventh-century English kingdom's north-eastern limit in geological terms, since the Tees marks an approximate boundary between what are often termed the 'lowland' and 'highland' zones of Britain (Salway, *Roman Britain*, pp. 4–5), but we should be wary of straightforward geographical determinism, not least because the English kingdom did later extend beyond the Tees.

however, indirect, being mediated by the fundamental but geographically limited administrative changes of the mid- to late tenth century: it was these that underpinned the idea that the land from the Channel to the Tees constituted a discrete political unit, distinct from the rest of Britain.

Commitment to the English Kingdom's Preservation

That the eleventh-century English kingdom was perceived as a unit did not mean that it would necessarily endure: we noted in Chapter 1 that there were various times when a lasting partition may only have been averted by the timely death of a member of one of the kingdom's ruling dynasties.[85] Indeed, this was recognized by at least one contemporary: the anonymous author of the *Encomium Emmae Reginae*, who wrote in 1041 or 1042, interpreted Edmund Ironside's demise in 1016 as God taking pity on 'the realm of the English' ('Anglorum... imperii'), since it ended the territorial split that he and Cnut had agreed, and thereby averted the risk of prolonged and destructive conflict.[86] Even after the Norman Conquest, division of the kingdom remained thinkable, with Hugh the Chanter alleging that Archbishop Lanfranc self-servingly told William the Conqueror that without Canterbury's primatial authority there would be a risk of the Archbishop of York establishing an alternative king in the north.[87] One might seek to account for the ongoing potential for division by invoking Frank Stenton's contention that the kingdom's coherence was undermined by a 'racial cleavage' between Danes and English, but it is now recognized that persons described by contemporaries as 'Danes' need not all have been of Scandinavian origin or descent.[88] It is, moreover, doubtful whether antagonism between those identified as Danish and English was fundamental to most (prospective) divisions of the kingdom in the late tenth and eleventh centuries, given that the Thames (rather than, say, Watling Street) was repeatedly used or contemplated as a line of partition.[89] Nonetheless, the point stands that the break-up of the new English kingdom remained a possibility throughout the eleventh century: whether or not regional particularism was linked to identification with Scandinavian origins (real or imagined) is of little consequence here.

There were, however, a significant number of contemporaries who considered the kingdom's preservation desirable: such sentiments are apparent in the encomiast's

---

[85] Above, pp. 37–8. See also below, pp. 245–8.

[86] *Encomium Emmae Reginae*, ii.14, ed. A. Campbell with supplementary introduction by S. Keynes (Cambridge, 1998), p. 30.

[87] Hugh the Chanter, *The History of the Church of York, 1066–1127*, ed. and trans. C. Johnson, M. Brett, C. N. L. Brooke, and M. Winterbottom (Oxford, 1990), p. 4. See also William of Jumièges, *Gesta Normannorum Ducum*, vii.19, ed. and trans. E. M. C. van Houts (2 vols, Oxford, 1992–5), ii, 178–80.

[88] F. M. Stenton, 'The Danes in England', *PBA*, 13 (1927), p. 241; M. Innes, 'Danelaw Identities: Ethnicity, Regionalism, and Political Allegiance', in D. M. Hadley and J. D. Richards (eds), *Cultures in Contact: Scandinavian Settlement in England in the Ninth and Tenth Centuries* (Turnhout, 2000), pp. 65–88; D. M. Hadley, *The Northern Danelaw: Its Social Structure, c.800–1100* (London, 2000), pp. 298–309; D. M. Hadley, 'Viking and Native: Re-thinking Identity in the Danelaw', *EME*, 11 (2002), pp. 45–70 especially 46–53.

[89] Above, pp. 29, 33–4, 35, 36, but note *ASC* CDE 1013.

interpretation of Edmund Ironside's death as a manifestation of divine beneficence, and comparable comments appear in a number of other late tenth- and eleventh-century texts.[90] Writing at some point between 964 and 984, Æthelwold criticized Eadwig for having 'dispersed this kingdom [*þis rice*] and divided its oneness [*annesse*]', before praising Edgar for bringing 'back to oneness [*annesse*] the divisions of this kingdom [*þæs rices twislunge*]' after he had 'obtained all the dominion of the English [*ealne Angelcynnes anweald*]'.[91] Ælfric appears to have so objected to any suggestion of joint rule that he explained in the Latin preface to his collection of saints' *Lives*, written around the turn of the tenth and eleventh centuries, that he would depart from his sources, and suppose that only one emperor had been concerned in the persecution of martyrs at any time, 'just as our people [*gens nostra*] is subject to one king, and is accustomed to speak of one king, not of two'.[92] In the same vein, Archbishop Wulfstan II of York (d. 1023) repeatedly called on people to support a single royal lord.[93] Similarly, the D text of the *Chronicle* and the anonymous *Life* of Edward the Confessor state that all-out armed conflict between the king and various magnate groupings was averted in 1051, 1052, and 1065 through horror at the prospect of civil strife among the English, or fear that fighting could make the kingdom vulnerable to attack; a desire to avoid violence would not necessarily require commitment to the kingdom's territorial integrity, but could well militate in such a direction.[94]

Insofar as there was an impetus to preserve the English kingdom, it was probably in part a product of the Benedictine reform movement that gained prominence during Edgar's reign. Those who desired royal enforcement of uniform monastic observance had reason to oppose division, since different kings could have promoted divergent practices, and Æthelwold even paired 'the customs of one rule and of one country [*patriae*]' in the preface to the *Regularis Concordia*.[95] Previously, there may well have been less religious objection to the possibility of partition: it is, for example, notable that Asser's account of the 850s expresses outrage

---

[90] *Encomium Emmae Reginae*, ii.14 (p. 30).

[91] *Councils and Synods with Other Documents Relating to the English Church, I, A.D. 871–1204*, ed. D. Whitelock, M. Brett, and C. N. L. Brooke (2 vols, Oxford, 1981), no. 33 (i, 146); D. Whitelock, 'The Authorship of the Account of King Edgar's Establishment of Monasteries', in J. L. Rosier (ed.), *Philological Essays: Studies in Old and Middle English Language and Literature in Honour of Herbert Dean Meritt* (The Hague, 1970), pp. 125–36. D. Pratt, 'The Voice of the King in "King Edgar's Establishment of Monasteries"', *ASE*, 41 (2012), pp. 157–62, 168–72 argues for a likely date of 966×c.970. On Æthelwold's relationships with Eadwig and Edgar, see above, pp. 189–92.

[92] Ælfric, *Lives of Saints*, ed. W. W. Skeat (2 vols, EETS, 76, 114, London, 1881–1900), i, 2–4. Ælfric did not make this point in the vernacular preface, presumably because only those capable of understanding Latin would have been in a position to detect that he had manipulated his sources.

[93] V Atr 1, 35; VI Atr 1.1; VIII Atr 44.1; IX Atr Expl.; Wulfstan of York, *Institutes of Polity*, ed. K. Jost, *Die «Institutes of Polity, Civil and Ecclesiastical». Ein Werk Erzbischof Wulfstans von York* (Bern, 1959), pp. 152, 165. See also Northu 67.1.

[94] *ASC* D 1051, CD 1052; *The Life of King Edward who Rests at Westminster Attributed to a Monk of Saint-Bertin*, i.7, ed. and trans. F. Barlow, 2nd edn (Oxford, 1992), p. 80. The *Life*'s first book appears to have been written in 1065–1066. Those who invoked ideas of English cohesion in this way appear to have been seeking to preserve the status quo, not to push for the kingdom's expansion to encompass all the English.

[95] *RC*, iv (p. 71).

at Æthelbald's rebellion against his father, but not at the division of Æthelwulf's kingdom per se.[96] Nonetheless, it is likely that in any period there would have been powerful figures in favour of preserving whatever was then the status quo. In particular, magnates with widely dispersed lands may well have been reluctant to support partition, lest their loyalties become divided between two or more potentially antagonistic kings, any one of whom could deprive them of a substantial proportion of their possessions. Such risks were illustrated in the Carolingian lands after the death in 840 of Louis the Pious. His demise precipitated a conflict that ended in a territorial partition between three of his sons, and we have a text in which a disappointed aristocrat lamented how fidelity to one of these (half-)brothers resulted in estates being confiscated by another.[97] The possibility that a division north of the Channel could have had comparable consequences may well have alarmed English magnates, and not just during the last century of the Anglo-Saxon period.[98] In particular, it is striking that Æthelstan Half-King ceased to attest royal charters and became a monk at the very point when a partition between Eadwig and Edgar was established on the line of the Thames.[99] This could be coincidental, but Æthelstan's interests straddled the Thames, and it is tempting to speculate that he either felt that the split so imperilled his position that he should renounce worldly affairs, or was coerced into being tonsured after unsuccessfully resisting it. In the light of this, we should be wary of the supposition that opposition to partitions between Cerdicings was altogether new in the late tenth century. What did, however, probably become increasingly pronounced from then onwards was a sense that the Cerdicings' kingdom comprised not the whole of Britain, nor indeed the entire area of English habitation, but the land between the Channel and (at least roughly) the Tees: by the eleventh century, the kingdom that might be either maintained or divided was coming to be defined by the geographical limits of mid- to late tenth-century administrative change.

THE 'CONSTITUTIONAL TRADITION'

The Substantive Limits of Reform

Just as the geographical parameters of administrative reform had important implications, so too did its substantive limits. In particular, it is significant that the

---

[96] *VA*, xii–xiii, xvi (pp. 9–11, 14–15); above, pp. 16–18.

[97] Nithard, *Histoire des fils de Louis le Pieux*, ed. P. Lauer (Paris, 1926), especially ii.2 (pp. 40–2); J. L. Nelson, 'Public *Histories* and Private History in the Work of Nithard', *Speculum*, 60 (1985), pp. 251–93 especially 269–82. Nithard was a grandson of Charlemagne, and thus a nephew of Louis. Many magnates did, however, manage to retain estates in more than one Carolingian kingdom: S. Airlie, 'The Aristocracy', in *NCMH2*, pp. 435–6. For another illustration of the problems potentially associated with holding lands in the territories of opposing rulers, see R. Bartlett, *England under the Norman and Angevin Kings, 1075–1225* (Oxford, 2000), pp. 13–17.

[98] C. Wickham, *Problems in Doing Comparative History* (Southampton, 2005), pp. 15–35.

[99] *VSO*, iii.14 (p. 84); *VSD*, xxiv.2 (p. 74); C. Hart, *The Danelaw*, pp. 569–604 especially 578, 580–2; S. Keynes, *An Atlas of Attestations in Anglo-Saxon Charters, c.670–1066* (Cambridge, 2002), Tables XXXII, L; above, pp. 33–4, 138 n. 98.

major (albeit far from total) shift in how the Cerdicings regulated the conduct of the general populace between the Channel and the Tees was not matched by a comparably profound change in their dealings with this area's greater inhabitants. That is not to say that the magnates of what would constitute Domesday *Anglia* were unaffected by mid- to late tenth-century administrative developments: they sometimes pursued disputes in shire and hundred meetings, their lands were taxed, their judicial rights may well have become subject to closer definition, and those based far from Wessex began to attend royal assemblies with much greater frequency.[100] There were, however, considerable continuities in the means by which kings exercised dominance over other powerful figures. The general pattern of royal itineration did not fundamentally change, although London and (from the 1040s) Gloucester became more prominent: kings still seem to have spent the bulk of their time in the southernmost part of Britain, where their lands were most densely concentrated.[101] So too the basic function of royal assemblies stayed much the same, although they were now consistently attended by great men from York, increasingly took place in towns, and may have involved more elaborate ceremonial: since kings did not try to keep up a frequent personal presence in all regions, it remained important that they should have their greater subordinates come to them.[102]

Similarly, kings' attempts to secure magnates' obedience continued to be based on a mixture of patronage and coercion. Indeed, far from rendering patronage redundant, administrative innovation could create new avenues for it. Thus, for example, kings began to favour people by exempting their estates from the *here-geld*, or by allowing them to profit through participation in its collection.[103] While there were some shifts in the forms that patronage took, there was an important underlying continuity: it remained necessary for magnates to cultivate the reigning king's favour, particularly if they wished to obtain major lay or ecclesiastical offices.[104] So too did royal support continue to be valuable in disputes, and kings could permit people to circumvent the judicial apparatus of shire and hundred in return

---

[100] J. Campbell, 'The Late Anglo-Saxon State: A Maximum View', *PBA*, 87 (1994), pp. 39–65, reprinted in his *The Anglo-Saxon State* (London, 2000), p. 25; P. Wormald, 'Giving God and King their Due: Conflict and its Regulation in the Early English State', *Settimane di studio del centro italiano di studi sull'alto medioevo*, 44 (1997), pp. 549–90, reprinted in his *Legal Culture*, pp. 342–52; S. Baxter, *The Earls of Mercia: Lordship and Power in Late Anglo-Saxon England* (Oxford, 2007), pp. 107–9; above, pp. 165, 166–7, 175–9, 197.

[101] D. H. Hill, *An Atlas of Anglo-Saxon England* (Oxford, 1981), pp. 90–1, 94, 101; M. Hare, 'Kings, Crowns and Festivals: The Origins of Gloucester as a Royal Ceremonial Centre', *Transactions of the Bristol and Gloucestershire Archaeological Society*, 115 (1997), pp. 41–78 especially 52–5, 65–7. *ASC* CDE 1006 may well record a visit to Shropshire by Æthelred II because it was unusual. Æthelred went to Shropshire to receive *feorm* (a food render); this may only have been necessary because, according to the same annal, viking forces had taken *feorm* in Hampshire and Berkshire, and generally inflicted destruction in the south.

[102] J. R. Maddicott, *The Origins of the English Parliament, 924–1327* (Oxford, 2010), pp. 41–9; above, pp. 177–9.

[103] Baxter, *Earls*, pp. 106–9; Pratt, 'Demesne Exemption', pp. 17–20, 33–4.

[104] The royal role in the appointment of bishops and ealdormen is especially clear in the mid-eleventh century: *ASC* CDE 1013, CE 1044, C 1045, 1047, 1049, CD 1050, E 1051, 1055, DE 1065; Baxter, *Earls*, pp. 68–71.

for payment: the Ramsey *Liber Benefactorum* records that the monastery's abbot decided that it would be imprudent to contest 'publicly' ('publice') a claim raised by a certain powerful man, and instead procured victory by purchasing Edward the Confessor's goodwill for 20 marks of gold.[105] Patronage continued to be coupled with the threat that the reigning king might inflict serious harm on anyone who displeased him. Edgar and Æthelred respectively laid waste Thanet and the diocese of Rochester, and later kings continued to use harrying as a punishment: Hartha-cnut had all Worcestershire ravaged, Edward the Confessor ordered that Godwine wreak destruction on Dover, and William the Conqueror devastated large parts of the north.[106] Furthermore, there are grounds to suspect that Edgar confiscated lands from certain persons who had been close to Eadwig, Æthelred is known to have deprived several laypeople and churches of estates, and Edward the Confessor expropriated his own mother.[107] Edward was, in addition, able to expel from the kingdom several of his greatest subordinates, at least temporarily, and Æthelred and Cnut are also known to have exiled ealdormen or earls.[108] There is, moreover, reason to think that Æthelred, Cnut, and Harthacnut were involved in the killings of men of such rank, and Æthelred is known to have had the sons of certain eal-dormen blinded.[109] Thus, while kings developed the capability to regulate in a standardized and impersonal manner the conduct of a substantial proportion of those dwelling between the Channel and the Tees, they continued to deal with members of the elite individually, and sometimes violently.

The Evidence for Attempts to Restrain Royal Arbitrariness

The foregoing characterization of the kingship of Edgar and his successors is rem-iniscent of that of some late eighth- and ninth-century Carolingians: Charlemagne, Louis the Pious, and Charles the Bald were able (at least intermittently) to impose standard prescriptions (notably coin reforms) on the general populace in substan-tial parts of their territories, but their domination over their greater subordinates was based on highly personalized rewards and punishments, including removal from office, expropriation, exile, blinding, and occasionally death.[110] There were,

---

[105] *Chronicon Abbatiæ Rameseiensis*, ciii, ed. W. D. Macray (RS, 83, London, 1886), pp. 169–71. The abbot also gave Edward's wife five marks of gold to induce her to use her influence over him.

[106] *ASC* DE 969, CDE 986, CD 1041, E 1051, DE 1069; Roger of Wendover, *Flores Historiarum*, ed. H. O. Coxe (5 vols, London, 1841–4), i, 414–15. Godwine refused to implement Edward's com-mand, but the king's intention is nonetheless notable.

[107] S. Jayakumar, 'Eadwig and Edgar: Politics, Propaganda, Faction', in D. Scragg (ed.), *Edgar, King of the English 959–975: New Interpretations* (Woodbridge, 2008), pp. 91–5; S 877, 883, 885, 886, 891, 892, 893, 896, 901, 916, 918, 926, 927, 934, 937; *ASC* CDE 1006, 1015, 1043; John of Worcester, *Chronicle*, 1006, ed. and trans. R. R. Darlington, P. McGurk, and J. Bray (2 vols so far, Oxford, 1995–), ii, 456.

[108] *ASC* CDE 985, 1002, 1020, 1021, D 1044, CDE 1046, C 1049, CDE 1051, 1055, D 1058; S 896, 916, 926, 937.

[109] *ASC* CDE 993, 1006, 1015, 1016, 1017, CD 1041; John of Worcester, *Chronicle*, 1006, 1016, 1017 (ii, 458, 482, 504).

[110] J. L. Nelson, 'Kingship and Royal Government', in *NCMH2*, pp. 383–430; Airlie, 'Aristoc-racy', especially pp. 443–7; J. L. Nelson, *Charles the Bald* (Harlow, 1992), especially pp. 41–74; above, pp. 133–4.

however, some notable attempts to restrict Carolingian kings' power during the ninth century. Most dramatically, Louis the Pious was, in effect, deposed in 833, amid accusations that he had committed manifold evil deeds, including sacrilege, perjury, and wrongfully depriving people of their lives and possessions. He returned to power the next year, after the fragmentation of the alliance that had ousted him, but subsequent decades saw further moves to circumscribe royal arbitrariness, especially in West Frankia following Louis's death and the ensuing war between his sons.[111] By virtue of the territorial division that ended the conflict, Charles the Bald became king in West Frankia in 843, whereupon he reached an agreement at Coulaines with his leading subordinates, ecclesiastical and lay. The king and his subjects pledged to maintain each other's *honor*, a term which appears to have encompassed office, lands, and status, and Charles specifically declared that no one should be deprived of *honor* without just and equitable judgement.[112] In 856, he gave comparable but more detailed guarantees to head off the defection of some of his leading magnates to one of his half-brothers.[113] Faced with renewed rebellion two years later, Charles again swore to treat his subordinates in accordance with law and justice.[114] In 869, when Charles was reconsecrated to mark his acquisition of Lotharingia, Archbishop Hincmar of Rheims revised the procedure for royal inauguration, such that unction was only administered after the king had affirmed principles similar to those agreed at Coulaines.[115] When Charles's successor, Louis the Stammerer, was installed in 877, Hincmar took the pre-consecration promise a stage further, requiring that the new king make a written profession that he would uphold ecclesiastical rules, and preserve the laws and statutes of his predecessors.[116] At no point did magnates form a wholly united front, and Charles's promises can reasonably be interpreted as attempts to shore up support, rather than terms that had been forced on him by his subordinates. Nonetheless, it is hard to avoid seeing such undertakings as responses to pressure, and it is notable that kings should agree to treat their subjects in accordance with stated norms.

The similarities between the ninth-century West Frankish and eleventh-century English kingdoms are underlined when one considers that the latter also saw collective attempts by some of its leading magnates to induce their rulers to accept restraints on royal arbitrariness, most clearly in 1013–1014.[117] Late in 1013, after Swein had received submissions in several parts of the kingdom, Æthelred was

---

[111] M. de Jong, *The Penitential State: Authority and Atonement in the Age of Louis the Pious, 814–840* (Cambridge, 2009), especially pp. 46–52, 214–59, 271–9. Note also pp. 42–4, 185–213, on the rebellion against Louis in 830.

[112] *CRF*, no. 254; Nelson, *Charles the Bald*, pp. 132–9; Nelson, 'Kingship and Royal Government', p. 427.

[113] *CRF*, no. 262; Nelson, *Charles the Bald*, pp. 183–5.

[114] *CRF*, no. 269; Nelson, *Charles the Bald*, pp. 185–6.

[115] *CRF*, no. 276; J. L. Nelson, 'Kingship, Law and Liturgy in the Political Thought of Hincmar of Rheims', *EHR*, 92 (1977), pp. 257–9, with references to other occasions when Coulaines was echoed at 255–7.

[116] *CRF*, no. 283; Nelson, 'Kingship, Law and Liturgy', pp. 260–3.

[117] What follows draws on P. Stafford, 'The Laws of Cnut and the History of Anglo-Saxon Royal Promises', *ASE*, 10 (1982), pp. 173–90; Maddicott, *Origins*, pp. 33–41.

exiled to Normandy.[118] He was allowed back a few months later, following Swein's death in February 1014, but only on condition that he address his subjects' grievances. The C, D, and E texts of the *Chronicle* relate:

> Then all the wise people [*witan*], ecclesiastical and lay, advised that King Æthelred should be sent for, and they said that no lord was dearer to them than their natural lord [*gecynda hlaford*] if he would rule them more justly than he did before [*gif he hi rihtlicor healdan wolde þonne he ær dyde*]. Then the king sent his son Edward here with his messengers, and bade them greet all his people, and said that he would be a faithful lord [*hold hlaford*] to them, and amend each of the things which they all hated [*ælc þæra ðinga betan þe hi ealle ascunudon*]; and that each of the things that had been done or said against him should be forgiven, on condition that they all resolutely turned to him without treachery. And full friendship was then established with word and pledge on either side, and they pronounced every Danish king an outlaw from *Engla lande* for ever. Then during the spring King Æthelred came home to his own people and he was gladly received by them all.[119]

That the magnates could act collectively in the absence of a king is interesting in itself, as an illustration of the coherence of the English kingdom. The nature of their action is, however, of particular significance, and indeed went beyond anything known to have happened in ninth-century West Frankia. Unlike Charles the Bald's attempts to respond to his subordinates' grievances, Æthelred's promises of reform cannot readily be construed as a primarily royal initiative, and the manner in which he regained power was quite different from Louis the Pious. Thus, while Æthelred accepted constraints on his rule and issued a blanket pardon to those who had deposed him, Louis triumphantly resumed his former position and forced Archbishop Ebo of Rheims from office for his part in the affair.[120] Indeed, when seeking parallels to the extraction of concessions from Æthelred, one might look at least as much to 1215 and Magna Carta: as in 1014, the magnates who rebelled against John coerced their king into renouncing practices that he had previously employed.[121]

Some indication of the likely nature of the undertakings that Æthelred gave in 1014 can be inferred from Cnut's legislation. Towards the end of the latter king's secular ordinance is a series of provisions that are described as a 'lihtingc' ('mitigation'), intended to protect people from various forms of oppression that they had suffered. This 'lihtingc' stipulated the levels of heriots (payments due on death), commanded reeves not to requisition goods without consent, proclaimed that

[118] *ASC* CDE 1013; Wulfstan of York, *Homilies*, ed. D. Bethurum, *The Homilies of Wulfstan* (Oxford, 1957), XX (B H), lines 66–71.

[119] *ASC* CDE 1014. The C text refers to those who recalled Æthelred as 'all the wise people who were in *Engla lande*, ecclesiastical and lay'. For 'gecynda', compare *ASC* ABCDE 867, CD 1042.

[120] de Jong, *Penitential State*, pp. 50–8, 249–59. Other prelates fled to avoid reprisals. Louis forgave leading lay rebels (including Lothar, his eldest son), on condition that they go to Italy and stay there.

[121] J. C. Holt, *Magna Carta*, 2nd edn (Cambridge, 1992). Magna Carta was a negotiated settlement, not a set of terms dictated to John, but he was clearly forced into making significant concessions. John obtained a papal annulment of Magna Carta, but it was re-issued (in modified form) by Henry III.

testamentary and inheritance rights should be respected, prohibited forced marriage, limited the circumstances in which a man's wife and children could be punished for his misdeeds, and guaranteed people the right to hunt on their own land.[122] Cnut expressed similar sentiments in his proclamation of 1027, in which he promised to rule justly, and to emend wrongful acts caused by negligence or youthful intemperance. Specifically, he ordered reeves and sheriffs not to employ unjust force, and to refrain from extracting wealth for him by unjust means.[123] While renouncing these various abuses, Cnut held up Edgar's reign as a benchmark of good practice, declaring in his proclamation of 1020 that everyone should 'steadfastly observe the law of Edgar, which all have chosen and sworn to at Oxford'; this echoes a statement in the D text of the *Chronicle* that in 1018 the English and the Danes reached an agreement at Oxford 'according to Edgar's law'.[124] Cnut's clear implication is that the types of oppression that he forbade had recently been prevalent, and that kings or their agents had been among the perpetrators: people had been unjustly deprived of their possessions, the levels of heriots had been set arbitrarily, inheritance had been denied, and women had been married against their will, probably for political or financial gain. In particular, it is likely that these abuses were associated in people's minds with Æthelred: we know from extant wills that he had increased heriots, and he was implicitly condemned by the choice of Edgar's reign as the source of good legal precedent.[125] In consequence, Cnut's 'lihtingc' probably provides at least a rough guide to the kind of things that Æthelred had been forced to renounce in 1014, and it may even be based on now-lost legislation issued that year.[126] A further possibility, in no way mutually exclusive with the last, is that the 'lihtingc' embodies undertakings that Cnut himself had given at the outset of his reign. He may have needed to make concessions to secure acceptance, especially while Edmund Ironside was still alive, and it is notable that John of Worcester says that after Æthelred's death Cnut promised to be a 'faithful lord' ('fidelis...dominus'), an echo of his predecessor's pledge in 1014.[127]

[122] II Cn 69–83.2.

[123] Cn 1027 10–12. The reference to youthful indiscretion echoes certain charters of Æthelred: S 876, 885, 891, 893.

[124] Cn 1020 13; *ASC* D 1018. See also Cn 1018 1. That Cnut committed to uphold Edgar's law may go some way towards explaining why so much of his known legislation is closely based on that of his predecessors: P. Wormald, *The Making of English Law: King Alfred to the Twelfth Century. Volume I: Legislation and its Limits* (Oxford, 1999), pp. 345–66.

[125] On heriots, see N. Brooks, 'Arms, Status and Warfare in Late-Saxon England', in D. H. Hill (ed.), *Ethelred the Unready: Papers from the Millenary Conference* (Oxford, 1978), pp. 87–90. The heriots stipulated in II Cn 71–71.5 are broadly consistent with those known to have been paid during Æthelred's reign: the point of the 'lihtingc' was to arrest an upward trend. The invocation of Edgar bears comparison to the way in which William the Conqueror passed over Harold II when identifying himself as Edward the Confessor's successor: G. Garnett, *Conquered England: Kingship, Succession, and Tenure, 1066–1166* (Oxford, 2007), pp. 9–24.

[126] That some legislation from 1014 has been lost is implied by the survival from that year of a set of ecclesiastical decrees, which are described as 'one of the ordinances' drawn up by the English king: VIII Atr Prol. The 'lihtingc' could have originated as a secular counterpart, and it should be noted that both Edgar and Cnut are known to have issued paired ordinances for religious and worldly matters. See Stafford, 'Laws of Cnut', pp. 180–1; Wormald, *Making*, pp. 361–2.

[127] John of Worcester, *Chronicle*, 1016 (ii, 484). Stafford, 'Laws of Cnut' suggests that the 'lihtingc' may have originated as a 'coronation charter' issued by Cnut. This is possible, but unprovable.

Whenever the 'lihtingc' was first promulgated, however, it represents a significant concession: while it is unlikely to have been forcibly wrung from Cnut, it is hard to believe that his abjuration of a set of potentially lucrative practices was entirely spontaneous, especially given how much he and his father extorted from the English kingdom.

There was a further effort to circumscribe royal arbitrariness in 1041, the penultimate year of Harthacnut's reign, when Edward the Confessor returned to the English kingdom from his exile in Normandy. According to the second preface of *Quadripartitus*, an early twelfth-century legal collection, Edward was met by 'the magnates of all *Anglia*' ('totius Angliæ baronibus'), who declared 'that he would be received as king only if he guaranteed to them upon oath that the laws of Cnut and his sons should continue in his time with unshaken firmness'.[128] Although late, the account contains a significant amount of plausible circumstantial detail, which suggests that it should be given credence. The reference to the laws of Cnut could have been a specific invocation of that king's declarations that his people should be spared from assorted types of oppression, or it could have denoted a more general commitment to maintain existing custom. Either way, the initiative apparently came from the English magnates, and it is implicit that Edward made the requisite promise, since he was installed as sole king after Harthacnut's death. No extant text of the *Chronicle* mentions the 1041 oath, but the C and E versions state that at Edward's consecration Archbishop Eadsige of Canterbury 'admonished him well for his own sake and for that of all the people'.[129] Previous records of royal consecrations in the various versions of the *Chronicle* had made no reference to such lectures, which suggests that the admonition of the incoming king was either an innovation, or particularly noteworthy on this occasion. Either way, this would be eminently consistent with the unusual circumstances of Edward's accession, which meant that he had already sworn to uphold the existing legal framework. In the decades and centuries after Edward became king, references to comparable royal undertakings can be multiplied: notable examples include Edward's pledge to all the people of 'full law' or 'good law' after his reconciliation with Godwine in 1052; his renewal of Cnut's law in response to the Northumbrian revolt of 1065; William the Conqueror's pre-coronation promise that 'he would rule this people as well as any king before him best did'; the same king's declaration that the inhabitants of London should be entitled to the rights they had had under Edward; Henry I's coronation edict; and of course Magna Carta and its various reissues.[130]

The idea that kings should rule in accordance with certain norms was not new in the early eleventh century, even in an English context. It was, for example, implicit in the proclamations that concluded the earliest known English royal consecration rite, which goes back to at least the first half of the ninth century.[131] We have, moreover, seen that interest in the moral responsibilities of kings intensified

---

[128] Quadr. Arg. 9; J. R. Maddicott, 'Edward the Confessor's Return to England in 1041', *EHR*, 119 (2004), pp. 650–66.

[129] *ASC* CE 1043.

[130] *ASC* CD 1052, DE 1065, D 1066; Wl Lond 2; C Hn cor; Holt, *Magna Carta*.

[131] Above, p. 188.

from the mid-tenth century, with coronation apparently becoming conditional on an oath to promote peace, forbid wrongdoing, and order justice and mercy.[132] But the events of 1013–1014 and the decades that followed appear to represent a significant change. The expulsion and conditional recall of Æthelred was, so far as we know, unprecedented.[133] Nor should we assume that such actions had been anticipated when the coronation promise was introduced: the requirement that an incoming king swear an oath need not have implied that he should be deprived of power if he broke his pledge. The undertakings given by early eleventh-century kings were, moreover, much more precise than the pre-consecration promise, or the moralizing declarations found in some earlier legislation. Rather than just making generic pledges to discharge the conventional responsibilities of a Christian king, Æthelred agreed to address his subjects' grievances, Cnut renounced a specific set of abuses, and both he and Edward swore to uphold the laws of one or more recent predecessors. We cannot exclude the possibility that earlier kings gave comparable commitments, without these being recorded in surviving sources. But even if the events of the early eleventh century had precursors, attempts to demarcate limits to royal power seem at very least to have acquired a new urgency then: in contrast to the silence (but not absence) of earlier sources, we find within the space of three decades a fair amount of evidence for efforts to circumscribe kings' arbitrariness. Moreover, this is not a matter of a single text (or kind of text) breaking its silence: our evidence comes from three quite different sources, namely *Chronicle* annals, Cnut's legislation, and the preface to a later compilation. It thus appears that the early eleventh century was of considerable importance in the development of what has been called the English kingdom's 'constitutional tradition': once the principle was established that a king's position might be conditional on his acceptance of certain restrictions, it is little surprise that later generations sought to obtain comparable undertakings from their rulers.[134]

The Causes of Attempts to Restrain Royal Arbitrariness

In seeking to explain why the early eleventh century saw what appear to have been (at least in an English context) novel attempts to set limits on kings, there are two obvious factors—motive and opportunity. On motive, many people probably resented that Æthelred had imposed unprecedentedly heavy burdens on his subjects, but failed to deliver security from Scandinavian attack. Indeed, the events of 1013–1014 can to some extent be seen as a reaction to the (probably) recent

---

[132] Above, pp. 187–8.

[133] *ASC* ABCDE 757 says that the West Saxons deprived Sigeberht of most of his kingdom on account of his unjust acts, but there is no mention of conditions being imposed on his replacement. Similar considerations apply to *VSD*, xxiv (p. 74), and to the implication in the *Old English Boethius* that an unrighteous ruler might legitimately be resisted: J. L. Nelson, 'The Political Ideas of Alfred of Wessex', in A. J. Duggan (ed.), *Kings and Kingship in Medieval Europe* (London, 1993), pp. 152–4. The connection between the *Old English Boethius* and Alfred is uncertain, and the text may be later than his reign: above, p. 168 n. 229.

[134] Maddicott, *Origins*, p. 40. Contrast J. C. Holt, 'The Origins of the Constitutional Tradition in England', in J. C. Holt, *Magna Carta and Medieval Government* (London, 1985), pp. 1–22.

intensification of Cerdicing domination, since certain of Æthelred's wealth extraction techniques (e.g. the *heregeld*) were based on the system of shires, hundreds, and wapentakes, although it should be noted that others (e.g. raised heriots) were not. Similarly, it is not hard to identify reasons for discontent with Louis the Pious and Charles the Bald: both caused the death or marginalization of members of the elite; Louis's wife and chamberlain were perceived as immoral and manipulative; and Charles extracted large sums from his subordinates to fund payments to the vikings.[135] Turning from motive to opportunity, Æthelred's military failure and expulsion, Cnut's need to secure acceptance, and Edward's return from exile gave English magnates chances to obtain concessions. Likewise, Louis and Charles were both vulnerable, since each had antagonistic relationships with close relatives, to whom discontented magnates could transfer (or threaten to transfer) their allegiance.[136] Such arguments only take us so far, however. While Æthelred's demands were probably unprecedentedly onerous, we know from Asser that previous royal exactions had not always been welcomed, and it is doubtful that earlier kings would have been able to overcome concerted opposition from their greatest subordinates, especially at times of military crises, minorities or succession disputes.[137] The question, therefore, is why early eleventh-century English magnates exploited comparable opportunities in ways that their predecessors seemingly had not.

One significant consideration is that concern with the duties of Christian rulers, already strong and deepening during the reigns of kings from Alfred to Edgar, became even more pronounced in the late tenth and early eleventh centuries, as it did over the course of the Carolingian period.[138] Ælfric distinguished a king ('rex') from a tyrant ('tyrannus') on the basis that the former guides his people with restraint, while the latter oppresses them with his power.[139] He also presented the position of a king as that of 'Christ's own vicar' ('Cristes sylfes speligend'), an echo of his teacher Æthelwold.[140] In addition to being the likely source for this idea, Æthelwold may well have introduced Ælfric to *On the Twelve Abuses of the World*, an early medieval Irish tract that had been seminal to much Carolingian thinking

---

[135] de Jong, *Penitential State*, pp. 28–9, 38–44, 148–53, 185–205, 234–41; Nelson, *Charles the Bald*, pp. 28–9, 35, 171–2, 184, 187–8.

[136] de Jong, *Penitential State*, pp. 31, 44–6; Nelson, *Charles the Bald*, pp. 71–4, 108–9, 139, 147, 156–7, 171, 178–81, 187.

[137] *VA*, xci (pp. 77–9). It should not, however, be assumed that royal demands were invariably resented, since many people may have been content to discharge moderate burdens if this helped them lay claim to social status: above, pp. 95–8.

[138] H. H. Anton, *Fürstenspiegel und Herrscherethos in der Karolingerzeit* (Bonn, 1968); W. Ullmann, *The Carolingian Renaissance and the Idea of Kingship* (London, 1969); Nelson, 'Kingship, Law and Liturgy'; Nelson, 'Kingship and Royal Government', pp. 422–30. One might also suggest that, since eleventh-century magnates were probably wealthier than their predecessors, they would have had more scope to put pressure on kings. Such a hypothesis has limited explanatory force, however, since kings were also greatly enriched during the late Anglo-Saxon period: above, pp. 183–5.

[139] Ælfric, *Grammar*, ed. J. Zupitza, *Ælfrics Grammatik und Glossar: Text und Varianten* (Berlin, 1880), pp. 293–4.

[140] Ælfric, *Homilies: A Supplementary Collection*, ed. J. C. Pope, *The Homilies of Ælfric: A Supplementary Collection* (2 vols, EETS, 259–60, Oxford, 1967–8), i, 380; S 745; M. J. Silverman, 'Ælfric's Designation of the King as "Cristes sylfes speligend"', *Review of English Studies*, 35 (1984), pp. 332–4; above, p. 191.

on royal responsibilities: Æthelwold is not known to have quoted this text, but he possessed a copy, and his pupil was strongly influenced by it.[141] Ælfric produced an English summary of the whole work, and elsewhere drew on its discussion of kingship, which listed a king's duties, declared that observance of such precepts would bring him both earthly prosperity and heavenly reward, and warned that neglect would cause his kingdom to suffer numerous afflictions.[142] Ælfric is not known to have expressed overt criticism of Æthelred, and often treated contemporary famine, disease, and viking attack as portents of the apocalypse or trials of faith, rather than punishments for sin.[143] He did, however, also raise the latter possibility, notably in his *On the Prayer of Moses*, where he explicitly identified the casting down of monastic life as the reason why the English were afflicted by pestilence, hunger, and a heathen army. His rebuke appears to have been directed against all those who had failed to maintain the honour in which monasticism had formerly been held, but it is likely that the reigning king was a particular target of his criticism. Ælfric was probably writing soon after Æthelred had publicly confessed to selling the abbacy of Abingdon, and among the various biblical references with which the homilist buttressed his admonition was the account of how God had punished the sins of King David by visiting death upon his people.[144] Moreover, Ælfric's vernacular version of the *Twelve Abuses* summarizes the consequences of unrighteous kingship as ravaging, hunger, pestilence, bad weather, and wild animals, a list that corresponds fairly closely to the disasters then befalling the English, and it is hard to resist the conclusion that he at least contemplated the possibility that Æthelred's own wickedness was a significant cause of these

---

[141] S 1448; R. Meens, 'Politics, Mirrors of Princes and the Bible: Sins, Kings and the Well-being of the Realm', *EME*, 7 (1998), pp. 345–57; de Jong, *Penitential State*, pp. 174–5, 181–2. What follows draws on M. Clayton, 'Ælfric and Æthelred', in J. Roberts and J. L. Nelson (eds), *Essays on Anglo-Saxon and Related Themes in Memory of Lynne Grundy* (London, 2000), pp. 65–88; M. Clayton, '*De Duodecim Abusiuis*, Lordship and Kingship in Anglo-Saxon England', in S. McWilliams (ed.), *Saints and Scholars: New Perspectives on Anglo-Saxon Literature and Culture in Honour of Hugh Magennis* (Cambridge, 2012), pp. 141–63 especially 153–61.

[142] *Pseudo-Cyprianus De XII Abusivis Saeculi*, ed. S. Hellmann (Leipzig, 1909–10), especially pp. 51–3; Ælfric, *De duodecim abusivis*, ed. and trans. M. Clayton, *Two Ælfric Texts: The Twelve Abuses and The Vices and Virtues* (Cambridge, 2013), pp. 109–37; Ælfric, *De octo vitiis et de duodecim abusivis gradus*, ed. and trans. Clayton, *Two Ælfric Texts*, 154–77; Ælfric, *Catholic Homilies: The Second Series*, ed. M. Godden (EETS, s.s., 5, Oxford, 1979), p. 183; Ælfric, *Grammar*, p. 293; Ælfric, *Lives of Saints*, i, 290–2; Ælfric, *Homilies: A Supplementary Collection*, i, 380–1. The Old English version of the text is attributed to Ælfric by Clayton, *Two Ælfric Texts*, pp. 23–30. If Clayton's attribution were wrong, this would only strengthen my argument, since it would indicate that another writer was also familiar with the text.

[143] M. Godden, 'Apocalypse and Invasion in Late Anglo-Saxon England', in M. Godden, D. Gray, and T. Hoad (eds), *From Anglo-Saxon to Early Middle English: Studies Presented to E. G. Stanley* (Oxford, 1994), pp. 131–42. See also L. Roach, 'Apocalypse and Atonement in the Politics of Æthelredian England', *English Studies*, 95 (2014), pp. 733–57.

[144] Ælfric, *Lives of Saints*, i, 282–306 especially 292–302. The text is dated c.995 by Godden, 'Apocalypse and Invasion', p. 133. For Æthelred's confession, see S 876, issued in 993. Jayakumar, 'Eadwig and Edgar', pp. 96–7 suggests that Ælfric saw the sins of Edgar, rather than Æthelred, as the cause of the tribulations that the English were suffering. This sits awkwardly with Ælfric's enthusiastic comments about Edgar at Ælfric, *Lives of Saints*, i, 468–70. See also *The Old English Heptateuch*, ed. R. Marsden, *The Old English Heptateuch and Ælfric's Libellus de Veteri Testamento et Novo* (EETS, 330, Oxford, 2008), p. 200.

afflictions.[145] Furthermore, it is interesting that two of Ælfric's later homilies allude briefly but negatively to 'various taxes' ('mislicum geldum') and 'all-new laws' ('eall-niwe gesetnyssa'): in neither case is wrongdoing specifically associated with a king, but such comments strongly suggest that Ælfric's disapproval of Æthelred was not confined to the latter's treatment of monastic institutions.[146]

The duties of a Christian king were also a major concern of Archbishop Wulfstan. This is especially clear in his *Institutes of Polity*, the earliest version of which dates from towards the end of Æthelred's reign, and opens with a summary of a king's obligations. The sentiments expressed were hardly novel, but Wulfstan declared with notable forcefulness that a king should love Christianity, shun heathenism, protect the Church, and uphold just law. He then listed eight pillars of a rightful kingdom, and seven attributes of just kingship, these lists deriving from Sedulius Scottus (who wrote at Liège in the mid-ninth century) and the *Collectio Canonum Hibernensis* (an early medieval Irish canon law compilation). In the present context, it is particularly notable that the seventh column supporting a rightful kingdom was 'lightness of tribute' ('leuitas tributi'), which Wulfstan rendered as 'lihtengnes', the same word as he would use to open the mitigatory section of Cnut's legislation.[147] The *Institutes of Polity* presents earthly prosperity as contingent on the right ordering of society, but does relatively little to spell out the consequences of unjust kingship, and Wulfstan's other writings suggest that he (like Ælfric) may not have been wholly certain about why the English were experiencing afflictions.[148] Wulfstan is, however, known to have been familiar with the ideas about kingship contained in the *Twelve Abuses*, since he made excerpts from a section of the *Collectio Canonum Hibernensis* into which they had been incorporated.[149] He was, moreover, quite possibly the author of a homiletic exposition of the royal consecration oath, composed at some point before Æthelred's death, which draws heavily (although perhaps indirectly) on the *Twelve Abuses*, and warns explicitly that a king who breached his inauguration promises could bring down punishment on himself and his people.[150] The intensifying concern with the obligations

---

[145] Ælfric, *De duodecim abusivis*, p. 130; Ælfric, *De octo vitiis et de duodecim abusivis gradus*, p. 170. Compare the longer list of afflictions at *Pseudo-Cyprianus De XII Abusivis Saeculi*, pp. 52–3.

[146] Ælfric, *Homilies: A Supplementary Collection*, ii, 500, 520; S. Keynes, 'An Abbot, an Archbishop, and the Viking Raids of 1006–7 and 1009–12', *ASE*, 36 (2007), pp. 160–70.

[147] Wulfstan, *Institutes of Polity*, pp. 40–2, 52–4; II Cn 69. Compare Sedulius Scottus, *De rectoribus Christianis*, x, ed. R. W. Dyson (Woodbridge, 2010), pp. 108–10; *Die irische Kanonensammlung*, ed. F. W. H. Wasserschleben, 2nd edn (Leipzig, 1885), p. 81. On Wulfstan's sources, see M. Clayton, 'The Old English *Promissio regis*', *ASE*, 37 (2008), pp. 138–40. The earliest extant version of the *Institutes of Polity* is that labelled D2 in Jost's edition. In subsequent versions, the section on a king's obligations is expanded, though a reference to his being Christ's vicar ('Cristes gespeliga') is dropped.

[148] Godden, 'Apocalypse and Invasion', pp. 142–62; Molyneaux, 'Did the English Really Think they were God's Elect in the Anglo-Saxon Period?', pp. 733–4 and n. 50; Roach, 'Apocalypse and Atonement', pp. 743–50. In the late recension of the *Institutes of Polity*, which postdates Æthelred's death, a reference is added to a people being afflicted on account of the misguidance ('misræde') of an unwise king: Wulfstan, *Institutes of Polity*, p. 47.

[149] *Die irische Kanonensammlung*, pp. 77–8; Clayton, 'Old English *Promissio regis*', pp. 115–16, 138.

[150] Clayton, 'Old English *Promissio regis*'. As with Ælfric and the Old English version of the *Twelve Abuses*, my argument would only be strengthened if Wulfstan were not the homily's author.

of Christian rulership very probably encouraged closer scrutiny of kings' behaviour, such that Æthelred would have been more liable to moral censure than his predecessors, even had he not exceeded them in predation and arbitrariness. Ælfric is not known to have called for attempts to depose sinful kings, and Wulfstan explicitly condemned Æthelred's expulsion.[151] The ideas that they articulated would, however, have contributed to an intellectual climate in which kings were judged on the righteousness or otherwise of their actions, and in which people could believe that the afflictions that they themselves suffered were caused by the moral inadequacy of their ruler.

The development of the idea that kings should be subject to constraints probably owed a considerable amount to the fact that it was not just churchmen who conceived of kingship in increasingly moralized terms: kings themselves expressed heightened concern with the rectitude and consequences of their own actions, or at least permitted such ideas to be articulated in their names. This is particularly marked in the case of Æthelred. His legislation, much of which appears to have been drafted by Wulfstan, asserts that a Christian king is Christ's vicar ('Cristes gespelia'), and repeatedly declares the importance of righteousness, mercy, and equality of access to justice.[152] Similarly, several of his diplomas do not merely state what he had decided to grant, but incorporate passages that justify how the land in question had come into his possession, or explain a rationale for his actions.[153] Especially striking is a charter of 993, in which Æthelred guaranteed the liberties of the abbey of Abingdon, having identified his previous sale of the abbacy as a reason why he and his people had been suffering frequent and manifold afflictions.[154] Thus, while Ælfric and (later) Wulfstan may well have thought that royal sins were a cause of collective suffering, Æthelred was far more overt, admitting his wrongdoing and its consequences in the presence of the leading magnates of his kingdom. Æthelred was not the first Cerdicing to confess to sinfulness: Asser

---

[151] Wulfstan, *Homilies*, XX (B H), lines 66–71. It has sometimes been thought that Ælfric explicitly denied the right of an unjust king's subjects to offer resistance, but see M. Godden, 'Ælfric and Anglo-Saxon Kingship', *EHR*, 102 (1987), pp. 911–15. Compare Nelson, 'Kingship, Law and Liturgy', pp. 263–79.

[152] Such sentiments are ubiquitous in Æthelred's legislation, but see especially V Atr 1.1–3.1, 32–33.1; VI Atr 8–10.3, 40–40.1, 52–3; VII Atr 6.1; VIII Atr 2.1, 5.2; X Atr 2. Compare Cn 1018 3–6, 24, 36; Cn 1020 2, 11; II Cn 1–3, 68–68.3.

[153] S. Keynes, *The Diplomas of King Æthelred 'the Unready', 978–1016: A Study in their Use as Historical Evidence* (Cambridge, 1980), pp. 95–8, 200–2; P. Stafford, 'Political Ideas in Late-Tenth-Century England: Charters as Evidence', in P. Stafford, J. L. Nelson, and J. Martindale (eds), *Law, Laity and Solidarities: Essays in Honour of Susan Reynolds* (Manchester, 2001), pp. 68–82. Explanatory passages were not unprecedented (e.g. S 362), but had not previously appeared with such frequency.

[154] S 876; S. Keynes, 'Re-Reading King Æthelred the Unready', in D. Bates, J. Crick, and S. Hamilton (eds), *Writing Medieval Biography, 750–1250: Essays in Honour of Professor Frank Barlow* (Woodbridge, 2006), pp. 89–96; C. Cubitt, 'The Politics of Remorse: Penance and Royal Piety in the Reign of Æthelred the Unready', *Historical Research*, 85 (2012), pp. 179–92; L. Roach, 'Penitential Discourse in the Diplomas of King Æthelred "the Unready"', *Journal of Ecclesiastical History*, 64 (2013), pp. 258–76; S. Keynes, 'Church Councils, Royal Assemblies, and Anglo-Saxon Royal Diplomas', in G. R. Owen-Crocker and B. W. Schneider (eds), *Kingship, Legislation and Power in Anglo-Saxon England* (Woodbridge, 2013), pp. 108–116. Æthelred also made penitent restorations of church lands in S 885, 891, 893, although these charters do not explicitly ascribe general tribulations to royal wrongdoing.

relates that Alfred prayed for an illness that would restrain his lust, and the New Minster Winchester refoundation charter (probably drafted by Æthelwold) presents Edgar as resolving to 'cease from all evil deeds', which implies some past wrongdoing.[155] Unlike in Æthelred's case, however, it is uncertain whether either Alfred or Edgar explicitly declared his own wickedness to be a cause of his people's suffering; they (and others) may have contemplated such a possibility, but it was to wider societal failings, namely neglect of wisdom and non-payment of tithes, that these kings most clearly ascribed viking attack and pestilence.[156] Æthelred did not absolve his subjects of blame, and sought in his Bath decrees (probably issued in 1009) to propitiate God by ordering a general programme of collective fasting and penance, but his admission of 993 is highly significant in explaining his vulnerability.[157] Since Æthelred had announced with what may well have been unprecedented clarity that royal misconduct had brought afflictions on the kingdom, he left no room for doubt about how dangerous it would be if his sinfulness were left unchecked.

While Edgar is not known to have attributed societal suffering to his own wrongdoing, he too was very much a contributor to the growth in concern about royal responsibilities. His legislation was less suffused with homiletic exhortation than Æthelred's would be, but he declared that he would be a 'hold hlaford' ('faithful lord'), that every person should receive justice, that compensations should be remitted, and that any person for whom justice was too oppressive should apply to the king for 'lihtinge' ('mitigation').[158] He also set a precedent for the idea that the rights of both a king and his subjects should be defined with reference to the time of an earlier ruler, in this case Edmund.[159] Edgar did not spell out what he meant by 'hold hlaford' or 'lihtinge', but it is notable that these expressions recur in Æthelred's 1014 promise and Cnut's legislation, both of which were associated with the renunciation of abuses: Edgar's successors, at least sometimes acting under

---

[155] *VA*, lxxiv (pp. 54–7); S 745; M. Lapidge, 'Æthelwold as Scholar and Teacher', in B. Yorke (ed.), *Bishop Æthelwold: His Career and Influence* (Woodbridge, 1988), pp. 95–8. Note also *Councils and Synods*, no. 33 (p. 149), where Æthelwold refers to Edgar considering how he could 'rectify his own life'. William of Malmesbury, *Gesta Regum*, ii.139.5 (i, 226) refers to Æthelstan submitting to a seven-year penance, but this may well be nothing more than legend. For a much earlier example, see S 1258.

[156] *King Alfred's West-Saxon Version of Gregory's Pastoral Care*, pp. 2–9; IV Eg Prolog–1. Three further points may heighten the contrast further. First, it is doubtful whether Alfred's confessional prayer was widely known: Asser states that it was made in secret, the *Life* may well have had a narrow circulation, and those present at Alfred's wedding were apparently perplexed about what could have caused the illness which struck him then. Second, Asser presents Alfred's illness not as a punishment, but as a means to minimize the risk of his acting on his desires. Third, while it is possible that Edgar confessed to specific grave sins (perhaps of a sexual nature, in view of later stories about him), his resolution to cease from evil deeds may just have been a conventional allusion to ordinary human shortcomings. For discussion, see D. Pratt, 'The Illnesses of King Alfred the Great', *ASE*, 30 (2001), pp. 39–90; Pratt, 'Voice of the King', especially pp. 149–57, whose interpretation is in some respects different from mine.

[157] VII Atr; VIIa Atr Poen. For comment, see Keynes, 'An Abbot, an Archbishop', pp. 179–89, who notes the probable Carolingian inspiration for these decrees.

[158] III Eg 1.1–1.2, 2.1; IV Eg 16. Æthelstan mandated mercy, but only in limited circumstances: III As 3; V As 3.1; VI As 12.1–12.3. Note also Af El 49, 49.7.

[159] IV Eg 2.2a.

duress, pledged to give practical effect to the principles that he had espoused in more general terms.[160] I argued in the previous chapter that Edgar's apparent implementation of administrative innovations may well have been prompted in large part by a desire to discharge what he regarded as the duties of a Christian king.[161] But even if one supposed that Edgar's reforms were simply driven by a wish (or need) to extract more resources, the fact that he presented his rule in moralizing terms would be of considerable significance. The key point is that he and (even more so) Æthelred raised expectations of the standards against which kings should be judged, while in practice employing many of the methods of their predecessors. So too the Carolingians set exalted moral standards for themselves and their people, and Louis the Pious openly admitted his sinfulness: he did public penance in 822 for having mistreated certain of his relatives, and in 828–829 attributed the various tribulations then being suffered by his kingdom to divine anger at himself and his subjects.[162] Given that both Æthelred and Louis presented royal rectitude as necessary for the assuaging of God's wrath, but were perceived to have failed to adhere to their own precepts, there was a strong logic for depriving them of power: if their sinfulness continued unabated, their peoples could not expect any remission from divine punishment.

There is, however, a further explanation, in no way mutually exclusive with the last, for why the eleventh century saw significant attempts to constrain the arbitrariness of the English kingdom's rulers. If the argument of the previous chapter be accepted, Æthelred's expulsion occurred after a half-century in which elements of the Cerdicings' domination between the Channel and the Tees became much more based on standardized institutions and predictable procedures. Their dealings with their greatest subordinates, on the other hand, remained highly personal, and a degree of fickleness in royal wrath and favour made it all the more necessary for magnates constantly to ingratiate themselves with the reigning king. But in a context where some aspects of kings' domination were becoming more uniform and predictable, continued royal arbitrariness may well have begun to seem increasingly incongruous, even to people who were not steeped in deliberations about the moral consequences of unjust kingship. Once again, one might draw a comparison with the Carolingians, who made significant efforts to systematize elements of their rule.[163] The parallels to the context of Magna Carta are, however, at least as striking.[164] Like Æthelred's expulsion and conditional recall, the revolt against John followed a period of vast royal demands to finance military action that ultimately failed. It also came after a half-century in which significant aspects of royal rule had been reformed, while others had been left little changed: the judicial

---

[160] *ASC* CDE 1014; Cn 1020 2; II Cn 69.   [161] Above, pp. 187–93.

[162] de Jong, *Penitential State*, pp. 36, 38–40, 122–31, 148–84. Louis's position was initially strengthened by his penance of 822, but the sins to which he had confessed then were among those cited when he was deprived of power in 833.

[163] K. F. Werner, '*Missus-Marchio-Comes*. Entre l'administration centrale et l'administration locale de l'Empire carolingien', in W. Paravicini and K. F. Werner (eds), *Histoire comparée de l'administration (IVᵉ–XVIIIᵉ siècles)* (Munich, 1980), pp. 191–239 especially 195–205, 225–7.

[164] What follows is indebted to Holt, *Magna Carta*, especially pp. 23–49, 123–87.

innovations of Henry II (r. 1154–1189) made standard writs for common legal actions readily available to most free men, but not to the king's own tenants. Such magnates resented that their exclusion from the new procedures left them highly dependent on the king's personal favour, and they demanded that John should adhere to stated standards in his dealings with them. Similar considerations applied in the early eleventh century. Kings had significantly increased the extent to which they dealt with ordinary people on a routine and impersonal basis. They had, moreover, taken responsibility for providing a framework in which disputes could be settled through relatively standardized procedures, without specific royal intervention. On the other hand, however, many of J. E. A. Jolliffe's general observations about the arbitrary dimension of Angevin kingship could be applied, *mutatis mutandis*, to the late tenth and eleventh centuries: the Cerdicings continued to deal individually with their greater subordinates, for whom royal favour or disfavour remained critical.[165] This conjunction of change and continuity does much to explain why the eleventh century saw moves to induce kings to accept restraints: for those who had suffered through Æthelred's personal attentions, the Cerdicings' increasingly standardized engagement with the bulk of the population probably did much to make it thinkable that kings should be constrained to treat all their subjects in accordance with defined norms.

The administrative reforms of the mid- to late tenth century resulted in a substantial intensification in the Cerdicings' domination, giving Edgar and his successors unprecedented scope to shape significant aspects of the lives of quite ordinary people across the land from the Channel to the Tees. There were, however, important geographical and substantive limits to the shift in how kings ruled, and these limits made the implications of reform somewhat paradoxical: the administrative changes which underpinned intensified royal domination also contributed to kings' titles becoming more modest, and their discretion less untrammelled. In neither case was there an immediate or total bouleversement: some people continued to entertain the possibility of a kingdom of Britain long after the Norman Conquest, and the similarities between Cnut's 'lihtingc', Henry I's coronation edict, and Magna Carta (and its re-issues) reflect that many perceived abuses continued to be perpetrated, as they would be for centuries.[166] Both developments were, however, of considerable long-term importance: the area that we think of as England is only a little larger than Domesday *Anglia*, and repeated attempts to impose constraints on kings ultimately resulted in significant curtailments of royal arbitrariness. The profound but limited administrative changes that appear to have been wrought around the time of Edgar's reign were thus fundamental to the definition of the English kingdom, and to its subsequent political history.

---

[165] J. E. A. Jolliffe, *Angevin Kingship*, 2nd edn (London, 1963); above, pp. 217–18. Note also above, p. 73 and n. 112.

[166] Stafford, 'Laws of Cnut', pp. 178–9; Davies, *First English Empire*, pp. 8, 16–17, 29, 31–53.

Conclusion: The Formation of the English Kingdom and the 'Anglo-Saxon State'

The central argument of this book is that the English kingdom of the eleventh and subsequent centuries owed its formation not only to the military campaigns of Alfred, his children, and grandchildren, but also to a series of administrative reforms that were most probably implemented in the mid- to late tenth century. It is doubtful whether those responsible for these apparent changes had the intention of constructing a realm confined to the land that would make up Domesday *Anglia*, and I am not proposing that any specific individual be celebrated as the English kingdom's creator. Nonetheless, the innovations that seem to have been implemented in or around Edgar's reign served to define the area from the Channel to the Tees as a unit, and thus to foster the idea that the great majority of what is now England constituted a single and discrete political entity. The implications of administrative change were therefore considerable, but this should not obscure that much remained the same throughout the late Anglo-Saxon period, and far beyond. Perhaps most importantly, kings' power long continued to be predicated on the wealth that enabled them to use patronage and coercion to maintain the loyalty of at least the bulk of the aristocracy. Nor should it be thought that the changes of the mid- to late tenth century came out of thin air, since much was probably based on the modification and standardization of a variety of existing practices. Moreover, what shifted was not so much the Cerdicings' overall aims, as certain of their means of pursuing them: in particular, while the administrative framework of hundreds and wapentakes gave kings more scope to specify how thieves were to be identified and treated, theft had been the single greatest concern of royal ordinances since the early tenth century, and the continuous tradition of written legislation went back to Alfred. Thus, I do not assert that the likes of Alfred and Æthelstan were unimportant, or that everything changed around the time of Edgar. Rather, my point is that those reforms which probably did take place in the mid- to late tenth century turned out to be of great significance: by fundamentally changing how kings dealt with the general populace of the land between the Channel and the Tees, the administrative innovations of this period were crucial to the formation of the English kingdom as a territorial unit, distinct both from the island of Britain, and from the full area of English habitation.

Some may mistake my arguments for an attack on the contention that there was a sophisticated 'Anglo-Saxon state', as portrayed by James Campbell and Patrick Wormald.[1] It is, however, only occasionally that I seek to refute a substantive proposition advanced by either of these scholars, notwithstanding my challenge to the latter's claim that the English kingdom was constructed on the basis of a vision derived from Bede.[2] Indeed, with regard to the last century or so of the Anglo-Saxon period, I accept the broad thrust (if not every specific detail) of their claims about the considerable administrative capabilities of pre-Norman kings. I also accept, as Campbell in particular has stressed, that some elements of eleventh-century royal administration were based on very long-standing practices, a notable example being the use of hides to assess obligations.[3] Moreover, my contention that very substantial changes to royal administration took place during the tenth century is consistent with statements made by both Campbell and Wormald. The former notes that it was sometime between the reigns of Edward the Elder and Æthelred II that the Midland shires were created, and suggests that it was 'not improbably in the late ninth or tenth century' that the hundredal system was established.[4] Similarly, while Wormald was sometimes keen to ascribe innovations to Alfred, he declared that it was through 'a "Tenth-Century Revolution in Government"' that shires became something more than units of military organization.[5] Both scholars are, however, far from specific about when these major changes are most likely to have occurred: my aim is therefore to refine, rather than refute, their interpretations of the late Anglo-Saxon period, by identifying the mid- to late tenth century as the key period for the development of relatively standardized administrative structures across the land from the Channel to the Tees.

There are, however, two broader issues on which I differ from Campbell and Wormald, at least to some extent. The first is that I attach no great significance to whether or not the pre-Conquest English kingdom should be called a 'state': under some definitions of this word it could, while under others it could not, and a definitional debate does nothing to illuminate our understanding of the Anglo-Saxon

---

[1] Among their many writings on this issue, see especially J. Campbell, 'The Late Anglo-Saxon State: A Maximum View', *PBA*, 87 (1994), pp. 39–65, reprinted in his *The Anglo-Saxon State* (London, 2000), pp. 1–30; P. Wormald, 'Pre-Modern "State" and "Nation": Definite or Indefinite?', in S. Airlie, W. Pohl, and H. Reimitz (eds), *Staat im frühen Mittelalter* (Vienna, 2006), pp. 179–89.

[2] Above, pp. 201–9.

[3] Campbell, 'Late Anglo-Saxon State', pp. 2–8; J. Campbell, 'Archipelagic Thoughts: Comparing Early Medieval Polities in Britain and Ireland', in S. Baxter, C. E. Karkov, J. L. Nelson, and D. Pelteret (eds), *Early Medieval Studies in Memory of Patrick Wormald* (Farnham, 2009), pp. 47–63; above, pp. 92–8. My hypotheses about how estates could have come to be assessed at particular numbers of hides are, however, rather different from Campbell's. On the possibility of pre-hundredal local assemblies, see also P. Wormald, 'Germanic Power Structures: The Early English Experience', in L. Scales and O. Zimmer (eds), *Power and the Nation in European History* (Cambridge, 2005), pp. 105–24; above, pp. 102–3, 148–9.

[4] Campbell, 'Late Anglo-Saxon State', pp. 16–17; J. Campbell, 'The United Kingdom of England: The Anglo-Saxon Achievement', in A. Grant and K. J. Stringer (eds), *Uniting the Kingdom: The Making of British History* (London, 1995), pp. 31–47, reprinted in his *Anglo-Saxon State*, p. 40.

[5] Wormald, 'Germanic Power Structures', p. 117.

period.[6] That is not to say that the noun 'state' should be expunged from work on the medieval period. In particular, it can, if explicitly and consistently conceptualized, be useful in comparative contexts, and might indeed prove helpful in a fuller treatment of some of the problems to which we are about to turn, since it would offer a category of analysis that could encompass both the English kingdom and (say) the Croatian duchy.[7] But when one is focused on a single political entity, as I have been in the bulk of this book, the semantic question is an avoidable distraction: it is far more important to analyse the nature of the Cerdicings' power in different periods than to argue about whether or not they ruled a 'state'.

ENGLISH EXCEPTIONALISM?

The second wider issue about which I may disagree with Campbell and Wormald is that of English exceptionalism, the idea that the history of the English diverged from some kind of wider trend. Four points need to be made at the outset. First, the words 'exceptional' and 'unique' are not synonymous: to say that a kingdom was exceptional implies not only that it was unlike anywhere else (i.e. unique), but also that it stood in contrast to an otherwise common standard. Second, it is not just the English who have often been presented as exceptional: analogous ideas are (or have been) prominent in various other historiographical traditions, notably those of Germany and Spain, and an accumulation of possible 'exceptions' must raise doubts about whether there was a norm.[8] Third, however, French historians have frequently taken a contrary approach, adopting the course of France's history as a paradigm for that of Europe as a whole, and thereby offering exceptionalists of all nationalities a supposed norm from which they can identify divergence.[9] Fourth,

---

[6] For particularly forceful pronouncements that the early English kingdom was a 'state', see Campbell, 'Late Anglo-Saxon State', p. 10; Wormald, 'Pre-Modern "State" and "Nation"'. For wider debate about the usefulness of the term, see S. Reynolds, 'The Historiography of the Medieval State', in M. Bentley (ed.), *Companion to Historiography* (London, 1997), pp. 117–38; R. R. Davies, 'The Medieval State: The Tyranny of a Concept?', *Journal of Historical Sociology*, 16 (2003), pp. 280–300; S. Reynolds, 'There were States in Medieval Europe: A Response to Rees Davies', *Journal of Historical Sociology*, 16 (2003), pp. 550–5; S. Foot, 'The Historiography of the Anglo-Saxon "Nation-State"', in Scales and Zimmer (eds), *Power and the Nation*, pp. 125–42.

[7] Reynolds, 'There were States in Medieval Europe'; C. Wickham, *Framing the Early Middle Ages: Europe and the Mediterranean, 400–800* (Oxford, 2005), especially pp. 6–7, 57, 303–4.

[8] P. Linehan, 'History in a Changing World: The Case of Medieval Spain', in P. Linehan, *Past and Present in Medieval Spain* (Aldershot, 1992), I, pp. 1–22; F. Fernández-Armesto, 'The Survival of a Notion of *Reconquista* in Late Tenth- and Eleventh-Century León', in T. Reuter (ed.), *Warriors and Churchmen in the High Middle Ages: Essays Presented to Karl Leyser* (London, 1992), pp. 123–5; T. Reuter, 'The Medieval German *Sonderweg*? The Empire and its Rulers in the High Middle Ages', in A. J. Duggan (ed.), *Kings and Kingship in Medieval Europe* (London, 1993), pp. 179–211; T. Reuter, 'Nur im Westen was Neues? Das Werden prämoderner Staatsformen im europäischen Hochmittelalter', in J. Ehlers (ed.), *Deutschland und der Westen Europas im Mittelalter* (Stuttgart, 2002), pp. 327–51.

[9] For an extreme case, see G. Bois, *The Transformation of the Year One Thousand: The Village of Lournand from Antiquity to Feudalism*, trans. J. Birrell (Manchester, 1992). Bois bases his argument on a single village in the Mâconnais, but avers that 'the feudal revolution was a European phenomenon' (p. 135). He barely mentions anywhere outside France, save for a vague allusion to 'the very variable degree of dissociation of the state structures of Italy and England' (p. 170).

it is far from clear that either Campbell or Wormald had a settled view on English exceptionalism, and it is for this reason that I say only that I *may* disagree with them. Each made comments which appear to suggest flirtation with exceptionalist ideas: the former writes of 'the determinative contrast between England and the other great states of Europe', and the latter referred approvingly to how historians had become 'increasingly aware that it is indeed England's that is the *Sonderweg* ["special path"]'.[10] On the other hand, however, Wormald explicitly denied that he was an English exceptionalist, although there must be a suspicion that he was protesting overmuch, and it is even more problematic to pigeon-hole Campbell in this way: he argues that the English kingdom differed from its neighbours in certain important respects, but has repeatedly raised the possibility that evidential imbalances have caused such contrasts to be overstated, and the capabilities of Continental rulers underrated.[11] My object here, however, is not to undertake exegesis of the works of Campbell and Wormald to pinpoint the nuances, ambiguities, and shifts in their thinking. Rather, what follows is an attempt to place the formation of the English kingdom in a broader comparative context, and to argue that it was neither typical nor exceptional.[12]

Comparisons with West Frankia and East Frankia

If one is going to argue for exceptionalism (or typicality), as opposed merely to asserting it, it is necessary to undertake comparisons. When historians of the early English kingdom compare it with anywhere else—and they usually just discuss it in isolation—they most often do so in relation to West Frankia, the forerunner of France.[13] Considerable attention has been devoted to the way in which the Cerdicings drew on Carolingian ideas about rulers' responsibility for promoting

---

[10] J. Campbell, 'Epilogue', in J. Campbell (ed.), *The Anglo-Saxons* (Oxford, 1982), p. 240; P. Wormald, '*Engla Lond*: The Making of an Allegiance', *Journal of Historical Sociology*, 7 (1994), pp. 1–24, reprinted in his *Legal Culture in the Early Medieval West: Law as Text, Image and Experience* (London, 1999), p. 360.

[11] J. Campbell, 'Observations on English Government from the Tenth to the Twelfth Century', *TRHS*, 5th series, 25 (1975), pp. 39–54, reprinted in his *Essays in Anglo-Saxon History* (London, 1986), pp. 155–70 especially 166–7, 170; J. Campbell, 'The Significance of the Anglo-Norman State in the Administrative History of Western Europe', in W. Paravicini and K. F. Werner (eds), *Histoire comparée de l'administration (IVe–XVIIIe siècles)* (Munich, 1980), pp. 117–34, reprinted in his *Essays*, pp. 171–89 especially 182–8; J. Campbell, 'Was it Infancy in England? Some Questions of Comparison', in M. Jones and M. Vale (eds), *England and her Neighbours, 1066–1453: Essays in Honour of Pierre Chaplais* (London, 1989), pp. 1–17, reprinted in his *Anglo-Saxon State*, pp. 197–9; Campbell, 'Late Anglo-Saxon State', especially pp. 28–30; J. Campbell, 'Introduction', in Campbell, *Anglo-Saxon State*, p. xii; Wormald, 'Pre-Modern "State" and "Nation"', p. 181. See also Wormald, 'Giving God and King their Due: Conflict and its Regulation in the Early English State', *Settimane di studio del centro italiano di studi sull'alto medioevo*, 44 (1997), pp. 549–90, reprinted in his *Legal Culture*, p. 354; P. Wormald, 'James Campbell as Historian', in J. R. Maddicott and D. M. Palliser (eds), *The Medieval State: Essays Presented to James Campbell* (London, 2000), pp. xix–xx; S. Baxter, 'The Limits of the Late Anglo-Saxon State', in W. Pohl and V. Wieser (eds), *Der frühmittelalterliche Staat—europäische Perspektiven* (Vienna, 2009), pp. 507–8.

[12] Compare Reynolds, 'Historiography', pp. 132–3.

[13] For references to literature exploring other comparisons, see below, pp. 237, 238–9.

moral reform, and the deluge of written royal legislation from Alfred to Cnut is widely recognized (thanks above all to Wormald) as a counterpart to the string of capitularies issued by kings from Pippin III (r. 751–768) to Carloman II (r. 879–884).[14] It has also quite frequently been pointed out, especially by Campbell, that some aspects of English royal administration may well have been modelled on Frankish precedents, possible examples including elements of hundredal organization, loyalty oaths, and the allocation to earls of one third of certain royal revenues.[15] Perhaps more important than the likelihood that certain individual practices were transplanted across the Channel, though, is that the political structure of the eleventh-century English kingdom had much in common with that of its ninth-century West Frankish predecessor. In both cases, as we saw in Chapter 5, kings maintained a personal domination over major magnates through coercion and patronage, while also having administrative systems that enabled some degree of routine and impersonal regulation of the behaviour of even fairly ordinary people.[16]

Prior to the mid-tenth century, however, the similarity between the Cerdicings' power and that of ninth-century West Frankish kings was probably somewhat looser. Alfred and his immediate successors (perhaps especially Æthelstan) aspired to emulate the Carolingians, and were able to maintain a reasonable grip on most of their greater subordinates, but probably had rather less capability than Louis the Pious or Charles the Bald to engage directly and routinely with the mass of the population.[17] Indeed, the Cerdicings' position in the late ninth and early tenth centuries may perhaps have been closer to that of the sixth- and seventh-century Visigoths or Merovingians (and perhaps the early Carolingians), the ninth-century East Frankish kings, or the rulers of tenth-century Germany or León. In all of these cases, kings used their considerable wealth to exercise a more or less effective hold

---

[14] P. Wormald, *The Making of English Law: King Alfred to the Twelfth Century. Volume I: Legislation and its Limits* (Oxford, 1999); D. Pratt, *The Political Thought of King Alfred the Great* (Cambridge, 2007). It is interesting that in each case the near-continuous stream of written legislation was of similar duration (i.e. somewhat over a century).

[15] See especially Campbell, 'Observations on English Government', pp. 159–67. Contrast H. Cam, *Local Government in Francia and England: A Comparison of the Local Administration and Jurisdiction of the Carolingian Empire with that of the West Saxon Kingdom* (London, 1912), who was more cautious about the possibility of borrowing from Frankia. See also above, pp. 64, 111 n. 113, 151–2.

[16] Above, pp. 218–20. Such structural resemblances mean that there is much to be said for Campbell's statement that 'late Anglo-Saxon England was a state of what might be called a Carolingian type' (Campbell, 'Epilogue', p. 241), but it should be noted that Carolingian kingdoms varied considerably, with contrasts between East and West Frankia being particularly marked. It might therefore be better to say that the English kingdom and the various Carolingian kingdoms were all 'of patrimonial type', and this would have the added benefit of facilitating a wider range of comparisons. Compare M. Weber, *Economy and Society: An Outline of Interpretive Sociology*, ed. G. Roth and C. Wittich (3 vols, New York, NY, 1968), iii, 1006–110; N. Elias, *The Court Society*, trans. E. Jephcott (Oxford, 1983). Note that a patrimonial society, as characterized by Weber and Elias, can have a significant bureaucratic element.

[17] M. Wood, 'The Making of King Aethelstan's Empire: An English Charlemagne?', in P. Wormald, D. Bullough, and R. Collins (eds), *Ideal and Reality in Frankish and Anglo-Saxon Society: Studies Presented to J. M. Wallace-Hadrill* (Oxford, 1983), pp. 250–72; Wormald, *Making*; Pratt, *Political Thought*.

over the aristocracy, but probably had fewer mechanisms for standardized local administration than the rulers of ninth-century western Frankia.[18]

The differences between the rule of Alfred or Æthelstan and that of Louis or Charles tend to be occluded in broad statements about similarities between the Cerdicings and the Carolingians, and many of the comparisons just suggested have received little or no attention. The historiographical emphasis is not, however, always on common features of the English and West Frankish kingdoms, since it is widely known that there were markedly divergent trends of political change north and south of the Channel between the late ninth and twelfth centuries. Indeed, English historians quite often point out, sometimes with a possible hint of pride, that while the Cerdicings were extending and consolidating their power, and becoming 'more Carolingian than the Carolingians', the West Frankish kingdom itself was fragmenting, with a variety of potentates appropriating former royal rights.[19]

Comparison between the Cerdicings and those ruling in western Frankia has been, and remains, highly fruitful. Indeed, the similarities between Edgar and Æthelred II on the one hand, and Louis the Pious and Charles the Bald on the other, have been an important theme in the last two chapters of this book. But it is problematic that this one comparison is so dominant: it should be supplemented by a much wider range of perspectives, since the disintegration of West Frankish royal power from the late ninth century is not representative of the Continent as a whole, despite its prominence in much of the French and French-inspired literature on Europe in this period.[20] The general narrative of tenth-century fragmentation works reasonably well for much of the Italian kingdom, as well as for large

---

[18] I. N. Wood, *The Merovingian Kingdoms, 450–751* (London, 1994), especially pp. 60–70, 88–101, 118–19, 140, 146–58, 221–38, 261–72; R. Collins, *Visigothic Spain, 409–711* (Oxford, 2004), pp. 38–143 especially 113–16; Wickham, *Framing*, pp. 93–115, 120–4; E. J. Goldberg, *Struggle for Empire: Kingship and Conflict under Louis the German, 817–876* (Ithaca, NY, 2006), especially pp. 186–230; below, pp. 237, 240–1. Visigothic Spain is a particularly interesting comparison: its kings also issued extensive moralizing legislation, and it too succumbed suddenly to external attack. The Carolingian period is often treated as a block, but there are grounds to posit a shift in the nature of royal rule around the turn of the eighth and ninth centuries: it appears to have been from 802 that *missi* were systematically appointed as standing representatives in particular regions, rather than as agents charged with one-off tasks, and from then on Charlemagne's legislation shows an increased focus on the detail of how his commands should be implemented. See K. F. Werner, '*Missus-Marchio-Comes*. Entre l'administration centrale et l'administration locale de l'Empire carolingien', in Paravicini and Werner (eds), *Histoire comparée*, pp. 195–205; R. McKitterick, *Charlemagne: The Formation of a European Identity* (Cambridge, 2008), pp. 213, 233–43, 256–63.

[19] Campbell, 'Epilogue', p. 241 and Wormald, *Making*, p. 483 are two instances where it is hard to avoid suspecting the influence of a certain pride in the perceived precocity of English development. For further discussion, see Campbell, 'Was it Infancy in England?'; P. A. Clarke, *The English Nobility under Edward the Confessor* (Oxford, 1994), pp. 147–52; T. Reuter, 'Debate: The "Feudal Revolution"', *P&P*, 155 (1997), pp. 191–2; C. Wickham, *Problems in Doing Comparative History* (Southampton, 2005), pp. 15–35. Wormald, 'Pre-Modern "State" and "Nation"', p. 184 refers to the Cerdicings as 'plus Carolingien que les Carolingiens'.

[20] The limitations of the Francocentric model are stressed by Reuter, 'Debate: The Feudal Revolution', pp. 187–95; J. L. Nelson, 'Rulers and Government', in *NCMH3*, pp. 95–129 especially 112–13; C. Wickham, *The Inheritance of Rome: A History of Europe from 400 to 1000* (London, 2009), pp. 444, 522–4.

parts of West Frankia.[21] It does not, however, as is increasingly recognized, fit East Frankia: the coercive power of the tenth-century Ottonian kings and emperors was at least as great as that of Louis the German (r. 817–876) had been, and they operated across a wider area, bringing a substantial part of the Italian peninsula under their hegemony.[22] The Ottonians thus resembled, indeed surpassed, the Cerdicings in extending the geographical range of their domination during the tenth century, and even at the start of this period they had a territory much larger than that of their West Saxon counterparts. It is, moreover, now quite well established that there were close contacts between the two dynasties, and similarities in some of the ways in which they ruled. In particular, a fair amount of attention has been devoted to Otto I's marriage to one of Æthelstan's half-sisters, reciprocal intellectual and artistic influences, and parallels in royal itineration, assembly-holding, and (possibly) ritual.[23] Carolingian domination east of the Rhine had, however, been considerably less intensive than in much of West Frankia, and there is little sign that tenth-century Germany saw a transformation in the means of royal rule akin to that (seemingly) effected across the North Sea: while the Ottonians' power over their greater magnates became somewhat more secure as the century progressed, they do not appear to have developed any widespread apparatus to systematize local administration.[24] The general pattern of political change in tenth-century East Frankia was thus rather different from what was then becoming the English kingdom, but neither had a trajectory like that of West Frankia in the same period.

The English Kingdom and 'Outer Europe'

A paradigm based on tenth- and eleventh-century West Frankia is also of little applicability to the contemporaneous history of many areas that had been on or

[21] C. Wickham, *Early Medieval Italy: Central Power and Local Society, 400–1000* (London, 1981), pp. 168–93, as modified by B. Rosenwein, 'The Family Politics of Berengar I, King of Italy (888–924)', *Speculum*, 71 (1996), pp. 247–89. There were some broad similarities in the patterns of change in West Frankia and Italy, but also significant differences: Wickham, *Inheritance*, pp. 435–44.

[22] Reuter, 'Debate: The Feudal Revolution', pp. 189–91 emphasizes differences from West Frankia. See also Reuter, 'Medieval German *Sonderweg?*'; Reuter, 'Nur im Westen was Neues?', and, more generally, T. Reuter, *Germany in the Early Middle Ages, 800–1056* (London, 1991).

[23] R. Deshman, '*Christus rex et magi reges*: Kingship and Christology in Ottonian and Anglo-Saxon Art', *Frühmittelalterliche Studien*, 10 (1976), pp. 367–405; K. J. Leyser, 'The Ottonians and Wessex', in K. J. Leyser, *Communications and Power in Medieval Europe: The Carolingian and Ottonian Centuries*, ed. T. Reuter (London, 1994), pp. 73–104; J. Sarnowsky, 'England und der Kontinent im 10. Jahrhundert', *Historisches Jahrbuch*, 114 (1994), pp. 47–75; T. Reuter, 'The Making of England and Germany, 850–1050: Points of Comparison and Difference', in A. P. Smyth (ed.), *Medieval Europeans: Studies in Ethnic Identity and National Perspectives in Medieval Europe* (Basingstoke, 1998), pp. 53–70; J. Barrow, 'Demonstrative Behaviour and Political Communication in Later Anglo-Saxon England', *ASE*, 36 (2007), pp. 127–50; D. Rollason, C. Leyser, and H. Williams (eds), *England and the Continent in the Tenth Century: Studies in Honour of Wilhelm Levison (1876–1947)* (Turnhout, 2010); L. Roach, 'Penance, Submission and *deditio*: Religious Influences on Dispute Settlement in Later Anglo-Saxon England (871–1066)', *ASE*, 41 (2012), pp. 343–71; L. Roach, *Kingship and Consent in Anglo-Saxon England, 871–978: Assemblies and the State in the Early Middle Ages* (Cambridge, 2013). On itineration, see also above, pp. 52–4.

[24] K. J. Leyser, *Rule and Conflict in an Early Medieval Society: Ottonian Saxony* (Oxford, 1979); K. J. Leyser, 'Ottonian Government', *EHR*, 96 (1981), pp. 721–53; Reuter, 'Making of England and Germany'.

(like the developing English kingdom) beyond the frontiers of the Carolingian empire. In Croatia, Bohemia, Hungary, Poland, Denmark, Norway, Scotland, and northern Iberia, this period saw not fragmentation, but the formation of larger and somewhat more stable political units. The common trend towards more coherent political structures in these areas is identified by Chris Wickham, whose survey of early medieval Europe groups them in a chapter on 'Outer Europe', a term of convenience for those polities situated on or beyond the limits of the former Carolingian empire.[25] Wickham's 'Outer Europe' does not, however, appear to include the English kingdom, which he treats in a separate chapter, entitled ' "Carolingian" England, 800–1000', and there is a similar organizational tactic in the tenth-century volume of the *New Cambridge Medieval History*: there, the territories that had been ruled by the Carolingians, plus the English kingdom, are grouped under the heading 'Post-Carolingian Europe', while the rest of the Continent is branded 'Non-Carolingian Europe'.[26] This latter label is problematic since, as we shall see, the English kingdom was not the only place beyond the Carolingian empire to draw directly or indirectly on its legacy. Indeed, rather than bracketing the English kingdom with the lands that the Carolingians had ruled, it may be more helpful to view it in conjunction with the various parts of Wickham's 'Outer Europe'. This is not to say that the early English kingdom was closely similar to anywhere else, or that the administrative achievements of its kings were matched by contemporary rulers in eastern Europe, Scandinavia, Scotland, or northern Iberia. Rather, my proposition is that the pattern of change in the developing English kingdom was but one manifestation of a general trend towards political consolidation around the fringes of what had been the Carolingian empire.

Comparisons between the English kingdom and certain other places on the peripheries of Latin Europe are not unprecedented, but have tended to focus on cases involving direct connections: in particular, it is relatively well known that various English practices, notably relating to coin production, were emulated in Denmark, Norway, and (somewhat later) Scotland, and that each of these kingdoms exhibited some tendencies towards greater coherence across the period from the tenth century to the twelfth.[27] The parallels between the early English

---

[25] Wickham, *Inheritance*, pp. 472–507. See also R. Bartlett, *The Making of Europe: Conquest, Colonization and Cultural Change, 950–1350* (London, 1993). I use territorial terms such as 'Croatia' and 'Hungary' reluctantly. As with 'England' and 'the English kingdom' (above, p. 6), it would be preferable to refer to 'the Croatian duchy', 'the Hungarian kingdom' and so on; to do this repeatedly would, however, be irritatingly cumbersome.

[26] *NCMH3*, pp. viii–ix; Wickham, *Inheritance*, pp. 453–71.

[27] Campbell, 'Late Anglo-Saxon State', p. 8; G. Williams, 'Hákon *Aðalsteins fóstri*: Aspects of Anglo-Saxon Kingship in Tenth-Century Norway', in T. R. Liszka and L. E. M. Walker (eds), *The North Sea World in the Middle Ages* (Dublin, 2001), pp. 108–26; P. H. Sawyer, 'English Influence on the Development of the Norwegian Kingdom', in S. Keynes and A. P. Smyth (eds), *Anglo-Saxons: Studies Presented to Cyril Roy Hart* (Dublin, 2006), pp. 224–9; G. Williams, 'Kingship, Christianity and Coinage: Monetary and Political Perspectives on Silver Economy in the Viking Age', in J. Graham-Campbell and G. Williams (eds), *Silver Economy in the Viking Age* (Walnut Creek, CA, 2007), pp. 177–214; T. Bolton, *The Empire of Cnut the Great: Conquest and the Consolidation of Power in Northern Europe in the Early Eleventh Century* (Leiden, 2009); A. Taylor, *The Shape of the State in Medieval Scotland, 1124–1290* (forthcoming); below, p. 245. For general surveys, see I. Skovgaard-Petersen, 'The Making of the Danish Kingdom', in K. Helle (ed.), *The Cambridge History of Scandinavia. Volume I: Prehistory to 1520*

kingdom and regions to which it was not geographically proximate have, however, been the subject of very little exploration.[28] It is impractical to undertake a detailed analysis of every part of eastern Europe, northern Iberia, Scandinavia, and Britain here, but there are two specific cases where the potential for comparison with the English kingdom appears particularly promising. The first is the northern Iberian kingdom known successively as Asturias (until 910), León (910–1037), and León-Castile (1037–1157), which expanded considerably in the second half of the ninth century, then largely maintained the resultant territorial gains, before beginning another spurt of growth in the second half of the eleventh.[29] The Astur-Leonese-Castilian and English kingdoms thus shared in a tenth- and eleventh-century trend towards the development of larger political entities, evident in an arc around the former Carolingian lands, but there are certain respects in which these two polities can be jointly contrasted with most parts of Scandinavia and eastern Europe. For one thing, their territories had been within the Roman empire, unlike the lands west and north of the Rhine and Danube.[30] This difference is, however, less significant than it may at first sight appear, since continuity into the medieval period of Romanized political, social, or economic structures appears to have been limited in northern Iberia and (even more so) Britain; indeed, the absence of a pervasive Roman legacy in Britain, northern Iberia, and the rest of Wickham's 'Outer Europe' is a feature that distinguishes all of these regions from Italy and West Frankia.[31] There are, however, other respects in which the Astur-Leonese-Castilian and English kingdoms were distinctive. Perhaps most significantly, the Cerdicings and the Asturian kings had been enlarging their territories and consolidating their positions for a considerable time by the tenth century, when the likes of Hungary, Poland, and Norway first began to develop as kingdoms. Similarly, Wessex and northern Iberia had long been Christian by the tenth century, again in contrast to most of Scandinavia and eastern Europe. Furthermore, in both the English and Spanish cases expansion took place partly at the expense of non-Christian rivals, in what

(Cambridge, 2003), pp. 168–83; I. Skovgaard-Petersen, 'The Danish Kingdom: Consolidation and Disintegration', in Helle (ed.), *Cambridge History of Scandinavia*, pp. 353–62; A. Woolf, *From Pictland to Alba, 789–1070* (Edinburgh, 2007); S. Bagge, *From Viking Stronghold to Christian Kingdom: State Formation in Norway, c.900–1350* (Copenhagen, 2010); R. Oram, *Domination and Lordship: Scotland, 1070–1230* (Edinburgh, 2011).

[28] Exceptions focus on northern Iberia: R. A. Fletcher, *Saint James's Catapult: The Life and Times of Diego Gelmírez of Santiago de Compostela* (Oxford, 1984), pp. 73–7; I. Álvarez Borge, *Comunidades locales y transformaciones sociales en la Alta Edad Media: Hampshire (Wessex) y el sur de Castilla, un estudio comparativo* (Logroño, 1999); Nelson, 'Rulers and Government', pp. 104, 106, 112, 114; Wickham, *Inheritance*, pp. 502, 504–5, 556.

[29] R. Collins, *Early Medieval Spain: Unity in Diversity, 400–1000*, 2nd edn (Basingstoke, 1995), pp. 222–45; R. Collins, 'The Spanish Kingdoms', in *NCMH3*, pp. 670–87; A. Isla Frez, *La Alta Edad Media. Siglos VIII–XI* (Madrid, 2002), pp. 13–40, 87–114; S. Barton, 'Spain in the Eleventh Century', in *NCMH4*, ii, 154–90.

[30] Wickham, *Inheritance*, pp. xiv–xv provides a map of the Roman empire.

[31] Wickham, *Framing*, pp. 227–32, 303–39, especially 338–9. There is debate about the extent to which Roman influence endured, especially in northern Iberia, but it is clear that there was a marked contrast with Italy and West Frankia.

is traditionally, but problematically, referred to as a 'reconquest'.[32] Thus, while one can group the Astur-Leonese-Castilian and English kingdoms with other polities around the edges of Latin Europe that were also expanded and consolidated in the tenth and eleventh centuries, these two regnal units are distinguished by sufficient common features that they may be treated as constituents of a subcategory.[33]

Turning from general similarities to the specific question of how the Astur-Leonese-Castilian kings ruled, detailed comparison with the Cerdicings is hampered by imbalances in the available evidence. On the English side, we have sizeable corpora of both legislation and charters, but few texts which contain much narrative. In tenth-century northern Iberia, on the other hand, there are numerous charters, which commonly incorporate substantial narrative sections, but kings do not appear to have issued written legislation; this probably reflects, at least in part, that they were less influenced than the Cerdicings by Carolingian models, instead drawing inspiration from the Visigoths, whose laws continued to be invoked.[34] Whatever the reasons for the evidential contrast, though, the difference poses interpretive problems, since an abundance of legislation often tempts historians to posit neat institutional structures, while narratives of specific events reveal the heterogeneity of actual practice. If we allow for the different kinds of evidence at our disposal, however, there is a reasonable likelihood that tenth-century Astur-Leonese kings' power was broadly similar in nature to that of Edward the Elder or Æthelstan, as analysed in Chapters 2 and 3 of this volume: there is little sign that rulers in northern Iberia had much capability to regulate routinely the conduct of ordinary people, but they were able to manipulate great magnates through land grants and confiscations, and sought to co-opt aristocratic strength by conferring the title of count on men who were already powerful.[35] As the tenth century progressed,

---

[32] R. A. Fletcher, 'Reconquest and Crusade in Spain, *c.*1050–1150', *TRHS*, 5th series, 37 (1987), pp. 31–47; above, p. 9, although Fernández-Armesto, 'Survival' seeks to rehabilitate the term.

[33] The Croatian duchy and the Scottish kingdom could potentially be added to this subcategory: they were reasonably coherent Christian entities by the second half of the ninth century, and the latter may have been similar in structure to the earlier Pictish kingdom. The Balkans had been within the Roman empire, but do not appear to have seen much structural continuity into the medieval period, and northern Britain had only ever been under loose Roman domination. For overviews, see F. Curta, *Southeastern Europe in the Middle Ages, 500–1250* (Cambridge, 2006), especially pp. 134–45; Woolf, *From Pictland to Alba*, especially pp. 312–50. There had been a fairly well-established (but only minimally Christian) Danish kingdom in the early ninth century, although the power of its kings may then have weakened seriously, before being reasserted from the middle of the tenth: B. Sawyer and P. H. Sawyer, *Medieval Scandinavia: From Conversion to Reformation circa 800–1500* (Minneapolis, MN, 1993), pp. 49–58, 100–2; Skovgaard-Petersen, 'Making of the Danish Kingdom'.

[34] R. Collins, '"*Sicut lex Gothorum continet*": Law and Charters in Ninth- and Tenth-Century León and Catalonia', *EHR*, 100 (1985), pp. 489–512; T. Deswarte, *De la destruction à la restauration. L'idéologie du royaume d'Oviedo-León (VIIIᵉ–XIᵉ siècles)* (Turnhout, 2003), but note Collins, *Early Medieval Spain*, pp. 229–30, 233 on Carolingian connections.

[35] Isla Frez, *Alta Edad Media*, pp. 137–93; S. Castellanos and I. Martín Viso, 'The Local Articulation of Central Power in the North of the Iberian Peninsula (500–1000)', *EME*, 13 (2005), pp. 19–42; W. Davies, *Acts of Giving: Individual, Community, and Church in Tenth-Century Christian Spain* (Oxford, 2007), especially pp. 14–16; Wickham, *Inheritance*, pp. 500–5; R. Portass, 'The Contours and Contexts of Public Power in Tenth-Century Liébana', *Journal of Medieval History*, 38 (2012), pp. 389–407; R. Portass, 'All Quiet on the Western Front? Royal Politics in Galicia from *c.*800 to *c.*950', *EME*, 21 (2013), pp. 283–306. Like English ealdormen (above, p. 112), Iberian counts were far from reliably pliant royal agents.

however, there probably came to be more pronounced differences in royal rule between the two kingdoms, as northern Iberia does not appear to have undergone major administrative changes like those which the Cerdicings seem to have wrought. There may have been some gradual increase in the capability of Astur-Leonese-Castilian kings to shape local practice, since there was a tendency for their charters to specify more closely what rights a grant included, and the inhabitants of certain places began to obtain written royal guarantees of their customs and privileges (*fueros*); as with English writ-charters, relatively precise royal statements about who was to enjoy what rights could reflect that kings were becoming more, not less, able to intervene in such matters.[36] Even at the end of the eleventh century, however, there is no reason to think that the kings of León-Castile had at their disposal a standardized administrative framework analogous to that constructed between the Channel and the Tees, and it is notable that they do not seem to have had coins minted (except perhaps on a very small scale) until the reign of Alfonso VI (r. 1065–1109).[37] There were thus important contrasts between the English and Astur-Leonese-Castilian kingdoms, but they nonetheless display certain broad similarities: the Cerdicings were not the only Christian dynasty in the peripheries of Latin Europe for which the period from the late ninth to the eleventh century was a time of expansion and consolidation.

The second case that offers especially interesting points for comparison is Hungary. At first sight, its development looks quite different from the English kingdom: in the mid-950s, when the Cerdicings had just gained what turned out to be lasting power at York, the Hungarians or Magyars were still heathen nomads raiding Germany and Italy, and they were decisively defeated by Otto I in 955. It was only in the late tenth and early eleventh centuries that a coherent and settled Hungarian kingdom began to take shape, with Géza (r. 971–997) and then István I (r. 997–1038), members of a dynasty known as the Árpáds, suppressing their internal enemies and introducing Christianity.[38] The particular interest of the comparison with the English situation arises because we have a fairly substantial body of written legislation issued by István and his successors. The corpus of their decrees is smaller than that for kings from Alfred to Cnut, but both English and Hungarian rulers showed particular concern with theft and conformity to Christian norms, and in each case there was a trend towards increasing specificity about the methods by

[36] Collins, *Early Medieval Spain*, pp. 244–5; W. Davies, 'Lordship and Community: Northern Spain on the Eve of the Year 1000', in C. Dyer, P. Coss, and C. Wickham (eds), *Rodney Hilton's Middle Ages: An Exploration of Historical Themes* (Oxford, 2007), pp. 24–5, 32; above, pp. 168–9.

[37] B. F. Reilly, *The Kingdom of León-Castilla under King Alfonso VI (1065–1109)* (Princeton, NJ, 1988), pp. 369–75; M. Crusafont, A. M. Balaguer, and P. Grierson, *Medieval European Coinage with a Catalogue of the Coins in the Fitzwilliam Museum, Cambridge. 6: The Iberian Peninsula* (Cambridge, 2013), pp. 209–25. Minting may have begun under Ferdinand I (r. 1037–1065), but the lack of surviving coins from his reign (with one possible exception) implies that the volume of any such output was low.

[38] K. Bakay, 'Hungary', in *NCMH3*, pp. 536–52; N. Berend, 'Hungary in the Eleventh and Twelfth Centuries', in *NCMH4*, ii, 304–16; N. Berend, J. Laszlovszky, and B. Zsolt Szakács, 'The Kingdom of Hungary', in N. Berend (ed.), *Christianisation and the Rise of Christian Monarchy: Scandinavia, Central Europe and Rus' c.900–1200* (Cambridge, 2007), pp. 319–68.

which royal injunctions were to be implemented.[39] General resemblances of this sort could be coincidental, or wholly unconnected responses to common circumstances, but such explanations become more strained when we turn to matters of detail, where three particular points stand out. First, there are repeated references in the Árpáds' legislation to *comites* ('counts') being allocated one third of various sources of royal income, presumably to incentivize them to collect revenues for the king, an obvious parallel with the earl's third share documented in Domesday.[40] Second, there appears to have been a separation between the personal possessions of a Hungarian *comes* and those which he held by virtue of his office, since the decrees ascribed to István state that:

> every person while living should have lordship [*dominetur*] of his own possessions [*propriorum*] and likewise of gifts of the king [*donorum regis*], except that which pertains to an episcopal and comital position [*ad episcopatum pertinet et comitatum*], and after his life his sons should succeed to similar lordship [*simili dominio succedant*].[41]

Much the same distinction probably applied in the English kingdom, since there are strong grounds to infer that earls' wealth, and hence their ability to enforce royal commands, derived in part from *ex officio* tenure of certain estates.[42] The third comparison arises from a passage in the legislation attributed to László I (r. 1077–1095), which commands that the king's messenger ('nuntius regis') should proceed to all the *civitates* (which means something like 'towns' or 'strongholds'), and there assemble the *centuriones* and *decuriones* of the *ewrii* (which means something like 'guards'), together with those committed to them. Those assembled were to be ordered to denounce thieves, who were then to be put to the ordeal; if any village was infamous for theft, its inhabitants were to be divided into groups of ten, with one representative undergoing the ordeal on behalf of the other nine. The messenger was also to announce that 'the magnates of all Hungary' ('totius Hungarie principes') had sworn not to aid thieves; to instruct the people of each village to make an equivalent oath; and to declare that any person detained since the time of 'the *descriptio* [survey] of judge Sarkas' should be presented to the king.[43] All of

---

[39] These observations are based on 'Decreta S. Stephani regis', 'Decreta S. Ladislai regis', 'Decretum Colomani regis', 'Constitutiones synodi in civitate Zabolch 20 Maii 1092', 'Decreta synodorum habitorum sub Colomanno rege', and 'Capitula Colomanni regis de iudeis', all edited in *The Laws of the Medieval Kingdom of Hungary. Volume 1: 1000–1301*, ed. J. M. Bak, G. Bónis, J. Ross Sweeney, and L. S. Domonkos, 2nd edn (Idyllwild, CA, 1999). In certain cases, decrees may have been issued (at least in the first instance) by a king other than the one to whom they are ascribed, but this does not fundamentally affect my arguments: *Laws*, ed. Bak et al., pp. 78, 83, 123–4.

[40] 'Decreta S. Stephani regis', ii.5; 'Decreta S. Ladislai regis', iii.13, iii.20; 'Decretum Colomani regis', 25, 78. Note also 'Decreta S. Ladislai regis', iii.27. For the English evidence, see above, p. 111 n. 113. Hungarian writers usually translate *comes* as *ispán*.

[41] 'Decreta S. Stephani regis', ii.2. It is interesting that this declaration was made after 'a petition of the whole council [*senatus*]', since confirmation of inheritance rights in response to a petition presents a possible parallel to Cnut's mitigatory legislation: II Cn 70–1, 78–9; above, pp. 220–2.

[42] See the literature cited above at p. 66 n. 84.

[43] 'Decreta S. Ladislai regis', iii.1–iii.2. Sarkas's *descriptio* is not extant, but it seems that it had included a record of royal dependants, and that any of them who had been removed from the king's service were now to be returned. 'Decreta S. Ladislai regis', ii.17 uses 'ewrii' to render 'custodes...confiniorum' ('guards of the frontiers').

this raises some very striking possible parallels with the English kingdom. For one thing, the Hungarian *decuriones* and *centuriones* may have been analogous to the tithingmen and hundredmen of the Hundred Ordinance, or to the leaders of ten- and 100-person bodies in the London peace regulations.[44] Likewise, the grouping of villagers into tens is reminiscent of the frankpledge system, and the oath concerning theft is closely similar to that which Cnut prescribed.[45] Perhaps most tantalizing of all, however, Sarkas's now-lost *descriptio* (the nature of which is uncertain) seems to have been sufficiently important and widely known to serve as a landmark in the past: in this respect at least, it appears to have resembled Domesday, the *descriptio totius Anglie*.[46]

It is not out of the question that one way in which the English and Hungarian kingdoms came to share certain characteristics was through direct borrowing between them: possible conduits for information include Edward *ætheling* (a son of Edmund Ironside whom Cnut exiled to Hungary) or people travelling to or from the Holy Land, although there is no evidence that legal texts from either kingdom were available in the other.[47] Probably more important as an explanation, however, is that similarities could have arisen because the Cerdicings and the Árpáds drew independently on the same Carolingian inheritance: Frankish *comites* received one third of certain royal revenues; the Carolingians' legislation contains a scattering of references to local figures known as *centenarii*; Charles the Bald sought to have his subordinates swear oaths abjuring theft; and it was on the basis of a *descriptio* of what had been Louis the Pious's lands that his sons established the partition of 843.[48] The last Carolingian king died in 987, ten years before István came to power, but both Hungarian and English rulers could have drawn on the Carolingians' example well after that dynasty's ninth-century heyday. For one thing, arrangements established or used by the Carolingians may well have outlasted them; thus, for example, there are occasional references to *centenae* and *centenarii* in eleventh-century and later sources, although the meanings of these terms

---

[44] VI As 3, 8.1; Hu 2, 4, 5; above, pp. 113–14, 144–5.   [45] II Cn 21; above, pp. 195–6.

[46] Above, p. 4. The parallels pointed out here are not exhaustive: others include attempts to require trade to take place in particular locations in the presence of particular people ('Decreta S. Ladislai regis', ii.7—compare above, pp. 106–9, 122), a restriction on the sale of horses outside the kingdom ('Decreta S. Ladislai regis', ii.15–ii.18; 'Decretum Colomani regis', 76—compare II As 18), the allocation of one third of forfeited property to the dependants of the person from whom it had been confiscated ('Decreta S. Ladislai regis', ii.8, ii.11; 'Decretum Colomani regis', 77—compare VI As 1.1), the use of a royal seal to initiate judicial procedures ('Constitutiones synodi in civitate Zabolch 20 Maii 1092', 42—compare above, p. 168 n. 229), and those discussed below at pp. 244–5.

[47] *ASC* D 1057, E 1096; John of Worcester, *Chronicle*, 1058, ed. and trans. R. R. Darlington, P. McGurk, and J. Bray (2 vols so far, Oxford, 1995–), ii, 584.

[48] *CRF*, nos. 20 (c. 19), 25 (c. 4), 33 (cc. 13, 25, 28, 39, 40), 44 (c. 12), 50 (cc. 3, 7), 60 (c. 3), 61 (c. 11), 64 (c. 3), 65 (c. 15), 73 (cc. 2, 3), 74 (c. 2), 77 (c. 5), 78 (c. 22), 80 (c. 4), 86 (c. 2, 4), 95 (c. 5), 97, 99 (c. 6), 103, 141 (cc. 14, 19, 20, 21), 152, 156 (c. 3), 192 (c. 10), 193 (c. 5), 260 (c. 4 and oath formulae on p. 274); F. L. Ganshof, 'On the Genesis and Significance of the Treaty of Verdun (843)', in F. L. Ganshof, *The Carolingians and the Frankish Monarchy*, trans. J. Sondheimer (London, 1971), pp. 289–302; S. Baxter, *The Earls of Mercia: Lordship and Power in Late Anglo-Saxon England* (Oxford, 2007), pp. 89–90. See also R. H. C. Davis, 'Domesday Book: Continental Parallels', in J. C. Holt (ed.), *Domesday Studies: Papers Read at the Novocentenary Conference of the Royal Historical Society and the Institute of British Geographers, Winchester, 1986* (Woodbridge, 1987), pp. 15–39.

are far from clear.[49] Even if practices used by the Carolingians rapidly fell into desuetude, however, both English and Hungarian kings (and their respective advisers) could have been inspired to emulate them through knowledge of texts in which they were mentioned or described: manuscripts containing Carolingian ordinances (or extracts therefrom) were available north of the Channel, and the Árpáds' legislation includes many echoes which indicate familiarity with Frankish legal sources.[50] The question of how the similarities between English and Hungarian legislation arose is not, however, crucial here: more important is that the Cerdicings were not the only rulers on or beyond the peripheries of the former Carolingian empire to make use of Carolingian-style practices in the tenth and eleventh centuries.

By the turn of the eleventh and twelfth centuries, the Árpáds may even have developed structures of local administration at least loosely analogous to those used by Edgar and his successors. The legislation ascribed to László's successor Kálmán (r. 1095–1116) stipulated that in every bishopric there should be twice annual assemblies, attended by the bishop and one or more *comites*: this is reminiscent of Edgar's and Cnut's orders that each year two shire meetings be held in the presence of a bishop and an ealdorman, and it appears that these Hungarian assemblies were similarly intended (at least in part) to handle judicial business, since it was stated that anyone neglecting a summons to one would be deemed guilty.[51] Perhaps even more interestingly, however, the same set of decrees declared that before Michaelmas each *comes* should send to Esztergom (the seat of the kingdom's principal archbishopric) the pennies 'which are collected throughout all parts of Hungary [*per universas Hungarie partes*]', noting how much had been obtained from each *centurionatus*.[52] This appears to refer to a system of kingdom-wide taxation, organized on the basis of a unit whose name was the Latin equivalent of 'hundred'.[53] There is too little evidence to ascertain how far a Hungarian *centurionatus* resembled an English hundred, or to assess the extent to which these various commands were implemented. It is, however, extremely interesting that the composition of coin hoards raises the possibility that King Solomon (r. 1063–1074) sought to increase the

[49] Ch.-E. Perrin, 'Sur le sens du mot «centena» dans les chartes lorraines du moyen âge', *Archivum Latinitatis Medii Aevi*, 5 (1930), pp. 167–98; L. Génicot, 'La *centena* et le *centenarius* dans les sources «belges» antérieures à 1200', in E. Magnou-Nortier (ed.), *Aux sources de la gestion publique. Tome I. Enquête lexicographique sur fundus, villa, domus, mansus* (Lille, 1993), pp. 85–102.

[50] F. Schiller, 'Das erste ungarische Gesetzbuch und das deutsche Recht', in *Festschrift Heinrich Brunner zum siebzigsten Geburtstag dargebract von Schülern und Verehrern* (Weimar, 1910), pp. 379–404; H. Gneuss, *Handlist of Anglo-Saxon Manuscripts: A List of Manuscripts and Manuscript Fragments Written or Owned in England up to 1100* (Tempe, AZ, 2001), nos. 29, 41, 73, 363, 379, 440, 592, 629, 879, 896, 922, 925, 926. The notes in *Laws*, ed. Bak et al. detail borrowings from elsewhere. It is particularly notable that Archbishop Wulfstan II of York appears to have annotated a copy of part of Ansegisus's capitulary collection: N. R. Ker, 'The Handwriting of Archbishop Wulfstan', in P. Clemoes and K. Hughes (eds), *England before the Conquest: Studies in Primary Sources Presented to Dorothy Whitelock* (Cambridge, 1971), pp. 328–30.

[51] 'Decretum Colomani regis', 2; III Eg 5.1–5.2; II Cn 18–18.1. For maps of Hungarian bishoprics, see Berend et al., 'Kingdom of Hungary', pp. 332, 342. Many of these bishoprics were larger than most English shires, but the procedural resemblance is still notable.

[52] 'Decretum Colomani regis', 79.

[53] For the use of hundreds and wapentakes to collect tax, see above, pp. 143, 165, 185.

uniformity of the circulating currency, and that László may have taken this further: these conclusions are not clear-cut, but, given the significance widely attached to the English numismatic evidence, we should be very wary of supposing that the Árpáds' legislation was a dead letter, or that they were incapable of regulating the conduct of ordinary people, at least from the late eleventh century.[54]

In a similar vein, it is notable that from the second half of the eleventh century Danish and Norwegian kings appear to have made some moves to homogenize the currencies circulating in their respective kingdoms, and that Polish rulers began to do likewise in the twelfth.[55] When considering tenth- and eleventh-century Denmark, Norway, and Poland, we are confronted with a near-absence of contemporary texts, but this need not mean that kings in these areas ruled in markedly different ways from their Hungarian counterparts.[56] In particular, it is important to bear in mind that they may well have issued decrees of which no record has survived, perhaps because they were never written down at all. Such observations are, however, no more than speculations, and it is possible that the paucity of tenth- and eleventh-century texts from most parts of eastern Europe and Scandinavia reflects that kings in these regions had only the most rudimentary of administrative systems at their disposal. Nonetheless, when one considers that at the turn of the ninth and tenth centuries there is little sign of any stable centralized power in (what would become) Hungary, Bohemia, Poland, Denmark, and Norway, it is arguable that the transformations that these places underwent between *c.*900 and *c.*1100 were even more profound than those effected by kings from Alfred to the Norman Conquest.[57] The basic point, however, is that during the tenth and eleventh centuries there was a trend towards the development of larger, more stable, and more centralized political units in many regions that had been on or beyond the fringes of the Carolingian empire. The formation of the English kingdom was thus part of a wider pattern of change, not an anomalous divergence from the increasing fragmentation of royal power in West Frankia and Italy.

The Durability of the English Kingdom

The kingdom to which Alfred succeeded in 871 was in important respects quite different from that which was then ruled by Charles the Bald: the former kingdom

---

[54] L. Kovács, 'A kora Árpad-kori pénzújításról', *Századok*, 130 (1996), pp. 823–60. I have relied on the English summary at 859–60. Minting had begun during István's reign.

[55] S. Suchodolski, 'Renovatio Monetae in Poland in the 12th Century', *Wiadomości Numizmatyczne*, supplement to vol. 5 (1961), pp. 57–75; S. H. Gullbekk, 'Renovatio monetae i Norge i middelalderen', *Nordisk Numismatisk Årsskrift* (1992–3), pp. 52–87; S. H. Gullbekk, 'Myntforringelse i Danmark og innføring av monopolmynt under Sven Estridsen (1047–74)', *Nordisk Numismatisk Årsskrift* (1994–6), pp. 111–29; J. Steen Jensen, 'Møntfornyelse (*Renovatio monetae*) i Danmark indtil år 1200', *Nordisk Numismatisk Unions Medlemsblad* (1996), pp. 130–6.

[56] A near-absence of contemporary texts is quite different from the situation in the kingdom of Edward the Elder and Æthelstan, from which extant legislation is relatively extensive, but says nothing about hundreds or wapentakes: above, pp. 144–6, 153–4.

[57] Sawyer and Sawyer, *Medieval Scandinavia*, pp. 54–8; J. Strzelczyk, 'Bohemia and Poland: Two Examples of Successful Western Slavonic State-Formation', in *NCMH3*, pp. 514–35; Skovgaard-Petersen, 'Making of the Danish Kingdom'; Bagge, *From Viking Stronghold to Christian Kingdom*.

was much smaller; probably had fewer standardized structures through which its king could seek to regulate routinely what happened at a local level; and had yet to see a major efflorescence of interest in either Benedictine monasticism or the restraint of royal arbitrariness. Given that there were substantial differences between the two kingdoms in 871, it is hardly surprising that they witnessed contrasting patterns of change during the period that followed. Somewhat more interesting is that, while the kingdom of Alfred and his successors underwent many developments similar to those which had taken place south of the Channel a century or two before, it did not go on to experience a prolonged and fundamental collapse in royal power, like that which occurred in West Frankia from the latter part of the ninth century until the twelfth. Indeed, the similarities between ninth-century West Frankia and the eleventh-century English kingdom sometimes appear to have made historians feel that the latter ought to have disintegrated too, and that some peculiar feature must be found to account for why it did not.[58] There are, however, various potential explanations, and there is no reason to fixate on one to the exclusion of others. An obvious first consideration is size: the eleventh-century English kingdom was smaller than West Frankia, and in consequence somewhat less difficult to control.[59] Another fairly simple point is that expropriation after the conquests of 1016 and (especially) 1066 forestalled trends towards the entrenchment of greater aristocrats, who might otherwise have begun to develop territorial principalities like those that formed south of the Channel.[60] A third possibility, plausible but unprovable, is that the Cerdicings may well have held a much greater proportion of the land in the English kingdom than the Carolingians had done in West Frankia; if so, this would have given the former more room for manoeuvre in securing and maintaining aristocratic loyalty.[61]

Furthermore, disputes between those seeking the English (previously West Saxon) throne were resolved decisively and fairly quickly, at least before the death of William the Conqueror: the splits or contested successions of 855–860, 899–903, 924, 957–959, 975–978, 1016, 1035–1040, and 1066 each lasted no more than a few years, often because one or more disputants soon died.[62] This is significant, since prolonged succession disputes could lead to contenders for the throne conceding royal lands and rights in efforts to buy support. Indeed, a major reason for the disintegration of West Frankish royal power is that after 887 there was a century of uncertainty about the royal succession: magnates could to a significant extent choose between the Carolingian and Capetian lines when deciding whom to recognize as king, and royal resources were dissipated in the resultant competition to gain and retain aristocratic loyalty.[63] The swift resolution of English succession disputes is therefore a matter of considerable importance, and one reason why the kingdom endured was

---

[58] Wormald, '*Engla Lond*', pp. 369–71 is a particularly clear example.

[59] Nelson, 'Rulers and Government', p. 105 is one of many to note this contrast.

[60] D. Bates, 'England and the «Feudal Revolution»', *Settimane di studio del centro italiano di studi sull'alto medioevo*, 47 (2000), pp. 617–19, 647–8; Wickham, *Problems*, pp. 27–8, 34. Compare Wormald, '*Engla Lond*', p. 370.

[61] Wickham, *Inheritance*, pp. 470–1. On the scale of Cerdicing landholding, see above, pp. 83–4.

[62] Above, pp. 16–18, 27, 29, 33–4, 35, 36, 37–8.

[63] J. Dunbabin, *France in the Making, 843–1180*, 2nd edn (Oxford, 2000), pp. 27–37.

because many members of its ruling families did not. These deaths may often have been fortuitous, but several kings or potential kings are known to have died otherwise than from natural causes; it is therefore significant that during the late Anglo-Saxon period the English appear to have been considerably more willing than their East or West Frankish contemporaries to kill members of their ruling dynasties.[64] It is also interesting that, whether by chance or by design, only six of the twelve Cerdicing kings who died between 899 and 1066 are known to have fathered children: this low fertility rate will have minimized the number of disappointed members of the royal dynasty, reducing the risk of damaging succession disputes.[65]

The importance of dynastic stability is underlined when one thinks about the English kingdom in relation to other regions that had likewise been outwith the Carolingian empire, and this comparison also highlights that the prolonged collapse in West Frankish royal power should not be taken as paradigmatic. In most parts of eastern Europe, Scandinavia, Britain, and northern Iberia, there were periods in or after the eleventh century when power became more fragmented, often in the wake of a contested royal succession. The English kingdom was no exception: the dispute between Stephen and Matilda (plus the future Henry II) that followed Henry I's death in 1135 saw barons appropriating royal rights and building castles, much as West Frankish magnates had been doing for over a century, although in the English case the trend was swiftly reversed after Henry II's accession in 1154.[66] In some places, there were significantly longer breakdowns in royal power. Thus, for example, the Polish kingdom was divided on Bolesław III's death in 1138, and there were then nearly two centuries of struggles between his descendants, who made numerous concessions to try to secure magnates' support.[67] The English kingdom was not, however, alone in escaping such lengthy eras of attenuated royal power: one can, for instance, point to Hungary, Norway, and Scotland, each of which saw significant periods of internal discord and royal weakness, without going the way of West Frankia in the longer term.[68] There is, moreover, again

[64] Above, pp. 27, 29–30, 34, 36, and contrast Leyser, *Rule and Conflict*, pp. 85–7, 106; J. G. Busch, 'Vom Attentat zur Haft. Die Behandlung von Konkurrenten und Opponenten der frühen Karolinger', *Historische Zeitschrift*, 263 (1996), pp. 561–88.

[65] Alfred, Edward the Elder, Edmund, Edgar, Æthelred II, and Edmund Ironside had children; Ælfweard, Æthelstan, Eadred, Eadwig, Edward the Martyr, and Edward the Confessor are not known to have done so. Of the four kings from Swein's family, two or three are known to have had children (Swein, Cnut, and possibly Harold Harefoot (see W. H. Stevenson, 'An Alleged Son of King Harold Harefoot', *EHR*, 28 (1913), pp. 112–17), but not Harthacnut). Nelson, 'Rulers and Government', p. 104 suggests that Æthelstan may have avoided fathering (or at least acknowledging) children in order to ease the succession of his half-brother, Edmund.

[66] G. J. White, *Restoration and Reform, 1153–1165: Recovery from Civil War in England* (Cambridge, 2000). The similarities between Stephen's reign and what had long been happening in West Frankia are examined by Campbell, 'Was it Infancy in England?', pp. 187–8; T. N. Bisson, *The Crisis of the Twelfth Century: Power, Lordship, and the Origins of European Government* (Princeton, NJ, 2009), especially pp. 60–2, 269–78.

[67] J. Lukowski and H. Zawadzki, *A Concise History of Poland*, 2nd edn (Cambridge, 2006), pp. 10–21.

[68] For surveys, see M. Molnár, *A Concise History of Hungary*, trans. A. Magyar (Cambridge, 2001); J. Wormald (ed.), *Scotland: A History* (Oxford, 2005); Bagge, *From Viking Stronghold to Christian Kingdom*. The constitutional crises of the thirteenth-century Hungarian and English kingdoms have some similarities.

an interesting comparison with León-Castile, where, as in the English kingdom, the first half of the twelfth century witnessed a serious diminution of royal power in the context of a succession dispute involving a female contender: many rights passed into aristocratic hands as Urraca and her estranged husband (Alfonso I of Aragon) competed for support between 1110 and 1117, and the Leonese-Castilian monarchy's hold on Portugal was so undermined that it soon became a separate kingdom. But, as in the English kingdom, the fragmentation of power in León-Castile's core territory was not especially prolonged, with some measure of cohesion being restored in the latter part of Urraca's reign, and under her son, Alfonso VII (r. 1126–1157).[69] Thus, when one broadens one's range of comparisons, the English kingdom appears far from anomalous in failing to splinter (except temporarily) along West Frankish lines. This does not, however, mean that what happened in West Frankia was an 'exception', especially given its similarities with Italy: there was no single standard path of political change across ninth-, tenth-, and eleventh-century Latin Europe.[70]

Final Observations

In arguing against the idea that the early English kingdom's development was exceptional, my claim is neither that it was very closely similar to anywhere else, nor that everywhere around the edges of Latin Europe was the same: such propositions would be at best simplistic, and probably downright wrong. Rather, my contention is that the general trajectories of political change in several regions on or beyond the frontiers of the former Carolingian empire, including the English kingdom, had sufficient shared features during the tenth and eleventh centuries that they can collectively be contrasted with what took place in many parts of West Frankia and Italy. Further, several of the political units on Latin Europe's peripheries had enough in common that it would be worth comparing them in detail to identify more precisely how and why they differed: the point of comparative history is to isolate and explain contrasts between phenomena that are in some important respects alike, not just to remark on similarity. Comparative analysis might, for example, permit the construction and testing of hypotheses about links between economic and political change, or about the reasons why there were prolonged fragmentations of power in some polities, but not in others. A serious comparative treatment would, however, need to be founded on detailed study of each part of eastern Europe, Scandinavia, Britain, and northern Iberia in its own right; it cannot simply be a coda to a book about the formation of the English kingdom. For now, it is enough to recognize that lowland southern Britain was not alone in

---

[69] P. Linehan, 'Spain in the Twelfth Century', in *NCMH4*, ii, 475–509; Bisson, *Crisis*, pp. 243–59. There was further discord after Alfonso VII's death, when one of his sons received Castile and the other León, but this did not precipitate a thoroughgoing collapse in royal power in either of the resultant kingdoms, which were rejoined from 1230. There is also a potential comparison to León in the late tenth century, for which see Collins, *Early Medieval Spain*, pp. 239–40; Collins, 'Spanish Kingdoms', pp. 681–6. Note too Portass, 'Contours and Contexts'.

[70] On Italy, see the literature cited above at p. 237 n. 21.

developing quite differently from much of West Frankia and Italy during the late ninth and subsequent centuries. Hence, while the English kingdom was unique, so, too, was each of its contemporaries. It is consequently very problematic to see this period in terms of any variety of exceptionalism: there was no Europe-wide norm from which a political entity could diverge.[71]

In the context of the early twenty-first century, when many on the British (and especially English) political right (and a few on the left) are deeply antipathetic towards institutions based in Brussels, it may not be too hard to persuade at least some of those tempted by exceptionalist notions that the early English kingdom should instead be seen as part of something labelled 'Outer Europe'. But if scepticism about the European Union is not enough to make this proposition palatable, there is another consideration that could prompt a change of tune: claims about the supposedly exceptional nature of English historical development might hold less appeal if it were appreciated that they rest on, and perhaps even help to perpetuate, a historiographical paradigm from France, of all places. English historians are right to react against those French scholars who treat West Frankia as typical, but any inference that the different pattern of historical development north of the Channel made the English kingdom exceptional implicitly accepts the claim (or assumption) that France's path was the norm. Propositions about French typicality and English exceptionalism are thus complementary, indeed mutually reinforcing, but both are flawed, at least with respect to the political trends of the late ninth, tenth, and eleventh centuries. There were many parts of Europe where developments during this period were quite different from those seen in West Frankia. What was in the process of becoming the English kingdom was one such region, and in the late tenth and eleventh centuries its rulers were probably more able than any of their counterparts elsewhere in Latin Europe to regulate routinely the conduct of the mass of the population under their domination. This does not, however, make the English kingdom an exception to some otherwise general common standard. Indeed, the broad trajectory of its development looks far from extraordinary if one widens one's gaze beyond the former Carolingian lands: the formation of the English kingdom was part of a wider pattern of ninth-, tenth-, and eleventh-century political consolidation around the peripheries of Latin Europe.

---

[71] Compare S. Reynolds, *Kingdoms and Communities in Western Europe, 900–1300*, 2nd edn (Oxford, 1997), p. 8, who criticizes the assumption that the Continent was 'the territory of that amorphous mass of foreigners who are all fundamentally much more like each other than they are like Us'. It would be rash to assert that there has never been an era in which any aspect of English historical development was exceptional, but my arguments may be applicable in certain other contexts for which exceptionalist claims have been made. One possible case is the avowedly exceptionalist view of English parliaments offered by J. R. Maddicott, *The Origins of the English Parliament, 924–1327* (Oxford, 2010), pp. 376–453. Maddicott shows that there were respects in which thirteenth-century English parliaments differed from assemblies held in certain other parts of Europe, especially France, but does not demonstrate that assembly practices across the Continent were sufficiently alike to constitute a norm from which the English case could be an 'exception'. Indeed, he points out at p. 408 that the absence of a system of local representation made France different not only from the English kingdom, but also from several other parts of western Europe.

Bibliography

MANUSCRIPTS

London, British Library, MS Cotton Faustina B.ix, consulted in facsimile in D. Broun and J. Harrison, *The Chronicle of Melrose Abbey: A Stratigraphic Edition. I: Introduction and Facsimile* (Woodbridge, 2007).

London, British Library, MS Cotton Nero D.iv, consulted in facsimile in T. D. Kendrick et al., *Evangeliorum quattuor Codex Lindisfarnensis* (2 vols, Olten and Lausanne, 1956–60).

London, British Library, MS Stowe 944, consulted in facsimile in S. Keynes, *The Liber Vitae of the New Minster and Hyde Abbey Winchester* (Copenhagen, 1996).

PRINTED PRIMARY SOURCES

Adam of Dryburgh, *De tripartito tabernaculo*, in *Patrologia Latina*, ed. J. P. Migne (221 vols, Paris, 1844–64), cxcviii, columns 609–796.

Adomnán, *Life of Columba*, ed. and trans. A. O. Anderson and M. O. Anderson (Oxford, 1991).

Ælfric, *Catholic Homilies: The First Series*, ed. P. Clemoes (Early English Text Society, supplementary series, 17, Oxford, 1997).

Ælfric, *Catholic Homilies: The Second Series*, ed. M. Godden (Early English Text Society, supplementary series, 5, Oxford, 1979).

Ælfric, *De duodecim abusivis*, ed. and trans. M. Clayton, *Two Ælfric Texts: The Twelve Abuses and The Vices and Virtues* (Cambridge, 2013), pp. 109–37.

Ælfric, *Glossary*, ed. J. Zupitza, *Ælfrics Grammatik und Glossar: Text und Varianten* (Berlin, 1880), pp. 297–322.

Ælfric, *Grammar*, ed. J. Zupitza, *Ælfrics Grammatik und Glossar: Text und Varianten* (Berlin, 1880), pp. 1–296.

Ælfric, *Homilies: A Supplementary Collection*, ed. J. C. Pope, *The Homilies of Ælfric: A Supplementary Collection* (2 vols, Early English Text Society, 259–60, Oxford, 1967–8).

Ælfric, *Lives of Saints*, ed. W. W. Skeat (2 vols, Early English Text Society, 76, 114, London, 1881–1900).

Ælfric, *De octo vitiis et de duodecim abusivis gradus*, ed. and trans. M. Clayton, *Two Ælfric Texts: The Twelve Abuses and The Vices and Virtues* (Cambridge, 2013), pp. 139–77.

Ælfric, *Pastoral Letters*, ed. B. Fehr, *Die Hirtenbriefe Ælfrics in altenglischer und lateinischer Fassung* (Hamburg, 1914).

Æthelweard, *Chronicle*, ed. and trans. A. Campbell (Edinburgh, 1962).

Alcuin, *Epistolae*, ed. E. Dümmler (*Monumenta Germaniae Historica, Epistolae Karolini Aevi*, ii, Berlin, 1895).

Alfred the Great: Asser's Life of King Alfred *and Other Contemporary Sources*, trans. S. Keynes and M. Lapidge (London, 1983).

Anglo-Saxon Charters, ed. and trans. A. J. Robertson, 2nd edn (Cambridge, 1956).

The Anglo-Saxon Chronicle: A Collaborative Edition. Volume 3: MS A, ed. J. M. Bately (Cambridge, 1986).

The Anglo-Saxon Chronicle: A Collaborative Edition. Volume 4: MS B, ed. S. Taylor (Cambridge, 1983).

The Anglo-Saxon Chronicle: A Collaborative Edition. Volume 5: MS C, ed. K. O'B. O'Keeffe (Cambridge, 2001).

The Anglo-Saxon Chronicle: A Collaborative Edition. Volume 6: MS D, ed. G. P. Cubbin (Cambridge, 1996).

The Anglo-Saxon Chronicle: A Collaborative Edition. Volume 7: MS E, ed. S. Irvine (Cambridge, 2004).

The Anglo-Saxon Chronicle: A Collaborative Edition. Volume 8: MS F, ed. P. S. Baker (Cambridge, 2000).

The Anglo-Saxon Chronicle: A Revised Translation, trans. D. Whitelock, D. C. Douglas, and S. I. Tucker (London, 1961).

The Anglo-Saxon Chronicles, trans. M. Swanton, revised edn (London, 2000).

Anglo-Saxon Wills, ed. and trans. D. Whitelock (Cambridge, 1930).

Anglo-Saxon Writs, ed. F. E. Harmer (Manchester, 1952, reprinted Stamford, 1989).

Annales Cambriae, A.D. 682–954: Texts A–C in Parallel, ed. D. N. Dumville (Cambridge, 2002).

Annales de Saint-Bertin, ed. F. Grat, J. Vielliard, and S. Clémencet (Paris, 1964).

The Annals of Clonmacnoise, ed. D. Murphy (Dublin, 1896).

Annals of Ulster, ed. and trans. S. Mac Airt and G. Mac Niocaill, *The Annals of Ulster (to A.D. 1131). Part I: Text and Translation* (Dublin, 1983).

The Anonymous Old English Legend of the Seven Sleepers, ed. H. Magennis (Durham, 1994).

Armes Prydein: The Prophecy of Britain from the Book of Taliesin, ed. I. Williams and trans. R. Bromwich (Dublin, 1982).

Asser, *Life of Alfred*, ed. W. H. Stevenson and revised D. Whitelock, *Asser's Life of King Alfred together with the Annals of Saint Neots Erroneously Ascribed to Asser* (Oxford, 1959), pp. 1–96.

B, *Life of St Dunstan*, ed. and trans. M. Winterbottom and M. Lapidge, *The Early Lives of St Dunstan* (Oxford, 2012), pp. 1–109.

The Battle of Maldon, ed. D. G. Scragg (Manchester, 1981).

Bede, *Ecclesiastical History of the English People*, ed. and trans. B. Colgrave and R. A. B. Mynors (Oxford, 1969).

Bede, *Letter to Ecgberht*, ed. and trans. C. Grocock and I. N. Wood, *Abbots of Wearmouth and Jarrow* (Oxford, 2013), pp. 123–61.

The Benedictional of Archbishop Robert, ed. H. A. Wilson (London, 1903).

Byrhtferth of Ramsey, *Life of St Oswald*, ed. and trans. M. Lapidge, *Byrhtferth of Ramsey. The Lives of St Oswald and St Ecgwine* (Oxford, 2009), pp. 1–203.

Capitularia regum Francorum, ed. A. Boretius and V. Krause (2 vols, *Monumenta Germaniae Historica, Legum II*, Hanover, 1883–97).

Charters of Abingdon Abbey, ed. S. E. Kelly (2 vols, Oxford, 2000–1).

Charters of Northern Houses, ed. D. A. Woodman (Oxford, 2012).

Charters of Sherborne, ed. M. A. O'Donovan (Oxford, 1988).

Charters of St Albans, ed. J. Crick (Oxford, 2007).

Chronicle of the Kings of Alba, ed. B. T. Hudson, 'The Scottish Chronicle', *Scottish Historical Review*, 77 (1998), pp. 129–61 at 148–51.

Chronicon Abbatiæ Rameseiensis, ed. W. D. Macray (Rolls Series, 83, London, 1886).

La chronique de Nantes, ed. R. Merlet (Paris, 1896).

The Claudius Pontificals, ed. D. H. Turner (Chichester, 1971).

'Cnut's Law Code of 1018', ed. A. G. Kennedy, *Anglo-Saxon England*, 11 (1983), pp. 57–81 at 72–81.

Cogitosus, *Life of St Brigit*, ed. I. Bollandus and G. Henschenius, *Acta Sanctorum Februarii* (3 vols, Antwerp, 1658), i, 135–41.

Councils and Ecclesiastical Documents Relating to Great Britain and Ireland, ed. A. W. Haddan and W. Stubbs (3 vols, Oxford, 1869–78).

Councils and Synods with Other Documents Relating to the English Church, I, A.D. 871–1204, ed. D. Whitelock, M. Brett, and C. N. L. Brooke (2 vols, Oxford, 1981).

Diplomatarium Anglicum Ævi Saxonici, ed. B. Thorpe (London, 1865).

Domesday Book, ed. J. Morris et al. (35 vols, Chichester, 1975–86).

Early Scottish Charters Prior to A.D. 1153, ed. A. C. Lawrie (Glasgow, 1905).

Encomium Emmae Reginae, ed. A. Campbell with supplementary introduction by S. Keynes (Cambridge, 1998).

English Episcopal Acta XI: Exeter, 1046–1184, ed. F. Barlow (Oxford, 1996).

English Historical Documents, i, c.500–1042, trans. D. Whitelock, 2nd edn (London, 1979).

Exon Domesday, ed. H. Ellis, *Libri censualis vocati Domesday-Book additamenta ex codic. antiquiss.* (London, 1816), pp. 1–493.

Feudal Documents from the Abbey of Bury St. Edmunds, ed. D. C. Douglas (London, 1932).

Flodoard, *Annals*, ed. P. Lauer, *Les annales de Flodoard* (Paris, 1905).

Folcwin of St-Bertin, *Gesta abbatum S. Bertini Sithiensium*, ed. O. Holder-Egger (*Monumenta Germaniae Historica*, Scriptores, 13, Hanover, 1881), pp. 607–35.

Fragmentary Annals of Ireland, ed. and trans. J. N. Radner (Dublin, 1978).

Gerald of Wales, *De principis instructione*, ed. G. F. Warner, in J. S. Brewer, J. F. Dimock, and G. F. Warner (eds), *Giraldi Cambrensis Opera* (Rolls Series, 21, 8 vols, London, 1861–91), viii, 3–329.

Die Gesetze der Angelsachsen, ed. F. Liebermann (3 vols, Halle, 1903–16).

Great Domesday, ed. R. W. H. Erskine, A. Williams, and G. H. Martin (6 cases, London, 1986–92).

Gregory, *Pastoral Care*, ed. F. Rommel, *Règle pastorale* (2 vols, Paris, 1992).

Gulathing Law, ed. B. Eithun, M. Rindal, and T. Ulset, *Den eldre Gulatingslova* (Oslo, 1994).

Heinrici IV. Diplomata, ed. D. von Gladiss and A. Gawlik (*Monumenta Germaniae Historica, Diplomata regum et imperatorum Germaniae*, 6, 3 vols, Weimar, 1952–3 and Hanover, 1978).

Hemingi Chartularium Ecclesiæ Wigorniensis, ed. T. Hearne (2 vols, Oxford, 1723).

Henry of Huntingdon, *Historia Anglorum*, ed. and trans. D. Greenway (Oxford, 1996).

Historia de Sancto Cuthberto, ed. T. Johnson South (Cambridge, 2002).

Historia Ecclesie Abbendonensis, ed. and trans. J. G. H. Hudson (2 vols, Oxford, 2002–7).

Historia Regum, ed. T. Arnold, *Symeonis Monachi Opera Omnia* (Rolls Series, 75, 2 vols, London, 1882–5), ii, 3–283.

Hugh the Chanter, *The History of the Church of York, 1066–1127*, ed. and trans. C. Johnson, M. Brett, C. N. L. Brooke, and M. Winterbottom (Oxford, 1990).

De iniusta vexatione Willelmi episcopi, ed. T. Arnold, *Symeonis Monachi Opera Omnia* (Rolls Series, 75, 2 vols, London, 1882–5), i, 170–95.

Inquisitio Comitatus Cantabrigiensis, ed. N. E. S. A. Hamilton (London, 1876).

Die irische Kanonensammlung, ed. F. W. H. Wasserschleben, 2nd edn (Leipzig, 1885).

John of Worcester, *Chronicle*, ed. and trans. R. R. Darlington, P. McGurk, and J. Bray (2 vols so far, Oxford, 1995–).

King Alfred's Version of St. Augustine's Soliloquies, ed. T. A. Carnicelli (Cambridge, MA, 1969).

King Alfred's West-Saxon Version of Gregory's Pastoral Care, ed. and trans. H. Sweet (Early English Text Society, 45, 50, London, 1871–2).

Lantfred of Winchester, *Translatio et Miracvla S. Swithvni*, ed. and trans. M. Lapidge, *The Cult of St Swithun* (Oxford, 2003), pp. 252–333.

The Laws of the Earliest English Kings, ed. and trans. F. L. Attenborough (Cambridge, 1922).

The Laws of the Kings of England from Edmund to Henry I, ed. and trans. A. J. Robertson (Cambridge, 1925).

The Laws of the Medieval Kingdom of Hungary. Volume 1: 1000–1301, ed. J. M. Bak, G. Bónis, J. Ross Sweeney, and L. S. Domonkos, 2nd edn (Idyllwild, CA, 1999).

Leges Edwardi Confessoris, ed. and trans. B. R. O'Brien, *God's Peace and King's Peace: The Laws of Edward the Confessor* (Philadelphia, PA, 1999), pp. 158–203.

Leges Henrici Primi, ed. and trans. L. J. Downer (Oxford, 1972).

The Leofric Missal, ed. N. Orchard (2 vols, London, 2002).

Liber Eliensis, ed. E. O. Blake (London, 1962).

Liber Pontificalis, ed. L. Duchesne (2 vols, Paris, 1886–92).

The Life and Miracles of St Kenelm, ed. and trans. R. C. Love, *Three Eleventh-Century Anglo-Latin Saints' Lives* (Oxford, 1996), pp. 49–89.

The Life of King Edward who Rests at Westminster Attributed to a Monk of Saint-Bertin, ed. and trans. F. Barlow, 2nd edn (Oxford, 1992).

The Life of St Cathroe, ed. J. Colgan, *Acta Sanctorum Hiberniae* (Leuven, 1645), pp. 494–501.

Matthew Paris, *Chronica Majora*, ed. H. R. Luard (Rolls Series, 57, 7 vols, London, 1872–83).

Monasticon Anglicanum, ed. W. Dugdale, J. Caley, H. Ellis, and B. Bandinel (6 vols in 8, London, 1817–30).

Nithard, *Histoire des fils de Louis le Pieux*, ed. P. Lauer (Paris, 1926).

De obsessione Dunelmi, ed. T. Arnold, *Symeonis Monachi Opera Omnia* (Rolls Series, 75, 2 vols, London, 1882–5), i, 215–20.

The Old English Boethius: An Edition of the Old English Versions of Boethius's De Consolatione Philosophiae, ed. M. Godden and S. Irvine (2 vols, Oxford, 2009).

The Old English Heptateuch, ed. R. Marsden, *The Old English Heptateuch and Ælfric's Libellus de Veteri Testamento et Novo* (Early English Text Society, 330, Oxford, 2008), pp. 3–200.

The Old English Martyrology, ed. and trans. C. Rauer (Cambridge, 2013).

The Old English Version of Bede's Ecclesiastical History of the English People, ed. and trans. T. Miller (Early English Text Society, 95–6, 110–11, 4 vols in 2, London, 1890–8).

Orderic Vitalis, *Ecclesiastical History*, ed. and trans. M. Chibnall (6 vols, Oxford, 1969–80).

Pliny, *Natural History*, ed. and trans. H. Rackham, W. H. S. Jones, and D. E. Eichholz (10 vols, Cambridge, MA, 1938–63).

De primo Saxonum adventu, ed. T. Arnold, *Symeonis Monachi Opera Omnia* (Rolls Series, 75, 2 vols, London, 1882–5), ii, 365–84.

Pseudo-Cyprianus De XII Abusivis Saeculi, ed. S. Hellmann (Leipzig, 1909–10).

Regesta Regum Anglo-Normannorum: The Acta of William I (1066–1087), ed. D. Bates (Oxford, 1998).

Regularis Concordia Anglicae Nationis, ed. T. Symons and D. S. Spath, in K. Hallinger (ed.), *Corpus Consuetudinum Monasticarum VII.3* (Siegburg, 1984), pp. 61–147.

Richer, *Historiae*, ed. H. Hoffmann (*Monumenta Germaniae Historica*, Scriptores, 38, Hanover, 2000).

Rituale Ecclesiae Dunelmensis: The Durham Collectar, ed. U. Lindelöf (Durham, 1927).

Roger of Howden, *Chronica*, ed. W. Stubbs (Rolls Series, 51, 4 vols, London, 1868–71).

Roger of Wendover, *Flores Historiarum*, ed. H. O. Coxe (5 vols, London, 1841–4).

The Sacramentary of Ratoldus, ed. N. Orchard (London, 2005).

Sedulius Scottus, *De rectoribus Christianis*, ed. R. W. Dyson (Woodbridge, 2010).

Select English Historical Documents of the Ninth and Tenth Centuries, ed. and trans. F. E. Harmer (Cambridge, 1914).

Smaragdus, *Via regia*, in *Patrologia Latina*, ed. J. P. Migne (221 vols, Paris, 1844–64), cii, columns 933–70.

Snorri Sturluson, *Heimskringla*, ed. F. Jónsson (4 vols, Copenhagen, 1893–1901).

Stephen of Ripon, *The Life of Bishop Wilfrid*, ed. and trans. B. Colgrave (Cambridge, 1927).

Strabo, *Geography*, ed. and trans. H. L. Jones (8 vols, Cambridge, MA, 1917–32).

Symeon of Durham, *Libellus de Exordio atque Procursu istius, hoc est Dunhelmensis, Ecclesie*, ed. and trans. D. Rollason (Oxford, 2000).

William of Jumièges, *Gesta Normannorum Ducum*, ed. and trans. E. M. C. van Houts (2 vols, Oxford, 1992–5).

William of Malmesbury, *Gesta Regum Anglorum*, ed. and trans. R. A. B. Mynors, R. M. Thomson, and M. Winterbottom (2 vols, Oxford, 1998–9).

William of Newburgh, *Historia rerum Anglicarum*, ed. R. Howlett, *Chronicles of the Reigns of Stephen, Henry II and Richard I* (Rolls Series, 82, 4 vols, London, 1884–9), i and ii, 415–500.

Wulfstan of Winchester, *Life of St Æthelwold*, ed. and trans. M. Lapidge and M. Winterbottom, *Wulfstan of Winchester. The Life of St Æthelwold* (Oxford, 1991), pp. 1–69.

Wulfstan of Winchester, *Narratio Metrica de S. Swithvno*, ed. and trans. M. Lapidge, *The Cult of St Swithun* (Oxford, 2003), pp. 372–551.

Wulfstan of York, *Homilies*, ed. D. Bethurum, *The Homilies of Wulfstan* (Oxford, 1957).

Wulfstan of York, *Institutes of Polity*, ed. K. Jost, *Die «Institutes of Polity, Civil and Ecclesiastical». Ein Werk Erzbischof Wulfstans von York* (Bern, 1959).

PUBLISHED SECONDARY WORKS

R. Abels, *Alfred the Great: War, Kingship and Culture in Anglo-Saxon England* (Harlow, 1998).

R. Abels, 'Household Men, Mercenaries and Vikings in Anglo-Saxon England', in J. France (ed.), *Mercenaries and Paid Men: The Mercenary Identity in the Middle Ages* (Leiden, 2008), pp. 143–65.

R. Abels, 'King Alfred's Peace-Making Strategies with the Vikings', *Haskins Society Journal*, 3 (1991), pp. 23–34.

R. Abels, *Lordship and Military Obligation in Anglo-Saxon England* (London, 1988).

L. Abrams, 'Edgar and the Men of the Danelaw', in D. Scragg (ed.), *Edgar, King of the English 959–975: New Interpretations* (Woodbridge, 2008), pp. 171–91.

L. Abrams, 'Edward the Elder's Danelaw', in N. J. Higham and D. H. Hill (eds), *Edward the Elder, 899–924* (London, 2001), pp. 128–43.

B. Ager and G. Williams, 'The Vale of York Viking Hoard: Preliminary Catalogue', in T. Abramson (ed.), *Studies in Early Medieval Coinage, Volume 2: New Perspectives* (Woodbridge, 2011), pp. 135–45.

W. M. Aird, 'Northumbria and the Making of the Kingdom of the English', in H. Tsurushima (ed.), *Nations in Medieval Britain* (Donington, 2010), pp. 45–60.

W. M. Aird, *St Cuthbert and the Normans: The Church of Durham, 1071–1153* (Woodbridge, 1998).

S. Airlie, 'The Aristocracy', in R. McKitterick (ed.), *The New Cambridge Medieval History II, c.700–c.900* (Cambridge, 1995), pp. 431–50.

M. Allen, *Mints and Money in Medieval England* (Cambridge, 2012).

I. Álvarez Borge, *Comunidades locales y transformaciones sociales en la Alta Edad Media: Hampshire (Wessex) y el sur de Castilla, un estudio comparativo* (Logroño, 1999).

M. Ammon, '"Ge mid wedde ge mid aðe": The Functions of Oath and Pledge in Anglo-Saxon Legal Culture', *Historical Research*, 86 (2013), pp. 515–35.

M. O. Anderson, 'Lothian and the Early Scottish Kings', *Scottish Historical Review*, 39 (1960), pp. 98–112.

O. S. Anderson, *The English Hundred-Names* (3 vols, Lund, 1934–9).

T. Andersson, 'Die schwedischen Bezirksbezeichnungen *hund* und *hundare*. Ein Beitrag zur Diskussion einer germanischen Wortfamilie', *Frühmittelalterliche Studien*, 13 (1979), pp. 88–124.

H. H. Anton, *Fürstenspiegel und Herrscherethos in der Karolingerzeit* (Bonn, 1968).

G. G. Astill, 'Towns and Town Hierarchies in Saxon England', *Oxford Journal of Archaeology*, 10 (1991), pp. 95–117.

T. H. Aston, 'The Origins of the Manor in England', *Transactions of the Royal Historical Society*, 5th series, 8 (1958), pp. 59–83.

S. Bagge, *From Viking Stronghold to Christian Kingdom: State Formation in Norway, c.900–1350* (Copenhagen, 2010).

K. Bakay, 'Hungary', in T. Reuter (ed.), *The New Cambridge Medieval History III, c.900–c.1024* (Cambridge, 1999), pp. 536–52.

J. Baker and S. Brookes, *Beyond the Burghal Hidage: Anglo-Saxon Civil Defence in the Viking Age* (Leiden, 2013).

J. Bannerman, *Studies in the History of Dalriada* (Edinburgh, 1974).

N. Banton, 'Monastic Reform and the Unification of Tenth-Century England', *Studies in Church History*, 18 (1982), pp. 71–85.

E. E. Barker, 'The Anglo-Saxon Chronicle Used by Æthelweard', *Bulletin of the Institute for Historical Research*, 40 (1967), pp. 74–91.

F. Barlow, *Edward the Confessor*, 2nd edn (New Haven, CT, 1997).

P. S. Barnwell, '*Hlafæta, ceorl, hid* and *scir*: Celtic, Roman or Germanic?', *Anglo-Saxon Studies in Archaeology and History*, 9 (1996), pp. 53–61.

G. W. S. Barrow, *The Anglo-Norman Era in Scottish History* (Oxford, 1980).

G. W. S. Barrow, 'The Anglo-Scottish Border', *Northern History*, 1 (1966), pp. 21–42, reprinted in his *The Kingdom of the Scots: Government, Church and Society from the Eleventh to the Fourteenth Century*, 2nd edn (Edinburgh, 2003), pp. 112–29.

G. W. S. Barrow, 'Midlothian—or the Shire of Edinburgh?', *Book of the Old Edinburgh Club*, 35 (1985), pp. 141–8.

G. W. S. Barrow, 'Pre-Feudal Scotland: Shires and Thanes', in G. W. S. Barrow, *The Kingdom of the Scots: Government, Church and Society from the Eleventh to the Fourteenth Century*, 2nd edn (Edinburgh, 2003), pp. 7–56.

G. W. S. Barrow, 'The Scots and the North of England', in E. King (ed.), *The Anarchy of King Stephen's Reign* (Oxford, 1994), pp. 231–53, reprinted in his *The Kingdom of the Scots: Government, Church and Society from the Eleventh to the Fourteenth Century*, 2nd edn (Edinburgh, 2003), pp. 130–47.

J. Barrow, 'The Community of Worcester, 961–*c.*1100', in N. Brooks and C. Cubitt (eds), *St Oswald of Worcester: Life and Influence* (London, 1996), pp. 84–99.

J. Barrow, 'Demonstrative Behaviour and Political Communication in Later Anglo-Saxon England', *Anglo-Saxon England*, 36 (2007), pp. 127–50.

R. Bartlett, *England under the Norman and Angevin Kings, 1075–1225* (Oxford, 2000).

R. Bartlett, *The Making of Europe: Conquest, Colonization and Cultural Change, 950–1350* (London, 1993).

S. Barton, 'Spain in the Eleventh Century', in D. Luscombe and J. Riley-Smith (eds), *The New Cambridge Medieval History IV, c.1024–c.1198* (2 vols, Cambridge, 2004), ii, 154–90.

S. Bassett, 'The Administrative Landscape of the Diocese of Worcester in the Tenth Century', in N. Brooks and C. Cubitt (eds), *St Oswald of Worcester: Life and Influence* (London, 1996), pp. 147–73.

S. Bassett, 'Anglo-Saxon Fortifications in Western Mercia', *Midland History*, 36 (2011), pp. 1–23.

S. Bassett, 'In Search of the Origins of Anglo-Saxon Kingdoms', in S. Bassett (ed.), *The Origins of Anglo-Saxon Kingdoms* (London, 1989), pp. 3–27.

S. Bassett, 'The Middle and Late Anglo-Saxon Defences of Western Mercian Towns', *Anglo-Saxon Studies in Archaeology and History*, 15 (2008), pp. 180–239.

D. Bates, 'England and the «Feudal Revolution»', *Settimane di studio del centro italiano di studi sull'alto medioevo*, 47 (2000), pp. 611–49.

S. Baxter, 'Archbishop Wulfstan and the Administration of God's Property', in M. Townend (ed.), *Wulfstan, Archbishop of York* (Turnhout, 2004), pp. 161–205.

S. Baxter, 'The Earls of Mercia and their Commended Men in the Mid Eleventh Century', *Anglo-Norman Studies*, 23 (2001), pp. 23–46.

S. Baxter, *The Earls of Mercia: Lordship and Power in Late Anglo-Saxon England* (Oxford, 2007).

S. Baxter, 'The Limits of the Late Anglo-Saxon State', in W. Pohl and V. Wieser (eds), *Der frühmittelalterliche Staat—europäische Perspektiven* (Vienna, 2009), pp. 503–13.

S. Baxter, 'Lordship and Justice in Late Anglo-Saxon England: The Judicial Functions of Soke and Commendation Revisited', in S. Baxter, C. E. Karkov, J. L. Nelson, and D. Pelteret (eds), *Early Medieval Studies in Memory of Patrick Wormald* (Farnham, 2009), pp. 383–419.

S. Baxter and J. Blair, 'Land Tenure and Royal Patronage in the Early English Kingdom: A Model and a Case Study', *Anglo-Norman Studies*, 28 (2006), pp. 19–46.

M. Becher, *Eid und Herrschaft. Untersuchungen zum Herrscherethos Karls des Großen* (Sigmaringen, 1993).

G. T. Beech, 'The Naming of England', *History Today*, 57 (10) (October, 2007), pp. 30–5.

N. Berend, 'Hungary in the Eleventh and Twelfth Centuries', in D. Luscombe and J. Riley-Smith (eds), *The New Cambridge Medieval History IV, c.1024–c.1198* (2 vols, Cambridge, 2004), ii, 304–16.

N. Berend, J. Laszlovszky, and B. Zsolt Szakács, 'The Kingdom of Hungary', in N. Berend (ed.), *Christianisation and the Rise of Christian Monarchy: Scandinavia, Central Europe and Rus' c.900–1200* (Cambridge, 2007), pp. 319–68.

J. W. Bernhardt, *Itinerant Kingship and Royal Monasteries in Early Medieval Germany, c.936–1075* (Cambridge, 1993).

M. Biddle, 'Towns', in D. M. Wilson (ed.), *The Archaeology of Anglo-Saxon England* (London, 1976), pp. 99–150.

M. Biddle and D. H. Hill, 'Late Saxon Planned Towns', *Antiquaries Journal*, 51 (1971), pp. 70–85.

M. Biddle and D. Keene, 'General Survey and Conclusions', in M. Biddle (ed.), *Winchester in the Early Middle Ages: An Edition and Discussion of the Winton Domesday* (Oxford, 1976), pp. 449–508.

M. Biddle and D. Keene, 'Winchester in the Eleventh and Twelfth Centuries', in M. Biddle (ed.), *Winchester in the Early Middle Ages: An Edition and Discussion of the Winton Domesday* (Oxford, 1976), pp. 241–448.

F. M. Biggs, 'Edgar's Path to the Throne', in D. Scragg (ed.), *Edgar, King of the English 959–975: New Interpretations* (Woodbridge, 2008), pp. 124–39.

D. A. Binchy, *Celtic and Anglo-Saxon Kingship* (Oxford, 1970).

T. N. Bisson, *The Crisis of the Twelfth Century: Power, Lordship, and the Origins of European Government* (Princeton, NJ, 2009).

M. A. S. Blackburn, 'Alfred's Coinage Reforms in Context', in T. Reuter (ed.), *Alfred the Great: Papers from the Eleventh-Centenary Conferences* (Aldershot, 2003), pp. 199–217.

M. A. S. Blackburn, 'Coinage and Currency', in E. King (ed.), *The Anarchy of King Stephen's Reign* (Oxford, 1994), pp. 145–205.

M. A. S. Blackburn, 'Currency under the Vikings. Part 1: Guthrum and the Earliest Danelaw Coinages', *British Numismatic Journal*, 75 (2005), pp. 18–43.

M. A. S. Blackburn, 'Currency under the Vikings. Part 2: The Two Scandinavian Kingdoms of the Danelaw, *c.*895–954', *British Numismatic Journal*, 76 (2006), pp. 204–26.

M. A. S. Blackburn, 'Currency under the Vikings. Part 3: Ireland, Wales, Isle of Man and Scotland in the Ninth and Tenth Centuries', *British Numismatic Journal*, 77 (2007), pp. 119–49.

M. A. S. Blackburn, 'Expansion and Control: Aspects of Anglo-Scandinavian Minting South of the Humber', in J. Graham-Campbell, R. Hall, J. Jesch, and D. N. Parsons (eds), *Vikings and the Danelaw: Select Papers from the Proceedings of the Thirteenth Viking Congress* (Oxford, 2001), pp. 125–42.

M. A. S. Blackburn, 'Gold in England during the "Age of Silver" (Eighth–Eleventh Centuries)', in J. Graham-Campbell and G. Williams (eds), *Silver Economy in the Viking Age* (Walnut Creek, CA, 2007), pp. 55–98.

M. A. S. Blackburn, 'The London Mint in the Reign of Alfred', in M. A. S. Blackburn and D. N. Dumville (eds), *Kings, Currency and Alliances: History and Coinage of Southern England in the Ninth Century* (Woodbridge, 1998), pp. 105–23.

M. A. S. Blackburn, 'Mints, Burhs, and the Grately Code, cap. 14.2', in D. H. Hill and A. R. Rumble (eds), *The Defence of Wessex: The Burghal Hidage and Anglo-Saxon Fortifications* (Manchester, 1996), pp. 160–75.

M. A. S. Blackburn, 'Money and Coinage', in R. McKitterick (ed.), *The New Cambridge Medieval History, II: c.700–c.900* (Cambridge, 1995), pp. 538–59.

M. A. S. Blackburn and K. Leahy, 'A Lincoln Mint-Signed Coin from the Reign of Edgar', *Numismatic Chronicle*, 156 (1996), pp. 239–41.

M. A. S. Blackburn and S. Lyon, 'Regional Die-Production in Cnut's *Quatrefoil* Issue', in M. A. S. Blackburn (ed.), *Anglo-Saxon Monetary History: Essays in Memory of Michael Dolley* (Leicester, 1986), pp. 223–72.

J. Blair, *Anglo-Saxon Oxfordshire* (Stroud, 1994).

J. Blair, *The Church in Anglo-Saxon Society* (Oxford, 2005).

J. Blair, 'Grid-Planning in Anglo-Saxon Settlements: The Short Perch and the Four-Perch Module', *Anglo-Saxon Studies in Archaeology and History*, 18 (2013), pp. 18–61.

C. E. Blunt, 'The Coinage of Athelstan, King of England, 924–939: A Survey', *British Numismatic Journal*, 42 (1974), pp. 35–160.

C. E. Blunt, 'A Penny of the English King Athelstan Overstruck on a Cologne Denier', in T. Fischer and P. Ilisch (eds), *Lagom. Festschrift für Peter Berghaus zum 60. Geburtstag am 20. November 1979* (Münster, 1981), pp. 119–21.

C. E. Blunt, B. H. I. H. Stewart, and C. S. S. Lyon, *Coinage in Tenth-Century England from Edward the Elder to Edgar's Reform* (Oxford, 1989).

G. Bois, *The Transformation of the Year One Thousand: The Village of Lournand from Antiquity to Feudalism*, trans. J. Birrell (Manchester, 1992).

T. Bolton, *The Empire of Cnut the Great: Conquest and the Consolidation of Power in Northern Europe in the Early Eleventh Century* (Leiden, 2009).

J. Bovendeert, 'Royal or Monastic Identity? Smaragdus' *Via regia* and *Diadema monachorum* Reconsidered', in R. Corradini, R. Meens, C. Pössel, and P. Shaw (eds), *Texts and Identities in the Early Middle Ages* (Vienna, 2006), pp. 239–51.

J. D. Brand, *Periodic Change of Type in the Anglo-Saxon and Norman Periods* (Rochester, 1984).

A. Breeze, 'Edgar at Chester in 973: A Breton Link?', *Northern History*, 44 (2007), pp. 153–7.

S. Brookes, 'The Lathes of Kent: A Review of the Evidence', in S. Brookes, S. Harrington, and A. Reynolds (eds), *Studies in Early Anglo-Saxon Art and Archaeology: Papers in Honour of Martin G. Welch* (Oxford, 2011), pp. 156–70.

S. Brookes and A. Reynolds, 'The Origins of Political Order and the Anglo-Saxon State', *Archaeology International*, 13/14 (2009–11), pp. 84–93.

N. Brooks, 'The Administrative Background to the Burghal Hidage', in D. H. Hill and A. R. Rumble (eds), *The Defence of Wessex: The Burghal Hidage and Anglo-Saxon Fortifications* (Manchester, 1996), pp. 128–50.

N. Brooks, 'Alfredian Government: The West Saxon Inheritance', in T. Reuter (ed.), *Alfred the Great: Papers from the Eleventh-Centenary Conferences* (Aldershot, 2003), pp. 153–73.

N. Brooks, ' "Anglo-Saxon Chronicle(s)" or "Old English Royal Annals"?', in J. L. Nelson, S. Reynolds, and S. M. Johns (eds), *Gender and Historiography: Studies in the Earlier Middle Ages in Honour of Pauline Stafford* (London, 2012), pp. 35–48.

N. Brooks, 'Arms, Status and Warfare in Late-Saxon England', in D. H. Hill (ed.), *Ethelred the Unready: Papers from the Millenary Conference* (Oxford, 1978), pp. 81–103.

N. Brooks, 'The Creation and Early Structure of the Kingdom of Kent', in S. Bassett (ed.), *The Origins of Anglo-Saxon Kingdoms* (London, 1989), pp. 55–74.

N. Brooks, 'The Development of Military Obligations in Eighth- and Ninth-Century England', in P. Clemoes and K. Hughes (eds), *England Before the Conquest: Studies in Primary Sources Presented to Dorothy Whitelock* (Cambridge, 1971), pp. 69–84.

N. Brooks, *The Early History of the Church of Canterbury: Christ Church from 597 to 1066* (Leicester, 1984).

N. Brooks, 'England in the Ninth Century: The Crucible of Defeat', *Transactions of the Royal Historical Society*, 5th series, 29 (1979), pp. 1–20.

N. Brooks, 'English Identity from Bede to the Millennium', *Haskins Society Journal*, 14 (2003), pp. 33–51.

N. Brooks, 'European Medieval Bridges: A Window onto Changing Concepts of State Power', *Haskins Society Journal*, 7 (1995), pp. 11–29.

N. Brooks, 'The Fonthill Letter, Ealdorman Ordlaf and Anglo-Saxon Law in Practice', in S. Baxter, C. E. Karkov, J. L. Nelson, and D. Pelteret (eds), *Early Medieval Studies in Memory of Patrick Wormald* (Farnham, 2009), pp. 301–17.

N. Brooks, 'Rochester Bridge, AD 43–1381', in N. Yates and J. M. Gibson (eds), *Traffic and Politics: The Construction and Management of Rochester Bridge, AD 43–1993* (Woodbridge, 1993), pp. 1–40, 362–9.

N. Brooks, 'The Unidentified Forts of the Burghal Hidage', *Medieval Archaeology*, 8 (1964), pp. 74–90.

N. Brooks, 'The West Saxon Hidage and the "Appendix"', in D. H. Hill and A. R. Rumble (eds), *The Defence of Wessex: The Burghal Hidage and Anglo-Saxon Fortifications* (Manchester, 1996), pp. 87–92.

D. Broun, 'Becoming Scottish in the Thirteenth Century: The Evidence of the Chronicle of Melrose', in B. Ballin Smith, S. Taylor, and G. Williams (eds), *West over Sea: Studies in Scandinavian Sea-Borne Expansion and Settlement before 1300. A Festschrift in Honour of Dr Barbara E. Crawford* (Leiden, 2007), pp. 19–32.

D. Broun, 'Defining Scotland and the Scots before the Wars of Independence', in D. Broun, R. J. Finlay, and M. Lynch (eds), *Image and Identity: The Making and Re-Making of Scotland through the Ages* (Edinburgh, 1998), pp. 4–17.

D. Broun, *Scottish Independence and the Idea of Britain from the Picts to Alexander III* (Edinburgh, 2007).

D. Broun, 'The Welsh Identity of the Kingdom of Strathclyde, *c*.900–*c*.1200', *Innes Review*, 55 (2004), pp. 111–80.

A. Burghart and A. Wareham, 'Was there an Agricultural Revolution in Anglo-Saxon England?', in J. Barrow and A. Wareham (eds), *Myth, Rulership, Church and Charters: Essays in Honour of Nicholas Brooks* (Aldershot, 2008), pp. 89–99.

J. G. Busch, 'Vom Attentat zur Haft. Die Behandlung von Konkurrenten und Opponenten der frühen Karolinger', *Historische Zeitschrift*, 263 (1996), pp. 561–88.

F. J. Byrne, *Irish Kings and High-Kings* (London, 1973).

T. C. Cain, 'An Introduction to the Rutland Domesday', in A. Williams and R. W. H. Erskine (eds), *The Northamptonshire and Rutland Domesday* (London, 1987), pp. 18–34.

H. Cam, 'Early Groups of Hundreds', in J. G. Edwards, V. H. Galbraith, and E. F. Jacob (eds), *Historical Essays in Honour of James Tait* (Manchester, 1933), pp. 13–26.

H. Cam, 'The Evolution of the Mediaeval English Franchise', *Speculum*, 32 (1957), pp. 427–42.

H. Cam, *Local Government in Francia and England: A Comparison of the Local Administration and Jurisdiction of the Carolingian Empire with that of the West Saxon Kingdom* (London, 1912).

H. Cam, '*Manerium cum Hundredo*: The Hundred and the Hundredal Manor', *English Historical Review*, 47 (1932), pp. 353–76.

J. Campbell, 'Archipelagic Thoughts: Comparing Early Medieval Polities in Britain and Ireland', in S. Baxter, C. E. Karkov, J. L. Nelson, and D. Pelteret (eds), *Early Medieval Studies in Memory of Patrick Wormald* (Farnham, 2009), pp. 47–63.

J. Campbell, 'Asser's *Life of Alfred*', in C. Holdsworth and T. P. Wiseman (eds), *The Inheritance of Historiography, 350–900* (Exeter, 1986), pp. 115–35, reprinted in his *The Anglo-Saxon State* (London, 2000), pp. 129–55.

J. Campbell, *Bede's Reges and Principes* (Jarrow, 1979), reprinted in his *Essays in Anglo-Saxon History* (London, 1986), pp. 85–98.

J. Campbell, 'Bede's Words for Places', in P. H. Sawyer (ed.), *Places, Names and Graves: Early Medieval Settlement* (Leeds, 1979), pp. 34–54, reprinted in his *Essays in Anglo-Saxon History* (London, 1986), pp. 99–119.

J. Campbell, 'The East Anglian Sees before the Conquest', in I. Atherton, E. Fernie, C. Harper-Bill, and H. Smith (eds), *Norwich Cathedral: Church, City and Diocese,*

1096–1996 (London, 1996), pp. 3–21, reprinted in his *The Anglo-Saxon State* (London, 2000), pp. 107–27.

J. Campbell, 'Epilogue', in J. Campbell (ed.), *The Anglo-Saxons* (Oxford, 1982), pp. 240–6.

J. Campbell, 'Introduction', in J. Campbell, *The Anglo-Saxon State* (London, 2000), pp. ix–xxix.

J. Campbell, 'The Late Anglo-Saxon State: A Maximum View', *Proceedings of the British Academy*, 87 (1994), pp. 39–65, reprinted in his *The Anglo-Saxon State* (London, 2000), pp. 1–30.

J. Campbell, 'Observations on English Government from the Tenth to the Twelfth Century', *Transactions of the Royal Historical Society*, 5th series, 25 (1975), pp. 39–54, reprinted in his *Essays in Anglo-Saxon History* (London, 1986), pp. 155–70.

J. Campbell, 'The Significance of the Anglo-Norman State in the Administrative History of Western Europe', in W. Paravicini and K. F. Werner (eds), *Histoire comparée de l'administration (IVᵉ–XVIIIᵉ siècles)* (Munich, 1980), pp. 117–34, reprinted in his *Essays in Anglo-Saxon History* (London, 1986), pp. 171–89.

J. Campbell, 'Some Agents and Agencies of the Late Anglo-Saxon State', in J. C. Holt (ed.), *Domesday Studies: Papers Read at the Novocentenary Conference of the Royal Historical Society and the Institute of British Geographers, Winchester, 1986* (Woodbridge, 1987), pp. 201–18, reprinted in his *The Anglo-Saxon State* (London, 2000), pp. 201–25.

J. Campbell, 'Stenton's *Anglo-Saxon England*, with Special Reference to the Earlier Period', in D. Matthew, A. Curry, and E. Green (eds), *Stenton's* Anglo-Saxon England *Fifty Years On* (Reading, 1994), pp. 49–59.

J. Campbell, 'The United Kingdom of England: The Anglo-Saxon Achievement', in A. Grant and K. J. Stringer (eds), *Uniting the Kingdom: The Making of British History* (London, 1995), pp. 31–47, reprinted in his *The Anglo-Saxon State* (London, 2000), pp. 31–53.

J. Campbell, 'Was it Infancy in England? Some Questions of Comparison', in M. Jones and M. Vale (eds), *England and her Neighbours, 1066–1453: Essays in Honour of Pierre Chaplais* (London, 1989), pp. 1–17, reprinted in his *The Anglo-Saxon State* (London, 2000), pp. 179–99.

S. Castellanos and I. Martín Viso, 'The Local Articulation of Central Power in the North of the Iberian Peninsula (500–1000)', *Early Medieval Europe*, 13 (2005), pp. 1–42.

H. M. Chadwick, *Studies on Anglo-Saxon Institutions* (Cambridge, 1905).

P. Chaplais, 'The Anglo-Saxon Chancery: From the Diploma to the Writ', *Journal of the Society of Archivists*, 3.4 (1966), pp. 160–76.

P. Chaplais, 'The Letter from Bishop Wealdhere of London to Archbishop Brihtwold of Canterbury: The Earliest Original "Letter Close" Extant in the West', in M. B. Parkes and A. G. Watson (eds), *Medieval Scribes, Manuscripts and Libraries: Essays Presented to N. R. Ker* (London, 1978), pp. 3–23.

P. Chaplais, 'The Origin and Authenticity of the Royal Anglo-Saxon Diploma', *Journal of the Society of Archivists*, 3.2 (1965), pp. 48–61.

P. Chaplais, 'The Royal Anglo-Saxon "Chancery" of the Tenth Century Revisited', in H. Mayr-Harting and R. I. Moore (eds), *Studies in Medieval History Presented to R. H. C. Davis*, (London, 1985), pp. 41–51.

P. Chaplais, 'William of Saint-Calais and the Domesday Survey', in J. C. Holt (ed.), *Domesday Studies: Papers Read at the Novocentenary Conference of the Royal Historical Society and the Institute of British Geographers, Winchester, 1986* (Woodbridge, 1987), pp. 65–77.

T. M. Charles-Edwards, 'Celtic Kings: "Priestly Vegetables"?', in S. Baxter, C. E. Karkov, J. L. Nelson, and D. Pelteret (eds), *Early Medieval Studies in Memory of Patrick Wormald* (Farnham, 2009), pp. 65–80.

T. M. Charles-Edwards, '"The Continuation of Bede", *s.a.* 750: High-Kings, Kings of Tara and "Bretwaldas"', in A. P. Smyth (ed.), *Seanchas: Studies in Early and Medieval Irish Archaeology, History and Literature in Honour of Francis J. Byrne* (Dublin, 2000), pp. 137–45.

T. M. Charles-Edwards, '*Críth Gablach* and the Law of Status', *Peritia*, 5 (1986), pp. 53–73.

T. M. Charles-Edwards, *Early Christian Ireland* (Cambridge, 2000).

T. M. Charles-Edwards, 'Kinship, Status and the Origins of the Hide', *Past and Present*, 56 (1972), pp. 3–33.

T. M. Charles-Edwards, 'The Making of Nations in Britain and Ireland in the Early Middle Ages', in R. Evans (ed.), *Lordship and Learning: Studies in Memory of Trevor Aston* (Woodbridge, 2004), pp. 11–37.

T. M. Charles-Edwards, 'The Pastoral Role of the Church in the Early Irish Laws', in J. Blair and R. Sharpe (eds), *Pastoral Care before the Parish* (Leicester, 1992), pp. 63–80.

T. M. Charles-Edwards, 'Some Celtic Kinship Terms', *Bulletin of the Board of Celtic Studies*, 24 (1971), pp. 105–22.

T. M. Charles-Edwards, *Wales and the Britons, 350–1064* (Oxford, 2013).

N. Christie, O. Creighton, M. Edgeworth, and M. Fradley, '"Have you Found Anything Interesting?" Exploring Late-Saxon and Medieval Urbanism at Wallingford: Sources, Results, and Questions', *Oxoniensia*, 75 (2010), pp. 35–47.

P. A. Clarke, *The English Nobility under Edward the Confessor* (Oxford, 1994).

M. Clayton, 'Ælfric and Æthelred', in J. Roberts and J. L. Nelson (eds), *Essays on Anglo-Saxon and Related Themes in Memory of Lynne Grundy* (London, 2000), pp. 65–88.

M. Clayton, '*De Duodecim Abusiuis*, Lordship and Kingship in Anglo-Saxon England', in S. McWilliams (ed.), *Saints and Scholars: New Perspectives on Anglo-Saxon Literature and Culture in Honour of Hugh Magennis* (Cambridge, 2012), pp. 141–63.

M. Clayton, 'The Old English *Promissio regis*', *Anglo-Saxon England*, 37 (2008), pp. 91–150.

R. Cleasby, G. Vigfusson, and W. A. Craigie, *An Icelandic–English Dictionary*, 2nd edn (Oxford, 1957).

R. Collins, *Early Medieval Spain: Unity in Diversity, 400–1000*, 2nd edn (Basingstoke, 1995).

R. Collins, '"*Sicut lex Gothorum continet*": Law and Charters in Ninth- and Tenth-Century León and Catalonia', *English Historical Review*, 100 (1985), pp. 489–512.

R. Collins, 'The Spanish Kingdoms', in T. Reuter (ed.), *The New Cambridge Medieval History III, c.900–c.1024* (Cambridge, 1999), pp. 670–91.

R. Collins, *Visigothic Spain, 409–711* (Oxford, 2004).

P. W. Conner, *Anglo-Saxon Exeter: A Tenth-Century Cultural History* (Woodbridge, 1993).

B. Cook, 'Foreign Coins in Medieval England', in L. Travaini (ed.), *Moneta locale, moneta straniera. Italia ed Europa XI–XV secolo* (Milan, 1999), pp. 231–84.

W. J. Corbett, 'The Tribal Hidage', *Transactions of the Royal Historical Society*, new series, 14 (1900), pp. 187–230.

M. Costambeys, M. Innes, and S. MacLean, *The Carolingian World* (Cambridge, 2011).

S. Coupland, 'L'article XI de l'Édit de Pîtres du 25 juin 864', *Bulletin de la société française de numismatique*, 40 (1985), pp. 713–14.

S. Coupland, 'Carolingian Single Finds and the Economy of the Early Ninth Century', *Numismatic Chronicle*, 170 (2010), pp. 287–319.

S. Coupland, 'Charlemagne's Coinage: Ideology and Economy', in J. Story (ed.), *Charlemagne: Empire and Society* (Manchester, 2005), pp. 211–29.

S. Coupland, 'The Coinage of Lothar I (840–855)', *Numismatic Chronicle*, 161 (2001), pp. 157–98.

S. Coupland, 'The Coinages of Pippin I and II of Aquitaine', *Revue numismatique*, 6ᵉ série, 31 (1989), pp. 194–222.

S. Coupland, 'The Early Coinage of Charles the Bald, 840–864', *Numismatic Chronicle*, 151 (1991), pp. 121–58.

S. Coupland, 'The Fortified Bridges of Charles the Bald', *Journal of Medieval History*, 17 (1991), pp. 1–12.

S. Coupland, 'Money and Coinage under Louis the Pious', *Francia*, 17 (1990), pp. 23–54.

J. Crick, 'Men, Women and Widows: Widowhood in Pre-Conquest England', in S. Cavallo and L. Warner (eds), *Widowhood in Medieval and Early Modern Europe* (Harlow, 1999), pp. 24–36.

M. Crusafont, A. M. Balaguer, and P. Grierson, *Medieval European Coinage with a Catalogue of the Coins in the Fitzwilliam Museum, Cambridge. 6: The Iberian Peninsula* (Cambridge, 2013).

C. Cubitt, '"As the Lawbook Teaches": Reeves, Lawbooks and Urban Life in the Anonymous Old English Legend of the Seven Sleepers', *English Historical Review*, 124 (2009), pp. 1021–49.

C. Cubitt, 'The Politics of Remorse: Penance and Royal Piety in the Reign of Æthelred the Unready', *Historical Research*, 85 (2012), pp. 179–92.

C. Cubitt, 'Review Article: The Tenth-Century Benedictine Reform in England', *Early Medieval Europe*, 6 (1997), pp. 77–94.

F. Curta, *Southeastern Europe in the Middle Ages, 500–1250* (Cambridge, 2006).

H. Dannenbauer, 'Hundertschaft, Centena und Huntari', *Historisches Jahrbuch*, 62–9 (1942–9), pp. 155–219.

H. C. Darby, *Domesday England* (Cambridge, 1977).

R. R. Darlington and P. McGurk, 'The "Chronicon ex Chronicis" of "Florence" of Worcester and its Use of Sources for English History before 1066', *Anglo-Norman Studies*, 5 (1982), pp. 185–96.

M. R. Davidson, 'The (Non)submission of the Northern Kings in 920', in N. J. Higham and D. H. Hill (eds), *Edward the Elder, 899–924* (London, 2001), pp. 200–11.

R. R. Davies, *Domination and Conquest: The Experience of Ireland, Scotland and Wales, 1100–1300* (Cambridge, 1990).

R. R. Davies, *The First English Empire: Power and Identities in the British Isles, 1093–1343* (Oxford, 2000).

R. R. Davies, *Lords and Lordship in the British Isles in the Late Middle Ages*, ed. B. Smith (Oxford, 2009).

R. R. Davies, 'The Medieval State: The Tyranny of a Concept?', *Journal of Historical Sociology*, 16 (2003), pp. 280–300.

W. Davies, *Acts of Giving: Individual, Community, and Church in Tenth-Century Christian Spain* (Oxford, 2007).

W. Davies, 'The Consecration of Bishops of Llandaff in the Tenth and Eleventh Centuries', *Bulletin of the Board of Celtic Studies*, 26 (1976), pp. 53–73.

W. Davies, 'Lordship and Community: Northern Spain on the Eve of the Year 1000', in C. Dyer, P. Coss, and C. Wickham (eds), *Rodney Hilton's Middle Ages: An Exploration of Historical Themes* (Oxford, 2007), pp. 18–33.

W. Davies, *Patterns of Power in Early Wales* (Oxford, 1990).

W. Davies, *Small Worlds: The Village Community in Early Medieval Brittany* (London, 1988).

W. Davies, '*Unciae*: Land Measurement in the *Liber Landavensis*', *Agricultural History Review*, 21 (1973), pp. 111–21.

W. Davies and H. Vierck, 'The Contexts of the Tribal Hidage: Social Aggregates and Settlement Patterns', *Frühmittelalterliche Studien*, 8 (1974), pp. 223–93.

R. H. C. Davis, 'Domesday Book: Continental Parallels', in J. C. Holt (ed.), *Domesday Studies: Papers Read at the Novocentenary Conference of the Royal Historical Society and the Institute of British Geographers, Winchester, 1986* (Woodbridge, 1987), pp. 15–39.

R. Deshman, *The Benedictional of Æthelwold* (Princeton, NJ, 1995), pp. 192–214.

R. Deshman, '*Benedictus monarcha et monachus*: Early Medieval Ruler Theology and the Anglo-Saxon Reform', *Frühmittelalterliche Studien*, 22 (1988), pp. 204–40.

R. Deshman, '*Christus rex et magi reges*: Kingship and Christology in Ottonian and Anglo-Saxon Art', *Frühmittelalterliche Studien*, 10 (1976), pp. 367–405.

T. Deswarte, *De la destruction à la restauration. L'idéologie du royaume d'Oviedo-León (VIIIᵉ–XIᵉ siècles)* (Turnhout, 2003).

J.-P. Devroey, *Puissants et misérables. Système social et monde paysan dans l'Europe des Francs (VIᵉ–IXᵉ siècles)* (Brussels, 2006).

F. H. Dickinson, 'Charter of William the Second, Granting Bath to Bishop John de Villula', *Proceedings of the Somersetshire Archaeological and Natural History Society*, 22 (1876), pp. 114–19.

J. McN. Dodgson, 'OE *Weal-stilling*', in D. H. Hill and A. R. Rumble (eds), *The Defence of Wessex: The Burghal Hidage and Anglo-Saxon Fortifications* (Manchester, 1996), pp. 176–7.

M. Dolley, 'Roger of Wendover's Date for Eadgar's Coinage Reform', *British Numismatic Journal*, 49 (1979), pp. 1–11.

R. H. M. Dolley and D. M. Metcalf, 'The Reform of the English Coinage under Eadgar', in R. H. M. Dolley (ed.), *Anglo-Saxon Coins: Studies Presented to F. M. Stenton on the Occasion of his 80th Birthday* (London, 1961), pp. 136–68.

C. Downham, 'The Chronology of the Last Scandinavian Kings of York, AD 937–954', *Northern History*, 40 (2003), pp. 25–51.

C. Downham, *Viking Kings of Britain and Ireland: The Dynasty of Ívarr to A.D. 1014* (Edinburgh, 2007).

S. Draper, 'The Significance of Old English *Burh* in Anglo-Saxon England', *Anglo-Saxon Studies in Archaeology and History*, 15 (2008), pp. 240–53.

R. Drögereit, 'Gab es eine angelsächsische Königskanzlei?', *Archiv für Urkundenforschung*, 13 (1935), pp. 335–436.

F. Dumas, 'Le début de l'époque féodale en France d'après les monnaies', *Cercle d'études numismatiques*, 10 (1973), pp. 65–77.

D. N. Dumville, 'St Cathróe of Metz and the Hagiography of Exoticism', in J. Carey, M. Herbert, and P. Ó Riain (eds), *Studies in Irish Hagiography: Saints and Scholars* (Dublin, 2001), pp. 172–88.

D. N. Dumville, 'The Terminology of Overkingship in Early Anglo-Saxon England', in J. Hines (ed.), *The Anglo-Saxons from the Migration Period to the Eighth Century: An Ethnographic Perspective* (Woodbridge, 1997), pp. 345–73.

D. N. Dumville, 'The Tribal Hidage: An Introduction to its Texts and their History', in S. Bassett (ed.), *The Origins of Anglo-Saxon Kingdoms* (London, 1989), pp. 225–30.

D. N. Dumville, *Wessex and England from Alfred to Edgar* (Woodbridge, 1992).

D. N. Dumville, 'The West Saxon Genealogical Regnal List: Manuscripts and Texts', *Anglia*, 104 (1986), pp. 1–32.

J. Dunbabin, *France in the Making, 843–1180*, 2nd edn (Oxford, 2000).

A. A. M. Duncan, 'The Battle of Carham, 1018', *Scottish Historical Review*, 55 (1976), pp. 20–8.

A. A. M. Duncan, 'Yes, the Earliest Scottish Charters', *Scottish Historical Review*, 78 (1999), pp. 1–38.

C. Dyer, *Lords and Peasants in a Changing Society: The Estates of the Bishopric of Worcester, 680–1540* (Cambridge, 1980).

C. Dyer, *Making a Living in the Middle Ages: The People of Britain, 850–1520* (New Haven, CT, 2002).

T. Dyson, 'King Alfred and the Restoration of London', *London Journal*, 15 (1990), pp. 99–110.

R. J. Eaglen and R. Grayburn, 'Gouged Reverse Dies in the Quatrefoil Issue of Cnut', *British Numismatic Journal*, 70 (2000), pp. 12–37.

B. Eagles, '"Small Shires" and *regiones* in Hampshire and the Formation of the Shires of Eastern Wessex', *Anglo-Saxon Studies in Archaeology and History* (forthcoming).

F. Edmonds, 'The Emergence and Transformation of Medieval Cumbria', *Scottish Historical Review*, 93 (2014), pp. 195–216.

N. Elias, *The Civilizing Process*, trans. E. Jephcott (2 vols, Oxford, 1978–82).

N. Elias, *The Court Society*, trans. E. Jephcott (Oxford, 1983).

P. Ettel, 'Frankish and Slavic Fortifications in Germany from the Seventh to the Eleventh Centuries', in J. Baker, S. Brookes, and A. Reynolds (eds), *Landscapes of Defence in Early Medieval Europe* (Turnhout, 2013), pp. 261–84.

R. Faith, *The English Peasantry and the Growth of Lordship* (London, 1997).

D. L. Farmer, 'Prices and Wages', in H. E. Hallam (ed.), *The Agrarian History of England and Wales. Volume II: 1042–1350* (Cambridge, 1988), pp. 715–817.

G. Fellows-Jensen, 'Scandinavian Settlement in Cumbria and Dumfriesshire: The Place-Name Evidence', in J. R. Baldwin and I. D. Whyte (eds), *The Scandinavians in Cumbria* (Edinburgh, 1985), pp. 65–82.

O. Fenger, 'The Danelaw and Danish Law: Anglo-Scandinavian Legal Relations During the Viking Period', *Scandinavian Studies in Law*, 16 (1972), pp. 83–96.

F. Fernández-Armesto, 'The Survival of a Notion of *Reconquista* in Late Tenth- and Eleventh-Century León', in T. Reuter (ed.), *Warriors and Churchmen in the High Middle Ages: Essays Presented to Karl Leyser* (London, 1992), pp. 123–43.

R. W. Finn, *An Introduction to Domesday Book* (London, 1963).

D. J. V. Fisher, 'The Anti-Monastic Reaction in the Reign of Edward the Martyr', *Cambridge Historical Journal*, 10 (1952), pp. 254–70.

R. Fleming, *Britain after Rome: The Fall and Rise, 400 to 1070* (London, 2010).

R. Fleming, *Kings and Lords in Conquest England* (Cambridge, 1991).

R. Fleming, 'Monastic Lands and England's Defence in the Viking Age', *English Historical Review*, 100 (1985), pp. 247–65.

R. A. Fletcher, 'Reconquest and Crusade in Spain, *c*.1050–1150', *Transactions of the Royal Historical Society*, 5th series, 37 (1987), pp. 31–47.

R. A. Fletcher, *Saint James's Catapult: The Life and Times of Diego Gelmírez of Santiago de Compostela* (Oxford, 1984).

S. Foot, *Æthelstan: The First King of England* (New Haven, CT, 2011).

S. Foot, 'The Historiography of the Anglo-Saxon "Nation-State"', in L. Scales and O. Zimmer (eds), *Power and the Nation in European History* (Cambridge, 2005), pp. 125–42.

S. Foot, 'The Making of *Angelcynn*: English Identity before the Norman Conquest', *Transactions of the Royal Historical Society*, 6th series, 6 (1996), pp. 25–49.

J. S. Forbes and D. B. Dalladay, 'Composition of English Silver Coins (870–1300)', *British Numismatic Journal*, 30 (1960–1), pp. 82–7.

J. E. Fraser, *From Caledonia to Pictland: Scotland to 795* (Edinburgh, 2009).

V. H. Galbraith, *The Making of Domesday Book* (Oxford, 1961).

A. Gannon, *The Iconography of Early Anglo-Saxon Coinage, Sixth to Eighth Centuries* (Oxford, 2003).

F. L. Ganshof, 'Charlemagne's Use of the Oath', in F. L. Ganshof, *The Carolingians and the Frankish Monarchy*, trans. J. Sondheimer (London, 1971), pp. 111–24.

F. L. Ganshof, 'Louis the Pious Reconsidered', *History*, 42 (1957), pp. 171–80.

F. L. Ganshof, 'On the Genesis and Significance of the Treaty of Verdun (843)', in F. L. Ganshof, *The Carolingians and the Frankish Monarchy*, trans. J. Sondheimer (London, 1971), pp. 289–302.

F. L. Ganshof, 'Les réformes judiciaires de Louis le Pieux', *Comptes-rendus des séances de l'Académie des Inscriptions et Belles-Lettres*, 109 (1965), pp. 418–27.

I. H. Garipzanov, 'Metamorphoses of the Early Medieval Ruler in the Carolingian World', *Early Medieval Europe*, 14 (2006), pp. 419–64.

G. Garnett, *Conquered England: Kingship, Succession, and Tenure, 1066–1166* (Oxford, 2007).

G. Garnett, 'The Origins of the Crown', *Proceedings of the British Academy*, 89 (1996), pp. 171–214.

M. Garrison, 'Divine Election for Nations—A Difficult Rhetoric for Medieval Scholars?', in L. B. Mortensen (ed.), *The Making of Christian Myths in the Periphery of Latin Christendom (c.1000–1300)* (Copenhagen, 2006), pp. 275–314.

M. Gelling, *The West Midlands in the Early Middle Ages* (Leicester, 1992).

L. Génicot, 'La *centena* et le *centenarius* dans les sources «belges» antérieures à 1200', in E. Magnou-Nortier (ed.), *Aux sources de la gestion publique. Tome I. Enquête lexicographique sur fundus, villa, domus, mansus* (Lille, 1993), pp. 85–102.

M. F. Giandrea, *Episcopal Culture in Late Anglo-Saxon England* (Woodbridge, 2007).

J. Gillingham, 'Chronicles and Coins as Evidence for Levels of Tribute and Taxation in Late Tenth- and Early Eleventh-Century England', *English Historical Review*, 105 (1990), pp. 939–50.

J. Gillingham, ' "The Most Precious Jewel in the English Crown": Levels of Danegeld and Heregeld in the Early Eleventh Century', *English Historical Review*, 104 (1989), pp. 373–84.

H. Gneuss, *Handlist of Anglo-Saxon Manuscripts: A List of Manuscripts and Manuscript Fragments Written or Owned in England up to 1100* (Tempe, AZ, 2001).

H. Gneuss, 'The Origins of Standard Old English and Æthelwold's School at Winchester', *Anglo-Saxon England*, 1 (1972), pp. 63–83.

M. Godden, 'Ælfric and Anglo-Saxon Kingship', *English Historical Review*, 102 (1987), pp. 911–15.

M. Godden, 'Apocalypse and Invasion in Late Anglo-Saxon England', in M. Godden, D. Gray, and T. Hoad (eds), *From Anglo-Saxon to Early Middle English: Studies Presented to E. G. Stanley* (Oxford, 1994), pp. 130–62.

M. Godden, 'Did King Alfred Write Anything?', *Medium Ævum*, 76 (2007), pp. 1–23.

J. Goebel, *Felony and Misdemeanor: A Study in the History of English Criminal Procedure* (New York, NY, 1937).

E. J. Goldberg, *Struggle for Empire: Kingship and Conflict under Louis the German, 817–876* (Ithaca, NY, 2006).

J. Gould, 'Third Report of the Excavations at Tamworth, Staffs., 1968—The Western Entrance to the Saxon Borough', *South Staffordshire Archaeological and Historical Society Transactions*, 10 (1969), pp. 32–42.

A. Gransden, 'Traditionalism and Continuity during the Last Century of Anglo-Saxon Monasticism', *Journal of Ecclesiastical History*, 40 (1989), pp. 159–207.

J. L. Grassi, 'The Lands and Revenues of Edward the Confessor', *English Historical Review*, 117 (2002), pp. 251–83.

M. Gretsch, 'Æthelwold's Translation of the *Regula Sancti Benedicti* and its Latin Exemplar', *Anglo-Saxon England*, 3 (1974), pp. 125–51.

M. Gretsch, *The Intellectual Foundations of the English Benedictine Reform* (Cambridge, 1999).

M. Gretsch, 'Winchester Vocabulary and Standard Old English: The Vernacular in Late Anglo-Saxon England', *Bulletin of the John Rylands University Library of Manchester*, 83 (2001), pp. 41–87.

P. Grierson, 'The *Gratia Dei Rex* Coinage of Charles the Bald', in M. T. Gibson and J. L. Nelson (eds), *Charles the Bald: Court and Kingdom*, 2nd edn (Aldershot, 1990), pp. 52–64.

P. Grierson, 'Numismatics and the Historian', *Numismatic Chronicle*, 2 (1962), pp. i–xvii.

P. Grierson and M. A. S. Blackburn, *Medieval European Coinage with a Catalogue of the Coins in the Fitzwilliam Museum, Cambridge. I: The Early Middle Ages (5th–10th Centuries)* (Cambridge, 1986).

S. H. Gullbekk, 'Myntforringelse i Danmark og innføring av monopolmynt under Sven Estridsen (1047–74)', *Nordisk Numismatisk Årsskrift* (1994–6), pp. 111–29.

S. H. Gullbekk, 'Renovatio monetae i Norge i middelalderen', *Nordisk Numismatisk Årsskrift* (1992–3), pp. 52–87.

D. M. Hadley, ' "And They Proceeded to Plough and to Support Themselves": The Scandinavian Settlement of England', *Anglo-Norman Studies*, 19 (1997), pp. 69–96.

D. M. Hadley, *The Northern Danelaw: Its Social Structure, c.800–1100* (London, 2000).

D. M. Hadley, 'Viking and Native: Re-thinking Identity in the Danelaw', *Early Medieval Europe*, 11 (2002), pp. 45–70.

D. M. Hadley, *The Vikings in England: Settlement, Society and Culture* (Manchester, 2006).

K. Halloran, 'Anlaf Guthfrithson at York: A Non-Existent Kingship?', *Northern History*, 50 (2013), pp. 180–5.

M. Hare, 'Kings, Crowns and Festivals: The Origins of Gloucester as a Royal Ceremonial Centre', *Transactions of the Bristol and Gloucestershire Archaeological Society*, 115 (1997), pp. 41–78.

E. J. Harris, 'Debasement of the Coinage', *Seaby's Coin and Medal Bulletin*, 524 (January 1962), pp. 5–7.

E. J. Harris, 'The Stuff of Coins', *Seaby's Coin and Medal Bulletin*, 521 (October 1961), pp. 389–90.

C. Hart, *The Danelaw* (London, 1992).

C. Hart, *The Hidation of Cambridgeshire* (Leicester, 1974).

C. Hart, *The Hidation of Northamptonshire* (Leicester, 1970).

C. Heighway, 'Gloucester and the New Minster of St Oswald', in N. J. Higham and D. H. Hill (eds), *Edward the Elder, 899–924* (London, 2001), pp. 102–11.

M. Herbert, '*Rí Éirenn, Rí Alban*, Kingship and Identity in the Ninth and Tenth Centuries', in S. Taylor (ed.), *Kings, Clerics and Chronicles in Scotland, 500–1297: Essays in Honour of Marjorie Ogilvie Anderson on the Occasion of her Ninetieth Birthday* (Dublin, 2000), pp. 62–72.

D. H. Hill, 'Athelstan's Urban Reforms', *Anglo-Saxon Studies in Archaeology and History*, 11 (2000), pp. 173–86.

D. H. Hill, *An Atlas of Anglo-Saxon England* (Oxford, 1981).

D. H. Hill, 'Gazetteer of Burghal Hidage Sites', in D. H. Hill and A. R. Rumble (eds), *The Defence of Wessex: The Burghal Hidage and Anglo-Saxon Fortifications* (Manchester, 1996), pp. 189–231.

D. H. Hill, 'The Shiring of Mercia—Again', in N. J. Higham and D. H. Hill (eds), *Edward the Elder, 899–924* (London, 2001), pp. 144–59.

D. H. Hill and A. R. Rumble, 'Introduction', in D. H. Hill and A. R. Rumble (eds), *The Defence of Wessex: The Burghal Hidage and Anglo-Saxon Fortifications* (Manchester, 1996), pp. 1–4.

D. A. Hinton, 'The Fortifications and their Shires', in D. H. Hill and A. R. Rumble (eds), *The Defence of Wessex: The Burghal Hidage and Anglo-Saxon Fortifications* (Manchester, 1996), pp. 151–9.

D. A. Hinton, 'The Large Towns, 600–1300', in D. M. Palliser (ed.), *The Cambridge Urban History of Britain. Volume I: 600–1540* (Cambridge, 2000), pp. 217–43.

W. Hofstetter, 'Winchester and the Standardization of Old English Vocabulary', *Anglo-Saxon England*, 17 (1988), pp. 139–61.

C. E. Hohler, 'Some Service Books of the Later Saxon Church', in D. Parsons (ed.), *Tenth-Century Studies: Essays in Commemoration of the Millennium of the Council of Winchester and Regularis Concordia* (London, 1975), pp. 60–83, 217–27.

C. W. Hollister, '1066: The "Feudal Revolution"', *American Historical Review*, 73 (1968), pp. 708–23.

C. W. Hollister, *Anglo-Saxon Military Institutions on the Eve of the Norman Conquest* (Oxford, 1962).

J. C. Holt, *Magna Carta*, 2nd edn (Cambridge, 1992).

J. C. Holt, *The Northerners: A Study in the Reign of King John* (Oxford, 1961).

J. C. Holt, 'The Origins of the Constitutional Tradition in England', in J. C. Holt, *Magna Carta and Medieval Government* (London, 1985).

R. Holt, 'The Urban Transformation in England, 900–1100', *Anglo-Norman Studies*, 32 (2010), pp. 57–78.

N. Hooper, 'Some Observations on the Navy in Late Anglo-Saxon England', in C. Harper-Bill, C. J. Holdsworth, and J. L. Nelson (eds), *Studies in Medieval History Presented to R. Allen Brown* (Woodbridge, 1989), pp. 203–13.

N. Howe, *Migration and Mythmaking in Anglo-Saxon England* (New Haven, CT, 1989; reprinted with new introduction, Notre Dame, IN, 2001).

B. T. Hudson, 'Cnut and the Scottish Kings', *English Historical Review*, 107 (1992), pp. 350–60.

J. G. H. Hudson, *The Oxford History of the Laws of England. Volume II: 871–1216* (Oxford, 2012).

N. D. Hurnard, 'The Anglo-Norman Franchises', *English Historical Review*, 64 (1949), pp. 289–327, 433–60.

P. R. Hyams, *Rancor and Reconciliation in Medieval England* (Ithaca, NY, 2003).

M. Innes, 'Danelaw Identities: Ethnicity, Regionalism, and Political Allegiance', in D. M. Hadley and J. D. Richards (eds), *Cultures in Contact: Scandinavian Settlement in England in the Ninth and Tenth Centuries* (Turnhout, 2000), pp. 65–88.

M. Innes, *State and Society in the Early Middle Ages: The Middle Rhine Valley, 400–1000* (Cambridge, 2000).

C. Insley, 'Athelstan, Charters and the English in Cornwall', in M. T. Flanagan and J. A. Green (eds), *Charters and Charter Scholarship in Britain and Ireland* (Basingstoke, 2005), pp. 15–31.

C. Insley, 'Charters, Ritual and Late Tenth-Century English Kingship', in J. L. Nelson, S. Reynolds, and S. M. Johns (eds), *Gender and Historiography: Studies in the Earlier Middle Ages in Honour of Pauline Stafford* (London, 2012), pp. 75–89.

C. Insley, 'Kings and Lords in Tenth-Century Cornwall', *History*, 98 (2013), pp. 2–22.

C. Insley, 'Southumbria', in P. Stafford (ed.), *A Companion to the Early Middle Ages: Britain and Ireland, c.500–c.1100* (Chichester, 2009), pp. 322–40.

A. Isla Frez, *La Alta Edad Media. Siglos VIII–XI* (Madrid, 2002).

J. Jarnut, 'Ludwig der Fromme, Lothar I. und das Regnum Italiae', in P. Godman and R. Collins (eds), *Charlemagne's Heir: New Perspectives on the Reign of Louis the Pious (814–840)* (Oxford, 1990), pp. 349–62.

B. Jaski, *Early Irish Kingship and Succession* (Dublin, 2000).

S. Jayakumar, 'Eadwig and Edgar: Politics, Propaganda, Faction', in D. Scragg (ed.), *Edgar, King of the English 959–975: New Interpretations* (Woodbridge, 2008), pp. 83–103.

S. Jayakumar, 'Reform and Retribution: The "Anti-Monastic Reaction" in the Reign of Edward the Martyr', in S. Baxter, C. E. Karkov, J. L. Nelson, and D. Pelteret (eds), *Early Medieval Studies in Memory of Patrick Wormald* (Farnham, 2009), pp. 337–52.

S. Jayakumar, 'Some Reflections on the "Foreign Policies" of Edgar "the Peaceable"', *Haskins Society Journal*, 10 (2001), pp. 17–37.

D. Jenkins and M. E. Owen, 'Glossary', in D. Jenkins and M. E. Owen (eds), *The Welsh Law of Women* (Cardiff, 1980), pp. 187–221.

P. A. Jewell (ed.), *The Experimental Earthwork on Overton Down, Wiltshire, 1960* (London, 1963).

E. John, *Orbis Britanniae and Other Studies* (Leicester, 1966).

J. E. A. Jolliffe, *Angevin Kingship*, 2nd edn (London, 1963).

J. E. A. Jolliffe, *Pre-Feudal England: The Jutes* (Oxford, 1933).

G. R. J. Jones, 'Multiple Estates and Early Settlement', in P. H. Sawyer (ed.), *Medieval Settlement: Continuity and Change* (London, 1976), pp. 15–40.

P. F. Jones, *A Concordance to the Historia Ecclesiastica of Bede* (Cambridge, MA, 1929).

M. de Jong, *The Penitential State: Authority and Atonement in the Age of Louis the Pious, 814–840* (Cambridge, 2009).

K. Jonsson, *The New Era: The Reformation of the Late Anglo-Saxon Coinage* (Stockholm, 1987).

K. Jonsson, 'The Pre-Reform Coinage of Edgar—The Legacy of the Anglo-Saxon Kingdoms', in B. Cook and G. Williams (eds), *Coinage and History in the North Sea World, c.500–1250: Essays in Honour of Marion Archibald* (Leiden, 2006), pp. 325–46.

K. Jonsson and G. van der Meer, 'Mints and Moneyers, c.973–1066', in K. Jonsson (ed.), *Studies in Late Anglo-Saxon Coinage in Memory of Bror Emil Hildebrand* (Stockholm, 1990), pp. 47–136.

E. Joranson, *The Danegeld in France* (Rock Island, IL, 1923).

E. H. Kantorowicz, *The King's Two Bodies: A Study in Mediaeval Political Theology* (Princeton, NJ, 1957).

W. E. Kapelle, *The Norman Conquest of the North: The Region and its Transformation, 1000–1135* (Chapel Hill, NC, 1979).

D. Keene, 'Text, Visualisation and Politics: London, 1150–1250', *Transactions of the Royal Historical Society*, 6th series, 18 (2008), pp. 69–99.

F. Kelly, *A Guide to Early Irish Law* (Dublin, 1988).

M. Kempshall, 'No Bishop, No King: The Ministerial Ideology of Kingship and Asser's *Res Gestae Aelfredi*', in R. Gameson and H. Leyser (eds), *Belief and Culture in the Early Middle Ages: Studies Presented to Henry Mayr-Harting* (Oxford, 2001), pp. 106–27.

A. Kennedy, 'Disputes about *bocland*: The Forum for their Adjudication', *Anglo-Saxon England*, 14 (1985), pp. 175–95.

A. Kennedy, 'Law and Litigation in the *Libellus Æthelwoldi Episcopi*', *Anglo-Saxon England*, 24 (1995), pp. 131–83.

N. R. Ker, *Catalogue of Manuscripts Containing Anglo-Saxon* (Oxford, 1957).

N. R. Ker, 'The Handwriting of Archbishop Wulfstan', in P. Clemoes and K. Hughes (eds), *England before the Conquest: Studies in Primary Sources Presented to Dorothy Whitelock* (Cambridge, 1971), pp. 315–31.

P. Kershaw, 'The Alfred-Guthrum Treaty: Scripting Accommodation and Interaction in Viking Age England', in D. M. Hadley and J. D. Richards (eds), *Cultures in Contact: Scandinavian Settlement in England in the Ninth and Tenth Centuries* (Turnhout, 2000), pp. 43–64.

S. Keynes, 'An Abbot, an Archbishop, and the Viking Raids of 1006–7 and 1009–12', *Anglo-Saxon England*, 36 (2007), pp. 151–220.

S. Keynes, 'The Æthelings in Normandy', *Anglo-Norman Studies*, 13 (1990), pp. 173–205.

S. Keynes, *An Atlas of Attestations in Anglo-Saxon Charters, c.670–1066* (Cambridge, 2002).

S. Keynes, 'Church Councils, Royal Assemblies, and Anglo-Saxon Royal Diplomas', in G. R. Owen-Crocker and B. W. Schneider (eds), *Kingship, Legislation and Power in Anglo-Saxon England* (Woodbridge, 2013), pp. 17–182.

S. Keynes, 'The Control of Kent in the Ninth Century', *Early Medieval Europe*, 2 (1993), pp. 111–31.

S. Keynes, 'County Hidage', in M. Lapidge, J. Blair, S. Keynes, and D. Scragg (eds), *The Wiley Blackwell Encyclopedia of Anglo-Saxon England*, 2nd edn (Chichester, 2014), pp. 128–9.

S. Keynes, 'Crime and Punishment in the Reign of King Æthelred the Unready', in I. Wood and N. Lund (eds), *People and Places in Northern Europe, 500–1600: Essays in Honour of Peter Hayes Sawyer* (Woodbridge, 1991), pp. 67–81.

S. Keynes, 'The Cult of King Alfred the Great', *Anglo-Saxon England*, 28 (1999), pp. 225–356.

S. Keynes, 'The Declining Reputation of King Æthelred the Unready', in D. H. Hill (ed.), *Ethelred the Unready: Papers from the Millenary Conference* (Oxford, 1978), pp. 227–53.

S. Keynes, *The Diplomas of King Æthelred 'the Unready', 978–1016: A Study in their Use as Historical Evidence* (Cambridge, 1980).

S. Keynes, 'The "Dunstan B" Charters', *Anglo-Saxon England*, 23 (1994), pp. 165–93.

S. Keynes, 'Edgar, *rex admirabilis*', in D. Scragg (ed.), *Edgar, King of the English 959–975: New Interpretations* (Woodbridge, 2008), pp. 3–59.

S. Keynes, 'Edward, King of the Anglo-Saxons', in N. J. Higham and D. H. Hill (eds), *Edward the Elder, 899–924* (London, 2001), pp. 40–66.

S. Keynes, 'England, 700–900', in R. McKitterick (ed.), *The New Cambridge Medieval History II, c.700–c.900* (Cambridge, 1995), pp. 18–42.

S. Keynes, 'England, *c.*900–1016', in T. Reuter (ed.), *The New Cambridge Medieval History III, c.900–c.1024* (Cambridge, 1999), pp. 456–84.

S. Keynes, 'The Fonthill Letter', in M. Korhammer (ed.), *Words, Texts and Manuscripts: Studies in Anglo-Saxon Culture Presented to Helmut Gneuss on the Occasion of his Sixty-Fifth Birthday* (Cambridge, 1992), pp. 53–97.

S. Keynes, 'King Alfred and the Mercians', in M. A. S. Blackburn and D. N. Dumville (eds), *Kings, Currency and Alliances: History and Coinage of Southern England in the Ninth Century* (Woodbridge, 1998), pp. 1–45.

S. Keynes, 'King Athelstan's Books', in M. Lapidge and H. Gneuss (eds), *Learning and Literature in Anglo-Saxon England: Studies Presented to Peter Clemoes on the Occasion of his Sixty-Fifth Birthday* (Cambridge, 1985), pp. 143–201.

S. Keynes, 'Manuscripts of the *Anglo-Saxon Chronicle*', in R. Gameson (ed.), *The Cambridge History of the Book in Britain. Volume I: c.400–1100* (Cambridge, 2012), pp. 537–52.

S. Keynes, 'Re-Reading King Æthelred the Unready', in D. Bates, J. Crick, and S. Hamilton (eds), *Writing Medieval Biography, 750–1250: Essays in Honour of Professor Frank Barlow* (Woodbridge, 2006), pp. 77–97.

S. Keynes, 'A Tale of Two Kings: Alfred the Great and Æthelred the Unready', *Transactions of the Royal Historical Society*, 5th series, 36 (1986), pp. 195–217.

S. Keynes, 'The West Saxon Charters of King Æthelwulf and his Sons', *English Historical Review*, 109 (1994), pp. 1109–49.

S. Keynes, 'Wulfstan I', in M. Lapidge, J. Blair, S. Keynes, and D. Scragg (eds), *The Wiley Blackwell Encyclopedia of Anglo-Saxon England*, 2nd edn (Chichester, 2014), pp. 512–13.

S. Keynes and R. Love, 'Earl Godwine's Ship', *Anglo-Saxon England*, 38 (2009), pp. 185–223.

H. Kleinschmidt, 'Die Titulaturen englischer Könige im 10. und 11. Jahrhundert', in H. Wolfram and A. Scharer (eds), *Intitulatio III. Lateinische Herrschertitel und Herrschertitulaturen vom 7. bis zum 13. Jahrhundert* (Vienna, 1988), pp. 75–129.

D. Knowles, *The Monastic Order in England*, 2nd edn (Cambridge, 1963).

L. Kovács, 'A kora Árpad-kori pénzújításról', *Századok*, 130 (1996), pp. 823–60.

J. Lafaurie, 'Numismatique. Des Carolingiens aux Capétiens', *Cahiers de civilisation médiévale*, 13 (1970), pp. 117–37.

H. H. Lamb, *Climate, History and the Modern World*, 2nd edn (London, 1995).

T. B. Lambert, 'Royal Protections and Private Justice: A Reassessment of Cnut's "Reserved Pleas"', in S. Jurasinski, L. Oliver, and A. Rabin (eds), *English Law before Magna Carta: Felix Liebermann and Die Gesetze der Angelsachsen* (Leiden, 2010), pp. 157–75.

T. B. Lambert, 'Theft, Homicide and Crime in Late Anglo-Saxon Law', *Past and Present*, 214 (2012), pp. 3–43.

M. Lapidge, 'Æthelwold as Scholar and Teacher', in B. Yorke (ed.), *Bishop Æthelwold: His Career and Influence* (Woodbridge, 1988), pp. 89–117.

M. Lapidge, 'Some Latin Poems as Evidence for the Reign of Athelstan', *Anglo-Saxon England*, 9 (1981), pp. 61–98.

L. M. Larson, *The King's Household in England Before the Norman Conquest* (Madison, WI, 1904).

R. E. Latham et al., *Dictionary of Medieval Latin from British Sources* (Oxford, 1975–2013).

R. Lavelle, '*Ine* 70.1 and Royal Provision in Anglo-Saxon Wessex', in G. R. Owen-Crocker and B. W. Schneider (eds), *Kingship, Legislation and Power in Anglo-Saxon England* (Woodbridge, 2013), pp. 259–73.

R. Lavelle, 'The Politics of Rebellion: The Ætheling Æthelwold and West Saxon Royal Succession, 899–902', in P. Skinner (ed.), *Challenging the Boundaries of Medieval History: The Legacy of Timothy Reuter* (Turnhout, 2009), pp. 51–80.

M. K. Lawson, *Cnut: England's Viking King* (Stroud, 2004).

M. K. Lawson, 'The Collection of Danegeld and Heregeld in the Reigns of Æthelred II and Cnut', *English Historical Review*, 99 (1984), pp. 721–38.

M. K. Lawson, 'Danegeld and Heregeld Once More', *English Historical Review*, 105 (1990), pp. 951–61.

M. K. Lawson, '"Those Stories Look True": Levels of Taxation in the Reigns of Æthelred II and Cnut', *English Historical Review*, 104 (1989), pp. 385–406.

M. Lessen, 'A Presumed "Hampshire" Hoard of Eadgar CC Coins', *Numismatic Circular*, 111 (2003), pp. 61–2.

W. Levison, *England and the Continent in the Eighth Century* (Oxford, 1946).

C. P. Lewis, 'An Introduction to the Lancashire Domesday', in A. Williams (ed.), *The Lancashire Domesday* (London, 1991), pp. 1–41.

K. J. Leyser, 'Ottonian Government', *English Historical Review*, 96 (1981), pp. 721–53.

K. J. Leyser, 'The Ottonians and Wessex', in K. J. Leyser, *Communications and Power in Medieval Europe: The Carolingian and Ottonian Centuries*, ed. T. Reuter (London, 1994), pp. 73–104.

K. J. Leyser, *Rule and Conflict in an Early Medieval Society: Ottonian Saxony* (Oxford, 1979).

P. Linehan, 'History in a Changing World: The Case of Medieval Spain', in P. Linehan, *Past and Present in Medieval Spain* (Aldershot, 1992), I, pp. 1–22.

P. Linehan, 'Spain in the Twelfth Century', in D. Luscombe and J. Riley-Smith (eds), *The New Cambridge Medieval History IV, c.1024–c.1198* (2 vols, Cambridge, 2004), ii, 475–509.

H. R. Loyn, 'Gesiths and Thegns in Anglo-Saxon England from the Seventh to the Tenth Century', *English Historical Review*, 70 (1955), pp. 529–49.

H. R. Loyn, *The Governance of Anglo-Saxon England, 500–1087* (London, 1984).

H. R. Loyn, 'The Hundred in England in the Tenth and Eleventh Centuries', in H. Hearder and H. R. Loyn (eds), *British Government and Administration: Studies Presented to S. B. Chrimes* (Cardiff, 1974), pp. 1–15.

H. R. Loyn, 'Numismatics and the Medieval Historian: A Comment on Recent Numismatic Contributions to the History of England, c.899–1154', *British Numismatic Journal*, 60 (1990), pp. 29–36.

H. R. Loyn, 'Progress in Anglo-Saxon Monetary History', in M. A. S. Blackburn (ed.), *Anglo-Saxon Monetary History: Essays in Memory of Michael Dolley* (Leicester, 1986), pp. 1–10.

J. Lukowski and H. Zawadzki, *A Concise History of Poland*, 2nd edn (Cambridge, 2006).

C. S. S. Lyon, '206', in M. Allen and S. Moorhead (eds), 'Coin Register 2010', *British Numismatic Journal*, 80 (2010), pp. 207–37 at 226.

C. S. S. Lyon, 'The Earliest Signed Penny of Cricklade: A Local Find of Edgar's "Circumscription Cross" Issue', in T. Abramson (ed.), *Studies in Early Medieval Coinage, Volume 2: New Perspectives* (Woodbridge, 2011), pp. 181–2.

S. Lyon, 'The Coinage of Edward the Elder', in N. J. Higham and D. H. Hill (eds), *Edward the Elder, 899–924* (London, 2001), pp. 67–78.

S. Lyon, 'Die-Cutting Styles in the *Last Small Cross* Issue of c.1009–1017 and Some Problematic East Anglian Dies and Die-Links', *British Numismatic Journal*, 68 (1998), pp. 21–41.

S. Lyon, 'Dr Michael Dolley, MRIA, FSA', *British Numismatic Journal*, 52 (1982), pp. 265–71.

S. Lyon, 'Variations in Currency in Late Anglo-Saxon England', in R. A. G. Carson (ed.), *Mints, Dies and Currency: Essays Dedicated to the Memory of Albert Baldwin* (London, 1971), pp. 101–20.

S. Lyon and S. Holmes, 'The Circumscription Cross Penny of Edgar from Middleton on the Wolds', *Numismatic Circular*, 110 (2002), p. 192.

A. W. Lyons and W. A. Mackay, 'The Coinage of Æthelred I (865–871)', *British Numismatic Journal*, 77 (2007), pp. 71–118.

A. W. Lyons and W. A. Mackay, 'The Lunettes Coinage of Alfred the Great', *British Numismatic Journal*, 78 (2008), pp. 38–110.

A. MacColl, 'The Meaning of "Britain" in Medieval and Early Modern England', *Journal of British Studies*, 45 (2006), pp. 248–69.

P. MacCotter, *Medieval Ireland: Territorial, Political and Economic Divisions* (Dublin, 2008).

J. R. Maddicott, 'Edward the Confessor's Return to England in 1041', *English Historical Review*, 119 (2004), pp. 650–66.

J. R. Maddicott, *The Origins of the English Parliament, 924–1327* (Oxford, 2010).

F. W. Maitland, *Domesday Book and Beyond: Three Essays in the Early History of England* (Cambridge, 1897).

L. Mariotti, *Italy, Past and Present* (2 vols, London, 1848).

L. Marten, 'The Shiring of East Anglia: An Alternative Hypothesis', *Historical Research*, 81 (2008), pp. 1–27.

K. L. Maund, *Ireland, Wales, and England in the Eleventh Century* (Woodbridge, 1991).

H. McKerrell and R. B. K. Stevenson, 'Some Analyses of Anglo-Saxon and Associated Oriental Silver Coinage', in E. T. Hall and D. M. Metcalf (eds), *Methods of Chemical and Metallurgical Investigation of Ancient Coinage* (London, 1972), pp. 195–209.

R. McKitterick, *Charlemagne: The Formation of a European Identity* (Cambridge, 2008).

R. McKitterick, 'Constructing the Past in the Early Middle Ages: The Case of the Royal Frankish Annals', *Transactions of the Royal Historical Society*, 6th series, 7 (1997), pp. 101–29.

B. Meehan, 'The Siege of Durham, the Battle of Carham and the Cession of Lothian', *Scottish Historical Review*, 55 (1976), pp. 1–19.

R. Meens, 'Politics, Mirrors of Princes and the Bible: Sins, Kings and the Well-being of the Realm', *Early Medieval Europe*, 7 (1998), pp. 345–57.

D. M. Metcalf, *An Atlas of Anglo-Saxon and Norman Coin Finds, c.973–1086* (London, 1998).

D. M. Metcalf, 'The Monetary Economy of Ninth-Century England South of the Humber: A Topographical Analysis', in M. A. S. Blackburn and D. N. Dumville (eds), *Kings, Currency and Alliances: History and Coinage of Southern England in the Ninth Century* (Woodbridge, 1998), pp. 167–97.

D. M. Metcalf, 'The Monetary History of England in the Tenth Century Viewed in the Perspective of the Eleventh Century', in M. A. S. Blackburn (ed.), *Anglo-Saxon Monetary History: Essays in Memory of Michael Dolley* (Leicester, 1986), pp. 133–57.

D. M. Metcalf, 'The Rome (Forum) Hoard of 1883', *British Numismatic Journal*, 62 (1992), pp. 63–96.

D. M. Metcalf, 'The Taxation of Moneyers under Edward the Confessor and in 1086', in J. C. Holt (ed.), *Domesday Studies: Papers Read at the Novocentenary Conference of the Royal Historical Society and the Institute of British Geographers, Winchester, 1986* (Woodbridge, 1987), pp. 279–93.

D. M. Metcalf, *Thrymsas and Sceattas in the Ashmolean Museum, Oxford* (3 vols, London, 1993–4).

D. M. Metcalf, 'Were Ealdormen Exercising Independent Control over the Coinage in Mid Tenth Century England?', *British Numismatic Journal*, 57 (1987), pp. 24–33.

D. M. Metcalf and J. P. Northover, 'Carolingian and Viking Coins from the Cuerdale Hoard: An Interpretation and Comparison of their Metal Contents', *Numismatic Chronicle*, 148 (1988), pp. 97–116.

D. M. Metcalf and J. P. Northover, 'Coinage Alloys from the Time of Offa and Charlemagne to c.864', *Numismatic Chronicle*, 149 (1989), pp. 101–20.

D. M. Metcalf and J. P. Northover, 'Debasement of Coinage in Southern England in the Age of King Alfred', *Numismatic Chronicle*, 145 (1985), pp. 150–76.

D. M. Metcalf and J. P. Northover, 'Interpreting the Alloy of the Later Anglo-Saxon Coinage', *British Numismatic Journal*, 56 (1986), pp. 35–63.

D. M. Metcalf and J. P. Northover, 'Sporadic Debasement in the English Coinage, c.1009–1052', *Numismatic Chronicle*, 162 (2002), pp. 217–36.

E. Miller, *The Abbey and Bishopric of Ely: The Social History of an Ecclesiastical Estate from the Tenth Century to the Early Fourteenth Century* (Cambridge, 1951).

M. Molnár, *A Concise History of Hungary*, trans. A. Magyar (Cambridge, 2001).

G. Molyneaux, 'Did the English Really Think they were God's Elect in the Anglo-Saxon Period?', *Journal of Ecclesiastical History*, 65 (2014), pp. 721–37.

G. Molyneaux, 'The *Old English Bede*: English Ideology or Christian Instruction?', *English Historical Review*, 124 (2009), pp. 1289–323.

G. Molyneaux, 'The *Ordinance Concerning the Dunsæte* and the Anglo-Welsh Frontier in the Late Tenth and Eleventh Centuries', *Anglo-Saxon England*, 40 (2012), pp. 249–72.

G. Molyneaux, 'Why were some Tenth-Century English Kings Presented as Rulers of Britain?', *Transactions of the Royal Historical Society*, 6th series, 21 (2011), pp. 59–91.

C. J. Morris, *Marriage and Murder in Eleventh-Century Northumbria: A Study of 'De obsessione Dunelmi'* (York, 1992).

W. A. Morris, *The Frankpledge System* (London, 1910).

W. A. Morris, *The Medieval English Sheriff to 1300* (Manchester, 1927).

E. Müller-Mertens, *Die Reichsstruktur im Spiegel der Herrschaftspraxis Ottos des Grossen* (Berlin, 1980).

J. Mumby, 'The Descent of Family Land in Later Anglo-Saxon England', *Historical Research*, 84 (2011), pp. 1–17.

A. C. Murray, 'From Roman to Frankish Gaul: "Centenarii" and "Centenae" in the Administration of the Merovingian Kingdom', *Traditio*, 44 (1988), pp. 59–100.

R. Naismith, 'The English Monetary Economy, *c.*973–1100: The Contribution of Single-Finds', *Economic History Review*, 66 (2013), pp. 198–225.

R. Naismith, 'Kings, Crisis and Coinage Reforms in the Mid-Eighth Century', *Early Medieval Europe*, 20 (2012), pp. 291–332.

R. Naismith, 'London and its Mint, *c.*880–1066: A Preliminary Survey', *British Numismatic Journal*, 83 (2013), pp. 44–74.

R. Naismith, *Money and Power in Anglo-Saxon England: The Southern English Kingdoms, 757–865* (Cambridge, 2012).

R. Naismith, 'Payments for Land and Privilege in Anglo-Saxon England', *Anglo-Saxon England*, 41 (2012), pp. 277–342.

R. Naismith, 'Prelude to Reform: Tenth-Century English Coinage in Perspective', in R. Naismith, M. Allen, and E. Screen (eds), *Early Medieval Monetary History: Studies in Memory of Mark Blackburn* (Farnham, 2014), pp. 39–83.

R. Naismith, 'The Social Significance of Monetization in the Early Middle Ages', *Past and Present*, 223 (2014), pp. 3–39.

C. Neff, 'Scandinavian Elements in the Wantage Code of Æthelred II', *Journal of Legal History*, 10 (1989), pp. 285–316.

J. L. Nelson, *Charles the Bald* (Harlow, 1992).

J. L. Nelson, 'The Earliest Surviving Royal *Ordo*: Some Liturgical and Historical Aspects', in B. Tierney and P. Linehan (eds), *Authority and Power: Studies in Medieval Law and Government Presented to Walter Ullmann* (Cambridge, 1980), pp. 29–48.

J. L. Nelson, 'The First Use of the Second Anglo-Saxon *Ordo*', in J. Barrow and A. Wareham (eds), *Myth, Rulership, Church and Charters: Essays in Honour of Nicholas Brooks* (Aldershot, 2008), pp. 117–26.

J. L. Nelson, 'Inauguration Rituals', in P. H. Sawyer and I. N. Wood (eds), *Early Medieval Kingship* (Leeds, 1977), pp. 50–71.

J. L. Nelson, ' "A King Across the Sea": Alfred in Continental Perspective', *Transactions of the Royal Historical Society*, 5th series, 36 (1986), pp. 45–68.

J. L. Nelson, 'Kingship and Royal Government', in R. McKitterick (ed.), *The New Cambridge Medieval History II, c.700–c.900* (Cambridge, 1995), pp. 383–430.

J. L. Nelson, 'Kingship, Law and Liturgy in the Political Thought of Hincmar of Rheims', *English Historical Review*, 92 (1977), pp. 241–79.

J. L. Nelson, 'The Political Ideas of Alfred of Wessex', in A. J. Duggan (ed.), *Kings and Kingship in Medieval Europe* (London, 1993), pp. 125–58.

J. L. Nelson, 'Public *Histories* and Private History in the Work of Nithard', *Speculum*, 60 (1985), pp. 251–93.

J. L. Nelson, 'Rulers and Government', in T. Reuter (ed.), *The New Cambridge Medieval History III, c.900–c.1024* (Cambridge, 1999), pp. 95–129.

J. L. Nelson, 'The Second English *Ordo*', in J. L. Nelson, *Politics and Ritual in Early Medieval Europe* (London, 1986), pp. 361–74.

T. F. X. Noble, 'The Monastic Ideal as a Model for Empire: The Case of Louis the Pious', *Revue bénédictine*, 86 (1976), pp. 235–50.

A. Nørgård Jørgensen, 'The Kanhave Canal on Samsø—New Investigations', *Château Gaillard*, 18 (1998), pp. 153–8.

B. R. O'Brien, *God's Peace and King's Peace: The Laws of Edward the Confessor* (Philadelphia, PA, 1999).

C. E. Odegaard, 'Carolingian Oaths of Fidelity', *Speculum*, 16 (1941), pp. 284–96.

C. T. Onions, G. W. S. Friedrichsen, and R. W. Burchfield, *The Oxford Dictionary of English Etymology* (Oxford, 1966).

R. Oram, *Domination and Lordship: Scotland, 1070–1230* (Edinburgh, 2011).

O. J. Padel, 'Cornwall', in M. Lapidge, J. Blair, S. Keynes, and D. Scragg (eds), *The Wiley Blackwell Encyclopedia of Anglo-Saxon England*, 2nd edn (Chichester, 2014), p. 124.

H. Pagan, 'Mints and Moneyers in the West Midlands and at Derby in the Reign of Eadmund (939–46)', *Numismatic Chronicle*, 155 (1995), pp. 139–61.

H. Pagan, 'The Pre-Reform Coinage of Edgar', in D. Scragg (ed.), *Edgar, King of the English 959–975: New Interpretations* (Woodbridge, 2008), pp. 192–207.

D. M. Palliser, 'An Introduction to the Yorkshire Domesday', in A. Williams and G. H. Martin (eds), *The Yorkshire Domesday* (London, 1992), pp. 1–38.

S. Patzold, 'Eine „loyale Palastrebellion" der „Reichseinheitspartei"? Zur 'Divisio imperii' von 817 und zu den Ursachen des Aufstands gegen Ludwig den Frommen im Jahre 830', *Frühmittelalterliche Studien*, 40 (2006), pp. 43–77.

D. Pelteret, 'An Anonymous Historian of Edward the Elder's Reign', in S. Baxter, C. E. Karkov, J. L. Nelson, and D. Pelteret (eds), *Early Medieval Studies in Memory of Patrick Wormald* (Farnham, 2009), pp. 319–36.

Ch.-E. Perrin, 'Sur le sens du mot «centena» dans les chartes lorraines du moyen âge', *Archivum Latinitatis Medii Aevi*, 5 (1930), pp. 167–98.

H. B. A. Petersson, *Anglo-Saxon Currency: King Edgar's Reform to the Norman Conquest* (Lund, 1969).

H. B. A. Petersson, 'Coins and Weights: Late Anglo-Saxon Pennies and Mints, c.973–1066', in K. Jonsson (ed.), *Studies in Late Anglo-Saxon Coinage in Memory of Bror Emil Hildebrand* (Stockholm, 1990), pp. 207–433.

R. Portass, 'All Quiet on the Western Front? Royal Politics in Galicia from c.800 to c.950', *Early Medieval Europe*, 21 (2013), pp. 283–306.

R. Portass, 'The Contours and Contexts of Public Power in Tenth-Century Liébana', *Journal of Medieval History*, 38 (2012), pp. 389–407.

D. Pratt, 'Demesne Exemption from Royal Taxation in Anglo-Saxon and Anglo-Norman England', *English Historical Review*, 128 (2013), pp. 1–34.

D. Pratt, 'The Illnesses of King Alfred the Great', *Anglo-Saxon England*, 30 (2001), pp. 39–90.

D. Pratt, *The Political Thought of King Alfred the Great* (Cambridge, 2007).

D. Pratt, 'The Voice of the King in "King Edgar's Establishment of Monasteries"', *Anglo-Saxon England*, 41 (2012), pp. 145–204.

D. Pratt, 'Written Law and the Communication of Authority in Tenth-Century England', in D. Rollason, C. Leyser, and H. Williams (eds), *England and the Continent in the Tenth Century: Studies in Honour of Wilhelm Levison (1876–1947)* (Turnhout, 2010), pp. 331–50.

H. Pryce, 'British or Welsh? National Identity in Twelfth-Century Wales', *English Historical Review*, 116 (2001), pp. 775–801.

J. A. Raftis, *The Estates of Ramsey Abbey: A Study in Economic Growth and Organization* (Toronto, 1957).

W. Rees, 'Survivals of Ancient Celtic Custom in Medieval England', in H. Lewis (ed.), *Angles and Britons* (Cardiff, 1963), pp. 148–68.

B. F. Reilly, *The Kingdom of León-Castilla under King Alfonso VI (1065–1109)* (Princeton, NJ, 1988).

T. Reuter, 'Debate: The "Feudal Revolution"', *Past and Present*, 155 (1997), pp. 177–95.

T. Reuter, 'The End of Carolingian Military Expansion', in P. Godman and R. Collins (eds), *Charlemagne's Heir: New Perspectives on the Reign of Louis the Pious (814–840)* (Oxford, 1990), pp. 391–405.

T. Reuter, *Germany in the Early Middle Ages, c.800–1056* (Harlow, 1991).

T. Reuter, 'The Making of England and Germany, 850–1050: Points of Comparison and Difference', in A. P. Smyth (ed.), *Medieval Europeans: Studies in Ethnic Identity and National Perspectives in Medieval Europe* (Basingstoke, 1998), pp. 53–70.

T. Reuter, 'The Medieval German *Sonderweg*? The Empire and its Rulers in the High Middle Ages', in A. J. Duggan (ed.), *Kings and Kingship in Medieval Europe* (London, 1993), pp. 179–211.

T. Reuter (ed.), *The New Cambridge Medieval History III, c.900–c.1024* (Cambridge, 1999).

T. Reuter, 'Nur im Westen was Neues? Das Werden prämoderner Staatsformen im europäischen Hochmittelalter', in J. Ehlers (ed.), *Deutschland und der Westen Europas im Mittelalter* (Stuttgart, 2002), pp. 327–51.

T. Reuter, 'Plunder and Tribute in the Carolingian Empire', *Transactions of the Royal Historical Society*, 5th series, 35 (1985), pp. 75–94.

A. Reynolds, *Anglo-Saxon Deviant Burial Customs* (Oxford, 2009).

S. Reynolds, *Fiefs and Vassals: The Medieval Evidence Reinterpreted* (Oxford, 1994).

S. Reynolds, 'The Historiography of the Medieval State', in M. Bentley (ed.), *Companion to Historiography* (London, 1997), pp. 117–38.

S. Reynolds, *Kingdoms and Communities in Western Europe, 900–1300*, 2nd edn (Oxford, 1997).

S. Reynolds, 'There were States in Medieval Europe: A Response to Rees Davies', *Journal of Historical Sociology*, 16 (2003), pp. 550–5.

A. Richards and A. Kuper (eds), *Councils in Action* (Cambridge, 1971).

M. Richter, 'Bede's *Angli*: Angles or English?', *Peritia*, 3 (1984), pp. 99–114.

L. Roach, 'Apocalypse and Atonement in the Politics of Æthelredian England', *English Studies*, 95 (2014), pp. 733–57.

L. Roach, *Kingship and Consent in Anglo-Saxon England, 871–978: Assemblies and the State in the Early Middle Ages* (Cambridge, 2013).

L. Roach, 'Law Codes and Legal Norms in Later Anglo-Saxon England', *Historical Research*, 86 (2013), pp. 465–86.

L. Roach, 'Penance, Submission and *deditio*: Religious Influences on Dispute Settlement in Later Anglo-Saxon England (871–1066)', *Anglo-Saxon England*, 41 (2012), pp. 343–71.

L. Roach, 'Penitential Discourse in the Diplomas of King Æthelred "the Unready"', *Journal of Ecclesiastical History*, 64 (2013), pp. 258–76.

L. Roach, 'Public Rites and Public Wrongs: Ritual Aspects of Diplomas in Tenth- and Eleventh-Century England', *Early Medieval Europe*, 19 (2011), pp. 182–203.

E. W. Robertson, *Historical Essays in Connexion with the Land, the Church &c* (Edinburgh, 1872).

N. Robertson, 'Dunstan and Monastic Reform: Tenth-Century Fact or Twelfth-Century Fiction?', *Anglo-Norman Studies*, 28 (2006), pp. 153–67.

E. Roesdahl, 'The Danish Geometrical Viking Fortresses and their Context', *Anglo-Norman Studies*, 9 (1987), pp. 208–26.

D. Roffe, 'The Lincolnshire Hundred', *Landscape History*, 3 (1981), pp. 27–36.

D. Roffe, 'The Yorkshire Summary: A Domesday Satellite', *Northern History*, 27 (1991), pp. 242–60.

D. Rollason, *Northumbria, 500–1100: Creation and Destruction of a Kingdom* (Cambridge, 2003).

D. Rollason, 'Symeon's Contribution to Historical Writing in Northern England', in D. Rollason (ed.), *Symeon of Durham: Historian of Durham and the North* (Stamford, 1998), pp. 1–13.

D. Rollason, C. Leyser, and H. Williams (eds), *England and the Continent in the Tenth Century: Studies in Honour of Wilhelm Levison (1876–1947)* (Turnhout, 2010).

B. Rosenwein, 'The Family Politics of Berengar I, King of Italy (888–924)', *Speculum*, 71 (1996), pp. 247–89.

J. H. Round, *Feudal England: Historical Studies on the XIth and XIIth Centuries* (London, 1909).

A. R. Rumble, 'An Edition and Translation of the Burghal Hidage, together with Recension C of the Tribal Hidage', in D. H. Hill and A. R. Rumble (eds), *The Defence of Wessex: The Burghal Hidage and Anglo-Saxon Fortifications* (Manchester, 1996), pp. 14–35.

A. R. Rumble, 'Edward the Elder and the Churches of Winchester and Wessex', in N. J. Higham and D. H. Hill (eds), *Edward the Elder, 899–924* (London, 2001), pp. 230–47.

A. R. Rumble, 'The Known Manuscripts of the Burghal Hidage', in D. H. Hill and A. R. Rumble (eds), *The Defence of Wessex: The Burghal Hidage and Anglo-Saxon Fortifications* (Manchester, 1996), pp. 36–59.

A. R. Rumble, 'OE *Waru*', in D. H. Hill and A. R. Rumble (eds), *The Defence of Wessex: The Burghal Hidage and Anglo-Saxon Fortifications* (Manchester, 1996), pp. 178–81.

P. Salway, *Roman Britain* (Oxford, 1981).

G. Sarah, 'Analyses élémentaires de monnaies de Charlemagne et de Louis le Pieux du Cabinet des Médailles. Le cas de Melle', in A. Clairand and D. Hollard (eds), *Numismatique et archéologie en Poitou-Charentes* (Paris, 2009), pp. 63–83.

G. Sarah, M. Bompaire, M. McCormick, A. Rovelli, and C. Guerrot, 'Analyses élémentaires de monnaies de Charlemagne et Louis le Pieux du Cabinet des Médailles. L'Italie carolingienne et Venise', *Revue numismatique*, 164 (2008), pp. 355–406.

J. Sarnowsky, 'England und der Kontinent im 10. Jahrhundert', *Historisches Jahrbuch*, 114 (1994), pp. 47–75.

B. Sawyer and P. H. Sawyer, *Medieval Scandinavia: From Conversion to Reformation circa 800–1500* (Minneapolis, MN, 1993).

P. H. Sawyer, *The Age of the Vikings*, 2nd edn (London, 1971).

P. H. Sawyer, *Anglo-Saxon Lincolnshire* (Lincoln, 1998).

P. H. Sawyer, 'The Charters of Burton Abbey and the Unification of England', *Northern History*, 10 (1975), pp. 28–39.

P. H. Sawyer, 'English Influence on the Development of the Norwegian Kingdom', in S. Keynes and A. P. Smyth (eds), *Anglo-Saxons: Studies Presented to Cyril Roy Hart* (Dublin, 2006), pp. 224–9.

P. H. Sawyer, 'The Royal *Tun* in Pre-Conquest England', in P. Wormald, D. Bullough, and R. Collins (eds), *Ideal and Reality in Frankish and Anglo-Saxon Society: Studies Presented to J. M. Wallace-Hadrill* (Oxford, 1983), pp. 273–99.

P. H. Sawyer, *The Wealth of Anglo-Saxon England* (Oxford, 2013).

A. Scharer, *Herrschaft und Repräsentation. Studien zur Hofkultur König Alfreds des Großen* (Vienna, 2000).

A. Scharer, 'The Writing of History at King Alfred's Court', *Early Medieval Europe*, 5 (1996), pp. 177–206.

F. Schiller, 'Das erste ungarische Gesetzbuch und das deutsche Recht', in *Festschrift Heinrich Brunner zum siebzigsten Geburtstag dargebract von Schülern und Verehrern* (Weimar, 1910), pp. 379–404.

E. J. Schoenfeld, 'Anglo-Saxon *Burhs* and Continental *Burgen*: Early Medieval Fortifications in Constitutional Perspective', *Haskins Society Journal*, 6 (1994), pp. 49–66.

R. Sharpe, *Norman Rule in Cumbria, 1092–1136* (Kendal, 2006).

R. Sharpe, 'The Use of Writs in the Eleventh Century', *Anglo-Saxon England*, 32 (2003), pp. 247–91.

M. J. Silverman, 'Ælfric's Designation of the King as "Cristes sylfes speligend"', *Review of English Studies*, 35 (1984), pp. 332–4.

I. Skovgaard-Petersen, 'The Danish Kingdom: Consolidation and Disintegration', in K. Helle (ed.), *The Cambridge History of Scandinavia. Volume I: Prehistory to 1520* (Cambridge, 2003), pp. 353–68.

I. Skovgaard-Petersen, 'The Making of the Danish Kingdom', in K. Helle (ed.), *The Cambridge History of Scandinavia. Volume I: Prehistory to 1520* (Cambridge, 2003), pp. 168–83.

A. H. Smith, *English Place-Name Elements* (2 vols, Cambridge, 1956).

P. Spufford, *Money and its Use in Medieval Europe* (Cambridge, 1988).

P. Squatriti, 'Digging Ditches in Early Medieval Europe', *Past and Present*, 176 (2002), pp. 11–65.

P. Stafford, 'The Anglo-Saxon Chronicles, Identity and the Making of England', *Haskins Society Journal*, 19 (2007), pp. 28–50.

P. Stafford, '"The Annals of Æthelflæd": Annals, History and Politics in Early Tenth-Century England', in J. Barrow and A. Wareham (eds), *Myth, Rulership, Church and Charters: Essays in Honour of Nicholas Brooks* (Aldershot, 2008), pp. 101–16.

P. Stafford, 'Archbishop Ealdred and the D Chronicle', in D. Crouch and K. Thompson (eds), *Normandy and its Neighbours, 900–1250: Essays for David Bates* (Turnhout, 2011), pp. 135–56.

P. Stafford, 'King and Kin, Lord and Community: England in the Tenth and Eleventh Centuries', in P. Stafford, *Gender, Family and the Legitimation of Power: England from the Ninth to the Early Twelfth Century* (Aldershot, 2006), VIII, pp. 1–33.

P. Stafford, 'The King's Wife in Wessex, 800–1066', *Past and Present*, 91 (1981), pp. 3–27.

P. Stafford, 'The Laws of Cnut and the History of Anglo-Saxon Royal Promises', *Anglo-Saxon England*, 10 (1982), pp. 173–90.

P. Stafford, 'Political Ideas in Late-Tenth-Century England: Charters as Evidence', in P. Stafford, J. L. Nelson, and J. Martindale (eds), *Law, Laity and Solidarities: Essays in Honour of Susan Reynolds* (Manchester, 2001), pp. 68–82.

P. Stafford, 'Political Women in Mercia, Eighth to Early Tenth Centuries', in M. P. Brown and C. A. Farr (eds), *Mercia: An Anglo-Saxon Kingdom in Europe* (London, 2001), pp. 35–49.

P. Stafford, *Queen Emma and Queen Edith: Queenship and Women's Power in Eleventh-Century England* (Oxford, 1997).

P. Stafford, 'The Reign of Æthelred II, a Study in the Limitations on Royal Policy and Action', in D. H. Hill (ed.), *Ethelred the Unready: Papers from the Millenary Conference* (Oxford, 1978), pp. 15–46.

P. Stafford, *Unification and Conquest: A Political and Social History of England in the Tenth and Eleventh Centuries* (London, 1989).

E. G. Stanley, 'The *Familia* in Anglo-Saxon Society: "Household", rather than "Family, Home Life" as now Understood', *Anglia*, 126 (2008), pp. 37–64.

J. Steen Jensen, 'Møntfornyelse (*Renovatio monetae*) i Danmark indtil år 1200', *Nordisk Numismatisk Unions Medlemsblad* (1996), pp. 130–6.

F. M. Stenton, *Anglo-Saxon England*, 3rd edn (Oxford, 1971).

F. M. Stenton, 'The Danes in England', *Proceedings of the British Academy*, 13 (1927), pp. 203–46.

W. H. Stevenson, 'An Alleged Son of King Harold Harefoot', *English Historical Review*, 28 (1913), pp. 112–17.

W. H. Stevenson, 'A Contemporary Description of the Domesday Survey', *English Historical Review*, 22 (1907), pp. 72–84.

W. H. Stevenson, 'Trinoda Necessitas', *English Historical Review*, 29 (1914), pp. 689–703.

W. H. Stevenson, 'Yorkshire Surveys and Other Eleventh-Century Documents in the York Gospels', *English Historical Review*, 27 (1912), pp. 1–25.

I. Stewart, 'Coinage and Recoinage after Edgar's Reform', in K. Jonsson (ed.), *Studies in Late Anglo-Saxon Coinage in Memory of Bror Emil Hildebrand* (Stockholm, 1990), pp. 456–85.

I. Stewart, 'English Coinage from Athelstan to Edgar', *Numismatic Chronicle*, 148 (1988), pp. 192–214.

J. A. Stodnick, 'The Interests of Compounding: *Angelcynn* to *Engla land* in the *Anglo-Saxon Chronicle*', in H. Magennis and J. Wilcox (eds), *The Power of Words: Anglo-Saxon Studies Presented to Donald G. Scragg on his Seventieth Birthday* (Morgantown, WV, 2006), pp. 337–67.

J. Strzelczyk, 'Bohemia and Poland: Two Examples of Successful Western Slavonic State-Formation', in T. Reuter (ed.), *The New Cambridge Medieval History III, c.900–c.1024* (Cambridge, 1999), pp. 514–35.

S. Suchodolski, 'Renovatio Monetae in Poland in the 12th Century', *Wiadomości Numizmatyczne*, supplement to vol. 5 (1961), pp. 57–75.

H. Summerson, 'Tudor Antiquaries and the *Vita Ædwardi regis*', *Anglo-Saxon England*, 38 (2009), pp. 157–84.

T. Talvio, 'Harold I and Harthacnut's *Jewel Cross* Type Reconsidered', in M. A. S. Blackburn (ed.), *Anglo-Saxon Monetary History: Essays in Memory of Michael Dolley* (Leicester, 1986), pp. 273–90.

A. Taylor, '*Lex Scripta* and the Problem of Enforcement: Anglo-Saxon, Welsh, and Scottish Law Compared', in F. Pirie and J. Scheele (eds), *Legalism: Community and Justice* (Oxford, 2014), pp. 47–75.

A. Taylor, *The Shape of the State in Medieval Scotland, 1124–1290* (forthcoming).

C. S. Taylor, 'The Northern Boundary of Gloucestershire', *Transactions of the Bristol and Gloucestershire Archaeological Society*, 32 (1909), pp. 109–39.

C. S. Taylor, 'The Origin of the Mercian Shires', *Transactions of the Bristol and Gloucestershire Archaeological Society*, 21 (1898), pp. 32–57.

P. Taylor, 'The Endowment and Military Obligations of the See of London: A Reassessment of Three Sources', *Anglo-Norman Studies*, 14 (1992), pp. 287–312.

A. Thacker, 'Chester and Gloucester: Early Ecclesiastical Organization in Two Mercian Burhs', *Northern History*, 18 (1982), pp. 199–211.

A. Thacker, 'Memorializing Gregory the Great: The Origin and Transmission of a Papal Cult in the Seventh and Early Eighth Centuries', *Early Medieval Europe*, 7 (1998), pp. 59–84.

F. Thorn, 'Hundreds and Wapentakes', in A. Williams and G. H. Martin (eds), *The Bedfordshire Domesday* (London, 1991), pp. 54–64.

F. Thorn, 'Hundreds and Wapentakes', in A. Williams and R. W. H. Erskine (eds), *The Cheshire Domesday* (London, 1991), pp. 26–44.

F. Thorn, 'Hundreds and Wapentakes', in A. Williams (ed.), *The Lancashire Domesday* (London, 1991), pp. 42–54.

F. Thorn, 'Hundreds and Wapentakes', in A. Williams and R. W. H. Erskine (eds), *The Nottinghamshire Domesday* (London, 1990), pp. 32–42.

F. Thorn, 'Hundreds and Wapentakes', in A. Williams and R. W. H. Erskine (eds), *The Sussex Domesday* (London, 1990), pp. 26–42.

F. Thorn, 'Hundreds and Wapentakes', in A. Williams and G. H. Martin (eds), *The Yorkshire Domesday* (London, 1992), pp. 39–70.

D. E. Thornton, 'Edgar and the Eight Kings, AD 973: *textus et dramatis personae*', *Early Medieval Europe*, 10 (2001), pp. 49–79.

F. Tinti, *Sustaining Belief: The Church of Worcester from c.870 to c.1100* (Farnham, 2010).

T. N. Toller, *An Anglo-Saxon Dictionary Based on the Manuscript Collections of the Late Joseph Bosworth* (Oxford, 1898), with *Supplement* (Oxford, 1921).

W. Ullmann, *The Carolingian Renaissance and the Idea of Kingship* (London, 1969).

A. Verhulst, *The Carolingian Economy* (Cambridge, 2002).

P. Vinogradoff, 'Sulung and Hide', *English Historical Review*, 19 (1904), pp. 282–6.

T. Vogtherr, 'Zwischen Benediktinerabtei und bischöflicher Cathedra. Zu Auswahl und Amtsantritt englischer Bischöfe im 9.–11. Jahrhundert', in F.-R. Erkens (ed.), *Die früh- und hochmittelalterliche Bischofserhebung im europäischen Vergleich* (Cologne, 1998), pp. 287–320.

A. W. Wade-Evans, *Vitae Sanctorum Britanniae et Genealogiae* (Cardiff, 1944).

J. M. Wallace-Hadrill, 'The Franks and the English in the Ninth Century: Some Common Historical Interests', *History*, 35 (1950), pp. 202–18.

M. Weber, *Economy and Society: An Outline of Interpretive Sociology*, ed. G. Roth and C. Wittich (3 vols, New York, NY, 1968).

K. F. Werner, '*Hludovicus Augustus*. Gouverner l'empire chrétien—idées et réalités', in P. Godman and R. Collins (eds), *Charlemagne's Heir: New Perspectives on the Reign of Louis the Pious (814–840)* (Oxford, 1990), pp. 3–123.

K. F. Werner, 'Important Noble Families in the Kingdom of Charlemagne—A Prosopographical Study of the Relationship between King and Nobility in the Early Middle Ages', trans. T. Reuter, *The Medieval Nobility: Studies on the Ruling Classes of France and Germany from the Sixth to the Twelfth Century* (Amsterdam, 1979), pp. 137–202.

K. F. Werner, '*Missus-Marchio-Comes*. Entre l'administration centrale et l'administration locale de l'Empire carolingien', in W. Paravicini and K. F. Werner (eds), *Histoire comparée de l'administration (IVe–XVIIIe siècles)* (Munich, 1980), pp. 191–239.

G. J. White, *Restoration and Reform, 1153–1165: Recovery from Civil War in England* (Cambridge, 2000).

D. Whitelock, 'The Authorship of the Account of King Edgar's Establishment of Monasteries', in J. L. Rosier (ed.), *Philological Essays: Studies in Old and Middle English Language and Literature in Honour of Herbert Dean Meritt* (The Hague, 1970), pp. 125–36.

D. Whitelock, 'The Dealings of the Kings of England with Northumbria in the Tenth and Eleventh Centuries', in P. Clemoes (ed.), *The Anglo-Saxons: Studies in Some Aspects of their History and Culture Presented to Bruce Dickins* (London, 1959), pp. 70–88.

D. Whitelock, 'Examination of the Will', in D. Whitelock, N. R. Ker, and F. Rennell (eds), *The Will of Æthelgifu: A Tenth-Century Anglo-Saxon Manuscript* (Oxford, 1968), pp. 18–37.

D. Whitelock, 'The Numismatic Interest of an Old English Version of the Legend of the Seven Sleepers', in R. H. M. Dolley (ed.), *Anglo-Saxon Coins: Studies Presented to F. M. Stenton on the Occasion of his 80th Birthday* (London, 1961), pp. 188–94.

J. Whybra, *A Lost English County: Winchcombeshire in the Tenth and Eleventh Centuries* (Woodbridge, 1990).

C. Wickham, *Early Medieval Italy: Central Power and Local Society, 400–1000* (London, 1981).

C. Wickham, *Framing the Early Middle Ages: Europe and the Mediterranean, 400–800* (Oxford, 2005).

C. Wickham, *The Inheritance of Rome: A History of Europe from 400 to 1000* (London, 2009).

C. Wickham, *Problems in Doing Comparative History* (Southampton, 2005).

A. Williams, *The English and the Norman Conquest* (Woodbridge, 1995).

A. Williams, *Kingship and Government in Pre-Conquest England, c.500–1066* (Basingstoke, 1999).

A. Williams, '*Princeps Merciorum gentis*: The Family, Career and Connections of Ælfhere, Ealdorman of Mercia, 956–83', *Anglo-Saxon England*, 10 (1982), pp. 143–72.

A. Williams, *The World Before Domesday: The English Aristocracy, 900–1066* (London, 2008).

G. Williams, 'Coinage and Monetary Circulation in the Northern Danelaw in the 920s in the Light of the Vale of York Hoard', in T. Abramson (ed.), *Studies in Early Medieval Coinage, Volume 2: New Perspectives* (Woodbridge, 2011), pp. 146–55.

G. Williams, 'Hákon *Aðalsteins fóstri*: Aspects of Anglo-Saxon Kingship in Tenth-Century Norway', in T. R. Liszka and L. E. M. Walker (eds), *The North Sea World in the Middle Ages* (Dublin, 2001), pp. 108–26.

G. Williams, 'Kingship, Christianity and Coinage: Monetary and Political Perspectives on Silver Economy in the Viking Age', in J. Graham-Campbell and G. Williams (eds), *Silver Economy in the Viking Age* (Walnut Creek, CA, 2007), pp. 177–214.

G. Williams, 'Military and Non-Military Functions of the Anglo-Saxon *burh*, c.878–978', in J. Baker, S. Brookes, and A. Reynolds (eds), *Landscapes of Defence in Early Medieval Europe* (Turnhout, 2013), pp. 129–63.

A. Wilmart, 'Magister Adam Cartvsiensis', in *Mélanges Mandonnet: Études d'histoire littéraire et doctrinale du moyen âge* (2 vols, Paris, 1930), ii, 145–61.

P. A. Wilson, 'On the Use of the Terms "Strathclyde" and "Cumbria"', *Transactions of the Cumberland and Westmorland Antiquarian and Archaeological Society*, new series, 66 (1966), pp. 57–92.

I. N. Wood, *The Merovingian Kingdoms, 450–751* (London, 1994).

M. Wood, 'The Making of King Aethelstan's Empire: An English Charlemagne?', in P. Wormald, D. Bullough, and R. Collins (eds), *Ideal and Reality in Frankish and Anglo-Saxon Society: Studies Presented to J. M. Wallace-Hadrill* (Oxford, 1983), pp. 250–72.

S. Wood, *The Proprietary Church in the Medieval West* (Oxford, 2006).

D. A. Woodman, '"Æthelstan A" and the Rhetoric of Rule', *Anglo-Saxon England*, 42 (2013), pp. 217–48.

A. Woolf, *From Pictland to Alba, 789–1070* (Edinburgh, 2007).

J. Wormald (ed.), *Scotland: A History* (Oxford, 2005).

P. Wormald, 'Æthelwold and his Continental Counterparts: Contact, Comparison, Contrast', in B. Yorke (ed.), *Bishop Æthelwold: His Career and Influence* (Woodbridge, 1988), pp. 13–42.

P. Wormald, 'Archbishop Wulfstan: Eleventh-Century State-Builder', in M. Townend (ed.), *Wulfstan, Archbishop of York* (Turnhout, 2004), pp. 9–27.

P. Wormald, 'Bede, the *Bretwaldas* and the Origins of the *Gens Anglorum*', in P. Wormald, D. Bullough, and R. Collins (eds), *Ideal and Reality in Frankish and Anglo-Saxon Society: Studies Presented to J. M. Wallace-Hadrill* (Oxford, 1983), pp. 99–129.

P. Wormald, 'Charters, Law and the Settlement of Disputes in Anglo-Saxon England', in W. Davies and P. Fouracre (eds), *The Settlement of Disputes in Early Medieval Europe* (Cambridge, 1986), pp. 149–68, reprinted in his *Legal Culture in the Early Medieval West: Law as Text, Image and Experience* (London, 1999), pp. 289–311.

P. Wormald, 'Courts', in M. Lapidge, J. Blair, S. Keynes, and D. Scragg (eds), *The Wiley Blackwell Encyclopedia of Anglo-Saxon England*, 2nd edn (Chichester, 2014), p. 129.

P. Wormald, '*Engla Lond*: The Making of an Allegiance', *Journal of Historical Sociology*, 7 (1994), pp. 1–24, reprinted in his *Legal Culture in the Early Medieval West: Law as Text, Image and Experience* (London, 1999), pp. 359–82.

P. Wormald, 'Frankpledge', in M. Lapidge, J. Blair, S. Keynes, and D. Scragg (eds), *The Wiley Blackwell Encyclopedia of Anglo-Saxon England*, 2nd edn (Chichester, 2014), pp. 197–8.

P. Wormald, 'Frederic William Maitland', *Law and History Review*, 16 (1998), pp. 1–25, reprinted in his *Legal Culture in the Early Medieval West: Law as Text, Image and Experience* (London, 1999), pp. 45–69.

P. Wormald, 'Germanic Power Structures: The Early English Experience', in L. Scales and O. Zimmer (eds), *Power and the Nation in European History* (Cambridge, 2005), pp. 105–24.

P. Wormald, 'Giving God and King their Due: Conflict and its Regulation in the Early English State', *Settimane di studio del centro italiano di studi sull'alto medioevo*, 44 (1997), pp. 549–90, reprinted in his *Legal Culture in the Early Medieval West: Law as Text, Image and Experience* (London, 1999), pp. 333–57.

P. Wormald, 'A Handlist of Anglo-Saxon Lawsuits', *Anglo-Saxon England*, 17 (1988), pp. 247–81, reprinted in his *Legal Culture in the Early Medieval West: Law as Text, Image and Experience* (London, 1999), pp. 253–87.

P. Wormald, 'James Campbell as Historian', in J. R. Maddicott and D. M. Palliser (eds), *The Medieval State: Essays Presented to James Campbell* (London, 2000), pp. xiii–xxii.

P. Wormald, '*Lex Scripta* and *Verbum Regis*: Legislation and Germanic Kingship from Euric to Cnut', in P. H. Sawyer and I. N. Wood (eds), *Early Medieval Kingship* (Leeds, 1977), pp. 105–38, reprinted in his *Legal Culture in the Early Medieval West: Law as Text, Image and Experience* (London, 1999), pp. 1–44.

P. Wormald, 'Living with King Alfred', *Haskins Society Journal*, 15 (2004), pp. 1–39.

P. Wormald, 'Lordship and Justice in the Early English Kingdom: Oswaldslow Revisited', in W. Davies and P. Fouracre (eds), *Property and Power in the Early Middle Ages* (Cambridge, 1995), pp. 114–36, reprinted in his *Legal Culture in the Early Medieval West: Law as Text, Image and Experience* (London, 1999), pp. 313–32.

P. Wormald, *The Making of English Law: King Alfred to the Twelfth Century. Volume I: Legislation and its Limits* (Oxford, 1999).

P. Wormald, 'Oaths', in M. Lapidge, J. Blair, S. Keynes, and D. Scragg (eds), *The Wiley Blackwell Encyclopedia of Anglo-Saxon England*, 2nd edn (Chichester, 2014), pp. 345–6.

P. Wormald, '*On þa wæpnedhealfe*: Kingship and Royal Property from Æthelwulf to Edward the Elder', in N. J. Higham and D. H. Hill (eds), *Edward the Elder, 899–924* (London, 2001), pp. 264–79.

P. Wormald, 'Pre-Modern "State" and "Nation": Definite or Indefinite?', in S. Airlie, W. Pohl, and H. Reimitz (eds), *Staat im frühen Mittelalter* (Vienna, 2006), pp. 179–89.

P. Wormald, 'The Venerable Bede and the "Church of the English"', in G. Rowell (ed.), *The English Religious Tradition and the Genius of Anglicanism* (Wantage, 1992), pp. 13–32.

P. Wormald, 'Viking Studies: Whence and Whither?', in R. T. Farrell (ed.), *The Vikings* (Chichester, 1982), pp. 128–53.

B. Yorke, 'Æthelwold and the Politics of the Tenth Century', in B. Yorke (ed.), *Bishop Æthelwold: His Career and Influence* (Woodbridge, 1988), pp. 65–88.

B. Yorke, 'Edward as Ætheling', in N. J. Higham and D. H. Hill (eds), *Edward the Elder, 899–924* (London, 2001), pp. 25–39.

B. Yorke, 'Edward, King and Martyr: A Saxon Murder Mystery', in L. Keen (ed.), *Studies in the Early History of Shaftesbury Abbey* (Dorchester, 1999), pp. 99–116.

B. Yorke, 'Joint Kingship in Kent, *c*.560 to 785', *Archaeologia Cantiana*, 99 (1983), pp. 1–19.

B. Yorke, *Wessex in the Early Middle Ages* (London, 1995).

T. Zotz, 'Kingship and Palaces in the Ottonian Realm and the Kingdom of England', in D. Rollason, C. Leyser, and H. Williams (eds), *England and the Continent in the Tenth Century: Studies in Honour of Wilhelm Levison (1876–1947)* (Turnhout, 2010), pp. 311–30.

UNPUBLISHED SECONDARY WORKS

N. Banton, 'Ealdormen and Earls in England from the Reign of King Alfred to the Reign of King Æthelred II' (D.Phil. thesis, University of Oxford, 1981).

S. E. Kelly, 'Royal Styles in Anglo-Saxon Diplomas'.

T. B. Lambert, 'Protection, Feud and Royal Power: Violence and its Regulation in English Law, *c*.850–*c*.1250' (PhD thesis, Durham University, 2009).

A. Pantos, 'Assembly-Places in the Anglo-Saxon Period: Aspects of Form and Location' (3 vols, D.Phil. thesis, University of Oxford, 2001).

ONLINE RESOURCES

J. Barrow, 'Oscytel (*d*. 971)', in H. C. G. Matthew and B. Harrison (eds), *Oxford Dictionary of National Biography* (Oxford, 2004), consulted at <http://www.oxforddnb.com/>

M. A. S. Blackburn, H. Pagan et al., *Checklist of Coin Hoards from the British Isles, c.450–1180*, consulted at <http://www-cm.fitzmuseum.cam.ac.uk/dept/coins/projects/hoards/index.list.html>

A. Cameron, A. C. Amos, and A. diP. Healey, *Dictionary of Old English* (Toronto, 1986–), consulted at <http://tapor.library.utoronto.ca/doe/>

A. diP. Healey, J. P. Wilkin, and X. Xiang, *Dictionary of Old English Web Corpus* (Toronto, 2009), consulted at <http://tapor.library.utoronto.ca/doecorpus/>

S. Keynes, 'Æthelred II (*c.*966×8–1016)', in H. C. G. Matthew and B. Harrison (eds), *Oxford Dictionary of National Biography* (Oxford, 2004), consulted at <http://www.oxforddnb.com/>

S. Keynes, 'Eadric Streona (*d.* 1017)', in H. C. G. Matthew and B. Harrison (eds), *Oxford Dictionary of National Biography* (Oxford, 2004), consulted at <http://www.oxforddnb.com/>

S. Keynes, 'Eadwig (*c.*940–959)', in H. C. G. Matthew and B. Harrison (eds), *Oxford Dictionary of National Biography* (Oxford, 2004), consulted at <http://www.oxforddnb.com/>

J. L. Nelson, S. Keynes, S. Baxter et al., *Prosopography of Anglo-Saxon England*, consulted at <http://www.pase.ac.uk/index.html>

M. Proffitt et al., *Oxford English Dictionary Online*, consulted at <http://www.oed.com>

P. H. Sawyer, *Anglo-Saxon Charters: An Annotated List and Bibliography* (London, 1968), revised S. E. Kelly, *The Electronic Sawyer*, consulted at <http://esawyer.org.uk/about/index.html>

A. Taylor, 'Common Burdens in the *Regnum Scottorum*: The Evidence of the Charter Diplomatic', in D. Broun (ed.), *The Reality behind Charter Diplomatic in Anglo-Norman Britain* (Glasgow, 2011), pp. 166–234, consulted at <http://paradox.poms.ac.uk/ebook/index.html>

P. Wormald, 'Papers Preparatory to *The Making of English Law: King Alfred to the Twelfth Century. Volume II: From God's Law to Common Law*', ed. S. Baxter and J. G. H. Hudson (London, 2014), consulted at <http://www.earlyenglishlaws.ac.uk/reference/wormald/>

These weblinks were all accessed on 9 October 2014.

Index